Repertoire for the
SOLO VOICE

A fully annotated guide to works for the solo voice
published in modern editions and covering material
from the 13th century to the present

by

NONI ESPINA

with a foreword by
Berton Coffin

VOLUME II

The Scarecrow Press, Inc.
Metuchen, N.J. 1977

CHAPTER VII

THREE GREAT GERMAN COMPOSERS

Introduction

77-2650

The user of this book may wonder why the author has chosen to iso-
late three names and present them in a separate chapter. The reasons are
simple. First, Johann Sebastian Bach, George Frideric Handel, and Christopher Willibald Gluck represent a near-perfect fatherhood in their respective
contributions to the development of avenues of expression with the voice. In
Bach we have music for the church in his passions, mass, and many cantatas; in Handel, the voice glories in his sacred and secular oratorios and operas; in Gluck, the voice has its consciousness of balance and equality of
lyric and dramatic styles. It is interesting to note that in this group of
three composers, Handel bridges the sacred and the secular, the church and
the theatre, which keep Bach and Gluck at opposite poles. Handel has, to
a great extent, used both sacred and secular subjects with great impact.
Opera was not Bach's main work and interest, neither were church cantatas
and passions Gluck's. It is also significant that there is some kind of unity
in time between them: Bach and Handel were born in the same year, and
Gluck was already forty-five years old and highly successful and controversial in the year Handel died.

Second, the music of the three men shared a feature of greatness:
universality. The homage the 20th century gives to them in many cultures
around the world is strong evidence of this fact. In the use of different
styles, in their breadth of musical expression, in their travels, and in their
association with artists in different locations, Handel and Gluck were already
international in their day. Bach, working in a small geographic area due to
his large family and devotion to local church traditions, became international
and universal after his death. His fame gathered momentum as appreciation
of his works fanned outward into all continents. The universality of the
works and accomplishments of these three great Germans is a force of great
power.

Third, the works of these three composers have influenced the musi-
cality and inspired the production of succeeding generations. The principles
they established in the forms that they were masters of helped to nurture
the professional growth of most of the great musicians who followed them.
We cannot ignore such an inheritance. Haydn, Mozart, Beethoven, and many
other greats have all learned from Bach, Handel, and Gluck, making them,
therefore, the direct "musical parents" in a long line of the world's greatest
Western composers.

Fourth, the musical accomplishments of the three composers have an
aesthetic impact and a high degree of retention in the international musical
scene. This is especially true with Bach and Handel, whose music has become permanent "musts" on the concert stage and in church sanctuaries. In
the case of Gluck, the impact of his work is felt in what he did for opera
since his ORFEO ED EURIDICE, whose approach and style were controversial

and revolutionary in its day.   The shock was felt throughout the world of
music for the stage--and the better that it was.

General Bibliography

Collections of works by various composers which include songs and arias by
Bach, Handel, and Gluck.   These titles appear before the first chapter of
this work, and are repeated here to facilitate reference.

AAP   Arie Antiche.   Three volumes: 30 songs each in volumes 1 & 2, 40
        songs in volume 3.   Edited by Alessandro Parisotti.   Milan: G.
        Ricordi.   (This collection has some fine notes about the composers.)

AIS   Anthology of Italian Song of the Seventeenth and Eighteenth Centuries.
        Two volumes, one key (medium and medium-high).   Edited by Ales-
        sandro Parisotti.   Italian texts, with English versions.   New York:
        G. Schirmer Inc.   (Note: This is perhaps the most popular collection
        of Italian airs.   It provides biographical notes.   The English versions
        are rather weak.)

AMB   Alte Meister des Bel Canto.   Two volumes, one key.   A collection
        mainly for soprano and contralto.   Edited by Ludwig Landshoff.   Ital-
        ian texts, with German versions.   Leipzig & Frankfurt: C. F.
        Peters.   (Note: Vol. I has two duets, and Vol. II has four.   The
        songs may be transposed for other voices.)

ARB   The Aria.   Renaissance and Baroque.   From the collection edited by
        Alessandro Parisotti.   Revised by Estelle Liebling, and edited by
        Ruggero Vené.   High, low.   Italian texts, with English versions.
        New York: Franco Colombo, Inc.

ASS   Anthology of Sacred Song.   Four volumes: Soprano, alto, tenor, bass.
        Edited by Max Spicker.   Texts are all in original English and English
        versions.   New York: G. Schirmer, Inc.

AUK   Arien und Kanzonetten des 17. und 18. Jahrhunderts.   Edited by Her-
        mann Keller.   Original texts, with English translations of the non-
        German songs and arias.   Basel: Bärenreiter Kassel.

CCF   Le Chant Classique.   Older title: Répertoire Classique de Chant
        Français.   Edited by François Auguste Gevaert.   The entire collection
        is a large monumental work, sometimes bound in 25 volumes.   Paris:
        Henry Lemoine.   (Note: Still one of the best editions of the French
        song.   Each song is available separately from the publisher.   Found
        in many libraries.   The numbers appearing after the codes in this
        work refer to the bound editions, and may differ in certain cases.)

CPS   Classic Period Songs.   Medium high, Medium low.   Edited by Van A.
        Christy and Carl Zytowski.   Original texts and English versions.
        Dubuque: William C. Brown Co.   (Note: Some of the music suffers
        from editing, and some of the English versions are not musically re-
        liable.)

DDK   Das Deutsche Kunstlied.   Three volumes, medium keys.   German texts only. Vol. 3 has songs by modern composers. Mainz & London: B. Schott's Söhne.

DLL   Das Leben in Liedern. High, Medium, Low. Edited by Paul Losse. Sixty songs by different composers. German texts only. Frankfurt: C. F. Peters.

EDF   Échos de France. Three volumes, no editor. Mostly high and medium keys. Reissued in 1957. Paris: Durand & Cie.

GAS   Great Art Songs of Three Centuries. High, Low. Compiled by Bernard Taylor. Original languages, with English versions. New York: G. Schirmer, Inc.

GSA   Gladys Swarthout Album of Concert Songs and Airs. New York: G. Schirmer, Inc.

GSB   The German Solo Song and the Ballad. Edited by Hans Joachim Moser. Fifty-six songs from Schein to Hindemith. German texts, with English versions. Köln: Arno Volk Verlag. (Note: Has very fine historical introduction and notes in English. Scholarly edition, with an extended bibliography.)

KAL   Kirchen-Arien und Lieder. Soprano (Tenor) and Organ (Piano). Edited by Georg Göhler. Original texts and German versions. Frankfurt: C. F. Peters.

KDL   Klassiker des Deutschen Liedes. Two volumes, edited by Hans Joachim Moser. High, Medium, Low. Frankfurt & New York: C. F. Peters, 1943. (Note: Vol. I: 45 songs from Albert to Schubert; Vol. II: 55 songs from Mendelssohn to Wolf.)

KLR   Klingende Lyrik. High voice. Edited by Ernst Reichert. A mixed collection, but mostly German composers. Vienna: Verlag Doblinger, 1957.

LFL   La Flora. Three volumes, generally in high keys. Edited by Knud Jeppessen. Notes in Italian, English, and German. Copenhagen: Wilhelm Hansen. (Note: Vol. I: 45 solos; Vol. II: 45 solos; Vol. III: 26 solos and 19 duets. A very fine and highly recommended edition.)

LIU   Das Lied im Unterricht. High, Medium (or Low). Edited by Paul Lohmann. German text only. Mainz & London: B. Schott's Söhne. (Note: 61 songs classified according to style.)

MAA   Marian Anderson Album of Songs and Spirituals. Edited by Franz Rupp. Low voice. New York: G. Schirmer, Inc. (Note: Songs in foreign languages are provided English translations.)

MLF   Master Lessons on Fifty Opera Arias. Vol. II: The Music. Edited by Weldon Whitlock. Milwaukee: Pro Musica Press. (Note: 27 arias for soprano; 4 for mezzo-soprano; 12 for tenor; 8 for baritone.)

OPA   Operatic Anthology. Five volumes: Soprano, mezzo-soprano and contralto, tenor, baritone, and bass. Edited by Kurt Adler. New York: G. Schirmer, Inc. (Note: The older edition, edited by Kurt Schindler, may be seen in libraries. It has a few arias not found in the newer edition.)

POS   Pathways of Song. Four volumes, revised. High, Low. Edited by
       Frank LaForge and Will Earhart. English songs, and songs in for-
       eign languages with English translations. New York: M. Witmark,
       Inc. (Note: POS-1 means Pathways of Song, Vol. 1.)

RES   Reliquary of English Songs. Two volumes, one key (medium high).
       Edited by Frank Hunter Potter. New York: G. Schirmer, Inc.
       (Note: Vol. I: from 1250-1700; Vol. II: from 1700 to 1800. Fine
       notes on the composers.)

SCS   Seven Centuries of Solo Song. High, low. Six volumes. Edited by
       James Woodside. Boston: Boston Music Co. (Note: Volume 4 is
       devoted to recital arrangements of folk songs. The material included
       is from the 13th to the 20th century.)

SGO   Solos from the Great Oratorios. One volume each for soprano and
       baritone or bass. Compiled by Bernard Taylor. New York: G.
       Schirmer, Inc. (Note: Some arias have both the original text and
       an English version. SGO-S means soprano volume.)

SVR   Standard Vocal Repertoire. High, low. Two volumes. Edited by
       R. D. Row. New York: R. D. Row, Inc.

UNT   Unterrichtslieder. High, Medium, Low. Edited by Paul Losse.
       German texts only. Leipzig & Frankfurt: C. F. Peters. (Note:
       60 songs, old and modern German composers.)

YAR   Young Artists' Repertoire. High, Low. Edited by John Toms. Orig-
       inal texts, with English translations. Evanston: Summy-Birchard Co.

56S   Fifty-Six Songs You Like to Sing. No editor. New York: G.
       Schirmer, Inc. (Note: A one-volume, mixed and general collection
       for different voices.)

A. JOHANN SEBASTIAN BACH, 1685-1750

The vocal solo output of Bach consists of excerpts from his large choral works and cantatas, solo cantatas, and sacred songs. His airs are full-blown arias which can only be handled by singers with advanced vocal training, while his sacred songs are generally as easy as the average church hymn. There is no in-between. Among his many cantatas are entire cantatas for one voice. Except his sacred songs, first published in a collection by Georg Christian Schemelli, his other material was written not with keyboard accompaniment alone, but for continuo and other instruments. In this combination, the solo voice performs frequently with an obbligato instrument. Bach airs are quite difficult musically, and for this reason they are not seen often on recital programs. Also, the popular concept that Bach airs must at all times be heard only with the indicated instruments has caused many a singer to feel out of step in attempting a Bach excerpt with only the piano. Such an attitude is often caused by the tirades of uncompromising purists and authenticists, music critics, and some frustrated musicians. As far as this author is concerned, one should not fear performance of any Bach air with piano alone, which is far better than not performing at all. Surely, it would be ideal and most artistically rewarding to have the complete and true instrumentation of Bach, but alas, one cannot always have this situation. Strict adherence to authenticity is the poison that kills the very life of music. If instruments are available, then a performance as Bach envisioned it will be a joy. If none is available, the use of the piano alone ought not to be a much lesser joy. There are some fine piano reductions of all Bach airs, and these can be useful. The most scholarly and authoritative, of course, are the voice-piano scores issued by Breitkopf & Härtel. Some of these cantatas are now issued with English versions to facilitate translation. Another fine and highly recommended edition is the set Bach Songs and Airs, edited by Ebenezer Prout, and published by Augener Ltd. All accompaniment ratings here are based on the reductions for piano from the instrumental ensemble scores.

One of the beauties of Bach solo literature is the fact that the composer gives almost equal importance to all the four accepted general types of solo voices. Operatic literature neglects the Mezzo-Soprano and Contralto voices in the number of arias compared to those for Soprano and Tenor. Not so in Bach. He wrote many fine solos for the voice types just mentioned. These arias and cantatas explore these voices and bring out their fullest bloom, putting to shame what operatic literature can offer. Bach arias generally require more vocal flexibility and control than any other form of vocal writing.

To especially allay the problem or task of performing a Bach air, a few considerations might be of some help.

1) Bach vocal lines, as in the true Baroque manner, are long. Florid passages are very extended and demanding of the singer's breath. The solution is not to sing them in one breath. Bach never intended them to be sung thus. There are places where breath may be taken without destruction of the vocal line, tempi, vowel purity, dynamics, and vocal quality. One place is the second member of a tied note as in a florid passage (♩ '♪♪♪♪ --apostrophe is where the breath may be taken). Another, and one which needs more practice than the other, is just before a pick-up note which appears

before a stressed note, such as in a string of 16ths (♪♪♪♪ | ♪♪♪♪).
In this pattern, the note that receives the stress is usually the highest in
the phrase such as the one indicated with an accent sign over it. This is,
of course, a very short breath, simply for reinforcement. A third is also
just before a pick-up note which is preceded by a dotted note (♪.♪♪ ♪♪♪♪).

2) All Bach airs are, technically, ensemble airs. In other words,
the vocal part is not much above the rest of the instruments in importance.
When an obbligato instrument is used, such as a violin, an oboe, or a trumpet, the solo instrument has the same importance as the voice. In the playing of the continuo, the bass melody must slightly predominate the part for
the right hand.

3) Rhythms and the flow of the notes in time must be very steady, almost metronomic, but flexible and without rigidity. Rubato, in the romantic
sense, is absolutely out of place.

4) Certain singers' idiosyncracies, which may be acceptable to some
degree in Romantic Period airs, are not applicable in Bach. Among these
are: (a) The tendency of some singers to "croon" or use "falsetto effects."
Tones in the performance of Bach must be solid, warm, and definite in approach, without being rigid and monotonous. (b) Sliding or slurring upward
or downward is very undesirable and causes the innate solidity of a Bach
line to fall apart. Attacks must be definite, precise and purposeful without
being overly dramatic or pompous unless the piece requires it. (c) Glottal
stops and attacks, catches in the voice, sobbing effects and their kind, made
common in dramatic situations in opera, are all out of place. All sentimental approaches to tone and phrase must be avoided.

5) Stresses or accents in Bach's music are differently placed in the
lines of different instruments. In other words, each instrument, including
the voice, must approach stresses as an individual soloist, and they must
never agree to coincide unless required so in the music, as in Bach's dance
movements. Some stresses do not occur on the barline; they may even be
on the weakest beats of the melodic lines of other instruments. Barlines are
generally ignored in properly accomplishing the strong beats of Bach's music.
This soloistic approach to Bach's music is the very essence of his polyrhyth-
mic technique.

6) Although soprani and alti airs were not originally intended by Bach
for women singers, women soloists must in no way try to imitate the tonal
and musical characteristics of boy soprani and alti, so much in use during
Bach's time.

7) Dynamics in Bach's music are approached more on the principle of
economy rather than generosity. Overuse or meticulous use of little bits of
shadings and subtleties are much against the character of the stretched and
long lines evident in Bach's music.

8) There must be no attempt to vocally dramatize the singing of a
Bach air. The approach instead is one of gently majestic lyricism, never
flamboyant or bombastic.

9) Lastly, Bach airs should not be sung in the manner popularly
thought of as resulting from deep piety or religious formality. Bach airs
should be sung as freely as one may feel moved by the vocal lines and with
the necessary lyric declamation of the texts. The manner of vocalization
must be one of lyric vibrance. Of course, anything can be overdone so that
it affects taste. But the popular practice of singing which results instead in
an apologetic Bach performance is anti-Bach. His music does not need
apology.

Bach airs ought to find their way again into recital programs, for the
master's solo repertoire is rich and the quality of many a recital would be
even more heightened by their presence.

BAS   Bach Arias for Soprano.   Compiled by Bernard Taylor.   Original
       texts, with English versions.   New York: G. Schirmer, Inc.

BSS   J. S. Bach Sacred Songs.   High, low.   Sixty-nine songs from the
       Schemelli Gesangbuch.   English texts, with an Appendix of the melod-
       ic lines and the original German texts.   St. Louis: Concordia Pub-
       lishing House.   Note: A very fine and practical collection, and is
       very highly recommended.

SSB   Sacred Songs.   Johann Sebastian Bach.   High voice, 25 songs.   Ed-
       ited by Herman Roth.   German texts, with English versions by
       Herbert Grossman in a separate insert.   New York: International
       Music Co.

40B   40 Songs and Airs.   Johann Sebastian Bach.   Edited by Ebenezer
       Prout.   Eight volumes, two for each voice.   London: Augener Ltd.
       (Note: Two volumes each for soprano (22 songs), contralto (18 songs),
       tenor (18 songs), and bass (22 songs).   German texts, and singable
       English versions.)

Note: The various vocal scores of cantatas, oratorios, passions, and mass
       are indicated in the entries themselves.   There are, of course, very
       many more solos from Bach cantatas.   See the catalog of Breitkopf
       & Härtel for a complete listing of individual vocal scores, all of
       which are available.

The Songs

(Selected from Various Collections)

A.   Sacred

5568. Ach, dass nicht die letzte Stunde   All Voices
       Poet: Erdmann Neumeister.   BWV 439.   e3-f#4   f#3-e4   Sustained
       in moderate tempo.   Sacred text.   Acc: 3 BSS

5569. Auf, auf! Die rechte Zeit ist hier   All Voices
       Poet: Martin Opitz.   BWV 440.   e3-f4   g3-d4   Sustained in moder-
       ate tempo.   Acc: 3 BSS

5570. Beglückter Stand getreuer Seelen   All Voices
       Poet: Ulrich Bogislaus von Bonin.   BWV 442.   d3-d4   e3-c4   Sus-
       tained in moderate tempo.   Somewhat slow; has a subdued ending.
       Acc: 3 BSS

5571. Brunnquell aller Gueter   All Voices
       Poet: Johann Franck.   BWV 445.   f#3-f4   g3-d4   Sustained in mod-
       erate tempo.   Acc: 3 BSS

5572. Der Tag mit seinem Lichte   All Voices
       Poet: Paul Gerhardt.   BWV 448.   d3-e4   f3-d4   Sustained in moder-
       ate tempo.   Climactic ending.   An evening song of praise.   Acc: 4
       BSS

5573. Die gold'ne Sonne, voll Freud' und Wonne   All Voices
      Poet: Paul Gerhardt. BWV 451. eb3-f4 ab3-eb4 Sustained in
      moderate tempo. Has some climactic passages, and a climactic end-
      ing. 2 verses. Acc: 3 POS-4, BSS, LIU

5574. Dir, dir, Jehova, will ich singen   All Voices
      Poet: Bartholomaeus Crasselius. BWV 452. f3-g4 a3-eb4 Ani-
      mated in moderate tempo. Joyous; a song of praise. Acc: 3 BSS

5575. Eins ist not   All Voices
      Poet: Johann Heinrich Schroeder. BWV 453. c3-e4 f3-d4 Sus-
      tained in moderate tempo. Low ending. Acc: 3 BSS

5576. Es ist vollbracht!   All Voices
      Poet: Johann Eusebius Schmidt. BWV 458. d3-f#4 a3-d4 Sus-
      tained in moderate slow tempo. Generally on MF level. The text
      refers to Christ's crucifixion. Acc: 2 BSS

5577. Gott lebet noch   All Voices
      Poet: Johann Friedrich Zihn. BWV 461. d3-f4 g3-e4 Slightly
      animated in moderate tempo. A graceful 3/4. Acc: 3 BSS

5578. Ich freue mich in dir   All Voices
      Poet: Kaspar Ziegler. BWV 465. eb3-f4 g3-eb4 Sustained in
      moderate tempo. Moving bass line in the accompaniment. Acc: 3
      BSS

5579. Ich halte treulich Still   High Voices
      Poet: J. H. Till. BWV 466. f3-g4 g3-d4 Sustained in moderate
      slow tempo. Gentle. May be transposed for lower voices. Acc:
      2 40B-S2, BSS

5580. Ich steh' an deiner Krippen hier   All Voices
      Poet: Paul Gerhardt. BWV 469. d3-eb4 g3-d4 Sustained in mod-
      erate tempo. Gentle. Has a running bass melody in the accompani-
      ment. Text is on Christmas. Acc: 3 BSS

5581. Komm, süsser Tod, komm, sel'ge Ruh'!   All Voices
      Poet: Johann Sebastian Bach. BWV 478. c3-g4 g3-eb4 Very sus-
      tained in slow tempo. Subdued and gentle. Acc: 3 40B-S2, BSS,
      LIU, KAL. (S)SC

5582. Liebster Herr Jesu   All Voices
      Poet: Anon. BWV 484. g3-f4 a3-d4 Sustained in slow tempo.
      Generally gentle, on MF level. Acc: 3 POS-4, BSS

5583. O liebe Seele, zieh' die Sinnen   All Voices
      Poet: Johann Sebastian Bach. BWV 494. d3-e4 g3-d4 Sustained
      in moderate slow tempo. Generally gentle, on MF level. Requires
      some flexibility. Acc: 3 40B-S2, BSS

5584. O Jesulein süss, O Jesulein mild   All Voices
      Poet: Valentin Thilo? BWV 493. g3-f4 g3-d4 Sustained in moder-
      ate slow tempo. Gentle. A well-known Bach song, it appears in
      several arrangements for choir. Acc: 3 BSS

5585. Steh' ich bei meinem Gott   All Voices
      Poet: Johann Daniel Herrenschmidt. BWV 503. e3-g4 g3-d4

Sustained in moderate tempo. Generally on MF level. Generally
gentle. Low ending. Acc: 3 BSS

5586. Vergiss mein nicht   All Voices
Poet: Anon. BWV 505. d♯3-g4 a3-f4 Sustained in moderate slow
tempo. Graceful. 2 verses given. Original key. A minor third
lower in DLL, and entitled "Aus Angst und Not," 3 verses. Acc: 3
UNT, DDK-2, BSS, DLL

B. Secular

5587. Bist du bei mir   All Voices
Poet: Anon. From Anna Magdalena Bach's Notebook, 1725. BWV
508. d3-ab4 ab3-g4 Sustained in moderate slow tempo. Requires
simplicity. Generally subdued and gentle. Original key. One of
Bach's best-known melodies. Matrimonial texts instead of religious.
In the Schott edition, this is published with "Komm, süsser Tod,"
German, with English. Acc: 3 (S)SC, GS-(high, medium, low),
DDK-3, KDL-1, LIU, POS-2

5588. Gedenke doch, mein Geist, zurücke   All Voices
Poet: Anon. BWV 509. d3-ab4 f3-eb4 Gently animated in moderate tempo. Requires some flexibility. Generally subdued. May be
transposed for lower voices. From Anna Magdalena Bach's Notebook,
1725. Acc: 3 KLR

5589. Gib dich zufrieden und sei stille   High Voices
Poet: Paul Gerhardt. BWV 510. d♯3-g4 g3-d4 Sustained in mod-
erate slow tempo. Requires some flexibility. Short. From Anna
Magdalena Bach's Notebook, 1725. Acc: 3 40B-S1

The Solo Cantatas

A. Sacred

CANTATA 35. Geist und Seele wird verwirret   Contralto
Text: Johann Sebastian Bach (?). (VS)BH

Part I.
NNA (1) Instrumental movement, full length.

5590. (2) Geist und Seele wird verwirret
b2-e4 e3-d4 Sustained in slow tempo. Has some florid passages.
Requires some flexibility. Has climactic passages. Scored for contralto solo, oboe 1 & 2, tenor oboe, violin 1 & 2, viola, organ obbligato, and continuo. Acc: 3-4

5591. (3) R: Ich wundre mich, denn Alles
c3-e4 e3-c4 Recitative with organ and continuo.

Part II.
NNA (4) Instrumental movement.

5592. (5) R: Ach, starker Gott
c3-e4 d3-c4 Short recitative with organ and continuo.

5593. (6) A: Ich wünsche mir bei Gott zu leben

c3-e4   d3-c4   Animated in moderate lively tempo. Has two florid
passages, some wide intervalic skips, and climactic passages. Requires flexibility. Descending ending line. Acc: 3-4

5594. (7) A: Gott hat Alles wohl gemacht
c3-e4   e3-c4   Animated in lively tempo. Generally energetic and
vigorous. Has florid passages, and requires flexibility. Climactic
ending. Scored for contralto, organ obbligato, and continuo. Continuo part is detached throughout. Acc: 3

CANTATA 53. Schlage doch, gewünschte Stunde   Contralto
Text: Anon. A solo cantata in one movement. (VS)BH

5595. Schlage doch, gewünschte Stunde
b2-e4   e3-c♯4   Quite sustained in moderate slow tempo. Grave,
warm, and generally subdued. Scored with chimes in g1 and d2,
strings, and continuo. Acc: 3

CANTATA 54. Widerstehe doch der Sünde   Contralto
Text: Anon. A solo cantata with two arias and one recitative.
Scored for strings and continuo. (VS)BH

5596. (1) A: Widerstehe doch der Sünde
f2-b♭3   c3-f3   Sustained vocal part in slow tempo. Grave, dark,
and warm. Has florid figures. Acc: 3-4   40B-C1

5597. (2) R: Die Art verruchter Sünden
g2-b♭3   c3-g3

5598. (3) Wer Sünde thut, der ist vom Teufel
f2-c4   c3-g3   Sustained in moderate tempo. Grave; has florid passages. Requires flexibility. Descending ending line. Acc: 4

CANTATA 55. Ich armer Mensch, ich Sündenknecht   Tenor
Text: Anon. This cantata ends with a chorale. (VS)BH

5599. (1) A: Ich armer Mensch, ich Sündenknecht
d2-b♭3   a2-g3   Sustained in moderate tempo. Graceful; has high
tessitura. Generally on MF level. Scored with flute, oboe d'amore,
violin 1 & 2, and continuo. Acc: 3-4

5600. (2) R: Ich habe wider Gott gehandelt
d2-a3   g2-e♭3   Recitative with continuo. Acc: 2

5601. (3) A: Erbarme dich
f2-b♭3   a2-f3   Generally sustained in moderate tempo, and on MF
level. Has some florid figures. Scored with flute and continuo.
Acc: 3

CANTATA 56. Ich will den Kreuzstab gerne tragen   Bass
Text: Johann Sebastian Bach (?). This cantata ends with a chorale.
(VS)BH

5602. (1) A: Ich will den Kreuzstab gerne tragen
g1-e3   c2-d3   Sustained in moderate slow tempo. Has extended,
florid passages. Requires flexibility and some fine high notes. High
tessitura in some passages. Descending ending line with g1 as the
last note. Extended instrumental prelude and postlude. Scored with

oboe 1 and violin 1 in unison, oboe 2 and violin 2 in unison, tenor
oboe, viola, and continuo. Acc: 3 40B-B2

5603. (2) R: Mein Wandel auf der Welt
a1-e3 c2-c3 A recitative with agitated accompaniment on violoncello
and continuo. Acc: 3

5604. (3) A: Endlich wird mein Joch
g1-e3 c2-c3 Animated in moderate lively tempo. Very florid. Requires considerable flexibility. Has climactic passages. Scored with
oboe solo and continuo. A short recitative separates this excerpt and
the final chorale. Acc: 3-4

NNA (4) Chorale: Komm, O Tod, du Schlafes Bruder.

CANTATA 82. Ich habe genug   Bass
Text: Anon. (VS)BH

5605. (1) A: Ich habe genug
g1-eb3 eb2-d3 Sustained in slow tempo. Dark and somber. Has
florid passages. Requires flexibility. Has extended instrumental prelude, interludes, and postlude. Scored with oboe, violin 1 & 2,
viola, organ, and continuo. Acc: 4

5606. (2) R: & Arioso: Ich habe genug!
bb1-eb3 eb2-c3 Recitative and one short arioso, with continuo.

5607. (3) A: Schlummert ein, ihr matten Augen
bb1-eb3 c2-c3 Sustained in moderate slow tempo. Generally gentle, warm, and subdued. Requires some flexibility. Extended instrumental prelude and postlude. Scored with two violins, viola,
organ, and continuo. Acc: 3-4 40B-B2

5608. (4) R: Mein Gott! wann kommt das schöne
ab1-eb3 d2-c3 Short recitative ending with a lyric passage marked
"arioso." Scored with organ and continuo.

5609. (5) A: Ich freue mich
g1-eb3 d2-c3 Animated in very lively tempo. Has florid passages
and several g1's. Requires flexibility. Extended instrumental prelude and postlude. Scored with oboe, violin 1 & 2, viola, organ, and
continuo. Acc: 4-5

CANTATA 84. Ich bin vergnügt mit meinem Glücke   Soprano
Text: Christian Friedrich Henrici (?) and Johann Sebastian Bach (?).
(VS)BH

5610. (1) A: Ich bin vergnügt mit meinen Glücke
d#3-g4 e3-f#4 Sustained in moderate tempo. Has climactic passages, one extended florid passage, and a few florid figures. Climactic high ending. Scored for voice, oboe, strings, and continuo. Acc:
3-4

5611. (2) R: Gott ist mir ja nichts schuldig
d3-a4 a3-e4 Recitative with continuo accompaniment.

5612. (3) A: Ich esse mit Freuden
d3-a4 g3-e4 Animated in moderate lively tempo. Graceful. Has

some florid figures.   Generally on MF level.   Scored for soprano
voice, violin solo, and continuo.   Acc: 3-4

5613.   (4) R: Im Schweisse meines Angesichts
        d3-g4   f♯3-d4 Recitative with sustained strings and continuo.

5614.   (5) Chorale: Ich leb' indess in der vergnügt

CANTATA 170.   Vergnügte Ruh', beliebte Seelenluft   Contralto
        Text: Johann Sebastian Bach (?).   (VS)BH

5615.   (1) A: Vergnügte Ruh', beliebte Seelenluft
        b2-e4   e3-d4 Sustained in moderate tempo.   Requires some flexibil-
        ity. Has climactic passages and a descending ending line.   Scored
        for contralto, oboe d'amore and violin 1 in unison, violin 2, viola,
        and continuo.   Acc: 4

5616.   (2) R: Die Welt, das Sündenhaus
        a2-e4   f♯3-c♯4 Recitative with continuo.

5617.   (3) A: Wie jammern mich doch die verkehrten Herzen
        b2-e4   c♯3-d4 Sustained in slow tempo.   Has some extremely florid
        passages.   Requires considerable flexibility, and some chromaticisms
        and climactic passages.   Acc: 4

5618.   (4) R: Wer sollte sich demnach
        c♯3-e4   e3-b3 Recitative with violin 1 & 2, viola, and continuo.

5619.   (5) A: Mir ekelt mehr zu leben
        c♯3-e4   e3-d4 Sustained in moderate lively tempo.   Has climactic
        passages.   Has extended instrumental interludes.   Scored with flute,
        organ obbligato, oboe d'amore and violin 1 in unison, violin 2, viola,
        and continuo.   Acc: 4

B.   Secular

CANTATA 202.   Weichet nur, betrübte Schatten   Soprano
        Text: Anon.   Other title: Hochzeitkantate.   English: Wedding can-
        tata.   (VS)BH

5620.   (1) A: Weichet nur, betrübte Schatten
        d3-a4   g3-g4 Sustained in slow tempo.   Slightly faster middle sec-
        tion. Has florid passages.   Scored with oboe, violin 1 & 2, viola,
        and continuo.   Acc: 4

5621.   (2) R: Die Welt wird wieder neu
        g3-f4   g3-e4 Short recitative with continuo.

5622.   (3) A: Phöbus eilt mit schnellen Pferden
        d3-g4   a3-f4 Animated in quite lively tempo.   Has florid passages.
        Requires some flexibility.   Has an active bass line in the instrumen-
        tal ensemble.   Scored with continuo.   Acc: 3-4

5623.   (4) R: D'rum sucht auch Amor sein vergnügen
        d♯3-g4   g3-e4 Short recitative.

5624.   (5) A: Wenn die Frühlingslüfte streichen
        d3-a4   g3-g4 Animated in lively tempo.   Has climactic passages, and

a descending ending line.   Scored with violin solo, and continuo.
Acc: 3-4

5625.   (6) R: Und dieses ist das Glücke
e3-a4 a3-e4 Short recitative with continuo.

5626.   (7) A: Sich üben im lieben
c♯3-g4 g3-f♯4 Sustained in moderate tempo.   Graceful.   Generally
on MF level.   Scored with oboe and continuo.   Acc: 3-4

5627.   (8) R: So sei das Band der keuschen Liebe
g3-g4 a3-e4 Short recitative with continuo.

5628.   (9) A: Sehet in Zufriedenheit
d3-a4 g3-e4 Sustained in moderate tempo.   Generally on MF level.
Short.   Scored with oboe, violin 1 & 2, viola, and continuo.   Acc: 3

CANTATA 203.   Amore traditore   Bass
Text: Anon.   A solo cantata for bass voice and cembalo (piano).
Italian text.   (VS)BH

5629.   (1) A: Amore traditore
b1-e3 c2-c3 Sustained in moderate tempo.   Generally lyric.   Has
climactic passages, florid passages, and some wide intervalic skips.
Acc: 3

5630.   (2) R: Voglio provar
d2-d3 e2-c3 Short recitative.

5631.   (3) A: Chi in amore
g1-e3 c2-c3 Sustained in moderate lively tempo.   Slightly slower
middle section.   Has climactic passages.   Acc: 3-4

CANTATA 204.   Von der Vergnügsamkeit   Soprano
Text: Anon.   (VS)BH

5632.   (1) R: Ich bin in mir vergnügt
d3-a4 f3-e♭4 Recitative with continuo.

5633.   (2) A: Ruhig und in sich zufrieden
c3-b♭4 g3-f4 Sustained in moderate lively tempo.   Has florid passages, some wide intervalic skips, and climactic passages and one
long-held note.   Descending ending line.   Requires flexibility.   Scored
with oboe 1 & 2, and continuo.   Acc: 3-4

5634.   (3) R: Ihr Seelen, die ihr ausser stets
c3-a4 f3-g4 An extended recitative in moderate and very fast tempi.
Scored with violin 1 & 2, and continuo.

5635.   (4) A: Die Schätzbarkeit der weiten Erden
c3-b♭4 f3-f4 Sustained in moderate tempo.   Has florid passages.
Requires flexibility.   Climactic ending with a "falling" note.   Scored
with violin solo, and continuo.   Acc: 3-4

5636.   (5) R: Schwer ist es zwar
c3-a♭4 f3-f4 An extended recitative with continuo.   Has two short
florid passages.

5637.   (6) A: Meine Seele sei vergnügt
        c3-bb4   f3-g4   Animated in moderate lively tempo.   Has florid pas-
        sages and climactic passages.   Requires flexibility.   Has some wide
        intervalic skips, and a descending ending line.   Scored with flute and
        continuo.   Acc: 3-4

5638.   (7) R: Ein edler Mensch
        c3-a4   f3-f4   Extended recitative with continuo.

5639.   (8) A: Himmlische Vergnügsamkeit
        c3-bb4   f3-g4   Sustained in moderate tempo.   Has some short florid
        figures.   Climactic ending.   Scored with flute, oboe 1 & violin 1 in
        unison, oboe 2 & violin 2 in unison, viola, and continuo.   Acc: 3-4

Excerpts from the Church Cantatas

I. Soprano

5640.   Auch mit gedämpften, schwachen Stimmen   Soprano
        CANTATA 36: Schwingt freudig euch empor.   Text: Christian Fried-
        rich Henrici.   d3-g4   f#3-e4   Animated in moderate tempo.   Middle
        section is florid.   Requires flexibility.   Extended instrumental pre-
        lude.   Scored for soprano, violin solo, organ, and continuo.   Acc:
        3-4 (VS)BH

5641.   Bereite dir, Jesu   Soprano
        CANTATA 147: Herz und Mund und Tat und Leben.   Text: Salomo
        Franck.   d3-bb4   a3-g4   Gently animated vocal part in moderate slow
        tempo.   Constantly agitated accompaniment.   Extended instrumental
        prelude and postlude.   Acc: 4 (VS)BH, CP

5642.   Bete, bete aber auch dabei   Soprano
        CANTATA 115: Mache dich, mein Geist, bereit.   Text: Johann
        Burchard Freystein.   d3-g#4   a3-f#4   Sustained in moderate slow
        tempo.   Has some short florid figures.   Descending ending line.
        Generally on MF level.   Acc: 3-4 (VS)BH

5643.   Die Armen will der Herr umarmen   Soprano
        CANTATA 186: Ärg're dich, o Seele, nicht.   Text: Salomo Franck.
        d3-g4   g3-eb4   Sustained in moderate tempo.   Requires some flexi-
        bility.   Generally on MF level.   Descending ending line.   Scored for
        soprano solo, violin 1 & 2 in unison, and continuo.   Acc: 3-4
        (VS)BH

5644.   Die Seele ruht in Jesu Händen   Soprano
        CANTATA 127: Herr Jesu Christ, wahr'r Mensch und Gott.   Text:
        Paul Eber.   c3-ab4   g3-f4   Sustained in slow tempo.   Has some
        short florid figures.   Requires flexibility.   Extended instrumental pre-
        lude.   Scored for soprano voice, two flutes, one oboe, two violins,
        viola, and continuo.   Acc: 4 40B-S2, (VS)BH

5645.   Es ist und bleibt der Christen Trost   Soprano
        CANTATA 44: Sie werden euch in den Bann thun.   Text: Christian
        Weise (?).   d3-a4   f3-f4   Animated in moderate tempo.   Florid, re-
        quires flexibility.   Has climactic passages and a climactic ending.
        Scored for soprano voice, oboe 1 and violin 1 in unison, oboe 2 &
        violin 2 in unison, viola, bassoon, and continuo.   Acc: 4 (VS)BH

5646.   Gedenk' an uns mit deiner Liebe   Soprano
        CANTATA 29: Wir danken dir, Gott.   Text: Anon.   f♯ 3-a4 a3-f♯ 4
        Gently animated vocal part in moderate slow tempo.   Graceful, and
        requires some flexibility.   Scored for one oboe, two violins, viola,
        and continuo.   Acc: 3-4 40B-S1, (VS)BH

5647.   Gelobet sei der Herr   Soprano
        CANTATA 129: Gelobet sei der Herr, mein Gott.   Poet: Johann
        Olearius.   e3-g4 g3-g4 Sustained in moderate tempo.   Has some
        florid passages and climactic and strong passages.   Strong ending
        section.   Scored for soprano voice, flute, violin solo, and continuo.
        Acc: 3-4 (VS)BH

5648.   Gott versorget alles Leben   Soprano
        CANTATA 187: Es wartet Alles auf dich.   Text: Anon.   d3-a♭4
        f3-f4 Generally sustained first part in slow tempo.   Graceful, slight-
        ly faster second and last part.   First part requires some flexibility.
        Scored for soprano voice, oboe solo, and continuo.   Acc: 3 (VS)BH

5649.   Gottes Engel weichen nie   Soprano
        CANTATA 149: Man singet mit Freuden vom Sieg.   Text: Anon.
        c♯ 3-a4 g♯ 3-f♯ 4 Sustained in moderate tempo.   Graceful, has some
        florid figures.   Generally gentle, requires some flexibility.   Extended
        instrumental prelude and postlude.   Scored for soprano voice, two
        violins, viola, and continuo.   Acc: 3-4 40B-S1, (VS)BH

5650.   Gottlob! gottlob!   Soprano
        CANTATA 28: Gottlob! Nun geht das Jahr zu Ende.   Text: Erdmann
        Neumeister.   d3-a4 g3-f4 Animated in moderate lively tempo.   En-
        ergetic and spirited.   Has florid passages; requires flexibility.
        Scored for soprano voice, oboe 1 & 2, violins 1 & 2, viola, and con-
        tinuo.   Acc: 4 (VS)BH.   BAS

5651.   Gottlob! Nun geht das Jahr zu Ende   Soprano
        CANTATA 28: Gottlob! Nun geht das Jahr zu Ende.   Text: Erdmann
        Neumeister.   d3-a4 g3-f4 Sustained in moderate slow tempo.   Has
        one extended florid passage and several florid figures.   Requires flex-
        ibility.   Extended instrumental prelude and postlude.   Scored for two
        oboes, tenor oboe, two violins, viola, and continuo.   Acc: 3-4
        (VS)BH.   40B-S1

5652.   Heil und Segen soll und muss zu aller Zeit   Soprano
        CANTATA 120: Gott, man lobet dich in der Stille.   Text: Christian
        Friedrich Henrici (?).   d3-g4 g3-e4 Sustained in slow tempo.   Has
        one extended florid passage.   Requires some flexibility.   Virtuostic
        violin solo.   Scored for soprano voice, solo violin, strings, and con-
        tinuo.   Acc: 3 (VS)BH

5653.   Herr deine Güte reicht   Soprano
        CANTATA 17: Wer Dank opfert, der preiset mich.   Text: Anon.
        e3-g♯ 4 f♯ 3-e4 Animated in moderate lively tempo.   Generally ener-
        getic.   Has florid passages and some wide intervalic skips.   Requires
        flexibility.   Climactic descending ending.   Scored for soprano voice,
        two violins, and continuo.   Acc: 3-4 (VS)BH

5654.   Herr, der du stark und mächtig bist   Soprano
        CANTATA 10: Meine Seel' erhebt den Herren.   Text: Luke 1:46-55.
        c3-a4 g3-g4 Animated in lively tempo.   Generally spirited, vigorous,

and bold. Has florid passages and some wide intervalic skips. Requires flexibility. Scored for soprano voice, two oboes, strings, and organ. Acc: 4 (VS)BH

5655. R: Wir beten zu dem Tempel an
       A: Höchster, Höchster, mache deine Güte   Soprano
       CANTATA 51: Jauchzet Gott in allen Landen. Text: Johann Sebastian Bach (?). e3-a4 g3-e4 Sustained in moderate tempo. Starts
       gently. Has some florid passages. Generally on MF level. Scored
       for soprano voice and continuo. Acc: 3 (VS)BH. SSM

5656. Höchster Tröster, heil'ger Geist   Soprano
       CANTATA 183: Sie werden euch in den Bann thun. Text: Marianne
       von Ziegler. d3-a4 g3-f4 Generally sustained in moderate tempo.
       Has one florid passage and several florid figures. Scored for soprano voice, oboe da caccia 1 & 2 in unison, violin 1 & 2, viola,
       and continuo. Acc: 3-4 (VS)BH

5657. Hört, ihr Augen, auf zu weinen   Soprano
       CANTATA 98: Was Gott thut, das ist wohlgethan. Text: Samuel
       Rodigast. c3-ab4 g3-eb4 Sustained in moderate tempo. Has a
       few short florid passages. Generally on MF level. Climactic ending. Scored for soprano voice, oboe solo, and continuo. Acc: 3
       (VS)BH

5658. Hört, ihr Völker, Gottes Stimme   Soprano
       CANTATA 76: Die Himmel erzählen die Ehre Gottes. Text: Christian Weise (?). d3-g4 g3-e4 Animated vocal part in moderate tempo. Abounds in dotted rhythms. Has some wide intervalic skips.
       Requires flexibility. Scored for soprano voice, violin solo, and continuo. Acc: 3-4 (VS)BH

5659. Ich ende behende mein irdisches Leben   Soprano
       CANTATA 57: Selig ist der Mann. Text: Christian Friedrich Henrici. d3-g4 g3-f4 Animated in lively tempo. Has some florid passages. Requires flexibility. Has extended instrumental prelude and
       interludes. Scored for soprano voice, violin solo, organ, and continuo. Acc: 3-4 (VS)BH

5660. Ich nehme mein Leiden mit Freuden auf mich!   Soprano
       CANTATA 75: Die Elenden sollen essen. Text: Christian Weise (?).
       c3-a4 g3-f4 Sustained in moderate slow tempo. Graceful, has
       florid passages. Requires flexibility. Extended instrumental prelude
       and postlude. Scored for soprano voice, oboe d'amore solo, and continuo. Acc: 3 40B-S1, (VS)BH

5661. Ich säe meine Zähren mit bangem Herzen   Soprano
       CANTATA 146: Wir müssen durch viel Trübsal in das Reich Gottes
       eingehen. Text: Anon. c3-g4 a3-e4 Sustained in moderate tempo.
       Has some short florid passages. Requires some flexibility. Descending ending line. Scored for soprano voice, flute, oboe d'amore 1 &
       2, and continuo. Acc: 3 (VS)BH. BAS

5662. Ich wünschte mir den Tod   Soprano
       CANTATA 57: Selig ist der Mann. Text: Christian Friedrich Henrici. c3-ab4 g3-f4 Sustained in slow tempo. Generally on MF
       level. Extended instrumental prelude and postlude. Scored for two
       violins, viola, and continuo. Somber and grave. Acc: 3-4 40B-S2,
       (VS)BH

5663. Ihm hab' ich mich ergeben   Soprano
       CANTATA 97: In allen meinen Thaten. Text: Paul Flemming. c3-
       g4 e3-c4 Animated in moderate tempo. Has some florid passages,
       and a few wide intervalic skips. Descending ending line. Scored for
       soprano voice, oboe 1 & 2, organ, and continuo. Acc: 3-4 (VS)BH

5664. Jauchzet Gott in allen Landen   Soprano
       CANTATA 51: Jauchzet Gott in allen Landen. Text: Johann Sebas-
       tian Bach (?). e3-c5 a3-f4 Animated in moderate lively tempo.
       Florid; requires considerable flexibility. Requires brilliance. Cli-
       mactic ending. Scored for soprano voice, strings, trumpet, and con-
       tinuo. Acc: 4 (VS)BH

5665. Jesus soll mein erstes Wort   Soprano
       CANTATA 171: Gott, wie dein Name, so ist auch dein Ruhm. Text:
       Georg Christian Eilmar. d3-g4 e3-f4 Sustained in moderate tempo.
       Has some florid passages and florid figures. Extended prelude and
       postlude in the instrumental ensemble. Scored for soprano voice,
       solo violin, and continuo. Acc: 4 40B-S1, (VS)BH

5666. Komm in mein Herzenshaus   Soprano
       CANTATA 80: Ein' feste Burg ist unser Gott. Text: Martin Luther.
       e3-a4 g3-g4 Sustained in moderate tempo. Has some extended
       florid passages. Requires flexibility and a very fine command of
       high notes. Scored for soprano voice, organ, and basses. Acc:
       3-4 40B-S2, BAS, (VS)BH

5667. Lass' der Spötter Zungen schmähen   Soprano
       CANTATA 70: Wachet, betet seid bereit allezeit. Text: Salomo
       Franck. d3-a4 g3-e4 Animated vocal part in moderate tempo. Re-
       quires some flexibility. Generally on MF level. Gently climactic
       ending. Scored for soprano voice, two violins, viola, bassoon, and
       continuo. Acc: 3-4 (VS)BH

5668. Lass uns, O höchster Gott, das Jahr vollbringen   Soprano
       CANTATA 41: Jesu, nun sei gepreiset. Text: Johann Heermann.
       d3-a4 a3-f4 Sustained in moderate tempo. Graceful, requires flex-
       ibility. Has florid passages in the second section. Joyous. Ex-
       tended instrumental prelude. Scored for soprano voice, three oboes,
       and continuo. Acc: 3-4 40B-S2, AUK, (VS)BH

5669. Lebens Sonne, Licht der Sinnen   Soprano
       CANTATA 180: Schmücke dich, o liebe Seele. Text: Johann Franck.
       d3-g4 f3-f4 Animated in moderate tempo. Joyous. Has florid fig-
       ures and one florid passage. Extended instrumental prelude and post-
       lude. Scored for soprano voice, flutes 1 & 2, oboi 1 & 2, violins 1
       & 2, viola, and continuo. Acc: 3-4 (VS)BH, GS

5670. Mein gläubiges Herze   Soprano
       CANTATA 68: Also hat Gott die Welt geliebt. Text: Marianne von
       Ziegler. f3-a4 a3-f4 Animated in lively tempo. Bright, joyous,
       generally on MF level. Requires flexibility. Slightly climactic end-
       ing. For the better English version, see ASS-1. Scored for soprano
       voice, violoncello, piccolo, and continuo. Acc: 4 40B-S2, ASS-1,
       KAL. (VS)BH, (S)GS-high, medium, low

5671. Mein Jesus will es thun   Soprano
       CANTATA 72: Alles nur nach Gottes Willen. Text: Salomo Franck.
       d3-a4 f3-e4 Generally animated in moderate lively tempo. Has

some sustained notes. Graceful, with a few florid figures. Scored
for soprano voice, oboe, strings, and continuo. Acc: 3-4 (VS)BH

5672. Mein Seelenschatz ist Gottes Wort   Soprano
CANTATA 18: Gleich wie der Regen und Schnee vom Himmel fällt.
Text: Erdmann Neumeister. e♭3-a♭4 g3-f4 Sustained in moderate
slow tempo. Has some slightly animated vocal passages. Climactic
ending. Extended instrumental prelude and postlude. Scored for soprano voice, two flutes in unison, four violas in unison, and continuo.
Acc: 3-4 40B-S1, BAS, (VS)BH

5673. Meinem Hirten bleib' ich Treu   Soprano
CANTATA 92: Ich hab in Gottes Herz und Sinn. Text: Paul Gerhardt. d3-a4 g3-e4 Sustained in moderate slow tempo. Has some
grace. Requires some flexibility. Generally on MF level. Scored
for soprano voice, oboe d'amore, strings, and continuo. Acc: 3
(VS)BH

5674. Öffne dich, mein ganzes Herze   Soprano
CANTATA 61: Nun komm, der Heiden Heiland. Text: Erdmann
Neumeister. d3-g4 g3-d4 Sustained in slow tempo. Generally subdued and gentle. Has simpler melody than most Bach arias. A fine
excerpt for young voices. Scored for soprano voice, and violoncelli
(or organ). Acc: 3 (VS)BH. KAL

5675. Sei Lob und Preis mit Ehren   Soprano
CANTATA 51: Jauchzet Gott in allen Landen. Text: Johann Sebastian Bach (?). c3-c5 g3-e4 First part is a solo choral section in
sustained moderato; second part is animated, and a florid "Alleluia."
Requires flexibility. Climactic ending. Scored for soprano voice,
strings, trumpet, and continuo. Acc: 4 (VS)BH

5676. Seufzer, Thränen, Kummer, Noth   Soprano
CANTATA 21: Ich hatte viel Bekümmerniss. Text: Salomo Franck
(?). d3-a♭4 g3-e♭4 Sustained in rather slow tempo. Requires
some flexibility. Graceful, generally gentle. Extended instrumental
prelude and postlude. Scored for soprano voice, oboe solo, and continuo. Acc: 3 40B-S1, BAS, (VS)BH

5677. Stein, der über alle Schätze   Soprano
CANTATA 152: Tritt auf die Glaubensbahn. Text: Salomo Franck.
d3-g4 g3-e4 Sustained in slow tempo. Requires some flexibility.
Generally on MF level. Extended instrumental prelude and postlude.
Scored for soprano voice, flute, viola d'amore, and continuo. Acc:
3-4 40B-S1, BAS, (VS)BH

5678. Süsser Trost, mein Jesus kommt   Soprano
CANTATA 151: Süsser Trost, mein Jesus kommt. Text: Anon.
e3-a4 a3-f♯4 Very sustained in slow tempo. Has some florid passages. Requires flexibility. Extended instrumental prelude and postlude. Scored for soprano voice, one flute, one oboe d'amore, two
violins, viola, and continuo. Acc: 4 40B-S2, (VS)BH

5679. Was die Welt in sich hält   Soprano
CANTATA 64: Sehet, welch' eine Liebe hat uns der Vater erzeiget.
Text: I John 3:1 and Johann Sebastian Bach (?). d3-g4 f♯3-f♯4
Sustained in slow tempo. Has some long-sustained notes. Generally
on MF level. Scored for soprano voice, violin 1 & 2, viola, organ,
and continuo. Acc: 3 (VS)BH

5680. Wie lieblich klingt es in den Ohren   Soprano
CANTATA 133: Ich freue mich in dir. Text: Kaspar Ziegler. e3-
a4 a3-g4 Sustained in moderate tempo. Slower middle section.
Requires flexibility and good command of high notes. Extended instrumental prelude. Scored for soprano voice, two violins, viola,
and continuo. Acc: 4 40B-S2, (VS)BH

5681. Wie zittern und wanken   Soprano
CANTATA 105: Herr, gehe nichts in's Gericht. Text: Anon. c3-
ab4 g3-f4 Animated in moderate tempo. Has florid passages, some
wide intervalic skips, and some climactic passages. Agitated accompaniment based on repeated notes. Scored for soprano voice, and
solo oboe, violins 1 & 2, and viola. Acc: 3 (VS)BH

5682. Wir beten zu dem Tempel an   Soprano
CANTATA 51: Jauchzet Gott in allen Landen. Text: Johann Sebastian Bach (?). e3-a4 g3-e4 Sustained in slow tempo. Has two
florid passages. Generally on MF level. Scored for soprano voice,
strings, and continuo. Acc: 3 (VS)BH

5683. Wirf Gott, wie lang' ach, lange?   Soprano
CANTATA 155: Mein Gott, wie lang', ach, lange. Text: Salomo
Franck. c3-a4 g3-g4 Rather strictly timed recitative, with one
florid passage and an animated aria in moderate tempo. Majestic;
has some short, florid passages. Slightly extended instrumental postlude. Scored for soprano voice, two violins, viola, and continuo.
Acc: 3-4 40B-S1, (VS)BH

II. Contralto & Mezzo-Soprano

5684. Ach Herr! was ist ein Menschenkind   Mezzo-Soprano, Contralto
CANTATA 110: Unser Mund sei voll Lachens. Text: Anon. c#3-
d#4 f#3-d4 Sustained in slow tempo. Requires some flexibility.
Extended instrumental prelude and postlude. Scored for contralto
voice, one oboe d'amore, and continuo. Acc: 3-4 40B-C2, (VS)BH

5685. Ach lege das Sodom der sündlichen Glieder Mezzo-Soprano, Contralto
CANTATA 48: Ich elender Mensch, wer wird mich erlösen. Text:
Anon. bb2-eb4 eb3-c4 Animated in moderate tempo. Graceful,
requires some flexibility. Short. Scored for contralto voice, oboe
solo, and continuo. Acc: 3 (VS)BH

5686. Ach, schläfrige Seele   Mezzo-Soprano, Contralto
CANTATA 115: Mache dich, mein Geist, bereit. Text: Johann
Burchard Freystein. a2-d4 e3-c4 Sustained in moderate slow tempo. Animated, lively, florid middle section. Extended instrumental
prelude, interlude, and postlude. Scored for contralto voice, one
oboe d'amore, two violins, viola, and continuo. Acc: 3-4 40B-C2,
(VS)BH

5687. Doch Jesus will auch beider Strafe   Mezzo-Soprano, Contralto
CANTATA 46: Schauet doch und sehet, ob irgend ein Schmerz sei.
Text: Anon. g2-eb4 d3-c4 Sustained in moderate tempo. Has
some florid passages and climactic passages. Scored for contralto
voice, flute 1 & 2, oboe da caccia 1 & 2. Acc: 3-4 (VS)BH

5688. Du, Herr, du krönst allein   Mezzo-Soprano, Contralto
CANTATA 187: Es wartet alles auf dich. Text: Anon. bb2-eb4
f3-d4 Animated in moderate tempo. Graceful, has florid passages.

Requires some flexibility. Extended instrumental prelude, interlude, and postlude. A simplified version of "Domine Fili unigenite," from MASS IN G MINOR. Scored for contralto voice, oboe, two violins, viola, and continuo. Acc: 3-4 40B-C1, (VS)BH

5689. Du machst, O Tod, mir nun nicht ferner
      bange   Mezzo-Soprano, Contralto
      CANTATA 114: Ach, lieber Christen, seid getrost. Text: Johann Gigas. bb2-eb4 eb3-c4 Animated in moderate tempo. Vigorous, has some florid figures. Requires some flexibility. Scored for contralto voice, oboe, two violins, viola, and continuo. Acc: 4 40B-C2, (VS)BH

5690. Ein unbarmherziges Gerichte   Mezzo-Soprano, Contralto
      CANTATA 89: Was soll ich aus dir machen, Ephraim? Text: Anon. c#3-e4 f#3-d4 Animated in moderate lively tempo. Requires some flexibility, and some fluent enunciation. Generally on MF level. Scored for contralto voice, and continuo. Acc: 3 (VS)BH

5691. Gelobet sei dir Herr   Mezzo-Soprano, Contralto
      CANTATA 129: Gelobet sei dir Herr. Text: Anon. c#3-e4 e3-d4 Gently animated vocal part in moderate tempo. Graceful. Has impressive florid passages. Extended instrumental prelude, interlude, and postlude. Scored for contralto voice, oboe d'amore, and continuo. Acc: 3 40B-C1, (VS)BH

5692. Getrost! es fasst ein heil'ger Leib Mezzo-Soprano, Contralto
      CANTATA 133: Ich freue mich in dir. Text: Kaspar Ziegler. a2-e4 e3-c#4 Animated in moderate lively tempo. Has florid passages, climactic passages, and a descending ending line. Requires flexibility. Spirited and energetic. Scored for contralto voice, oboe d'amore 1 & 2, and continuo. Acc: 3-4 (VS)BH

5693. Gott ist unser Sonn' und Schild   Mezzo-Soprano, Contralto
      CANTATA 79: Gott, der Herr, ist Sonn' und Schild. Text: Anon. c#3-e4 e3-d4 Animated in moderate tempo. Spirited, has some short florid figures. Extended instrumental prelude, interlude, and postlude. Slightly agitated accompaniment. Scored for contralto voice, oboe, and continuo. Acc: 3-4 40B-C2, (VS)BH

5694. Gott, man lobet dich in der Stille   Mezzo-Soprano, Contralto
      CANTATA 120: Gott, man lobet dich in der Stille. Text: Christian Friedrich Henrici (?). a2-e4 e3-d4 Sustained in slow tempo. Has fast-moving florid passages. Requires considerable flexibility. Climactic ending. Difficult. Scored for contralto voice, oboe d'amore 1 & 2, violin 1 & 2, viola, and continuo. Acc: 3-4 (VS)BH

5695. Halleluja, Stärk' und Macht   Mezzo-Soprano, Contralto
      CANTATA 29: Wir danken dir, Gott, wir danken dir. Text: Anon. a2-e4 d3-b3 Animated in lively tempo. Spirited and vigorous. Has some florid figures. Bright and joyous. Requires some flexibility. Scored for contralto voice, organ obbligato, and continuo. See the tenor aria version under the same title. Acc: 3-4 (VS)BH

5696. Herr, was du willst, soll mir gefallen Mezzo-Soprano, Contralto
      CANTATA 156: Ich steh' mit einem Fuss im Grabe. Text: Christian Friedrich Henrici. a2(f2)-eb4 d3-d4 Sustained in moderate tempo. Has some animated passages. Vigorous and florid. Extended instru-

mental prelude and postlude. Scored for contralto voice, oboe, violins in unison, and continuo. Acc: 4 40B-C1, (VS)BH

5697. Hochgelobter Gottes Sohn   Mezzo-Soprano, Contralto
CANTATA 6: Bleib' bei uns, denn es will Abend werden. Text: Christian Friedrich Henrici (?). bb2-eb4 eb3-c4 Sustained in moderate tempo. Requires flexibility. Has some wide intervalic skips and some short florid figures. Scored for contralto voice, oboe da caccia, and continuo. Acc: 3-4 (VS)BH

5698. Ich sehe schon im Geist   Mezzo-Soprano, Contralto
CANTATA 43: Gott fähret auf mit Jauchzen. Text: Anon. b2-e4 e3-c4 Animated in moderate tempo. Has some florid passages. Requires flexibility. Climactic ending. Scored for contralto voice, oboe 1 & 2, and continuo. Acc: 3-4 (VS)BH

5699. Ich will dich all mein Leben lang   Mezzo-Soprano, Contralto
CANTATA 117: Sei Lob und Ehr' dem höchsten Gut. Text: Johann Jacob Schütz. a2-e4 e3-c#4 Animated in moderate lively tempo. Abounds in triplet figures. Requires flexibility. Has climactic passages and a climactic, descending ending line. Scored for contralto voice, flute, strings, and continuo. Acc: 3-4 (VS)BH

5700. In Jesu Demuth kann ich Trost   Mezzo-Soprano, Contralto
CANTATA 151: Süsser Trost, mein Jesus kommt. Text: Anon. a2-e4 d3-d4 Sustained in moderate tempo. Has some florid figures; requires some flexibility. Subdued ending. Extended instrumental prelude and postlude. Scored for contralto voice, oboe d'amore, two violins and viola in unison, and continuo. Acc: 3-4 40B-C2, (VS)BH

5701. R: Immanuel! Du wollest dir gefallen lassen
A: Jesu, dir sei Preis   Mezzo-Soprano, Contralto
CANTATA 142: Uns ist ein Kind geboren. Text: Erdmann Neumeister. c3-c4 d3-c4 Recitative and sustained aria in moderate tempo. Has a few florid figures. Generally on MF level. Scored for contralto voice, flute 1 & 2, and continuo. Acc: 3 (VS)GS-with English, BH

5702. Jesus, lass dich finden   Mezzo-Soprano, Contralto
CANTATA 154: Mein liebster Jesus ist verloren. Text: Christian Weise (?). b2-d#4 e3-b3 Sustained in moderate tempo. Graceful, and generally subdued. Has two short florid passages. Slightly climactic ending. Scored for contralto voice, oboe d'amore 1 & 2, violin 1 & 2 and viola in unison, and continuo. Acc: 3 40B-C1, (VS)BH

5703. Jesus schläft, was soll ich hoffen?   Mezzo-Soprano, Contralto
CANTATA 81: Jesus schläft, was soll ich hoffen? Text: Christian Weise (?). a2-d4 bb2-c4 Sustained in slow tempo. Subdued. Has two long-held b2's. A descending contour abounds in the melody. Extended instrumental prelude and postlude. Scored for contralto voice, two flutes, two violins, viola, and continuo. Acc: 3-4 40B-C1, MAA, (VS)BH

5704. Kein Arzt ist ausser dir zu finden   Mezzo-Soprano, Contralto
CANTATA 103: Ihr werdet weinen und heulen. Text: Marianne von Ziegler (?). b2-d#4 c#3-c#4 Animated in moderate tempo. Requires some flexibility. Has one florid figure. Generally on MF level. Scored for contralto voice, concert violin or flute solo, and

708 Solo Voice Repertoire

continuo. Acc: 3-4 (VS)BH

5705. Komm, leite mich, es sehnet sich mein
Geist   Mezzo-Soprano, Contralto
CANTATA 175: Er rufet seinen Schafen mit Namen. Text: Mari-
anne von Ziegler. b2-e4 e3-b3 Sustained in moderate tempo.
Graceful, generally on MF level. Scored for contralto voice, flute
1, 2, & 3, and continuo. Acc: 3 (VS)BH

5706. Kommt, ihr angefocht'nen Sünder   Mezzo-Soprano, Contralto
CANTATA 30: Freue dich, erlöste Schaar. Text: Christian Friedrich Henrici (?). a2-e4 e3-c4 Sustained in moderate tempo.
Graceful, with an interesting combination of syncopation and triplet
figures. Generally on MF level. Climactic ending. Scored for contralto voice, violin 1 & 2, organ, and continuo. Acc: 3-4 (VS)BH

5707. Leg' ich mich späte nieder   Mezzo-Soprano, Contralto
CANTATA 97: In allen meinen Thaten. Text: Paul Fleming. b2-
eb4 eb3-c4 Sustained in moderate tempo. Has florid passages; requires flexibility. Grave, generally on MF level. Climactic high
ending. Scored for contralto voice, violin 1 & 2, viola, organ, and
continuo. Acc: 3 (VS)BH

5708. Leget euch dem Heiland unter   Mezzo-Soprano, Contralto
CANTATA 182: Himmelskönig, sei willkommen. Text: Salomo
Franck (?). a2-d4 d3-b3 Sustained in slow tempo. Requires some
flexibility. Has some wide intervalic skips. Vocal line has some
suggestions of strong chromaticism. Scored for contralto voice, flute
solo, and continuo. Acc: 3 (VS)BH

5709. Liebt, ihr Christen, in der That   Mezzo-Soprano, Contralto
CANTATA 76: Die Himmel erzählen die Ehre Gottes. Text: Christian Weise (?). b2-d4 e3-c4 Sustained in slow tempo. Dark,
grave, and subdued. Scored for contralto voice, oboe d'amore, viola
da gamba, and continuo. Acc: 3 (VS)BH

5710. Mein Jesu, ziehe mich nach dir   Mezzo-Soprano, Contralto
CANTATA 22: Jesus nahm zu sich die Zwölfe. Text: Johann Sebastian Bach (?). bb2-eb4 g3-c4 Sustained in moderate tempo. Graceful, and moves along. Generally on MF level; no strong contrasts in
dynamics. Descending ending line. Scored for contralto voice, oboe
solo, and continuo. Acc: 3 (VS)BH

5711. Meine Seele, auf! erzähle   Mezzo-Soprano, Contralto
CANTATA 69: Lobe den Herrn, meine Seele. Text: Psalm 103:2
and parts of Psalm 67. d3-e4 g3-d4 Sustained in moderate tempo.
Graceful. Has florid passages. Slightly climactic ending. Scored
for contralto voice, oboe, violin, bassoon, and continuo. Acc: 3
(VS)BH

5712. Menschen, glaubt doch dieser Gnade   Mezzo-Soprano, Contralto
CANTATA 7: Christ unser Herr zum Jordan kam. Text: Martin
Luther (?). b2-e4 e3-c#4 Vigorous, in moderate slow tempo. Has
one florid passage. Slightly extended instrumental postlude. Scored
for contralto voice, oboi d'amore 1 & 2, two violins, viola, and continuo. Acc: 3-4 40B-C2, (VS)BH

5713. R: O sel'ger Christ

Ao: Herr so du willt
A: "Mit Allem, was ich hab' und bin"   Mezzo-Soprano, Contralto
CANTATA 72: Alles nur nach Gottes Willen. Text: Salomo Franck.
bb2-e4 e3-c4 Recitative, a sustained arioso, and an animated aria
in very fast tempo. Has some wide intervalic skips.   Requires flexibility. Has some florid figures. Descending ending line. Scored
for contralto voice, violins 1 & 2, and continuo. Acc: 4 (VS)BH

5714. Mund und Herze steht dir offen   Mezzo-Soprano, Contralto
CANTATA 148: Bringet dem Herrn Ehre seines Namens. Text:
Christian Friedrich Henrici. b2-e4 e3-d4 Sustained in moderate
slow tempo. Requires some flexibility. Graceful. Extended instrumental prelude and postlude. Scored for contralto voice, oboi 1 & 2,
tenor oboe, and continuo. Acc: 3-4 40B-C1, (VS)BH

5715. Murre nicht, lieber Christ   Mezzo-Soprano, Contralto
CANTATA 144: Nimm, was dein ist, und gehe hin. Text: Christian
Friedrich Henrici. a2-e4 e3-d4 Sustained in moderate slow tempo.
Graceful. Has some low tessitura in some passages. Extended in-
strumental prelude and postlude. Scored for contralto voice, two vio-
lins, and continuo. Acc: 3 40B-C1, (VS)BH

5716. Nichts kann mich erretten   Mezzo-Soprano, Contralto
CANTATA 74: Wer mich liebet, der wird mein Wort halten. Text:
Marianne von Ziegler. g2-e4 d3-c4 Animated in lively tempo.
Generally strong and energetic. Has florid passages; requires flexi-
bility. Scored for contralto voice, oboi 1 & 2, oboe da caccia, vio-
lin solo, strings, and continuo. Acc: 4 (VS)BH

5717. O Mensch, errette deine Seele   Mezzo-Soprano, Contralto
CANTATA 20: O Ewigkeit, du Donnerwort. Text: Johann Rist.
c#3-e4 f3-c4 Sustained in slow tempo. Grave and short. Has two
florid figures. Generally from P to MF level. Scored for contralto
voice, violins 1 & 2, viola, and continuo. Acc: 3 (VS)BH

5718. Schäme dich, o Seele   Mezzo-Soprano, Contralto
CANTATA 147: Herz und Mund und Tat und Leben. Text: Salomo
Franck. c3-e4 e3-d4 Sustained in moderate tempo. Has a few
florid figures. Generally on MF level. Extended instrumental prelude. Scored for contralto voice, oboe d'amore, and continuo. Acc:
3 (VS)BH

5719. Schläfert aller Sorgen Kummer   Mezzo-Soprano, Contralto
CANTATA 197: Gott ist unsere Zuversicht. Text: Anon. a2-e4
e3-d4 Very sustained in moderate slow tempo. Has animated, florid
middle section. Requires flexibility. Low and subdued ending. Extended instrumental prelude and postlude. Scored for contralto voice,
oboe d'amore, two violins, viola, and continuo. Acc: 3-4 40B-C2,
(VS)BH

5720. Schlage doch, gewünschte Stunde   Mezzo-Soprano, Contralto
CANTATA 53: Schlage doch, gewünschte Stunde. Text: Anon. b2-
d#4 e3-c#4 Sustained in moderate slow tempo. Extended instrumental prelude and postlude. Scored for contralto voice, two bells in E
and B, two violins, viola, and continuo. Acc: 3-4 40B-C1, (VS)BH

5721. Unerforschlich ist der Weise   Mezzo-Soprano, Contralto
CANTATA 187: Es wartet Alles auf dich. Text: Anon. c3-e4

      e3-d4 Sustained in moderate tempo. Has florid passages and synco-
pated figures. Requires considerable flexibility. Has climactic passages. Scored for contralto voice, violoncello, and organ obbligato.
Acc: 3-4 (VS)BH

5722. Vergib, O Vater   Mezzo-Soprano, Contralto
CANTATA 87: Bisher habt ihr nichts gebeten. Text: Marianne von
Ziegler. b♭2-e4 d3-c4 Sustained in slow tempo. Requires some
flexibility. Generally on MF level. Scored for contralto voice, oboe
da caccia 1 & 2, and continuo. Acc: 3 (VS)BH

5723. Von der Welt verlang' ich nichts   Mezzo-Soprano, Contralto
CANTATA 64: Sehet, welch' eine Liebe hat uns der Vater erzeiget.
Text: I John 3:1 and Johann Sebastian Bach (?). b2-e4 e3-c4 Sustained in moderate tempo. Has some wide intervalic skips and a few
florid figures. Requires some flexibility. Graceful, and generally
on MF level. Scored for contralto voice, oboe d'amore, organ, and
continuo. Acc: 3-4 (VS)BH

5724. Was Gott thut, das ist wohlgethan   Mezzo-Soprano, Contralto
CANTATA 100: Was Gott thut, das ist wohlgethan. Text: Anon.
a2-e4 e3-d4 Animated in slightly lively tempo. Graceful. Has
some slightly florid figures. Subdued ending. Extended instrumental
prelude and postlude. Scored for contralto voice, oboe d'amore, and
continuo. Acc: 3-4 40B-C2, (VS)BH

5725. Weh! der Seele   Mezzo-Soprano, Contralto
CANTATA 102: Herr, deine Augen sehen nach dem Glauben. Text:
Christian Friedrich Henrici (?). b2-e♭4 f3-c4 Sustained in slow
tempo. Generally dark, grave, and intense. Has some florid figures.
Scored for contralto voice, solo oboe, and continuo. Acc: 3
(VS)BH

5726. Wenn kommt der Tag   Mezzo-Soprano, Contralto
CANTATA 70: Wachet, betet, seid bereit allezeit. Text: Salomo
Franck. a2-d4 d3-b3 Sustained in moderate tempo. Has triplet
figures, one florid passage, and three florid figures. Generally on
MF level. Scored for contralto voice, violoncello obbligato, bassoon,
and continuo. Acc: 3 (VS)BH

5727. Wer Gott bekennt aus wahrem Herzensgrund Mezzo-Soprano, Contralto
CANTATA 45: Es ist dir gesagt, Mensch, was gut ist. Text: Anon.
b#2-d#4 e3-c#4 Sustained in moderate slow tempo. Has florid passages. Requires flexibility. Grave. Florid ending line. Scored for
contralto voice, flute, and continuo. Acc: 3-4 (VS)BH

5728. Widerstehe, doch der Sünde   Mezzo-Soprano, Contralto
CANTATA 54: Widerstehe, doch der Sünde. Text: Anon. f2-b♭3
c3-a♭3 Gently animated vocal part in slow tempo. Rather low tessitura, best for contralto. Extended instrumental prelude and postlude.
Agitated accompaniment. Scored for contralto voice, two violins, two
violas, and continuo. Acc: 4 40B-C1, (VS)BH

5729. Wie furchtsam wankten meine Schritte   Mezzo-Soprano, Contralto
CANTATA 33: Allein zu dir, Herr Jesu Christ. Text: Konrad Hu-
bert. a2-d4 d3-b3 Sustained in moderate tempo. Requires flexibility for the frequent intervalic skips. Generally on MF level. Scored
for contralto voice, violin 1 & 2, organ, and continuo. Acc: 3-4
(VS)BH

5730. Wo Zwei und Drei versammelt sind in
    Jesu theurem Namen   Mezzo-Soprano, Contralto
CANTATA 42: Am Abend aber desselbigen Sabbaths. Text: Paraphrase of Biblical verses by Johann Sebastian Bach or Christian Friedrich Henrici (?). b2-e4 e3-c4 Animated in moderate tempo. Slower middle section. Has florid passages and some wide intervalic
skips. Requires considerable flexibility. Scored for contralto voice,
oboe 1 & 2, bassoon, violin 1 & 2, viola, organ, and continuo. Acc:
3-4 (VS)BH

5731. Wohl euch, ihr auserwählten Seelen   Mezzo-Soprano, Contralto
CANTATA 34: O ewiges Feuer, o Ursprung der Liebe. Text: Johann Sebastian Bach (?). b2-e4 e3-d4 Sustained in moderate slow
tempo. Requires some flexibility. Gentle in certain passages. Extended instrumental prelude and postlude. Scored for contralto voice,
two flutes, two violins, viola, and continuo. Acc: 3-4 40B-C2,
(VS)BH

5732. Zum reinen Wasser er mich weist   Mezzo-Soprano, Contralto
CANTATA 112: Der Herr ist mein getreuer Hirt. Text: Psalm 23,
paraphrased by Wolfgang Musculus. b2-e4 d3-c4 Sustained in moderate tempo. Graceful. Has florid passages. Generally on MF
level. Scored for contralto voice, solo oboe d'amore, and continuo.
Acc: 3-4 (VS)BH

III. Tenor

Note: All range and tessitura indications are understood to sound one
octave lower than indicated.

5733. Ach, schlage doch bald, sel'ge Stunde   Tenor
CANTATA 95: Christus, der ist mein Leben. Text: Anon. c3-a4
g3-g4 Sustained in slow tempo. One step lower than the original.
Sad text. Extended instrumental prelude and interlude. Scored for
tenor voice, two oboi d'amore, two violins, viola, and continuo. Acc:
3-4 40B-T2, (VS)BH

5734. Adam muss in uns verwesen   Tenor
CANTATA 31: Der Himmel lacht, die Erde Jubiliret. Text: Salomo
Franck. c3-g4 g3-e4 Animated in moderate lively tempo. Generally on MF level. Short. Scored for tenor voice, violins 1 & 2,
viola 1 & 2, violoncello 1 & 2, and continuo. Acc: 3-4 (VS)BH

5735. An irdische Schätze das Herze   Tenor
CANTATA 26: Ach wie flüchtig, ach wie nichtig. Text: Michael
Franck. g2-e4 d3-b3 Animated in moderate lively tempo. Has two
florid passages, and climactic passages. Has instrumental interlude.
Scored for tenor voice, oboi 1, 2, & 3, organ, and continuo. Acc:
3 (VS)BH

5736. R: Ein Herz, das seinen Jesum lebend weiss
    A: Auf, auf, Gläubige!   Tenor
CANTATA 134: Ein Herz, das seinen Jesum lebend weiss. Text:
Anon. d3-b♭4 f3-f4 A short recitative and an animated aria in live-
ly tempo. Energetic and spirited. Generally climactic and strong.
Climactic ending. Scored for tenor voice, oboe 1 & 2, violin 1 & 2,
viola, and continuo. Acc: 4-5 (VS)BH

5737. R: Wie, hast du dich, mein Gott
       A: Bäche von gesalznen Zähren   Tenor
       CANTATA 21: Ich hatte viel Bekümmerniss. Text: Salomo Franck
       (?). c3-g4 g3-f4 Sustained aria in slow tempo. Slightly faster
       second section. Has florid passages. Generally subdued recitative.
       Scored for tenor voice, two violins, viola, and continuo. Acc: 3-4
       40B-T1, (VS)BH

5738. Bewundert, o Menschen   Tenor
       CANTATA 62: Nun komm, der Heiden Heiland. Text: Johann Sebas-
       tian Bach (?). c3-a4 a3-f4 Animated in moderate lively tempo.
       Has florid passages; requires flexibility. Has climactic passages.
       Scored for tenor voice, oboe 1 & violin 1 in unison, oboe 2 & violin
       2 in unison, viola, and continuo. Acc: 3-4 (VS)BH

5739. Der schädlichen Dornen unendliche   Tenor
       CANTATA 181: Leichtgesinnte Flattergeister. Text: Anon. c3-a4
       f3-f4 Animated in moderate tempo. Has florid passages. Requires
       flexibility. Graceful, with a florid ending. Scored for tenor voice,
       and continuo. Acc: 3 (VS)BH

5740. Die schäumenden Wellen von Belial's Bächen   Tenor
       CANTATA 81: Jesus schläft, was soll ich hoffen? Text: Christian
       Weise (?). d3-a4 g3-g4 Animated in lively tempo. Florid, re-
       quires flexibility. Very agitated and thick instrumental parts. Ex-
       tended instrumental prelude. Scored for tenor voice, two violins,
       viola, and continuo. Acc: 5 40B-T1, (VS)BH

5741. Die Welt kann ihre Lust und Freud'   Tenor
       CANTATA 94: Was frag' ich nach der Welt. Text: George Michael.
       c♯3-b4 f3-f4 Animated in moderate lively tempo. Has florid pas-
       sages and dotted rhythms. Requires flexibility. Has climactic pas-
       sages and a descending ending line. Scored for tenor voice, strings,
       organ, and continuo. Acc: 3-4 (VS)BH

5742. Die Welt sucht Ehr' und Ruhm   Tenor
       CANTATA 94: Was frag' ich nach der Welt. Text: George Michael.
       d3-a4 g3-g4 Alternating recitative and arioso section. Generally
       subdued. Slightly extended instrumental prelude and postlude. Scored
       for tenor voice, two oboi, and continuo. Acc: 3-4 40B-T2, (VS)BH

5743. Drum ich mich ihm ergebe   Tenor
       CANTATA 107: Was willst du dich betrüben. Text: Johann Heer-
       mann. f♯3-a4 a3-g4 Sustained in moderate tempo. Has one ex-
       tended florid passage. Generally on MF level. High tessitura.
       Scored for tenor voice, two flutes in unison, organ, and continuo.
       Acc: 3 (VS)BH

5744. Erfreue dich Seele   Tenor
       CANTATA 21: Ich hatte viel Bekümmerniss. Text: Salomo Franck
       (?). c3-a4 a3-f4 Animated in lively tempo. Energetic; has climac-
       tic passages. Requires flexibility. Scored for tenor voice, organ,
       and continuo. Acc: 3-4 (VS)BH

5745. Ermunt're dich   Tenor
       CANTATA 180: Schmücke dich, o liebe Seele. Text: Johann Franck.
       d3-a4 g3-g4 Animated in moderate tempo. Florid, requires flexi-
       bility. Has some octave intervalic skips. Extended instrumental

prelude, interludes, and postlude. Scored for tenor voice, flute, and continuo. Acc: 3-4 (VS)BH, GS

5746. Ewigkeit, du machst mir bange   Tenor
CANTATA 20: O Ewigkeit, du Donnerwort. Text: Johann Rist.
c3-ab4 g3-eb4 Sustained in slow tempo. Grave, intense, and has florid passages. Requires some flexibility. Scored for tenor voice, violins 1 & 2, viola, and continuo. Acc: 3 (VS)BH

5747. Gott, dem der Erdenkreis zu klein   Tenor
CANTATA 91: Gelobet seist du, Jesu Christ. Text: Martin Luther.
e3-g4 g3-e4 Animated in moderate tempo. Abounds in dotted rhythms. Energetic, in declamatory style. Climactic ending. Scored for tenor voice, oboi 1, 2, & 3, and continuo. Acc: 3-4 (VS)BH

5748. Halleluja, Stärk' und Macht   Tenor
CANTATA 29: Wir danken dir, Gott, wir danken dir. Text: Anon.
e3-a4 g♯3-f♯4 Animated in lively tempo. Spirited, vigorous, bright, and joyous. Broader second section. Has climactic passages. Scored for tenor voice, violin solo, organ, and continuo. See the contralto setting under the same title. Acc: 3-4 (VS)BH

5749. Handle nicht nach deinen Rechten   Tenor
CANTATA 101: Nimm von uns, Herr, du treuer Gott. Text: Martin Moller. d3-ab4 g3-e4 Sustained in moderate tempo. Has florid passages and long-sustained notes. Descending ending line. Virtuostic violin solo. Scored for tenor voice, solo violin, and continuo. Acc: 3 (VS)BH

5750. Hasse nur, hasse mich recht   Tenor
CANTATA 76: Die Himmel erzählen die Ehre Gottes. Text: Christian Weise (?). c3-g4 g3-e4 Sustained in moderate tempo. Energetic and spirited. Has extended florid passages. Requires some flexibility. Scored for tenor voice, viola da gamba, and continuo. Acc: 3 (VS)BH

5751. Hebt euer Haupt empor   Tenor
CANTATA 70: Wachet, betet, seid bereit allezeit. Text: Salomo Franck. c3-g4 g3-e4 Sustained in moderate slow tempo. Extended instrumental prelude and postlude. Scored for tenor voice, two violins, viola, and continuo. Acc: 3-4 40B-T1, (VS)BH

5752. Hilf, Jesu hilf   Tenor
CANTATA 147: Herz und Mund und Tat und Leben. Text: Salomo Franck. e3-a4 g3-f4 Sustained in moderate slow tempo. Florid. Has some wide intervalic skips. Scored for tenor voice, and continuo. Acc: 4 (VS)BH, CP

5753. R: Es kann mir nichts geschehen
A: Ich traue seiner Gnaden   Tenor
CANTATA 97: In allen meinen Thaten. Text: Paul Fleming. d3-ab4 g3-eb4 Sustained aria in slow tempo. Has florid passages; requires flexibility. Generally on MF level. Scored for tenor voice, violin solo, organ, and continuo. Acc: 3-4 (VS)BH

5754. Ich weiss dass mein erlöser lebt   Tenor
CANTATA 160: Ich weiss das mein erlöser lebt. Text: Erdmann

Neumeister. d3-g4 g3-e4 Animated in lively tempo. Majestic.
Has some short florid passages. Climactic ending. Extended instrumental prelude and postlude. Scored for tenor voice, solo violin,
bassoon, and continuo. Acc: 3-4 40B-T1, (VS)BH

5755. Ich will leiden, Ich will schweigen   Tenor
CANTATA 87: Bisher habt ihr nichts begeten in meinem Namen.
Text: Anon. f3-b♭4 g3-g4 Sustained in slow tempo. Has some
wide intervalic skips. High tessitura in some passages. Graceful.
Extended instrumental prelude and postlude. Scored for tenor voice,
two violins, viola, and continuo. Acc: 3-4 40B-T2, (VS)BH

5756. Ihr Menschen, rühmet Gottes Liebe   Tenor
CANTATA 167: Ihr Menschen, rühmet Gottes Liebe. Text: Anon.
d3-a4 g3-f4 Animated in moderate lively tempo. Has two florid
passages. Has some grace and some climactic passages. Descending ending line. Scored for tenor voice, violin 1 & 2, viola, and
continuo. Acc: 3 (VS)BH

5757. R: Es will der Höchste sich ein Siegsgepräng' bereiten
A: Ja tausendmal Tausend begleiten den Wagen   Tenor
CANTATA 43: Gott fähret auf mit Jauchzen. Text: Anon. d3-a4
f♯3-f♯4 Very animated in very lively tempo. Has one extended
florid passage. Has some wide intervalic skips. Requires flexibility.
Descending ending line. Scored for tenor voice, violin 1 & 2 in unison, and continuo. Acc: 3-4 (VS)BH

5758. Jesu, dir sei Dank   Tenor
CANTATA 142: Uns ist ein Kind geboren. Text: Erdmann Neumeister. g♯3-g4 a3-g4 Sustained in moderate tempo. Fairly high
tessitura. Short; requires flexibility. Scored for tenor voice, oboi
1 & 2, and continuo. Acc: 3 (VS)BH, GS

5759. Jesu, lass durch Wohl und Weh   Tenor
CANTATA 182: Himmelskönig, sei willkommen. Text: Salomo
Franck (?). d3-g4 f♯3-e4 Generally sustained in moderate tempo.
Has two florid passages. Generally on MF level. Descending ending
line. Scored for tenor voice, and continuo. Acc: 3 (VS)BH

5760. Jesus Christus, Gottes Sohn   Tenor
CANTATA 4: Christ lag in Todesbanden. Text: Martin Luther.
d♯3-f♯4 g3-e4 Sustained in moderate lively tempo. Majestic; ends
with "hallelujah" passages. A chorale. Scored for tenor voice, two
violins in unison, and continuo. Acc: 4 40B-T1, (VS)BH

5761. Kann ich nur Jesum mir zum Freunde machen   Tenor
CANTATA 105: Herr, gehe nichts in's Gericht. Text: Anon. d3-
a♭4 f3-e♭4 Sustained in moderate tempo. Has some wide intervalic
skips. Requires some flexibility. Generally on MF level. Scored
for tenor voice, horn, violins 1 & 2, viola, and continuo. Acc: 3-4
(VS)BH

5762. R: Der Heiland ist gekommen
A: Komm, Jesu, komm zu deiner Kirche   Tenor
CANTATA 61: Nun komm, der Heiden Heiland. Text: Erdmann
Neumeister. c3-f4 f3-d4 A recitative and sustained aria in moder-
ate tempo. Graceful and generally subdued. Scored for tenor voice,
violins 1 & 2, viola 1 & 2, organ, and continuo. Acc: 3 (VS)BH

5763. Kommt! eilet! stimmet Sait' und Lieder   Tenor
      CANTATA 74: Wer mich liebet, der wird mein Wort halten. Text:
      Marianne von Ziegler. d3-a4 a3-f♯4 Animated in fast tempo.
      Quite florid; requires considerable flexibility. Has climactic passages.
      Scored for tenor voice, strings, and continuo. Acc: 4 (VS)BH

5764. Man halte nur ein wenig stille   Tenor
      CANTATA 93: Wer nur den lieben Gott lässt walten. Text: Georg
      Neumark. d3-b♭4 a♭3-f4 Sustained in moderate slow tempo.
      Graceful, and generally subdued. Has one extended florid passage.
      Scored for tenor voice, strings, and continuo. Acc: 3 40B-T2,
      (VS)BH

5765. Mein Alles in Allem, mein ewiges Gut   Tenor
      CANTATA 22: Jesus nahm zu sich die Zwölfe. Text: Johann Sebas-
      tian Bach (?). d3-g4 f3-d4 Generally sustained in moderate tempo.
      Graceful. Has two short florid passages. Requires some flexibility.
      Climactic ending. Scored for tenor voice, violins 1 & 2, viola, and
      continuo. Acc: 3-4 (VS)BH

5766. Mein Jesus ist erstanden   Tenor
      CANTATA 67: Halt' im Gedächtniss Jesum Christ. Text: Christian
      Weise or Johann Sebastian Bach (?). e3-a4 b3-g♯4 Animated in
      moderate lively tempo. Majestic. Has some short florid figures.
      Climactic ending. Extended instrumental prelude and postlude.
      Scored for tenor voice, oboe d'amore, strings, and continuo. Acc:
      4 40B-T2, (VS)BH

5767. Mein Jesus soll mein Alles sein!   Tenor
      CANTATA 75: Die Elenden sollen essen. Text: Christian Weise (?).
      d3-g4 g3-e4 Animated in lively tempo. Has a few florid figures.
      Graceful. Scored for tenor voice, oboe, strings, and continuo. Acc:
      3 (VS)BH

5768. Mein liebster Jesus ist verloren   Tenor
      CANTATA 154: Mein liebster Jesus ist verloren. Text: Christian
      Weise (?). f♯3-a4 b3-g4 Sustained in moderate slow tempo. Agi-
      tated accompaniment in the middle section. Extended instrumental
      prelude and postlude. Scored for tenor voice, two violins, viola, and
      continuo. Acc: 3-4 40B-T1, (VS)BH

5769. R: Welt, deine Lust ist Last
      A: Mein Verlangen ist   Tenor
      CANTATA 161: Komm, du süsse Todesstunde. Text: Salomo Franck.
      c3-g4 f3-e4 Recitative and very sustained aria in moderate slow
      tempo. Has two short florid passages. Generally on MF level.
      Scored for tenor voice, violin 1 & 2, viola, and continuo. Acc: 3
      (VS)BH

5770. Meine Seufzer, meine Thränen   Tenor
      CANTATA 13: Meine Seufzer, meine Thränen. Text: Anon. d3-a♭4
      g3-e4 Sustained in moderate slow tempo. Grave. Has one florid
      passage. Generally subdued. Scored for tenor voice, flute 1 & 2,
      oboe da caccia, and continuo. Acc: 3-4 (VS)BH

5771. Nimm mich dir zu eigen hin   Tenor
      CANTATA 65: Sie werden aus Saba all kommen. Text: Christian
      Weise (?). d3-a4 g3-e4 Sustained in moderate tempo. Second sec-
      tion has florid passages. Extended instrumental prelude, interlude,

and postlude. Scored for tenor voice, two flutes, oboi da caccia, two horns, two violins, viola, and continuo. Acc: 3-4 40B-T1, (VS)BH

5772. O Seelen-Paradies   Tenor
CANTATA 172: Erschallet, ihr Lieder. Text: Salomo Franck (?). c3-g4 g3-f4 Sustained in moderate slow tempo. Has some slow-moving melismas. Extended instrumental prelude. Scored for tenor voice, two violins & viola in unison, and continuo. Acc: 3 40B-T1, (VS)BH

5773. Seht! was die Liebe thut!   Tenor
CANTATA 85: Ich bin ein guter Hirt. Text: Marianne von Ziegler (?). d3-bb4 ab3-g4 Sustained in moderate slow tempo. Tranquil, generally subdued, and lyric in style. Requires fine control of high notes. Scored for tenor voice, two violins & viola in unison, and continuo. Acc: 3-4 40B-T2, AUK, (VS)BH

5774. R: Was Gott den Vätern alter Zeiten
       A: Sein Same musste sich so sehr   Tenor
CANTATA 10: Meine Seel'erhebt den Herren. Text: Luke 1:46-55. d3-g4 a3-g4 Recitativo secco, and a sustained, short aria. Scored for tenor voice, violin 1 & 2, viola, and continuo. Acc: 3 (VS)BH

5775. Stürmt nur, stürmt, ihr Trübsalswetter   Tenor
CANTATA 153: Schau', lieber Gott, wie meine Feind'. Text: Johann Sebastian Bach (?). e3-a4 g3-f4 Animated in moderate lively tempo. Has some wide intervalic skips, and very fast-moving florid passages. Requires considerable flexibility. Strong and accented. Scored for tenor voice, violins 1 & 2, viola, and continuo. Acc: 4 (VS)BH

5776. Tröste mir, Jesu, mein Gemüthe   Tenor
CANTATA 135: Ach Herr, mich armen Sünder. Text: Christoph Demantius (?). c3-a4 g3-g4 Sustained in moderate slow tempo. Has one slightly extended florid passage. Extended instrumental prelude, interlude, and postlude. Scored for tenor voice, two oboi, and continuo. Acc: 3-4 40B-T2, (VS)BH

5777. Was des Höchsten Glanz erfüllt   Tenor
CANTATA 194: Höchsterwünschtes Freudenfest. Text: Anon. d3-g4 g3-f4 Sustained in moderate slow tempo. Majestic; has some florid passages. Requires flexibility. Scored for tenor voice, oboe, two violins, viola, and continuo. Acc: 3-4 40B-T1, (VS)BH

5778. Welch Übermaass der Güte   Tenor
CANTATA 17: Wer Dank opfert, der preiset mich. Text: Anon. d3-a4 a3-g4 Sustained in moderate tempo. Has some wide intervalic skips. Requires flexibility. Has one extended florid passage. Extended instrumental prelude and postlude. Scored for tenor voice, two violins, viola, and continuo. Acc: 3-4 40B-T2, (VS)BH

IV.   Baritone & Bass

5779. Ächzen und erbärmlich Weinen   Baritone, Bass
CANTATA 13: Meine Seufzer, meine Thränen. Text: Anon. g1-eb3 eb2-c3 Sustained in moderate tempo. Has climactic passages and one short florid passage. Descending ending line. Requires

flexibility. Scored for bass voice, solo violin, flute in unison with
violin, and continuo. Acc: 3-4 (VS)BH

5780. Auf, auf, mit hellem schall   Baritone, Bass
CANTATA 128: Auf Christi Himmelfahrt allein. Text: Marianne von
Ziegler. f♯ 1-e3 c♯ 2-d3 Animated in moderate lively tempo. Majestic, vigorous, and florid. Ends with a recitative section. Extended instrumental prelude and postlude. Scored for bass voice,
trumpet, two violins, viola, and continuo. Acc: 4-5 40B-B2,
(VS)BH

5781. Beglückte Heerde Jesu Schafe   Baritone, Bass
CANTATA 104: Du Hirte Israel, höre. Text: Christian Weise (?).
f♯ 1-d3 c♯ 2-c♯ 3 Gently animated, with low tessitura. The vocal
part moves in moderate slow tempo. Slightly extended instrumental
prelude. Scored for bass voice, oboe d'amore, two violins, viola,
and continuo. Acc: 3-4 40B-B1, (VS)BH

5782. Darum sollt ihr nicht sorgen   Baritone, Bass
CANTATA 187: Es wartet Alles auf dich. Text: Anon. g1-e♭3
d2-d3 Animated in moderate lively tempo. Vigorous. Has two florid
passages, and passages with high tessitura. Extended instrumental
prelude and postlude. Scored for bass voice, two violins, and continuo. Acc: 3-4 40B-B2, (VS)BH

5783. Das Brausen von den rauhen Winden   Baritone, Bass
CANTATA 92: Ich hab' in Gottes Herz und Sinn. Text: Paul Gerhardt. a1-e3 c2-c3 Animated in fast tempo. Very florid; requires
flexibility. Has some wide intervalic skips. Generally strong.
Scored for bass voice, and continuo. Acc: 3-4 (VS)BH

5784. Dein Geburrtstag' ist erschienen   Baritone, Bass
CANTATA 142: Uns ist ein Kind geboren. Text: Erdmann Neumeister. b1(e1)-c3 e2-b2 Animated in moderate tempo. Generally on
MF level. Has some florid passages; requires flexibility. Extended
instrumental prelude and postlude. The e1 is the last note, and may
be sung one octave higher. Scored for bass voice, violin 1 & 2, and
continuo. Acc: 3 (VS)BH, GS

5785. Dein Wetter zog sich auf von Weitem   Baritone, Bass
CANTATA 46: Schauet doch und sehet, ob irgend ein Schmerz sei.
Text: Anon. b♭1-e3 e♭2-c3 Sustained in moderate tempo. Majestic, has climactic passages. Has two extended florid passages, and
a climactic ending. Requires flexibility and agility. Scored for bass
voice, trumpet, violin 1 & 2, viola, and continuo. Acc: 4 (VS)BH

5786. Doch weichet, ihr tollen vergeblichen Sorgen   Baritone, Bass
CANTATA 8: Liebster Gott, wann werd' ich sterben. Text: Kaspar
Neumann (?). a1-e3 e2-c♯ 3 Animated in moderate lively tempo. Has
florid passages and some long-sustained notes. Requires flexibility
and fluent enunciation. Generally graceful. Extended instrumental
prelude. Scored for bass voice, flute, two violins, viola, and continuo. Acc: 4-5 40B-B1, (VS)BH

5787. Es ist vollbracht, das Leid ist alle   Baritone, Bass
CANTATA 159: Sehet, wir geh'n hinauf gen Jerusalem. Text:
Christian Friedrich Henrici. g1-e♭3 d2-d3 Very sustained in slow
tempo. Has florid passages. Generally gentle. Requires warmth

and very fine vocal control. Scored for bass voice, oboe, two violins, viola, and continuo. Acc: 3-4 40B-B1, (VS)BH

5788. R: Erwünschter Tag! sei Seele wider froh
       A: Fürst des Lebens, starker Streiter   Baritone, Bass
       CANTATA 31: Der Himmel lacht, die Erde jubiliret. Text: Salomo
       Franck. f1-d3 c2-a2 Animated in slow tempo. Has some wide in-
       tervalic skips, several short florid figures, and dotted rhythms.
       Dotted, agitated bass line in the accompaniment. Scored for bass
       voice, violoncello, and continuo. Acc: 3-4 (VS)BH

5789. Gewaltige, Gewaltige stösst Gott vom Stuhl hinunter   Baritone, Bass
       CANTATA 10: Meine Seel' erhebt den Herren. Text: Luke 1:46-55.
       f1-eb3 c2-c3 Animated in moderate lively tempo. Energetic and
       vigorous. Has some dramatic intensity. Has some florid figures.
       Requires flexibility and some fluent enunciation. Scored for bass
       voice and continuo. Acc: 3-4 (VS)BH

5790. Gute Nacht, du Weltgetümmel   Baritone, Bass
       CANTATA 27: Wer weiss, wie nahe mein Ende. Text: Johann G.
       Albinus and Johann Sebastian Bach. g1-eb3 c2-d3 Very sustained
       in slow tempo. Has short, florid passages. Descending ending line
       of close to two octaves with g1 as the last note. Extended instrumen-
       tal prelude. Scored for bass voice, two violins, viola, and continuo.
       Acc: 3 40B-B1, (VS)BH

5791. R: Wer mich liebet
       A: Heiligste Dreieinigkeit, grosser Gott   Baritone, Bass
       CANTATA 172: Erschallet, ihr Lieder. Text: Salomo Franck (?).
       g1-d3 c2-c3 Recitative with florid passages, and a majestic aria in
       moderate tempo. Has climactic passages. Scored for bass voice,
       trumpets 1, 2, and 3, timpani, and continuo. Acc: 3-4 40B-B1,
       (VS)BH

5792. R: Ach, unser Wille bleibt verkehrt
       A: Herr, so du willt   Baritone, Bass
       CANTATA 73: Herr, wie du willt, so schicks mit mir. Text:
       Christian Friedrich Henrici (?). g1-eb3 d2-d3 Slightly sustained
       recitative and sustained aria in moderate slow tempo. Somewhat
       grave, and generally subdued. Scored for bass voice, two violins,
       viola, and continuo. Acc: 3 40B-B1, (VS)BH

5793. Hier, in meines Vaters Stätte   Baritone, Bass
       CANTATA 32: Liebster Jesu, mein Verlangen. Text: Anon. g1-e3
       d2-d3 Sustained in moderate slow tempo. Graceful; requires some
       flexibility. Gentle, and generally subdued. Extended instrumental
       prelude and postlude. Scored for bass voice, solo violin, and contin-
       uo. Acc: 3-4 40B-B2, (VS)BH

5794. Hier ist das rechte Osterlamm   Baritone, Bass
       CANTATA 4: Christ lag in Todesbanden. Text: Martin Luther.
       e1-e3 e2-b2 Sustained in slow tempo. Grave; has a sustained e#1
       for 7 beats. Majestic, climactic, and has a "falling" ending with a
       full two-octave range in less than two measures. Scored for bass
       voice, violin 1 & 2, viola 1 & 2, and continuo. Acc: 3 (VS)BH

5795. Höllische Schlange, wird dir nicht bange?   Baritone, Bass
       CANTATA 40: Dazu ist erschienen der Sohn Gottes. Text: Johann

Sebastian Bach (?). g1-e3 d2-c3 Animated in lively tempo. Strong,
vigorous, and climactic. Has one short florid passage. Scored for
bass voice, oboe 1 & 2, violin 1 & 2, and continuo. Acc: 4
(VS)BH

5796. Ich will von Jesu Wunden singen   Baritone, Bass
CANTATA 147: Herz und Mund und Tat und Leben. Text: Salomo
Franck. g1-e3 d2-d3 Animated in moderate lively tempo. Florid;
has some long lines. Extended instrumental prelude and postlude.
Scored for bass voice, trumpet, oboe 1 & 2 (or violin 1 & 2), violin
1 & 2, viola, and continuo. Acc: 4-5 (VS)BH, CP

5797. Ja, ja, ich kann die Feinde schlagen   Baritone, Bass
CANTATA 57: Selig ist der Mann. Text: Christian Friedrich Henrici. g1-eb3 d2-d3 Animated in very lively tempo. Requires flexibility and fluent enunciation. Florid, vigorous, and outgoing. Extended instrumental prelude; agitated accompaniment. Scored for bass
voice, two violins, viola, and continuo. Acc: 4-5 40B-B2, (VS)BH

5798. R: Man kann hier von ein schön
A: Jesus ist ein Schild der Seinen   Baritone, Bass
CANTATA 42: Am Abend aber desselbigen Sabbaths. Text: From
the Bible, paraphrase by Johann Sebastian Bach and Christian Friedrich Henrici (?). a1-e3 c#2-d3 Short recitative and animated aria
in lively tempo. Energetic; has climactic passages. Quite florid;
requires considerable flexibility. Climactic ending. Scored for bass
voice, violin, bassoon, organ, and continuo. Acc: 4 (VS)BH

5799. Johannis freudenvolles Springen   Baritone, Bass
CANTATA 121: Christum wir sollen loben schon. Text: Martin
Luther or Christian Friedrich Henrici (?). g1-e3 c2-c3 Animated
in moderate lively tempo. Energetic, has florid passages. Requires
flexibility. Several phrases start with g1. Mainly a bass aria.
Scored for bass voice, violin 1 & 2, viola, and continuo. Acc: 4
(VS)BH

5800. R: Es bricht das Grab
A: Lasset dem Höchsten   Baritone, Bass
CANTATA 66: Erfreut euch, ihr Herzen. Text: Johann Sebastian
Bach (?). a1-e3 d2-c3 Animated in lively tempo. Energetic, and
generally strong. Has florid passages. Requires flexibility. Has
climactic passages. Scored for bass voice, oboi 1 & 2, bassoon,
strings, and continuo. Acc: 3-4 (VS)BH

5801. Mein Erlöser und Erhalter   Baritone, Bass
CANTATA 69: Lobe den Herrn, meine Seele. Text: Psalm 103:2
and from Psalm 67. a1-e3 e2-b2 Sustained in moderate slow tem-
po. Grave. Has some florid passages. Semi-climactic ending.
Scored for bass voice, oboe d'amore, strings, bassoon, and continuo.
Acc: 3 (VS)BH

5802. Meinen Jesum lass' ich nicht   Baritone, Bass
CANTATA 98: Was Gott thut, das ist wohlgetan. Text: Samuel
Rodigast. a1-eb3 eb2-c3 Animated in lively tempo. Vigorous.
Has some short florid passages, climactic passages, and a descending
ending line. Scored for bass voice, violin 1 & 2, and continuo. Acc:
3-4 (VS)BH

5803. Merke, mein Herze, beständig nur dies   Baritone, Bass
       CANTATA 145: So du mit deinem Munde bekennest Jesum. Text:
       Christian Friedrich Henrici. a1-e3 e2-d3 Animated in moderate
       lively tempo. Majestic and vigorous. Strongly rhythmic, florid, and
       requires flexibility. Extended instrumental prelude and postlude.
       Scored for bass voice, flute, two oboi d'amore, trumpet, two violins,
       and continuo. Acc: 4 40B-B1, (VS)BH

5804. O Menschen, die ihr täglich sündigt   Baritone, Bass
       CANTATA 122: Das neugebor'ne Kindelein. Text: Cyriacus
       Schneegass and Johann Sebastian Bach (?). c2(g1)-eb3 c2-c3 Ani-
       mated in moderate tempo. Has florid passages and passages with
       high tessitura. Requires flexibility. Descending ending line. Scored
       for bass voice, and continuo. Acc: 3-4 (VS)BH

5805. Schweig', aufgethürmtes Meer!   Baritone, Bass
       CANTATA 81: Jesus schläft, was soll ich hoffen? Text: Christian
       Weise (?). g1-e3 b1-c3 Animated in lively tempo. Has florid pas-
       sages and some long, sustained lines. Requires flexibility. Vigor-
       ous. Scored for bass voice, two oboi d'amore, two violins, viola,
       and continuo. Acc: 4-5 40B-B1, (VS)BH

5806. Selig ist der Mann   Baritone, Bass
       CANTATA 57: Selig ist der Mann. Text: Christian Friedrich Hen-
       rici. g1-eb3 e2-c3 Sustained in moderate slow tempo. Has some
       long sustained notes and long lines. Has florid passages, and a "fall-
       ing" ending. Extended instrumental prelude and postlude. Scored for
       bass voice, oboe 1 and violin 1 in unison, oboe 2 and violin 2 in uni-
       son, horn, viola, organ, and continuo. Acc: 3-4 (VS)BH

5807. R: Ach, soll nicht dieser grosse Tag
       A: Seligster Erquickungs Tag   Baritone, Bass
       CANTATA 70: Wachet, betet, seid bereit allezeit. Text: Salomo
       Franck. g1-f3 c2-d3 Extended recitative in moderate slow tempo,
       with a florid passage. Sustained aria in moderate slow tempo. Aria
       has a very florid and animated middle section. Requires flexibility.
       Scored for bass voice, trumpet, two violins, viola, bassoon, and con-
       tinuo. Acc: 4 40B-B1, (VS)BH

5808. So loschet im Eifer   Baritone, Bass
       CANTATA 90: Es reifet euch ein schrecklich Ende. Text: Anon.
       bb1-eb3 d2-b2 Animated in moderate lively tempo. Majestic and
       generally strong. Has one short florid passage. Descending ending
       line. Scored for bass voice, trumpet, violin 1 & 2, viola, and con-
       tinuo. Acc: 3-4 (VS)BH

5809. R: Siehe, siehe, ich komme
       A: Starkes Lieben, das dich, grosser Gottes Sohn   Baritone, Bass
       CANTATA 182: Himmelskönig, sei willkommen. Text: Salomo
       Franck (?). e1-c3 c2-b2 Animated in moderate tempo. Has some
       low notes and some wide intervalic skips. Mainly a bass aria.
       Scored for bass voice, violin, viola 1 & 2, and continuo. Acc: 3-4
       (VS)BH

5810. Streite, siege, starker Held!   Baritone, Bass
       CANTATA 62: Nun komm, der Heiden Heiland. Text: Martin Luther
       or Christian Friedrich Henrici. a1-e3 e2-c#3 Animated in moder-
       ate tempo. Florid, requires flexibility. Has climactic passages.

One-line accompaniment. Scored for bass voice, strings, and continuo. Acc: 3-4 (VS)BH

5811. Tag und Nacht   Baritone, Bass
CANTATA 71: Gott ist mein König. Text: Georg Christian Eilmar.
f1-e3 c2-c3 Sustained in slow tempo. Florid and animated middle
section, which also requires flexibility. Scored for bass voice,
flutes 1 & 2, violoncello, oboi 1 & 2, bassoon, and organ. Acc: 3
(VS)BH

5812. Verachtest du den Reichthum seiner Gnade   Baritone, Bass
CANTATA 102: Herr, deine Augen sehen nach den Glauben. Text:
Christian Friedrich Henrici (?). g1-eb3 eb2-d3 Spirited, has parts
that are marked. Has some short florid passages. Slightly climactic
ending. Generally animated in very fast tempo. Extended instrumental prelude. Scored for bass voice, two violins, viola, and continuo.
Acc: 3-4 40B-B1, (VS)BH

5813. Verstumme, Höllenheer   Baritone, Bass
CANTATA 5: Wo soll ich fliehen hin. Text: Johann Heermann.
a1-e3 c2-c3 Animated in very fast tempo. Vigorous, has florid
figures. Extended instrumental prelude, interlude, and postlude.
Scored for bass voice, two oboes, trumpet, two violins, viola, and
continuo. Acc: 5 40B-B2, (VS)BH

5814. Wacht auf, ihr Adern und ihr Glieder   Baritone, Bass
CANTATA 110: Unser Mund sei voll Lachens. Text: Anon. f#1-e3
d2-d3 Animated in moderate lively tempo. Majestic, vigorous, and
florid. Climactic. Extended instrumental prelude and postlude.
Scored for bass voice, two oboes, oboe da caccia, trumpet, two violins, viola, and continuo. Acc: 4 40B-B2, (VS)BH

5815. Wacht auf, wacht auf, verlorne Schafe   Baritone, Bass
CANTATA 20: O Ewigkeit, du Donnerwort. Text: Anon. g1-e3
c2-c3 Animated in moderate tempo. Vigorous, and majestic. Has
florid passages. Requires flexibility. Extended instrumental prelude
and postlude. Scored for bass voice, three oboi, trumpet, two violins, viola, and continuo. Acc: 4 40B-B1, (VS)BH

5816. Wahrlich, wahrlich, ich sage euch   Baritone, Bass
CANTATA 86: Wahrlich, wahrlich, ich sage euch. Text: Christian
Weise (?). g#1-d3 d2-b2 Sustained in moderate tempo. Energetic,
majestic, and broad. Scored for bass voice, violin 1 & 2, viola, and
continuo. Acc: 3 (VS)BH

5817. Warum willst du so zornig sein   Baritone, Bass
CANTATA 101: Nimm von uns, Herr, du treuer Gott. Text: Martin
Luther. g1-e3 c2-d3 Animated in very fast tempo. Has a few
florid passages, and some climactic passages. Descending ending
line. The interpolation of the chorale melody "Vater unser im Him-
melreich" is the interesting feature of this aria. Scored for bass
voice, oboi 1 & 2, viola, and continuo. Acc: 4 (VS)BH

5818. Was Gott thut, das ist wohlgethan   Baritone, Bass
CANTATA 100: Was Gott thut, das ist wohlgethan. Text: Samuel
Rodigast. a1-e3 e2-c3 Animated in moderate lively tempo. Has
climactic passages and some florid passages. Requires flexibility.
Climactic ending. Scored for bass voice, strings, and continuo.
Acc: 3-4 (VS)BH

5819. Weicht all', ihr Übelthäter   Baritone, Bass
CANTATA 135: Ach Herr, mich armen Sünder. Text: Christoph
Demantius (?). a1-e3 d2-d3 Animated in lively tempo. Has some
unusual florid passages. Requires flexibility. Descending ending line.
Extended instrumental prelude and postlude. Scored for bass voice,
two violins, viola, and continuo. Acc: 3-4 40B-B2, (VS)BH

Solo Excerpts from the Large Choral Works

See the very first entry of each large work for a fuller description.

I. Soprano

5820. Aus Liebe will mein Heiland sterben   Soprano
Work: MATTHÄUS PASSION, BWV 244. Texts arr. from the Bible
by Christian Friedrich Henrici. English title: The Passion According to St. Matthew. First English line: In love my Saviour now is
dying. e3-a4 a3-f4 Sustained in slow tempo. Has florid passages.
Requires fine P. Has climactic passages, and requires fine vocal
control. Scored for soprano voice, flute, and oboi da caccia 1 & 2.
Acc: 4 (VS)BH, CP-German; (VS)GS-English. KAL

5821. Blute nur, du liebes Herz   Soprano
Work: MATTHÄUS PASSION, BWV 244. First English line: Bleed
and break, thou loving heart. e3-g4 g3-e4 Sustained in moderate
tempo. Generally subdued and dark. The descending contour of
melodic phrases is an interesting feature. Scored for soprano voice,
flutes 1 & 2, strings, organ, and continuo. Acc: 3-4 (VS)BH, CP-
German; (VS)GS-English

5822. Flösst, mein Heiland flösst dein Namen   Soprano
Work: WEIHNACHTS-ORATORIUM, BWV 248. Texts arr. by Christian Friedrich Henrici from Luke and Matthew. English title: Christmas Oratorio. First English line: Ah! my Saviour! d3-g4 g3-e4
Gently moving vocal part in moderate tempo. Graceful; has some
florid passages. Requires some flexibility. May be performed without the choral excerpt. This aria has an "echo voice" (soprano).
Scored for soprano voice, echo voice, solo oboe, organ, and continuo.
Acc: 3 (VS)BH, CP-German; (VS)GS, NO-English

5823. Ich folge dir gleichfalls   Soprano
Work: JOHANNESPASSION, BWV 245. Texts by Barthold Heinrich
Brockes, after the Bible. English title: The Passion According to
St. John. First English line: I follow Thee also. d3-ab4 g3-g4
Animated in moderate lively tempo. Florid, bright, and gently joyous.
Requires flexibility. Extended instrumental prelude and postlude.
Often done too fast and in a flambuoyant manner. Scored for soprano
voice, flute 1 & 2 in unison, organ, and continuo. Acc: 3-4 (VS)BH,
CP-German; (VS)GS Mendel-English

5824. R: Wie wohl mein Herz in Thränen schwimmt
A: Ich will dir mein Herze schenken
Work: MATTHÄUS PASSION, BWV 244. First English line: R--
Although both heart and eyes overflow; A--Lord, to Thee my heart I
proffer. c3-g4 e3-e4 Animated in moderate tempo. Has florid
passages and some climactic passages. Requires flexibility. Scored
for soprano voice, oboe d'amore 1 & 2, organ, and continuo. Acc:

3-4 (VS)BH, CP-German; (VS)GS-English. KAL

5825. Laudamus te   Soprano
Work: MASS IN B MINOR, BWV 232. Texts: Liturgical Latin.
c♯3-e4 e3-d4 Sustained in moderate slow tempo. Florid; requires
flexibility. Has some long lines. Extended instrumental prelude.
With violin obbligato. Scored for soprano voice, violin solo, violins
1 & 2, viola, and continuo. Acc: 5 (VS)GS, BA, BH, CP

5826. Nur ein Wink von seinen Händen   Soprano
Work: WEIHNACHTS-ORATORIUM, BWV 248. First English line:
Naught against the power He wieldeth. c♯3-a4 a3-f♯4 Sustained in
moderate slow tempo. Requires flexibility. Has some florid figures.
Generally on MF level. Scored for soprano voice, oboe d'amore,
strings, organ, and continuo. Acc: 3-4 (VS)CP, BH-German texts;
(VS)GS, NO-English

5827. Quia respexit humilitatem   Soprano
Work: MAGNIFICAT, BWV 243. Texts: Luke 1:48 in Latin. d3-
f♯4 f♯3-e4 Sustained in slow tempo. Gentle, requires fine P and
PP. Extended instrumental prelude. Scored for soprano voice, vio-
lins 1 & 2, viola, organ, and continuo. Acc: 3-4 (VS)CP, GS, NO,
BH

5828. Zerfliesse, mein Herze   Soprano
Work: JOHANNESPASSION, BWV 245. First English line: Release,
O my spirit. c3-ab4 g3-g4 Generally sustained in moderate slow
tempo. Florid, requires flexibility. Requires fine command of high
notes. Sad text; requires straightforward approach instead of the already common sentimental tone. Extended instrumental prelude.
Scored for soprano voice, flutes 1 & 2, oboe da caccia 1 & 2, organ,
and continuo. Acc: 4-5 (VS)BH, CP-German; (VS)GS Mendel-English

II. Mezzo-Soprano and Contralto

5829. Agnus Dei   Mezzo-Soprano, Contralto
Work: MASS IN B MINOR, BWV 232. Texts: Liturgical Latin. a2-
eb4 d3-c4 Sustained in slow tempo. Subdued. Tessitura stays high
in several passages. Extended instrumental postlude. With violin
obbligato. Scored for contralto voice, violins 1 & 2 in unison, and
continuo. Acc: 3 (VS)GS, BA, BH, CP

5830. R: Nun wird mein liebster Bräutigam
A: Bereite dich, Zion   Mezzo-Soprano, Contralto
Work: WEIHNACHTS-ORATORIUM, BWV 248. Texts arr. from Luke
and Matthew. English title: Christmas Oratorio. First English line:
Prepare thyself, Zion. b2-e4 e3-c4 Animated in moderate lively
tempo. Graceful; has one florid passage. Scored for contralto voice,
oboe d'amore, violin, bassoon, organ, and continuo. Acc: 3 (VS)BH,
CP-German; (VS)GS, NO-English

5831. R: Du lieber Heiland du
A: Buss und Reu   Mezzo-Soprano, Contralto
Work: MATTHÄUS PASSION, BWV 244. Texts arr. from the Bible
by Christian Friedrich Henrici. English title: The Passion According
to St. Matthew. First English line: R--O blessed Saviour; A--
Bleed and break. b2-e4 f♯3-d4 Sustained in slow tempo. Scored
for contralto voice, flutes 1 & 2, organ, and continuo. Acc: 3

(VS)BH, CP-German;   (VS)GS-English

5832. Erbarme dich, mein Gott   Mezzo-Soprano, Contralto
       Work: MATTHÄUS PASSION, BWV 244. First English line: Have
       mercy, Lord, on me. c♯3-e4 f♯3-d4 Very sustained in slow tem-
       po. Has a few florid figures. Requires some flexibility. Has some
       slightly climactic passages. Scored for contralto voice, violin solo,
       strings, organ, and continuo. Acc: 3-4 (VS)BH, CP-German;
       (VS)GS-English

5833. Es ist vollbracht   Mezzo-Soprano, Contralto
       Work: JOHANNESPASSION, BWV 245. Texts by Barthold Heinrich
       Brockes, after the Bible. English title: The Passion According to
       St. John. First English line: It is fulfilled. b2-d4 d3-d4 Sus-
       tained, subdued, and quite slow section, followed by a vigorous, ani-
       mated, joyous, and florid section. Requires flexibility. Short ending
       phrase, repeated, as in the first section. Scored for contralto
       voice, viola da gamba, organ, and continuo. Acc: 5 (VS)BH, CP-
       German;   (VS)GS Mendel-English

5834. Esurientes implevit bonis   Low Mezzo-Soprano, Contralto
       Work: MAGNIFICAT, BWV 243. Text: Luke 1:53 in Latin. g♯2-
       d4 b2-c♯4 Sustained in moderate slow tempo. Florid. Requires
       flexibility. Has some passages with low tessitura. Extended instru-
       mental prelude and postlude. Scored for contralto voice, flutes 1 &
       2, organ, and continuo. Acc: 4 (VS)CP, GS, NO, BH

5835. Et exultavit spiritus meus   Mezzo-Soprano
       Work: MAGNIFICAT, BWV 243. Text: Luke 1:47 in Latin. c♯3-
       f♯4 f♯3-e4 Sustained in moderate tempo. Has gently-moving melod-
       ic figures and passages. Requires some flexibility. Extended instru-
       mental prelude and postlude. Scored for mezzo-soprano voice, vio-
       lins 1 & 2, organ, and continuo. Acc: 3-4 (VS)CP, GS, NO, BH

5836. R: Erbarm' es Gott!
       A: Können Thränen meiner Wangen   Mezzo-Soprano, Contralto
       Work: MATTHÄUS PASSION, BWV 244. First English line: R--O
       gracious God; A--If my tears be unavailing. c3-e♭4 g3-d4 Sus-
       tained and slow recitative with animated accompaniment in dotted
       rhythms. Sustained aria in moderate slow tempo. Abounds in dotted
       rhythms. Requires flexibility. Intense. Scored for contralto voice,
       strings, organ, and continuo. Acc: 3-4 (VS)BH, CP-German;
       (VS)GS-English

5837. Laudamus te   Mezzo-Soprano, Contralto
       Work: MASS IN B MINOR, BWV 232. c♯3-e4 e3-d4 Sustained in
       moderate slow tempo. Florid, requires flexibility. Has some long
       lines. Extended instrumental prelude. With violin obbligato in the
       full score. Scored for mezzo-soprano voice, violin solo, violins 1 &
       2, viola, and continuo. Acc: 5 (VS)GS, BA, BH, CP

5838. Qui sedes ad dexteram patris   Mezzo-Soprano, Contralto
       Work: MASS IN B MINOR, BWV 232. c♯3-e4 d3-d4 Sustained in
       moderate tempo. Florid, requires flexibility. Has some wide inter-
       valic skips. Generally from P to MF level. Extended instrumental
       prelude and interlude. With oboe d'amore obbligato in the full score.
       Scored for contralto voice, oboe d'amore, violins 1 & 2, viola, and
       continuo. Acc: 4 (VS)GS, BA, BH, CP

5839. Schlafe, mein Liebster   Mezzo-Soprano, Contralto
Work: WEIHNACHTS-ORATORIUM, BWV 248. First English line:
Slumber, beloved. a2-e4 e3-c4 Very sustained in slow tempo.
Has florid passages. Generally gentle and subdued. Scored for con-
tralto voice, flute, oboe d'amore, violins 1 & 2, viola, organ, and
continuo. Acc: 3-4 (VS)BH, CP-German; (VS)GS, NO-English

5840. Schliesse, mein Herze, dies selige, Wunder Mezzo-Soprano, Contralto
Work: WEIHNACHTS-ORATORIUM, BWV 248. First English line:
Keep, O my spirit. b2-e4 e3-d4 Sustained in moderate tempo.
Has climactic and strong passages. Descending ending line. Scored
for contralto voice, violin solo, organ, and continuo. Acc: 3
(VS)BH, CP-German; (VS)GS, NO-English

5841. R: Ach Golgotha, unsel'ges Golgotha!
A: Sehet, sehet, Jesus hat die Hand   Mezzo-Soprano, Contralto
Work: MATTHÄUS PASSION, BWV 244. First English lines: R--
Ah, Golgotha! unhappy Golgotha!; A--Look ye, Jesus waiting stands.
g2-eb4 eb3-db4 Very sustained in slow tempo. Emotionally intense and warm. Has florid passages. Requires flexibility. With
choral background: "Where? come where?" in the full score. Scored
for contralto voice, choir, oboi 1 & 2, strings, organ, and continuo.
Acc: 3-4 (VS)BH, CP-German; (VS)GS-English

5842. Von der Stricken meiner Sünden   Mezzo-Soprano, Contralto
Work: JOHANNESPASSION, BWV 245. First English line: From the
tangle of my transgressions. bb2-eb4 d3-c4 Sustained in moderate
slow tempo. Has some short florid figures. Requires some flexibility. Generally subdued, with a subdued, low ending. Scored for contralto voice, oboi 1 & 2, organ, and continuo. Acc: 3-4 (VS)BH,
CP-German; (VS)GS Mendel-English

III. Tenor

5843. Ach, mein Sinn, wo willt du endlich hin   Tenor
Work: JOHANNESPASSION, BWV 245. Texts by Barthold Heinrich
Brockes, after the Bible. English title: The Passion According to
St. John. First English line: O my soul, where wilt thou find thy
goal. e3-a4 g3-g4 Sustained in moderate slow tempo. Requires
fine high notes. In lyric style, generally subdued. Has extended prelude. Scored for tenor voice, violins 1 & 2, viola, organ, and continuo. Acc: 3-4 (VS)BH, CP-German; (VS)GS Mendel-English

5844. Benedictus qui venit   Tenor
Work: MASS IN B MINOR, BWV 232. Texts: Liturgical Latin. e3-
a4 g3-g4 Sustained in moderate slow tempo. Requires fine high
notes and flexibility. Mainly lyric, with no strong contrasts in dynamics. Extended instrumental prelude and postlude. With violin obbligato in the full score. Scored for tenor voice, violin solo, and continuo. Acc: 4 (VS)GS, BA, BH, CP

5845. Deposuit potentes   Tenor
Work: MAGNIFICAT, BWV 243. Texts: Luke 1:52 in Latin. c#3-
a4 f#3-f#4 Sustained in moderate lively tempo. Strong entrance.
Florid, requires flexibility. Has dramatic passages. Extended instrumental prelude and postlude. Scored for tenor voice, violins in unison, organ, and continuo. Acc: 4 (VS)CP, GS, NO, BH

5846.   Erwäge, wie sein blutgefärbter Rücken   Tenor
        Work: JOHANNESPASSION, BWV 245. First English line: Behold
        then how each living stripe. e3-a4 g3-g4 Sustained in moderate
        slow tempo. Requires very fine high notes and flexibility. Florid,
        with some passages rather extended. Difficult. Extended instrumen-
        tal prelude, interlude, and postlude. Scored for tenor voice, viola
        d'amore 1 & 2, organ, and continuo. Acc: 4 (VS)BH, CP-German;
        (VS)GS Mendel-English

5847.   Frohe Hirten eilt, ach eilet   Tenor
        Work: WEIHNACHTS-ORATORIUM, BWV 248. Texts arr. from Luke
        and Matthew. English title: Christmas Oratorio. First English line:
        Haste, ye shepherds. d3-a4 g3-e4 Animated in moderate tempo.
        Graceful. Has florid passages; requires flexibility. Ends with florid
        passages. Scored for tenor voice, flute, organ, and continuo. Acc:
        4 (VS)BH, CP-German; (VS)GS, NO-English

5848.   R: Mein Jesus schweigt
        A: Geduld, Geduld! wenn mich falsche Zungen   Tenor
        Work: MATTHÄUS PASSION, BWV 244. Texts from the Bible by
        Christian Friedrich Henrici. English title: The Passion According
        to St. Matthew. First English lines: He holds His peace; A--Be
        still, be still! if lying lips assail thee. e3-a4 a3-f4 Generally ani-
        mated vocal part in slow tempo. Generally on MF level. Slightly
        climactic ending. Animated accompaniment. Scored for tenor voice,
        oboi 1 & 2, organ, and continuo. Acc: 3-4 (VS)BH, CP-German;
        (VS)GS-English

5849.   Ich will nur dir zu Ehren leben   Tenor
        Work: WEIHNACHTS-ORATORIUM, BWV 248. First English line:
        'Tis Thee I would be praising. c3-g4 f3-d4 Animated in moderate
        lively tempo. Has florid passages, requires flexibility. Climactic
        ending. Scored for tenor voice, violins 1 & 2, organ, and continuo.
        Acc: 4 (VS)BH, CP-German; (VS)GS, NO-English

5850.   Nun mögt ihr stolzen Feinde schrecken   Tenor
        Work: WEIHNACHTS-ORATORIUM, BWV 248. First English line:
        Ye foes of man. d3-a4 a3-f#4 Sustained in moderate tempo. Has
        some short florid figures. Requires flexibility. Climactic passages.
        Scored for tenor voice, oboe d'amore 1 & 2, organ, and continuo.
        Acc: 3-4 (VS)BH, CP-German; (VS)GS, NO-English

5851.   Sanfte soll mein Todeskummer   Tenor
        Work: OSTER-ORATORIUM, BWV 249. Texts: Anon. English title:
        Easter Oratorio. c#3-a4 d3-f#4 Sustained in slow tempo. Has
        several long-held notes. Extended prelude, interlude, and postlude.
        Scored for tenor voice, two flutes, two violins, bassoon, and continuo.
        Acc: 4 40B-T2, (VS)BH-German & English; (VS)SC-German

                        IV.   Baritone and Bass

5852.   Betrachte, mein Seel'   Baritone, Bass
        Work: JOHANNESPASSION, BWV 245. Texts: Barthold Heinrich
        Brockes, after the Bible. English title: The Passion According to
        St. John. First English line: Bethink thee, O my soul. bb1-eb3
        eb2-d3 Sustained in moderate slow tempo. Mainly lyric in style,
        with no strong contrasts in dynamics. Short. "Bethink thee" is best
        substituted with "Consider." Scored for bass voice, viola d'amore

1 & 2, lute organ, and continuo. Acc: 3-4 (VS)BH, CP-German;
(VS)GS Mendel-English

5853. Eilt, eilt ihr angefocht'nen Seelen   Baritone, Bass
Work: JOHANNESPASSION, BWV 245. First English line: Run, run,
ye souls whom care oppresses. g1-e3 a1-d3 Animated in moderate
fast tempo. Florid. Has passages with low tessitura. Has treble
choral background in the full score. Extended instrumental prelude
and postlude. Scored for bass voice, mixed choir, violins 1 & 2,
viola, organ, and continuo. Acc: 4 (VS)BH, CP-German; (VS)GS
Mendel-English

5854. Erleucht' auch meine finstre   Baritone, Bass
Work: WEIHNACHTS-ORATORIUM, BWV 248. Texts arr. from Luke
and Matthew. English title: Christmas Oratorio. First English line:
O Lord, my darkened soul enlighten. b1-e3 e2-d3 Sustained in moderate slow tempo. Has florid passages. Requires flexibility. Scored
for bass voice, oboe d'amore solo, organ, and continuo. Acc: 3
(VS)BH, CP-German; (VS)GS, NO-English

5855. Et in spiritum sanctum   Baritone, Bass
Work: MASS IN B MINOR, BWV 232. Texts: Liturgical Latin.
f♯1-e3 c♯2-d3 Sustained in moderate slow tempo. Uses a wide
range considerably. Difficult. Has florid passages and long lines.
Low ending on a1. Extended instrumental prelude and postlude. With
oboe d'amore obbligato in the full score. Scored for bass voice, oboi
d'amore 1 & 2, and continuo. Acc: 3-4 (VS)GS, BA, BH, CP

5856. Gebt mir meinen Jesum wieder   Baritone, Bass
Work: MATTHÄUS PASSION, BWV 244. Texts arr. from the Bible
by Christian Friedrich Henrici. English title: The Passion According
to St. Matthew. First English line: Bring him back, is all my
prayer. g1-e3 d2-c3 Sustained in moderate tempo. Has some florid
figures and some wide intervalic skips. Requires flexibility. The violin solo is virtuostic. Scored for bass voice, solo violin, strings,
organ, and continuo. Acc: 4 (VS)BH, CP-German; (VS)GS-English

5857. R: Der Heiland fällt vor seinem Vater nieder
A: Gerne will ich mich bequemen   Baritone, Bass
Work: MATTHÄUS PASSION, BWV 244. First English lines: R--
The Saviour low before His Father bending; A--Gladly would I be en-
during. g1-e♭3 d2-c3 A descriptive recitative and a sustained and
graceful aria in moderate slow tempo. Requires a fine command of
high notes. Requires flexibility. Generally on MF level. Scored for
bass voice, violins 1 & 2 in unison, organ, and continuo. Acc: 3
(VS)BH, CP-German; (VS)GS-English

5858. Grosser Herr und starker König   Baritone, Bass
Work: WEIHNACHTS-ORATORIUM, BWV 248. First English line:
Mighty Lord, and King all-glorious. a1-e3 e2-d3 Animated in mod-
erate tempo. Majestic and vigorous. Has some short florid figures.
Climactic passages. Scored for bass voice, trumpet, flute, strings,
bassoon, organ, and continuo. Acc: 3-4 (VS)BH, CP-German;
(VS)GS, NO-English

5859. R: Ja! freilich will in mir
A: Komm süsses Kreus   Baritone, Bass
Work: MATTHÄUS PASSION, BWV 244. First English lines: R--

In truth, to bear the cross; A--Come, healing cross. a1-e3 d2-d3
Very sustained in moderate slow tempo. Requires some flexibility.
Has some florid passages, and climactic passages. Scored for bass
voice, viola da gamba, organ, and continuo in the aria. Acc: 4
(VS)BH, CP-German; (VS)GS-English

5860. R: Am Abend da es kühle war
       A: Mache dich mein Herze rein   Baritone, Bass
       Work: MATTHÄUS PASSION, BWV 244. First English lines: R--
       At evening, hour of calm and rest; A--Make thee clean my heart
       from sin. g1-eb3 c2-c3 Sustained in moderate slow tempo. Gen-
       erally gentle. Requires some flexibility and a fine command of high
       notes. Has some climactic passages. Scored for bass voice, oboe
       da caccia 1 & violin 1 in unison, oboe da caccia 2 & violin 2 in uni-
       son, viola, organ, and continuo. Acc: 3-4 (VS)BH, CP-German;
       (VS)GS-English

5861. Mein teurer Heiland   Baritone, Bass
       Work: JOHANNESPASSION, BWV 245. First English line: O Thou
       my Saviour. g1-e3 c2-d3 Gently animated vocal part in moderate
       slow tempo. Has some wide intervalic skips and some florid pas-
       sages. With choral background in the full score. Scored for bass
       voice, mixed choir, organ, and continuo. Acc: 3 (VS)BH, CP-
       German; (VS)GS Mendel-English

5862. Quia fecit mihi magna   Baritone, Bass
       Work: MAGNIFICAT, BWV 243. Texts: Luke 1:49 in Latin. g#1-
       d#3 c#2-c#3 Sustained in moderate tempo. Florid, has some
       strong passages, wide range, and a "falling" ending. "Mihi" is pro-
       nounced "miki," and "magna" is "manya." Scored for bass voice,
       organ, and continuo. Acc: 3-4 (VS)CP, GS, NO, BH

5863. Quoniam tu solus sanctus   Baritone, Bass
       Work: MASS IN B MINOR, BWV 232. g#1-e3 b1-c#3 Sustained in
       slow tempo. Has florid passages. Requires flexibility. Tessitura
       stays low in some passages. Mainly lyric, does not have strong con-
       trasts in dynamics. Extended instrumental prelude and postlude.
       With corno da caccia obbligato in the full score. Scored for bass
       voice, horn, bassoons 1 & 2, and continuo. Acc: 3-4 (VS)GS, BA,
       BH, CP

Excerpts from the Secular Cantatas

Listed according to the title of the excerpt. A fuller description of
the cantata is found in the very first entry of each work.

5864. R: Der Herr is gut
       A: Ach Herr Schösser   Baritone, Bass
       CANTATA 212 (BWV): Mer hahn en neue Oberkeet. English title:
       The Peasant Cantata. Texts: Picander (Christian Friedrich Henrici).
       d2-e3 e2-c#3 Animated in moderate tempo. Humorous text. Scored
       for bass voice, violin, viola, and continuo. Acc: 3 (VS)BH, EK

5865. Das ist galant   Soprano
       CANTATA 212 (BWV): Mer hahn en neue Oberkeet. Texts: Picander.
       d3-g4 g3-d4 Animated in moderate lively tempo. Slightly humorous
       text. Extended instrumental prelude. Scored for soprano voice,

violin, viola, and continuo. Acc: 3-4 (VS)BH, EK

5866. R: Du hast wohl recht
       A: Dein Wachstum sei feste   Baritone, Bass
       CANTATA 212 (BWV): Mer hahn en neue Oberkeet. Texts: Picander.
       b1-e3 e2-e3 Short recitative and an allegro aria with a middle sec-
       tion in moderate tempo. Has some short, florid passages. Scored
       for bass voice, violin, and continuo. Acc: 3-4 (VS)BH, EK

5867. Ei! wie schmeckt der Kaffee süsse   Soprano
       CANTATA 211 (BWV): Schweigt stille, plaudert nicht. Texts: Pi-
       cander. English title: Coffee Cantata. Part of Lizzie. d3-a4 a3-
       f4 Gently animated in moderate lively tempo. Graceful. Requires
       some flexibility. Humorous texts. Best for light voices. Scored
       for soprano voice, flute, and continuo. Acc: 3-4 (VS)BH, EK

5868. R: Und unsre gnäd'ge Frau
       A: Fünfzig Thaler baares Geld   Baritone, Bass
       CANTATA 212 (BWV): Mer hahn en neue Oberkeet. Text: Picander.
       b♭1-e♭3 e2-c3 Animated in moderate lively tempo. Bright, has
       humorous text. Scored for bass voice, violin, viola, and continuo.
       Acc: 3 (VS)BH, EK

5869. Hat man nicht mit seinen Kindern   Bass, Baritone
       CANTATA 211 (BWV): Schweigt stille, plaudert nicht. Texts: Pi-
       cander. Part of Schlendrian. b1-e3 d2-d3 Animated in moderate
       lively tempo. Requires fluent enunciation and flexibility. Has some
       high tessitura. Humorous text. Scored for bass voice, violins 1 &
       2, viola, continuo. Acc: 4 40B-B2, (VS)BH, EK

5870. Heute noch, lieber Vater   Soprano
       CANTATA 211 (BWV): Schweigt stille, plaudert nicht. Texts: Pi-
       cander. Part of Lizzie. d3-a4 g3-g4 Animated in moderate lively
       tempo. Requires flexibility. Has some florid figures, and humorous
       texts. Scored for soprano voice, violins 1 & 2, viola, cembalo, and
       continuo. Acc: 3-4 (VS)BH, EK

5871. R: Im Ernst ein Wort!
       A: Klein-Zschocher müsse so zart   Soprano
       CANTATA 212 (BWV): Mer hahn en neue Oberkeet. Texts: Picander.
       e3-a4 g#3-f#4 Sustained in slow tempo. Graceful; has some short
       florid figures. Extended instrumental interludes. Scored for soprano
       voice, flute, violins 1 & 2, and continuo. Acc: 3-4 (VS)BH, EK

5872. Mit verlangen   Bass, Baritone
       CANTATA 201 (BWV): Geschwinde, geschwinde, ihr wirbelnden Winde.
       Other title: Der Streit zwischen Phoebus und Pan. Texts: Picander.
       Part of Phoebus. b2-f#3 e2-d3 Sustained in slow tempo. Florid,
       requires flexibility. High tessitura. Somewhat thick accompaniment.
       Extended instrumental prelude, interlude, and postlude. Scored for
       bass voice, flute, oboe d'amore, two violins, viola, and continuo.
       Acc: 4 40B-B2, (VS)BH

5873. Patron, das macht der Wind!   Soprano
       CANTATA 201 (BWV): Geschwinde, geschwinde, ihr wirbelnden Winde.
       Texts: Picander. Part of Momus. d3-a4 g3-f#4 Animated in live-
       ly tempo. Requires fluent enunciation. Generally on MF level.
       Scored for soprano voice, and continuo. Acc: 3-4 40B-S1, (VS)BH

5874. Ruhet hie, matte Sinne   Soprano
       CANTATA 210a (BWV): O angenehme Melodei. Texts: Picander (?).
       d♯3-a4 f♯3-f♯4 Sustained in moderate slow tempo. Graceful, gen-
       erally gentle, generally on MF level. Extended instrumental prelude
       and postlude. Scored for soprano voice, oboe d'amore, violin, and
       continuo. Acc: 3-4 40B-S2, (VS)BH

5875. Schafe können sicher weiden   Soprano
       CANTATA 208 (BWV): Was mir behagt, ist nur die muntre Jagd.
       Other title: Geburtstag Kantate. English title: Birthday Cantata.
       Written for Prince Ernst August von Sachsen-Weissenfels. Texts:
       Salomo Franck. f3-ab4 bb3-f4 Sustained in moderate tempo. Gen-
       erally on MF level. Delicate and short. Scored for soprano voice,
       flutes 1 & 2, and continuo. Acc: 3 (VS)BH

5876. R: Es bleibt dabei
       A: Unser trefflicher lieber Kammerherr   Soprano
       CANTATA 212 (BWV): Mer hahn en neue Oberkeet. Texts: Picander.
       e3-a4 a♯3-f♯4 Sustained in moderate slow tempo. Joyous and
       bright. Scored for soprano voice, violin, viola, and continuo. Acc:
       3 (VS)BH, EK

5877. Wie will ich lustig lachen   Bass
       CANTATA 205 (BWV): Zerreisset, zersprenget, zertrümmert die
       Gruft. Other title: Der zufriedengestellte Aeolus. Texts: Christian
       Friedrich Henrici. f♯1-f♯3 e2-e3 Animated in moderate lively tem-
       po. Strong, florid, and vigorous. Requires considerable flexibility.
       Dramatic ending with a "falling" final syllable. Scored for bass voice,
       violins 1 & 2, viola, and continuo. Acc: 4 (VS)BH

Note: Edwin F. Kalmus issued a collection of J. S. Bach arias with an ob-
       bligato instrument for each:

5878. Arias from Church Cantatas for soprano, with an Obligato [sic] Instru-
       ment and Piano or Organ. German texts, with an English version by
       Jane May.

       (1) Auch mit gedämpften, schwachen Stimmen. Violin obbligato.
       From CANTATA 36: Schwingt freudig euch empor.

       (2) Die Armen will der Herr umarmen. Unison violins obbligato.
       From CANTATA 186: Ärgre dich, o Seele nicht.

       (3) Es halt' es mit der blinden Welt. Oboe obbligato. From CAN-
       TATA 94: Was frag' ich nach der Welt.

       (4) Gerechter Gott, ach, rechnest du. Oboe obbligato. From CAN-
       TATA 89: Was soll ich aus dir machen, Ephraim.

       (5) Gott versorget alles Leben. Oboe obbligato. From CANTATA
       187: Es wartet alles auf dich.

       (6) Höchster, was ich habe. Unison flutes. From CANTATA 39:
       Brich dem Hungrigen dein Brot.

       (7) Hört, ihr Augen, auf zu weinen. Oboe obbligato. From CANTA-
       TA 98: Was Gott tut, das ist wohlgetan.

(8) Ich bin vergnügt in meinem Leiden.   Violin obbligato.   From CANTATA 58: Ach Gott, wie manches Herzeleid.

(9) Ich ende behende mein irdisches Leben.   Violin obbligato.   From CANTATA 57: Selig ist der Mann.

(10) Ich nehme mein Leiden mit Freuden auf mich.   Oboe obbligato. From CANTATA 75: Die Elenden sollen essen.

(11) Ich will auf den Herren schau'n.   Oboe obbligato.   From CANTATA 93: Wer nur den lieben Gott lässt walten.

(12) Seufzer, Tränen, Kummer, Not.   Oboe obbligato.   From CANTATA 21: Ich hatte viel Bekümmernis.

B.   GEORGE FRIDERIC (GEORG FRIEDRICH) HANDEL (HÄNDEL), 1685-1759

Handel, international musician in background, practice and reputation, is also one of the most written-about composers in history.   Numerous books and articles about him and his works attest to his importance as a figure in the world of music.

Handel wrote in many forms, and in them he used or fused his German, Italian, and English influences.   In the area of music for the solo voice, the bulk of his production is in his stage works and oratorios.   Handel was mainly a dramatic composer, and in the dramatic form are found his very best solo compositions.   Although he wrote songs--airs and Lieder-- they have not become as well-known as his dramatic excerpts.

Handel was one of the most practical musicians for the simple fact that he wrote music for his day and age.   It is the type of music that easily became popular and highly regarded.   He also accommodated the needs of all voices, from coloratura sopranos to coloratura basses.   He wrote for some of the virtuoso voices of his time as well as for the average musician.   The diatonic character of his melodies goes extremely well with the voice and provides for rewarding artistic experiences.   Student singers in slightly advanced stages of development will find many Handelian airs that suit their voices.   Another practical aspect of Handel airs is the fact that most of them can be conveniently transposed to other voices and be made to sound well.   This is because the ranges of Handel's airs are not vocally demanding. Today, when excerpts from most of his operas are no longer closely associated with the large works to which they belong, most of them may be sung separately by any man's or woman's voice that would textually suit its character.   The operas of Handel's day move much too slowly for the 20th century appetite for action, and for this reason most of them have not been revived.

There are numerous editions of Handel arias and they vary considerably in editorial scholarship.   The editions included in this chapter are among the most reliable.   When there are some editorial flaws or intentioned changes, one can set them straight by simply referring to copies of complete editions such as the Handel Gesselschaft.   Very recently, Gregg International of London reprinted the Handel complete works.   This new complete edition is smaller in size and clear in format.   Most music libraries own this edition. Vocal scores of Handel oratorios are available in many modern editions, mainly German, British, and American.

Some pointers in the performance of Handel arias may be of help:

1)   As in the music of his great contemporary, Johann Sebastian Bach, Handel's melodies are composed of the long and stretched Baroque lines. This form must be kept in performance whether or not the lines are punctuated with frequent pauses or rest signs for the purpose of dramatic interpretation.   Please see references to "Where'er you walk" and "Lascia ch'io pianga" in the Preface of this book.

2)   The Romantic Period type of rubato must be avoided, as well as ritards at the ends of sections or entire aria, if they are not indicated. Sometimes the privilege to control any performance is abused.   Usually

Handel writes an "Adagio" at the end. This "Adagio" is his ritard, and one should not ritard some more on the "Adagio" itself. There is also a tendency of many singers to execute a ritard on the last phrase when the instrumental part (or piano) has material that moves, sometimes urgently, into a brief section that forms the instrumental postlude. This should also be avoided. Rhythms and tempi must be kept steady though not rigid.

3) Handel melodies require a type of vocalization that is basically Italianate, with pure vowels and exultant lyricism. Handel's writing for the voice clearly shows his Italian training and exposure, and it is this one aspect that helps to keep his vocal music in the limelight to this day. His melodies are all very singable, and must always be allowed to emote with artistic freedom. There is much also that is majestic and follows a semblance of formal dignity. This is due to his German upbringing. Again, these aspects must never be so exaggerated as to sound ponderous and overbearing.

The many-faceted Handel knew how to write well music in varied moods. One can find contrasts even when considering just a few examples: the tenderness of "O sleep, why dost thou leave me" from SEMELE, the pathos of "Ah! mio cor" from ALCINA, the quiet dignity of "Ombra mai fu" from SERSE, the glorious exultation of "Rejoice" from MESSIAH, and the deep-felt penitence of "Vouchsafe, O Lord" from DETTINGEN TE DEUM.

Every singer, amateur and professional, active or not so active musically, should have in his repertoire or knowledge a few arias by Handel. It is unfortunate that generally Handel is credited only for MESSIAH, but great as this work is, it barely touches the mark of his genius. When considering his entire career, one finds that Handel was more of an operatic or dramatic composer than a church musician. In fact, his MESSIAH was not even written for the church but for the concert hall.

The solo works of Handel included in this reference are classified under the following divisions:
I. Solo Excerpts from the Operas
II. Solo Excerpts from Secular Choral Works
III. Solo Excerpts from the Oratorios
IV. Solo Excerpts from Passions and Extended Anthems
V. Solo Cantata
VI. Incidental Music for "Alceste," a Play
VII. Works of Doubtful Authenticity

CSH   A Collection of Songs. G. F. Handel. Seven volumes, one each for the following: I--Light Soprano; II--Dramatic Soprano; III--Mezzo-Soprano; IV--Contralto; V--Tenor; VI--Baritone; VII--Bass. Edited and arranged by Walter Ford and Rupert Erlebach. Original keys, except "Subtle love." London: Boosey & Hawkes. (Note: Has fine notes on the arias and an appendix entitled "Some Hints on the Singing of Handel." "The Triumph of Time and Truth" is simply listed as "Time and Truth." CSH-1 means light soprano volume, etc.)

WGH   The Works of George Frederic Handel. Complete edition, with notes and translations in English. Ninety-seven volumes printed as 84. Original keys. Printed for the German Handel Society, Leipzig. Republished 1965 by Gregg Press, Inc., Ridgewood, New Jersey. (In this monumental edition, some of the excerpts can be directly read from these scores since pianoforte parts often duplicate the notation

734 Solo Voice Repertoire

of other instruments. Reference to the code of this edition is limited
here to only the few materials for which separate editions have not
been made available. It is of course understood that all the entries
reviewed are found in this edition of the complete works in their full
scores.)

6IA   6 Italian Arias for Soprano & Piano (or Soprano, Violin Obbligato and
       Piano). Two volumes. George Frederick Handel. Italian texts only.
       Frankfurt & New York: C. F. Peters.

15A   15 Arias for High Voice. George Frederick Handel. Edited by Wolff.
       New York: G. Schirmer, Inc. (Note: English versions accompany
       the Italian texts.)

45A   45 Arias from Operas and Oratorios. Three volumes. High, Low.
       George Frederick Handel. Edited by Sergius Kagen. New York:
       International Music Co. (Note: English translations are printed un-
       under the titles.)

(VS)-JC MESSIAH. George Frederick Handel. Vocal score edited by Jacob
         Maurice Coopersmith. New York: Carl Fischer, Inc. (Includes
         notes and explanations. The Appendix is a collection of different ver-
         sions of the arias used in Handel's time. A very fine, scholarly,
         and authoritative edition. Highly recommended.)

(VS)-WS MESSIAH. George Frederick Handel. Vocal score edited by Wat-
         kins Shaw. London: Novello & Co. , Ltd. (Note: This edition in-
         cludes notes and explanations, several versions of the arias and reci-
         tatives with as little editing as possible, ornamentation of arias, etc.
         A very fine edition, scholarly and authoritative. It also gives some
         facts regarding performance of the work not mentioned in other edi-
         tions.)

Note: Other editions of MESSIAH are published by G. Schirmer, C. F.
       Peters, and other firms.

I. Solo Excerpts from the Operas

A. Soprano

AGRIPPINA
Opera 1708 or 1709, libretto by Vincenzo Grimani.

5879. Bel piacere è godere   Soprano
       Part of Poppea, Act III. d3-g4 g3-e4 Animated in moderate lively
       tempo. Requires some flexibility. In the full score, this air is pre-
       ceded by a brief recitative: Piega pur del mio cor. Acc: 3 (S)IM

5880. Pensieri, voi mi tormentate   Soprano
       Part of Agrippina, Act II. e3-g4 g3-f4 Sustained in moderate tem-
       po. Slightly faster middle section. Has one recitative passage and
       two long-sustained, only slightly florid passages. Acc: 3 15A

ALCINA
Opera 1735, libretto by Antonio Marchi, after Lodovico Ariosto's
Orlando Furioso.

5881. Ama, sospira, ma non ti offende   Soprano
Part of Morgana, Act II. e3-a4 a3-g4 Sustained in moderate slow
tempo. Has some long-held high notes and slightly florid figures.
Somewhat climactic ending. Acc: 3-4 LFL-3

ARIODANTE
Opera 1734, libretto by Antonio Salvi, based on Lodovico Ariosto's
Orlando Furioso.

5882. Il mio crudel martoro   Soprano
Part of Ginevra, Act II. e3-g4 g3-e4 Sustained in slow tempo. In
quasi-recitative. Generally subdued. Descending and slow ending line.
Acc: 3 6IA-2

ARMINIO
Opera 1736, libretto by Antonio Salvi, with alterations.

5883. Al furor che ti consiglia   Soprano
Part of Tusnelda, Act II. e3-a4 g3-e4 Sustained in moderate slow
tempo. Starts gently. Has strong middle section. Acc: 3 6IA-1

ATALANTA
Opera 1736, libretto adapted from Belisario Valeriani's La Caccia in
Etolia.

5884. Care selve   Soprano
Part of Meleagro, Act I. f#3-a4 a3-f#4 Very sustained in very
slow tempo. Gentle and very lyric in quality. A favorite Handel air.
Acc: 3 45A, POS-3, SVR-2, 15A. (S)IM-high, low

5885. Un cenno leggiadretto   Soprano
Part of Atalanta, Act I. d#3-g#4 f#3-e4 Animated in lively tempo.
Requires fluent enunciation. Has a couple of florid figures. Requires
some flexibility. A recitative precedes the aria in the full score:
Per rapir quel tesoro. Acc: 3 15A

DEIDAMIA
Opera 1740, libretto by Paolo Rolli.

5886. Se il timore   Soprano
Part of Deidamia, Act II. e#3-g#4 g#3-e4 Sustained in slow tempo. Generally gentle. Has some climactic passages. Preceded by
a recitative in the full score: Lusinghe allettatrici. Acc: 3 6IA-2

FLORIDANTE
Opera 1721, libretto by Paolo Rolli.

5887. R: Servasi alla mia bella
A: Amor commanda   Soprano
Part of Timante, Act III. f#3-a4(bb4) a3-g4 Animated vocal part
in moderate tempo. Has some high tessitura, florid figures, and
some wide intervalic skips. Has an alternate section in the full score.
Acc: 3-4 (S)IM

GIULIO CESARE
Opera 1724, libretto by Nicola Francesco Haym.

5888. R: E pur cosi in un giorno
A: Piangerò la sorte mia
                                                                     Soprano

Part of Cleopatra, Act III.   e3-a4   g#3-e4   Recitative and a Da Capo
air, first very slow and sustained, then lively, animated, and florid.
Acc: 3-4 54A-3, AAP-3, 15A

5889. Svegliatevi nel core   Soprano
Part of Sesto, Act I. c3-f4(g4) g3-eb4 Slightly animated vocal part
in moderate tempo. Requires some flexibility. Has some octave intervalic skips. Agitated accompaniment. This appears with recitative in the full score: Vani sono i lamenti. Acc: 3-4 15A

5890. V'adoro, pupille, saette d'Amore   Soprano
Part of Cleopatra, Act II. f3-g4 a3-g4 Sustained in slow tempo.
Generally gentle, graceful, on MF level. Descending ending line.
Acc: 3-4 (S)IM. OAR-S1(Ch. XI)

MUZIO SCEVOLA

Opera 1721, libretto by Paolo Rolli. Handel composed only Act III.
Acts I and II are by Bononcini and Mattei, respectively, and all the
three acts were submitted for a music contest.

5891. Dimmi, crudele Amore   Dramatic Soprano
Part of Clelia, Act III. bb2-g4(ab4) d3-eb4 Animated in lively
tempo. Requires considerable flexibility. Has some wide intervalic
skips, florid passages, extended piano prelude, and agitated accompaniment. In the full score this is accompanied by a recitative: Io
d'altro regno. Acc: 3-4 15A

5892. Non ti fidar   Soprano
Part of Fidalma, Act III. f3-bb4 f3-eb4 Animated in lively tempo.
Graceful. Has two florid figures and some wide intervalic skips.
Acc: 3-4 15A

ORLANDO

Opera 1732, libretto by Grazio Braccioli, based on Lodovico Ariosto's
Orlando Furioso.

5893. Se fedel vuoi ch'io ti creda   Soprano
Part of Angelica, Act I. f#3-a4 a3-g4 Sustained in slow tempo.
Has some octave intervalic skips, and a few florid figures. Requires
some flexibility. Short. In the full score, this is preceded by a recitative: (Oh soccorso opportun'). Acc: 3 15A

OTTONE

Opera 1723, libretto by Nicola Francesco Haym.

5894. Affanni del pensier   Soprano
Part of Teofanio, Act I. eb3-ab4 ab3-eb4 Sustained in slow tem-
po. Requires some flexibility. A Da Capo air. Best for high voices.
Acc: 3 45A-3, AIS-1, AAP-1

5895. Benchè mi sia crudele   Soprano
Part of Teofane, Act III. f#3-a4 a3-g4 Sustained in moderate tempo. Has some extended florid passages. Requires some flexibility.
Descending ending line. In the full score, this is preceded by a recitative in slow tempo: Dir li potessi vedi. Acc: 3 6IA-1

PARTENOPE

Opera 1730, libretto by Silvio Stampiglia.

5896. Io ti levo l'impero dell' armi   Soprano
       Part of Partenope, Act I. f♯3-b4 g3-g4 Generally animated vocal
       part in moderate slow tempo. Florid. Has some wide intervalic
       skips. Requires fluent enunciation and flexibility. Has triplet figures.
       Acc: 4 15A

RADAMISTO
Opera 1720, libretto by Nicola Haym, altered from L'amor tirannico,
perhaps by Domenico Lalli.

5897. Sommi Dei   Soprano
       Part of Polissena, Act I. g3-a4 g3-e4 Sustained in very slow tem-
       po. Short. Acc: 3 45A-2 (S)IM-high, low

RINALDO
Opera 1711, libretto by Aaron Hill, translated by Giacomo Rossi.

5898. R: Armida, dispietata
       A: Lascia ch'io pianga   Soprano
       Part of Almirena, Act II. f3-g4 a3-f4 Recitative and a Da Capo
       aria. Sustained in slow tempo. Subdued aria, gentle, tranquil. The
       breaking of the word "cruda" is as the composer wrote and must al-
       ways be performed as such. No recitative in LFL-1. Acc: 3
       45A-1, POS-2, LFL-1, 15A, OAR-S1(Ch. XI), KAL. (S)IM-high,
       low; GS-high, medium

SERSE
Opera 1738, libretto by Nicolò Minato, with alterations.

5899. Caro voi siete   Soprano
       Part of Romilda, Act III. e3-a4 g♯3-f♯4 Sustained in moderate
       slow tempo. Requires fine high P. Climactic ending. Acc: 3
       LFL-2

5900. Di tacere e di schernirmi   Soprano
       Part of Serse, soprano or mezzo-soprano, Act I. d3-g4 g3-g4
       Gently animated vocal part in moderate slow tempo. Has some dra-
       matic passages. Climactic ending. Acc: 3 LFL-1. (VS)BA

5901. Ne men con l'ombre   Soprano
       Part of Romilda, Act I. e3-a4 g♯3-f♯4 Sustained in slow tempo.
       Very subdued, requires very fine PP. Has florid passages. Re-
       quires flexibility. Acc: 3 LFL-2

5902. Non so se sia la speme   Soprano
       Part of Arsamene, soprano or mezzo-soprano, Act I. d3-e4 e3-c4
       Sustained in slow tempo. Generally subdued. Strong ending on mid-
       dle register. Acc: 3 LFL-2

5903. R: Frondi tenere
       A: Ombra mai fù   Soprano
       Part of Serse, soprano or mezzo-soprano, Act I. c3-f4 f3-d4
       Originally for soprano, now sung mostly by tenor. Very sustained
       and slow. Mistakenly labelled "largo"; the real tempo by Handel is
       "larghetto." Generally on MF level. Requires elegance and dignity.
       A well-known Handel air, it is corrupted in the present day with so
       many adaptations, including religious. Requires simplicity, and a
       straightforward treatment. No recitative in LFL-1. Acc: 3 45A-2,

LFL-1, POS-2, OAR-M(Ch. XI), KAL.   (S)GS-high

5904. Quella che tutta fe   Soprano
       Part of Arsamene, soprano or mezzo-soprano, Act II.   The part is
       now usually sung by tenor.   c3-f4 f3-eb4 Gently animated in slow
       tempo. Graceful and subdued.   Acc: 3 LFL-2

5905. Và godendo   Soprano
       Part of Romilda, Act I.   e3-a4 a3-e4 Slightly animated and graceful.
       Requires flexibility. Light. Has one long and florid passage. Ex-
       tended instrumental postlude.   Acc: 3 45A-1

5906. Voi mi dite   Soprano
       Part of Atalanta, Act II.   f3-g4 g3-f4 Sustained in moderate slow
       tempo. Has dramatic passages.   Acc: 3 LFL-2

SIROE
Opera 1728, libretto by Pietro Metastasio, altered by Nicola Haym.

5907. Ch'io mai vi possa   Soprano
       Part of Emira, Act III.   d#3-g4 g3-e4 Sustained in lively tempo.
       Has florid passages.   Requires flexibility, and some fluent enuncia-
       tion. A Da Capo air. See the setting by Nicolo Porpora.   Acc:
       3-4 45A-1

SOSARME
Opera 1732, libretto by Matteo Noris.

5908. R: Rasserena, o Madre
       A: Rend'il sereno al ciglio   Soprano
       Part of Elmira, Act I.   f#3-g#4 g#3-e4 The recitative, formed out
       of the alto and soprano parts, may be omitted. Sustained in very
       slow aria. Subdued throughout, gentle.   Acc: 3 45A-2, POS-1,
       SVR-2, (S)IM-high, low

TAMERLANO
Opera 1724, libretto by Nicola Haym, adapted from Agostino Piovene.

5909. Deh! Lasciatemi   Soprano
       Part of Asteria, Act I.   e#3-g#4 f#3-g#4 Gently animated vocal
       part in somewhat slow tempo. Requires very fine high P. Has some
       gently florid passages.   Acc: 3 LFL-3. (VS)BH

TESEO
Opera 1712, libretto by Nicola Haym.

5910. Quell' amor, ch'è nato a forza   Soprano
       Part of Medea, Act II.   eb3-g4 g3-eb4 Sustained in moderate tem-
       po. Has one long sustained note, and a couple of florid figures. In
       the full score this is preceded by a recitative: L'infelice Medea!
       Acc: 3 6IA-1

B. Mezzo-Soprano & Contralto

ADMETO
Opera 1727, libretto by Nicola Haym or Paolo Rolli, from Aurelio
Aureli's L'Antigona Delusa da Alceste.

5911. Cangiò d'aspetto   Mezzo-Soprano, Contralto
Part of Admeto, contralto, Act I. b2-d4 d3-b3 Original key. Animated in lively tempo. Requires fluent enunciation and flexibility.
Has one long florid passage. Best for medium or low voices. The
autograph and conducting score of this opera were lost. Acc: 3
45A-2

ALCINA
Opera 1735, libretto by Antonio Marchi, after Lodovico Ariosto's
Orlando Furioso.

5912. Ah! mio cor   Mezzo-Soprano, Contralto
Part of Alcina, mezzo-soprano or soprano, Act II. c3-eb4 e3-d4
Sustained in moderate slow tempo. Sad texts. Extended instrumental
prelude and postlude. The middle part of the aria is omitted in the
Parisotti editions (G. Schirmer, Franco Colombo, etc.). Four steps
higher in the original for soprano. Acc: 3 AIS-1, AAP-1

5913. Verdi prati   Mezzo-Soprano, Contralto
Part of Ruggiero, Act II. Sustained in slow tempo. Climactic end-
ing. Fine for medium or low voices. Acc: 3-4 45A-2, LFL-1,
POS-1, OAR-M(Ch. XI)

AMADIGI DI GAULA
Opera 1715, libretto by John James Heidegger (?).

5914. Ah! Spietato!   Mezzo-Soprano, Contralto
Part of Melissa, soprano or mezzo-soprano, Act I. b2-d4(L) d3-c4
Sustained in very slow tempo, followed by a lively section with some
florid passages. First part has chordal accompaniment. A Da Capo
air. Acc: 3 45A-1. (S)IM-high, low

5915. R: D'un sventurato amante
A: Pena tiranna io sento   Mezzo-Soprano, Contralto
Part of Dardano, contralto, Act II. c3-eb4 e3-d4 Very sustained
in very slow tempo. Recitative and a Da Capo air. Best for medium or low voices. Acc: 3 45A-3

BERENICE
Opera 1737, libretto by Antonio Salvi.

5916. Sì, tra i ceppi   Mezzo-Soprano, Contralto
Part of Demetrio, contralto, Act II. b2-d4 d3-c4 Animated with
some florid passages. Requires flexibility and fluent enunciation.
Listed as Version B. Fine for medium or low voices. Acc: 3
45A-2, GAS. (S)GS-medium

FLORIDANTE
Opera 1721, libretto by Paolo Rolli.

5917. Alma mia   Mezzo-Soprano, Contralto
Part of Floridante, Act I. c#3-e4 d3-d4 Sustained in slow tempo.
Generally on MF level. Short. Original key. Acc: 3 (S)IM-high,
low

5918. Notte cara, deh!   Mezzo-Soprano, Contralto
Part of Elmira, Act II. bb2-eb4 db3-db4 Sustained in slow tempo.
Arioso and recitative. Fragmentary phrases in the vocal part.

Descending ending line with b♭2 as the final note. Acc: 3 15A

ORLANDO
Opera 1732, libretto by Grazio Braccioli, based on Lodovico Ariosto's
Orlando Furioso.

5919. Ah! stigie larve   Mezzo-Soprano, Contralto
Part of Orlando, Act II. a♭2-d4 d3-b♭3 Animated in varied tempi.
An extended solo recitative and rondo. Requires flexibility and some
fluent enunciation. Has extended florid passages. Agitated accompaniment. In SC, the texts are in Italian, with German and English
versions. Acc: 4 (S)SC

OTTONE
Opera 1723, libretto by Nicola Haym.

5920. Ah! tu non sai   Mezzo-Soprano, Contralto
Part of Matilda, contralto, or mezzo-soprano, Act II. c3-d4 e3-c4
Original key. Sustained in slow tempo. Sad texts. Best for medium
or low voices. Acc: 3 45A-2

PARTENOPE
Opera 1730, libretto by Silvio Stampiglia.

5921. Furibondo spira il vento   Mezzo-Soprano, Contralto
Part of Arsace, contralto, Act II. b2-e4 d3-d4 Animated and very
florid. Requires considerable agility and flexibility. May also be
sung by baritone or bass as a single song. Acc: 4-5 45A-1

PORO
Opera 1731, libretto by Pietro Metastasio, from his Alessandro nell'
Indie.

5922. Son confusa pastorella   Contralto
Part of Erissene, Act III. a2-d4 d3-b3 Original key. Alto is the
original range. Sustained in moderate slow tempo. Graceful. Descending ending. Transposed for high voice in 15A. Acc: 3 15A

RADAMISTO
Opera 1720, libretto by Nicola Haym, altered from L'amor Tirannico,
perhaps by Domenico Lalli.

5923. Ombra cara   Mezzo-Soprano, Contralto
Part of Radamisto, Act II. Version I is for soprano; Version II is
for contralto. c3-e4 d3-d4 Very sustained in very slow tempo.
Extended instrumental prelude. Best for medium or low voices.
Acc: 3 45A-1

RINALDO
Opera 1711, libretto by Aaron Hill, translated by Giacomo Rossi.

5924. Cara sposa   Mezzo-Soprano, Contralto
Part of Rinaldo, soprano or mezzo-soprano, Act I. a2-d4 d3-d4
Sustained in very slow tempo. The first part is followed by a shorter,
animated and lively section which requires flexibility. A Da Capo air.
Acc: 3 45A-1, OPA-2 (see opera)

5925. R: Armida dispietata
A: Lascia ch'io pianga   Mezzo-Soprano, Contralto

Part of Almirena, soprano or mezzo-soprano, Act II.   d3-e4   e3-d4
Very sustained in slow tempo.   Elegant.   Very lyric in style.   The
breaking of the word "cruda" is intended by the composer and must
be performed as such.   No recitative in LFL-1.   Acc: 3   45A-1,
LFL-1, POS-2.   (S)IM-high, low; GS-high, medium

5926.   Scorta Rea   Mezzo-Soprano, Contralto
Part of Eustazio, contralto, Act II.   bb2-c4   c3-c4   Slightly animated
vocal line in moderate lively tempo.   Has florid passages.   Generally
graceful.   Acc: 3   LFL-3

5927.   Sorge nel petto   Mezzo-Soprano, Contralto
Part of Goffredo, contralto, Act III.   b2-d4   d3-c# 4   Sustained in
slow tempo.   Generally subdued and gentle.   Somewhat low ending.
Fine for medium or low voices.   Acc: 3   LFL-3

RODELINDA
Opera 1725, libretto by Nicola Haym, adapted from Antonio Salvi.

5928.   Con rauco mormorio   Mezzo-Soprano, Contralto
Part of Bertarido, contralto, Act II.   bb2-d4   d3-c4   Sustained in
slow tempo.   The movement and musical character of this aria may
remind one of "He shall feed His flock" from MESSIAH.   Best for
medium or low voices.   Acc: 2-3   45A-3

5929.   R: Pompe vane di morte
A: Dove sei? amato bene!   Mezzo-Soprano, Contralto
Part of Bertarido, contralto, Act I.   b2-e4   d# 3-b3   Sustained in
very slow tempo, in 3/4 time.   Gentle and graceful.   No recitative
in 45A-3.   Acc: 3   45A-3, GAS-low

SCIPIONE
Opera 1726, libretto by Paolo Rolli, based on Apostolo Zeno's Scipione
nelle Spagne.

5930.   R: Nulla temer
A: Generoso chi sol drama   Mezzo-Soprano, Contralto
Part of Rosalba, contralto, supplementary aria.   b2-d# 4   d# 3-c# 4
Recitative and a Da Capo air.   Sustained air in slightly lively tempo,
abounds in triplet rhythmic figures.   Requires flexibility.   Acc: 3
45A-1

5931.   Tutta raccolta ancor   Mezzo-Soprano, Contralto
Part of Berenice, soprano, Act II.   c3-eb4   f3-bb3   Generally sus-
tained in very slow tempo.   Short.   Best for the heavier voices.
May also be sung by a bass voice.   Acc: 3   45A-3

SERSE
Opera 1738, libretto by Nicolò Minato, with alterations.

5932.   Non so se sia la speme   Mezzo-Soprano, Contralto
Part of Arsamene, soprano or mezzo-soprano, Act I.   The part is
now sung by tenor.   d3-e4   e3-c4   Sustained in slow tempo.   Generally subdued.   Strong ending in the middle range.   Acc: 3   LFL-2

TAMERLANO
Opera 1724, libretto by Nicola Haym, adapted from Agostino Piovene.

5933.   R: Il Tartaro ama Asteria

A: Bella Asteria   Mezzo-Soprano, Contralto
Part of Andronico, contralto, Act I.   a2-d4   c#3-c#4 Recitative and
a gently animated aria in slow tempo.   Florid, requires some flexibility. Requires fine P. Climactic ending. Acc: 3-4 LFL-2,
(VS)BH

5934. Dammi pace   Mezzo-Soprano, Contralto
Part of Tamerlano, contralto, Act I.   Original part is for contralto;
more recently given to bass-baritone.   c3-d4 d3-c4 Animated in
lively tempo.   Has some short, florid passages.   Best for medium
or low voices.   Acc: 3-4 LFL-3, (VS)BH

TOLOMEO
Opera 1728, libretto by Nicola Haym.

5935. Non lo dirò col labbro   Mezzo-Soprano, Contralto
Part of Alessandro, contralto, Act I.   b2-c#4 d#3-c#4 Sustained
in moderate slow tempo.   Requires some flexibility.   Acc: 2-3
45A-2

5936. R: Inumano fratel
A: Stille amare   Mezzo-Soprano, Contralto
Part of Tolomeo, contralto, Act III.   b♭2-d♭4 e♭3-c4 Recitative
and sustained, slow aria.   Vocal line has an unfinished ending as a
dramatic device of a person dying.   Fine for men's voices.   Acc: 3
45A-1

C. Tenor

ALCINA
Opera 1735, libretto by Antonio Marchi, after Lodovico Ariosto's
Orlando Furioso.

5937. Un momento di contento   Tenor
Part of Oronte, tenor, Act III.   e3-g#4 f#3-f#4 Animated in moderate lively tempo.   Florid, requires flexibility.   No strong contrasts
in dynamics.   Acc: 3 LFL-3

RADAMISTO
Opera 1720, libretto by Nicola Haym, altered from L'amor Tirannico,
perhaps by Domenico Lalli.

5938. Ombra cara   Tenor
Part of Radamisto, soprano (contralto), Act II.   e♭3-g4 f3-e♭4
Very sustained in very slow tempo.   Extended instrumental prelude.
Acc: 3 45A-1

SERSE
Opera 1738, libretto by Nicolò Minato, with alterations.

5939. Non so se sia la speme   Tenor
Part of Arsamene, tenor, Act I.   Original part for soprano.   d3-e4
e3-c4 Sustained in slow tempo.   Generally subdued.   Strong ending
on middle range.   Acc: 3 LFL-2

5940. R: Frondi tenere e belle
A: Ombra mai fù   Tenor
Part of Serse, originally soprano, now tenor, Act I.   c3-f4   f3-d4

Recitative and very sustained, slow aria. Mistakenly labeled "largo"; the original and intended tempo is "larghetto." Requires simplicity, elegance, and straightforward approach. A well-known Handel air, issued in corrupted adaptations, including religious. No recitative in LFL-1. Acc: 3 45A-2, LFL-1, POS-2, OAR-M(Ch. XI), KAL-aria only, (S)GS-high

5941. Quella che tutta fè   Tenor
Part of Arsamene, tenor, Act II. Originally for soprano. c3-f4 f3-eb4 Gently animated in slow tempo. Graceful. Generally sub-dued. Acc: 3 LFL-2

TAMERLANO
Opera 1724, libretto by Nicola Haym, adapted from Agostino Piovene.

5942. Figlia mia, non pianger   Tenor
Part of Bajazet, tenor, Act III. d3-f4 g3-db4 May also be sung by high baritone. Sustained in moderate slow tempo. Subdued through-out. Requires fine P and PP. Gentle. Acc: 3 LFL-3, AUK, (VS)BH

D. Baritone and Bass

Note: All baritone and bass range and tessitura indications have been tran-scribed, for this section only, into the pitches as they would sound even if they appear in treble clef in the editions reviewed.

EZIO
Opera 1732, libretto by Pietro Metastasio.

5943. Nasce al bosco   Baritone, Bass
Part of Varo, bass, Act II. f1(a1)-f3 d2-e3 Sustained in moderate lively tempo. Has a full two-octave range, but substitute notes are also provided by the editor. Has some long-sustained as well as florid passages. Requires considerable flexibility. Acc: 3-4 45A-3

FLORIDANTE
Opera 1721, libretto by Paolo Rolli.

5944. Finchè lo strale   Baritone, Bass
Part of Oronte, bass, Act I. bb1-f3 eb2-eb3 Original key. Ani-mated in lively tempo. Has florid figures. Light and graceful. Acc: 3 45A-2

ORLANDO
Opera 1732, libretto by Grazio Braccioli, based on Lodovico Ariosto's Orlando Furioso.

5945. Sorge infausta una procella   Baritone, Bass
Part of Zoroastro, bass, Act III. g1-eb3 d1-d3 Animated in lively tempo. Has florid passages. Requires flexibility. Spirited, with agitated accompaniment. Extended instrumental prelude. Acc: 4 45A-3

OTTONE
Opera 1723, libretto by Nicola Haym.

5946. Del minacciar del vento   Baritone, Bass
       Part of Emireno, bass, Act I.   a1-f3   d2-d3 Original key. Ani-
       mated in lively tempo.   Florid, requires flexibility and fluent enuncia-
       tion. Wide range. Has some wide intervalic skips. Acc: 4
       45A-3, OAR-Br(Ch. XI)

                              PARTENOPE
       Opera 1730, libretto by Silvio Stampiglia.

5947. Furibondo spira il vento   Baritone, Bass
       Part of Arsace, originally contralto, Act II. b1-e3 d2-d3 Animated
       in very lively tempo. Extremely florid, requires considerable flexi-
       bility and agility. Difficult. Acc: 4-5 45A-1

                               SCIPIONE
       Opera 1726, libretto by Paolo Rolli, based on Apostolo Zeno's Scipi-
       one nelle Spagne.

5948. Tutta raccolta ancor   Baritone, Bass
       Part of Berenice, originally soprano, Act II.   Aria is performed
       separately by men.   c2-eb3 f2-bb2 Generally sustained in very
       slow tempo. Has one climactic high passage, but is generally sub-
       dued. Short. Best for the heavier voices. Acc: 3 45A-3

                              TAMERLANO
       Opera 1724, libretto by Nicola Haym, adapted from Agostino Piovene.

5949. Dammi pace   Baritone, Bass
       Part of Tamerlano, originally contralto, Act I.   Later, the part was
       given to bass-baritone. c2-d3 d2-c3 Animated in lively tempo.
       Has some short florid figures. Acc: 3-4 LFL-3. (VS)BH

5950. Figlia mia, non pianger   Baritone, Bass
       Part of Bajazet, originally tenor, Act III. d2-f3 g2-db3 Sustained
       in moderate slow tempo. Subdued throughout. Gentle. Requires
       fine P and PP. Acc: 3 LFL-3. (VS)BH

                               TOLOMEO
       Opera 1728, libretto by Nicola Haym.

5951. R: Inumano fratel
       A: Stille amare   Baritone, Bass
       Part of Tolomeo, originally for contralto, Act III.   bb1-db3   eb2-c3
       Recitative and sustained, slow aria. Sad text. Generally subdued.
       The vocal part has an unfinished ending used as a dramatic device for
       the death of the character. Acc: 3 45A-1

                 II. Solo Excerpts from Secular Choral Works

                            A. Soprano

                              HERCULES
       Choral work 1745, texts by Thomas Broughton, based on Sophocles
       and Ovid.

5952. Ah, think what ills   Lyric Soprano
       Part of Iole. d3-ab4 g3-f4 Sustained in moderate slow tempo.

Requires flexibility. Has some fast-moving florid passages. Accompaniment in the second half is agitated. Acc: 4 CSH-1

5953. Banish love from thy breast   Lyric Soprano
Part of Iole. d3-a4 e3-g4 Animated in lively tempo. Has fast-moving florid passages, and some wide intervalic skips. Requires considerable flexibility. Acc: 4 CSH-1

5954. R: Alas! Erastea
A: Daughter of gods   Lyric Soprano
Part of Iole. d3-g4 f3-f4 Slightly dramatic secco recitative, and a sustained aria in slow tempo. Aria has some extended florid passages. Requires flexibility. Generally on MF level. Acc: 3 CSH-1

5955. My father! ah! methinks I see   Lyric Soprano
Part of Iole, Act I. c3-f4 f3-eb4 Sustained in slow tempo. Generally tranquil and somewhat subdued. Subdued and low ending. Acc: 3 ASS-S

5956. My heart with tender pity swells   Lyric Soprano
Part of Iole, Act III. d#3-a4 f#3-e4 Sustained in slow tempo. Gently graceful. Generally on MF level. Descending ending. Original title: My breast with tender pity swells. Acc: 3 CSH-1

        L'ALLEGRO, IL PENSEROSO, ED IL MODERATO
Choral work 1740, texts by John Milton (I & II), adapted by Charles Jennens (III).

5957. Come and trip it   Soprano, Tenor
eb3-ab4 g3-eb4 Slightly animated in moderate lively tempo. Graceful and light. Requires some flexibility. Has florid passages. One of the best-known Handel airs. Acc: 3-4 45A-1, SCS-2

5958. R: Come, pensive nun
A: Come, but keep thy wonted state   Dramatic Soprano
f3-ab4 g3-eb4 Sustained in slow and moderate slow tempi. Generally on MF level. Short. Acc: 3 CSH-2

5959. R: Me, when the sun begins to fling
A: Hide me from day's garish eye   Lyric Soprano
eb3-ab4 f3-eb4 Short secco recitative and a sustained aria in slow tempo. Aria is subdued, gentle, and graceful. Acc: 3 CSH-1

5960. Let me wander not unseen   Soprano, Tenor
d3-f4 a3-f4 Sustained in moderate tempo. A graceful Siciliana. Generally on MF level. Has a recitative in the full score: If I give thee honour due. Descending ending line. Short. Acc: 3 15A

5961. May at last my weary age   Dramatic Soprano
d3-a4 f3-f4 Sustained in slow tempo. Has a few florid figures. Generally on MF level. Descending ending line. Acc: 3 CSH-2

5962. Oft, on a plot of rising ground   Lyric Soprano
f3-g4 a3-f4 Sustained in slow tempo. Generally subdued. Requires some flexibility. Descending ending line. Acc: 3 CSH-1

5963. There, held in holy passion still   Dramatic Soprano
bb2-bb4 f3-eb4 Sustained in slow tempo. Generally on MF level,

with some high climactic passages. Descending ending line after high climax. Acc: 3 CSH-2

5964. Straight, mine eye hath caught new pleasures   Lyric Soprano
d3-g4 f♯3-e4 Generally sustained in moderate slow tempo. Has some florid passages. Generally on MF level. Requires some flexibility. Acc: 3 CSH-1

ODE ON ST. CECILIA'S DAY
Choral work 1739, texts by John Dryden.

5965. The soft complaining flute   Soprano
d3-g4 f♯3-f♯4 Sustained in moderate slow tempo. Requires very fine high P. Florid, requires flexibility. Extended instrumental prelude and postlude. Acc: 3-4 ASS-S

SEMELE
Choral work 1744, texts by William Congreve.

5966. Endless pleasures, endless love   Lyric Soprano
Part of Semele. e3-a4 g3-g4 Animated in moderate lively tempo. In gavotte style. Has some florid passages, climactic passages, and a few wide intervalic skips. Descending ending line. Acc: 3-4 CSH-1

5967. No, no, I'll take no less   Lyric Soprano
Part of Semele. d3-g4 f♯3-f♯4 Animated in lively tempo. Has extended florid passages. Requires considerable flexibility and some fluent enunciation. Has some climactic passages. Descending ending line. Acc: 4 CSH-1

5968. O sleep, why dost thou leave me?   Soprano
Part of Semele, Act II. d♯3-g♯4 e3-e4 Sustained in very slow tempo. Generally subdued. Has one extended florid passage and a few short florid figures. Requires simplicity and quiet dignity. Acc: 3 45A-2, POS-3. (S)GS-high, medium, low

THE CHOICE OF HERCULES
Choral work 1751, texts by Thomas Morell or Tobias Smollett, after Joseph Spence.

5969. R: See, Hercules
A: Come, beauteous boy   Dramatic Soprano
Part of pleasure. e3-a4 g3-f4 This work was produced as a new act for ALEXANDER'S FEAST. A slightly extended secco recitative, and a sustained aria in moderate slow tempo. Generally on MF level. Descending ending line. Acc: 3 CSH-2

B. Mezzo-Soprano and Contralto

HERCULES
Choral work 1745, texts by Thomas Broughton, based on Sophocles and Ovid.

5970. Begone, my fears   Mezzo-Soprano, Contralto
Part of Dejanira. a2-f♯4 e3-e4 Animated in lively tempo. Has florid passages in the first section. Requires flexibility. Has climactic passages. Slightly climactic adagio ending. Acc: 3-4 CSH-3

5971.   He, who for Atlas   Mezzo-Soprano, Contralto
Part of Lichas. b♭2-d4 d3-c4 Gently animated vocal part in moderate slow tempo. Has three florid passages and several florid figures. Low ending, sustained b♭2. Acc: 3 CSH-4

5972.   R: Forgive me, generous victor
A: My father!   Mezzo-Soprano
Part of Iole. c3-f4 e♭3-e♭4 Short secco recitative and a sustained
aria in slow tempo. Generally subdued. Somewhat inwardly intense.
Very subdued, descending ending line. Acc: 3 CSH-3

5973.   R: See, with what sad dejection
A: No longer, fate, relentless frown   Contralto
Part of Lichas. b♭2-e♭4 e♭3-c4 Sustained in slow tempo. Has a
few florid figures. Generally on MF level. Descending ending line.
Acc: 3 CSH-4

5974.   The smiling hours, a joyful train   Mezzo-Soprano, Contralto
Part of Lichas, Act I. b♭2-d4 d3-c4 Animated in lively tempo.
Graceful, florid, requires flexibility. Generally light. Acc: 3-4
ASS-A

5975.   R: O Hercules!
A: The world, when day its course has run   Mezzo-Soprano
Part of Dejanira. c3-g4 e3-e4 Secco recitative in moderate slow
tempo, and a sustained aria in slow tempo. Has a few florid figures,
some wide intervalic skips, and a descending ending line. Generally
on MF level. Acc: 3 CSH-3

5976.   R: O dreadful oracle!
A: There in myrtle shades reclined   Mezzo-Soprano
Part of Dejanira. c3-g4 f3-e4 A secco recitative and a sustained
aria in slow tempo. Has florid passages, some wide intervalic skips,
and climactic passages. Requires some flexibility. Descending ending
line. Acc: 3-4 CSH-3

5977.   Where shall I fly?   Mezzo-Soprano, Contralto
Part of Dejanira. a2-g4 d3-d4 Has recitative and arioso sections.
A dramatic aria, requiring intensity. Generally strong. Has some
extended florid passages. Requires flexibility. Dramatic ending with
a falling final note. Acc: 4 CSH-3

SEMELE
Choral work 1744, texts by William Congreve.

5978.   Above measure is the pleasure   Contralto
Part of Juno. c3-d4 d3-c4 Sustained, first in moderate slow tempo,
then slightly slower tempo. Has some florid figures. More sustained
second part. Acc: 3 CSH-4

5979.   Despair no more shall fright me   Contralto
Part of Athamas. b♭2-c4 c3-c4 Animated in lively tempo. Has
florid passages. Requires flexibility. Low ending after extended
florid passage. Acc: 3-4 CSH-4

5980.   R: She weeps! the gentle maid
A: Your tuneful voice my tale would tell   Contralto
Part of Athamas. a♯2-b3 c♯3-b3 Secco recitative, and a sustained

aria in slow tempo. Has a fairly low tessitura and some florid figures. Acc: 3 CSH-4

THE CHOICE OF HERCULES
Choral work 1751, texts by Thomas Morell and Tobias Smollett, after
Joseph Spence. This work was produced as a new act for ALEX-
ANDER'S FEAST.

5981. Yet can I hear that dulcet lay?   Contralto
Part of Hercules. b2-d4 d# 3-c# 4 Sustained in slow tempo. Has
florid passages. Requires some flexibility. Slightly climactic, descending ending. Acc: 3 CSH-4

C. Tenor

ACIS AND GALATEA
Choral work 1718-1720, texts attributed to John Gay, additions by
John Dryden, Alexander Pope, and John Hughes.

5982. Would you gain the tender creature?   Tenor
Part of Damon. e3-g4 g3-f4 Sustained in moderate tempo. Marked
"allegro" by the editor, which is too fast for the style of the excerpt.
Graceful, generally on MF level. Descending ending line. Acc: 3
CSH-5

ALEXANDER'S FEAST
Choral work 1736, texts by John Dryden, with additions by Newburgh
Hamilton.

5983. R: The mighty master
A: Softly sweet in Lydian measures   Tenor
In the original score, the recitative is for tenor, the arioso is for
soprano. d3-g4 g3-f# 4 Secco recitative and sustained aria in slow
tempo. Abounds in dotted rhythms. Generally on MF level. Climactic ending. Acc: 3-4 CSH-5

5984. R: Give the vengeance due
A: The Princes applaud   Tenor
e3-a4 a3-f4 Animated in lively tempo. Has florid passages. Requires flexibility. Has dramatic passages. Extended instrumental
prelude. Acc: 4 CSH-5

5985. War, he sung, is toil and trouble   Tenor
For soprano voice in the original. e3-a4 a3-g4 Animated in lively
tempo. Energetic and spirited. Has florid passages, climactic passages, and a dramatic ending. Slightly legato second ending. Acc:
4 CSH-5

HERCULES
Choral work 1745, texts by Thomas Broughton, based on Sophocles
and Ovid.

5986. From celestial seats descending   Tenor
Part of Hyllus, Act II. c3-g4 g3-f4 Animated in moderate tempo.
Graceful. Has some wide intervalic skips. Requires flexibility.
Slightly climactic ending. Acc: 3-4 ASS-T

5987. R: Despair not
A: Where, congealed the northern streams   Tenor

Part of Hyllus. e3-a4 g3-g4 Secco recitative and a sustained aria
in moderate slow tempo. Has two extended and one short florid passages. Requires some flexibility. Descending ending line after a
high climax. Acc: 3-4 CSH-5

L'ALLEGRO, IL PENSEROSO, ED IL MODERATO
Choral work 1740, texts by John Milton (I & II), adapted by Charles
Jennens (III).

5988. Come and trip it   Tenor
eb3-ab4 g3-eb4 Slightly animated in moderate lively tempo. Graceful, light, and requires some flexibility. Has florid passages. One
of Handel's best-known airs. Acc: 3-4 45A-1, SCS-2

5989. Let me wander not unseen   Tenor or Soprano
d3-f4 a3-f4 Sustained in moderate tempo. A graceful Siciliana.
Generally on MF level. Has a recitative in the full score: If I give
thee honour due. Descending ending line. Short. Acc: 3 15A

SEMELE
Choral work 1744, texts by William Congreve.

5990. O sleep, why dost thou leave me?   Tenor
Originally part for Semele, Act II. The air is beautifully fitting for
light tenor. d#3-g#4 e3-e4 Sustained in very slow tempo. Generally subdued. Has one extended florid passage and a few short
florid figures. Requires simplicity and quiet dignity. Acc: 3 45A-
2, POS-3. (S)GS-high, medium, low

5991. Where'er you walk   Tenor
Part of Jupiter, tenor, Act II. Now sung by all voices as a single
song, but especially performed by men. f3-g4 g3-d4 Sustained in
very slow tempo. Generally on MF level. Many corrupted editions
ignore the intended rest signs in the florid extension of the word
"shade." Must be performed as Handel intended. Second section is
mistakenly sung at a faster tempo, which is a wrong approach. Acc:
3 45A-1, 56S, SVR-1, 15A. (S)GS-high, medium, low

D. Baritone and Bass

ACIS AND GALATEA
Choral work 1718-1720, texts attributed to John Gay, additions by
John Dryden, Alexander Pope, and John Hughes.

5992. R: I rage, I melt, I burn!
A: O ruddier than the cherry   Bass
Part of Polyphemus, bass, Act II. f1-f3 c2-d3 Somewhat pompous
recitative and an animated aria. Has florid passages, wide range,
and wide intervalic skips. Requires flexibility and fluent enunciation.
Acc: 3-4 45A-1

ALEXANDER'S FEAST
Choral work 1736, texts by John Dryden, with additions by Newburgh
Hamilton. Other title: THE POWER OF MUSIC.

5993. Bacchus ever fair and young   Baritone, Bass
c2-f3 f2-d3 Sustained in moderate slow tempo. Bright, with high
tessitura--several f3's. This work is designated as an Ode in honor
of St. Cecilia. Acc: 2 45A-3

5994. Revenge, Timotheus cries   Baritone, Bass
       g1-e3 d2-d3 Animated in moderate lively tempo. Florid, requires
       flexibility and fluent enunciation. Accented, strong, and bold. Acc:
       4 45A-2

                                    HERCULES
       Choral work 1745, texts by Thomas Broughton, based on Sophocles
       and Ovid.

5995. Alcides' name in latest story   Bass
       Part of Hercules. g1-d3 c2-c3 Animated in lively tempo. Has
       some low tessitura and florid passages. Generally on MF level. De-
       scending ending. Acc: 3-4 CSH-7

5996. Oh Jove! What land is this?   Baritone
       Part of Hercules. g1-f3 eb2-d3 Animated in moderate lively tem-
       po. Strong and florid. Requires considerable flexibility. Strong and
       descending ending. Very agitated accompaniment. Acc: 4-5 CSH-6

5997. R: Now farewell arms!
       A: The god of war   Bass
       Part of Hercules. bb1-eb3 d2-d3 Secco recitative and animated
       aria in lively tempo. Has some florid passages. Generally on MF
       level, with some climactic passages. Descending ending. Acc: 3
       CSH-7

              L'ALLEGRO, IL PENSEROSO, ED IL MODERATO
       Choral work 1740, texts by John Milton (I & II), adapted by Charles
       Jennens (III).

5998. Mountains, on whose barren breast   Baritone
       b1-e3 e2-c#3 An accompanied recitative. Has two short florid pas-
       sages. Agitated accompaniment. Short. Acc: 3 CSH-6

                                    SEMELE
       Choral work 1744, texts by William Congreve.

5999. Leave me, loathsome light   Bass
       Part of Somnus. a1-d3 d2-b2 Very sustained in moderate slow tem-
       po. Subdued, somewhat dark, and requires fine vocal control. De-
       scending ending line. Acc: 3 CSH-7, GAS-L

6000. More sweet is that name   Baritone, Bass
       Part of Somnus. a1-d3 d2-c3 Animated in lively tempo. Has
       florid passages. Generally on MF level. Has climactic passages.
       Acc: 3 CSH-7

                III.   Solo Excerpts from the Oratorios

       In this section, entries are arranged alphabetically by title of oratorio
       for easier reference.

                              A.   Soprano

                            ALEXANDER BALUS
       Oratorio 1748, texts by Thomas Morell.

6001. Here amid the shady woods   Soprano
       d3-f4   f3-d4 Sustained in moderate slow tempo. Moves gently and
       gracefully. Has some slightly climactic passages. Acc: 3 POS-4

ATHALIA
Oratorio 1733, texts by Samuel Humphreys, based on Jean Racine.

6002. R: Oh! Killing shock of unexpected pain!
       A: Faithful cares in vain extended   Lyric Soprano
       Part of Josabeth. f3-g4 a3-g4 A dramatic recitative, and a sus-
       tained aria in slow tempo. Aria is slightly subdued. Sad and in-
       tense text. Acc: 3-4 CSH-1

6003. My vengeance awakes me   Dramatic Soprano
       Part of Athalia. d3-g4 f3-f4 Animated in lively tempo. Intense,
       generally strong, and dramatic. Acc: 3-4 CSH-2

6004. Soothing tyrant   Dramatic Soprano
       Part of Josabeth. f♯3-a4 a3-f♯4 Sustained in moderate slow tempo.
       Has two slowly-moving florid passages. Generally on MF level.
       Acc: 3 CSH-2

BELSHAZZAR
Oratorio 1745, texts by Charles Jennens.

6005. R: O sentence too severe
       A: Alternate hopes and fears   Soprano
       Part of Nitocris. d3-ab4 g3-g4 Recitative and generally sustained
       aria in slow tempo. Requires fine high notes. Has one florid pas-
       sage. Climactic ending. Acc: 3-4 SGO-S, (VS)NO

6006. R: Vain fluctuating state
       A: Thou God most high   Dramatic Soprano
       Part of Nitocris. d3-g4 f3-f4 Extended dramatic recitative in
       varied slow tempi. Sustained in slow tempo. Has dramatic passages.
       Descending line after a high climax. Acc: 3 CSH-2, (VS)NO

DEBORAH
Oratorio 1733, texts by Samuel Humphreys.

6007. Choirs of angels, all around thee   Dramatic, Lyric Soprano
       Part of Deborah. f3-g4 a3-f4 Sustained in moderate lively tempo.
       Has two florid and fast-moving passages, some climactic passages,
       and a descending ending line. Acc: 3 CSH-2

6008. In Jehovah's awful sight   Dramatic Soprano
       Part of Deborah. f3-g4 g3-f4 Very sustained in slow tempo. Gen-
       erally on MF level. Descending ending line. Chordal accompaniment.
       Acc: 3 CSH-2

ESTHER
Oratorio 1733, second version, texts by Alexander Pope and John
Arbuthnot, after Racine; other texts by Samuel Humphreys.

6009. R: O King of Kings
       A: Alleluia   Dramatic Soprano
       Part of Esther. e3-a4 g3-g4 Short and majestic recitative, and an
       animated, florid alleluia in very rapid tempo. Joyous, bright, and

requires considerable flexibility.   An extended alleluia aria.   Climactic ending.   Acc: 3-4 CSH-2

ISRAEL IN EGYPT
Oratorio 1739, texts compiled from Exodus.

6010.   Thou didst blow   Soprano
eb3-bb4 g3-f4 Sustained in moderate slow tempo. Florid, requires
flexibility. Descending ending phrase after high climax. Acc: 3-4
(VS)GS. SGO-S

JEPHTHA
Oratorio 1752, texts by Thomas Morell, after the Bible.

6011.   R: Ye sacred Priests!
A: Farewell, ye limpid springs and floods   Soprano
Part of Iphis, Part 3.   d#3-g4 f#3-e4 Recitative and sustained aria
in slow tempo. Requires fine P and PP. Descending ending line
after a high climax. Slightly extended instrumental postlude. Acc:
3 ASS-S

JOSEPH AND HIS BRETHREN
Oratorio 1744, texts by James Miller.

6012.   O lovely youth   Lyric Soprano
Part of Asenath.   d3-g4 eb3-f4 Sustained in slow tempo. Starts
gently on ascending phrase. Has a few short florid passages. Generally on MF level. Descending ending line. Acc: 3 CSH-1

6013.   Together, lovely innocents   Lyric Soprano
Part of Asenath.   e3-g4 a3-e4 Sustained in slow tempo. Generally
on MF and P levels. Has two short florid passages. Acc: 3 CSH-1

JOSHUA
Oratorio 1748, texts by Thomas Morell.

6014.   As cheers the sun   Lyric Soprano
Part of Achsah.   d3-g4 f3-g4 Sustained in slow tempo. Has climac-
tic passages. Exultant, joyous, and bright. Descending ending line.
Acc: 4 CSH-1

6015.   Hark, hark, 'tis the linnet   Soprano
Part of Achsah.   d3-g4 f#3-e4 Animated in lively tempo. Has
florid passages. Requires flexibility. Bright, joyous, and has climactic passages. Descending and strong ending line. Acc: 3-4
SGO-S

6016.   Oh! had I Jubal's lyre   Soprano
Part of Achsah.   d#3-f#4 g#3-e4 Animated in lively tempo. Bright,
florid, and requires flexibility. Slightly climactic ending. Extended
instrumental prelude and postlude. Acc: 3-4 ASS-S, KAL

6017.   R: Matrons and virgins
A: Oh, who can tell   Soprano
Part of Achsah.   d3-g4 f#3-f#4 Recitative and sustained aria in
slow tempo. Has some long, florid passages, and requires flexibility.

Has climactic passages. Acc: 4 SGO-S

JUDAS MACCABAEUS
Oratorio 1747, texts by Thomas Morell, after the Bible.

6018. R: Oh, let eternal honors
       A: From mighty kings he took the spoil   Soprano
       Part of the Israelite woman, Part II. e3-a4 g#3-e4 Strong secco
       recitative and a slightly animated aria in moderate slow tempo. Has
       florid passages; requires flexibility. Has dramatic passages. Acc:
       3-4 (VS)GS

6019. R: To heaven's almighty king
       A: O liberty, thou choicest treasure   Soprano
       Part of the Israelite woman, Part I. e3-f#4 g#3-d4 Secco recita-
       tive and sustained aria is slow tempo. Requires some flexibility.
       Generally gentle, somewhat subdued. Acc: 3-4 (VS)GS. SGO-S

6020. R: Oh grant it, heaven
       A: So shall the lute and harp awake   Soprano
       Part of the Israelite woman, Part 3. d3-g4 g3-f4 Subdued secco
       recitative and animated aria in lively tempo. Has long, florid pas-
       sages. Requires flexibility. Climactic ending. Acc: 3-4 (VS)GS.
       SGO-S

MESSIAH
Oratorio 1742, texts compiled and adapted from the Bible by Charles
Jennens.

6021. R: Thy rebuke....Behold and see.... He was cut off
       A: But Thou didst not leave his soul   Soprano
       d#3-g4 e3-e4 Three short recitatives and a gently animated air.
       The air is graceful, but incisive. Agitated accompaniment. Acc:
       3-4 (VS)JC, WS, GS, NO, CP

6022. But who may abide   Soprano
       Version C. c3-a4 g3-g4 First part is very sustained, subdued, in
       slow tempo. Second part is very rapid, animated, florid, and
       spirited. Agitated accompaniment in the fast sections. In the Appen-
       dix, Coopersmith edition. Version II in the Watkins Shaw edition.
       Acc: 5 (VS)JC, WS

6023. Come unto Him   Soprano
       Version B, Part II. Part I "He shall feed His flock" is sung by the
       contralto. f3-g4 g3-f4 Sustained in slow tempo. Moves gently;
       generally subdued. Acc: 3 (VS)JC, WS, GS, NO, CP. ASS-S

6024. R: Comfort ye my people
       A: Every valley   Soprano
       e3-g#4 e3-e4 Sustained recitative and very florid aria in moderate
       slow tempo. Requires considerable flexibility. Has long lines and a
       climactic ending. Acc: 4 (VS)CF, WS, GS, NO, CP

6025. R: Then shall the eyes
       A: He shall feed His flock   Soprano
       Version A. f3-g4 g3-f4 Recitative and sustained, gently moving
       aria, incorporating all material in the more popular Version B for

contralto and soprano. Generally gentle and subdued. Acc: 3
(VS)JC, WS. KAL-aria only

6026. He was despised   Soprano
Version B. f3-g4 g3-e4 Sustained, very slow first part; animated,
rhythmic, dramatic second part. Acc: 3 (VS)JC

6027. How beautiful are the feet   Soprano
Version A: d3-a4 g3-g4; Version B: f3-g4 g3-eb4 Sustained in
moderate slow tempo. Often sung too slowly. Tempo must flow, in
gentle movement. Generally on MF level. Second part of Version A
uses different material and texts: Their sound is gone out. Version
B is the more well-known. Acc: 3 (VS)JC, WS. Version B only:
(VS)GS, NO, CP. ASS-S

6028. I know that my Redeemer liveth   Soprano
e3-g♯4 e3-e4 Sustained in moderate tempo. Requires majestic approach. Must move along with quiet dignity and majesty. Acc: 3
(VS)JC, WS, GS, NO, CP. ASS-S, KAL

6029. If God be for us   Soprano
eb3-ab4 g3-g4 Sustained in moderate slow tempo. Has some long,
sustained and florid passages. Textwise, one of the most dynamic
solos in MESSIAH. Acc: 3 (VS)JC, WS, GS, NO, CP

6030. Rejoice   Soprano
Version A: d3-ab4 g3-f4; Version B: eb3-ab4 g3-f4 Animated in
lively tempo. Bright, joyous, and very florid. Requires considerable
flexibility. Middle section is oftentimes sung too slowly and sentimen-
tally. Version A is in 12/8 time, with triplet figures in the florid
passages. Accompaniment in this version is simpler than that of Version B, the better-known version. Acc: Version A: 3-4; Version B:
4-5 (VS)JC, WS; Version B only: (VS)GS, NO, CP. ASS-S

6031. Their sound is gone out   Soprano
f3-g4 f3-f4 Version C. Animated in moderate tempo. Short. Acc:
3 (VS)JC

6032. Thou art gone up on high   Soprano
Version D. d3-a4 g3-f4 Sustained in moderate slow tempo. Long
lines with slowly moving melismas. One of the finest arias in MES-
SIAH. In the Appendix section of the Coopersmith edition. Acc: 3-4
(VS)JC, WS

OCCASIONAL ORATORIO
Oratorio 1746, texts by Thomas Morell, from Milton, Spenser, etc.

6033. How great and many perils   Dramatic Soprano
d3-g4 e3-e4 Sustained in slightly slow tempo. Has two florid passages. Generally on MF level. Descending ending line. Acc: 3
CSH-2

6034. Prophetic visions   Dramatic Soprano
c3-a4 g3-f4 Animated in lively tempo. Has fast-moving florid passages. Requires flexibility. Has dramatic passages. Descending ending. Acc: 3-4 CSH-2

SAMSON
Oratorio 1743, texts by Newburgh Hamilton, adapted from John Milton's Samson Agonistes, and other works.

6035. Great Dagon has subdued our foe   Soprano
Part of a Philistine, tenor or soprano, Act II. d♯3-g4 g3-f4 Animated in lively tempo. Rhythmic in 3/4 meter. Has some short florid passages. Joyous, and outgoing. Descending ending line. Acc: 3 (VS)GS

6036. Let the bright Seraphim   Soprano
Part of the Israelite woman, Act III. d3-a4 a3-f♯4 Vigorous and animated in moderate lively tempo. Florid, requires flexibility. Exultant and bright. Descending ending line. Acc: 3-4 (VS)GS.
ASS-S

6037. My faith and truth   Soprano
Part of Dalila, Act II. e3-g♯4 a3-f♯4 Sustained in moderate slow tempo. Gentle and graceful. Air ends unaccompanied. Acc: 3 (VS)GS

6038. With plaintive notes and am'rous moan   Soprano
Part of Dalila, Act II. c♯3-g4 g3-e4 Sustained in moderate slow tempo. Florid, requires flexibility. Light throughout. Extended instrumental prelude and postlude. Acc: 3-4 (VS)GS. SGO-S

6039. Ye men of Gaza   Soprano
Part of the Philistine woman, Act I. e3-a4 a3-f♯4 Sustained in moderate tempo. Has two florid passages, the second more lengthy than the first. Joyous, with some animated passages. Acc: 3 (VS)GS

SAUL
Oratorio 1739, texts by Charles Jennens.

6040. Author of peace   Lyric Soprano
Part of Merab. f3-b♭4 g3-g4 Sustained in slow tempo. Has florid passages. Requires flexibility. Generally on MF level. Descending ending line. Acc: 3-4 CSH-1

6041. Capricious man, in humour lost   Lyric Soprano
Part of Merab. c3-a4 g3-g4 Animated in lively tempo. Has climactic passages, florid passages, some florid figures, and some wide intervalic skips. Requires flexibility. Acc: 4 CSH-1

SOLOMON
Oratorio 1749, texts by unknown author.

6042. R: No more shall armed bands
A: Beneath the vine   Lyric Soprano
Part of the First Woman. d3-g4 g3-e4 Short recitative, and a sustained and graceful aria in moderate tempo. In pastoral style. Generally on MF level. Descending ending. Acc: 3 CSH-1

6043. Blessed the day   Lyric Soprano
Part of the Queen. d♯3-a4 g♯3-e4 Animated in lively tempo. Has some fast-moving florid passages. Bright, requires flexibility. Acc: 3-4 CSH-1

6044. With thee th'unsheltered moor I'd tread   Dramatic Soprano
Part of the Queen.   d3-g4   g3-e4   Sustained in slightly slow tempo.
Generally on MF level.   Graceful.   Acc: 3 CSH-2

SUSANNA
Oratorio 1749, texts by unknown author.

6045. Ask if yon damask rose be sweet   Soprano
Part of the Attendant, soprano, Act II.   d3-g4   g3-e♭4 Gently animated in moderate lively tempo.   Generally light, graceful.   Published
in Clio and Euterpe, Vol. II, 1759.   Acc: 3 YAR, RES-2

6046. R: I know the pangs
A: Beneath the cypress' gloomy shade   Soprano
Part of the Attendant, soprano, Act II.   d3-f4   a3-d4   Generally subdued recitative and sustained aria in slow tempo.   Requires fine P
and PP.   Graceful, in Siciliana style.   Sad text.   Acc: 3 ASS-S

6047. Guilt trembling spoke my doom   Dramatic Soprano
Part of Susanna.   b2-a4   e3-f♯4   Animated in lively tempo.   Has
some slightly extended florid passages.   Requires some flexibility.
Acc: 4 CSH-2

THE TRIUMPH OF TIME AND TRUTH
Oratorio 1708 & 1757, texts by Cardinal Benedetto Panfili, English
translation by Thomas Morell.

6048. Guardian angels, O protect me   Lyric Soprano
e3-g♯4   g♯3-g♯4   Sustained in slow tempo.   Has one florid passage.
Requires some flexibility.   Generally on MF level.   Climactic high
ending.   Acc: 3 CSH-1

THEODORA
Oratorio 1749, texts by Thomas Morell.

6049. R: O worse than death indeed!
A: Angels, ever bright and fair   Soprano
Part of Theodora, Act I.   e3-f4   a3-f4   Sustained in slow tempo.
Dramatic recitative and gentle aria.   Generally on MF level.   Descend-
ing ending line.   Acc: 3-4 (S)GS-high, medium

B.   Mezzo-Soprano and Contralto

ALEXANDER BALUS
Oratorio 1748, texts by Thomas Morell.

6050. R: Calm thou my soul
A: Convey me to some peaceful shore   Mezzo-Soprano
Part of Cleopatra.   e3-f♯4   g3-e4   Slow, subdued and contemplative
recitative, and a sustained aria in slow tempo.   Generally on MF
level.   Acc: 3 CSH-3

6051. Here amid the shady woods   Mezzo-Soprano
Part of Cleopatra.   d3-f4   f3-e4   Sustained in slow tempo.   Graceful,
generally on MF level.   Descending ending line.   Acc: 3 CSH-3

6052. O Mithra, with thy brightest beams   Mezzo-Soprano
Part of Alexander.   c3-f4   f3-d4   Animated in moderate lively tempo.

Has three florid passages.   Generally on MF level.   Descending ending line.   Gently graceful.   Acc: 3 CSH-3

6053.   Subtle love, with fancy viewing   Mezzo-Soprano
Part of Aspasia.   d3-e4 e3-d4 Animated vocal part in slow tempo.
Has florid passages.   Requires flexibility.   Generally on MF level.
Slightly climactic ending.   Acc: 3-4 CSH-3

ATHALIA
Oratorio 1733, texts by Samuel Humphreys, based on Jean Racine.

6054.   R: O Judah, Judah! chosen seed!
A: O Lord, whom we adore   Mezzo-Soprano, Contralto
Part of Joad, Act I.   b♭2-c4 d3-b♭3 Generally subdued recitative
and sustained aria in slow tempo.   Slightly animated second section.
Subdued, descending ending line.   Acc: 3 ASS-A

6055.   R: Great Prophetess!
A: In the battle, fame pursuing   Mezzo-Soprano, Contralto
Part of Barak, Act II.   a2-d4 d3-b3 Short recitative and slightly
spirited and animated aria.   Florid, requires flexibility.   Extended
instrumental prelude.   Acc: 3-4 ASS-A

BELSHAZZAR
Oratorio 1745, texts by Charles Jennens.

6056.   Great God, who yet but darkly known   Contralto
Part of Cyrus.   c3-d4 e3-c4 Sustained in slow tempo.   Graceful in
3/4 time.   Generally on MF level.   Short.   Acc: 3 CSH-4, (VS)NO

DEBORAH
Oratorio 1733, texts by Samuel Humphreys.

6057.   Impious mortal   Mezzo-Soprano, Contralto
Part of Barak.   b♭2-e♭4 e♭3-c4 Animated vocal part in slow tempo.   In quasi-majestic style.   Has climactic passages.   Agitated accompaniment.   Acc: 3-4 CSH-4

ESTHER
Oratorio 1733, second version, texts by Alexander Pope and John
Arbuthnot, after Jean Racine, other texts by Samuel Humphreys.

6058.   Hope, thou pure and dearest treasure   Mezzo-Soprano
Part of Mordecai.   b2-e4 e3-e4 Sustained in slow tempo.   Generally
on MF level.   Has some slightly climactic passages.   Acc: 3 CSH-3

6059.   R: Guards sieze the traitor
A: Through the nation he shall be   Mezzo-Soprano, Contralto
Part of Ahasuerus.   b2-c♯4 d♯3-c♯4 Dramatic recitative and sustained, majestic aria in moderate slow tempo.   Has florid passages,
one of which is extended.   Requires flexibility.   Descending ending
line.   Acc: 4 CSH-4

ISRAEL IN EGYPT
Oratorio 1739, texts compiled from Exodus.

6060.   Thou shalt bring them in   Mezzo-Soprano, Contralto
b2-c♯4(e4) e3-b3 Sustained in slow tempo.   Generally on MF level.

Has some florid passages, and requires flexibility. Acc: 3-4
(VS)GS. ASS-A

JOSHUA
Oratorio 1748, texts by Thomas Morell.

6061. R: But who is this?
A: Awful, pleasing being, say   Mezzo-Soprano, Contralto
Part of Othniel, contralto, Act I. b2-e4 e3-c♯4 Slightly animated
recitative and sustained, slow aria. Has two florid passages and
some climactic passages. Acc: 3 ASS-A

6062. R: Now give the army breath
A: Heroes, when with glory burning   Mezzo-Soprano, Contralto
Part of Othniel, contralto, Act II. c3-f4 e3-c4 Animated recitative
and aria. Marked, strong in passages. Has a few short florid passages. Extended instrumental prelude. Acc: 3 ASS-A

JUDAS MACCABAEUS
Oratorio 1747, texts by Thomas Morell, after the Bible.

6063. Father of heaven   Mezzo-Soprano, Contralto
Part of the Priest, Part 3. c3-f4 d3-d4 Sustained in moderate slow
tempo. Has some florid figures. Requires flexibility. A solemn
prayer. Has a few climactic passages. Acc: 3-4 (VS)GS. ASS-A

MESSIAH
Oratorio 1742, texts compiled and adapted from the Bible by Charles
Jennens.

6064. But who may abide the day of His coming?   Mezzo-Soprano, Contralto
g2-e4 c3-d4 Alternating slow-sustained and very rapid-animated sections. Florid, requires considerable flexibility, and some fluent enunciation. Climactic ending. This version was composed in 1750 for
the male alto, Gaetano Guadagni. Handel had it sung also by a woman
alto and transposed it also for soprano. There is no evidence that it
was done by a bass during Handel's time. Acc: 5 (VS)WS

6065. R: Then shall the eyes of the blind
A: He shall feed His flock   Mezzo-Soprano, Contralto
c3-d4 d3-c4 Version B, Part I. Recitative and sustained air in
slow tempo. Gentle, generally on MF level. Part II "Come unto
Him" is sung by the soprano. Acc: 3 (VS)JC, WS, GS, NO, CP

6066. He was despised   Mezzo-Soprano, Contralto
b♭2-c3 d3-b♭3 Version A. Sustained in slow tempo. Faster and
more agitated middle section, with dramatic energy, and incisive
rhythm. Intense. Acc: 3-4 (VS)JC, WS, GS, NO, CP. ASS-A

6067. How beautiful are the feet   Mezzo-Soprano, Contralto
b♭2-d4 c3-c4 Version C. Sustained in moderate slow tempo. Flowing, and must not be sung too slowly. Gentle and graceful. Version
II in the Watkins Shaw edition. Acc: 3-4 (VS)JC, WS

6068. If God be for us   Mezzo-Soprano, Contralto
a♭2-d♭4 c3-c4 Version II for contralto. Sustained in moderate slow
tempo. Has some extended and florid passages. Textwise, one of
the most dynamic solos in MESSIAH. Acc: 3-4 (VS)WS

6069. R: Behold, a Virgin shall conceive
       A: O thou that tellest good tidings   Mezzo-Soprano, Contralto
       a2-b3 d3-a3 Short recitative and a sustained air. Has florid pas-
       sages and graceful movement. If used as a solo, omit the choral
       section. Acc: 3-4 (VS)JC, WS, GS, NO, CP. ASS-A

6070. Thou art gone up on high   Mezzo-Soprano, Contralto
       Version B: c3-f4 e3-e4 Version C: a2-e4 d3-c4 Sustained in
       moderate slow tempo. Long lines, and slowly moving melismas.
       One of the finest arias in MESSIAH. In the Appendix of the Cooper-
       smith edition. Acc: 3-4 (VS)JC, WS

                                 SAMSON
       Oratorio 1743, texts by Newburgh Hamilton, adapted from John Mil-
       ton's Samson Agonistes, and other works.

6071. Return, oh God of Hosts!   Mezzo-Soprano, Contralto
       Part of Micah, Act II. bb2-eb4 d3-c4 Sustained in very slow tem-
       po. On MF level in the first half; stronger and fuller sounding sec-
       ond half. The text is a prayer. Acc: 3-4 45A-3, ASS-A. (VS)GS

6072. The Holy One of Israel   Mezzo-Soprano, Contralto
       Part of Micah, contralto, Act III. a2-b3 d3-b3 Animated in lively
       tempo. Has florid passages. Has phrases with low tessitura. Sub-
       dued, low ending. Acc: 3-4 (VS)GS

6073. Then long eternity   Contralto
       Part of Micah. a2-d4 d3-c#4 Generally sustained, first in slow
       tempo, then in moderate slow tempo. Has florid passages. Requires
       flexibility. Slightly climactic ending. Acc: 3 CSH-4. (VS)GS

6074. Ye sons of Israel, now lament   Mezzo-Soprano, Contralto
       Part of Micah, contralto, Act III. bb2-db4 eb3-c4 Sustained in
       slow tempo. Subdued and short. Acc: 3 (VS)GS

                                  SAUL
       Oratorio 1739, texts by Charles Jennens.

6075. Oh Lord, whose mercies numberless   Mezzo-Soprano, Contralto
       Part of David, contralto, Act I. bb2-d4 f3-c4 Sustained in slow
       tempo. Has some short, florid figures. The rest marks must be
       followed as written. Acc: 3 ASS-A

                                SOLOMON
       Oratorio 1749, texts by unknown author.

6076. Haste to the cedar grove   Mezzo-Soprano
       Part of Solomon. b2-f#4 e3-d4 Sustained in moderate slow tempo.
       Has some florid passages and figures. Generally on MF level. De-
       scending ending line. Acc: 3-4 CSH-3

6077. R: Gold now is common
       A: How green our fertile pastures look Mezzo-Soprano, Contralto
       Part of Solomon. a2-e4 e3-d4 Secco recitative and an animated
       aria in moderate tempo. Has florid passages. Requires flexibility.
       Requires some fluent enunciation. Acc: 3-4 CSH-4

6078. What though I trace each herb and flower   Mezzo-Soprano, Contralto

Part of Solomon, contralto, Act I. c#3-e4 e3-c#4 Sustained in
moderate slow tempo. Requires some flexibility. Acc: 3-4 ASS-A

SUSANNA
Oratorio 1749, texts by unknown author.

6079. Beneath the cypress' gloomy shade   Mezzo-Soprano, Contralto
Part of the Attendant. d3-f4 a3-d4 Sustained in moderate tempo.
In Siciliana style; generally on MF level. Descending ending line.
Short. Acc: 3 CSH-3

6080. R: What means this weight?
A: Bending to thy throne   Mezzo-Soprano, Contralto
Part of Susanna. c#3-e4 e3-d4 Recitative on MF level, and a sustained aria in slow tempo. Generally on MF level. Slightly climactic ending. Acc: 3 CSH-3

6081. R: Lead me, Oh lead me
A: Crystal strains in murmurs flowing   Mezzo-Soprano, Contralto
Part of Susanna. d3-g4 f#3-e4 Short secco recitative and a sustained aria in moderate slow tempo. Slightly subdued. Some gently
animated vocal lines. Requires some flexibility. Descending ending
line. Agitated accompaniment. Acc: 3-4 CSH-3

6082. Gold within the furnace tried   Contralto
Part of Joachim. b2-e4 d#3-c#4 Animated in lively tempo. Has
two extended and florid passages, and a few florid figures. Requires
some fluent enunciation. Acc: 3-4 CSH-4

6083. R: Frost nips the flowers
A: On fair Euphrates' verdant side   Contralto
Part of Joachim. b2-e4 e3-c#4 Secco recitative and a sustained
aria in slow tempo. Has florid passages. Slightly climactic ending.
Acc: 3-4 CSH-4

6084. The bird that flies in search of food   Contralto
Part of Joachim. b2-e4 e3-d4 Sustained in slow tempo. Generally
on MF level. Has a few florid figures. Acc: 3 CSH-4

6085. R: A love like mine
A: When first I saw my lovely maid   Contralto
Part of Joachim, contralto, Act I. c#3-e4 f#3-d4 Somewhat sub-
dued recitative, and a gently animated, graceful aria in slow tempo.
Strong descending ending. May also be sung by tenor. Acc: 3
ASS-A

THE TRIUMPH OF TIME AND TRUTH
Oratorio 1708 & 1757, texts by Cardinal Benedetto Panfili, English
translation by Thomas Morell.

6086. Dryads, Sylvans, with fair Flora   Mezzo-Soprano
Part of Pleasure. bb2-f4 eb3-eb4 Sustained in moderate slow tempo. Has grace, in 12/8 meter. Has some florid passages. Generally on MF level. Acc: 3 CSH-3

6087. Mortals think that Time is sleeping   Contralto
Part of Counsel. b2-d4 d3-c4 Sustained in slow tempo. Lively
second section. Has four extended and florid passages. Requires
flexibility. Acc: 3-4 CSH-4

6088.   Pleasure's gentle zephyrs play   Contralto
        Part of Deceit. b2-e4 d2-c4 Sustained in moderate slow tempo.
        Has some florid passages. Graceful. Descending ending line. Acc:
        3 CSH-4

6089.   Sorrow darkens every feature   Mezzo-Soprano
        Part of Beauty. b2-f♯4 e3-e4 Sustained in moderate slow tempo.
        Has two florid figures, and an abundance of dotted rhythms. Re-
        quires some flexibility. Descending ending line. Acc: 3 CSH-3

THEODORA
Oratorio 1749, texts by Thomas Morell.

6090.   As with rosy steps   Contralto
        Part of Irene. c3-e4 e3-c4 Sustained in slow tempo. Has some
        short florid passages; an almost syllabic treatment of texts. Slightly
        majestic. Acc: 3-4 CSH-4

6091.   R: Oh bright example
        A: Bane of virtue   Contralto
        Part of Irene. b2-e4 e3-c♯4 Secco recitative and an animated aria
        in moderate slow tempo. Has florid passages and dotted rhythms.
        Requires flexibility. Has climactic passages. Descending ending line.
        Acc: 4 CSH-4

6092.   Deeds of kindness to display   Contralto
        Part of Didimus. b2-d4 e3-c♯4 Sustained in slow tempo. Has ex-
        tended prelude. Generally on MF level. Acc: 3 CSH-4

6093.   R: The clouds begin!
        A: Defend her, heaven!   Mezzo-Soprano
        Part of Irene. d3-f♯4 e3-d4 Secco recitative and sustained aria in
        slow tempo. Has some slow-moving florid passages. Generally on
        MF level. Acc: 3 CSH-3

6094.   Lord, to Thee, each night and day   Mezzo-Soprano, Contralto
        Part of Irene, Act III. c♯3-e4 f♯3-d4 Sustained in slow tempo.
        Moderately animated, stronger second section with one florid passage.
        Acc: 3-4 ASS-A

6095.   The pilgrim's home   Mezzo-Soprano
        Part of Theodora. d3-f4 g3-e4 Sustained in slow tempo. Generally
        on MF level. Graceful. Descending ending. Acc: 3 CSH-3

6096.   R: O thou bright sun!
        A: With darkness deep   Mezzo-Soprano
        Part of Theodora. d♯3-f♯4 f♯3-d4 Secco recitative and sustained
        aria in slow tempo. Has some agitated accompaniment in the aria.
        Slightly climactic ending. Acc: 3-4 CSH-3

C. Tenor

ALEXANDER BALUS
Oratorio 1748, texts by Thomas Morell.

6097.   To God, who made the radiant sun   Tenor
        Part of Jonathan. e3-f4 f3-f4 Sustained in slow tempo. Generally
        on MF level. Bright; an exultation. Descending ending line. Acc:
        3 CSH-5

ATHALIA
Oratorio 1733, texts by Samuel Humphreys, based on Jean Racine.

6098. R: Great Queen!
      A: Gentle airs, melodious strains   Tenor
Part of Mathan, Act I. e3-f♯4 g♯3-e4 Short recitative and an aria
with gently animated vocal part in slow tempo. Has some florid figures, dotted rhythms. With violoncello obbligato. Acc: 3-4 ASS-T

BELSHAZZAR
Oratorio 1745, texts by Charles Jennens.

6099. Let the deep bowl   Tenor
Part of Belshazzar. d3-a4 f♯3-g4 Animated in lively tempo. Generally strong. Has two florid passages. Climactic ending. A drinking song. Acc: 3-4 CSH-5, (VS)NO

ESTHER
Oratorio 1733, second version, texts by Alexander Pope and John
Arbuthnot, after Jean Racine, other texts by Samuel Humphreys.

6100. R: Who dares intrude?
      A: Come, beauteous Queen   Tenor
Part of Ahasuerus; second version. f3-g4 g3-f4 Secco recitative
and sustained aria in moderate slow tempo. In pastoral style. Requires simplicity. Descending ending line. Acc: 3 CSH-5

ISRAEL IN EGYPT
Oratorio 1739, texts compiled from Exodus.

6101. The enemy said, I will pursue   Tenor
d3-a4 g3-e4 Animated in moderate slow tempo. Florid, requires
flexibility. Energetic and spirited. Extended instrumental prelude
and postlude. Acc: 3-4 (VS)GS

JEPHTHA
Oratorio 1752, texts by Thomas Morell, after the Bible.

6102. For ever blessed   Tenor
Part of Jephtha. g3-g4 b♭3-e♭4 Sustained in slow tempo. Generally on MF level. Slightly climactic ending. Short. Acc: 3 CSH-5

6103. R: Horror! Confusion!
      A: Open thy marble jaws   Tenor
Part of Jephtha. c3-a♭4 f3-e♭4 Dramatic secco recitative and an
animated aria in lively tempo. Slightly dramatic and intense. Has
climactic passages. Acc: 3 CSH-5

6104. R: Deeper, and deeper still
      A: Waft her, angels, through the skies   Tenor
Part of Jephtha, Part II. d3-a4 g3-g4 An extended and dramatic
recitative which was not originally intended to precede the aria. Sustained aria in moderate slow tempo. Has florid passages. Gently
agitated accompaniment. Acc: 4 45A-1, ASS-T, AUK

JOSHUA
Oratorio 1748, texts by Thomas Morell.

6105.   R: So long the memory shall last
        A: While Kedron's brook   Tenor
        Part of Joshua. e3-g4 a3-f4 Short secco recitative and a sustained
        aria in moderate slow tempo. Has extended florid passages. Re-
        quires flexibility. Has some slightly climactic passages. Acc: 3-4
        CSH-5

                        JUDAS MACCABAEUS
        Oratorio 1747, texts by Thomas Morell, after the Bible.

6106.   R: 'Tis well, my friends!
        A: Call forth thy powers, my soul   Tenor
        Part of Judas, Part I. d3-a4 a3-f♯4 Secco recitative and animated
        aria in lively tempo. Florid. Requires flexibility. Has dramatic
        passages, and a climactic ending. Acc: 3-4 (VS)GS

6107.   R: Thanks to my brethren!
        A: How vain is man   Tenor
        Part of Judas, Part II. d3-g4(a4) f3-f4 Secco recitative and sus-
        tained aria in moderate tempo. Has florid and dramatic sections.
        Subdued, more gentle middle section. Acc: 3-4 (VS)GS

6108.   R: Sweet flow the strains
        A: No unhallowed desire   Tenor
        Part of Judas, Part III. f3-g4 g3-f4 Subdued secco recitative and
        an animated aria in lively tempo. Marked; has two florid and also
        climactic passages. Acc: 3-4 (VS)GS

6109.   R: My arms! against this Gorgias will I go!
        A: Sound an alarm   Tenor
        Part of Judas, Part II. d3-a4 f♯3-f♯4 Dramatic secco recitative,
        and an animated aria in lively martial tempo. Strong, dramatic, and
        florid. Dramatic ending. Acc: 3-4 (VS)GS. ASS-T

                            MESSIAH
        Oratorio 1742, texts compiled and adapted from the Bible by Charles
        Jennens.

6110.   R: Thy rebuke....Behold, and see.... He was cut off
        A: But thou didst not leave his soul   Tenor
        d♯3-g♯4 e3-e4 Three short recitatives and a gently animated air.
        The air is graceful, but incisive. Vibrant. Agitated accompaniment.
        Acc: 3-4 (VS)JC, WS, GS, NO, CP

6111.   R: Comfort ye my people
        A: Every valley   Tenor
        d♯3-g♯4 e3-e4 Sustained recitative and a very florid aria. Re-
        quires considerable flexibility. Sustained, in long lines. Climactic
        ending. Acc: 4 (VS)JC, WS, GS, NO, CP. ASS-T

6112.   Rejoice   Tenor
        Version A: d3-ab4 g3-f4; Version B: eb3-ab4 g3-f4 Animated in
        lively tempo. Bright, joyous, very florid. Requires considerable
        flexibility. The middle section is oftentimes sung too slowly and in a
        sentimental manner, which is the wrong approach. Version A is in
        12/8 time, with triplet figures in the florid passages. The accom-
        paniment in this version is simpler than that of the more popular ver-
        sion B. Acc: Version A: 3-4; Version B: 4-5. (VS)JC, WS.

Version B only: (VS)GS, NO, CP

6113. Their sound is gone out   Tenor
        f3-g4 f3-f4 Version C. Animated in moderate tempo. Short.
        Version II in the Watkins Shaw edition. Acc: 3 (VS)JC, WS

6114. R: He that dwelleth in heaven
        A: Thou shalt break them   Tenor
        e3-a4 g3-g4 Version A. Recitative and a sustained air in moderate
        slow tempo. Has florid passages. Quasi-dramatic. Traditionally,
        the aria is ended on a4. Acc: 4 (VS)JC, WS, GS, NO, CP. ASS-T

OCCASIONAL ORATORIO
Oratorio 1746, texts by Thomas Morell, from Milton, Spenser, etc.

6115. He has His mansion fixed on high   Tenor
        e3-g4 f♯3-f♯4 Sustained in slow tempo. Generally on MF level.
        Has two florid passages and slightly climactic passages. Slightly cli-
        mactic ending. Acc: 3 CSH-5

6116. Jehovah! to my words give ear   Tenor
        d♯3-f♯4 f♯3-e4 Sustained in moderate slow tempo. Has some
        slightly climactic passages. Extended instrumental prelude and post-
        lude. With violin obbligato. Acc: 3 ASS-T

6117. O Lord, how many are my foes!   Tenor
        d3-g4 g3-e4 Sustained in slow tempo. Generally on MF level.
        Syllabic treatment of the text. Acc: 3 CSH-5

SAMSON
Oratorio 1743, texts by Newburgh Hamilton, adapted from John Milton's Samson Agonistes, and other works.

6118. Great Dagon has subdued our foe   Tenor
        Part of the Philistine. d♯3-g4 g3-g4 Animated in lively tempo.
        Generally strong, energetic, jovial, in praise of the pagan god. Has
        two florid passages. Descending ending line. Acc: 3-4 CSH-5

6119. Thus when the sun in his watery bed   Tenor
        Part of Samson, Act III. d3-g4 g3-e4 Slightly animated vocal part
        in moderate slow tempo. Has florid passages. Generally on MF
        level. Extended instrumental prelude. Descriptive text. Acc: 3-4
        (VS)GS

6120. Total eclipse!   Tenor
        Part of Samson, tenor, Act I. e3-g4 g3-e4 Sustained in somewhat
        slow tempo. Generally subdued. Short. Rather sombre. Acc: 3
        (VS)GS. ASS-T

6121. Why does the God of Israel sleep?   Tenor
        Part of Samson, Act I. d3-ab4 g3-g4 Animated in lively tempo.
        Florid, requires flexibility. Has some climactic passages, and a cli-
        mactic ending. Extended instrumental prelude and postlude. Acc: 4
        (VS)GS. ASS-T

SOLOMON
Oratorio 1749, text by unknown author.

6122. R: From morn to eve
A: See yonder palm   Tenor
Part of Zadok. e3-a4 g3-g4 Secco recitative and an animated aria
in lively tempo. Has florid passages. Generally on MF level. Descending ending line. Acc: 3-4 CSH-5

SUSANNA
Oratorio 1749, texts by unknown author.

6123. Ask if yon damask rose be sweet   Tenor
Part of the Attendant, Act II. Originally for soprano. d3-g4 g3-
eb4 Gently animated in moderate lively tempo. Generally light and
graceful. Acc: 3 YAR, RES-2

6124. R: A love like mine
A: When first I saw my lovely maid   Tenor
Part of Joachim, originally for contralto, Act I. c#3-e4 f#3-d4
Slightly subdued recitative and a gently animated and graceful aria in
moderate slow tempo. Strong descending ending. Acc: 3 ASS-A

6125. R: Tyrannic love!
A: Ye verdant hills, ye balmy vales   Tenor
Part of the First Elder, Act I. d3-f#4 f#3-e4 Extended dramatic
recitative and a sustained aria in moderate slow tempo. Requires
fine P and PP. A short and simple air. No recitative in CSH.
Acc: 3-4 ASS-T, CSH-5

THE TRIUMPH OF TIME AND TRUTH
Oratorio 1708 & 1757, texts by Cardinal Benedetto Panfili, English
translation by Thomas Morell.

6126. As clouds from the rage of the tempest   Tenor
Part of Pleasure. d3-a4 g3-g4 Animated in lively tempo. Slower
middle section. Has florid passages. Requires flexibility. Has
some climactic and intense passages. Dramatic ending. Generally
agitated accompaniment. Acc: 4 CSH-5

6127. Pensive sorrow   Tenor
Part of Pleasure. e3-a4 a3-f#4 Sustained in moderate slow tempo.
Has florid passages. Requires flexibility. Generally on MF level.
Acc: 3 CSH-5

D. Baritone and Bass

ALEXANDER BALUS
Oratorio 1748, texts by Thomas Morell.

6128. R: Ungrateful child
A: O sword and thou, all-daring hand   Baritone, Bass
Part of Ptolemy. g1-e3 c2-d3 Secco recitative and an animated
aria in lively tempo. Has florid passages. Generally strong. Has
some low tessitura. Descending ending with a1 as the last note.
Acc: 3-4 CSH-6

6129. R: And thus let happy Egypt's king
A: Thrice happy the monarch   Baritone, Bass
Part of Ptolemy. a1-f3 eb2-eb3 Secco recitative and animated aria
in lively tempo. Bright. Requires flexibility. Has florid passages

and a descending ending.   Generally agitated accompaniment.   Acc:
4   CSH-6

6130.   R: Thus far my wishes thrive
        A: Virtue, thou ideal name   Baritone, Bass
        Part of Ptolemy.   a1-e3 c♯2-d3 Extended secco recitative and an
        animated aria in lively tempo.   Florid, requires flexibility.   Has
        some fairly low tessitura.   Low ending on a1.   Agitated accompani-
        ment.   Acc: 4   CSH-6

ATHALIA
Oratorio 1733, texts by Samuel Humphreys, based on Jean Racine.

6131.   When storms the proud   Bass
        Part of Abner.   g1-f3   c2-d3 Animated in lively tempo.   Has florid
        passages and some low tessitura.   Requires flexibility.   Has climac-
        tic passages, extended instrumental prelude, and agitated accompani-
        ment.   Acc: 4   CSH-7

BELSHAZZAR
Oratorio, 1745, texts by Charles Jennens.

6132.   Behold the monstrous human beast   Baritone, Bass
        Part of Gobrias, bass, Act I.   g1-f3   d2-d3 Animated in lively tem-
        po.   Has florid passages, and passages with high tessitura.   Requires
        some fine high P and flexibility.   Agitated accompaniment.   Acc: 4
        SGO-B, (VS)NO

6133.   R: O memory, still bitter to my soul!
        A: Oppressed with never ceasing care   Baritone, Bass
        Part of Gobrias.   b♭1-e♭3   d2-d3 Secco recitative and a sustained
        air in slow tempo.   Has florid passages, climactic passages, and
        some wide intervalic skips.   Intense.   Acc: 3-4   CSH-6, (VS)NO

6134.   To power immortal   Baritone, Bass
        Part of Gobrias.   a1-e3   d2-c3 Sustained in slow tempo.   Generally
        on MF level.   Has two florid figures, and a descending ending line.
        See the other version in 12/8 time.   Acc: 3-4   CSH-6, (VS)NO

6135.   To power immortal   Baritone, Bass
        Part of Gobrias.   g1-d3   d2-c3 Sustained in slow tempo.   In Siciliana
        style.   Generally subdued, with a low ending.   Best for bass.   See
        the other version above which is in 3/4 time.   Acc: 3   CSH-7,
        (VS)NO

DEBORAH
Oratorio 1733, texts by Samuel Humphreys.

6136.   Tears such as tender fathers shed   Baritone, Bass
        Part of Abinoam, Act III.   b♭1-e♭3   e♭2-c3 Sustained in slow tem-
        po.   Generally gentle and subdued.   Descending ending line.   Short.
        Acc: 3   ASS-B

ESTHER
Oratorio 1732, first version, texts by Alexander Pope and John
Arbuthnot, after Racine.

6137.   How thou art fallen   Baritone, Bass

Part of Haman. c2-e3 e2-d3 Sustained in slow tempo. Has wide
intervalic skips and some climactic passages. Descending ending line.
Acc: 3 CSH-6

6138. Turn not, O Queen   Baritone, Bass
Part of Haman. c2-d3 d2-c3 Sustained in slow tempo. Generally
on MF level. Short. Chordal accompaniment. Acc: 3 CSH-6

JEPHTHA
Oratorio 1752, texts by Thomas Morell, after the Bible.

6139. R: Let me congratulate
A: Laud her, all ye virgin train   Baritone, Bass
Part of Zebul. c#2-d3 d2-d3 Secco recitative and animated aria in
lively tempo. Has two florid passages. Bright and joyous. Acc:
3 CSH-6

JOSEPH AND HIS BRETHREN
Oratorio 1744, texts by James Miller.

6140. Since the race of time has run   Bass
Part of Pharaoh. g1-e3 d2-d3 Animated in moderate lively tempo.
Florid, with some wide intervalic skips. Requires flexibility. Has
climactic passages. Generally agitated accompaniment. Acc: 4
CSH-7

JOSHUA
Oratorio 1748, texts by Thomas Morell.

6141. See the raging flames   Baritone, Bass
Part of Caleb, bass, Act II. a1-e3 c2-c3 Animated in lively tempo.
Florid, energetic, and requires flexibility. Climactic ending on a1.
Acc: 4-5 45A-1, SGO-B

6142. R: My cup is full
A: Shall I in Mamre's fertile plain   Baritone, Bass
Part of Caleb, bass, Act III. g1-eb3 eb2-c3 Short recitative and
sustained aria in slow tempo. Generally on MF level. Subdued ending, no climactic passages. Acc: 3 SGO-B

JUDAS MACCABAEUS
Oratorio 1747, texts by Thomas Morell, after the Bible.

6143. R: I feel the deity within
A: Arm, arm, ye brave!   Baritone, Bass
Part of Simon, bass, Part I. b1-e3 c2-d3 Majestic recitative and
a lively, dramatic aria. Has some short florid figures and strong
rhythm. Marked and energetic. Climactic ending. Acc: 3-4
45A-2, ASS-B. (VS)GS. (S)GS-medium, low

6144. R: Not vain is all this storm of grief
A: Pious orgies, pious airs   Baritone, Bass
Part of Simon, Part I. g1-eb3 eb2-c3 Secco recitative and sus-
tained aria in slow tempo. Requires some flexibility. Generally gen-
tle and subdued. Subdued ending. Best for bass. Acc: 3 ASS-B,
(VS)GS

6145. Rejoice, oh Judah!   Baritone, Bass

Part of Simon, Part III. a1-e3 e2-d3 Sustained in moderate tempo.
Has climactic passages. This part directly precedes a chorus. Climactic ending. Acc: 3-4 (VS)GS. SGO-B

LA RESURREZIONE
Oratorio 1708, texts by Carlo Sigismondo Capece.

6146. R: Ha! what vision effulgent
       A: Haste! Fiends of Erebus   Baritone
       Part of Lucifer. g1-f3 eb2-eb3 A slightly extended accompanied
       recitative, and an animated aria in moderate tempo. Generally
       strong. Has some florid passages. Generally agitated accompani-
       ment. Acc: 3-4 CSH-6

MESSIAH
Oratorio 1742, texts compiled and adapted from the Bible by Charles
Jennens.

6147. R: Thus saith the Lord
       A: But who may abide   Baritone, Bass
       Version A: a1-f3 c2-d3; Version B: g1(a1)-e3 c2-d3 Sustained in
       slow and fast tempi. Majestic, florid recitative in moderate tempo.
       In the aria, alternating very subdued and slow section with very rapid,
       animated, very florid, and spirited section. Version A is in the Ap-
       pendix of the Coopersmith edition; Version B is the better-known.
       Accompaniment is agitated in the fast sections. In the Watkins Shaw
       edition, the aria is for contralto, another version. Acc: 5 (VS)JC,
       WS. Version B only: (VS)GS, NO, CP. ASS-B

6148. R: For, behold, darkness
       A: The people that walked in darkness   Baritone, Bass
       f#1(a1)-e3 c#2-c#3 Sustained in moderate slow tempo. Long lines.
       Requires flexibility. Shows more chromaticism than most Handel airs.
       Often done too slowly. The lines must move gently. Acc: 3 (VS)JC,
       WS, GS, NO, CP. ASS-B

6149. R: Behold, I tell you a mystery
       A: The trumpet shall sound   Baritone, Bass
       a1-e3 d1-d3 Subdued recitative and majestic, broad, and energetic
       aria with long-sustained notes and florid passages. Unfortunately the
       second section of the aria is sometimes omitted in most performances.
       Extended instrumental prelude. Acc: 4 (VS)JC, WS, GS, NO, CP.
       ASS-B

6150. Thou art gone up on high   Baritone, Bass
       bb1-e3 d2-d3 Version A. Sustained in moderate slow tempo. Long
       lines, slowly moving melismas. One of the finest arias in MESSIAH.
       In the Watkins Shaw edition, this aria is in Appendix. Acc: 3-4
       (VS)WS, JC, GS, NO, CP

6151. Why do the nations so furiously rage together   Baritone, Bass
       b1-e3 d2-d3 Versions A and B. Animated in rapid tempo. Strong,
       dramatic, and very florid. Requires considerable flexibility. Agi-
       tated accompaniment. This is originally not a Da Capo aria. Ver-
       sion A is the one used often. Section two of Version B is brief, and
       not florid. Acc: 5 (VS)JC, WS. Version A only: (VS)GS, NO, CP.
       ASS-B

OCCASIONAL ORATORIO
Oratorio 1746, texts by Thomas Morell, from Milton, Spenser, etc.

6152. R: Humbled with fear
A: His scepter is the rod of righteousness   Bass
f♯1-e3 c♯2-c♯3 Slightly extended secco recitative, and an animated
aria in lively tempo. Strong, climactic, and florid. Requires flexibility. Has some very low tessitura. Climactic ending. Requires
some fluent enunciation. Extended instrumental prelude and postlude.
Acc: 4 CSH-7, ASS-B, SGO-B

6153. To God, our strength   Baritone, Bass
a1-e3 d2-d3 Sustained in moderate slow tempo. Slightly faster middle section. Generally strong and exultant. Has florid passages.
Requires flexibility. Descending ending line. Acc: 3-4 CSH-6

6154. Why do the gentiles tumult?   Baritone, Bass
a1-e3 d2-c3 The text is similar to the one used in MESSIAH, "Why
do the nations so furiously rage." Animated in lively tempo. Requires some fluent enunciation, and some flexibility. Has florid passages. Generally strong and climactic. Extended instrumental prelude, and agitated accompaniment. Acc: 4 CSH-7

SAMSON
Oratorio 1743, texts by Newburgh Hamilton, adapted from John Milton's Samson Agonistes, and other works.

6155. Honor and arms   Baritone, Bass
Part of Harapha, bass, Act II. g1-e♭3 b♭2-d3 Energetic, rhythmic,
somewhat on the pompous side, in lively tempo. Florid, with a climactic ending. Requires flexibility and a fine command of the high
register. Acc: 3-4 45A-3, ASS-B. (VS)GS

6156. How willing my paternal love   Baritone, Bass
Part of Manoah, bass, Act III. b1-e3 c♯2-c♯3 Sustained in slightly
slow tempo. Has some short florid figures. Generally on MF level.
Short. Acc: 3-4 45A-2. (VS)GS

6157. Presuming slave! to move their wrath!   Baritone, Bass
Part of Harapha, bass, Act III. g1-e♭3 c2-d3 Animated in moderate lively tempo. Outgoing and somewhat pompous. Has florid passages and a descending ending line. Extended instrumental postlude.
Acc: 3-4 (VS)GS

6158. Thy glorious deeds inspired my tongue   Baritone, Bass
Part of Manoah, bass, Act I. b♭1-f3 c2-d3 Sustained in lively tempo. Has some long and florid lines. Majestic. Requires some flexibility and a fine command of high tessitura. Ends with a sustained,
quite slow, and subdued section over chordal accompaniment. Best
for baritone. Acc: 3-4 45A-3, SGO-B. (VS)GS

SAUL
Oratorio 1739, texts by Charles Jennens.

6159. A serpent in my bosom warmed   Baritone, Bass
Part of Saul. b♭1-e♭3 e♭2-d3 Animated in lively tempo. Generally
on MF level. Has florid passages. Requires flexibility. Extended instrumental prelude; and agitated accompaniment. Acc: 4 CSH-7

SOLOMON
Oratorio 1749, text by unknown author.

6160. R: Great prince, thy resolution's just
       A: Thrice blest that wise discerning king   Bass
       Part of the Levite. g1-d3 c2-c3 Secco recitative and an animated
       aria in lively tempo. Has some florid passages, some low tessitura,
       and some climactic passages. Low ending. Acc: 3-4 CSH-7

SUSANNA
Oratorio 1749, texts by unknown author.

6161. Peace, peace crowned with roses   Bass
       Part of Chelsias. a1-e3 d2-c3 Very sustained in slow tempo.
       Slightly subdued. Has two florid figures. Descending ending. Short.
       Acc: 3 CSH-7

6162. The oak that for a thousand years   Bass
       Part of the 2nd Elder. f1-e3 d2-c3 Animated in moderate lively
       tempo. Has florid passages with some wide intervalic skips, and
       some low tessitura. Generally agitated accompaniment. Low ending.
       Acc: 3-4 CSH-7

THE TRIUMPH OF TIME AND TRUTH
Oratorio 1708 & 1757, texts by Cardinal Benedetto Panfili, English
translation by Thomas Morell.

6163. R: You hoped to call in vain
       A: False, destructive ways of pleasure   Baritone
       Part of Time. a♭1-f3 c2-e♭3 Secco recitative and an animated
       aria in lively tempo. Has florid passages. Requires flexibility. De-
       scending ending. Acc: 3-4 CSH-6

6164. From the heart that feels my warning   Baritone, Bass
       Part of Time. a♯1-d3 d2-d3 Sustained in moderate slow tempo.
       Has florid passages. Requires flexibility. Descending ending. Acc:
       3 CSH-6

6165. Like the shadow   Bass
       Part of Time. a1-d3 d2-c♯3 Sustained in moderate slow tempo.
       Generally on MF level. Has one passage with low tessitura. Short.
       Descending ending. Acc: 3 CSH-7

THEODORA
Oratorio 1749, texts by Thomas Morell.

6166. R: 'Tis Dioclesian's natal day
       A: Go, my faithful soldier, go   Baritone, Bass
       Part of Valens. a1-e3 d2-d3 Secco recitative and sustained aria in
       moderate tempo. Pompous and somewhat majestic. Has some florid
       passages. Generally strong. Climactic descending ending. For some
       unknown reason, Handel replaced this aria with a four-bar recitative.
       Acc: 3-4 CSH-6

6167. Wide spread his name   Baritone, Bass
       Part of Valens. a1-d3 c2-c3 Animated in moderate lively tempo.
       Has florid passages, some wide intervalic skips, and climactic pas-
       sages. Strong, descending ending. Acc: 3 CSH-7

IV. Solo Excerpts from Passions and Extended Anthems

Note: Due to the brevity of this section, the excerpts are arranged alphabetically by aria titles.

A. Soprano

6168. Ah! the pains that now afflict Him   Soprano
Work: Der für die Sünden der Welt gemarterte und sterbende Jesus. Passion 1716, texts by Barthold Heinrich Brockes. Part of the Daughter of Zion. d3-f♯4 f♯3-e4 Sustained in slow tempo. Generally subdued. Has one florid passage. Acc: 3 CSH-2

6169. And shall my sin-stained soul   Soprano
Work: Der für die Sünden der Welt gemarterte und sterbende Jesus. Passion 1716, texts by Barthold Heinrich Brockes. Part of the Daughter of Zion. d3-g4 g3-e♭4 Sustained in slow tempo. Generally subdued. Slightly somber. Includes the part of the Believer. Acc: 3 CSH-1

6170. Break, my heart   Dramatic Soprano
Work: Der für die Sünden der Welt gemarterte und sterbende Jesus. Passion 1716, texts by Barthold Heinrich Brockes. Part of the Daughter of Zion. e♭3-g4 f3-f4 Sustained in slow tempo. Generally subdued. Descending ending line. Sad texts. Acc: 3 CSH-2

6171. Excelsus super omnes   Soprano
Work: Psalm 112, Laudate Puere Dominum. Latin text. g3-g4 g3-g4 Animated in lively tempo. Graceful; has florid passages. Climactic ending. Extended instrumental prelude and postlude. Acc: 3 (VS)CP

6172. Laudate pueri Dominum   Dramatic Soprano
Work: 113th Psalm, 1702. c3-a4 f3-f4 Animated in moderate lively tempo. Has fast-moving florid passages, and some wide intervalic skips. Bright and joyous. Requires considerable flexibility and agility. Acc: 3-4 CSH-2

6173. O magnify the Lord   Soprano
Work: Chandos Anthem No. 8: O come, Let Us Sing Unto the Lord. Texts: Psalm 34:4, paraphrase by Handel. e3-g♯4 g♯3-e4 Animated in moderate tempo. Bright and joyous. Has florid passages and dotted figures. Requires flexibility. Descending ending line. Has climactic passages. Acc: 3 CSH-2

6174. Qui habitare facit   Soprano
Work: Psalm 112, Laudate Pueri Dominum. Latin text. e3-a4 f♯3-e4 Animated in lively tempo. Bright and joyous. Quite florid. Climactic ending. Slightly extended prelude and postlude. Acc: 3 (VS)CP

6175. Sinners lift your eyes and tremble   Soprano
Work: Der für die Sünden der Welt gemarterte und sterbende Jesus. Passion 1716, texts by Barthold Heinrich Brockes. Part of the Daughter of Zion. f3-g4 a3-f4 Sustained in moderate slow tempo. Has florid passages. Requires flexibility. Generally on MF level. Descending ending line. Acc: 3 CSH-1

B.   Mezzo-Soprano and Contralto

6176.   Getrost, mein Herz   Mezzo-Soprano, Contralto
Work: JOHANNESPASSION, 1704, aria texts by Christian Heinrich
Postel. Composed when Handel was 19 years old. a2-d4 f3-c4
Sustained in slow tempo. Generally on MF level. The accompani-
ment can be read directly from the full score. Acc: 3 WGH-72

6177.   I will magnify Thee, O God my King   Mezzo-Soprano, Contralto
Work: Chandos Anthem No. 5b: I will magnify Thee. Text: Psalm
145:1. b2-d4 e3-b3 Sustained in moderate slow tempo. Has some
florid figures. Requires some flexibility. Generally on MF level.
Descending ending phrase. Not a Da Capo air. May be read directly from the full score. Acc: 3-4 WGH-54

6178.   My tears are my daily food   Mezzo-Soprano, Contralto
Work: Chandos Anthem No. 6b: As Pants the Hart for Cooling
Streams. Texts: Psalm 42:3. g2-b3 d3-a3 Very sustained in slow
tempo. Somber. Has some low tessitura. Generally subdued; has a
subdued ending. May be read directly from the full score. Acc: 3
WGH-54

6179.   Righteousness and equity   Mezzo-Soprano, Contralto
Work: Chandos Anthem No. 5b: I Will Magnify Thee. Text: Psalm
145, paraphrase. c♯3-d4 f♯3-c♯4 Sustained in slow tempo. Generally on MF level. Descending ending phrase. The piano accompaniment may be read directly from the full score. Acc: 3 WGH-54

6180.   Tears are my daily food   Mezzo-Soprano, Contralto
Work: Chandos Anthem No. 6c: As Pants the Hart for Cooling
Streams. Texts: Psalm 42:3. c3-c4 d3-b3 Very sustained in mod-
erate slow tempo. Subdued and short. Accompaniment which re-
quires pianoforte may be read directly from the full score. Acc: 3
WGH-54

C.   Tenor

6181.   Beatus vir   Tenor
Work: Nisi Dominus, 1707. Latin texts. e♯3-a4 a3-f♯4 Sustained
in moderate slow tempo. Has passages with high tessitura, and some
climactic passages. Acc: 3 CSH-5

6182.   Blessed are they that consider the poor   Tenor
Work: Foundling Hospital Anthem. Psalm 41:1-2. d3-g4 g3-f4
Sustained on MF level. Requires flexibility. Climactic ending. Ex-
tended instrumental prelude. Acc: 3-4 CSH-5

6183.   R: But how? must I then perish in despair?
A: Bow'd with grief   Tenor
Work: Der für die Sünden der Welt gemarterte und sterbende Jesus.
Passion 1716, texts by Barthold Heinrich Brockes. Part of Peter.
d3-g4 g3-f♯4 Short secco recitative and sustained aria in slow tempo. Has dramatic passages. Intense. Descending ending line. Acc:
3-4   CSH-5

6184.   God is a constant sure defense   Tenor
Work: Chandos Anthem No. 2: In the Lord Put I My Trust. Text:
Psalm 48:3, paraphrase by Handel. d3-a4 g3-f4 Sustained in mod-

erate slow tempo. Has two florid passages and some passages with
high tessitura. Generally on MF level, with some climactic passages. Acc: 3 CSH-5

6185. Though bound and helpless   Tenor
Work: Der für die Sünden der Welt gemarterte und sterbende Jesus.
Passion 1716, texts by Barthold Heinrich Brockes. Part of the Believer. e3-g4 a3-f4 Sustained in moderate slow tempo. Generally
on MF level. Short. Acc: 3 CSH-5

D. Baritone and Bass

6186. Die ihr Gottes Gnad'versäumet   Baritone, Bass
Work: THE PASSION OF CHRIST, texts by Barthold Heinrich Brockes.
This air is better-known by its Italian title: Chi sprezzando. d2-e3
e2-d3 Very sustained in moderate slow tempo. Somewhat intense.
Accompaniment mainly in full chords. Acc: 3 45A-1, AAP-3

6187. My father, look upon my anguish   Baritone, Bass
Work: THE PASSION OF CHRIST, texts by Barthold Heinrich Brockes.
Part of Jesus. b♭1-e♭3 d2-c3 Sustained vocal part in slow tempo.
Generally subdued, but intense. Has recitative in the middle. Agi-
tated, rhythmically intense accompaniment. Acc: 3-4 ASS-B

6188. O praise the Lord   Baritone, Bass
Work: O praise the Lord ye Angels of His (Included by Arnold as
Chandos No. 12). Texts: Psalm 103:21. b1-e3 e2-d3 Sustained
in moderate tempo. Exultant, has climactic passages. Has one
short florid passage. Low ending. Acc: 3 CSH-7

6189. O work sublime   Baritone
Work: JOHANNESPASSION, the arias by Christian Heinrich Postel,
original texts in German. Composed when Handel was 19 years old.
b♭1-f3 d2-e♭3 Sustained in slow tempo. Grave, dark, has florid
passages, and some wide intervalic skips. Requires flexibility.
Abounds in dotted rhythmic figures. Descending ending line. Text is
based on Jesus' statement, "It is finished." Acc: 3-4 CSH-6

6190. That God is great   Baritone
Work: Chandos Anthem No. 9: O praise the Lord With One Consent.
Texts: Psalm 135:5. a1-f3 d2-e♭3 Animated in rapid tempo.
Strong and climactic. Has florid passages and dotted figures. Re-
quires flexibility. Low ending. A song of exultation. Acc: 3-4
CSH-6

6191. Vouchsafe, O Lord   Baritone, Bass
Work: DETTINGEN TE DEUM. Texts: Latin hymn, translated.
d2-d♯3 e2-c♯3 Very sustained in slow tempo. Majestic, serious,
intense. Slightly climactic ending passage. Chordal accompaniment.
Appears in several transposed editions. Acc: 3 45A-2, POS-4,
MAA, CSH-7. (VS)NO, EK. (S)MW

6192. R: Ye heavens what is this?
A: When nature groans   Bass
Work: THE PASSION OF CHRIST, texts by Barthold Brockes. The
part of the Centurion. g1-e3 e♭2-d3 Slightly extended recitative and
an animated aria in moderate lively tempo. Has florid passages, with
dotted rhythms. Requires flexibility. Generally strong and climactic.

Descending ending. Acc: 3 CSH-7

6193. When Thou tookest upon Thee to deliver man   Baritone, Bass
       Work: DETTINGEN TE DEUM. Texts: Latin hymn, translated.
       d# 2-e3 e2-d3 Sustained in slow tempo. Has florid as well as cli-
       mactic passages. Requires some flexibility. Slightly climactic end-
       ing. Acc: 3 (VS)NO, EK

V. Solo Cantata

Il Gelsomino. English: The Jasmine. A solo cantata in three movements,
       two arias and a recitative, for Soprano and Basso Continuo. Anony-
       mous poet. SSM

6194. (1) A: Son gelsomino   Soprano
       d3-f4 f3-eb4 Animated in moderate lively tempo. Graceful and gen-
       erally on MF level. Has one short florid passage. One fine feature
       is the use of hemiolas. Acc: 3

NNA   (2) R: Tremolante e leggi   Soprano
       g3-e4 g3-c4 A secco recitative with gently descriptive texts. Acc:
       2

6195. (3) A: Spesso mi sento dir   Soprano
       d3-a4 a3-f4 Sustained in moderate tempo. Graceful, with some
       high tessitura. Has some slightly climactic passages. Descending
       ending phrase. Acc: 3

VI. Incidental Music for "Alceste," a Play

6196. Enjoy the sweet Elysian grove   Tenor
       Work: Alceste, 1750, texts by Tobias Smollett. The play was never
       performed. Handel used this composition in THE CHOICE OF HER-
       CULES. d3-a4 g# 3-f# 4 Animated in moderate lively tempo. Has
       fast-moving florid passages. Requires flexibility. Bright. Semi-
       climactic ending. Acc: 4 CSH-5

6197. Ye fleeting shades   Baritone
       Work: Alceste, 1750, texts by Tobias Smollett. Handel used this
       composition in THE CHOICE OF HERCULES. Part of Charon. a1-
       eb 3 d2-d3 Animated vocal part in moderate slow tempo. Has florid
       passages and frequent intervalic skips. Requires flexibility. Agitated
       accompaniment. Acc: 3-4 CSH-6

VII. Works of Doubtful Authenticity

6198. Alleluja-Amen   High Voices
       Text: Alleluja and Amen. d3-g4 g3-e4 Animated in lively tempo.
       Florid, with climactic passages. Requires some flexibility. Source
       of this song has not been established. Acc: 3 KLR

6199. Dank sei Dir, Herr   All Voices
       Text: Anon. e3-g4 g3-e4 Very sustained and slow. Majestic,
       best for the heavier voices. Sacred texts, chordal accompaniment.
       Authorship of this song has been attributed to Handel, but as of now
       quite spurious. Acc: 3 45A-3, GAS. (S)SC

Other Modern Edition of Interest

NNA   Look down, harmonious saint.
       Solo cantata for tenor, strings, and harpsichord or piano. Text:
       Anon. Edited by Denis Stevens. University Park, Pa: Pennsylvania
       State University.

C. CHRISTOPHER WILLIBALD (VON) GLUCK, 1714-1787

Gluck, an international master like Handel and Mozart, was a German composer of Bohemian parentage whose works were mostly written to French and Italian texts. He wrote very few works to German texts; to be specific, the nine odes of Friedrich Gottlieb Klopstock. Mainly a dramatist, his life work centered in the field of opera, and in several of them he reaped his greatest successes. His role in the reform of the operatic form established a consciousness of balance between drama and music, which later was also to be the principle behind Richard Wagner's music dramas. Herein, therefore, is a clue to the performance of Gluck's works.

Declamation is of supreme importance in the performance of Gluck solo excerpts, as it is in Monteverdi and Wagner. Elegance and a majestic impulse throughout are required in the recitation of his lines, whose texts and melodies are closely related.

Most of Gluck's solo writing is generally limited to dramatic soprano, high tenor, and high baritone, with fine command of high tessitura. Some of the airs seem to be pitched too high for better word projection if one merely follows the notation. This is due to the fact that pitch in Gluck's time was lower than it is today. With this consideration, therefore, it is permissible and more practical to sing them transposed down even as much as a whole step. The transposed airs would then serve musical and dramatic purposes better than the often resulting strained vocal performance or non-performance in order to please advocates of perfect authenticity.

Gluck's writing was greatly influenced by the literature with which he worked. Many of his operas are on mythological subjects, and it would help performers to get acquainted with this background. Gluck's best-known work, ORFEO ED EURIDICE, is still being heard today, and interest in the revival of lesser-known ones is evident.

DMA Deux Morceaux de Rôle d'Admète. Christopher Willibald Gluck. Paris: Henry Lemoine.

DMR Deux Morceaux de Rôle d'Agamemnon. Christopher Willibald Gluck. Paris: Henry Lemoine.

DSA Deux Scènes d'Alceste. Christopher Willibald Gluck. Paris: Henry Lemoine.

TAG Trois Ariettes de Gluck. Christopher Willibald Gluck. Paris: Henry Lemoine.

TMA Trois Petits Morceaux d'Iphigénie en Aulide. For soprano or mezzo-soprano. Paris: Henry Lemoine.

Note: Codes of general collections in which songs and arias by Gluck appear are described in the bibliographies of the chapters listed below:

Chapter IV-A (Italian):	AMB, AIS, ARB, AAP
Chapter V-A (French):	EDF-1 & 2, CCF-4

Chapter VI-A (German):   KLR, KDL, GSB, LIU
Chapter XI-A & B (Opera):   MLF(A), OPA-1(A & B),
                                OPA-2(B), OPA-5(I)

I. Soprano

ALCESTE
Opera 1767, libretto by Raniero da Calzabigi. Also performed in
French, translation by Francois Lebland du Roullet.

6200. O ciel! quel supplice quelle douleur!   Soprano
       Part of Alceste, Act II. g3-a4 c3-a4 Sustained in moderate slow
       tempo. Extremely high tessitura. Dramatic; has a dramatic high
       ending. Agitated accompaniment. Acc: 4 (VS)EC

ARMIDE
Opera 1777, libretto by Philippe Quinault.

6201. Ah! Si la liberté   Soprano
       Part of Armide, Act III. e3-g4 g3-e4 Sustained in moderate slow
       tempo. Has dramatic passages. Slightly slower middle section. Re-
       quires some flexibility. One tone lower in EDF and CCF. Acc:
       3-4 (VS)EC, HL, AD. EDF-1, CCF-1a

6202. R: Helas! c'est mon coeur que je crains
       A: De mes plus doux regards   Soprano
       Part of Armide, Act III. g3-g4 a3-f4 Dramatic recitative and sus-
       tained air in moderate tempo. Air is quite lyric, on the subdued
       side. Acc: 3-4 (VS)EC, HL, AD

6203. Jamais dans ces beaux lieux   Soprano
       Part of Lucinde, Act IV. f3-f4 bb3-f4 Sustained in moderate tem-
       po. Graceful and short air, which, in the score, precedes a choral
       section, the character singing with the sopranos. Acc: 3 (VS)EC,
       HL, AD

6204. Jeunes coeurs! tout vous est favorable   Soprano
       Part of "a soprano," Act V. d3-e4 g3-d4 Gently animated in mod-
       erate tempo. Generally light. The air follows the Sicilienne section.
       Acc: 3 (VS)EC, HL, AD

6205. La chaine de l'Hymen m'étonne   Soprano
       Part of Armide, Act I. f#3-f#4 g#3-e4 Sustained in moderate slow
       tempo. Graceful and generally light. Acc: 3-4 (VS)EC, HL, AD

6206. Les enfers ont prédit cent fois   Soprano
       Part of Armide, Act I. f3-ab4 a3-f4 Sustained in moderate tempo.
       Has dramatic climaxes and a climactic ending. Agitated accompani-
       ment. Acc: 3 (VS)EC, HL, AD

6207. On s'étonnerait moins   Soprano
       Part of the Shepherd, Act II. f#3-a4 a3-g4 Animated in minuet
       style. Generally light; requires some flexibility. Three steps lower
       in CCF and EDF-2. Acc: 3 (VS)EC, HL, AD. CCF, EDF-2, TAG

6208. Si je dois m'engager un jour   Soprano
       Part of Armide, Act I. g3-g4   a3-f♯4 Sustained in moderate tempo.
       Majestic and short. Has climactic ending. Acc: 3 (VS)EC, HL,
       AD

6209. Voici la charmante retraite   Soprano
       Part of Lucinde, Act IV. f3-f4 g3-d4 Animated in moderate tempo.
       Graceful. This air is joined to a choral section. Acc: 3 (VS)EC,
       HL, AD. EDF-2

6210. Vous troublez-vous   Soprano
       Part of Sidonie, Act I. g3-ab4 bb3-eb4 Sustained in moderate slow
       tempo. Short. Has some high climaxes and a climactic ending.
       Acc: 3 (VS)EC, HL, AD

                         IL PARNASO CONFUSO
       Opera 1765, libretto by Pietro Metastasio; French version by G.
       Antheunis.

6211. Di questa cetra in seno   Soprano
       Part of Erato, one-act opera. First French line: Au sein de cette
       lyre. d3-g4 g3-d4 Sustained in moderate slow tempo. Graceful
       and generally light. Requires fine P and PP. Issued with French
       and Italian texts. Acc: 3-4 (S)HL

                         IL TRIONFO DI CLELIA
       Opera 1763, libretto by Pietro Metastasio.

6212. Ah, ritorna età dell' oro   Soprano
       Part of Larissa. d3-b4 g3-f4 Sustained in minuet style. Graceful.
       Requires fine P and flexibility. Subdued ending. Acc: 3-4 AMB-2,
       (S)HL

                         IPHIGÉNIE EN AULIDE
       Opera 1774, libretto by Francois Lebland du Roullet, after Racine's
       tragedy based on Euripides.

6213. Adieu, conservez dans votre âme   Soprano
       Part of Iphigénie, Act III. d3-ab4 g3-f4 Sustained in slow tempo.
       Generally gentle, lyric, and requires some flexibility. Slow ending
       phrases. Acc: 3 (VS)NO. TMA, (S)HL

6214. Armez vous d'un noble courage   Soprano
       Part of Clytemnestra, Act I. bb2-g4 eb3-eb4 Animated in moder-
       ate lively tempo. Generally strong, accented, and dramatic. Re-
       quires some flexibility. Strong, descending ending line. Acc: 3-4
       (VS)NO. (S)AD

6215. Heureux guerriers, volez à la victoire   Soprano
       Part of a Greek Woman, Act III. g3-a4 a3-e4 Sustained in moder-
       ate slow tempo. Starts gently. Has dramatic passages and a climac-
       tic ending. Has some wide intervalic skips. Acc: 3 (VS)NO

6216. Il faut de mon destin subir la loi   Soprano
       Part of Iphigénie, Act III. bb2-g4 f3-eb4 Sustained in moderate
       slow tempo. Generally gentle and short. Acc: 3 (VS)NO

6217. Iphigénie, helas! vous a trop fait connaître   Soprano

Part of Iphigénie, Act I. f♯ 3-f♯ 4 g♯ 3-d4 Sustained in moderate tempo. Has some climactic passages. Intense. Strong, descending ending line. Acc: 3-4 (VS)NO

6218. Les voeux dont ce peuple   Soprano
Part of Iphigénie, Act I. f3-g4 a3-e4 Sustained in moderate slow tempo. Generally gentle and short. Acc: 3 (VS)NO. TMA

6219. R: Vous essayes en vain de bannir mes alarmes
A: Par la crainte et par l'espérance   Soprano
Part of Iphigénie, Act II. d3-a4 f3-f4 Gentle recitative and a sustained aria in generally moderate tempo. Has dramatic passages, one long-sustained note of 19 beats, and a dramatic descending ending line. Acc: 3 (VS)NO

6220. R: L'ai-je bien entendu?
A: Parjure! et tu moses trahir   Soprano
Part of Iphigénie, Act I. f3-g4 g3-f4 Generally sustained in varied tempi. Slow recitative and aria which starts moderately slow. Dramatic, strong, and accented. Climactic ending. Acc: 3-4 (VS)NO. (S)HL

6221. Que j'aime à voir ces Hommages   Soprano
Part of Clytemnestra, Act I. g3-e4 g3-e4 Sustained in moderate slow tempo. Graceful and short. Acc: 3 (VS)NO

6222. Son front est couronne   Soprano
Part of a Greek Woman, Act I. d3-f♯ 4 g♯ 3-d4 Sustained in moderate tempo. Generally on MF level. Short. Descending ending line. Acc: 3 (VS)NO

6223. Vivez, vivez pour Oreste   Soprano
Part of Iphigénie, Act III. e3-e4 g3-d4 Sustained in slow tempo. Generally gentle, short, and lyric. Acc: 3 (VS)NO. TMA

IPHIGÉNIE EN TAURIDE
Opera 1779, libretto by François Guillard, based on Euripides.

6224. R: Je cède à vos desires
A: D'une image, hélas! trop chérie   Soprano
Part of Iphigénie, Act III. f3-g4 g3-eb4 Recitative in moderate lively tempo, and a sustained, generally subdued and gentle aria in moderate slow tempo. Graceful and lyric. Acc: 3 (VS)EC, HL, NO

LA CYTHÈRE ASSIÉGÉE
Opera 1759, libretto by Charles-Simon Favart.

6225. Sous un ormeau   Soprano
Part of Carite. eb3-ab4 eb3-eb4 Sustained in moderate tempo. Generally subdued with climactic passages. Descending ending line after high climax. Acc: 3-4 TAG

LES PÈLERINS DE LA MECQUE
Opera 1764, libretto by L. H. Dancourt. Other title: LA RECONTRE IMPRÉVUE.

6226. Je cherche à vous faire   Soprano

Part of Amine, Act II.   c#3-g4   g3-d4   Animated in moderate lively
tempo. Graceful. Generally on MF level. Requires some flexibility.
Extended instrumental prelude. Acc: 3 TAG

ORFEO ED EURIDICE
Opera 1762, libretto by Ranieri da Calzabigi. Also performed in
French, with translations by Pierre-Louis Moline.

6227.   R: Ah, dovess' io saper
        A: Che fiero momento   Soprano
        Part of Euridice, Act III, Nos. 40 & 41.   French titles: R--Mais
        d'ou vient qu'il persiste; A--Fortune ennemie, quelle barbarie! e3-
        ab4 g3-f4 Extended recitative and sustained aria.   Middle section
        of the aria is a duet with Orfeo. Climactic ending. Acc: 4
        (VS)GR-Italian; NO-Italian & English; CP-French & German; GS-
        French & English

6228.   Gli sguardi trattieni   Soprano
        Part of Amor, Act I, No. 15. French first line: Soumis au silence.
        f#3-g4 g3-e4 Sustained in slow tempo. Graceful. Slower middle
        section. Acc: 3 (VS)GR-Italian; NO-Italian & English; CP-French
        & German; GS-French & English

6229.   Questo asilo di placide e grato   Soprano
        Part of Euridice or a Blessed Spirit, Act II, No. 32. French first
        line: Cet asile aimable et tranquille.   e3-a4 g3-f4 Animated in
        moderate lively tempo. Graceful 6/8 time. With chorus in the
        score. Acc: 3-4 (VS)GR-Italian; NO-Italian & English; CP-French
        & German; GS-French & English

6230.   R: Amore, assisterà
        A: Se il dolce suon de la tua lira   Soprano
        Part of Amor, Act I, Nos. 12 & 13. French first lines: R--L'amour
        vient; A--Si les doux accords de ta lyre. e3-a4 g3-f4 Animated in
        moderate lively tempo. Graceful. Requires some flexibility. Acc:
        3-4 (VS)GR-Italian; NO-Italian & English; CP-French & German; GS-
        French & English

PARIDE ED ELENA
Opera 1770, libretto by Ranieri da Calzabigi.

6231.   O del mio dolce ardor   Soprano
        Part of Paride (Paris), Act I.   b2-f#4 e3-e4 Very sustained in mod-
        erate slow tempo. Requires simplicity and a thoroughly lyric approach.
        Gluck's best-known air, now usually sung by all voices. Original Ital-
        ian texts, and an English version. Acc: 3 AIS-1, SOS-2, ARB,
        AAP-1, OAR-M(Ch. XI). (S)GS-high, low in Italian & English; HL-
        Italian & French

II. Dramatic Soprano

Most of the airs in the Soprano section are basically suited for the Dramatic
Soprano voice. The entries below are airs which are very best suited for
the true dramatic voice.

ALCESTE
Opera 1776 in French. Also performed in the original Italian version.

Libretto by Ranieri da Calzabigi; French version by François Louis Lebland du Roullet.

6232. R: Grands Dieux! soutenez mon courage!
       A: Ah! Divinitéz implacables!   Dramatic Soprano
       Part of Alceste, Act III. e3-a4 g3-g4 Extended dramatic recitative
       and a sustained air in moderate slow tempo. Has two choral interpo-
       lations. Climactic ending. Acc: 3-4 (VS)EC

6233. R: Dérobez-moi vos pleurs
       A: Ah! Malgré moi   Dramatic Soprano
       Part of Alceste, Act II. e3-a4 g3-a4 Short, subdued recitative and
       a very sustained, quite slow aria. Slightly faster second half. Gen-
       erally subdued. Has dramatic climaxes and a dramatic ending. Agi-
       tated accompaniment. Acc: 3-4 (VS)EC. OAR-S1 (Ch. XI), (S)HL

6234. Divinités du Styx   Dramatic Soprano
       Part of Alceste, Act I. e3(c3)-b♭4 f3-f4 Dramatic aria in varied
       tempi. Starts gently in moderate slow tempo. Strong, energetic,
       and majestic. Climactic ending. Best for the heavier voices. Acc:
       3-4 (VS)EC. OPA-1, AUK, EDF-1, DSA, OAR-S1(Ch. XI)

6235. R: Hélas! dans ce malheur extrême
       A: Et sur l'excès de mon malheur   Dramatic Soprano
       Part of Alceste, Act I. e3-b♭4 g3-f4 Majestic recitative and slight-
       ly animated aria in moderate tempo. Has some dramatic climaxes
       and a dramatic ending. Acc: 3-4 (VS)EC. (S)HL

6236. R: Les dieux ont entendu
       A: Je n'ai jamais chéri la vie   Dramatic Soprano
       Part of Alceste, Act II. d3(c♯3)-a4 a3-f♯4 Subdued recitative and
       sustained aria in moderate slow tempo. Requires some flexibility.
       Acc: 3-4 (VS)EC

6237. R: Où suis-je? O malheureuse Alceste!
       A: Non, ce n'est point un sacrifice   Dramatic Soprano
       Part of Alceste, Act I. f♯3-a4 g3-f♯4 Slow, generally subdued
       recitative and a sustained aria in generally moderate slow tempo.
       Has tempi changes, dramatic passages, and a climactic ending. Acc:
       3 (VS)EC. CCF, EDF-1(aria only), DSA

ARMIDE
Opera 1777, libretto by Philippe Quinault.

6238. Ah! Si la liberté   Dramatic Soprano
       Part of Armide, Act III. e3-g4 g3-e4 Sustained in moderate slow
       tempo. Has dramatic passages. Slightly slower middle section.
       Acc: 3 (VS)EC

6239. Amour, sors pour jamais   Dramatic Soprano
       Part of Haine (Hate), Act IV. g3-g4 a3-e4 Sustained in moderate
       tempo. The short air has a dramatic ending section. Agitated ac-
       companiment. Acc: 3 (VS)EC

6240. Le perfide Renaud me fuit   Dramatic Soprano
       Part of Armide, Act V. g3-a4 a3-g4 Dramatic scena and aria,
       which ends the opera. Extended excerpt with several high climactic
       passages and a dramatic ending. Energetic. Generally in moderate

tempo. Acc: 3-4 (VS)EC

6241. Les enfers ont prédit cent fois   Dramatic Soprano
Part of Armide, Act I. f3-ab4 a3-f4 Sustained in moderate tempo.
Has dramatic climaxes. Climactic ending. Agitated accompaniment.
Acc: 3 (VS)EC

6242. R: Enfin il est en ma puissance
A: Venez, secondez mes désirs   Dramatic Soprano
Part of Armide, Act II. e3-a4 g3-f♯4 Extended dramatic scena
and sustained aria. Dramatic; has a climactic ending. Aria ends
Act II. Acc: 3-4 (VS)EC

6243. R: Il m'aime, quel amour!
A: Venez, venez, haine implacable!   Dramatic Soprano
Part of Armide, Act III. f3-a4 g3-g4 Slightly extended recitative
and sustained aria in moderate tempo. Has dramatic high passages
and agitated accompaniment. Acc: 3-4 (VS)EC

IPHIGÉNIE EN AULIDE
Opera 1774, libretto by François Lebland du Roullet.

6244. R: L'ai-je bien entendu?
A: Hélas! mon coeur sensible et tendre   Dramatic Soprano
Part of Iphigénie, Act I. f3-g4 g3-f4 Generally sustained in varied
tempi. Slow recitative and moderate slow start of the aria. Dramatic, strong, and accented. Climactic ending. Acc: 3-4 (VS)NO

6245. Heureux guerriers, volez a la victoire   Dramatic Soprano
Part of a Greek Woman, Act III. g3-a4 a3-e4 Sustained in moderate slow tempo. Starts gently. Has dramatic passages and a climactic ending. Has some wide intervalic skips. Acc: 3 (VS)NO

6246. R: Dieux puissants, que j'atteste!
A: Jupiter, lance ta foudre   Dramatic Soprano
Part of Clytemnestra, Act III. d3-g4 g3-e4 A dramatic scena and
a dramatic aria. Energetic and vocally demanding. Interpretatively
not easy. Dramatic ending. Agitated accompaniment. Acc: 3-4
(VS)NO

6247. R: Vous essayes en vain de bannir mes alarmes
A: Par la crainte et par l'espérance   Dramatic Soprano
Part of Iphigénie, Act II. d3-a4 f3-f4 Gentle recitative and sus-
tained aria in generally moderate tempo. Has dramatic passages, one
long-sustained note of 19 beats, and a dramatic descending ending line.
Acc: 3-4 (VS)NO

6248. R: Seigneur! j'embrasse vos genoux
A: Par son père cruel, à la mort condamnée   Dramatic Soprano
Part of Clytemnestra, Act II. e3-g4 f♯3-d4 Generally animated in
moderate tempo. Has slower sections and dramatic passages. Climactic ending. Generally simple accompaniment. In CCF, three
steps lower. Acc: 3 (VS)NO. EDF-1, CCF-4

IPHIGÉNIE EN TAURIDE
Opera 1779, libretto by François Guillard, based on Euripides.

6249. R: Non, cet affreux devoir
A: Je t'implore et je tremble   Dramatic Soprano

Part of Iphigénie, Act IV. d#3-a4 a3-e4 Short and animated recitative, and an animated aria in moderate lively tempo. Dramatic and
vocally demanding. Thick and agitated accompaniment. Climactic
ending with extended instrumental postlude. Acc: 4-5 (VS)EC, HL,
NO

6250. O malheureuse Iphigénie   Dramatic Soprano
Part of Iphigénie, Act II. b2-a4 g3-g4 Sustained aria in moderate
tempo. Has dramatic climaxes. Majestic. Requires fine high P.
Subdued, descending ending. Acc: 3 (VS)EC, HL, NO. (S)HL

6251. R: Cette nuit j'ai revu le palais de mon père
A: Ô toi, qui prolongeas mes jours   Dramatic Soprano
Part of Iphigénie, Act I. f3-a4 a3-f#4 Extended, difficult, and
dramatic scena, and a sustained aria. Has some dramatic passages
in the aria; also requires fine P and PP. Descending ending line.
A short chorus by treble voices between the recitative and aria. Acc:
4 (VS)EC, HL, NO. (S)HL. OAR-S1(Ch. XI)

III. Mezzo-Soprano

ALCESTE
Opera 1776 in French. Also performed in the original Italian version.
Libretto by Ranieri da Calzabigi; French version by François Louis
Lebland du Roullet.

6252. R: Les Dieux ont entendu
A: Je n'ai jamais chéri la vie   Mezzo-Soprano, Contralto
Part of Alceste, Act II. a2-f4 d3-d4 Subdued recitative and a sustained aria in moderate slow tempo. Requires some flexibility. A
transposed edition of the original soprano key. Acc: 3 CCF

ARMIDE
Opera 1777, libretto by Philippe Quinault.

6253. Jeunes coeurs! tout vous est favorable   Mezzo-Soprano
Part for "a soprano," Act V. d3-e4 g3-d4 Gently animated in mod-
erate tempo. Generally light. This air follows the Sicilienne section.
Acc: 3 (VS)EC

IPHIGÉNIE EN AULIDE
Opera 1774, libretto by François Lebland du Roullet.

6254. R: Allez! Il faut sauver notre gloire opprimée
A: Armez-voux d'un noble courage   Dramatic Soprano
Part of Clytemnestra, Act I. bb2-g4 eb3-eb4 Animated in moder-
ate lively tempo. Generally strong, accented, and dramatic. Re-
quires some flexibility. Strong, descending ending line. Acc: 3-4
(VS)NO. (S)HL

6255. Il faut de mon destin subir la loi suprême   Dramatic Soprano
Part of Iphigénie, Act III. bb2-g4 f3-eb4 Sustained in moderate
slow tempo. Generally gentle and short. Acc: 3 (VS)NO

6256. R: Dieux puissants qu j'atteste
A: Jupiter, lance ta foudre   Dramatic Soprano
Part of Clytemnestra, Act III. d3-g4 g3-e4 A dramatic scena and
a dramatic aria. Energetic and vocally demanding. Interpretatively

not easy. Dramatic ending. Agitated accompaniment. Acc: 3-4
(VS)NO

6257. Que j'aime a voir   Dramatic Soprano
Part of Clytemnestra, Act I. g3-e4 g3-e4 Sustained in moderate
slow tempo. Graceful and short. Acc: 3 (VS)NO

LA CYTHÈRE ASSIÉGÉE
Opera 1759, libretto by Charles-Simon Favart. An opera-ballet.

6258. Sous un ormeau   Dramatic Soprano
Part of Carite. e♭3-a♭4 e♭3-e♭4 Sustained in moderate tempo.
Generally subdued with climactic passages. Descending ending line
after a high climax. Acc: 3-4 TAG

ORFEO ED EURIDICE
Opera 1762, libretto by Ranieri da Calzabigi. Also performed in
French, with translations by Pierre-Louis Moline.

6259. R: Che disse! ch'ascoltai?
A: Addio, o miei sospiri   Dramatic Soprano
Part of Orfeo, Act I, Nos. 16 & 17. First French lines: R--
Qu'entends-je? qu'atil dit?; A--Amour, viens rendre à mon âme.
b♯2-g4 e3-e4 Grave scena and an animated aria in moderate lively
tempo. Very florid, with long lines. Requires flexibility. Climac-
tic ending. This aria ends Act I. Difficult. Acc: 3-4 (VS)GR-
Italian; NO-Italian & English; CP-French & German; GS-French &
English

6260. R: Ove trascorsi, ohimè
A: Che farò senza Euridice?   Dramatic Soprano
Part of Orfeo, Act III (Act IV in some editions), Nos. 42b & 43.
First French lines: R--C'est moi, qui lui ravis le jour; A--J'ai
perdu mon Euridice. Also known as "Orfeo's lament." b2-f4 e3-e4
Dramatic recitative and a sustained aria in moderate tempo. Re-
quires some flexibility. Dramatic ending. Sad text. Acc: 3-4
(VS)GR-Italian; NO-Italian & English; CP-French & German; GS-French
& English. CCF-4, EDF-1, OPA-2, OAR-M(Ch. XI-French)

6261. Che puro ciel! che chiaro sol!   Dramatic Soprano
Part of Orfeo, Act I, No. 33. First French line: Quel nouveau
ciel. c3-e♭4 e3-c4 A sustained, quasi-recitative in moderate slow
tempo. Has a very agitated, but light accompaniment. Climactic and
low ending. Extended instrumental prelude. Acc: 4 (VS)GR-Italian;
NO-Italian & English; CP-French & German; GS-French & English

6262. R: Lasciatemi! quel luogo convien
A: Chiamo il mio ben così   Dramatic Soprano
Part of Orfeo, Act I, Nos. 5, 7, 8-11. First French lines: R--
Eloignezvous; ce lieu convient..; A--Objet de mon amour... a2-f4
f3-c4 An air thrice sung (to different texts), each time preceded by
a recitative. Sustained in moderate slow tempo. Abounds in descending vocal passages, thus expressing the sadness of the texts. Acc:
3-4 (VS)GR-Italian; NO-Italian & English; CP-French & German; GS-
French & English. OAR-M(Ch. XI-French)

6263. Deh! placatevi con me!   Contralto, Mezzo-Soprano
Part of Orfeo, Act II, No. 22. First French line: Laissezvous

toucher par mes pleurs. b♭2-g4 e♭3-e♭4 Sustained in slow tempo.
Has some wide intervalic skips and one florid passage. Strong and
energetic. Descending ending line. An air with a chorus. Acc: 3
(VS)GR-Italian; NO-Italian & English; CP-French & German; GS-
French & English. EDF-2(Ch. V), OAR-M(Ch. XI-French)

6264. Men tiranne, voi sareste   Contralto, Mezzo-Soprano
       Part of Orfeo, Act II, No. 26. First French line: La tendresse qui
       me pres se. c3-d♭4 f3-c4 Sustained in moderate slow tempo.
       Short, and generally subdued. Acc: 3 (VS)GR-Italian; NO-Italian &
       English; CP-French & German; GS-French & English

6265. Mille pene, ombre sdegnose   Contralto, Mezzo-Soprano
       Part of Orfeo, Act II, No. 24. First French line: Ah! la flamme
       qui me dévore. c3-e♭4 f3-c4 Sustained in moderate tempo. Lyric
       and short. Descending ending line. Acc: 3 (VS)GR-Italian; NO-
       Italian & English; CP-French & German; GS-French & English

PARIDE ED ELENA
Opera 1770, libretto by Ranieri da Calzabigi.

6266. Spiagge amate   Mezzo-Soprano
       Part of Paride (Paris), Act I. b2-e4(L) d3-d4 Sustained in very
       slow tempo. Generally tranquil and light. One of Gluck's charming
       melodies. Acc: 3 POS-3

SEMIRAMIDE RICONOSCIUTA
Opera 1748, libretto by Pietro Metastasio.

6267. Vieni, che poi sereno   Contralto
       b2-e4 e3-d4 Sustained in moderate tempo. Graceful. Requires
       some flexibility. Has some climactic passages. Subdued ending.
       Acc: 3 GSA

IV. Tenor

ALCESTE
Opera 1776 in French. Also performed in the original Italian version.
Libretto by Ranieri da Calzabigi; French version by François Louis
Lebland du Roullet.

6268. R: Vivre sans toi! moi? vivre sans Alceste?
       A: Alceste, au nom des Dieux   Tenor
       Part of Admète, Act III. f3-a4 a3-g4 Recitative and sustained aria
       in moderate slow tempo. Has climactic high passages, high tessitura,
       and agitated accompaniment. Requires some flexibility. Climactic
       ending. Has an intervalic skip of a 10th. Acc: 3-4 (VS)EC. DMA

6269. R: O moment délicieux!
       A: Bannis la crainte et les alarmes   Tenor
       Part of Admète, Act II. g3-a4 a3-a4 Recitative and sustained aria
       in moderate slow tempo. Mainly lyric in style, with some dramatic
       climaxes. Descending ending line on "plaît à mon coeur. " Acc: 3
       (VS)EC. DMA

6270. R: Tu veux mourir
       A: Barbare, non, sans toi je ne puis vivre   Tenor

Part of Admète, Act II. e3-a4 a3-a4 Scena and a sustained aria
in moderate tempo. Has dramatic high climaxes, a high tessitura,
and agitated accompaniment. Brisk final section. Climactic descending ending. Acc: 4 (VS)EC

6271. Que votre main barbare   Tenor
       Part of Admète, Act III. bb3-bb4 bb3-ab4 Sustained vocal part in
       lively tempo. Dramatic, with extremely high tessitura. Quite agi-
       tated accompaniment. Climactic ending. Sounds better transposed.
       Acc: 3-4 (VS)EC

ARMIDE
Opera 1777, libretto by Philippe Quinault.

6272. Allez éloignez-vous de moi   Tenor
       Part of Renaud, Act V. g3-a4 b3-g4 Sustained in moderate slow
       tempo. Lyric with one high climactic passage. Somewhat subdued
       ending section. Acc: 3 (VS)EC, HL, AD

6273. Par une heureuse indifférence   Tenor
       Part of Renaud, Act II. g3-a4 bb3-f4 Slightly animated in moder-
       ate tempo. Quite high tessitura. Generally on MF level. This air
       sounds better transposed down one step. Acc: 3 (VS)EC, HL, AD

6274. Plus j'observe ces lieux   Tenor
       Part of Renaud, Act II. g3-a4 b3-g4 Sustained in moderate slow
       tempo. Has dramatic high passages. Subdued and calm ending.
       Acc: 3 (VS)EC, HL, AD

IPHIGÉNIE EN AULIDE
Opera 1774, libretto by François Lebland du Roullet, after Jean
Racine's tragedy based on Euripides.

6275. R: Eh bien! obéissez barbares!
       A: Calchas, d'un trait mortel blessé   Tenor
       Part of Achilles, Act III. g#3-b4 b3-g4 Dramatic recitative and
       aria in lively tempo. Requires fluent enunciation, flexibility, and a
       fine command of high notes. Vocally demanding and energetic. Has
       several a4's and b4's. Dramatic ending. Agitated accompaniment.
       This air sounds better transposed to a lower key. Acc: 4-5 (VS)NO

6276. Cours et dislui   Tenor
       Part of Achilles, Act II. f#3-b4 a3-g4 Generally sustained in
       varied tempi. Has dramatic passages and ending. Short. Acc: 3
       (VS)NO

6277. R: S'il était vrai
       A: Cruelle, non, jamais votre insensible coeur   Tenor
       Part of Achilles, Act I. g#3-b4 a3-f4 Generally strong recitative
       and sustained aria in moderate slow tempo. Has dramatic passages.
       Requires fine command of high notes and tessitura. Slightly faster
       and climactic ending. Acc: 3-4 (VS)NO

IPHIGÉNIE EN TAURIDE
Opera 1779, libretto by François Guillard, based on Euripides.

6278. Ah! mon ami: j'implore ta pitié   Tenor
       Part of Pylade, Act III. a3-ab4 bb3-eb4 Sustained vocal part in

moderate lively tempo. Has some dramatic climaxes. Acc: 3
(VS)EC, HL

6279. Divinité des grandes âmes!   Tenor
Part of Pylade, Act III. g3-a4 b3-e4 Sustained vocal part in moderate lively tempo. Majestic, with some dramatic passages. Climactic ending. Agitated accompaniment. Acc: 3-4 (VS)EC, HL

6280. R: Quel langage accablant pour un ami qui t'aime
A: Unis dès la plus tendre enfance   Tenor
Part of Pylade, Act II. f♯3-a4 a3-e4 Somewhat subdued, gentle
recitative and sustained aria in moderate slow tempo. Gentle. Acc:
3-4 (VS)EC, HL. EDF-1(Ch. V), OAR-T(Ch. XI). (S)HL

ORFEO ED EURIDICE

Note: All arias of ORFEO may also be sung by tenor voice. For
the excerpts from this opera, refer to the Mezzo-Soprano section.

PARIDE ED ELENA
Opera 1770, libretto by Ranieri da Calzabigi.

6281. O del mio dolce ardor   Tenor
Part of Paride (Paris), Act I. b2-f♯4 e3-e4 Very sustained in
moderate slow tempo. Requires simplicity and a thoroughly lyric ap-
proach. Issued with Italian and English texts. Considered one of
Gluck's most beautiful melodies, also his best-known. Acc: 3
AIS-1, SCS-2, ARB, AAP-1, (S)GS-high, low with Italian & English;
HL-Italian & French. OAR-M(Ch. XI)

V. Baritone

AÉTIUS
Opera 1750, libretto by G. Antheunis.

6282. R: Dans ta fureur enfin j'ai lu mon triomphe!
A: En cet instant suprême   Baritone
Part of Aétius. Italian first line: Ecco alle mie catene. b1-e3
e2-c♯3 Semi-dramatic recitative and sustained aria in moderate tempo. Has some high climaxes and dramatic passages. Requires fine
high tessitura. Semi-dramatic and descending ending line. Acc: 3
(S)HL

ALCESTE
Opera 1776, in French. Also performed in the original Italian version.
Libretto by Ranieri da Calzabigi; French version by François Louis
Lebland du Roullet.

6283. Caron t'appelle, entends sa voix   Baritone
Part of Tanato, Act III. c♯2-e3(f♯4) d2-d3 Generally sustained in
moderate tempo. Has some strong climaxes and incisive rhythms.
Mostly octaves in the accompaniment. Acc: 3 (VS)EC

6284. R: Au pouvoir de la Mort je saurai la ravir
A: C'est en vain que l'enfer compte sur sa victime   Baritone
Part of Hercule, Act III. e2-e3 g♯2-e3 Strong recitative and sus-
tained aria in moderate tempo. Majestic. High tessitura. Has

788   Solo Voice Repertoire

some tempi variations.   Climactic ending.   May be transposed lower.
Acc: 3-4 (VS)EC

6285. R: Tes destins sont remplis!
       A: Déjà la mort s'apprête   Baritone
       Part of the High Priest (Grand Prêtre), Act I.   c2-f3   eb2-eb3
       Very brief recitative and sustained aria with moderate tempo in the
       first half and slightly faster in the second half.   Majestic, with high
       tessitura.   Acc: 3 (VS)EC

                              ARMIDE
               Opera 1777, libretto by Philippe Quinault.

6286. R: Armide, que le sang qui m'unit avec vous
       A: Je vois de près la mort   Baritone
       Part of Hidraot, Act I.   d2-f3   g2-d3 Sustained in moderate slow
       tempo. Quite high tessitura.   Acc: 3 (VS)EC.   (S)HL

6287. Pour vous, quand il vous plaît   Baritone
       Part of Hidraot, Act I.   e2-f3   g2-e3 Animated in moderate tempo.
       Quite high tessitura; may be transposed lower.   Climactic ending.
       Acc: 3 (VS)EC

                        IPHIGÉNIE EN AULIDE
       Opera 1774, libretto by François Lebland du Roullet, after Racine's
       tragedy based on Euripides.

6288. R: Diane impitoyable!
       A: Brillant auteur de la lumiere   Baritone
       Part of Agamemnon, Act I.   c2-e3   f#2-d3 Sustained recitative and
       aria. Has dramatic passages.   Aria ends with recitative section.
       Acc: 3 (VS)NO.   DMR

6289. R: Tu décides son sort
       A: O toi, l'objet le plus aimable   Baritone
       Part of Agamemnon, Act II.   c2-f#3   e2-d3 An extended dramatic
       and vocally demanding scena, and sustained aria in moderate tempo.
       High tessitura; may be transposed lower.   Has several f3's and f#3's.
       Livelier and dramatic ending section.   Aria may be performed alone.
       Agitated accompaniment.   Acc: 3-4 (VS)NO.   (S)HL

6290. Peuvent-ils ordonner qu'un père   Baritone
       Part of Agamemnon, Act I.   d2-f3   g2-d3 Strong, dramatic, and in-
       tense.   Sustained in moderate slow tempo.   Dramatic ending.   Agi-
       tated accompaniment.   Acc: 3 (VS)NO.   DMR

                        IPHIGÉNIE EN TAURIDE
       Opera 1779, libretto by François Guillard, based on Euripides.

6291. R: Le ciel, par d'éclatants miracles
       A: De noirs pressentiments   High Baritone
       Part of Thoas, Act I.   e#2-g3   a2-e3 Recitative and sustained aria
       in moderate slow tempo.   Dramatic and vocally demanding.   Heavy
       and agitated accompaniment.   Extremely high tessitura; this aria
       sounds best transposed lower.   Acc: 4 (VS)EC, HL, NO.   MLF,
       OPA-5, OAR-Br(Ch. XI).   (S)HL

6292. R: Je t'ai donné la mort!
       A: Dieu qui me poursuivez!   High Baritone

Part of Oreste, Act II.   f♯ 2-f♯ 3 a2-e3 Dramatic recitative and animated aria in lively tempo.   Dramatic, strong, and with high tessitura.   Has several f♯ 3's.   Climactic ending.   Agitated accompaniment. May be transposed to a lower key where it would sound better.   Acc: 4 (VS)EC, HL, NO. OAR-Br(Ch. XI)

6293.   R: Dieux! protecteurs de ces affreux rivages
A: La calme rentre dans mon coeur   Baritone
Part of Oreste, Act II.   d2-f♯ 3 a2-d3 Dramatic recitative and sustained aria in moderate slow tempo.   High tessitura; may be transposed to a lower key where it would sound better.   Generally on MF level, with some dramatic climaxes.   Acc: 3-4 (VS)EC, HL, NO. OAR-Br(Ch. XI)

ORFEO ED EURIDICE

Note: All arias of ORFEO may also be sung by baritone voice.   For all the entries of this part, refer to the Mezzo-Soprano section.

VI.   All Voices

6294.   Die frühen Gräber   All Voices
Text: Friedrich Gottlieb Klopstock.   First line: Willkommen, o silberner Mond.   d3-f4 g3-e4 Sustained in moderate slow tempo. Short melody on three verses.   May be transposed for lower voices. Acc: 3 GSB, KDL-1

6295.   Die Maienkönigin   Women
Text: Charles Simon Favart, translated into German by Max Kalbeck. Other title: Ariette der Helene.   First line: Gern beim Morgenscheine.   d3-g4 g3-eb4 Sustained vocal part in moderate tempo. Has climactic passages.   Also requires fine P.   Climactic and descending ending line.   May be transposed for the lower voices.   Acc: 3 KLR

6296.   Die Sommernacht   Men
Text: Friedrich Gottlieb Klopstock.   eb3-f4 g3-eb4 Original key, but may be transposed for the lower voices.   Very sustained in moderate tempo.   Generally gentle, subdued, and calm.   3 verses, best for tenors.   First line: Wenn die Schimmer.   There are two settings of this song, dated 1773 and 1785.   May be transposed for lower voices.   Acc: 3 CPS, LIU

6297.   O del mio dolce ardor   All Voices
Work: PARIDE ED ELENA, opera 1770, libretto by Ranieri da Calzabigi.   Part of Paride (Paris), Act I.   b2-f♯ 4 e3-e4 Very sustained in moderate slow tempo.   Requires simplicity and a thoroughly lyric treatment.   Gluck's best-known air, now sung by all voices.   Issued with Italian and English texts.   Acc: 3 AIS-1, SCS-2, ARB, AAP-1. (S)GS-high, low, with Italian & English; HL-Italian & French.   OAR-M(Ch. XI)

6298.   Spiagge amate   All Voices
Work: PARIDE ED ELENA, opera 1770, libretto by Ranieri da Calzabigi.   Part of Paride (Paris), Act I.   b2-e4(L) d3-d4 Sustained in very slow tempo.   Generally tranquil.   One of Gluck's best-known airs.   Acc: 3 POS-3

CHAPTER VIII

SCANDINAVIAN SOLO VOICE REPERTOIRE

Denmark, Finland, Norway, Sweden

The music of Denmark, Finland, Norway, and Sweden is, in general, not as well known as it ought to be. Much less known are the musical backgrounds before the adaptation of Gregorian chant in the early days of recorded history. Most of our standard references either completely ignore or merely dart through any mention of music before the full establishment of Christian music. Several questions are therefore left unanswered. It is quite disconcerting that in several music references the music of Scandinavian countries is slighted and mention is meager.

It can only be surmised that early Scandinavian music, like that of other geographical areas, belongs to the folk tradition, and that there were songs of different types, mostly fitted to the functions of the people's daily lives. Of musical instruments, the lur, a long S-shaped trumpet, and harps were used by the Danes. The Finns had their kantele, which is a kind of psaltery. Finland has a wealth of ancient songs. One of the earliest-known types is called joiku, an improvised lament sung to legendary verses. These have been collected by Elias Lönnrot and used as the basis for both vocal and instrumental music.

In the 12th and 13th centuries, several Danish musician-priests journeyed to Notre Dame in Paris and there exposed themselves to the music of the Middle Ages French composers. Danish folk melodies as well as composed songs were collected as well, and some manuscripts from the early 14th century are extant. English lutenist-composer John Dowland was one of those employed in the Danish court in the 16th century. Among the earliest-known formal composers are Mogens Pedersøn and Hans Nielson.

Although musical activities in Denmark during the 17th and 18th centuries were dominated by Italian, French, and German musicians, the country produced one of the greatest musicians of the time: Dietrich Buxtehude, whose organ playing and other musical activities attracted the attention of young Johann Sebastian Bach.

Toward the end of the 18th century and in the 19th, several native composers of vocal music came into prominence, among them, Christoph E. F. Weyse, Peter Arnold Heise, Friedrich Kuhlau, Niels Gade, and John Hartmann. At this time the writing of German-style Singspiel was taken over by Danish composers and developed in their own way.

In recent times we have Carl Nielsen, an important and prominent composer, who has written songs although his main output was instrumental. Other song composers are Peter Lange-Müller, Hakon Børresen, and Knud Jeppesen, who is known to the outside world mainly for his editing of La Flora, a fine collection of Italian airs.

In Finland, religious songs were well-known from the 12th to the 16th centuries. In the 18th century and the early 19th, a Finnish composer of importance named Bernhard Crusell became known. Although mainly a clarinet virtuoso and instrumental composer, he also wrote some songs and choral music. His best-known songs are 12 settings of Tegner's poems, a work which has not been made available for this book. Richard Faltin, German-born and naturalized Finnish, made his contributions with a few song compositions and the collection and publication of many Finnish folk songs. Other composers who have produced some songs and who lived into the 20th century are: Robert Kajanus, Martin Wagelius, Oskar Merikanto, Armas Järnefelt, Erkki Melartin, and Selim Palmgren.

Jean Sibelius was the first Finnish composer to attain international reputation. He is credited for establishing a national style of music for his country. He wrote a few songs, while his tune, "Finlandia," is widely known through the hymn adaptation in most Protestant church hymnals. Finland's principal song composer and one of the greatest writers in this genre is Yrjö Kilpinen. Amazingly, very few recitalists and teachers of voice outside Scandinavia are acquainted with the songs of this great composer. In Finland he is known by many musicians as "the Finnish Schubert."

Norway's folk song literature is perhaps the most extensive in all of Scandinavia. The folk style has influenced much of the song writing in the country. The land itself provides much of nature's beauty to inspire, and, like Grieg, one can be affected by it. Solo singing has always been encouraged by folk traditions, and in this wise the solo art song saw some high degree of development.

Some of the oldest composed music in Norway were chants honoring St. Olaf in the 12th century. Some were part songs, others were for solo or unison voices. Norway has also its share of Latin hymns honoring patron saints, but in the days of the Reformation in the 16th century they were forbidden.

Among the first important native composers were a family team, Johan Daniel Berlin and his son, Johan Henrich in the 18th century. Movements which led to political independence in the early part of the 19th century also encouraged nationalism in the arts, and among the most significant works of the new consciousness was a Singspiel by Waldemar Thrane, entitled "Fjeldeventyret," first performed in 1850.

The first important Norwegian composer of songs was Halfdan Kjerulf in the 19th century. Then followed Martin Udbye and Rikard Nordraak. But the person who won international fame for Norway's music was Edvard Grieg. Among his contemporaries were Johan Svendsen and Christian Sinding. Moving from the late 19th to the 20th century we encounter more names in the area of song: Agathe Backer-Gröndahl and her son, Fridtjof Backer-Gröndahl, and Johan Backer-Lunde, who is credited with over 300 songs.

As in the other Scandinavian countries, early Swedish music was founded on the folk song. Much of Sweden's vocal folk music is associated with dancing. Some of the folk tunes became sources of themes of Grieg and other Scandinavian composers.

Hymns and sequences were the Gregorian chant influences of 13th- and 14th-century Swedish monophonic songs. Church music, monophonic and polyphonic, achieved some moderate use. Some of the more freely composed religious songs of the 14th and 15th centuries were adaptations of known folk melodies. Some collections of songs in one to four parts were used in the schools, and even adapted in neighboring Finland.

The first-known Swedish composer of repute was Helmich Roman, a contemporary of Handel, who wrote in Handel's style. In the 18th century, solo vocal activities were given some importance with the construction of opera houses. Gustaf III was a monarch who championed the growth of interest in opera. German opera composers and conductors were active in Sweden in the 18th and 19th centuries.

Prominent among the composer-performers was the well-known poet, Carl Mikael Bellman, who set his own poems to music and performed them in many public places. He had the patronage of Gustavus III, and to the present, Bellman is honored with a celebration every July 26 by the Swedish people.

Among the song composers in the 19th century may be counted Ivar Hallström and Johan August Söderman. In the late 19th and early 20th centuries, Johan Andreas Hallén, Wilhelm Stenhammar, Hugo Alfven, Natanael Berg, Ture Rangström, and Emil Sjögren, who is credited with about 200 songs, are among those who have helped elevate the art song.

Contemporary or mid-century Swedish music is represented by the works of Hilding Rosenberg who, at the outset, was influenced by the style of Schönberg, Knut Bäck, Ingvar Lidholm, and Gösta Nyström, whose initial influence was the French school of Ravel and Debussy. Nyström's style changed in later years, and today he is considered one of the highest ranking Swedish composers.

It is both natural and admirable that Scandinavian composers' texts in their songs come from the writings of some of their famous poets who have attained international reputation. Among the favorite poets for song settings are: Danish writers Jens Peter Jacobsen, Holger Drachmann, Hans Christian Andersen; Norwegians Henrik Ibsen, Otto Benson, Aasmund O. Vinje, Vilhelm Krag, Andreas Munch, and Björnstjerne Björnson.

Most entries in this chapter are given in the English translations provided by the publications reviewed. Original Scandinavian titles are given in parentheses following the English translations. At present we must rely on translations because Scandinavian languages are not as well known to most singers and audiences as English, German, Italian, French, and Spanish. Non-Scandinavians who have Scandinavian diction specialists within easy availability would best use the original languages of the texts. There is much to be desired in the way of English translations of Scandinavian songs. Those that are generally available are not musically and textually adequate. A translation that fully meets artistic requirements is difficult to come by, simply because the work of translation, bound by musical accents and melodic flow, is a most difficult job. It is this author's belief that singers should be given the freedom to edit any of the translations if they can find more suitable words and phrases to substitute for some of those that appear awkward in the published score. But in no case must the vocal melody be edited or altered to fit a translation. The statements in this paragraph also apply to Russian songs.

Bibliography of Scandinavian Songs

MSS   <u>Modern Scandinavian Songs</u>. Two volumes. High, low. Edited by
Reinald Werrenrath. Original texts, with English versions. Vol. I:
Alfvén to Kjerulf; Vol. II: Lange-Müller to Winge. Bryn Mawr:
Oliver Ditson, c/o Theodore Presser. (For a long time the best
available collection of Scandinavian songs. Vol. I is now out of print,
but the entire set of two volumes is found in most libraries.)

SFS   <u>Songs from Scandinavia</u>. Medium, High. Edited by Ella Hjertaas
Roe. Original texts, with English versions. Park Ridge, Ill.:
Pallma Music Co.

A. DENMARK

HAKON AXEL EINAR BØRRESEN, 1876-1954

6299. If you have kindly feelings (Hvis du har varme tanker)   All Voices
Poet: Helen Nyblom.   c♯3-e4(g♯4)   f♯3-d♯4   Original key.   Sustained in moderate slow tempo.   Has climactic passages.   Subdued,
descending ending line.   English version: Aretta Werrenrath.   Acc:
3-4   MSS-1

6300. Landscape (Landskab)   All Voices
Poet: Jens Peter Jacobsen.   f3-g♭4   a♭3-f4   Original key.   Sustained in somewhat slow tempo.   Gentle first part; dramatic and energetic middle section.   The third section is similar to the first.   English version: Aretta Werrenrath.   Acc: 3   MSS-1

DIDERIK (German: DIETRICH) BUXTEHUDE, 1637-1707

Note: See the author's Vocal Solos for Protestant Services.

NIELS VILHELM GADE, 1817-1890

6301. March violets (Martsviolerne)   All Voices
Poet: Hans Christian Andersen.   d3-g♭4   g3-e♭4   Original key.
Animated in moderate lively tempo.   Generally light.   Requires some
fluent enunciation.   English version: Aretta Werrenrath.   Acc: 3-4
MSS-1

6302. The birch-tree (Birken)   Women
Poet: Johannes Carsten Hauch.   e3-f4   a3-d4   Original key.   Sus-
tained in moderate slow tempo.   Requires simplicity.   4 verses.
English version: Aretta Werrenrath.   Acc: 3   MSS-1

JOHN PEDER EMILIUS HARTMANN, 1805-1900

6303. My thoughts (Mine tanker)   All Voices
Poet: Wilhelm Gregersen.   c3-g4   g3-e4   Original key.   Gently animated vocal part in moderate tempo.   Generally on MF level.   English version: Aretta Werrenrath.   Acc: 3-4   MSS-1

PETER ARNOLD HEISE, 1830-1879

6304. Ah, who once wore a fine bonnet (Ak, hvem der havde en hue)   Women
Poet: Holger Drachmann.   e3-a4   a3-f4   Original key.   Animated in
lively tempo.   Marked; narrative.   Has climactic passages.   Requires fine P.   Subdued ending after high climax.   Acc: 3-4   MSS-1

6305. It rises (Det stiger)   Men
Poet: Holger Drachmann.   c3-a♭4   g3-e♭4   Original key.   Animated
in lively tempo.   Dramatic.   Interpretatively not easy.   Descending

ending line after dramatic climax. Not for light voices. English
version: Aretta Werrenrath. Acc: 3-4 MSS-1

6306. When I was a little tiny boy (Dengang jeg var kun saa stor som saa) Men
Poet: William Shakespeare, from his Twelfth Night; Danish version
by C. Newman. c3-f4 a3-f4 Original key. Animated in very fast
tempo. Requires fluent enunciation. Joyous, outgoing, and humorous.
Requires simplicity. Generally strong. 4 verses. See the setting
by Mario Castelnuovo-Tedesco, and "Hey, ho, the wind and the rain"
by Jean Sibelius. Acc: 4 MSS-1

CHARLES KJERULF, 1858-1919

6307. All the bells bring far-off word (Alle klokker bringer
        fjaernt)   All Voices
Poet: Holger Drachmann. d3-e4 f♯ 3-d4 Sustained in moderate
slow tempo. Very subdued, gentle, and tranquil. English version:
Aretta Werrenrath. Acc: 3 MSS-1

PETER ERASMUS LANGE-MÜLLER, 1850-1926

6308. Autumn (Efteraar)   All Voices
Poet: Ludvig Holstein. f3-d4 a3-c4 Sustained in moderate tempo.
On recitative style, with vocal line centered on and around one note
in the high key, c4. Subdued. Requires some characterization.
Acc: 3 MSS-2

6309. Late in the night in frost cold (Silde ved nat hin kolde)   All Voices
Poet: Flemish folksong; Danish by Thor Lange. f♯ 3-g4 a3-e4 Ani-
mated in quite lively tempo. Has some strong, dramatic passages.
Climactic ending. Agitated accompaniment. Acc: 4 MSS-2

6310. Shine, bright and clear, O sunshine (Skin ud, du klare
        solskin)   All Voices
Poet: Thor Lange. b2-f♯ 4 e3-d4 Animated in moderate lively tem-
po. Generally on MF level. Subdued ending. Acc: 3-4 MSS-2,
SFS

6311. The maples their leaves are shedding (Nu faelder sit løv den ahorn) Men
Poet: Slovak folksong; Danish by Thor Lange. c♯ 3-g♯ 4 g♯ 3-d♯ 4
Gently animated vocal part in moderate slow tempo. Generally sub-
dued with two climactic passages. Acc: 3 MSS-2

CARL (AUGUST) NIELSEN, 1865-1931

Nielsen, this century's greatest Danish composer, wrote a variety of works,
among them operas, incidental music, symphonies, chamber pieces, piano
and organ music, choral pieces, and songs. His music shows some stylistic
independence in the use of a variety of devices such as polytonality, modern
rhythms, contrasting tonal formulas, and others. Although his songs are
quite popular in Denmark, they are not as widely-known as they should be
elsewhere. Recital repertoire would be enriched by the inclusion of some
Nielsen songs. His settings show keen sensitivity to textual content. In this
wise Nielsen continued the tradition started in Denmark by Weyse and Heise.
Nielsen's first collection of songs which appeared in 1894 consists of settings

of poems by Ludvig Holstein. His music has been greatly admired by
Arthur Honegger.

NSN   9 Songs. Carl Nielsen. Danish texts, with English versions. Copen-
        hagen: Wilhelm Hansen.

SLN   Sange-Lieder, Op. 10. Carl Nielsen. Danish texts, with German
        versions by Eugen von Ensberg. Six songs. Copenhagen: Wilhelm
        Hansen.

Note: For other compositions by Carl Nielsen, see the catalog of Wilhelm
        Hansen, Denmark, for an exhaustive list which includes Nielsen's ar-
        rangements of Danish folksongs.

————————

6312.   An Erinnerungsee's Strand (Erindringens Sø)   Tenor, Baritone
        Poet: Ludvig Holstein. Original text: Danish. c♯3-f♭4 e♭3-d♭4
        Sustained in slow tempo. Requires fine P and PP. Has quasi-recita-
        tive passages. Very subdued ending after the climax. Acc: 3 SLN

6313.   Bow thy corolla, thou bloom (Saenk kun dit hoved, du
           blomst)   All Voices
        Poet: Johannes Jørgensen. f3-e4 g3-d4 Sustained in moderate tem-
        po. Generally subdued and gentle. Requires simplicity. Subdued
        ending. Acc: 3 NSN

6314.   Gruss (Hilsen)   Men
        Poet: Ludvig Holstein. d3-g4 f♯3-d4 Animated in rather fast tem-
        po. Generally light. Has some climactic passages. Requires fluent
        enunciation. Subdued ending. Acc: 3 SLN

6315.   Heut Abend (I Aften)   Medium, Low Voices
        Poet: Ludvig Holstein. c3-d4 f3-c4 Sustained in moderate slow
        tempo. Requires straightforward approach and a fine PP. Generally
        subdued. Subdued ending on descending melodic line. Acc: 3 SLN

6316.   Irmaleen rose (Irmelin rose)   All Voices
        Poet: Jens Peter Jacobsen. a2-e4 c3-d4 Animated in martial tem-
        po. Accented, with some strong passages. Has humor. Narrative
        text. NSN: medium or low keys; MSS: high (c3-g4). Acc: 3-4
        NSN, MSS-2. (S)WH

6317.   Sang hintern Pflug (Sang bag Ploven)   Medium, Low Voices
        Poet: Ludvig Holstein. b2-d4 e3-c4 Animated in moderate lively
        tempo. Has climactic passages. Requires simplicity. 3 verses.
        Acc: 3 SLN

6318.   Sommerlied (Sommersang)   High Voices
        Poet: Ludvig Holstein. d3-f♯4 e3-e4 Animated in lively tempo.
        Requires fluent enunciation, very fine high PP, and some flexibility.
        Subdued ending. Agitated accompaniment. Acc: 3-4 SLN

6319.   Song behind the plough (Sang bag ploven)   Men
        Poet: Ludvig Holstein. b2-d4 e3-c4 Slightly animated in moderate
        lively tempo. Generally strong and bold. Acc: 3 NSN

6320.   Summer song (Sommersang)   High, Medium Voices
        Poet: Ludvig Holstein. d3-f♯4 e3-e4 Animated in lively tempo.

Graceful. Requires very fine high PP. Acc: 4 NSN

6321. The apple blossom (Aebleblomst)   High Voices
Poet: Ludvig Holstein.   d3-g4   g♯3-e4 Animated in moderate lively
tempo. Requires some fluent enunciation. Agitated accompaniment.
Acc: 3-4 NSN, SLN

6322. The eagle (Høgen)   All Voices
Poet: Jeppe Aakjaer. d3-a4 a3-g4 Animated in lively tempo. Requires fluent enunciation. Has dramatic passages. Generally strong,
with a climactic ending. Not for light voices. Original key. Acc:
4 MSS-2

6323. Wondrous fragrance in the evening (Underlige aftenlufte)   All Voices
Poet: Jeppe Aakjaer. e♭3-e♭4 e♭3-c4 Sustained in moderate slow
tempo. Requires simplicity, has a folk-like melody. Nationalistic
text, 9 verses. Acc: 3 NSN

B. FINLAND

ARMAS (EDVARD) JÄRNEFELT, 1869-1958

6324. Sing thou, sing (Laula, laula!)   All Voices
Poet: K. Killinen. d3-g4 g3-e4 Original key. Alternating slow
and fast tempi. Has some florid passages. Generally blithe and
exultant. A fine opening song for a Scandinavian or Finnish group.
Best for high and medium voices. English version: Constance Purdy.
Acc: 3 MSS-1

6325. To the harp (Kanteleelle)   All Voices
Poet: K. Killinen. b2-f4 g3-e♭4 Original key. Generally sustained in moderate lively tempo. Has sections in gentle recitative
style. Subdued low ending. English version: Constance Purdy.
Acc: 3 MSS-1

YRJÖ (HENRIK) KILPINEN, 1892-1959

Kilpinen is Finland's greatest song composer. His songs, in quality and output, rank among the finest in contemporary repertoire anywhere, and should
be better known than they are at present. Considered in several countries
as "the Finnish Schubert," he wrote more than 700 songs, exceeding Schubert,
in whose footsteps he seemed to have followed. Stylistically, however, he
leans more strongly to Hugo Wolf, especially in his sensitive treatment of
texts and musical declamation. The piano parts in Kilpinen songs are generally transparent, although harmonically they have great vitality and dramatic power and imagination. He uses dissonances only to reinforce dramatic
imagination rather than for a driving impulse to keep the music sound contemporary, as is often heard in the works of many other composers. Most
of Kilpinen's songs were written for the medium voices, and not all of them
offer any serious musical or vocal difficulties. Their words require a mature and sensitive delivery. Most of his songs are settings to German, Finnish, and Swedish poetry, and his best writing may be heard in the Morgenstern poems. Lieder um den Tod (Songs About Death) are considered the

best examples of Kilpinen's writing; the treatment of its poetry offers a chal-
lenge to the imagination of the singer.   Arrangements of Finnish and Swedish
folksongs number among some of Kilpinen's musical achievements.

LMK   Lieder nach Gedichten von Christian Morgenstern.   Four volumes.
        Vol. I: Op. 59; Vol. II: Op. 60, Lieder der Liebe I; Vol. III: Op.
        61, Lieder der Liebe II; Vol. IV: Op. 62, Lieder um den Tod.
        Berlin: Ed. Bote & G. Bock.

VMK   Visor och Melodier.   Op. 43.   Yrjö Kilpinen.   Texts by Thor Cnat-
        tingius.   Swedish, Finnish, and German texts.   High, medium, low.
        Copenhagen: Wilhelm Hansen.

20K   20 Sänger till dikter av Anders Österling.   20 Lieder.   Op. 40.
        Yrjö Kilpinen.   Swedish, Finnish, and German texts.   Copenhagen:
        Wilhelm Hansen.

Note: For other published songs by Kilpinen, refer to the catalogs of Bote
        & Bock and Wilhelm Hansen.

_____

Lieder der Liebe I.   (Songs of Love.)   Yrjö Kilpinen.   Op. 60.   Poems by
        Christian Morgenstern.   German texts, with English versions by Olive
        Burnaby.   Medium voice and piano.   Berlin: Ed. Bote & G. Bock.

6326.   (1) Mein Herz ist leer   Medium Voices
        c3-e4 g3-c4 Sustained in slow tempo.   Has quasi-recitative pas-
        sages, climactic passages, and requires fine P and PP.   Has some
        frequent meter changes.   Acc: 3 LMK-2

6327.   (2) Es ist Nacht   Medium Voices
        g3-f4 bb3-f4 Sustained vocal part in very rapid tempo.   High tessi-
        tura.   Requires very fine high P and PP.   Very agitated accompani-
        ment in the first part.   Acc: 4 LMK-2

6328.   (3) Unsere Liebe   Medium Voices
        f3-fb4 ab3-db4 Sustained in slow tempo.   Has climactic passages.
        Requires fine P.   Subdued ending.   Acc: 3-4 LMK-2

6329.   (4) Wir sitzen im Dunkeln   Medium Voices
        c3-f4 g3-d4 Sustained in slow tempo.   Calm, gentle, and subdued.
        Descending ending line.   Short, one page.   Acc: 3 LMK-2

6330.   (5) Schicksal der Liebe   Medium Voices
        d3-f#4 g#3-d#4 Animated in quite lively tempo.   Requires fine P
        and PP.   Has one climactic passage.   Slow, subdued, and contempla-
        tive ending.   Agitated accompaniment.   Acc: 4-5 LMK-2

Lieder der Liebe II.   (Songs of Love.)   Yrjö Kilpinen.   Op. 61.   Poems by
        Christian Morgenstern.   German texts, with English versions by Olive
        Burnaby.   Medium voice and piano.   Berlin: Ed. Bote & G. Bock.

6331.   (1) Heimat   Medium Voices
        English: Home.   f#3-d#4 f#3-c#4 Sustained in slow tempo.   Sub-
        dued starting.   Requires fine P and PP.   Generally subdued and short.
        Acc: 3 LMK-3

6332.   (2) Kleines Lied   Medium Voices

English: Little song. d3-e4 d3-d4 Sustained in slow tempo. Requires simplicity. Subdued starting. Generally on MF level. Gentle.
Has some frequent meter changes. Sustained octaves in the left hand
accompaniment. Acc: 3 LMK-3

6333. (3) Deine Rosen an der Brust   Medium Voices
English: The roses on my breast. eb3-f4 f3-c4 Gently animated
in moderate slow tempo. Requires fine P and fine high PP. Graceful and gentle. No strong dynamics. Has some frequent meter
changes. Gently agitated right hand accompaniment. Short song.
Acc: 3 LMK-3

6334. (4) Über die tausend Berg   Medium Voices
English: Over the thousand mountains. f# 3-f# 4 f# 3-e4 Animated
in very fast tempo. Requires agility and flexibility. The last two
pages require dramatic energy. Has dramatic climaxes. A truly climactic song. Arpeggiated accompaniment. Acc: 4 LMK-3

6335. (5) Anmutiger Vertrag   Medium Voices
English: Sweet bargain. d# 3-f# 4 g# 3-d# 4 Very animated in quite
rapid tempo. Requires fluent enunciation and flexibility. Light and
delicate. Dynamics range only from P to MF. Joyous, but requires
well-controlled volume of sound. Interpretatively not easy. Subdued
ending. Very agitated and light accompaniment. Acc: 4-5 LMK-3

Lieder um den Tod. (Songs About Death.) Yrjö Kilpinen. Op. 62. Poems
by Christian Morgenstern. Six songs for medium voice and piano.
German texts, with English versions by Olive Burnaby. All interpretatively difficult. Berlin: Bote & Bock.

6336. (1) Vöglein Schwermut   Medium Voices
d3-f4 g3-d4 Sustained in moderate lively tempo. Requires fine P
and very fine treatment of the language. Atmospheric, requires some
characterization. Sparse accompaniment. Acc: 3 LMK-4

6337. (2) Auf einem verfallenen Kirchhof   Medium Voices
c# 3-fb 4 ab 3-db 4 Sustained in slow tempo. Sad, somewhat grave.
Requires some flexibility and fine P and PP. No dynamics above MF.
Acc: 3 LMK-4

6338. (3) Der Tod und der einsame Trinker   Medium Voices
c3-f4 f3-c4 Generally animated in generally lively tempo, with variations. Requires fine P. Dramatic ending section with sustained
f4's. Interpretatively difficult; requires characterization. More suitable for men's voices. Falling ending. A conversation between two
characters: death and the drinker. Acc: 4 LMK-4

6339. (4) Winternacht   Medium Voices
eb 3-f4 f3-d4 Sustained in moderate slow tempo. Requires fine P
and PP, and simplicity. Subdued. Sparse accompaniment. Acc: 3
LMK-4

6340. (5) Der Säemann   Medium Voices
f3-f4 f3-db 4 Animated in very lively tempo. Dramatic final section
with sustained f4's. Generally strong and dramatic. Very agitated
accompaniment throughout. Acc: 4-5 LMK-4

6341. (6) Unverlierbare Gewähr   Medium Voices

c♯3-e4 f♯3-d4 Very sustained in moderate slow tempo. Requires
fine P and PP. Contemplative, with one climactic passage. Generally gentle and tranquil. Requires simplicity. Introspective. Subdued, calm hanging ending. Acc: 3 LMK-4

Spielmanns-Lieder. Yrjö Kilpinen. Op. 77. Poems by Albert Sergel.
German texts. Medium voice and piano. Eight songs. Berlin: Ed.
Bote & G. Bock.

6342. (1) Ihr ewigen Sterne   Medium Voices
f♯3-c♯4 f♯3-c♯4 Sustained vocal part in moderate lively tempo.
Slower ending section. Subdued, contemplative throughout. Gently
moving top line in accompaniment. Acc: 3

6343. (2) Eingeschneite Stille Felder   Medium Voices
c♯3-f♯4 c♯3-d4 Very sustained in moderate slow tempo. Grave.
Generally subdued with a dramatic section before the subdued ending.
Requires some flexibility. Has some wide intervalic skips. Acc: 3

6344. (3) Spiel ich wo zum Tanze auf   Medium Voices
e♭3-f♯4 a3-d4 Animated in lively tempo. Generally light with some
high climactic passages. Rhythmic accompaniment with dotted figures
moving with animation. Acc: 3-4

6345. (4) Tanzlied   Medium Voices
f3-f♯4 f3-e♭4 Animated in moderate lively tempo in waltz rhythm.
Outgoing, with some climactic passages. Climactic ending. Acc: 3

6346. (5) Spielmannssehnen   Medium Voices
c♯3-f4 a3-d4 Animated in moderate slow tempo. Generally subdued
with one climactic high note. Has graceful sections. Acc: 3

6347. (6) Vor Tau und Tag   Medium Voices
f♯3-d♯4 f♯3-c♯4 Sustained in moderate slow tempo. Generally subdued, with a subdued ending. Chordal accompaniment except for a
swaying top line in the middle section. Acc: 3

6348. (7) Wenn der Wein nicht wär....   Medium Voices
c3-e4 f♯3-c♯4 In varied moods and tempi. Has some sudden contrasts of dynamics. Strong ending. Acc: 3-4

6349. (8) Ich sang mich durch das deutsche Land   Medium Voices
d♭3-f4 g3-d4 Animated in varied tempi and moods. Has dramatic
passages. Tranquil, subdued, and sustained ending section. Acc:
3-4

Single Songs

6350. An einem Brunnen (Vid en brunn)   Medium Voices
Poet: Anders Österling. Finnish title: Lähteelä. e3-f♯4 f♯3-c♯4
Sustained in moderate slow tempo. Generally subdued with a very
sustained ending section. Has one quasi-recitative passage. Detached
accompaniment for the most part. Best for men's voices. Acc: 3
20K

6351. Die Drossel (Trasten)   Medium Voices
Poet: Anders Österling. Finnish title: Rastas. e3-f♯4 f♯3-d♯4
Animated in lively tempo. Graceful. Has slower and tranquil middle

Scandinavian   801

section. Dramatic ending. Agitated accompaniment. Acc: 4 20K

6352. Die Dryade I   Medium Voices
Poet: Anders Österling. First line: Du, die bei Jasminen. Finnish title and first line: Sinipiika I--Sa, ken yölla hiljaa. d3-e4
e3-d4 Animated in moderate lively tempo. Generally subdued. Has
a slower section. Best for men's voices. Acc: 3 20K

6353. Die Dryade II   Medium Voices
Poet: Anders Österling. First line: Die ersten Tränen. Finnish
title and first line: Sinipiika II--Kun vuoksein kyynel vuosi sun. e3-
e4 a3-d4 Sustained in moderate slow tempo. Requires simplicity;
generally subdued. Unusual accompaniment. Acc: 2-3 20K

6354. Die Dryade III   Medium Voices
Poet: Anders Österling. First line: Nun wohn' bei mir gleich der
Dryade. Finnish title: Sinipiika III. e3-e4 f♯3-c♯4 Sustained in
slow tempo. Gentle, subdued, requires simplicity. Subdued ending.
Arpeggiated accompaniment. Acc: 2 20K

6355. Die Fusswaschung   Medium Voices
Poet: Christian Morgenstern. e3-f♯4 a3-d4 Sustained in slow tempo. Starts very gently, then moves into stronger phrases. Intense.
Dramatic high ending section with sustained f♯4's. Chordal accompaniment. Acc: 3 LMK-1

6356. Ein Lenzrefrain   Medium Voices
Poet: Anders Österling. Finnish title: Kevätkerto. e3-e4 g3-d4
Animated in rapid tempo. Joyous, has climactic passages. Climac-
tic ending section, with e4 as final note. Arpeggiated accompaniment.
Acc: 4 20K

6357. Eine kleine Frühlingsweise   High Voices
Poet: Thor Cnattingius. Finnish title: Pieni kevätlaulu. a3-f♯4
a3-d4 Animated in very fast tempo. Bright, requires fluent enunciation. Climactic high ending. Agitated accompaniment. Acc: 4
VMK

6358. Kleines Mädchen (Liten jungfru)   Men
Poet: Thor Cnattingius. Finnish title: Pieni neito. a3-e4 a3-d4
Animated in moderate slow tempo. Simple, gentle, and subdued
throughout. Graceful. 3 verses. German version by Grete Lieht-
werk. Acc: 3 VMK

6359. Little Ola's song (Lilla Olles visa)   Soprano
Poet: Thor Cnattingius. f♯3-f4 a3-d4 Sustained and animated sec-
tions in slow and lively tempi, respectively. Slow ending phrase.
Generally light, with gently agitated accompaniment. Acc: 3-4 SFS

6360. O Nacht   Medium Voices
Poet: Christian Morgenstern. c♯3-f♯4 e♭3-c4 Sustained in slow
tempo. Generally in quasi-recitative style. Subdued, with one dramatic high passage. Very subdued ending. Short, one page. Acc:
3 LMK-1

6361. Siehe, auch ich-lebe   Medium Voices
Poet: Christian Morgenstern. f♯3-f♯4 f♯3-d4 Quite animated in
lively tempo. Generally on MF level. Dramatic high ending on f♯4.

Strong final section.   Acc: 3-4   LMK-1

6362. Sprich, Geliebte, o sprick....   Medium Voices
       Poet: Anders Österling.   Finnish title: Armahain, puhu mulle...
       e3-d4 f♯3-c4 Very sustained in moderate slow tempo.   Has some
       frequent meter changes.   Slower middle section.   Subdued; requires
       fine P and PP.   Acc: 3   20K

6363. Thalatta!   Medium Voices
       Poet: Christian Morgenstern.   d♯3-f♯4 f♯3-f♯4 Animated in mod-
       erate lively tempo.   Dramatic, energetic, and vocally demanding.
       Dramatic last section with a "falling" ending.   Has large, full-sound-
       ing chords in the accompaniment.   Acc: 3-4   LMK-1

6364. Von zwei Rosen   Medium Voices
       Poet: Christian Morgenstern.   e♭3-g4 a3-e♭4 Sustained vocal part
       in moderate lively tempo.   Light and flowing.   Has one dramatic high
       passage.   Subdued, descending ending.   Agitated accompaniment.
       Acc: 3   LMK-1

6365. Wie vieles ist denn Wort geworden   Medium Voices
       Poet: Christian Morgenstern.   d3-e♭4 g3-d4 Sustained in somewhat
       slow tempo.   Requires very fine P and PP.   Contemplative, and gen-
       erally subdued.   Has a "falling" ending on a full octave.   Acc: 3
       LMK-1

6366. Wünschekranz (Önskekransen)   High Voices
       Poet: Thor Cnattingius.   e♭3-f4 a♭3-e♭4 Finnish title: Toivon
       seppel.   Animated in lively tempo.   Generally strong and outgoing.
       Climactic ending.   Animated accompaniment.   Acc: 3-4   VMK

Note: See also the following:

       Sommersegen.   Op. 75.   Six songs to texts by Albert Sergel.   Berlin:
       Ed. Bote & G. Bock.

       7 Songs to Texts by Hans Fritz von Zwehl.   Op. 79.   Berlin: Ed.
       Bote & G. Bock.

ERKKI (ERIK GUSTAF) MELARTIN, 1875-1937

6367. Farewell (Afsked)   All Voices
       Poet: Adapted from Heinrich Heine.   d3-g4 g3-d4 Sustained in mod-
       erate tempo.   Requires simplicity.   Strong entrance, then sustains on
       MF level.   Subdued and low ending.   Acc: 3   MSS-2

6368. O master (O Herre)   All Voices
       Poet: Vilhelm Krag.   c♯3-g♯4 g♯3-d♯4 Sustained in slow tempo.
       Calm, generally subdued.   Requires very fine high PP.   Subdued, de-
       scending ending line.   Best for the darker voices.   Acc: 3   MSS-2

(FRANS) OSKAR MERIKANTO, 1868-1924

6369. Lullaby (Pai, pai, paitaresseu)   Women
       Poet: Mustakallio.   c3-g4 f3-e♭4 Sustained in moderate tempo.
       Generally subdued.   Requires fine P and flexibility.   Very subdued

ending. Gentle. Acc: 3-4 MSS-2

6370. Melancholy (Onneton)					All Voices
Poet: Kaarlo Kramsu. d3-ab4 f♯3-f4 Sustained in moderate tempo. Has dramatic passages. Subdued ending passages. Agitated accompaniment in the middle section. Acc: 4 MSS-2

6371. That hymn that we sang (Säg, minnes du Psalmen)	All Voices
Poet: Eino Leino. c3-d4 f3-d4 Sustained in moderate slow tempo. Generally subdued. Sustained chordal accompaniment. A favorite throughout Finland. English version by Ella H. Roe. Acc: 2-3 SFS

SELIM PALMGREN, 1878-1951

SSP	Six Songs by Selim Palmgren. Edited, with English words by Carl Engel. High, low. Boston: Boston Music Co.

6372. Autumn (Höst)						All Voices
Poet: Cäsar Flaischlen. b2-g4 f♯3-d4 Sustained in slow tempo. Generally subdued. Starts slowly and softly. Not for light and high voices. Subdued low ending. Acc: 3-4 MSS-2, SSP

6373. By the kiln						All Voices
Poet: Anon. d3-a4 f3-f4 Sustained in moderate slow tempo. Has one climactic passage. Requires fine high P and PP. Subdued final section. Subdued ending. Best for men. Acc: 3 SSP

6374. Darker grow the shadows				All Voices
Poet: Anon. db3(bb2)-a4 f3-eb4 Sustained in slow tempo. Subdued first and ending sections. Has climactic passages. Generally on MF level. Descending ending line. Agitated accompaniment. Acc: 3 SSP

6375. In the willows						All Voices
Poet: Oswald Sirén. d3-f4 f♯3-d4 Sustained in moderate tempo. Rhythmic. Generally on MF level. Very subdued ending section with descending final line. Acc: 3-4 MSS-2

6376. Lily of the valley (Liljekonvalje)			All Voices
Poet: Oswald Sirén. d♯3-f♯4 f♯3-e4 Sustained in slow tempo. Quite subdued; marked "dreamily." Best for high and medium voices. Acc: 3 MSS-2

6377. Midsummer-day's dream				All Voices
Poet: Anon. f♯3-g4 a3-e4 Sustained vocal part in lively tempo. Requires fine high P. Generally light and subdued. Extended piano prelude. Accompaniment requires very fine control. Acc: 4 SSP

6378. Mother						High Voices
Poet: Selim Palmgren (?). e3-g4 g3-g4 Sustained in very slow tempo. Very subdued; requires fine high P and PP. English version by Carl Engel. Acc: 3 50A, SSP

6379. The rose-bud						All Voices
Poet: Anon. d3-g4 f♯3-e4 Sustained in slow tempo. Starts and

ends very gently. Slightly agitated middle section with gently agitated accompaniment. Acc: 3 SSP

JEAN (JOHAN JULIUS CHRISTIAN) SIBELIUS, 1865-1957

Sibelius, Finland's first important composer, was mainly a symphonist. His songs, written as a side line, are of minor importance. He wrote many, mainly on Swedish texts, and they cover a variety of subjects. Grove's Dictionary of Music and Musicians lists 93 individual titles. Sibelius' songs are melodic, and in the piano accompaniments he avoids his symphonic style. Among the best known are "Black roses" (Svarta rosor), "The tryst" (Flickan kom ifran), and "A maiden yonder sits" (Tuol laulaa neitonen). The songs of Sibelius were mildly popular for only a short time. It is unfortunate that today they are seldom heard in performance, and many of them are not readily available in print. There are strong reasons why they should be brought back into the singer's repertoire.

15L   15 Ausgewählte Lieder. Jean Sibelius. High, low. Original texts, with German and English versions. Wiesbaden: Breitkopf & Härtel, 1966.

6380. A floweret by the wayside (En blomma stod vid vagen)   All Voices
Poet: Ernst Josephson. g3-f4 a3-eb4 Sustained in moderate tempo. Generally light and subdued. Slow ending phrase. Narrative text. Best for light voices. Acc: 3 MSS-2

6381. A maiden yonder sings (Tuol laulaa neitonen)   All Voices
Poet: Margarete Susman. f3-f4 gb3-eb4 Sustained in slow tempo. Generally on MF level. Requires fine P. Subdued ending. Acc: 3 MSS-2

6382. Arioso   Soprano
Poet: Johan Ludvig Runeberg. b2-a4 f#3-f#4 Sustained in moderate slow tempo. Has dramatic passages. Subdued low ending. Published in Swedish, Finnish, German, and English. Acc: 3 (S)SM

6383. Black roses (Svarta rosor)   All Voices
Poet: Ernst Josephson. German title: Schwarze Rosen. d3-a#4 f#3-f#4 Sustained vocal part in moderate tempo. Generally subdued with a dramatic high ending line, with f4 as the last note. Has quasi-recitative passages and arpeggiated accompaniment. Best for high voices. See the setting by Frederick Delius. Acc: 4 15L, SVR-2. (S)EM-one step lower; English & German

6384. Come away, death! (Kom nu hit, död!)   All Voices
Poet: William Shakespeare, from his Twelfth Night, translated into Finnish. b2-e4 e3-c4 Sustained in slow tempo. In quasi-recitative style. Subdued, requires fine P and PP. Sustained chordal accompaniment. A piano reduction from the orchestral score. See the settings by John Koch, Gerald Finzi, Roger Quilter, Mario Castelnuovo-Tedesco, and Welford Russell. Acc: 3-4 15L

6385. From the north (Norden)   High Voices
Poet: Johan Ludvig Runeberg. d#3-g4 a3-f4 Sustained in moderate tempo. Has passages with high tessitura. Generally on MF level. English version by Theodore Baker is fair. Acc: 3 50A

6386. Hey, ho, the wind and the rain (Hållilå, uti storm och i regn)   Men
Poet: William Shakespeare, from his Twelfth Night, translated into
Finnish. Subtitle: When that I was a little wee boy. d♯ 3-e4 e3-
d♯ 4 Animated in moderate lively tempo. Energetic, bright, and climactic. Narrative. Ends strongly on e4. A piano reduction from
the orchestral score. See the following settings: When I was but a
tiny little boy by Peter Heise and Mario Castelnuovo-Tedesco. Acc:
3-4 15L

6387. Sigh, waves, slumber (Säf, säf, susa)   High Voices
Poet: Gustaf Fröding. b♭ 2-g4 f3-d♭ 4 Generally sustained in moderate slow tempo. Has some slower tempi. A dramatic setting with
quite agitated accompaniment. May be transposed for lower voices,
but musically inadvisable. English version by Ella H. Roe. Acc:
4 SFS, 15L

6388. Sunrise (Soluppgång)   All Voices
Poet: Tor Hedberg. d3-g4 f♯ 3-d4 Sustained in moderate tempo.
Starts gently. Has some climactic passages. Subdued high ending
on e4. May be transposed for lower voices. Acc: 3 (S)BH

6389. Swift the springtime passes (Våren flyktar hastigt)   All Voices
Poet: John Ludvig Runeberg. e3-g4 g3-d4 Animated in very fast tem-
po. Requires fluent enunciation. Best for high and medium voices.
Acc: 3-4 MSS-2, 15L

6390. The diamond in the snow (Demanten på marssnön)   All Voices
Poet: Josef Julius Wecksell. e3-f4 f3-d4 Sustained in moderate
tempo. Generally on MF level. Descriptive text. Acc: 3 15L

6391. The kiss (Kyssens hopp)   Men
Poet: Johan Ludvig Runeberg. c3-f4 g3-d4 Animated vocal part
in moderate slow tempo. Has faster middle section. Generally on
MF level. Very agitated accompaniment. Acc: 4-5 15L

6392. The silent city (Hiljainen kaupunki)   Medium, Low Voices
Poet: Anon. e♭ 3-e4 g3-d4 Sustained in moderate tempo. General-
ly on MF level. Requires fine PP. Arpeggiated accompaniment.
Subdued ending. Acc: 3 MSS-2

6393. The tryst (Flickan kom ifrån sin älsklings möte)   All Voices
Poet: Johan Ludvig Runeberg. c♯ 3-g♯ 4 f3-e4 Generally sustained
in moderate tempo. Has some quasi-recitative passages, an agitated
middle section, and some climactic passages. Subdued ending line.
Acc: 4 15L

6394. Then I ceased to ask those questions (Se'n har jag frågat mera) Women
Poet: Johan Ludvig Runeberg. d3-f♯ 4 e3-d4 Sustained in slow,
grave tempo. Subdued, with one climactic passage. Descending ending line. Chordal accompaniment. Acc: 3 15L

6395. Was it a dream? (Var det en Dröm?)   High Voices
Poet: Josef Julius Wecksell. b2-g♯ 4 e3-e4 Sustained vocal part in
moderate tempo. Long lines, and an agitated accompaniment. Has
climactic passages. Subdued, descending ending line. English version
by Ella H. Roe. Original text: Swedish. Acc: 4 SFS

6396. Wood on the water (Spånet på vattnet)   Women

Poet: Ilmari Calamnius. eb 3-f4 a3-d4 Sustained in moderate tempo. Generally on MF level. Agitated accompaniment which starts in syncopated rhythm. Acc: 3 15L

C. NORWAY

NOS   Norway Sings. English-Norwegian Edition. Mostly folk music. Oslo: Norsk Musikforlag.

EYVIND ALNAES, 1872-1932

6397. Spring longings (Vårlengsler)   Tenor
Poet: Nils Collett Vogt. b2(g# 2)-g# 4 f# 3-e4 Animated in lively tempo. Slower, gentler middle section. Has climactic passages. Requires very fine high P and PP. Dramatic ending section. Generally agitated accompaniment. Best for the heavier voices. English version by Ella H. Roe. Acc: 4 SFS

6398. Sunlight (Sol)   All Voices
Poet: Per Sivle. d3-f4 a3-e4 Original key. Sustained in moderate slow tempo. Requires simplicity, in the style of a gentle recitative. Subdued ending. Acc: 3 MSS-1

6399. The sailor's last voyage (Siste Reis)   All Voices
Poet: Henrik Wergeland. c# 3-d4 f# 3-d4 Animated in moderate lively tempo. Generally gentle and subdued. Has climactic passages in the middle. Used as a funeral song in Norway. This edition does not give the original Norwegian text for the often-repeated refrain, "Sing, sailor, oh!". Acc: 3 SFS

6400. Yuletide (Jul)   All Voices
Poet: Per Sivle. c3-f4(ab 4) e3-d4 Original key, one step lower. Sustained in moderate tempo. Requires very fine high P and PP. Has passages in the style of a gentle recitative. Very calm, subdued, low ending phrase. English version by John Lekberg. Acc: 3 MSS-1

AGATHE BACKER-GRÖNDAHL, 1847-1907

6401. At sea (Tilsjös)   All Voices
Poet: Hans Reynolds. d3-g4 g# 3-e4 Animated in moderate lively tempo. Strong, energetic, outgoing, and climactic. Dramatic ending. Extended piano postlude. Original key: 1/2 step higher. Acc: 3-4 MSS-1

6402. Now sleeps the wave (Nu somnar vågen)   All Voices
Poet: Zachris Topelius. d3-f4 f3-d4 Original key: two steps lower. Sustained in moderate slow tempo. Generally tranquil, with subdued ending. Has some short climactic passages. English version by John Koren. Acc: 2-3 MSS-1

6403. The linden (Lind)   All Voices

Poet: Anon. d# 3-f# 4 f# 3-d4 Sustained in moderate slow tempo.
Gentle, generally subdued, and contemplative. Gently agitated accompaniment. Original key. Acc: 3-4 MSS-1

FRIDTJOF BACKER-GRØNDAHL

TSB Tre Sanger. Op. 14. Fridtjof Backer-Grøndahl. Norwegian texts,
with English versions. Oslo: Norsk Musikforlag.

7SB-2 7 Sange. Op. 16. Part II. Fridtjof Backer-Grøndahl. German
texts only. Oslo: Norsk Musikforlag. (Admirable settings of poems
by Christian Morgenstern in the modern idiom.)

6404. Auf einem verfallenen Kirchhof   High Voices
Poet: Christian Morgenstern. b2-f4 e3-c4 Sustained in slow tempo. Subdued throughout except the ending phrase which moves in ascending, climactic crescendo. A most warm and beautiful setting.
See the setting by Yrjö Kilpinen in the cycle "Lieder um den Tod."
Acc: 3-4 7SB-2

6405. Cradle-song in the northern Winter   High Voices
Poet: Nordahl Grieg. Norwegian title: Vuggesang i mørketiden.
b2-g4 f# 3-e4 Sustained in moderate slow tempo. Generally subdued
and tranquil. Subdued high ending. Acc: 3 TSB

6406. Der Blick   High Voices
Poet: Christian Morgenstern. b2-a4 f# 3-e4 Sustained in moderate
tempo. Starts gently and subduedly. Has climactic passages. Requires some fine high P. Subdued ending. Accompaniment in sustained chords. Acc: 3 7SB-2

6407. I loved thee well   High, Medium Voices
Poet: Alexander S. Pushkin. Norwegian title: Du var mig Kjaer.
b# 2-f# 4 f# 3-d# 4 Sustained in slow tempo. Starts low and in gentle
manner. Generally on MF level. Subdued, descending ending line.
The text is a translation from the Russian. Acc: 3 TSB

6408. The third foot-print   High Voices
Poet: Nordahl Grieg. Norwegian title: Det tredje Fottrin. c3-g4
f# 3-e4 Generally sustained vocal part in lively tempo. Strong entrance and ending sections. Generally chordal accompaniment. Acc:
3 TSB

6409. Zeit und Ewigkeit   High, Medium Voices
Poet: Christian Morgenstern. db 3-f4 f3-db 4 Sustained in moderate
tempo. Grave, and somewhat intense. Has a climactic high passage.
Starts gently and contemplatively. Right hand accompaniment is in
steadily moving repeated figures. Acc: 3 7SB-2

JOHAN BACKER-LUNDE

6410. Goodnight, beloved (Godnatt)   Medium, Low Voices
Poet: Anon. a# 3-d4 f3-c4 Sustained in slow tempo. Tranquil,
gentle, and subdued. Requires very fine P and PP. Has low tessitura in some passages. English version by Ella H. Roe. Acc: 3 SFS

6411. Idyl (Genrebillede)   All Voices
      Poet: Jens Peter Jacobsen.   c3-f4 g3-d4 Original key.   Animated
      in moderate lively tempo.   Very strong, dramatic middle section.
      Agitated accompaniment.   English version by John Lekberg.   Acc: 3
      MSS-1

6412. Lady moon   High Voices
      Poet: Lord Houghton.   Norwegian title: Lille Måne.   b2-a4 e3-e4
      Sustained in moderate slow tempo.   Generally subdued and gentle.
      Requires very fine P to PP and high PP.   Fine for light voices.
      Chordal accompaniment.   Has English and Norwegian texts.   Acc: 3
      (S)NM

6413. Longing (Laengsel)   All Voices
      Poet: Anna Ritter.   d3(b2)-bb4 g3-f4 Original key.   Sustained in
      varied tempi.   Starts majestically.   Dramatic, energetic, and intense.
      Dramatic high ending.   Not for light voices.   English version by John
      Lekberg.   Acc: 3 MSS-1

FRANTZ BEYER, 1851-1918

6414. Amid roses (Millom rosor)   All Voices
      Poet: Kristofer Janson.   f3-f4 a3-d4 Original key.   Gently ani-
      mated vocal part in moderate tempo.   Generally on MF level.   De-
      scriptive text.   English version by John Lekberg.   Acc: 3 MSS-1

6415. Autumn (Höst)   All Voices
      Poet: Frantz Beyer.   d3-g4 f3-eb4 Original key is two steps low-
      er.   Sustained in moderate slow tempo.   Generally subdued.   Synco-
      pated rhythm in the accompaniment.   Best for warmer voices.   Eng-
      lish version by John Lekberg.   Acc: 3 MSS-1

OLE BULL, 1810-1880

6416. The herdgirl's Sunday (Saetergjentens Söndag)   Women
      Poet: Jörgen Moe.   c3-g4 f3-d4 Original key.   Animated vocal part
      in moderate slow tempo.   Requires simplicity, 3 verses.   English
      version by Constance Purdy.   Acc: 3 MSS-1

CATHERINUS ELLING, 1858-1942

6417. The fisherman to his son (Fiskeren til sønnen)   Men
      Poet: Kristofer Janson.   c#3-f#4 f#3-d4 Original key is two steps
      lower.   Sustained in slow tempo.   Generally on MF level.   English
      version by Greta Torpadie.   Acc: 3 MSS-1

EDVARD HAGERUP GRIEG, 1843-1907

Although Grieg wrote a variety of compositions, he excels best in his many
songs.   Considered one of the most distinguished of 19th-century song composers, the poems of his songs are chosen from outstanding lyrics in Danish,
German, and Norwegian.   Grieg was gifted with melodic inventiveness.   His
songs flow easily with attractive melodies that are not only pleasant to hear,
but also well-placed in interpreting the emotional content of the poetry.   His

style, simple, so right with the voice, and never demanding, was influenced by Norwegian folksongs, which he loved. The individuality of his genius is shown not only in his exquisite melodies, but also in their harmonic variety and imagination. Many of his songs were made known through the performances of his wife, Nina Grieg, an accomplished singer. His song cycle, Haugtussa, was among Grieg's own favorites, and for some time it was popular among recitalists. "A swan," "The first meeting," "With a water lily," "Ein Traum," and "Spring" have been among the best-known recital favorites. The songs of Grieg ought to be performed more. They would offer a refreshing sound to many a worn-out and over-used so-called "standard" recital repertoire.

FSG   Fifty Songs by Edvard Grieg. Edited by Henry T. Finck. Mostly original keys. German and English texts. Bryn Mawr: Oliver Ditson, c/o Theodore Presser.

GSS   Selected Songs. Edvard Grieg. High, low. Thirty-six songs. English and German texts. New York: G. Schirmer, Inc.

RSG   Romancer og Sange af Edvard Grieg. Ten volumes. Copenhagen: Wilhelm Hansen.

18S   18 Selected Songs by Edvard Grieg. Book 2. Norwegian texts with English versions. London: Enoch and Sons.

20S   20 Selected Songs by Edvard Grieg. Book 1. Norwegian texts with English versions. Edited by R. H. Elkin. London: Enoch and Sons.

Other collections:
       Selected Songs and other albums, published by C. F. Peters. Sixty songs. High, medium, low. Only German songs and translations. Some have both German and English versions.

6418. Haugtussa. Op. 67. Song cycle of 8 movements for medium voice and piano. Best for mezzo-soprano. Poems by Arne Garborg. Norwegian texts. Copenhagen: Wilhelm Hansen. Overall range: b2-gb4. Generally in the quasi-recitative style. Very comfortable for the voice. In different moods, has gentle lyric as well as dramatic styles. Acc: 5 (SC)WH. RSG-8 Titles:
       Det syng (The singing)
       Veslemøy (Little maiden)
       Blaarbaerli (Bilberry slopes)
       Møte (Meeting)
       Elsk (Love)
       Killingdans (Kidlings' dance)
       Vond dag (Evil day)
       Vel gjaetle-bekken (At the brook)
Single songs are also included in the following collections: Song No. 2 in 50M, Song No. 4 in FSG, Song No. 5 in FSG

Single Songs

6419. A mother's sorrow (Moderdorg)   Women
       Poet: Christian Richardt. Op. 15, No. 4. f3-f4 a3-db4 Sustained in slow tempo. Tranquil, gentle, and subdued. Gently agitated accompaniment. 2 verses. Acc: 3 20S, GSS, RSG-1

6420. A swan (En svane)   All Voices
       Poet: Henrik Ibsen. Op. 25, No. 2. d3-f4 f3-e4 Original key.
       Sustained in moderate slow tempo. Has gentle, somewhat spoken
       style. Subdued ending. One of Grieg's best-known songs. Acc: 3
       MSS-1, FSG, GSS, 50M, ART-2, RSG-3

6421. A vision (Et syn)   Men
       Poet: Aasmund O. Vinje. Op. 33, No. 6. c♯3-f♯4 f♯3-d4 Origi-
       nal key. Animated in lively tempo. Has climactic passages. Re-
       quires fine P and PP. Acc: 3 FSG, 20S, MSS-1, RSG-4

6422. Autumnal gale (Efteraarsstormen)   All Voices
       Poet: Christian Richardt. Op. 18, No. 4. a2-f4 d3-d4 Animated
       in lively tempo. Animated, dramatic, and powerful. Also requires
       some fine P. Has slower tempo in the middle. Descending ending
       line. Best for the heavier voices. English version by Nathan H.
       Dole. Acc: 3-4 GSS, FSG, 18S, RSG-2

6423. Be greeted, ye ladies (Vaer hilset, i damer)   Men
       Poet: Holger Drachmann. Op. 49, No. 3. d3-f4 a3-e♭4 Original
       key. Animated in moderate lively tempo. Strong, energetic, in quasi-
       recitative style. Outgoing. Requires fluent enunciation. Not for
       light voices. English version: Aretta Werrenrath. Acc: 3-4 MSS-
       1, RSG-6

6424. Boat song (Mens jeg venter)   Men
       Poet: Vilhelm Krag. Op. 60, No. 3. c3-d♯4(M) g3-c4 Animated
       in moderate lively tempo. Graceful and light. Extended piano post-
       lude. 3 verses. English version: Sigmund Spaeth. Acc: 3 55A,
       FSG, RSG-7

6425. By the brook (Langs en å)   High, Medium Voices
       Poet: Aasmund O. Vinje. Op. 33, No. 5. e3-e4 g3-d4 Sustained
       in moderate slow tempo. Requires fine P and PP. Has some dra-
       matic passages. Original key. English version: Frederic Field Bul-
       lard. Acc: 3 FSG, 50A, MSS-1, 50M, 18S, RSG-4

6426. Cradle song (Vuggesang)   Men
       Poet: Andreas Munch. Op. 9, No. 2. Original text: Danish. b2-
       d♯4 d♯3-b3 Sustained in slow tempo. Subdued. 4 verses and Coda.
       Best for medium or low men's voices. A man's lullaby; text implies
       that the mother is dead. English version: Nathan H. Dole. Acc:
       3-4 GSS, 20S, RSG-1

6427. Dreams (Drømme)   All Voices
       Poet: Otto Benzon. Op. 69, No. 5. b♭2-g4 g3-f♯4 Sustained in
       moderate lively tempo. Starts subdued. Requires fine P and PP.
       Has dramatic passages. Climactic ending. English version by Nathan
       H. Dole. Acc: 3 FSG, RSG-9

6428. Eros   All Voices
       Poet: Otto Benzon. Op. 70, No. 1. c3-f4 e3-d4 Animated vocal
       part in moderate slow tempo. In quasi-recitative style. Has dramat-
       ic passages and a climactic ending. Requires fine P. English ver-
       sion by Nathan H. Dole. Acc: 3-4 FSG, GAS, RSG-9

6429. Faith (Tro)   All Voices
       Poet: Anon. Op. 33, No. 5. d♭3-g♭4 a♭3-d♭4 Sustained in

moderate slow tempo.   Somewhat majestic.   Chordal accompaniment.
Sacred overtones in the text.   2 verses.   Acc: 3 18S, RSG-4

6430. Friendship   Men
Poet: Aasmund O. Vinje.   e3-f4(H) g3-db4 Sustained in moderate
slow tempo.   Requires simplicity and fine P and PP.   English version by Nathan H. Dole.   Acc: 2-3 FSG

6431. From an autograph album (Stamboksrim)   All Voices
Poet: Henrik Ibsen. Op. 25, No. 3.   e3-d4 e3-c4 Sustained in
moderate slow tempo.   Has some climactic passages and a subdued
ending.   English version: Ella H. Roe.   Acc: 3 SFS, RSG-3

6432. From Monte Pincio (Fra Monte Pincio)   All Voices
Poet: Björnstjerne Björnson.   Op. 39, No. 1.   bb2-gb4 gb3-f4
Original key.   In varied moods and tempi.   Requires fine P and PP,
as well as some dramatic strength.   Interpretatively not easy.   Text
is descriptive of Italian scenery.   English version: F. Corder.   Acc:
4 50M, FSG, RSG-4

6433. Gone (Borte)   Men
Poet: Henrik Ibsen.   Op. 25, No. 5.   e3-f4 e3-c4 Original key.
Sustained in moderate slow tempo.   In gentle recitative style.   Gen-
erally subdued.   English version: Reinald Werrenrath.   Acc: 2-3
MSS-1, RSG-3

6434. Good morning! (God morgen!)   All Voices
Poet: Björnstjerne Björnson.   Op. 21, No. 2.   Original text: Danish.
d3-f#4 f#3-f#4 Animated in fast tempo.   Vigorous and exultant.
Climactic ending.   Best for high voices.   English version: Nathan H.
Dole, for FSG.   Acc: 3 FSG, GSS, 20S, POS-4, RSG-2

6435. Hidden love (Dulgt kjaerlighed)   All Voices
Poet: Björnstjerne Björnson.   Op. 39, No. 2.   f#3-g4 f#3-f#4
Sustained in moderate slow tempo.   Requires fine P and PP, and
some flexibility.   Very subdued, ascending ending.   Best for high and
medium voices.   English version by Nathan H. Dole.   Acc: 3 FSG,
RSG-4

6436. Hunter's song   Men
Poet: Anon.   Original text: Danish.   bb2-f4(bb4) eb3-eb4 Animated in very fast tempo.   Energetic and climactic.   Requires fluent
enunciation.   Climactic and exultant ending.   Acc: 3 GSS

6437. I love thee (Jeg elsker Dig)   All Voices
Poet: Hans Christian Andersen.   Op. 5, No. 3.   Original text:
Danish.   e3-f4 e3-e4 Original key.   Sustained in moderate slow tempo.   Climactic ending.   Grieg's most well-known song.   English version by Auber Forestier.   Acc: 3 GSS, FSG, 20S, MSS-1, SVR-1,
56S, RSG-1.   (S)GS-high, medium, low

6438. Love (Kjaerlighed)   All Voices
Poet: Hans Christian Andersen.   Op. 15, No. 2.   Original text:
Danish.   db3-f4 ab3-eb4 Sustained in moderate slow tempo.   Re-
quires fine high P.   Ends softly on a high note.   3 verses.   Acc: 4
GSS, 20S, RSG-1

6439. Marguerite's cradle-song (Margretes Vuggesang)   Women

Poet: Henrik Ibsen. Op. 15, No. 1. Original text: Danish. c3-
f4 f3-c4 Sustained in slow tempo. Gentle, tranquil, and short. A
lullaby. English version: Arthur Westbrook. Acc: 3 FSG, GSS,
20S, RSG-1

6440.   Minstrel's song (Spillemaend)   All Voices
        Poet: Henrik Ibsen. Op. 25, No. 1. Original text: Norwegian.
        c3-g4 eb3-eb4 Sustained in slow tempo. In declamatory style.
        Has dramatic climaxes and passages with agitated accompaniment.
        In GS, the title is "The sorrowful minstrel." Acc: 3-4 FSG,
        RSG-3

6441.   My mind is like a peak snow-crowned (Min Tanke er et
            maegtigt Fjeld)   All Voices
        Poet: Hans Christian Andersen. Op. 5, No. 4. d3-gb4 f3-eb4
        Animated in lively tempo. Joyful. Not suitable for light soprano.
        Ends on low notes of the melody. English version: Nathan H. Dole.
        Acc: 4 FSG, GSS, 20S, RSG-1

6442.   My song shall be thine, sweet spring-time (Jeg giver mit
            digt til våren)   All Voices
        Poet: Björnstjerne Björnson. Op. 21, No. 3. b2-f4(L) e3-d4 Ani-
        mated in very fast tempo. Jovial, requires flexibility. Best for all
        voices, except bass. Original text: Danish. Acc: 3 GSS, FSG,
        18S, RSG-2

6443.   On the waters a boat is playing (Der gynger en Båd på Bølge)   Tenor
        Poet: Otto Benzon. Op. 69, No. 1. c3-f4 e3-e4 Animated in
        lively tempo. Graceful. Has dramatic passages; also requires fine
        P and PP. Subdued, low ending after high climax. Generally agi-
        tated accompaniment. May be transposed for lower voices. English:
        Ella H. Roe. Acc: 4 SFS, RSG-9

6444.   One summer night   All Voices
        Poet: John Paulsen. Original text: Norwegian. c#3-f#4 g#3-e4
        Animated in moderate lively tempo. Requires some flexibility, and
        simplicity. 3 verses. English version: Charles Manney. Acc: 3
        FSG, GSS

6445.   Outward bound (Udfarten)   Men
        Poet: Andreas Munch. Op. 9, No. 4. Original text: Danish. c3-
        g4 e3-e4 Animated in moderate lively tempo. Has climactic pas-
        sages. Requires some flexibility. Very subdued last section with
        low, sustained ending. Acc: 3-4 GSS, 18S, RSG-1

6446.   Radiant night   All Voices
        Poet: Otto Benzon. c#3-f4 e3-e4 Sustained in moderate tempo.
        Slightly faster middle section. Very subdued ending. Mostly subdued.
        English version: Nathan H. Dole. Acc: 3 FSG

6447.   Rosebud (Rosenknoppen)   Men
        Poet: Björnstjerne Björnson. Op. 18, No. 4. Original text: Danish.
        d3-e4(L) d3-d4 Animated in moderate tempo. Light, requires fine
        PP and some flexibility. 4 verses. Acc: 3-4 GSS, 20S, RSG-2

6448.   See the fellow that passed just now (Saa du knøsen, som strøg
            forbi)   Men
        Poet: Holger Drachmann. Op. 49, No. 1. c3-a4 a3-g4 Original

key: two steps lower. Animated in lively tempo. Generally strong, with climactic high ending on g4. Not for light tenor. English version: Aretta Werrenrath. Acc: 3-4 MSS-1, RSG-6

6449. She is so white (Hun er saa hvid)   Men
Poet: Hans Christian Andersen. Op. 18, No. 2. Original text: Danish. d♯ 3-d4 f3-c4 Gently animated in moderate lively tempo. Requires simplicity. Gentle, generally subdued. Acc: 3 GSS, 20S, MSS-1, RSG-2

6450. Snail, snail, come out of your house (Snegl, snegl, kom
    ud af dit hus!)   All Voices
Poet: Otto Benzon. Op. 69, No. 4. b2-f4 e3-e4 Animated in lively tempo. Requires some fluent enunciation. Has climactic passages. Requires fine P and PP. Interpretatively not easy. Very subdued, high ending. May be transposed for lower voices. English version: Ella H. Roe. Acc: 3 SFS, RSG-9

6451. Solvejg's slumber song (Solveigs Vuggevise)   Women
Poet: Henrik Ibsen. Op. 23, No. 2. c♯ 3-f♯ 4 e3-e4 Sustained in slow tempo. Gentle and tranquil. Slightly stronger ending phrase. English version: Charles F. Manney. Acc: 3 FSG, 20S, RSG-3

6452. Solvejg's song (Solveigs Sang)   All Voices
Poet: Henrik Ibsen. Op. 23, No. 1. e3-a4 g♯ 3-f♯ 4 Sustained in moderate slow tempo. Requires flexibility. The second verse ends with a gently florid cadenza. Melody was borrowed from folk material. One of Grieg's best-known settings. English version: Westbrook. Acc: 3 FSG, 20S, GSS, ART-2, 56S, RSG-3

6453. Song of hope   All Voices
Poet: None stated. e♭ 3-g4 g3-e♭ 4 Animated in very fast tempo. Joyous, with a climactic ending. 2 verses. Extended piano postlude. Acc: 3-4 GSS

6454. Spring (Vaaren)   All Voices
Poet: Aasmund O. Vinje. Op. 33, No. 2. d♯ 3-f♯ 4 g♯ 3-e♯ 4 Sustained in moderate slow tempo. In gentle recitative style. Requires fine P and PP. Has two climactic, strong passages. English version: Willis Wager. Acc: 3 GAS, SFS, 20S, RSG-4

6455. Strolling minstrel's song   Men
Poet: Henrik Ibsen. c3-e4 e3-c4 Sustained in slow tempo. Subdued, then moves on to a more dramatic section. Has agitated middle section with vocal line in recitative style. In FSG: 1-1/2 steps higher. English version: Nathan H. Dole. Acc: 3 GSS, FSG

6456. Sunset (Solnedgang)   All Voices
Poet: Andreas Munch. Op. 9, No. 3. Original text: Danish. b2-b3 d♯ 2-a3 Sustained in slow tempo. Gentle, generally subdued. 3 verses. Best for medium or low voices. Acc: 3 GSS, 20S, RSG-1

6457. Thanks for thy counsel (Tak for dit Rad)   Men
Poet: Björnstjerne Björnson. Op. 21, No. 4. Original text: Danish. c3-a4 f♯ 3-f♯ 4 Animated in fast tempo. Has dramatic passages. Generally strong and spirited. Not for light tenors. Climactic ending. English version: Reinald Werrenrath. Acc: 3-4 MSS-1, GSS, SFS, RSG-2

6458. The first meeting (Det første mode)   All Voices
       Poet: Björnstjerne Björnson. Op. 21, No. 1. c3-ab4 db3-db4
       Sustained in moderate slow tempo. Requires very fine P and PP.
       Climactic ending. English version by F. Corder. Acc: 3-4 GSS,
       FSG, 18S, POS-3, RSG-2

6459. The first primrose (Med en Primula veris)   Men
       Poet: John Paulsen. Op. 26, No. 4. db3-gb4 f3-eb4 Sustained
       in moderate lively tempo. Graceful and light. Requires some flexi-
       bility. English version by F. Corder. Acc: 3 FSG, GSS, MSS-1,
       50M, POS-1, RSG-3

6460. The harp (Harpen)   All Voices
       Poet: Andreas Munch. Op. 9, No. 1. c3-f4 f3-db4 Sustained in
       moderate slow tempo. Generally on MF level. Gentle. Has some
       gently agitated accompaniment. 3 verses. Acc: 3 18S, RSG-1

6461. The Odalisk (Okalisken synger)   All Voices
       Poet: Carl Brunn. No opus number. d3-f#4 e3-d4 Animated in
       lively tempo. Requires flexibility and fluent enunciation. Narrative,
       with Arabic basis for the text. Original text: Norwegian. Climactic
       ending. Acc: 4 GSS, RSG-3

6462. The old mother (Gamle mor)   Tenor, Baritone
       Poet: Aasmund O. Vinje. Op. 33, No. 1. Original text: Norwegian.
       d3-f#4 f#3-d4 Animated in moderate lively tempo. Requires sim-
       plicity. One step lower in NOS. English version by F. Corder.
       Original key. Acc: 3 20S, 50M, NOS, RSG-4

6463. The poet's heart (En Digters Bryst)   All Voices
       Poet: Hans Christian Andersen. Op. 5, No. 2. b#2-f#4 c#3-e4
       Animated in fast and agitated tempo. Requires fluent enunciation and
       flexibility. Has climactic passages, and a subdued, low ending. Eng-
       lish version: Nathan H. Dole. Acc: 4 GSS, FSG, 20S

6464. The poet's last song (En Digters Sidste sang)   All Voices
       Poet: Hans Christian Andersen. Op. 18, No. 3. Original text:
       Danish. c#3-e#4 d#3-d#4 Sustained in moderate tempo. Requires
       simplicity. Generally strong. Subdued ending. 2 verses. Acc: 3
       GSS, 18S, RSG-2

6465. The princess (Prinsessen)   Women
       Poet: Björnstjerne Björnson. No opus number. Original text:
       Danish. d3-g4 f3-eb4 Sustained in moderate lively tempo. Narra-
       tive. English version: Nathan H. Dole. Acc: 3 FSG, GSS, RSG-3

6466. The wanderer's return (Ved ronderne)   All Voices
       Poet: Aasmund O. Vinje. Op. 33, No. 3. First line: No ser eg
       atter slike fjell og dalar. db3-f4 f3-eb4 Sustained in moderate
       slow tempo. Tranquil, generally subdued, and requires fine PP. 2
       verses. The same song as "Memories of childhood" in NOS, 1/2
       step lower. Acc: 3 20S, NOS, POS-4, RSG-4

6467. Two brown eyes (Tø brune Øine)   All Voices
       Poet: Hans Christian Andersen. Op. 5, No. 1. c3-d4(L) e3-c4
       Animated in moderate lively tempo. Graceful. Acc: 3-4 20S, GSS,
       RSG-1

6468. Why with tears softly shimmering? (Hvorfor svömmer
       dit oge?)   **All Voices**
       Poet: John Paulsen.   Op. 59, No. 4.   e3-f4 a3-c4 Sustained in
       moderate slow tempo.   Starts gently.   Has one climactic passage.
       Requires fine P and PP.   Gently syncopated accompaniment.   English
       version by James Woodside.   Acc: 3 SCS-5, RSG-7

6469. With a water lily (Med en vandlilje)   **Women**
       Poet: Henrik Ibsen.   Op. 25, No. 4.   d♯3-f4 f♯3-e4 Gently ani-
       mated in lively tempo.   Graceful.   Requires flexibility.   Has delicate
       staccato passages.   Climactic ending.   Agitated accompaniment.   Eng-
       lish version: Nathan H. Dole.   Acc: 4 FSG, GSS, POS-3, RSG-3

                          Songs to German Texts

6470. Die Verschwiegene Nachtigall (Nattergalen)   **Women**
       Poet: Walther von der Vogelweide.   Op. 48, No. 4.   d3-e4 g3-e4
       Sustained in moderate lively tempo.   Subdued throughout.   Requires
       fine P and PP, and some flexibility.   Very subdued ending.   English
       version by Nathan H. Dole.   Acc: 3 FSG, RSG-5

6471. Ein Traum (En Drøm)   **Men**
       Poet: Friedrich von Bodenstedt.   Op. 48, No. 6.   Original key.
       g♭3-a♭4 a♭3-f4 Sustained in moderate slow tempo.   Requires very
       fine P and PP.   Has climactic passages and a climactic ending.   Agi-
       tated accompaniment.   English version by Charles F. Manney.   Acc:
       3-4 FSG, RSG-5

6472. Gruss (Hilsen)   **Men**
       Poet: Heinrich Heine.   Op. 48, No. 1.   English: Greeting.   e3-f♯4
       f♯3-e4 Animated in lively tempo.   Starts gently then becomes more
       exultant.   Climactic ending.   English version: Charles F. Manney.
       Acc: 4 FSG, RSG-5

6473. Lauf der Welt (Verdens Gang)   **Men**
       Poet: Ludwig Uhland.   Op. 48, No. 3.   English: The way of the
       world.   d3-f♯4 f♯3-e4 Animated in moderate lively tempo.   Light;
       requires fine P and PP.   Requires fluent enunciation.   Generally sub-
       dued.   English version by Charles F. Manney.   Acc: 3-4 FSG,
       RSG-5

6474. Morgenthau   **Medium, Low Voices**
       Poet: Adalbert von Chamisso.   Op. 4, No. 2.   English: Morning
       dew.   a2-e4 e3-e4 Animated vocal part in fairly fast tempo.   Exult-
       ant.   Uses much of the low range and tessitura.   Ends on lowest note
       of the song.   Acc: 3-4 GSS, FSG, RSG-1

LEIF HALVORSEN

6475. Mend me my strings (Hel mig mine strenge)   **All Voices**
       Poet: Vilhelm Krag.   e♯3-f♯4 f♯3-f♯4 Original key: one step low-
       er.   Animated in generally fast tempo.   In quasi-recitative.   Slightly
       joyous and outgoing.   2 verses.   English version by Greta Torpadie.
       Acc: 3-4 MSS-1

IVER PAUL FREDRIK HOLTER, 1850-1941

6476. On frost-cold Norway's moorlands (På Norges kolde vidder) All Voices
       Poet: After Heinrich Heine.   d3-e♭4 g♯3-c♯4 Original key. Sus-
       tained in moderate slow tempo. Generally subdued. Descriptive.
       Best for the darker voices. English version: Greta Torpadie. Acc:
       3 MSS-1

SVERRE JORDAN

6477. Finland (Finnland)   All Voices
       Poet: Viggo Stuckenberg.   d3-g4   a3-d4 Original key. Sustained in
       moderate slow tempo. Generally subdued, with climactic ending.
       Short. English version: Constance Purdy. Best for the darker
       voices. Acc: 2-3 MSS-1

6478. Herbstgang   Men
       Poet: Paul Remer. Original text: German. c3-a♭4(d4) g3-e4
       Sustained in moderate slow tempo. Generally subdued. Requires fine
       P. Has one climactic passage. Subdued ending. Acc: 3 MSS-1

HALFDAN KJERULF, 1815-1868

6479. A bridal party of the Hardanger Fjord (Brudeferden i
           Hardanger)   All Voices
       Poet: Andreas Munch.   a2-f4 f3-c4 Slightly sustained in moderate
       slow tempo. Has some strong passages. Joyous. Climactic ending.
       5 verses and refrain. Acc: 3 NOS

6480. Ingrid's song (Jngrids vise)   Women
       Poet: Björnstjerne Björnson.   c3-f4   g3-d4 Original key. Animated
       in moderate lively tempo. Joyful and rhythmic. 2 verses. Extended
       piano postlude. English version by Constance Purdy. Acc: 3 MSS-1

6481. Last night   All Voices
       Poet: Christian Winther.   c3-e4 c3-c4 Animated in moderate lively
       tempo. Graceful. 2 verses. A once well-known song. Acc: 2-3
       55A

6482. My heart and lute (Mit hjerte og min lyre)   All Voices
       Poet: Thomas Moore, translated.   d3-f♯4(a4) g3-e4 Original key.
       Sustained in moderate slow tempo. Generally on MF level. Descend-
       ing ending line. Acc: 3 MSS-1, SFS

6483. Synnöve's song (Synnöve's Sang)   All Voices
       Poet: Björnstjerne Björnson.   c3-f4 f3-e♭4 Original key. Sus-
       tained in moderate slow tempo. Generally subdued. Starts and ends
       with very gently vocalized passages. English version: Auber Fores-
       tier. Acc: 2-3 MSS-1

6484. The long day (Den langa dagen)   Women
       Poet: Nino Runeberg.   g3-f4(g4) a3-d4 Original key. Sustained in
       moderate tempo. Generally in gentle recitative style. Contemplative
       and subdued ending. Slightly extended piano postlude. English ver-
       sion: Greta Torpadie. Acc: 3 MSS-1

6485. Twilight musing (Aftenstemning)   All Voices
       Poet: Björnstjerne Björnson. d3-f4 g3-d4 Original key. Animated
       in moderate lively tempo. Graceful. Requires simplicity. Narrative
       text, 3 verses. English version: Nathan H. Dole. Acc: 3 MSS-1

SIGURD LIE, 1871-1904

6486. Fain would I saddle (Jeg vilde sadle)   Men
       Poet: Vilhelm Krag. c3-g4 g3-eb4 Animated in lively tempo. Re-
       quires fluent enunciation. Strong beginning and ending sections. Cli-
       mactic ending. Acc: 3-4 MSS-2

6487. Snow (Sne)   All Voices
       Poet: Helge Rode. f3-g4 g3-e4 Gently animated vocal part in mod-
       erate slow tempo. Requires some flexibility. Has some short florid
       figures. Generally gentle. Best for high voices. Acc: 3-4 MSS-2

SIGNE LUND, 1868-1950

6488. Night (Nat)   All Voices
       Poet: Sophus Michaëlis. c3-e4(g#4) e3-d4 Original key: one step
       lower. Sustained in moderate slow tempo. Has some climactic pas-
       sages. Subdued low ending. Chordal accompaniment. Acc: 3
       MSS-2

6489. The wanderer (Vandraren)   All Voices
       Poet: John Sverdrup Holt. c3-f#4(a4) e3-e4 Sustained in moderate
       slow tempo. Has dramatic passages. Very sustained, low ending.
       Somber text. Best for men's voices. Acc: 3 MSS-2

EDMUND NEUPERT, 1842-1888

6490. Sing me home (Syng mig hjaem!)   All Voices
       Poet: Björnstjerne Björnson. d#3-f#4 f#3-d4 Sustained in moder-
       ate slow tempo. Has one climactic passage. Subdued ending. Best
       for the darker voices. Acc: 3 MSS-2

RIKARD NORDRAAK, 1842-1866

6491. Tonen   All Voices
       Poet: Björnstjerne Björnson. First line: I skogen smågutten gikk
       dagen lang. d3-f#4 g3-d4 Sustained in moderate slow tempo. Short
       melody with piano postlude. 8 verses. Acc: 3 SSO

OLE OLSEN, 1850-1927

6492. Sailing (Baadfart)   All Voices
       Poet: Ole Olsen (?). f#3-f#4 g#3-d#4 Gently animated vocal part
       in moderate slow tempo. Requires simplicity. Subdued, gentle.
       Best for light voices. Acc: 3-4 MSS-2

6493. The sun is hid by the mountains nearly (Når solen
          faller bak topp og tinde)   All Voices

Poet: Nordahl Rolfsen.   d3-c4   g3-c4   Sustained in moderate tempo.
Simple, short melody.   5 verses.   An excerpt from the fairy tale
comedy "Svein Uraed. "   Acc: 3 NOS

SPARRE OLSEN, 1903-1929

6494. A heaven-blue day in March (Vår-blå himmel i Mars)   All Voices
Poet: Olav Aukrust.   d3-f#4   f#3-d4   Animated in moderate lively
tempo.   Generally light and gently joyous.   Best for men's voices.
2 verses.   May be transposed for the lower voices.   English version:
Ella H. Roe.   Acc: 3 SFS

CHRISTIAN SINDING, 1856-1941

SIN   Six Songs by Christian Sinding.   Medium voice and piano.   English
version only.   Boston: Boston Music Co.

6495. A lonely bird cried out (Der Skreg en Fugl)   All Voices
Poet: Vilhelm Krag.   bb2-f4   f3-c4   Sustained in moderate slow tempo.   Has climactic passages toward the end.   Descending, but strong
ending line.   Short.   May be transposed for lower voices.   English
version: Esther Gulbrandson.   Acc: 3 SFS

6496. A thought of spring (Ein vaartankje)   All Voices
Poet: Hans Utbö.   db3-g4   g3-eb4   Sustained in moderate slow tempo.   Requires simplicity and elegance.   Acc: 3 MSS-2

6497. Bring us songs of cheer and joy (Kom med sange og
helst af dem)   All Voices
Poet: Gustav Hetsch.   e3-g4   a3-e4   Animated in moderate lively
tempo.   Generally strong.   Best for high and medium voices.   Acc:
3-4 MSS-2

6498. Come to us with songs of glee   All Voices
Poet: Anon.   d3-e4   f#3-d4   Animated in moderate lively tempo.
Requires some fluent enunciation.   Has some climactic passages.   De-
scending ending line.   Acc: 3 SIN

6499. Faith (Tro)   All Voices
Poet: Holger Drachmann, from "Poems from the Levant. "   e3-f4
a3-e4   Animated in moderate lively tempo.   Has some dramatic passages.   Subdued ending.   Philosophic text.   Acc: 3-4 MSS-2

6500. Holy Mother, sweet and mild   High Voices
Poet: Edvard Brandes.   Original text: Danish.   db3-ab4   eb3-eb4
Sustained in moderate slow tempo.   Requires simplicity and elegance.
Has one climactic passage.   English version by Charles Wharton
Stork.   Acc: 3 SIN

6501. I'll show thee stars (Der gives stjerner)   All Voices
Poet: Anon.   e3-g#4   g#3-d4   Sustained in moderate slow tempo.
Lively ending phrases.   Gently agitated accompaniment.   Original key:
1-1/2 steps lower.   Acc: 3-4 MSS-2

6502. Life and blessedness (Liv og salighed)   All Voices

Poet: Ivar Mortenson. e3-f♯4 f♯3-e4 Sustained in moderate slow tempo. Generally subdued with some climactic passages. Best for men's voices. Acc: 3 MSS-2

6503. Light (Ljos) All Voices
Poet: Per Sivle. Original text: Norwegian. d3-a4 f3-e4 Sustained in moderate slow tempo. First section in quasi-recitative. Stronger, more climactic second section. Climactic high ending on a4. Best for the heavier voices. Acc: 3-4 MSS-2, SIN

6504. Sylvelin All Voices
Poet: Vetle Vislie. First line in English: O Sylvelin, God's own blessing be on you. e3-e4 a3-e4 Sustained in moderate slow tempo. Generally subdued, in quasi-recitative. Accompaniment has very gentle glissandos. English version: F. H. Martens. Acc: 4 56S, ART-2, SIN

6505. The maiden went where poppies grow All Voices
Poet: Carl Ewald. Original text: Danish. c♯3-f♯4 f♯3-e4 Animated in moderate lively tempo. Generally light, with a slightly climactic ending. Narrative text, with English version by Charles Wharton Stork. Acc: 3 SIN

6506. The new moon (Ny-mane) All Voices
Poet: Igbal, Swedish version from the original Hindustani. Original key. d3-g4 f♯3-d4 Gently animated vocal part in moderate slow tempo. Generally subdued. Best for light voices. Descriptive text. Acc: 3-4 MSS-2

6507. To voice my thoughts All Voices
Poet: Anon. d3-e4 f♯3-d4 Sustained in moderate slow tempo. Generally gentle with two climactic passages. Chordal accompaniment. Acc: 3 SIN

JOHN SVENDSEN, 1840-1911

6508. Waiting (Längsel) Men
Poet: Björnstjerne Björnson. d3-g4 g3-d4 Sustained in slow tempo. Requires very fine P and PP. Has some climactic passages. Very subdued ending section. Acc: 3-4 MSS-2

PER WINGE

6509. A maiden's thoughts (Pigetanker) Women
Poet: Kristofer Randers. e3-f♯4 e3-d4 Animated in moderate lively tempo. Graceful and generally light. Fine for light voices. Has many repeated notes. Acc: 3 MSS-2

D. SWEDEN

SWS Sweden Sings. Swedish texts, with English versions. Stockholm: Nordiska Musikförlaget.

HUGO ALFVÉN, 1872-1960

6510. The look (Blicken)   All Voices
       Poet: Emil Aarestrup.   c♯3-g4   f3-c4   Original key: one step low-
       er. Sustained in moderate slow tempo. Climactic and marked end-
       ing line. Short. English version: Greta Torpadie. Acc: 2-3
       MSS-1

6511. Anguish (Angest)   All Voices
       Poet: Emil Aarestrup.   d3-f♯4   a3-f♯4   Original key. Animated in
       fast tempo. Slightly slower middle section. Dramatic high ending.
       Agitated accompaniment. English version: Greta Torpadie. Acc:
       3-4 MSS-1

6512. Black roses (Svarta rosor)   All Voices
       Poet: Ellen Lundberg. Other title: Tristi amori.   c♭3-f♯4   f3-e4
       Original key. Sustained in slow tempo. Has some wide intervalic
       skips and dramatic passages. Slower, quite subdued ending. English
       version: Greta Torpadie. Acc: 3 MSS-1

BROR BECKMAN, 1866-1929

6513. A tune in three keys (En låt i tri toner)   All Voices
       Poet: Hjalmar Wallander.   e♭3-f4   g3-d4   Animated in moderate
       tempo. In passages requires some fluent enunciation. Requires sim-
       plicity. Has touch of folkish humor. English version: Greta Torpa-
       die. Acc: 3 MSS-1

6514. Three promises (Tre löften)   Women
       Poet: from Des Knaben Wunderhorn.   g♭3-g♭4   g♭3-f4   Sustained in
       moderate tempo. Requires fine P and simplicity. Original key: one
       step lower. English version: Greta Torpadie. Acc: 3 MSS-1

JOHAN ANDREAS HALLÉN, 1848-1925

6515. And many thousand ducats (Och många tusen kronor)   All Voices
       Poet: Anon.   e3-a4   a3-f♯4   Original key. Animated in lively tem-
       po. Joyous. Has climactic passages as well as subdued section.
       Climactic high ending on a4. Rhythmic accompaniment. English ver-
       sion: Greta Torpadie. Best for high voices. Acc: 3-4 MSS-1

6516. There is a laddie and he is mine (Det fins en gosse och
           han är min)   Women
       Poet: Gellerstedt.   e3-g4   a3-f♯4   Original key. Animated in mod-
       erate lively tempo. Requires fine PP. Has climactic passages and
       climactic high ending on g4. Generally agitated accompaniment. Eng-
       lish version: Greta Torpadie. Acc: 3-4 MSS-1

IVAR HALLSTRÖM, 1826-1901

6517. Black swans (Svarta svanor)   All Voices
       Poet: Carl Snoilsky.   d3-a♭4   g3-g4   Original key: two steps higher.
       Sustained in moderate slow tempo. Slightly faster middle section with
       agitated accompaniment. Has dramatic climaxes. Descending ending
       line after high climax. Best for the darker voices. English version:
       Greta Torpadie. Acc: 3-4 MSS-1

GUSTAV NORDQVIST, 1886-1949

6518. Drift snow (Drivsnö)   All Voices
Poet: Bertel Gripenberg. c♯3-e4 d♯3-c♯4 Sustained in slow tempo. Generally gentle with gently agitated accompaniment. English
version: C. A. Clausen. Acc: 3 SFS

OLOF WILHELM PETERSON-BERGER, 1867-1942

6519. Titania   All Voices
Poet: Gustaf Fröding. d3-eb4 a3-d4 Animated in lively tempo.
Gentle, delicate, and requires fine P and PP, and fluent enunciation.
Subdued ending. Best for light voices. Acc: 3-4 MSS-2

6520. To the bride (Till bruden)   All Voices
Poet: Werner von Heidenstam. d3-g4 g3-d4 Sustained in moderate
tempo. Majestic, has dramatic passages and a climactic ending.
Agitated, full-sounding accompaniment. Best for the heavier voices.
Acc: 3-4 MSS-2

6521. Twilight (Aftonstämning)   All Voices
Poet: Daniel Fallström. d3-g4 g3-eb4 Sustained in moderate slow
tempo. Very tranquil, with subdued ending. Best for the darker
voices. Acc: 3-4 MSS-2

TURE RANGSTRÖM, 1884-1947

6522. Adagio   All Voices
Poet: Bo Hjalmar Bergman. c♯3-g4 f♯3-e4 Sustained in somewhat
slow tempo. Subdued, requires very fine P and PP. Very subdued
ending. Acc: 3 MSS-2

6523. Ego (Jag)   All Voices
Poet: Ernst Josephson. c♯3-f♯4 f♯3-c♯4 Sustained in moderate
tempo. Rather intense on MF level. Descending ending line. Not
for light voices. Acc: 3 MSS-2

6524. Melody (Melodi)   All Voices
Poet: Bo Hjalmar Bergman. d♯3-f♯4 e3-e4 Sustained vocal part
in moderate lively tempo. Requires very fine P and PP. Very lyric
without climactic passages. Subdued, low ending. Arpeggiated accompaniment. May be transposed for lower voices. English version:
Ella H. Roe. Acc: 3-4 SFS

6525. Star-eyes (Stjärnöga)   All Voices
Poet: Bo Hjalmar Bergman. f3-f4 f3-eb4 Sustained in moderate
slow tempo. Requires simplicity and fine P and PP. In quasi-recitative style. Subdued. Original key: 2-1/2 steps lower. Acc: 3
MSS-2

6526. The peonies (Pionerna)   All Voices
Poet: Anders Österling. e3-ab4 ab3-eb4 Sustained in moderate
tempo. Very subdued and very delicate. Light. Best for light, high
voices. Original key: two steps lower. Acc: 3 MSS-2

EMIL SJÖGREN, 1853-1914

6527. A dream (Dröm)   All Voices
       Poet: Jens Peter Jacobsen. d3-f4 g3-d4 Sustained in quite slow
       tempo. Generally subdued, with a subdued, low ending. Starts in
       quasi-recitative style. Acc: 3 MSS-2

6528. Hab' ein Röselein dir gebrochen   All Voices
       Poet: Julius Wolff. Original text: German. e3-a4 bb3-f4 Ani-
       mated in moderate lively tempo. Generally light, requires simplicity.
       Best for light high and medium voices. Acc: 3-4 MSS-2

6529. Lehn' deine Wang'   All Voices
       Poet: Heinrich Heine. Original text: German. d3-g4 g3-d4 Sus-
       tained in moderate slow tempo. Starts gently and subduedly. Cli-
       mactic second half with full-sounding accompaniment. Acc: 3-4
       MSS-2

6530. Little prince a-cradled (Liten prins i vaggan)   All Voices
       Poet: Tor Hedberg. d3-f4 f♯3-d4 Sustained in moderate tempo.
       Subdued, requires fine P. Gentle. Subdued, low ending. Acc: 3
       MSS-2

6531. Sleepest thou, my soul? (Sover du, min Sjael?)   Medium, Low Voices
       Poet: Anon. e3-f4 a3-d4 Sustained in slow tempo. Grave and
       dark. Subdued, requires fine P and PP. Best for the darker voices.
       Acc: 2-3 MSS-2

6532. Suspiria (Suckarna)   All Voices
       Poet: Henry Wadsworth Longfellow, translated into Swedish. e3-g4
       g3-eb4 Sustained in moderate slow tempo. First and last sections
       in quasi-recitative style. Has climactic passages. Subdued ending.
       Acc: 3-4 MSS-2

6533. Weil' auf mir, du dunkles Auge   High, Medium Voices
       Poet: Nikolaus Lenau. Original text: German. c♯3-f♯4 a3-d4
       Sustained in moderate slow tempo. Requires very fine high P. Gen-
       erally subdued, gentle, and light. Arpeggiated accompaniment. Best
       for light voices. Acc: 3-4 MSS-2

JOHAN AUGUST SÖDERMAN, 1832-1876

6534. When the stars shed their light (Ser jag stjarnorna
          Längtan)   All Voices
       Poet: H. Sätherberg. a2-e4 f3-d4 Animated in moderate lively
       tempo. Requires some fine P and PP. Subdued ending. Acc: 3
       SWS

WILHELM EUGEN STENHAMMAR, 1871-1927

6535. At sunset (När sol går ner)   All Voices
       Poet: K. A. Melin. d3-g♯4 a3-e4 Sustained in moderate slow tem-
       po. Very tranquil. Subdued, requires very fine P and PP. Acc:
       2-3 MSS-2

6536. Ein Fichtenbaum steht einsam   All Voices

Poet: Heinrich Heine. Original text: German. e3-g#4 g3-b3
Very sustained in slow tempo. In recitative style. Generally sub-
dued. Very subdued, somewhat low ending. Not for light voices.
Acc: 3 MSS-2

6537. My grandsire, he had a pewter cup (Min stamfar hade
           en stor pokal)   All Voices
       Poet: Werner von Heidenstam. c#3-e4 g3-d4 Sustained in moder-
       ate tempo. Majestic and short. Descending ending line after climax.
       Acc: 3 SWS

6538. On Saint John's eve (Flickan knyter)   All Voices
       Poet: Johan Ludvig Runeberg. c3-f#4 f3-d4 Gently animated vocal
       part in moderate slow tempo. Requires simplicity and gentleness.
       Best for light voices. Acc: 3 MSS-2

6539. Sie liebten sich beide   All Voices
       Poet: Heinrich Heine. Original text: German. c3-g4 e3-d4 Gen-
       tly animated in moderate tempo. Gentle and light. Requires excel-
       lent P and PP. Subdued ending on e4. Best for light voices. Acc:
       3 MSS-2

6540. Star maiden (Stjärnöga)   Men
       Poet: Bo Hjalmar Bergman. c3-f4 f3-db4 Slightly animated in
       moderate slow tempo. Requires simplicity. Descending ending line.
       May be transposed for lower voices. Acc: 3 SWS

CHAPTER IX

RUSSIAN SOLO VOICE REPERTOIRE

Introduction

The music of Russia is deeply founded upon love for nature and the earth which provides the source of livelihood. Russian songs have, in general, an aura of melancholy and nostalgia that is different from those of other countries west of her boundary. Some of its atmosphere is drawn from thoughts of bleak and extremely cold winters. There is also its contact with Oriental influences, which adds mysticism to its melancholy. Folk songs are many, and they provide the true musical life of the country's population. One needs only to read Russia's poetry, old and new, to discern the elements that have dominated the temperament of the people. But the melancholy is enjoyed. One who does not understand the psychological background of the Russian type of life will never be able adequately to perform its songs.

All of the musical activity that was not connected with folk music before the 18th century belonged to the church. Its hymns and chants came from the country's exposure to the Byzantine culture. Russian chant developed and was greatly appreciated, and then elaborated into quite florid pieces, often with long melismas. Conflicts as to their continuous adaptation or reforms brought out opposing sides. But the Russian chant became both an institution and a way of life.

There is a great lack of information regarding the developments in music at the time of Peter the Great. However, the most drastic change happened during his rule when he tried to completely Westernize the country. He introduced Western opera in the 17th and 18th centuries by inviting foreign companies and artists to his kingdom. It was also at this time that the solo art song first received some public attention, through the publication by Grigory Nikolaevich Teplov of 17 of his own songs under the long title which starts with Mezhdu delom bezdel'e...

Catharine II, wife of Peter I's grandson, continued to encourage Western music. In her time several Italian composers lived and worked in St. Petersburg and managed the Imperial Opera there. Early professional Russian composers learned and wrote operas in the Italian style. Among them were Maximus Beresovsky, Dimitry Bortniansky, Evstigney I. Fomin, and Alexei Titov, whose model was Mozart.

Among Russian song composers from the 18th to the 19th century may be mentioned Mikhailovich Dubyansky, Jósef Koslowski, who was actually from Poland, A. S. Kozlyaninof, A. Shaposhnikof, the blind composer Alexei Dmitrievich Zhilin, Daniil Nikitich Kashin, and Dmitry Bortniansky. Because of Russia's constant cultural contact with the West and the attraction it had for German and Italian opera, a number of native composers wrote songs to the original languages of foreign poets.

Several important collections of Russian folk music were published in the 18th and 19th centuries. One of the earliest collections was issued in four volumes by V. Trutovsky. This was followed by an even better-known collection entitled Sobranie Narodn'ikh Russkikh Pesen (Collection of Russian Folk Songs), published close to the 19th century by Ivan Prach, a Czech immigrant.

Russian folk songs are the foundation on which the country's art songs grew. Even after the maturity of the art form, the folk idiom continued to show itself, affecting the mood and atmosphere of even the most sophisticated art songs, with a few exceptions such as the fully Western style of Anton Rubinstein, who was of German descent and musical preference.

In the 19th century, song and opera composing were in the hands of Alexander Alabief, Yakovlef, Mikhail Vielgorsky, Nikolai A. Titof, Mikhail Titof, Nikolai S. Titof, Nikolai Alekseevich, Alexander Varlamof, Gurilef, and Alexei Verstovsky, who was recognized for his unusual dramatic art. Of the names mentioned, perhaps that of Alabief stands out as one person who contributed the most in giving the Russian art song full identity.

However, a peak in the Russian art song was first reached in the works of Mikhail Glinka, the man generally regarded the "the father of Russian music." His work in creating a traditional Russian nationalism in music was ably continued by Alexander Dargomyzhsky.

The second half of the 19th century was a golden period for the Russian song as well as for its music in general, for it was a time when the country presented to the world an array of great names. A strong national spirit pervaded the ideals of a group of composers known as the "mighty five," all of whom wrote songs of great impact and charm. In the group were Mily Balakiref, César Cui, Alexander Borodin, Nikolai Rimsky-Korsakof, and the greatest of them all, Modest Mussorgsky. To this list may be added an outstanding but fairly unknown song composer, Nikolai Lodïzhensky, whose reputedly beautiful songs number only ten.

Nineteenth-century Russian composers for the voice were favored with a wealth of great literature from their countrymen. Fine poetry always helps to inspire and bring out fine songs, and at this time text sources were provided by the works of the following: Alexander Pushkin, Alexei Tolstoi, Mikhail Lermontof, Nikolai Nekrasof, Nestor Kukolnik, Alexei Koltzof, Leo Mey, Alexei Komiakof, Fyodor Tyutchef, Afanasi Fet, Arsenyi Golenischef-Kutusof, and Alexei Apukhtin. Many composers also used German, French, and translations of English poetry.

The establishment of conservatories in Petersburg and Moscow by Anton Rubinstein brought about a new movement in Russian song. Its first noted alumnus was Peter I. Tchaikovsky. Following closely into the 20th century were Anton Arensky, Alexander Glazounof, and Sergei Taneyef. More names were added to this list of the finest Russian song composers. Prominent in the first half of the present century are Alexander Glazounof, Reinhold Glière, Alexander Gretchaninof, Nikolai Medtner, Nikolai Miaskovsky, Sergei Rakhmaninof, Nikolai Tcherepnin, Sergei Vassilenko, Igor Stravinsky, and Sergei Prokofief. Interest in the fine texts by native Russian poets was also matched, although in a much smaller degree, by interest in songs without words, that is, vocal pieces sung to certain chosen vowels. The most well-known is Rakhmaninof's "Vocalise," Op. 34, No. 14, which today appears on many recital programs. Other examples are Medtner's "Sonate-Vocalise" and "Suite-Vocalise," Op. 41; Gretchaninof's "Polka-Vocalise"; Prokofief's "5 Melodies without Words," Op. 35; A. Tcherepnin's "Vocalise";

N. Tcherepnin's "Vocalise"; Glière's "Concerto for Coloratura Soprano and Orchestra," Op. 82; and Stravinsky's "Pastorale."

The best-known and most accomplished composers of the Soviet regime also wrote songs. Among them may be numbered Dmitry Kabalevsky, Aram Khachaturian (an Armenian by birth), Dimitri Shostakovich, Alexander Tcherepnin, Ivan Dzerzhinsky, Tikhon Khrennikof, Vissarion Shebalin, Georgy Svidirof, and Yuri Shaporin. Shostakovich is the most renowned of the composers under Soviet rule.

Change in the style of composition in Russia came in the early 1930s, when Soviet philosophy intruded into the realm of the arts and dictated that all art must serve society and conform to its nature. Among the taboos set forth were those aimed at all forms of modernism, classicism, abstract formalism, and subjectivism. First to control the arts was the Russian Association of Proletarian Musicians, and then, with some changes, the Central Committee of the Communist Party of the USSR, which, in 1949, specifically made accusations against Prokofief and Shostakovich.

In the 1960s, the strict rules against style in the arts were relaxed, and several of the young Soviet composers started using serial and some aleatory techniques in their works. With some kind of opposition, certain compositions of this type were allowed to be performed in Russia. It has not as yet affected compositions for the voice as much as the instrumental in terms of quantity. It may be significant, however, that on his visit to the United States (Los Angeles, January 1972) Khatchaturian claimed that there are no more restrictions on music in Russia. If this is true, then perhaps the rest of the world may expect significant musical contributions from Russia during the last part of this century.

Alexander Pushkin is still the favorite Russian poet of mid-century composers. Practically every great Russian composer has set some of his poetry to music. He is followed by Mikhail Lermontof, Konstantin Balmont, the Scottish poet Robert Burns, and others.

Bibliography

ATS   Album of Ten Songs by Russian Composers. High, low. English, French, and German versions only. Boston: Boston Music Co.

MRS   Modern Russian Songs. High, low. Edited by Ernest Newman. Vol. I: Alpheraky to Mussorgsky; Vol. II: Mussorgsky to Wihtol. Bryn Mawr: Oliver Ditson, c/o Theodore Presser. (Note: The spelling of Russian names in this edition is not consistent.)

RSB   The Russian Song Books. Edited and translated by Rosa Newmarch. French versions by G. Jean-Aubry. Two volumes each for soprano, alto, tenor, and bass. London: J. & W. Chester.

50R   50 Russian Art Songs from Glinka to Shostakovich. Three volumes, one key only. Edited by Nicolas Slonimsky. Russian texts and an English translation. New York: Leeds Music Corp. (Has fine notes at the beginning of each volume.)

Russian   827

ALEXANDER ALEXANDROVICH ALABIEF, 1787-1851

6541. Die Nachtigall   Soprano
       Poet: Russian folk verse. f3-a4 a3-f4 First part is sustained in
       moderate tempo. Second part is animated in lively tempo. Requires
       simplicity; has climactic passages and a climactic ending. Slightly
       extended piano postlude. 3 verses. Acc: 3-4 KAS

ACHILLES NIKOLAYEVICH ALFERAKY, 1846-1920 (Greek origin)

6542. Spring   All Voices
       Poet: Afanasi A. Fet. f♯3-g♯4 b3-f♯4 Animated in lively tempo.
       Requires fluent enunciation. Exultant and joyous. Climactic ending.
       Agitated accompaniment. English version: Frederick H. Martens.
       Acc: 4 MRS-1

6543. The bouquet   Men
       Poet: Velikho. c♯3-g♯4 f♯3-c♯4 Sustained in slow tempo. Short,
       with climactic ending. Text is an adaptation of a poem by Hafiz.
       English version: Constance Purdy. Acc: 3 MRS-1

6544. When leaves are falling sere   All Voices
       Poet: A. Umanetz. d3-f♯4 f♯3-d4 Sustained in moderate slow tem-
       po. Graceful. Subdued first half, strong second half with climactic
       ending. English version: Frederick H. Martens. Acc: 3 MRS-1

6545. When nocturnal shadows gliding   Women
       Poet: The Song of Solomon, Chapter 3, paraphrased in Russian.
       c♯3-f♯4(a4) e3-e4 Gently animated in moderate slow tempo. Strong
       last section; climactic high ending. English translation from the Rus-
       sian: Frederick H. Martens. Acc: 3 MRS-1

ANTON STEPANOVICH ARENSKY, 1861-1906

6546. A fable   All Voices
       Poet: G. Jean-Aubry. d3-e4 f3-c4 Animated in moderate lively
       tempo. Requires some fluent enunciation. Descending ending line.
       Narrative and amusing text. Acc: 3 YAR

6547. Berceuse   High Voices
       Poet: Tsepkinoi-Kupernik. d♯3-g♯4 e3-c4 Animated in moderate
       lively tempo. Requires some fluent enunciation. Generally subdued,
       with one climactic passage. Very subdued high ending. Requires
       very fine high PP. Acc: 3-4 RSB-S1

6548. But lately in dance I embraced her   Men
       Poet: Afanasi A. Fet. e♭3-g♭4 e♭3-b♭3 Animated in waltz tempo.
       Has climactic passages. Graceful. Has repeated notes and some
       passages with narrow range. Very subdued ending section. Extended
       piano postlude. Acc: 3 ATS

6549. Deep hidden in my heart   All Voices
       Poet: Arsenyi Golenischef-Kutusof. e3-g4(H) g3-e4 Animated in
       moderate lively tempo. Requires some fine P and PP. Has dramatic
       climaxes. English version: Constance Purdy. Acc: 3-4 MRS-1

6550. Oh, do not light that lamp   All Voices
       Poet: D. M. Rathaus. c3-a4 e3-d4 Animated in moderate lively
       tempo. Has one climactic passage. Subdued low ending. Best for
       high and medium-high voices. English version: Nicolas Slonimsky.
       Original key. Acc: 3-4 50R-2, RSB-S2

6551. Revery   All Voices
       Poet: L. Munschtein. d♯3-f♯4 f♯3-d♯4 Sustained in moderate slow
       tempo. Has some slightly strong passages. Subdued low ending.
       English version: Constance Purdy. Acc: 3 MRS-1

6552. Song of the little fish   All Voices
       Poet: Mikhail Y. Lermontof. d3-a4 a3-g4 Sustained vocal part in
       moderate lively tempo. Has dramatic passages, climactic ending
       with a long-sustained last note, and agitated accompaniment. Best
       for high voices. English version: Robert H. Hamilton. Acc: 5
       MRS-1

6553. The eagle   All Voices
       Poet: Arsenyi Golenischef-Kutusof. b2-a4 e3-f♯4 Generally sus-
       tained in moderate slow tempo. Has some slightly faster passages.
       Descriptive and dramatic. Subdued, low ending after climax. Not
       suitable for light, high voices. English version: Frederick H. Mar-
       tens. Acc: 4 MRS-1

6554. The spirit of poesy   High Voices
       Poet: Semyon Yakovlevich Nadson. b♭2-g4 f3-d4 Sustained in mod-
       erate slow tempo. Requires fine P. Dramatic toward the end. Sub-
       dued, descending ending line. Acc: 3 RSB-B1

6555. The wolves   Bass
       Poet: Aleksei Konstantinovich Tolstoi. a1-e♭3 c2-b♭2 Generally in
       moderate tempo. A dramatic ballad. Generally in recitative style.
       Has dramatic passages and a climactic ending. Interpretatively diffi-
       cult. Dedicated to Shaliapin. Op. 58. Acc: 3-4 RSB-B1

M. BAGRINOFSKI

6556. All the bells, the little bells   All Voices
       Poet: Skitaletz (Stepan Gavrilovich Petróf). f♯3-g4(b4) g3-g4 Ani-
       mated in fast tempo. Slightly slower middle section. Has dramatic
       passages as well as gentle P. Mostly agitated accompaniment. Best
       for high and medium-high voices. Acc: 4-5 MRS-1

MILY ALEXEYEVICH BALAKIREF, 1837-1910

Balakiref, an important figure in modern Russian music, comes directly
from the line of Glinka, especially in the treatment of solo music and the
folk song. Most of his songs are lyric in structure, but with more important pianoforte parts than Glinka's. A strong advocate of national music, he
developed interest (again Glinka's influence) in arranging folk songs. However, he also freely used western facets in his music. With his orientalism
and near-eastern traits are fused some aspects and techniques identified with
Schumann, Chopin, and Liszt. His favorite Russian poets are Lermontof,
Koltsof, and Khomiakof.

Balakiref's many outstanding songs need to be known and performed more.
The difficulty, however, is in securing them with adequate English translations. "A song of Georgia" is considered by many as Balakiref's masterpiece.

6557. A song of Georgia   High Voices
       Poet: Alexander S. Pushkin. eb 3-ab 4 gb 3-f4 Sustained in moder-
       ate slow tempo. Has florid passages. Requires flexibility. Strong
       contrasts in dynamics. Has quasi-recitative passages and a strong
       descending ending. Russian, German, French, and English texts.
       Acc: 4   (S)B-H

6558. Burning out is the sunset's red flame   All Voices
       Poet: V. Kulchinsky. c# 3-f# 4 f# 3-e4 Sustained in moderate slow
       tempo. Requires fine P. Generally subdued; subdued low ending.
       Gently agitated accompaniment. English version: Constance Purdy.
       Acc: 4 MRS-1

6559. Lullaby   Women
       Poet: A. Arsenief. f3-f4 f3-d4 Sustained in moderate slow tempo.
       Subdued, gentle, and light. Gently agitated accompaniment. Russian,
       German, French, and English texts. Acc: 3   (S)B-H

6560. Nocturne   All Voices
       Poet: Anon. Russian poet. b# 2-f# 4 f# 3-e4 Gently animated in
       moderate slow tempo. Slightly faster middle section. Subdued, low
       ending following a climax. English version: Frederick H. Martens.
       Acc: 3-4 MRS-1

6561. The knight   Medium, Low Voices
       Poet: Ch. Wilde. bb 2-eb 4 f3-c4 Animated in lively march tempo.
       Starts strongly. Has marking of P to PP, and F to FFF. Subdued
       ending section. Russian, German, French, and English texts. Acc:
       3   (S)B-H

6562. The pine-tree   All Voices
       Poet: Mikhail Y. Lermontof. c# 3-f# 4 f# 3-d4 First part is sus-
       tained in slow tempo. Second part is slightly animated. First sec-
       tion is in quasi-recitative. Generally subdued. Best for medium or
       low voices. English version: Constance Purdy. Acc: 3-4 MRS-1

6563. Vision   All Voices
       Poet: Alexei Stepanovich Khomyakof. d3-a4 f3-eb 4 Sustained in
       varied tempi and moods. Climactic, strong ending section. Best for
       heavier voices. May be transposed for lower voices. English ver-
       sion: Nicolas Slonimsky. Acc: 3-4 50R-1

JULIUS IVANOVICH BLEICHMANN, 1868-1909

6564. The convoy   Bass, Baritone
       Poet: Aleksei Konstantinovich Tolstoi. c# 2-e3 c# 2-c# 3 In slow
       march tempo. Short recitative in the middle. Has dramatic pas-
       sages. Majestic, with a subdued ending. Full-sounding accompani-
       ment. A favorite of Shaliapin. Op. 26, No. 2. Acc: 3-4 RSB-B1

6565. Wenn ich in deine Augen seh'   All Voices
       Poet: Heinrich Heine, translated into Russian. a3-g4 a3-f# 4

Sustained in moderate slow tempo. Requires very fine high PP.
Subdued throughout. Ends in gentle recitative style. See the settings
by Hugo Wolf and Robert Schumann.   Acc: 3-4 MRS-1

ALEXANDER PORPHYRIEVICH BORODIN, 1833-1887

Borodin, member of "the mighty five," was one of the most versatile of
Russian composers. His musical career was punctuated with activities in
science, chemistry, medicine, education, and poetry. As a composer, Borodin produced several operas, chamber music, piano music, vocal quartets,
and solo songs. His few art songs cover a wide range of styles. Some ex-
hibit his fine sense of humor; some his use of bold harmonies, and others
his dramatic seriousness. Borodin is credited for giving to Russian song
literature what is perhaps one of its great descriptive ballads in the song
"The Sea" (More), which he later orchestrated.

6566. A dissonance   All Voices
       Poet: Alexander Borodin.   e3-f#4 f3-db4 Sustained in moderate
       slow tempo. Generally subdued, with one slightly climactic passage.
       In quasi-recitative style. Short. English version: Frederick H.
       Martens. Acc: 3 MRS-1, 56S, RSB-S2, (S)OX

6567. Arabian melody (Arabakaya melodiya)   All Voices
       Poet: Alexander Borodin.   f3-d4 f3-c4 Animated and sustained sec-
       tions. Generally gentle, with a subdued ending. Extended piano post-
       lude. A true Arabian melody is used here. English version: James
       Woodside. Acc: 3 SCS-5

6568. Haughtiness (Spes')   Medium, Low Voices
       Poet: Aleksei Konstantinovich Tolstoi.   bb2-f4 f3-c4 Animated in
       moderate lively tempo. In martial style. Has climactic passages
       and humorous text. In this edition, it is printed with "A dissonance."
       English version: David Brown. Acc: 3 (S)OX

6569. My songs are envenomed and bitter   All Voices
       Poet: Heinrich Heine, Russian version by Borodin.   c3-g#4 g3-f4
       Animated in moderate tempo. Short; ends with descending vocal line
       in diminuendo. Original key: one step lower. English version:
       Charles F. Manney. Issued with French version. Acc: 3 MRS-1

6570. Poisoned   All Voices
       Poet: Heinrich Heine, Russian version by Borodin.   bb2-f#4 eb3-
       eb4 Sustained in moderate tempo. Generally strong and intense.
       Descending ending line. Original text: German. English version:
       Nathan H. Dole. Acc: 3 ATS

6571. The fair garden   All Voices
       Poet: Alexander Borodin.   e3-e4 g#3-c#4 Sustained in moderate
       tempo. Generally subdued, requires fine P and PP. Gently but con-
       stantly moving accompaniment. Original key: 1-1/2 steps lower.
       English version: Constance Purdy. Acc: 3 MRS-1

6572. The sea (More)   All Voices
       Poet: Alexander Borodin.   db3-g#4 f3-f4 Animated in lively tempo.
       Has strong, dramatic passages, and a full-sounding and agitated ac-
       companiment. Climactic ending, and an extended piano postlude.
       Best for the heavier, warmer voices. English version: Grace Hall.
       Acc: 5 MRS-1

6573. The sleeping princess   All Voices
Poet: Alexander Borodin, based on the story of The Sleeping Beauty.
e♭3-g4 f3-e♭4 Sustained in moderate slow tempo. Has slightly animated passages. Very subdued ending. Syncopated accompaniment,
but not deliberate. Original key: one step lower. English version:
Constance Purdy. Acc: 3-4 MRS-1, 50A, RSB-S1, SSO (Russian
& French)

6574. Your native land (Dlya beregov otchizni dal'noy)   Men
Poet: Alexander S. Pushkin. Correct translation of the Russian:
For the shores of thy distant fatherland. d3-a4 g3-a4 Sustained in
moderate tempo. Has climactic passages and a subdued, low ending
vocal line. Agitated and constantly moving accompaniment. May be
transposed for lower voices. Acc: 3-4 50R-1

CÉSAR ANTONOVICH CUI, 1835-1918

Cui was a miniaturist, for it is in his smaller works, such as songs and
small voice combinations, that he shows his best form. Although a successful and highly regarded opera composer, he was not at home with the art of
orchestration. Cui wrote in different styles, but basically he was a lyricist.
He was adept at composing music to French, German, and Polish poetry.
His French songs are settings of poems by Hugo, Musset, Richepin, and
others. Among his most outstanding are his "25 Poems by Pushkin," Op.
57. "The Statue of Tsarkoe Selo" is regarded as Cui's masterpiece, as
well as the favorite Russian song of many recitalists.

CSS   Six Songs by César Cui. High, low. English version only. Boston:
Boston Music Co.

6575. Ah, if Mother Volga   All Voices
Poet: Aleksei Konstantinovich Tolstoi. e3-g4 g3-f4 Animated vocal
part in moderate tempo. In gentle, declamatory style. Has strong
passages. Climactic ending. English version: Constance Purdy.
Acc: 3 MRS-1

6576. Dusk fallen   Men
Poet: Anon. Russian poet. e3-g♯4 g♯3-f♯4 Gently moving vocal
part in moderate slow tempo. Subdued, requires fine P and PP.
English version: Constance Purdy. Title in CSS: Mirage. Acc:
3-4 MRS-1, CSS

6577. Hunger song   All Voices
Poet: Nikolai A. Nekrasof. c3-f4 e3-e4 Sustained in moderate
slow tempo. Requires some characterization. In quasi-recitative
style. Descriptive, narrative text. Best for men's voices. English
version: Deems Taylor. Acc: 3 MRS-1

6578. If I only could forget   Men
Poet: Anon. d3-f4 f3-e4 Sustained in moderate lively tempo.
Graceful. Has climactic passages. Climactic high ending. Mainly
chordal accompaniment. English version: Nathan H. Dole. Acc: 3
CSS

6579. Oh, gentle wind   Men
Poet: Anon. d3-g4 e3-f♯4 Animated in moderate slow tempo.
Generally smooth and lyric. Has climactic passages and a descending

ending line. Generally agitated accompaniment. English version:
Nathan H. Dole. Acc: 3-4 CSS

6580. Separation   All Voices
       Poet: Anon. c3-f4 f3-eb4 Animated in moderate lively tempo.
       Generally on MF level. Rhythmic accompaniment. Has climactic
       passages and a climactic ending. English version: Nathan H. Dole.
       Acc: 3 CSS

6581. The dream   All Voices
       Poet: Anon. e♯3-g♯4 f♯3-e4 Sustained in first moderate slow
       tempo, then faster, with arpeggiated accompaniment. Starts gently;
       generally on MF level. English version: Nathan H. Dole. Acc: 3
       CSS

6582. The sower   High Voices
       Poet: Nikolai A. Nekrasof. db3-g4 g3-eb4 Sustained in moderate
       slow tempo. Has climactic passages. Starts strongly. Climactic
       and majestic ending. Op. 62, No. 11. Acc: 3 RSB-S1

6583. The statue of Tsarskoye Selo (Tsarskosel'skaya statuya) All Voices
       Poet: Alexander S. Pushkin. db3-eb4 f3-bb3 Sustained in moder-
       ate slow tempo. Short, with a subdued ending. Gently agitated ac-
       companiment. Narrative text. English version: Nicolas Slonimsky.
       Acc: 3 50R-1, GSA

6584. The wish   High Voices
       Poet: Alexander S. Pushkin. e3-ab4 f3-eb4 Gently animated vocal
       part in moderate slow tempo. Requires fine P. Has climactic pas-
       sages. Starts gently. Climactic ending. Op. 57, No. 25. Acc:
       3 RSB-S2

French Text

6585. Les trois oiseaux   Men
       Poet: François Coppée. c3-ab4(bb4) f3-f4 Sustained in moderate
       slow tempo. In gentle recitative style. Requires fine P and PP.
       Has some climactic passages. Subdued ending. English version:
       L. Louise Baum. Acc: 3 CSS, ATS

ALEXANDER SERGEYEVICH DARGOMIZHSKY, 1813-1869

6586. I will tell no one   All Voices
       Poet: Alexei V. Koltzóf. d3-g4 a3-d4 Animated in moderate lively
       tempo. Descending vocal part. Agitated accompaniment. English
       version by Nicolas Slonimsky. Acc: 3-4 50R-1

6587. Knight-errant   High Voices
       Poet: Arkady Joukovsky. f3-gb4 a3-f4 Animated in lively tempo.
       Requires fluent enunciation. Generally in quasi-recitative style. Has
       dramatic passages. Subdued ending. Acc: 3-4 RSB-S2

6588. Look, darling girl   Women
       Poet: Anon. d3-g4 g3-d4 Animated in moderate lively tempo. Re-
       quires some flexibility. Rhythmic and graceful. May be transposed
       for lower voices. English version: Nicolas Slonimsky. Acc: 3
       50R-1

6589. O thou rose-maiden   High, Medium Voices
Poet: Alexander S. Pushkin. e3-g4 g3-e4 Sustained in moderate
slow tempo. Has short florid figures. Requires fine high P. Best
for light voices. English version: Constance Purdy. Acc: 3-4
MRS-1

ALEXANDER (KONSTANTINOVICH) GLAZUNOF, 1865-1936

6590. Oriental romance   Low, Medium Voices
Poet: Alexander S. Pushkin. b2-eb4 d3-b3 Sustained in moderate
slow tempo. Has florid figures. In Eastern chant-style. Requires
some free declamation. Low, subdued ending. Best for men. Original key. English version: Nikolas Slonimsky. Acc: 3 50R-2

REINHOLD (MORITZOVICH) GLIÈRE, 1875-1956

6591. Ah, twine no blossoms   All Voices
Poet: D. M. Rathaus. d3-ab4 f3-f4 Gently animated in moderate
slow tempo. Has dramatic passages. The last long phrase is a
gradual descending vocal line. Best for the heavier voices. English
version: Deems Taylor. Acc: 3-4 MRS-1

6592. Awakening   Coloratura Soprano
Poet: Vladimir Lakond. f3-c5 ab3-g4 Generally sustained in moderate slow tempo. Has florid passages; requires flexibility and fine
high P. Has climactic passages and trills. Subdued high ending.
Generally agitated accompaniment. A show piece. Acc: 4 (S)SM

6593. Deserted garden   All Voices
Poet: Alexei Merzliakof. c3-g4 g3-d4 Sustained in moderate slow
tempo. Generally on MF level. Has climactic passages and some
quasi-recitative passages. Subdued high ending on g4. English version: Vladimir Lakond. Issued with Russian and English texts, high
and low keys. Acc: 3 (S)EM

6594. Forlorn love   High Voices
Poet: Vladimir Lakond. d3-a4 g3-e4 Sustained in slow tempo.
Very tranquil first part. Has climactic high passages. Climactic
high ending. Slightly agitated accompaniment. Acc: 3 (S)SM

6595. My little star   High Voices
Poet: Vladimir Lakond. c#3-a4 f#3-e4 Animated in moderate tem-
po. Requires fine P. Starts gently. Has one strong high climax.
Subdued ending section. Agitated accompaniment. Acc: 3-4 (S)SM

6596. Sweetly sang a gentle nightingale   High Voices
Poet: Alexei Merzliakof. c3-g4 f3-d4 Sustained in moderate slow
tempo. Has some climactic passages. Requires very fine high PP.
Ends very subdued on sustained g4. May be sung by medium voices,
but best for high voices. English version: Nicolas Slonimsky. Original key. Acc: 3 50R-2

6597. Today is mine   All Voices
Poet: G. Galina. c#3-a4 g3-f4 Animated in lively tempo. Starts
strongly. Has climactic high passages. Also requires fine P. Agitated accompaniment. A fine song for ending a recital group.

834   Solo Voice Repertoire

English version: Vladimir Lakond. Issued in Russian and English,
high, medium, low keys. Acc: 4 (S)EM

German Text

6598. Die heil'gen drei Kön'ge aus Morgenland   All Voices
Poet: Heinrich Heine. e3-f♯4 a3-e4 Sustained in moderate slow
tempo. In pastoral style. Generally on MF level. Has quasi-recitative passages. Climactic ending. Mainly chordal accompaniment.
Acc: 3 ATS

MIKHAIL IVANOVICH GLINKA, 1804-1857

Of the first classic song composers of Russia, Glinka was the most gifted
craftsman. Several of his art songs and arrangements of folk songs were
used as models by succeeding generations of Russian song composers.
Glinka does not strive to impress hearers with musical eloquence; rather, his
works attract listeners with simplicity and unaffected sincerity. He encouraged nationalism, and throughout his life sought to fully establish a Russian
national music. Yet, he also drew forth from other cultures what he felt
were their best and combined them in his music. Widely traveled, his visits
to Italy, Germany, France, and Spain were musically rewarding for his technique. Glinka wrote different types of songs, and his compositions about
other lands sounded more "authentic" than those by some of the real nation-
als. Not many songs of Glinka's are presently available, but the few reviewed here will help acquaint those interested in his music.

6599. Doubt   All Voices
Poet: Nestor V. Kukolnik. d3-g4 g3-d4 Sustained in moderate tempo. Requires fine PP. Has some climactic passages. Extended piano prelude and postlude. May be transposed for lower voices. English version: Nicolas Slonimsky. Acc: 3 50R-1

6600. So clearly I remember seeing   All Voices
Poet: Alexander S. Pushkin. e3-f4 g3-d4 Animated in moderate
lively tempo. Requires some fluent enunciation. Has some climactic
passages. May be transposed for lower voices. English version by
Nicolas Slonimsky. Acc: 3-4 50R-1

6601. Star of the north   All Voices
Poet: Rostopchine. e3-g4 f♯3-e4 Sustained in moderate slow tempo. Requires some majestic delivery. Generally on MF level. Descriptive, and narrative text. English version: Constance Purdy.
Acc: 3 MRS-1

6602. The journey   All Voices
Poet: Anon. Russian poet. f3-g4 g3-f4 Animated in very fast tempo. Requires fluent enunciation. Slightly slower, light, and more
reflective middle section. Descriptive text. Strong ending. English
version: Constance Purdy. Acc: 4 MRS-1

6603. Traveler's song (Poputnaya pesnya)   All Voices
Poet: Nestor V. Kukolnik. e3-g4 g3-f4 Animated in very fast tempo. Requires fluent enunciation. Has some climactic passages. May
be transposed for lower voices. English version: Nicolas Slonimsky.
Acc: 4 50R-1

6604. Vigil   High Voices

Poet: Anon. f# 3-f4 g3-eb 4 Sustained vocal part in moderate lively tempo. Requires fine P and PP. Has climactic passages. 2
verses. Acc: 2-3 RSB-S1

ALEXANDER TIKHONOVICH GRETCHANINOF, 1864-1956

Gretchaninof's songs are perhaps the best of his musical production. They
cover a wide range of subjects, and are mostly in the lyric style. They are
often known as romances after the French style of love song. Gretchaninof
left Russia, lived in Paris, and in 1939 settled in New York where he became an American citizen.

6605. Another little hour I begged   Men
Poet: Aleksei Nikolayevich Plescheyef. c3-g4 g3-d4 Declamatory
style in moderate lively tempo. Dramatic ending. English version:
Constance Purdy. Acc: 3 MRS-1

6606. My native land   All Voices
Poet: Aleksei Konstantinovich Tolstoi. e3-g4 g3-e4 Two allegro
sections, each preceded by a quasi-recitative largo, sung forte. Gently climactic ending on high note. May be transposed for lower
voices. Original key. English version: Nicolas Slonimsky. Acc:
3 50R-2

6607. Over the steppe   All Voices
Poet: Aleksei Nikolayevich Plescheyef. c3-g4 d3-d4 Sustained in
moderate slow tempo. Has some dramatic passages, and a strong,
sustained last note. In declamatory style. Best for the heavier
voices. English version: Deems Taylor and Kurt Schindler. Acc:
3 (S)GS. MRS-1

6608. Palm branches   All Voices
Poet: Alexander A. Blok. eb 3-f4 ab 3-db 4 Gently moving vocal
part in moderate lively tempo. In recitative style. Descriptive, narrative text. Short. English version: Grace Hall. Acc: 3 MRS-1

6609. Slumber reigns   All Voices
Poet: Afanasi A. Fet. e3(d3)-b4 g3-f4 Animated in lively tempo.
Has some dramatic passages. Subdued ending. Agitated accompani-
ment. English version: Frederick H. Martens. Acc: 4-5 MRS-1

6610. Slumber song   Women
Poet: Mikhail Y. Lermontof. b2-g# 4 f# 3-e4 Sustained in moderate
slow tempo. Gentle, requires fine P. Gently moving accompaniment.
Very fine for light, high voices. In this edition only the English and
French versions are included. English version by Charles F. Manney.
Acc: 3 ART-1, 50A, 55A, ATS

6611. Snowflakes   All Voices
Poet: Valéry Yakovlevich Brüssof. ab 3-f4 bb 3-eb 4 Animated in
lively tempo. Light and graceful. Best for high and medium voices.
English version: Constance Purdy. Acc: 3 MRS-1

6612. The captive   All Voices
Poet: Alexander S. Pushkin. b# 2-f# 4 f# 3-e4 Sustained in moderate
tempo, with slight variations. Starts in recitative style. Has
dramatic passages and a climactic ending. English version: Grace
Hall. Acc: 3-4 MRS-1

6613.   The siren   All Voices
        Poet: Konstantin Dmitrievich Balmont.   e♯ 3(c♯ 3)-a4(b4)   f♯ 3-f♯ 4
        Animated in lively tempo.   Has dramatic passages and ending.   Agi-
        tated accompaniment.   English version: Frederick H. Martens.
        Acc: 4 MRS-1

MIKHAIL MIKHAILOVICH IPPOLITOF-IVANOF, 1859-1935

6614.   Far on the road we two journeyed together   All Voices
        Poet: D. U. Tsertelev.   e3-f4   f3-f4   Sustained in quite slow tem-
        po.   Generally subdued, with subdued high ending.   English version
        by Constance Purdy.   Acc: 3   MRS-1, RSB-S1

6615.   Once there lived a king   All Voices
        Poet: Anon. Russian poet.   e3-f4   a3-f4   Sustained in moderate tem-
        po.   Requires fine P and PP.   Slow and subdued ending section.
        Narrative text.   English version: Constance Purdy.   Acc: 3   MRS-1

6616.   Romance   Men
        Poet: Anon. Spanish, translated into Russian.   e3-g♯ 4(b4)   f♯ 3-f♯ 4
        Animated in moderate lively tempo.   Graceful and dance-like, in
        Spanish style.   Climactic ending.   English version: Constance Purdy.
        Acc: 3-4 MRS-1

6617.   When we parted   All Voices
        Poet: D. M. Rathaus.   e♭ 3-e♭ 4   f3-c4   Animated in lively tempo.
        Has climactic passages.   Generally on MF level.   Staccati accom-
        paniment in the right hand.   Extended piano postlude.   English ver-
        sion: Nathan H. Dole.   Acc: 3-4 ATS

MYRON JACOBSON

6618.   You brought me flowers   All Voices
        Poet: Loukianof.   f♯ 3-g♯ 4   b3-e4   Sustained in moderate tempo.
        Starts gently.   Has dramatic climax close to the end.   English ver-
        sion: Deems Taylor.   Acc: 3-4 MRS-1

DMITRY BORISOVICH KABALEVSKY

6619.   Seven Merry Songs.   A set of songs for high voice or medium-high
        voice and piano.   Based on nursery rhymes.   Text by S. Marshak,
        with English versions by Nancy Bush.   Russian text.   Overall range
        and tessitura: c3-g4   e3-e4   New York: Leeds Music Corp.   Titles:
                1. Old King Cole
                2. If all the seas were one sea
                3. I saw a ship a-sailing
                4. There was an old woman
                5. For want of a nail the shoe was lost
                6. The little pigs
                7. The key of the kingdom

6620.   To her son   Women
        Poet: A. Bolaev-Kubatiev.   d3-g4   f3-d4   Animated vocal part in
        moderate slow tempo.   Majestic, has climactic passages.   Nationalis-
        tic texts, inspired by World War II events between the Russians and
        Germans.   Acc: 3-4 50R-3

BASIL SERGEIVICH KALINNIKOF, 1866-1901

6621. Stars ethereal   All Voices
Poet: Konstantin Mikhailovich Fofanof. b♯2-g♯4 g♯3-e4 Gently
animated vocal part in moderate tempo. Slightly slower middle section. Subdued and gentle vocal part throughout. English version:
Constance Purdy. Acc: 3-4 MRS-1

ARAM ILYICH KHACHATURIAN

6622. Nina's song   Women
Poet: Mikhail Y. Lermontof. f3-ab4 ab3-eb4 Sustained in moderate tempo. Generally on MF level with gently agitated accompaniment. Original key. English version: Nicolas Slonimsky. Acc:
3-4 50R-3

NIKOLAI RAZUMNIKOVICH KOCHETOF, 1864-dnk

6623. Tell, o tell her   Tenor
Poet: Aleksei Nikolayevich Apukhtin. e3-a4 g3-f♯4 Animated in
very fast tempo. Slower middle section. Dramatic high ending after
a gradual, long crescendo. Agitated accompaniment. English version: Louis Untermeyer. Acc: 4 50A

THEODOR KOENEMAN

6624. The blacksmith   Bass
Poet: Skitaletz (Stepan Gavrilovich Petrov). b1-e♯3 e2-c♯3 Ani-
mated in moderate tempo. Generally in recitative style. Dramatic.
Climactic ending. Dedicated to Shaliapin. Acc: 3-4 RSB-B1

ALEXANDER ALEXANDROVICH KOPILOF, 1854-1911

6625. The laborer's plaint   Men
Poet: Alexei V. Koltsóf. d3-g4 f3-e4 Sustained in moderate slow
tempo. Subdued, low ending. Sad text. English version: Grace
Hall. Acc: 3 MRS-1

ARSENI NIKOLAYEVICH KORESTCHENKO, 1870-1921

6626. The smith   Men
Poet: Anon. Russian poet. e3-g4(ab4) f3-f4 Animated in moderate
tempo. Has dramatic passages and a dramatic ending. Generally
strong and outgoing. Not for light voices. English version: Constance Purdy. Acc: 3-4 MRS-1

MARIAN VICTOROVICH KOVAL

6627. Blind existence   All Voices
Poet: Alexander S. Pushkin. db3-g4 f3-f4 Gently animated vocal
part in moderate slow tempo. Generally on MF level. Somber texts.
Original key. English version: Nicolas Slonimsky. Acc: 3 50R-3

ALEXANDER ABRAMOVICH KREIN, 1883-1951

6628. Why?   All Voices
       Poet: Mikhail Y. Lermontof. c3-g4 f3-eb4 Sustained in moderate
       slow tempo. In quasi-recitative style. Generally subdued. May be
       transposed for lower voices. Original key. English version: Nico-
       las Slonimsky. Acc: 3 50R-3

SERGEI MIKHAILOVICH LIAPOUNOF, 1859-1924

6629. Christmas song   High, Medium Voices
       Poet: Apollon Apollonovich Korinfsky. f3-g4(a4) g3-f4 Gently ani-
       mated in moderate slow tempo. Slightly animated middle section.
       Requires fine P. Has some strong passages. Climactic ending.
       English version: Constance Purdy. Acc: 3-4 MRS-1

6630. Nocturne   All Voices
       Poet: Alexei Stepanovich Khomiakof. d3-g4 f3-f4 Very sustained
       in moderate tempo. Subdued, tranquil until the climactic ending.
       Gentle, but constantly moving accompaniment until the end when re-
       placed with full-sounding chords. English version: Constance Purdy.
       Acc: 3-4 MRS-1

NINA VLADIMIROVNA MAKAROVA

6631. The werewolf   Mezzo-Soprano
       Poet: Alexander S. Pushkin. a2-ab4 c#3-d4 Generally sustained
       in varied tempi. Has dramatic passages and a climactic ending. In-
       terpretatively not easy. Descriptive. Extended piano prelude. Orig-
       inal key. Not for light voices. English version by Nicolas Slonimsky.
       Composer is Aram Kachaturian's wife. Acc: 3-4 50R-3

NICOLAI MEDNIKOF

6632. The hills of Gruzia   All Voices
       Poet: Alexander S. Pushkin. d3-a4 g3-e4 Generally sustained in
       slow tempo, with variations. Has dramatic and animated passages.
       Requires some fine high P. Has quasi-recitative passages. Subdued,
       descending ending. This edition has both the Russian and English
       texts. Acc: 3-4 (S)CF-high, low

NIKOLAI KARLOVICH MEDTNER, 1880-1951

Medtner adheres to the classic tradition, although he was not at all unsympa-
thetic to modern ideas, some of which filtered cautiously into his music.
The poetry of his songs is almost equally German and Russian. His love
for German poetry had caused contemporaries to accuse him of not being nationalistic. But his passion for Russian poetry did not lessen; in fact he was
more comfortable with it. His Russian songs are actually considered his
best song writing. His favorite German poets are Goethe, Heine, and Eichendorff. Pushkin, Tyutchef, and Fet are his Russian preferences. Being first
of all a pianist, many of his songs bear heavy piano parts, most of which
are far from being easy. There is very little attempt at interpreting poetic
meanings in meticulous ways. His style leans toward the abstract in

representing sound. Among his most interesting works for the voice is "Sonate-Vocalise," which is introduced by a motto, "Geweihter Platz," by Goethe. The entries below are arranged in two sections, first his songs to Russian poetry, and second those to German.

TSS   Twenty-Six Selected Songs. Nicholas Medtner. High key. Original texts with English versions by Henry S. Drinker. New York: G. Schirmer, Inc.

6633.   A poet's epitaph   High Voices
Poet: Andrej Biely. c3-a4 e3-e4 Animated in moderate tempo. Has slightly faster, animated middle section. Dramatic ending. Full-sounding accompaniment. Op. 13, No. 2. Acc: 3-4 RSB-S1

6634.   Dawn   All Voices
Poet: Afanasi A. Fet. bb2-eb4 eb3-cb4 Sustained in moderate slow tempo. Graceful, delicate, and generally subdued. Very subdued ending. Short. Best for medium voices. Original text: Russian. Acc: 3 TSS

6635.   Day and night   All Voices
Poet: Fyodor Ivanovich Tyutchef. c3-gb4 eb3-eb4 Sustained in generally slow tempo. Has dramatic passages and a strong ending. Narrative text. Best for the heavier voices. Acc: 3-4 TSS

6636.   Dear love   All Voices
Poet: Anon. German poet. c3-g4 f3-eb4 Animated in lively, restless tempo. Has some strong passages and a climactic ending. The composer used a Russian translation of the original German. English version: Constance Purdy. Acc: 3-4 MRS-1

6637.   Elegy   High, Medium Voices
Poet: Alexander S. Pushkin. b2-g4 g3-f#4 Sustained in moderate slow, fast, and moderate tempi. Has dramatic passages and a dramatic high ending on sustained g4. Requires fine P and PP, and flexibility. Rhythmically difficult, with 5 x 4 meter. Extended instrumental postlude. Acc: 4-5 TSS

6638.   Elegy   All Voices
Poet: Fyodor Ivanovich Tyutchef. bb2-f4 eb3-db4 Sustained in moderate slow tempo. Requires breadth, fine P and PP, tranquility, and gentleness. Low ending. Extended piano prelude and postlude. Best for the darker voices. Acc: 3-4 TSS

6639.   I have come to say good morning   All Voices
Poet: Afanasi A. Fet. c#3-g4 e3-f#4 Animated in moderate lively tempo. Requires fluent enunciation. Generally light. Climactic ending and an extended piano postlude. English version: George Harris, Jr. Acc: 4 MRS-1

6640.   Midday   Medium, Low Voices
Poet: Fyodor Ivanovich Tyutchef. bb2-f4 f3-eb4 Sustained in moderate slow tempo. Tranquil and generally subdued. Ends subdued in descending cadenza. Text is descriptive of nature. Acc: 4 TSS

6641.   Sleepless   High, Medium Voices
Poet: Fyodor Ivanovich Tyutchef. a2-ab4 eb3-f4 Sustained in

moderate tempo. Requires fine P and flexibility. Has dramatic passages and a vocalized ending section. Subdued, sustained low ending.
Acc: 4 TSS

6642. Spanish romance   High, Medium-high Voices
       Poet: Alexander S. Pushkin. db3-a4 gb3-gb4 Animated in very
       lively tempo. Requires fluent enunciation, fine P, and flexibility.
       Light, with a climactic ending. Acc: 4-5 TSS

6643. The angel   All Voices
       Poet: Alexander S. Pushkin. d#3-g4 g3-g4 Sustained in moderate
       tempo. Requires very fine high P. Has agitated passages. Agi-
       tated accompaniment throughout. Best for light voices. Narrative
       text. Acc: 4 TSS

6644. The butterfly (Babochka)   High, Medium-high Voices
       Poet: Afanasi A. Fet. db3-gb4 gb3-eb4 Animated in lively tem-
       po. Has some sustained, vocalized phrases. Requires lightness and
       flexibility. Extended piano prelude. Light and agitated accompani-
       ment. Acc: 4 TSS

6645. The coach of life   High, Medium Voices
       Poet: Alexander S. Pushkin. d3-ab4 g3-eb4 Animated in lively
       tempo. Requires fluent enunciation, flexibility, and fine P. General-
       ly strong, dramatic, and resolute. Subdued ending on long-held, un-
       measured note. Agitated accompaniment. Acc: 4-5 TSS

6646. The muse   Men
       Poet: Alexander S. Pushkin. c3-g4 e3-e4 Gently animated vocal
       part. Starts subdued and very tranquil. Requires fine high P and
       PP. Dramatic final section with slightly florid passages. Gently
       agitated accompaniment. Acc: 4-5 TSS

6647. The rose (Roza)   All Voices
       Poet: Alexander S. Pushkin. a2-eb3 d3-c4 Sustained in moderate
       slow tempo. Requires fine PP. Short. Slightly extended piano post-
       lude. Not for light voices. Acc: 3 TSS

6648. The singer   All Voices
       Poet: Alexander S. Pushkin. d3-f#4 g3-e4 Animated in moderate
       lively tempo. Generally subdued and light. Has a recitative-style
       passage. Acc: 3-4 TSS

6649. The willow   All Voices
       Poet: Fyodor Ivanovich Tyutchef. c#3-g#4 f#3-d4 Sustained in
       moderate slow tempo. Requires fine P. Generally subdued, short.
       Rather thick accompaniment which requires gentleness. Acc: 3-4
       TSS

6650. Waves and thoughts   All Voices
       Poet: Fyodor Ivanovich Tyutchef. c#3-g4 f3-d4 Sustained in slow
       tempo. Starts very gently. Has dramatic passages. Short, with a
       subdued ending. Acc: 3-4 TSS

6651. Waltz   Tenor
       Poet: Afanasi A. Fet. f3-bb4 g3-g4 Animated in waltz style.
       Graceful. Requires flexibility, and very fine high P and PP. Very
       subdued ending section. Acc: 3-4 TSS

6652. When roses fade   High Voices
Poet: Alexander S. Pushkin. c♯3-a4 f♯3-e4 Sustained in slow
tempo. Requires fine high P. Starts subdued and tranquil. Ends
with short florid passage. Gently agitated accompaniment. Acc: 4
TSS

6653. Winter evening   Tenor, High Baritone
Poet: Alexander S. Pushkin. c3-g4 f3-eb4 Animated in moderate
lively tempo. Has climactic passages. Dramatic high ending. Agitated accompaniment. Acc: 4-5 TSS

German Texts

6654. Alt Mütterlein   All Voices
Poet: Friedrich Nietzsche. bb2-gb4 eb3-db4 Sustained in moder-
ate slow tempo. Tranquil and subdued. Requires fine high PP.
Gently agitated accompaniment. Narrative text. Acc: 3-4 TSS

6655. Der untreue Knabe   High Voices
Poet: Johann Wolfgang von Goethe. c3-a4 f3-eb4 Animated in lively tempo. Requires fluent enunciation. Has climactic passages. Extended piano postlude. Best for high voices. Narrative text with
slight humor. Acc: 3-4 TSS

6656. Einsamkeit   All Voices
Poet: Johann Wolfgang von Goethe. a2-d4 d3-b3 Sustained in mod-
erate tempo. Has climactic passages and a subdued low ending.
Graceful. Has dramatic climaxes. Best for low voices. Acc: 3-4
TSS, MRS-1

6657. Erster verlust   All Voices
Poet: Johann Wolfgang von Goethe. c♯3-a4 e3-e4 Animated in
moderate lively tempo. Has some dramatic passages. Slightly extended piano postlude. Sad text. Acc: 3-4 MRS-1

6658. Gleich und Gleich   All Voices
Poet: Johann Wolfgang von Goethe. db3-db4 eb3-db4 Animated in
lively tempo. Requires fluent enunciation. Climactic vocal ending.
Short. Extended piano prelude and postlude. Acc: 3-4 TSS

6659. Glückliche Fahrt   All Voices
Poet: Johann Wolfgang von Goethe. c♯3-f♯4 f♯3-d♯4 Sustained
vocal part in somewhat lively tempo. Strong, majestic, and dramatic.
Climactic high ending. Agitated accompaniment. Extended piano prelude and postlude. Not for light voices. Acc: 4 TSS

6660. Lieb Liebchen   All Voices
Poet: Heinrich Heine. bb2-f4 f3-d4 Animated in lively tempo.
Requires fluent enunciation. Generally light and rhythmic. Acc:
3-4 TSS

6661. Mailied   Men
Poet: Johann Wolfgang von Goethe. c3-c♯4 ab3-ab4 Animated in
moderate lively tempo. Has dramatic passages. Climactic ending.
Acc: 4 MRS-1

6662. Meeresstille   All Voices
Poet: Johann Wolfgang von Goethe. b2-f♯4 f♯3-e4 Sustained in

moderate slow tempo. Tranquil, requires fine high PP. The rather thick-sounding accompaniment requires considerable gentleness and control. Extended piano prelude and postlude. See the settings by Robert Franz and Franz Schubert. Acc: 3-4 TSS

6663. Motto: "Geweihter Platz"   High Voices
Poet: Johann Wolfgang von Goethe. d3-a4 e3-f4 An introduction to "Sonate-Vocalise," Op. 41. Gently animated vocal part in moderate slow tempo. Requires very fine P and PP. Has climactic passages. Acc: 3-4 (S)JZ

6664. Selbstbetrug   Men
Poet: Johann Wolfgang von Goethe. d3-g4 e3-d4 Animated in moderate lively tempo. Requires flexibility, fluent enunciation, and fine P. Subdued ending. Agitated accompaniment. Acc: 3-4 TSS

6665. Sonate-Vocalise   Lyric Soprano
Poet: None, mostly "ah" vowel. c3-ab4 g3-g4 Introduced by the "Moto: Geweihter Platz. " An extended vocalise in generally moderate lively tempo. Starts and ends very gently and subduedly. Not to be attempted by less than well trained sopranos. Acc: 4 (S)JZ

NIKOLAI YAKOVLEVICH MIASKOVSKY, 1881-1950

6666. At times it seems to me   All Voices
Poet: Stepan Stchipatchef. f3-ab4 a3-e4 Sustained in moderate tempo. Has climactic passages. Descending ending line. May be transposed for lower voices. Original key. English version: Nicolas Slonimsky. Acc: 3 50R-3

6667. Elbrud and the airplane   All Voices
Poet: Stepan Stchipatchef. e3-g4 f3-e4 Sustained in moderate lively tempo. Generally strong. High climactic ending. Slightly extended piano postlude. May be transposed for the lower voices. Original key. Best for the heavier voices. English version: Nicolas Slonimsky. Acc: 3-4 50R-3

6668. Her picture   All Voices
Poet: Mikhail Y. Lermontof. d3-f4 gb3-f4 Gently animated vocal part in moderate slow tempo. Graceful, generally light. May be transposed for lower voices. Best for men. Original key. English version: Nicolas Slonimsky. Acc: 3 50R-3

ALEXANDER VASSILIEVICH MOSSOLOF

6669. Mountain summits   All Voices
Poet: Mikhail Y. Lermontof. c3-f4 f3-d4 Sustained in slow tempo. Somewhat subdued and tranquil. Extended piano prelude. Original key. May be transposed for lower voices. English version: Nicolas Slonimsky. Acc: 3 50R-3

MODEST PETROVICH MUSSORGSKY, 1839-1881

If a sculptor were to carve the bust of a man from a piece of massive stone by using Mussorgsky's philosophic ideas about art and life and his approach to musical composition, the result would not reveal a craftsmanship akin to that of the ancient Greeks or of Michelangelo. It would be a creation with rugged features roughly hewn and without attempts to smoothen lines and surface, but as if weathered by cruel sand and rain. At close distance, the work appears shocking and frightful. From a distance, the whole thing takes on a different look--and suddenly, everything makes sense. This is Mussorgsky.

Mussorgsky was a dramatic genius created of a different fiber from other Russian composers. He stood alone; he is a class in himself. The greatness of his talents is revealed especially in his ability for creating varied emotional pictures and atmospheres--stark, bold, and never apologetic. Dynamic realism dominates and the master touch is evident in all that he has written, whether it be about nonsense or the grim drama of death's visitations. Mussorgsky wrote some of his own poems, providing him with the wholeness necessary for artistic impact.

The solo works of Mussorgsky do not offer serious vocal and musical problems. They stay within the comfortable range of the voices to which they were assigned. But the work and attention in preparing them for performance are centered and required more in the area of interpretation and declamation. Both singer and accompanist have considerable responsibility.

CWM   Complete Works of Mussorgsky. Edited by Paul Lamm. Original
      Russian texts, with German translations. Commack, NY: Edwin F.
      Kalmus.

Songs and Dances of Death. German title: Lieder und Tänze des Todes.
      A cycle of four songs first published posthumously. Poems by Arsenyi Arkadyevich Golenischef-Kutusof. Original key: Medium. Edition reviewed here: International Music Co. in high, medium, low. Russian text, with English version by Marion Farquhar. Other edition: CWM-15 (Note: the cycle is definitely not for light voices.)

6670. (1) Lullaby   All Voices
       a2-f#4 c#3-c#4 Sustained in generally slow tempo. Has some faster passages. Dramatic narrative in declamatory style. Requires characterization. Interpretatively difficult. Subdued, low ending with a2 as final note. Acc: 3-4 MRS-1 (2 steps higher)

6671. (2) Serenade   All Voices
       cb3-f4 f3-eb4 Sustained in moderate tempo. Has some climactic passages. Requires fine P and PP. Starts with agitated accompaniment. Dramatic ending. High, climactic ending following a subdued passage. Acc: 3-4 MRS-2

6672. (3) Trepak   All Voices
       Other title: Russian dance. d3-f4 e3-d4 Sustained in generally slow tempo. Has tranquil as well as dramatic and strong passages. Interpretatively difficult. Subdued and reflective ending. Agitated accompaniment. Acc: 4-5 MRS-2

6673. (4) Commander-in-Chief   All Voices
       d3-f#4 f#3-e4 Sustained vocal part starting with rapid tempo. Has some slower, grave and martial tempi. Dramatic, strong, narrative, with some bold and accented sections. Vocally demanding. Interpretatively difficult. Dramatic ending. Full sounding accompaniment.

English version in 50R: Nicolas Slonimsky.   Best for men's voices.
Acc: 4-5 50R-1

The Nursery.   A cycle of seven songs with text and music by the composer.
Original key: high.   Edition used in this review: International Mu-
sic Co.   Original Russian text, with English version by Edward Agate.
Other editions: (SC)J. & W. Chester--English & French; CWM-12
(Note: German title: Die Kinderstube. The poetry is centered
around the activities and impressions of children in the nursery.
Some are humorous, but all are light, and are best for soprano voice.
The songs may be performed singly.)

6674.   (1) With nursey   Soprano, High Mezzo-Soprano
c# 3-f4 eb 3-db 4 Animated in moderate tempo.   Somewhat difficult.
Interpretatively not easy.   Acc: 4

6675.   (2) In the corner   Soprano, High Mezzo-Soprano
c3-f4 f3-d4 Animated in fast tempo.   Requires some flexibility and
fluent enunciation.   Interpretatively not easy.   Acc: 5

6676.   (3) The beetle   Soprano, High Mezzo-Soprano
db 3-f4 a3-e4 Animated in moderate lively tempo.   Interpretatively
not easy.   Requires some fluent enunciation.   Acc: 4

6677.   (4) With the doll   Soprano, High Mezzo-Soprano
eb 3-eb 4 g3-db 4 Sustained in moderate tempo.   Subdued.   Acc: 3

6678.   (5) Evening prayer   All Voices
c3-e4 eb 3-c4 Sustained in moderate tempo.   Requires some fluent
enunciation.   Interpretatively not easy.   Best for high and medium
voices.   Acc: 3-4

6679.   (6) The hobby horse   Soprano, High Mezzo-Soprano
c# 3-g4 ab 3-eb 4 Animated in fast tempo.   Requires fluent enunciation.   Interpretatively not easy.   Acc: 5

6680.   (7) The naughty puss   Soprano
c# 3-g# 4 a3-f# 4 Animated in fast tempo.   Light, somewhat delicate.
Interpretatively not easy.   Requires fluent enunciation.   Acc: 4

Without Sun.   German title: Ohne Sonne.   A cycle of six songs composed in
1874.   Poems by Arsenyi Arkadyevich Golenischef-Kutusof.   Edition
reviewed here: International Music Co.   Original key: Medium low.
Original Russian text, English version by Humphrey Procter-Gregg.
Other edition: CWM-13 (German only).   (Note: Not for light voices.
Generally somber texts, as the title indicates.)

6681.   (1) Within four walls   Medium, Low Voices
c# 3-d4 d3-bb 3 Sustained in moderate slow tempo.   Tranquil and
subdued.   In gentle recitative style.   Low ending.   Somber text.   English version in 50R: Nicolas Slonimsky.   Acc: 3 50R-1

6682.   (2) In the crowd   Medium, Low Voices
a2-eb 4 d3-a3 Sustained in moderate tempo.   Has one climactic passage.   Generally in quasi-recitative style.   Subdued ending.   Acc:
2-3

6683.   (3) An end at last to senseless day   Medium, Low Voices

b2-e4   e3-c4   Sustained in moderate tempo.   Slightly slower ending
section with moving vocal line.   Starts strongly; has climactic passages.   Subdued ending.   Acc: 3

6684.   (4) Ennui   Medium, Low Voices
b2-d# 3   f# 3-c4   Sustained in moderate slow tempo.   Has some quasi-
recitative passages.   Low ending.   Sad texts.   Acc: 3

6685.   (5) Elegy   Medium, Low Voices
c# 3-e4   e3-c4   Alternating andantino and allegro sections.   Has some
climactic passages.   Generally agitated accompaniment.   Acc: 4

6686.   (6) On the river   Medium, Low Voices
c# 3-d# 4   e# 3-c# 4   Sustained in moderate slow tempo.   Starts very
gently, in subdued manner, and contemplative.   Requires some fine
PP.   Subdued, low ending.   Agitated accompaniment.   Acc: 4

Single Songs

6687.   Ah, not with God's thunder   Medium, Low Voices
Poet: Aleksei Konstantinovich Tolstoi.   d3-f4   f3-e4   Sustained in
moderate tempo.   Strong, in majestic style.   Climactic ending.
Chordal accompaniment.   English version: Constance Purdy.   Acc:
3 (S)OD.   MRS-1

6688.   Children's song   Soprano
Poet: Leo Alexandrovich Mey.   c# 3-f# 4   b3-d# 4   Sustained in mod-
erate tempo.   Calm, simple and short.   English version: Nicolas
Slonimsky.   Acc: 2-3 50R-1, CWM-10

6689.   Cradlesong of the poor   Mezzo-Soprano, Contralto
Poet: Nikolai A. Nekrasof.   a2-c# 4   c# 3-b3   Sustained in slow tempo.   Generally subdued and gentle.   Very subdued ending.   Requires
sensitive treatment of text.   English version: Sigmund Spaeth.   Acc:
3   55A

6690.   Darling Savishna   All Voices
Poet: Modest Petrovich Mussorgsky.   eb 3-g4   f3-eb 4   Animated in
lively tempo.   Has strong passages, but generally on MF level.   Subdued ending.   Original key: 1-1/2 steps lower.   English version:
Constance Purdy.   Acc: 3 MRS-1, CWM-9

6691.   Hopak   Women
Poet: Leo Alexandrovich Mey.   c# 3-f# 4   f# 3-d4   Animated in lively
tempo.   Accented and joyous, in the style of a Russian dance.   Requires fluent enunciation.   Outgoing and rhythmic.   Climactic ending.
English version: Constance Purdy.   Acc: 4 MRS-1, CWM-9

6692.   Jeremouschka's cradle song   Women
Poet: Nikolai A. Nekrasof.   d3-f# 4   f# 3-e4   Sustained in moderate
slow tempo.   Dynamics from P to PPP.   English version: Constance
Purdy.   Acc: 3 MRS-1, CWM-10

6693.   Little star, where art thou?   Men
Poet: Modest Petrovich Mussorgsky.   d3-f# 4   f# 3-d4   Sustained in
slow tempo.   Has short, florid figures and slightly strong passages.
Short.   Best for tenor or high baritone.   English version: Constance
Purdy.   Acc: 3 MRS-2, SCS-5, CWM-8

6694. Song of the flea   Baritone, Bass
       Poet: Johann Wolfgang von Goethe, from his Faust, translated into
       Russian by Alexander Strugovschikof. a# 2-g4 d3-d4 Animated in
       moderate tempo. A dramatic, humorous narrative. Has many strong
       passages. Descending ending line. Requires flexibility. Interpreta-
       tively not easy. A favorite concert piece of many baritones and
       basses. Issued by GS in English, Russian, and French. Acc: 4
       (S)GS, RO

6695. Song of the Hebrew maiden   Women
       Poet: Leo Alexandrovich Mey. c×3-f#4 f#3-c#4 Gently animated
       in moderate slow tempo. Has contrasting strong and gentle passages.
       Subdued, descending ending line. English version: Nathan H. Dole.
       Acc: 3 ATS

6696. The seminarian   Men
       Poet: Modest Petrovich Mussorgsky. d3-g4 g3-eb4 Animated in
       moderate lively tempo. Requires fluent enunciation. Has some Latin
       words and phrases. Humorous; requires flexibility. Has strong sec-
       tions and a climactic ending. English version: Deems Taylor and
       Kurt Schindler. Acc: 3-4 GAS, CWM-9

6697. The song of Khivria   Women
       Poet: Anon. d3-a4 f3-f4 Animated in moderate lively tempo. Has
       some varied slower tempi before the last section. Climactic ending.
       Best for soprano. English version: Deems Taylor and Kurt Schind-
       ler. Acc: 3-4 GAS

NICOLAS NABOKOF

6698. The return of Pushkin   High Voices
       Poet: Alexander S. Pushkin. c3-b4 g3-g4 An elegie in three move-
       ments for high voice and orchestra. Thirty pages. The piano score
       is the one reviewed here. Original Russian texts, with German and
       English version. English version by Vladimir Nabokov. In varied
       tempi, moods, and styles. Has dramatic high passages. Also re-
       quires very fine, sustained P on a4. Third movement ends in sub-
       dued parlando on f3, unmeasured. First lines:
           (1) I have seen again that corner of the earth
           (2) On the border of my ancestral land
           (3) I remember at various times
       Edition: (S)Edition M. P. Belaieff

LEONID NIKOLAYEF

6699. Dawn of night   All Voices
       Poet: A. Struve. d3-g4 a3-e4 Animated in moderate lively tempo.
       Generally light. Requires fluent enunciation. Short, with syncopated
       accompaniment. Subdued ending on medium-high range. English ver-
       sion: Nathan H. Dole. Acc: 3-4 ATS

SERGEI SERGEYEVICH PROKOFIEF, 1891-1953

Prokofief, one of this century's most noted Russian composers, wrote some
admirable songs which need to be heard more often. Among his first songs,

and perhaps his best-known, is "The ugly duckling," whose texts are a
shortened version of the Hans Christian Andersen tale. Generally, Prokofief's first compositions were approached in a straightforward manner, avoid-
ing as conveniently as possible chromaticisms which tend to cloud the texture.
In later years, he slowly turned to lyricisms not only in his songs, but also
in his operas.

PBP Cinq Poêsies de C. Balmont. Op. 36. A collection of five songs
     for high voice and piano. Poems by Konstantin Dmitrievich Balmont.
     Texts in Russian, with French, German, and English versions.
     French version by Lina Llubera and Sergei Prokofief. Leipzig:
     Breitkopf & Härtel. (Note: Issued singly, as well as an entire set.)

Three Children's Songs. Sergei Prokofief. A set, not a cycle, of songs
     for medium or high voices. English versions by W. H. Easterbrook.
     New York: Leeds Music Corp.

6700. (1) The chatterbox   Soprano, Mezzo-Soprano
       Poet: A. Barto. c♯3-e4 e3-e4 Generally animated in alternating
       moderate and lively tempi. Requires fluent enunciation. Interpreta-
       tively not easy. Slightly sustained ending section. An extended song;
       has humor. Best for light voices. Acc: 3

6701. (2) Lollipop song   High, Medium Voices
       Poet: N. Sakonska. f3-f4 g3-f4 Animated vocal part in moderate
       slow tempo. Generally light, has many staccati figures. Acc: 3

6702. (3) The little pigs   High, Medium Voices
       Poet: Kvito. e3-f4 g3-e4 Animated in moderate lively tempo.
       Has humor; 2 verses. Acc: 3

Single Songs

6703. An incantation for fire and water   High, Medium Voices
       Poet: Konstantin Dmitrievich Balmont. French title: Une incanta-
       tion du feu et de l'eau. Other English title: A Malayan incantation.
       d3-g♯4 f♯3-f4 Animated in moderate lively tempo. Requires fine
       P. Has climactic passages. Very subdued ending. Acc: 3-4 PBP,
       (S)BH

6704. Greeting!   Medium Voices
       Poet: Anna Akhmatova. Op. 27, No. 4. French title: Bonjour!
       c♯3-f♯4 f♯3-d4 Generally sustained in varied tempi. Has element
       of declamation. Requires very fine P and PP. Only one climactic
       passage; generally subdued. Interpretatively not easy. Subdued end-
       ing, with the very last four notes in staccati. Issued singly or in
       complete opus of five songs. Acc: 3-4 (SC)BH; (S)BH

6705. In garden bed   High Voices
       Poet: Konstantin Dmitrievich Balmont. Op. 23, No. 4. French
       title: Dans mon jardin. c♭3-a4 f♯3-f♯4 Sustained in varied tempi
       and moods. Starts gently in moderate slow tempo. Has dramatic
       high passages, and chromatic figures. Requires fine high P and PP.
       Very subdued high ending. Texts in the original Russian, with Eng-
       lish, French, and German versions. Acc: 4 (S)BH

6706. Into your chamber   All Voices

Poet: Alexander S. Pushkin.   d3-g4   g3-eb4   Sustained in moderate
slow tempo.   Generally on MF level.   Subdued ending.   May be transposed for lower voices.   English version by Nicolas Slonimsky.
Original key.   Acc: 3   50R-3

6707. On the Arctic Ocean   All Voices
Poet: Mikhail Svetlof.   e3-f4   g3-e4   Sustained in moderate slow
tempo.   Generally tranquil, somewhat subdued.   May be transposed
for lower voices.   English version by Nicolas Slonimsky.   Original
key.   Acc: 3   50R-3

6708. Snowdrops   High Voices
Poet: Traditional Russian poem.   e3-a4   g#3-f#4   An arrangement
of a traditional melody rather than an original composition.   Animated
in lively tempo.   Strong beginning and ending sections.   Requires very
fine high P for the middle section.   Climactic high ending on a4.
English version in 50A is by Lorraine Noel Finley.   The Boosey &
Hawkes edition (Edition Russe de Musique) is in Russian, German,
French, and English.   Acc: 3-4   50A, (S)B-H

6709. Snowflakes   High Voices
Poet: Traditional Russian poem.   e3-g4   f#3-f#4   An arrangement
of a traditional melody rather than an original composition.   Sustained
in moderate slow tempo.   Gentle, delicate, and generally subdued.
Best for light, high voices.   May be transposed for lower voices.
The English version in 50A is by Lorraine Noel Finley.   The Boosey
& Hawkes edition (Edition Russe de Musique) is in Russian, French,
English, and German.   Acc: 3   50A, (S)B-H

6710. The butterfly   Soprano
Poet: Konstantin Dmitrievich Balmont.   e3-g4(c5)   g3-g4   French
title: Le papillon.   Animated in moderate lively tempo.   Graceful,
light, and best for light voices.   Climactic ending on sustained high
note.   Acc: 3-4   PBP, (S)BH

6711. The garret dweller   High Voices
Poet: Valentine Goryansky.   Op. 23, No. 1.   French title: Sous le
toit.   b2-a4   e3-f4   An extended song (21 pages) in varied tempi and
moods.   Starts in moderate tempo.   Has dramatic passages, recitative
passages, and some agitated accompaniment.   Requires fine high P
and PP, and some fluent enunciation.   Not for light voices.   Very
subdued ending section.   Acc: 4-5   (S)BH

6712. The pillars   High Voices
Poet: Konstantin Dmitrievich Balmont.   French title: Les granits.
c3-g4   f3-d4   Sustained in moderate slow tempo.   In quasi-recitative
style.   Has dramatic passages.   Strong, low ending.   Descriptive text.
Acc: 3-4   PBP, (S)BH

6713. The ugly duckling   High Voices
Poet: Hans Christian Andersen.   Russian title: Gadkiy utenok.   b2-
a4   e3-e4   An extended narrative, 28 pages, based on the famous
fairy tale.   A large part of the song is in recitative manner, requiring
sensitive textual delivery and interpretation.   A subdued, descending
ending line after the high climax.   French text by V. Janacopulos and
Sergei Prokofief.   English version by Robert Burness.   Acc: 4-5
(S)B-H

6714.   The voice of birds   High Voices
        Poet: Konstantin Dmitrievich Balmont.   French title: La voix des
        oiseaux.   db3-bb4 g3-g4 Sustained vocal part in moderate slow tem-
        po.   Requires simplicity and fine high P.   Gently agitated accompani-
        ment.   Acc: 4 PBP, (S)BH

6715.   Think on me!   High Voices
        Poet: Konstantin Dmitrievich Balmont.   French title: Pensi à moi!
        d3-b4 a3-f4 Sustained in moderate slow tempo.   Has dramatic pas-
        sages and a climactic ending.   Requires flexibility and some fluent
        enunciation.   Agitated accompaniment.   Other titles: A Malayan in-
        cantation; (French) Une incantation Malaise.   Acc: 4 PBP, (S)BH

6716.   With morning's first glow   High Voices
        Poet: Alexander S. Pushkin.   d3-g4 f3-e4 Animated in lively tem-
        po.   Requires fluent and crisp enunciation.   Graceful, mostly in 3/4
        meter.   Climactic high ending on g4.   Narrative text.   Published with
        the original Russian text.   English version by Ephim G. Fogel.   Acc:
        3-4 (S)LM

SERGEI VASSILIEVICH RAKHMANINOF, 1873-1943

Rakhmaninof's escape in 1918 from the Russian Revolution brought to him international recognition as one of the best concert pianists in his time.   As
a song composer, his lush romantic style and lyric exuberance are more
closely akin to Tchaikovsky than to any Russian composer before him.   His
songs are provided with highly polished, difficult, and overloaded piano parts
which need to be handled with great care by the accompanist so that they do
not obscure the voice.   Many of Rakhmaninof's songs are available in good
English versions.

FRS   Four Rachmaninov Songs.   Medium voice and piano.   English version
        by M. C. H. Collet.   London: J. & W. Chester Ltd.

SSR   Selected Songs.   Serge Rachmaninoff.   Twelve songs for high voice
        and piano.   Texts are Russian, with English, French, and German
        versions.   London: Boosey & Hawkes.

6717.   Before my window   All Voices
        Poet: G. Galina.   Op. 26, No. 10.   e3-a4(b4) a3-f#4 Sustained in
        slow tempo.   Starts in gentle declamatory style.   Requires very fine
        high P.   Subdued ending.   English version: Constance Purdy.   Acc:
        3 MRS-2, SSR

6718.   By a new-made grave   All Voices
        Poet: Semyon Yakovlevich Nadson.   Op. 21, No. 2.   eb3-g4(H) g3-
        eb4 Sustained in slow tempo.   Has some strong passages.   Starts
        in declamatory style.   Reflective, sad texts.   English version: Con-
        stance Purdy.   Acc: 3-4 MRS-2

6719.   Field beloved   All Voices
        Poet: Aleksei Konstantinovich Tols oi.   Op. 4, No. 5.   f#3-g4 f#3-
        e4 Sustained in slow tempo.   Has dramatic passages and agitated ac-
        companiment in the middle of the song.   Intense.   Ends with strong
        vocalized passage or cadenza.   English version by Robert H. Hamilton
        in MRS.   Title in FRS: The harvest of sorrow.   Acc: 3-4 MRS-2,
        FRS, SSR

850 Solo Voice Repertoire

6720. Floods of spring   All Voices
Poet: Fyodor Ivanovich Tyutchef. Op. 14, No. 11. db3-g#4 f3-
db4 Animated in lively tempo. Joyous, exultant, and bright. Has
strong and dramatic passages, and a full-sounding and heavy accompaniment. Climactic ending. Best for the heavier voices. English
version: in MRS: Constance Purdy. Title in FRS: Spring waters.
Acc: 5 MRS-2, FRS, SSR   (S)GS-high

6721. Forsake me not, my love, I pray   All Voices
Poet: Dmitri S. Mereschovsky. Op. 4, No. 1. c#3-g4 g3-e4
Animated in lively tempo. Has sudden contrasts in dynamics. Dra-
matic high ending. Agitated accompaniment. English version:
Bernard Taylor. Acc: 3-4 GAS, MRS-2, SSR

6722. How fair is this spot   All Voices
Poet: G. Galina. Op. 21, No. 7. c3(bb2)-g4 e3-d4 Sustained in
moderate tempo. Generally calm and subdued. Requires fine P.
Descending ending. Acc: 3 SVR-2

6723. In the silence of night   All Voices
Poet: Afanasi A. Fet. Op. 4, No. 3. d3-a4 f3-f4 Sustained in
slow tempo. Has dramatic passages. Very lyric. Very subdued
high ending. Agitated accompaniment. The composer's best-known
song. English version: Carl Engel. Title in FRS: In the silent
night. Acc: 3-4 50A, FRS, SSR, SVR-1   (S)GS-high, low

6724. Lilacs   All Voices
Poet: E. Beketova. Op. 21, No. 5. eb3-g4 g3-eb4 Generally
gentle and subdued. Requires fine high P and PP. Subdued ending.
Very gently agitated accompaniment. Original key. Best for high
and medium high voices. English version: Nicolas Slonimsky. Acc:
3-4 50R-2, SSR, 56S   (S)GS-high

6725. O, do not grieve for me!   High Voices
Poet: Aleksei Nikolayevich Apuchtin. Op. 14, No. 8. d3-b4(c5)
f3-f4 Sustained in moderate slow tempo. Has dramatic high passages. Slightly faster middle section. Descending ending line. Acc:
3 SSR, GSA

6726. Sorrow in spring   All Voices
Poet: G. Galina. Op. 21, No. 12. d3-bb4 g3-eb4 Animated in
lively tempo. Has some dramatic passages. Requires fine P. Extended piano postlude. Sad text. English version: Arthur Westbrook.
Acc: 4 MRS-2, SSR

6727. The island   All Voices
Poet: Alexei S. Khomyakof. Op. 14, No. 2. db3-f4 a3-d4 Sustained in quite slow tempo. In quasi-recitative style. Generally subdued, requires fine P and PP. Delicate. Very subdued ending. English version: Carl Engel. Acc: 3 50A, SSR

6728. The soldier's wife   Soprano, Mezzo-Soprano
Poet: Aleksei N. Plescheyef. f#3-g4 g3-eb4 Sustained in moderate slow tempo. Slightly faster middle section. Has dramatic passages. Ends with vocalized passage in one long diminuendo. Sad
text. English version: M. C. H. Collet. Acc: 3-4 FRS

6729. To the children   All Voices

Poet: Alexei S. Khomyakof. Op. 26, No. 7. f♯3-g4 g3-e4 Gently
moving vocal part in slow tempo. Generally subdued. Also has a
few strong passages. In quasi-recitative style. English version by
Rosa Newmarch. Acc: 3 MRS-2, SSR

6730. Vocalise   Soprano
Vowels ah, oh and u or a mixture of these sounds. Op. 34, No. 4.
c♯3-g♯4(c♯5) g♯3-e4 Sustained in slow tempo. Very lyric. Has
some climactic passages. Subdued ending. Acc: 3-4 GAS, SSR
(S)GS-high, medium, low

6731. We shall have peace!   All Voices
Poet: Anton Pavlovich Chekhov. c3-f4 f3-c4 Sustained in slow
tempo. Has one climactic passage, but generally subdued. Low ending. For all voices except the light, high. May be transposed for
all voices. Text: peace in our time. Acc: 3 50R-2

Sacred Song

6732. Christ is risen!   High, Medium Voices
Poet: Dmitri S. Mereschkovsky. Op. 26, No. 6. d3-f4 f3-e♭4
Sustained in moderate tempo. Dramatic, strong, marked, and intense.
Has dramatic high passages. Not for light voices. One step higher
in SSR (g4, highest note). Acc: 3 (S)GA. SSR

NICOLAS RAKOF

6733. Elegy   High Voices
Poet: Nikolai Mikháylovich Yazykof. e3-a4 g3-e4 Sustained in generally moderate tempo. Has climactic passages and a subdued ending.
Has slightly agitated accompaniment. Original key. English version
by Nicolas Slonimsky. Acc: 3-4 50R-3

NIKOLAI ANDREYEVICH RIMSKY-KORSAKOF, 1844-1908

Rimsky-Korsakof composed about 80 songs to works by Russian poets and
translations of Byron and Heine. He has set to music poetry of Pushkin,
Tolstoi, Mey, Maikof, and Lermontof more than any other Russian writers.
His songs are of a high quality; they are very well written for the voice.
Mainly lyric in style, they are well supported with fine piano accompaniments
which help to heighten their picturesque quality. There is some Oriental
flavor in his music, as shown in his best-known song, "The nightingale and
the rose." Rimsky-Korsakof's songs need to be known and performed more.

RKS   Six Songs by Rimsky-Korsakov. High, low. English version only.
       Boston: Boston Music Co.

6734. A flight of passing clouds   Soprano
Poet: Alexander S. Pushkin. e3-a4 f♯3-f♯4 Sustained in slow tempo. Gently moving vocal part. Has some climactic passages. Subdued ending. Agitated accompaniment. English version: Nicolas
Slonimsky. Acc: 4 50R-1

6735. Believe me not   All Voices
Poet: Aleksei Konstantinovich Tolstoi. e♭3-f4 g3-e♭4 Gently

animated in moderate tempo. Gently agitated accompaniment. Extended postlude. English version: Constance Purdy. Acc: 3-4
MRS-2

6736. Come to the realm of roses and wine   High Voices
Poet: Afanasi A. Fet. f♯ 3-f♯ 4 f♯ 3-d♯ 4 Animated in moderate
lively tempo. Joyous, with a climactic section. Requires fine high
P and PP. Very subdued low ending. Arpeggiated accompaniment.
Acc: 4 RSB-S2

6737. I have come to you this morning   All Voices
Poet: Afanasi A. Fet. e3-a4 a3-g4 Animated in moderate lively
tempo. Exultant, with inner joy. Climactic high ending. May be
transposed for lower voices, although best for high or medium. A
fine ending song for a Russian group. English version: Nicolas
Slonimsky. See the setting by Nikolai Medtner. Acc: 3 50R-1,
MRS-2

6738. Like mountains the waves   All Voices
Poet: Aleksei Konstantinovich Tolstoi. d3-g4 g3-e♭4 Sustained in
moderate tempo. Long lines in the last section. Agitated accompaniment throughout. English version: Constance Purdy. Acc: 4-5
MRS-2

6739. On Georgian hills   All Voices
Poet: Alexander S. Pushkin. d♯ 3-f♯ 4 f♯ 3-c♯ 4 Sustained in moderate tempo. Has some climactic passages. Subdued ending. May
be transposed for lower voices. English version: Nicolas Slonimsky.
Acc: 3 50R-1

6740. Song of Zuleïka   Men
Poet: George Gordon Byron, translated into Russian. e♯ 3-e4 g♯ 3-
d4 Gently moving vocal part in moderate slow tempo. In gentle recitative style. Short and light. Narrative text. English version:
Charles F. Manney. Acc: 3 MRS-2

6741. Southern night   All Voices
Poet: Scherbina. d♯ 3-f♯ 4 f♯ 3-c♯ 4 Sustained in moderate lively
tempo. Generally on MF level. Has some climactic passages. The
last half is in quasi-recitative style. Ends strongly on the lowest
note of the song. Agitated and arpeggiated accompaniment. English
version: P. C. Warren. Acc: 3 RKS

6742. The maid and the sun   Women
Poet: Apollon Nikolayevich Maikof. c♯ 3-a4 g♯ 3-e4 Animated in
moderate lively tempo. Has some climactic passages. Best for high
or medium-high voices. English version: Charles F. Manney. Acc:
3 MRS-2

6743. The nightingale and the rose   All Voices
Poet: Alexei V. Koltzóf. Other title: Oriental romance. f♯ 3-f♯ 4
g♯ 3-d4 Sustained in moderate tempo. Light and plaintive. Requires
simplicity. In the style of a gentle recitative. Extended prelude and
postlude. English version: Deems Taylor. See the setting by Anton
Rubinstein. Acc: 3 MRS-2, 55A-medium, RKS, SCS-5

6744. The octave   All Voices
Poet: Apollon Nikolayevich Maikof. e3-a4 g3-e4 Sustained in slow

tempo. Very lyric in style, with climax of melody at the end. The
text is in praise of the sounds of nature. English version: Constance
Purdy. Title in RKS: Nature's voice--its English version is unlike
the original theme of the text. Acc: 3 MRS-2, RKS

6745. The phantom ship   All Voices
Poet: Anon. e3-a4 g3-g4 Animated in moderate lively tempo.
Starts gently. Has climactic passages. Requires fine high P. Gen-
tle ending. Gently agitated accompaniment. Extended piano postlude.
English version: P. C. Warren. Acc: 3-4 RKS

6746. The rainy day is past   All Voices
Poet: Alexander S. Pushkin. c♯3-f♯4 f♯3-d♯4 Gently moving vocal
part in slow tempo. Generally subdued and gentle. Has recitative-
style sections and ending. English version: Constance Purdy. Acc:
3 MRS-2

6747. The singer   All Voices
Poet: Apollon Nikolayevich Maikof. f3-g4 g3-g4 Sustained in slow
tempo. Requires some fine P. Generally gentle. English version:
George Harris, Jr. Text is from the collection, New Greek Songs.
Acc: 3 MRS-2

6748. Waves dashing and breaking   All Voices
Poet: Aleksei Konstantinovich Tolstoi. d3-g4 f3-e♭4 Sustained in
moderate tempo. Majestic. Starts strongly on the highest note of
the song. Climactic ending. Not for light high voices. English version: Constance Purdy. Title in RKS: The wooing of the waters.
Acc: 3-4 MRS-2, RKS

ANTON GRIGOREVICH RUBINSTEIN, 1829-1894

Rubinstein founded the St. Petersburg Conservatory in 1862, and its first distinguished product was Peter I. Tchaikovsky. A brilliant concert pianist,
Rubinstein gained fame from his concerts in foreign countries. As a composer, he wrote for almost every type of music. His about 200 songs are
outstanding only for the fact that they were beautifully written in a style close
to Schumann's or Mendelssohn's, but they do not have the originality to elevate Rubinstein with the better composers. Many of his settings are of German poems, and this is due to his love for the German culture rather than
his German-Jewish ancestry. The best-known of his songs are "Der Asra,"
"Es blinkt der Tau," and "Die Waldhexe." His Persian songs, Op. 34, were
popular for some time, but like most of the others are now seldom performed
except in Russia. The few included here are basically the best representatives of his style of writing.

59S   Fifty-nine Songs by Anton Rubinstein. German texts, with English
       versions by William Stigand and Constance Bache. High voice and
       piano. London: Boosey & Hawkes.

                              _____

6749. An den Frühling   All Voices
Poet: Nikolaus Lenau. d3-g4 g3-d4 Gently animated in moderate
tempo. Has some climactic passages and some long-held high notes.
Bright, somewhat climactic. Acc: 3-4 59S

6750. Clärchens Lied   All Voices

Poet: Johann Wolfgang von Goethe.   c3-f4   g3-eb4   Sustained in
moderate tempo.   Has some varied tempi in the middle part and a
climactic passage.   Subdued ending.   Gently agitated accompaniment.
Best for women.   Text is from the author's "Egmont."   Acc: 3
59S

6751. Der Asra   All Voices
Poet: Heinrich Heine.   c3-gb4   f3-eb4   Sustained in moderate tempo.   Has one climactic passage.   Requires some gentle characterization.   Strong ending section.   Once a well-known song.   Narrative.
One step higher in MRS-2.   Acc: 3   59S, MRS-2

6752. Desire   Men
Poet: Mikhail Y. Lermontof.   c3-g4   f3-d4   Animated in moderate
lively tempo.   Strong, bold, climactic with the theme of "personal
freedom."   Requires fluent enunciation.   Climactic ending on slightly
slower and broader section.   English version: Nicolas Slonimsky.
Original key.   Acc: 3-4   50R-2

6753. Die helle Sonne leuchtet   All Voices
Poet: Mirza Schaffy.   d3-g4   g3-e4   Animated in moderate tempo.
Has florid passages.   Vocal part ends with descending florid line.
Extended piano prelude and postlude.   Acc: 3   59S

6754. Die Lerche   All Voices
Poet: Th. von Sacken.   eb3-g4   g3-eb4   Animated in moderate lively tempo.   Bright, has climactic passages.   Arpeggiated and agitated
accompaniment, requiring virtuosity.   Acc: 4-5   59S

6755. Die Nachtigall und die Rose   All Voices
Poet: Alexei V. Koltzof.   A German version from the Russian by
Von Viedert.   d3-d4   f3-c4   Sustained in moderate tempo.   Generally
subdued.   Narrative text.   See the setting by Rimsky-Korsakof.
Acc: 3   59S

6756. Du bist wie eine Blume   All Voices
Poet: Heinrich Heine.   d3-f4   g3-c4   Very sustained in moderate
tempo.   Gentle, generally on MF level.   Subdued, low ending.   Other
title: Lied.   See the settings by Schumann, Wolf, Liszt, and Chad-
wick's "Thou art so like a flower."   Acc: 3   59S

6757. Ein Traum   All Voices
Poet: Anon.   e3-f4   f3-d4   Generally sustained in moderate slow
tempo.   Has some climactic passages and agitated accompaniment.
Subdued low ending.   Acc: 3   59S

6758. Es blinkt der Thau   All Voices
Poet: G. von Boddien.   db3-fb4   g3-eb4   Animated in moderate tempo.   Has climactic passages.   Subdued ending after a climax.   Narrative text.   Acc: 3   59S, MRS-2 (one step higher)

6759. Es war ein alter König   All Voices
Poet: Heinrich Heine.   c3-f4   g3-eb4   Sustained in moderate tempo.
Generally subdued with a subdued ending.   In quasi-recitative style.
Narrative, tragic texts.   Acc: 3   59S

6760. Fliehe hin, Nachtigall   Men
Poet: Alexei V. Koltzof.   c3-f4   f3-f4   Animated in moderate tempo.

Has some climactic passages.   High tessitura in some sections.
Low ending.   German version from the Russian by Von Viedert.
Acc: 3   59S

6761. Frühlingslied   All Voices
Poet: Heinrich Heine.   First line: Die blauen Frühlingsaugen.   c# 3-
f# 4   e3-c# 4   Animated in moderate lively tempo.   Has some climactic passages.   Climactic ending.   Starts gently.   Acc: 3   59S

6762. Frühmorgens   All Voices
Poet: Emanuel von Geibel.   d3-g4   g3-d4   Animated in moderate
lively tempo.   Requires some fluent enunciation.   Has climactic passages.   Generally subdued.   Acc: 3   59S

6763. Gelb rollt mir zu Füssen   Men
Poet: Mirza Schaffy.   d3-g4   f3-eb 4   Animated in moderate slow
tempo.   Has some slightly florid figures.   Requires some flexibility.
Bright, with rhythmic chordal accompaniment.   Acc: 3   59S

6764. Lebewohl   Men
Poet: Alexei V. Koltzóf.   c# 3-g4   f# 3-d4   Slightly animated vocal
line in moderate tempo.   Has climactic passages.   Descending ending
phrase.   Translated from the Russian by Von Viedert.   Acc: 3
59S

6765. Mein Herz schmückt sich mit dir   All Voices
Poet: Mirza Schaffy.   e3-a4   e3-e4   Animated in lively tempo.   Requires fluent enunciation.   Has some florid passages.   Slightly climactic ending on a4.   2 verses.   Acc: 3-4   59S

6766. Nicht mit Engeln   Men
Poet: Mirza Schaffy.   eb 3-f4   ab 3-f4   Animated in moderate slow
tempo.   Requires some flexibility.   Has florid passages.   Bright and
exultant.   Climactic ending.   Generally agitated accompaniment.   Acc:
4   59S, MRS-2

6767. Nun die Schatten dunkeln   All Voices
Poet: Emanuel von Geibel.   db 3-f4   f3-eb 4   Sustained in moderate
tempo.   Slightly faster middle section.   Generally subdued and gentle.
See the setting by Robert Franz.   Acc: 3   59S

6768. Siehe, der Frühling währet nicht lang   All Voices
Poet: Hoffmann von Fallersleben.   d# 3-f# 4   g# 3-e4   Animated in
lively tempo.   Bright and exultant.   Has climactic passages; also requires fine P.   Strong, descending ending line.   Acc: 3-4   59S

G. SACKNOFSKY

6769. Spring   All Voices
Poet: G. Novikof.   d3-a4(b4)   g3-g4   Animated in lively tempo.
Joyous and bright.   Dramatic, climactic ending verse.   Ends on sus-
tained b4 marked FF.   English version: Constance Purdy.   Acc: 4
MRS-2

YURI ALEXANDROVICH SHAPORIN

6770. Invocation   High Voices

Poet: Alexander S. Pushkin. c♯3-g♯4 g♯3-e4 Animated in moderate lively tempo. Has dramatic passages and agitated accompaniment.
Original key. English version: Nicolas Slonimsky. Acc: 4-5
50R-3

VISSARION YAKOVLEVICH SHEBALIN, 1902-1963

6771. 'Tis time   All Voices
Poet: Alexander S. Pushkin. Original key. c♯3-f♯4 e3-d4 Sustained in moderate slow tempo. Generally subdued, with one climactic passage. May be transposed for lower voices. English version:
Nicolas Slonimsky. Acc: 3 50R-3

IVAN PETROVICH SHISHOF, 1888-1947

6772. The songster   All Voices
Poet: Alexander S. Pushkin. d♭3-d♭4 f3-d♭4 Sustained in moderate tempo. Has two slightly slower passages. Subdued, requires
fine P and PP. Subdued low ending. Original key. English version:
Nicolas Slonimsky. Acc: 3 50R-3

DIMITRI SHOSTAKOVICH, 1906-1975

Shostakovich, a significant composer, belongs to the new generation of musicians who work under the shadow of conformity to artistic principles laid
down by the state. It is difficult to say if his style would be different without the pressure of ideologies. However, the following songs are presented
as representatives of his genius. He has not written many songs, but those
included here are available, and should be tried by any enterprising singing
artist. For want of English versions, the songs on poems by Pushkin are
listed in German.

RUM Romanzen und Monologe nach Pushkin. Op. 46 & 91. Dimitri Schos-
      takowitsch. Low voice and piano. Russian texts, with German ver-
      sions by Christoph Hellmundt, Erwin J. Bach, and Johannes von
      Guenther. Leipzig: Edition Peters, 1966.

6773. Abschied   Low Voices
Poet: Alexander S. Pushkin. Op. 91, No. 4. a♭2-c4 c3-c4 Ani-
mated in moderate lively tempo. Has some recitative-style passages.
Subdued, low ending with c3 sustained for four measures. Acc: 3
RUM

6774. Bitterly sobbing   All Voices
Poet: Alexander S. Pushkin. e3-f4 g3-e♭4 Original key. Animated in moderate lively tempo. Generally subdued, requires fine
PP. May be transposed for lower voices. Narrative text. English
version: Nicolas Slonimsky. Acc: 3-4 50R-3

6775. Coming through the rye   All Voices
Poet: Robert Burns, translated into Russian. d3-e♭4 e♭3-c4 Gently animated vocal part in moderate tempo. Generally light. Extended piano prelude and postlude. Acc: 3 50R-3

6776. Eifersüchtig das Mägdlein schalt, bitterlich weinend   Low Voices
Poet: Alexander S. Pushkin. Op. 46, No. 2. c♯3-d4 f♯3-c4 Animated in moderate lively and moderate slow tempi. Generally on
MF level. Very subdued, descending ending. Agitated accompaniment. Slightly extended piano prelude and postlude. Acc: 3 RUM

6777. Fragment   Low Voices
Poet: Alexander S. Pushkin. Op. 91, No. 1. a2-d♭4 b2-g3 In
recitative style in moderate slow tempo. Requires simplicity. Generally subdued. Interpretatively not easy. Acc: 3 RUM

6778. MacPherson's farewell   Tenor
Poet: Robert Burns, Russian version by S. Marshak. b♭2-a♭4 a3-
f4 Animated in moderate lively tempo. Generally strong with some
high climactic passages. Not for light, high voices. Extended piano
prelude and postlude. Acc: 3-4 50R-3

6779. Oh, wert thou in the cauld blast   Men
Poet: Robert Burns, Russian version by S. Marshak. d3-g4 f♯3-d4
Gently, gracefully animated in moderate tempo. Requires fine PP.
Generally subdued and gentle. Acc: 3 50R-3

6780. Renaissance   All Voices
Poet: Alexander S. Pushkin. c3-f4 f3-d4 Sustained in moderate
tempo. Starts in quasi-recitative style. Generally subdued. Very
subdued ending. Requires very fine P and PP. Original key. English version: Nicolas Slonimsky. Acc: 3 50R-3

6781. Sendschreiben nach Sibirien   Low Voices
Poet: Alexander S. Pushkin. Op. 81, No. 3. d3-e♭4 d3-d4 Very
sustained in slow tempo. In quasi-recitative style. Has dramatic
passages. Subdued ending. Acc: 3 RUM

6782. Stanzen   Low Voices
Poet: Alexander S. Pushkin. Op. 46, No. 4. a♯2-e♭4 e3-c4 Generally sustained in slow tempo. Faster middle section. Has some
climactic passages. Beginning and ending sections are in quasi-recitative style. Very subdued ending. Generally agitated accompaniment.
Acc: 3 RUM

6783. Vorahnung   Low Voices
Poet: Alexander S. Pushkin. Op. 46, No. 3. b2-e4 d3-c4 Somewhat sustained vocal part in lively tempo. Graceful and generally
subdued. Requires fine high PP. Extended piano postlude. Acc: 3
RUM

6784. Was liegt dir wohl am Namen mein?   Low Voices
Poet: Alexander S. Pushkin. Op. 91, No. 2. b♭2-d4 e♭3-c4
Somewhat sustained vocal part in lively tempo. Rhythmic in 3/4.
Generally on MF level. Acc: 3 RUM

6785. Wiedergeburt   Low Voices
Poet: Alexander S. Pushkin. Op. 46, No. 1. a2-d4 e3-b3 Sustained in moderate tempo. In quasi-recitative style. Subdued throughout. Very subdued ending. Gently moving accompaniment. Acc: 3
RUM

NIKOLAI ALEXANDROVICH SOKOLOF, 1859-1922

6786.   How abundant and warm is the spring!   All Voices
Poet: Myrrha Lókhvitsky.   d3-g4   g3-e4   Animated in moderate lively tempo.   Graceful and rhythmic.   No strong dynamics.   English
version: George Harris, Jr.   Acc: 3 MRS-2

V. SOKOLOF

6787.   Through the fields in winter   Low Voices
Poet: Ivan S. Nikítin.   b2-e4   e3-c♯4   Sustained in moderate slow
tempo.   Has lively middle section.   Narrative, descriptive text.
Slightly extended and animated piano postlude.   Acc: 3-4 RSB-B1

MIKHAIL LEONIDOVICH STAROKADOMSKY, 1901-1954

6788.   An inscription in a bower   Tenor
Poet: Alexander S. Pushkin.   Original key.   d3-b♭4   a3-e4   Sustained in slow tempo.   Very subdued ending.   Strictly chordal accompaniment.   May be transposed for baritone.   English version by
Nicolas Slonimsky.   Acc: 3 50R-3

IGOR FEODOROVICH STRAVINSKY, 1882-1971

Stravinsky's position as one of the foremost composers of the 20th century
and in the entire history of music cannot be questioned.   His works and musical philosophy have affected the path of music more than most people real-
ize.   It is not that all he wrote is accepted without question; it is not.
Rather, it is the controversy surrounding his works that makes his name
survive.   Added to this are all the innovations and new approaches in composition that have influenced succeeding generations of composers and their
works.

Stravinsky's fame rests more on his instrumental and larger works than on
any other compositions.   His accomplishments in the area of solo song are
not outstanding.   Like his other works, his songs are very diverse in style
and treatment, covering the gamut from the ordinary to the near eloquent.
His settings are mostly of Russian, French, and English poetry.   Some of
them are musically simple, while others are complex and difficult.

Although Stravinsky settled in the United States of America at the outbreak
of World War II and became an American citizen, his soul was still definitely Russian.   This is evidenced in a direct quotation from him upon his visit
to Russia in 1962, after an absence of 48 years: "You see a very happy
man.   The smell of Russian earth is different ... a man has one birthplace,
one fatherland, one country."

Igor Stravinsky died in his New York apartment on April 6, 1971 at the age
of 88.

QCR   Quatre Chants Russes.   Igor Stravinsky.   Traditional Russian texts,
with French version by C. F. Ramuz.   London: J. & W. Chester.

Berceuses du Chat.   Igor Stravinsky.   A suite of four songs for contralto

and three clarinets.   Composed 1915-1916.   Original Russian:
Koshach'i kolʼbel'nʼie pesni.   English: Cat's lullabies.   Piano reduction by the composer.   The French version is reviewed here.   London: J. & W. Chester.

6789.   (1) Sur le poêle   Contralto, Mezzo-Soprano
Texts: Traditional Russian.   a2-g3   d3-f3   Sustained in moderate
slow tempo.   Subdued, very short, gentle, and with a narrow range.
Has a long-sustained final note.   Acc: 3

6790.   (2) Intérieur   Contralto, Mezzo-Soprano
Texts: Traditional Russian.   g2-a3   a2-e3   Gently animated vocal
part in moderate tempo.   Generally on MF level.   Has florid figures.
Short and gentle.   Acc: 3

6791.   (3) Dodo....   Contralto, Mezzo-Soprano
Texts: Traditional Russian.   c3-b3   d3-g3   Animated vocal part in
moderate slow tempo.   Subdued, short, and gentle.   Acc: 3

6792.   (4) Ce qu'il a, le chat....   Contralto, Mezzo-Soprano
Texts: Traditional Russian.   g3-e4   a3-c4   Sustained in moderate
slow tempo.   Subdued and gentle.   4 short verses.   Acc: 2-3

Le Faune et la Bergère.   Igor Stravinsky.   Original Russian: Favn i Pas-
tushka.   English: Faun and Shepherdess.   Poems by Alexander S.
Pushkin.   A cycle of three songs for high voice and orchestra.   Pi-
ano reduction available.   Op. 2.   The original Russian texts, with
French and German versions.   The French version is reviewed here.
Bonn: M. P. Belaieff.

6793.   (1) La bergère   High Voices
b2-f4   f3-eb4   Sustained in moderate slow tempo.   Has some climactic passages.   Subdued ending section with long, sustained final note.
Agitated accompaniment in the last part.   Acc: 4

6794.   (2) Le faun   High Voices
d3-g4   g3-e4   Sustained in moderate tempo, with faster middle section.   Has climactic passages.   Dramatic high ending on sustained g4.
Generally agitated accompaniment.   Acc: 4

6795.   (3) Le torrent   High Voices
d3-a4   f#3-e4   Sustained in first moderate slow tempo, then lively
tempo.   Has dramatic passages, and a dramatic ending.   Very agitated
accompaniment.   Acc: 5

Pribautki.   Igor Stravinsky.   French title: Chanson Plaisantes.   Composed
1914.   A set of four songs for medium voice and eight instruments.
Piano reduction available.   Texts are traditional Russian verses.
French version, reviewed here, is by C. F. Ramuz.   London: J. &
W. Chester Ltd.

6796.   (1) L'oncle Armand   Medium Voices
c3-db4   eb3-g3   Gently animated vocal part starting with moderate
tempo, then becomes slower.   Some frequent meter changes.   Descending ending line following climax.   Strong.   Acc: 3

6797.   (2) Le four   Medium Voices
d3-e4   f3-d#4   Animated in first lively, then slower tempi.   Requires

fluent enunciation and some flexibility. Strong and short. Acc: 3-4

6798. (3) Le colonel   Medium Voices
       e3-g4   e3-c♯4 Animated in moderate lively tempo. Has frequent
       meter changes. Descending ending line after high climax. Requires
       fluent enunciation. Acc: 4

6799. (4) Le vieux et le lièvre   Medium Voices
       d3-d4   d3-b3 Animated vocal part in slow tempo. Requires flexibil-
       ity. Generally on MF level. Strong and animated postlude. Acc: 4

Three Songs from William Shakespeare. Igor Stravinsky. A set of songs
       for mezzo-soprano and flute, clarinet, and viola. Piano reduction
       available. London: Boosey & Hawkes.

6800. (1) Musick to heare   Mezzo-Soprano
       c3-e♭4 c3-d4 Text is from Sonnet 8:1. Sustained and rhythmically
       complex. Requires flexibility. Acc: 5

6801. (2) Full fadom five   Mezzo-Soprano
       b♭2-e♭4 e♭3-d♭4 Text is from The Tempest. Animated, requires
       flexibility. Has rhythmic complexities. Acc: 5

6802. (3) When dasies pied   Mezzo-Soprano
       c3-e♭4 e♭3-d4 Text is from Love's Labour's Lost. Animated, re-
       quires flexibility. Has some florid figures, and rhythmic complexi-
       ties. Acc: 5

Trois Histoires pour Enfants. Igor Stravinsky. Original Russian: Tri
       istrii dlya detey. English: Three Stories for Children. Traditional
       Russian rhymes, translated into French by C. F. Ramuz. London:
       J. & W. Chester Ltd.

6803. (1) L'ours   Medium, Low Voices
       c3-g3 c3-f3 This is a narration with the song part set in the middle
       of the composition. Sustained in moderate tempo. Accompaniment is
       a one-line bass part. Composed 1915. Acc: 1-2

6804. (2) Les canards, les cygnes, les oies....   Medium Voices
       d3-d4 d3-a3 Animated in lively tempo. Requires fluent enunciation.
       Low ending. Composed 1917. Acc: 3-4

6805. (3) Tilim-bom   High, Medium Voices
       g3-d4 a3-d4 Animated in lively tempo. Requires fluent enunciation.
       Best for light voices. Text is a "mother goose" type rhyme song.
       English version by Rosa Newmarch. Acc: 3-4 (S)CH

Trois Poèsies de la Lyrique Japonaise. Igor Stravinsky. Original Russian:
       Tri stikhotvoreniya iz yaponskoy liriki. English: Three Japanese
       Lyrics. A set of songs for soprano and instruments. Piano reduc-
       tion by the composer. Russian, French, and English texts. London:
       Boosey & Hawkes.

6806. (1) Descendons au jardin   Soprano
       Poet: Akahito, translated into Russian. c♭3-b♭b♭4 c3-g4 Sustained
       in moderate tempo. Very high tessitura. Generally on MF level.
       Short, one page. Acc: 3

6807.   (2) Avril paraît   Soprano
        Poet: Mazatsumi, translated into Russian. a♯3-a4 b3-e4 After a
        rapid, extended instrumental introduction, the voice part sings a slow-
        er tempo and in sustained style. Strong and climactic. Acc: 5

6808.   (3) Qu'aperçoiton si blanc au loin?   Soprano
        Poet: Tsaraiuku, translated into Russian. g♯3-a♭4 a♯3-e♭4 Sus-
        tained in slow tempo. Tranquil and subdued. High ending. Acc: 3

Single Songs

6809.   Canard   High Voices
        Poet: Traditional Russian. Other title: Ronde. a♭3-a♯4 b3-f4
        Animated in lively tempo. Quite high tessitura. Requires some flex-
        ibility and fluent enunciation. Best for light and high voices. Com-
        posed 1918. Acc: 3-4 QCR

6810.   Chanson pour compter   High Voices
        Poet: Traditional Russian. b3-f♯4 b3-e4 Animated in very lively
        tempo. Requires fluent enunciation. Starts with unmeasured, free
        introduction. High tessitura. Strong and energetic spoken ending.
        Has several glissandos on the piano. Composed 1919. Acc: 4
        QCR

6811.   Chant dissident   High, Medium Voices
        Poet: Traditional Russian. f♯3-f♯4 g3-d4 Animated in moderate
        tempo. Requires flexibility and fluent enunciation. Has some florid
        figures. Rather free, unmeasured ending. Composed 1919. Acc: 4
        QCR

6812.   Con queste paroline   Bass
        Work: PULCINELLA, a ballet on music by Pergolesi. Unknown
        source of text. g1-e3 d2-d3 Sustained vocal part in lively tempo.
        Has some short florid figures. Requires flexibility for the octave in-
        tervalic skips. Semi-climactic ending. Piano reduction is by the
        composer. Acc: 3-4 (S)CH

6813.   La bonne chanson   Baritone
        Poet: Paul Verlaine. e♭2-e♭3 f2-c3 Generally sustained in moder-
        ate slow tempo. Generally on MF level, with occasionally high tessi-
        tura. Subdued beginning. Generally calm. Has some agitated but
        delicate accompaniment. See Fauré's "La lune blanche luit dans les
        bois" in his La Bonne Chanson; "La lune blanche" by Poldowski and
        Szulc; "Appaisement" by Chausson; and "L'Heure exquise" by Hahn.
        Acc: 4   (S)B-H

6814.   Le moineau est assis....   High Voices
        Poet: Traditional Russian. a3-g4 a3-e4 Animated in moderate live-
        ly tempo. Requires fluent enunciation and flexibility. High tessitura.
        Has contrasts of gentle and strong passages. Climactic high ending.
        Composed 1919. Acc: 4 QCR

6815.   Pastorale   High Voices
        Text: None, the vowels used are "ah" and "ah-oo." A vocalise
        c♯3-f♯4 e♯3-f♯4 Sustained in slightly slow tempo. Florid, requires
        flexibility. Generally gentle and subdued. Requires very fine P and
        PP. Gently agitated accompaniment. Graceful and delicate. Acc:
        3-4 50A

6816. Song of the dew   All Voices
       Poet: Sergei Gorodetsky. Original key. c♯3-f♯4 g3-e4 Sustained
       in slow tempo until the ending when the tempo becomes lively and the
       style animated. Strong ending section. Generally agitated accompani-
       ment. Best for medium voices. Not recommended for light high
       voices. English version: Nicolas Slonimsky. Acc: 4 50R-2

6817. The cloister   Women
       Poet: Sergei Gorodetsky. Op. 6, No. 1. d♯3-f♯4 g♯3-f♯4 Ani-
       mated in lively tempo. Slower middle section. Requires fine P.
       Has dramatic passages and a cadenza. Extended piano prelude. Eng-
       lish text, with French version by M. D. Calvocoressi. Acc: 4
       MRS-2

6818. The owl and the pussy-cat   All Voices
       Poet: Edward Lear. b2-d♯4 d3-c♯4 Animated in moderate tempo.
       Unmeasured, requires some fluent enunciation, and some characteriza-
       tion. On MF level. Single line accompaniment for right and left
       hands. Amusing narrative. Acc: 3 (S)B-H

Note: See also:
       Elegy for J. F. K. Texts by W(ystan) H(ugh) Auden. For baritone
       voice and three clarinets. Range: d2-e3 London: Boosey &
       Hawkes, Ltd.

SERGEI IVANOVICH TANEYEF, 1856-1915

6819. Minuet   All Voices
       Poet: Charles D'Orias. e3-ab4 f3-f4 Animated in minuet tempo.
       Faster middle section. Has dramatic passages and a very subdued
       ending. Has some narrative element. Acc: 3-4 MRS-2

6820. The birth of the harp   All Voices
       Poet: Thomas Moore, from his Irish Melodies. e3-g4 g3-g4 Sus-
       tained, in moderate slow tempo. First part is in recitative style,
       with long-held phrase ending. Requires fine P and PP. Narrative
       text. Acc: 4 MRS-2

PETER (PIOTR) ILYICH TCHAIKOVSKY, 1840-1893

Tchaikovsky belongs to the realm of romantic lyricism. Generally speaking,
his songs are all very attractive and they can easily win an audience as they
have done so many times before. They are very fine vehicles for the singer's sentiment as well as an encouraging factor in the use of beautiful tone.
If many of them are deficient in some way--in form, variety of expression,
and subtle word-painting--they nevertheless attract merely for the sake of
something "beautiful" to sing. Tchaikovsky wrote more than 100 songs, and
only a few of these, by close and careful analysis, can be classified as
great pieces. They cannot, for example, be classed in the same rank as
those of Schubert, Schumann, or Brahms, but they can survive on their own
merits as something audiences would enjoy hearing. Barring any prejudices
against Tchaikovsky's music, it is to be admitted that they reflect charm,
sweetness, and nostalgic sadness mingled together. These are his own personal temperaments which are accepted as being very human by those who
appreciate and enjoy his works.

Tchaikovsky's best-known song is "Nur wer die Sehnsucht kennt," often translated as "None but the lonely heart." Among the songs which represent his
best writing are "Was I not a blade of grass," "A legend" (considered by
many as his very best), "Pimpinella," "Cradle song," "Don Juan's serenade,"
and "By chance in the ballroom."

SFT   Forty Songs by Peter Ilyitch Tchaikovsky. High, low. Edited by
James Hunekar. Bryn Mawr: Oliver Ditson, c/o Theodore Presser
Co. (Note: The texts of these songs are almost all German and
English versions.)

TST   Twelve Songs. Peter Ilyitch Tchaikovsky. High, low. New York:
G. Schirmer, Inc. (Note: The texts of these songs are mostly English and German versions.)

6821. A legend   All Voices
Poet: Aleksei Nikolayevich Plescheyef. Op. 54, No. 5. e3-f#4
f#3-f#4 Sustained in moderate tempo. Generally subdued. A quasi-
religious text. English version: Charles F. Manney. Acc: 3
SFT, 50A

6822. A night of stars   All Voices
Poet: Jakov Petrovich Polonski. Op. 60, No. 12. c3-g♭4 d3-d4
Sustained in moderate slow tempo. Has some climactic passages.
Best for medium voices. English version: Frederick H. Martens.
Acc: 3-4 SFT

6823. By chance in the ballroom   All Voices
Poet: Aleksei Konstantinovich Tolstoi. Op. 38, No. 3. b2-e4 f#3-
d4 Gently animated in moderate tempo. Gentle waltz, graceful and
generally subdued. A charming and simple song. Original key.
English version in 50R is by Nicolas Slonimsky. In SFT the title is
"At the ball," English by Nathan H. Dole. Acc: 3 50R-2, SFT,
50A, 55A

6824. Cradle song   Women
Poet: Apollon N. Maikof. Op. 16, No. 1. d3-g4 g3-e♭4 Sustained with gentle movement in moderate slow tempo. Subdued
throughout; requires fine P and PP. Requires simplicity and calm-
ness. English version: Charles F. Manney. Acc: 3-4 SFT, TST

6825. Death   All Voices
Poet: Dmitri S. Mereskovsky. Op. 57, No. 5. d3-g4 f3-e4 Sus-
tained in moderate tempo. Has strong pseudo-dramatic passages.
Subdued ending. Not for very light voices. English version: Isidora
Martinez. Acc: 3 SFT

6826. Deception   All Voices
Poet: Paul Collin. Op. 65, No. 2. c3(b2)-f4 f3-e♭4 French text.
Sustained in moderate tempo. Starts calmly. Intense, climactic ending. Extended piano postlude. Best for medium voices. Original
key: 1/2 step lower. Acc: 3 SFT, 50M

6827. Did my mother give me life   Women
Poet: Adam Mickiewicz, Polish poet, translated into Russian. Op.
27, No. 5. b2-g♭4 f3-f4 Animated in lively tempo. Descending
ending after slightly climactic passage. Best for mezzo-soprano.

English version by Frederick H. Martens. Acc: 3-4 SFT

6828. Don Juan's serenade   Men
Poet: Aleksei Konstantinovich Tolstoi. Op. 38, No. 1. b2-e4(f♯4)
f♯3-d4 Animated in lively tempo. Has climactic passages. In joyous, fast waltz rhythm. Climactic ending. Extended piano prelude
and postlude. English version: Isabella G. Parker. Acc: 4 SFT

6829. Endless love   All Voices
Poet: Aleksei Konstantinovich Tolstoi. Op. 6, No. 4. f3-a♭4(H)
f3-g♭4 Sustained in moderate tempo. Has some climactic passages.
Also requires fine high P. Original key: two steps lower. English:
Isabella G. Parker. Acc: 3-4 SFT, MRS-2

6830. Farewell   All Voices
Poet: Nikolai A. Nekrasof. Op. 60, No. 8. c3-a4 d3-d4 Sustained in moderate tempo. Has dramatic passages. Low, strong
ending. Best for the heavier voices. Extended piano prelude. English: Frederick H. Martens. Acc: 3 SFT

6831. Farewell, fond visions!   All Voices
Poet: Grand Duke Constantine. Op. 63, No. 3. d3-f4 f3-f4 Sustained in moderate tempo. Slightly animated middle section. Has
some climactic passages and subdued ending. English version: Frederick H. Martens. Acc: 3-4 SFT

6832. He truly loved me so!   Women
Poet: Aleksi Nikolayevich Apuchtin. Op. 28, No. 4. d3-a4 d3-f4
Sustained in moderate tempo. Has gentle recitative style passages,
especially evident in the repeated notes. Subdued, low ending after
dramatic climax. Acc: 3 SFT, TST

6833. If you but know   Men
Poet: Paul Collin. Op. 60, No. 3. Translated into Russian. e♭3-
a♭4 f3-e♭4 Animated in lively tempo. Requires fluent enunciation.
Generally strong, with some dramatic passages. Climactic and sus-
tained ending. Slightly extended piano postlude. English version:
Samuel R. Gaines. Acc: 4 SFT

6834. Les larmes   Medium, Low Voices
Poet: A. M. Blanchecotte. The text is wrongly attributed to Paul
Collin in the Ditson edition. Op. 65, No. 5. d3-e4 d3-e4 French
text. Sustained in moderate slow tempo. Requires fine P. Has
some strong, dramatic, and intense passages. Sad texts. Acc: 3
SFT

6835. Linger yet!   All Voices
Poet: Grekow, inspired by the balcony scene of Shakespeare's Romeo
and Juliet. Op. 16, No. 2. d♯3-f4 f3-e♭4 Gently animated vocal
part in moderate tempo. Subdued, requires fine P and PP. Calm
and gentle. English version: Arthur Westbrook. Acc: 3-4 SFT

6836. Mignon's Lied   Women
Poet: Johann Wolfgang von Goethe. First line: Kennst du das Land.
Op. 25, No. 3. d3-g♭4 f3-f4 Animated in moderate lively tempo.
Has dramatic passages and a climactic ending. Slightly extended piano
prelude and postlude. Best for high and medium voices. In the Dit-
son, the text is unfortunately rearranged by F. Gumbert. See the

Russian   865

following settings: "Mignon" by Beethoven and Wolf; "Mignon's Lied"
by Liszt; "Mignon's Gesang" by Schubert; "Kennst du das Land" by
Zelter and Schumann. Acc: 4 SFT

6837. No, whom I love I'll never reveal   Men
Poet: Alfred de Musset. Original text of the setting is Russian,
translated from Musset. Op. 28, No. 1. e♭3-a♭4 f3-f4 Sustained
in moderate slow tempo. Gentle, subdued first section. Has some
climactic passages. Subdued, falling ending after climax. Best for
tenor. German and English versions by Charles F. Manney. Acc:
3-4 SFT

6838. No word from thee   Men
Poet: Aleksei Konstantinovich Tolstoi. Op. 28, No. 1. c3-f4 g3-
e♭4 Sustained in moderate slow tempo. Has some climactic passages. Slightly extended piano postlude. Best for heavy tenor or
baritone. English version: Isabella G. Parker. Acc: 3 SFT

6839. None but the lonely heart   All Voices
Poet: Johann Wolfgang von Goethe, translated into Russian. Op. 6,
No. 6. d3-g4(H) e♭3-e♭4 Very sustained in moderate slow tempo.
Requires fine P and PP. Has climactic passages. Best for medium
and low voices. Sad text. Care must be taken not to accentuate the
syncopated rhythm in the accompaniment. Original key: one step
lower. Slow, subdued ending. See the following settings: "Sehnsucht" by Loewe and Zelter; "Lied der Mignon" by Schubert; "Nur
wer die Sehnsucht kennt" by Beethoven and Schumann. Acc: 3-4
SFT, MRS-2, 50M, TST, 50R-2, 56S, HBS-3 (S)GS-high, medium,
low

6840. Not at once did I yield to love's yearning   All Voices
Poet: Grand Duke Constantine. Op. 63, No. 1. f3-g4 f3-d4 Gen-
tly animated in moderate tempo. Subdued ending after strong climax.
English version: Frederick H. Martens. Acc: 3 SFT

6841. O my child, in the silence of night   Men
Poet: Grand Duke Constantine. Op. 63, No. 6. d3-a4 f3-e4 Animated in moderate lively tempo. Has climactic passages and lyric
treatment. Extended piano prelude and postlude. A serenade. English version: Frederick H. Martens. Acc: 3 SFT

6842. Oh, leave me not, friend of mine   All Voices
Poet: Afanasi A. Fet. Op. 27, No. 3. c3(a2)-f4 g3-f4 Sustained
in moderate slow tempo. Generally subdued. Subdued, low ending.
Gently agitated accompaniment. Best for medium or low voices.
English version: Frederick H. Martens. Acc: 3 SFT

6843. One small word   Men
Poet: Peter Ilyich Tchaikovsky. The Russian text source "N.N." re-
fers to the composer himself. Op. 28, No. 6. c♯3-g♯4 e3-e4
Sustained in moderate slow tempo. Generally subdued. Subdued end-
ing. Requires fine P. English version: Frederick H. Martens.
Acc: 3 SFT

6844. Pilgrim's song   All Voices
Poet: Aleksei Konstantinovich Tolstoi. Other title: I bless you,
forests. Op. 47, No. 5. d3-g4 g3-f4 Sustained in moderate slow
tempo. Has dramatic sections. Extended piano prelude and postlude.

Best for the heavier voice, perferably men.   English version: Paul
England.   Acc: 4 (S)GS-high, medium, low

6845.   Pimpinella   Men
        Poet: Peter Ilyich Tchaikovsky.   Russian text was written by the
        composer himself.   This song was written when he was in Florence.
        Music is based on folk songs heard in Italy.   Op. 38, No. 6.   c3-
        ab4(H) f3-f4 A graceful waltz.   Has some climactic passages.   Gen-
        erally on MF level.   Original key: 1-1/2 steps lower.   Italian text.
        English version: Nathan H. Dole.   Acc: 3 SFT

6846.   Sérénade   Men
        Poet: Édouard Turquetiz.   Op. 65, No. 1.   b2-f#4 f#3-e4 French
        text.   Gently animated in moderate tempo.   Graceful and generally
        light.   Has some slightly climactic passages.   Very subdued ending.
        Acc: 3 SFT

6847.   So fearful, so joyful   High Voices
        Poet: Countess Rostopchin.   Op. 6, No. 3.   c#3-g#4(b4) g#3-g#4
        Animated in lively tempo.   Requires fluent enunciation and flexibility.
        Has dramatic high passages.   Requires fine P and PP.   Dramatic
        ending.   Intense.   Not for light voices.   English version: Theodore
        Baker.   Acc: 4 TST

6848.   So soon forgotten   All Voices
        Poet: Aleksei Nikolayevich Apukhtin.   No opus number.   Original
        key.   f3-ab4 f3-eb4 Sustained in generally moderate tempo, with
        some variations.   In quasi-recitative style.   Has dramatic passages.
        Best for high and medium-high voices.   English version: Nicolas
        Slonimsky.   Acc: 3 50R-2

6849.   Someone said unto the fool   All Voices
        Poet: Leo Alexandrovich Mey.   Op. 25, No. 6.   e3-g4(H) a3-f4
        Animated in lively tempo.   Requires simplicity.   Slightly climactic
        ending.   Original key: one step lower.   Jovial and bright.   English
        version: Isidora Martinez.   Acc: 3 SFT

6850.   Song of the gipsy girl   Women
        Poet: Jakov Petrovich Polonski.   Op. 60, No. 7.   d3-f4 e3-e4 Ani-
        mated in moderate lively tempo.   Slightly slower middle section.   Sub-
        dued ending.   Extended piano prelude and postlude.   Best for the dark-
        er voice.   English version: Frederick H. Martens.   Acc: 3-4 SFT

6851.   Speak not, O beloved   All Voices
        Poet: M. Hartmann, translated into Russian by A. Plescheyef.   Op.
        6, No. 2.   d#3-g4 e3-e4 Gently animated vocal part in moderate
        slow tempo.   In quasi-recitative style.   Generally gentle, subdued,
        except the slightly climactic middle section.   English version:
        Charles F. Manney.   Acc: 3 SFT, TST

6852.   That simple old ballad, O sing me   All Voices
        Poet: Aleksei Nikolayevich Plescheyef.   Op. 16, No. 4.   d3-g4 g3-
        f#4 Animated vocal part in moderate lively tempo.   In graceful 3/4.
        Stronger, somewhat climactic ending section.   Best for high or medi-
        um voices.   English version: Nathan H. Dole.   Acc: 3 SFT, TST

6853.   The canary   All Voices
        Poet: Leo Alexandrovich Mey.   Op. 25, No. 4.   c3-g4 g3-eb4

Sustained in moderate tempo. Requires fine P. Starts gently then becomes stronger and a little more agitated. Subdued ending. Best for medium voices. English version: Charles F. Manney. Acc: 3-4 SFT, MRS-2

6854. The veil of night has fallen   All Voices
       Poet: Adam Mickiewicz, translated by N. V. Berg. Other title:
       Dusk fell on the earth. Op. 47, No. 3. e3-f4 g3-e4 Sustained in
       moderate lively tempo. Has dramatic passages and a climactic end-
       ing. Extended piano prelude and postlude. Best for medium or low
       voices. English version: Theodore Baker. Acc: 3 TST

6855. To sleep   All Voices
       Poet: Nicolas Platónovich Ogaréf. Op. 27, No. 1. c3-g4 g3-f4
       Animated and very subdued first section; sustained second section in
       moderate slow tempo. Strong second half of the song. Subdued, fall-
       ing ending. Extended piano postlude. English: Isidora Martinez.
       Best for the darker voices. Acc: 4 SFT

6856. 'Twas you alone   All Voices
       Poet: A. Kristen, translated into Russian. Op. 57, No. 6. c3-a4
       f3-eb4 Gently animated in moderate tempo. In gentle declamatory
       style. Starts gently, then becomes stronger. Low, subdued ending
       after a dramatic climax. English version: Frederick H. Martens.
       Acc: 4 SFT

6857. Was I not a blade of grass   Women
       Poet: Ivan Zakharovich Surikof. Op. 47, No. 7. b2-b4 f#3-e4
       Sustained in moderate tempo. Has some short florid figures, and
       dramatic climaxes. Climactic, falling ending. Extended piano post-
       lude. English version: Charles F. Manney. Acc: 4 SFT, TST

6858. When spring was in the air   All Voices
       Poet: Aleksei Konstantinovich Tolstoi. Op. 38, No. 1. eb3-g4
       f3-eb4 Animated in moderate lively tempo. Joyful, has strong dra-
       matic passages. Slightly extended piano postlude. English version by
       Nicolas Slonimsky. Original key. The title in SFT: It was in early
       days of spring. Acc: 3-4 50R-2, SFT

6859. Whether day dawns   All Voices
       Poet: Aleksei Nikolayevich Apukhtin. Op. 47, No. 6. d#3-a4 g#3-
       d#4 Animated in very lively tempo. Requires fluent enunciation.
       Has dramatic passages. Imposing and very climactic ending. Ex-
       tended piano prelude and postlude. Best for the heavier voices. Eng-
       lish version: Charles F. Manney. Acc: 4-5 SFT, TST

6860. Why?   All Voices
       Poet: Heinrich Heine, translated by Mey from "Warum sind denn die
       Rosen so blass." Op. 6, No. 5. e3-a4 a3-f4 Animated in moder-
       ate tempo. Starts softly, then builds toward a climax. Dramatic end-
       ing. Extended piano postlude. Agitated accompaniment in full-sound-
       ing chords. Acc: 4 SFT, TST

ALEXANDER NIKOLAYEVICH TCHEREPNIN

SMT   Six Melodies. Alexander Tcherepnine. A set of songs for high voice

and piano.   Texts by Sergei Gorodetsky.   French version by André
G. Block.   A. Durand.

———————————

6861.   Ah, si j'avais toute vierge   High Voices
Poet: Sergei Gorodetsky.   d♯3-f♯4   g♯3-d♯4   Animated in lively
tempo.   Subdued beginning and ending.   Strong middle section.   Gently agitated accompaniment.   Acc: 3-4   SMT

6862.   Dieu toutpuissant   High Voices
Poet: Sergei Gorodetsky.   e♭3-g4   g3-e♭4   Sustained in moderate
tempo.   Starts and ends gently.   Has climactic high passage in the
middle.   Very subdued, ending on sustained e♭4.   Acc: 3   SMT

6863.   Je vous aime   High Voices
Poet: Tran van Tung, translated from the Chinese.   c3-g4   e3-d4
Sustained in moderate slow tempo.   In quasi-recitative style.   Gen-
erally on MF level.   Slightly climactic ending.   Acc: 3   (S)AD

6864.   L'afflux des mots   High Voices
Poet: Sergei Gorodetsky.   e♭3-g4   g3-e♭4   Animated in moderate
lively tempo.   Generally subdued, requires fine P.   Ends on g4
marked P.   Gently agitated, "swaying" style accompaniment.   Acc:
3   SMT

6865.   Les meules froides   High Voices
Poet: Sergei Gorodetsky.   d♭3-d4   f3-c4   Animated in moderate lively tempo.   Subdued throughout, rather delicate.   Acc: 3   SMT

6866.   Nuit, adieu! le jour se lève   High Voices
Poet: Sergei Gorodetsky.   g3-f4   a3-d4   Animated in very lively
tempo.   Strong, with dramatic ending on sustained f4 marked FF.
Agitated accompaniment.   Acc: 4   SMT

6867.   Pourrais-je aimer   High Voices
Poet: Sergei Gorodetsky.   g3-g4   b♭3-g4   Animated in lively tempo.
Strong throughout.   Ends with sustained g4 marked FF.   Short.   Acc:
3-4   SMT

6868.   Printemps annamite   Coloratura Soprano
Poet: Tran van Tung, translated from the Chinese.   b2-b4   g3-g4
Animated in lively tempo.   Requires fluent enunciation and flexibility.
Has climactic passages and trills.   Extremely high ending on a row
of florid and trilled b4's.   Acc: 4   (S)AD

NIKOLAI NIKOLAYEVICH TCHEREPNIN, 1873-1945

6869.   Cradle song   Women
Poet: Mikhail Y. Lermontof.   f3-g4   b♭3-f4   Sustained in slow tem-
po.   Subdued, requires fine P and PP.   Tranquil.   English version:
Constance Purdy.   Acc: 3   MRS-2

6870.   Dark are now the candles   All Voices
Poet: Konstantine Mikhailovich Fofanof.   d3-f♯4   g3-f♯4   Gently flowing vocal part in moderate slow tempo.   Has some dramatic as well
as tranquil and subdued passages.   Very subdued high ending.   English version: George Harris, Jr.   The title is better listed with:

Dark now are the candles. Acc: 4 MRS-2

6871. I would kiss you   Men
Poet: Apollon N. Maikof.   d3-a4 g3-g4 Original key.   Animated in
moderate lively tempo, with variations in the middle of the song.
Has some climactic passages.   English version: Nicolas Slonimsky.
The title in MRS: A kiss.   The title in RSB: The tell-tale stars.
Acc: 3-4 50R-2, MRS-2, RSB

6872. Menaeceus   Bass
Poet: Apollon N. Maikof.   g1-eb3 d2-c3 Very sustained in moderate slow tempo.   Generally tranquil in quasi-recitative style.   Generally subdued.   Has one climactic passage.   Subdued ending.   Op. 26,
No. 2.   Acc: 3 RSB-B1

6873. Quiet night   All Voices
Poet: Fyodor Ivanovich Tyutchef.   eb3-ab4 ab3-f4 Sustained in
moderate slow tempo.   Tranquil and generally subdued.   Requires
very fine high PP, and simplicity.   Best for high and medium voices.
English version: Constance Purdy.   Acc: 3-4 MRS-2

6874. Stars of radiant night   All Voices
Poet: Konstantine Mikhailovich Fofanof.   d3-g4 a3-e4 Sustained in
moderate tempo.   Tranquil and generally subdued.   Gently graceful.
Very subdued ending.   English version: Constance Purdy.   Acc: 3
MRS-2

6875. To music   All Voices
Poet: Percy Bysshe Shelley, translated into Russian.   bb2-f4(ab4)
g3-eb4 Sustained in moderate slow tempo.   Tranquil and generally
subdued.   Requires very fine high PP.   Very subdued high ending.
Requires delicate handling of the accompaniment.   Acc: 3 ATS

A. TINIAKOF

6876. At twilight   All Voices
Poet: Aleksei Konstantinovich Tolstoi.   b2-g4 f#3-e4 Sustained in
moderate slow tempo.   Starts and ends in recitative style.   Generally
subdued with one climactic passage before the ending section.   English version: Constance Purdy.   Acc: 3 MRS-2

SERGEI NIKIFOROVICH VASSILENKO, 1872-1956

6877. In the cathedral a girl sang prayers   All Voices
Poet: Alexander A. Blok.   d#3-g4 e3-e4 Sustained in moderate
tempo.   Requires simplicity and fine P.   Generally subdued with slight
variation in dynamics.   Original key.   English version: Nicolas Slonimsky.   Title in MRS: A maiden sang.   Acc: 3 50R-2, MRS-2

6878. In the tomb   All Voices
Poet: V. Bruce.   d3-g4 g3-eb4 Sustained in moderate slow tempo.
Slightly faster middle section.   Mostly in recitative style.   Has dra-
matic passages.   English version: Robert H. Hamilton.   Acc: 3
MRS-2

6879. Longing   All Voices

Poet: Konstantin Dmitrievich Balmont. e3-a4 a3-a4 Gently animated vocal part in moderate slow tempo. Requires very fine high
P and PP. Has some climactic passages. Sustained high ending on
a4, marked PP. Best for high or medium-high voices. English version: Deems Taylor. Acc: 4 MRS-2

6880. O my beloved one   High Voices
Poet: Konstantin Dmitrievich Balmont. e3-c5 g3-a4 Sustained
vocal part in moving tempo. Requires fine high P and PP, as well
as dramatic power. Has some long-held high notes. Subdued and
tranquil ending. English version: Constance Purdy. Acc: 3-4
MRS-2

6881. Tar   All Voices
Poet: Sergei Gorodetsky. c3-ab4 g3-eb4 Animated in moderate
lively tempo. Slower, more sustained middle section. Climactic
ending. Extended piano prelude and postlude. Agitated accompaniment. English version: Constance Purdy. Acc: 4 MRS-2

6882. The reapers   Tenor
Poet: Jakov Petrovich Polonski. f♯3-a4 f♯3-e4 Sustained in moderate tempo. Starts gently. Has dramatic passages. Subdued ending after high climax. Extended piano prelude. Op. 2, No. 2.
Acc: 3-4 RSB-S2

JOSEPH WIHTOL, 1863-1948

6883. Beggar's song   Men
Poet: Vieting. db3-gb4 eb3-eb4 Sustained in moderate tempo.
Has passages in recitative style and some climactic passages. Subdued ending section. English version: Charles F. Manney. Acc:
3 MRS-2

B. ZOLOTARIEF

6884. Canzonetta   All Voices
Poet: Fyodor Ivanovich Tyutchef. d3-eb4 g3-d4 Slightly animated
in moderate lively tempo. Graceful. Generally subdued, gentle, and
short. Op. 12, No. 4. Acc: 3 RSB-S1

CHAPTER X

SOLO VOICE REPERTOIRE OF OTHER MUSICAL CULTURES

Belgium	Israel
Canada	Japan
Czechoslovakia	The Netherlands
Greece	Philippines
Hungary	Poland
Switzerland	

Introduction

The vocal repertoire from several countries is grouped in this chapter for reasons that are obvious. A total of eleven countries, selected at random, is represented. This chapter has the widest variety of musical style, and culturally it is the most interesting. The vocal repertory of these countries is not extensive, but possibilities for development are certainly unlimited. This list is by no means fully representative of all musical cultures that have art songs for recital performance. As mentioned earlier, this work depended mainly upon the availability of materials and the cooperation of composers and music publishers. It may be a modest start in building a repertoire reference of still unexplored sources of material for the solo voice.

It is to be recognized that in the last fifteen to twenty years, interest especially in non-Western repertoire and in the inclusion of the non-usual songs and cycles from distant lands has grown and is still growing. This is because some singers and teachers of singing have the adventurous spirit to try out something new and to inject more variety and imagination into the presentation of recitals. This interest in music has grown alongside the interest in other nations and cultures, thus creating a broader and more universal outlook. This does not mean that interest in and use of non-Western ideas, images, styles and atmospheres have not been tried before. They have, but to a limited degree. To mention some of the few, we have Claude Debussy (Javanese music), Francesco Santoliquido (Persian and Arabian), Alexander Tcherepnin (Chinese), Gustav Holst (Hindu), John Alden Carpenter (Hindu), and Charles Griffis (Chinese). We also have the field of opera which explores the exotic from ancient times to the present for greater dramatic impact.

The performance of songs, and sometimes arias, that bear descriptive texts of faraway places and cultures seems now to be more challenging to the singer's imagination and artistic talents. They may need a little bit of research, but this age has grown more scholarship-conscious. The singer's repertoire can be tremendously enriched by including some of what we may label "unusual" or "out of the ordinary." Singers have to accept them first, however, as something that can contribute to their artistic personality and stature.

The reader will also find in this chapter material that is partially or

completely Western in style, but coming from backgrounds which have been
enriched by non-Western influences. We have, of course, Dvořak, Chopin,
Liszt, among several others.

     Belgium and The Netherlands share with other middle and western
European countries in the development of music through the Middle Ages,
Baroque, and the present. Because of geographical proximity, they were
closely involved in the musical developments of their neighbors.

     Belgium is affected by Dutch influence in the north and French in the
south. Its musicians played a great role in the shaping of music in Europe
in the 15th and 16th centuries. Early known and recorded vocal music of
Belgium and The Netherlands were Latin hymns, although some secular music, in simple forms, also existed though of little historical importance.
Situated at the crossroads of active cultures such as Great Britain and France,
these two countries shared with them the practice of the trouvères and the
English lutenists. But it was not until the 15th and 16th centuries that Belgium (Southern Netherlands at that time) became the most prominent and important artistic center in Europe. The country became the cradle of the
great Flemish development in the arts, from which most of the great composers in Europe at that time originated.

     Not much is said of vocal solo music of the Burgundian and Flemish
schools. However, some of the early known songs were written by Gilles
Joye and Hayne van Ghizeghem. Guillaume Dufay, Gilles Binchois, Antoine
Busnois, and Johannes Ockeghem wrote sacred and secular part songs as
well as songs for one voice and instruments. A good number of Belgian and
Dutch composers journeyed to other lands in pursuit of outlets for their musical talents.

     Among song composers of the 18th century are François Gossec and
André Ernest Grétry. In the 19th century we have the names of César
Franck, François van Campenhout, Peter Benoit, Henri Waelput, Christian
Urhan, Jan van den Eeden, Théodore Radoux, Edgar Tinel, and Fernand Le
Borne. Their music is not conveniently available in modern print, and for
this reason is relatively unknown.

     The early 20th century brought to attention Guillaume Lekeu, Joseph
Jongen, and Emiel Hullebroeck. Well into the first half of this century we
have Jean Absil, Paul Gilson, Marcel Poot, and Victor Vreuls.

     The Netherlands composers had monophonic songs in the 14th century.
Among the most famous collection is the Gruythuyser Manuscript, which con-
tains 147 monophonic songs. French influence is evident in much of the music of the Dutch. In the 15th century, Jacob Obrecht was recognized as The
Netherlands' most prominent composer. Both sacred and secular vocal
pieces were produced.

     Among 16th- and 17th-century composers we have Jan Pieterszoon
Sweelinck, whose style leaned more to the international, perhaps because of
his contact with German organists who studied under him. Constantijn
Huygens, a man even more accomplished in the field of solo song than
Sweelinck, composed perhaps the first important Dutch works for the solo
voice. He was also a poet who wrote in several languages. In the 17th and
18th centuries, Italian and French influences were particularly strong, somewhat obscuring any efforts for a national style.

In the 19th century, considerable German influence was felt. Prominent among composers were Johannes Verhulst, Richard Hol, Willem Nicolai, Alfons Diepenbrock, who wrote numerous songs and some stage music, Johan Wagenaar, and François Gossec, who migrated to France.

Born close to the 20th century were such men as Hendrik Andriessen, Alexander Voormolen, Daniel Ruyneman, and Willem Pijper. Much more recently we have Henk Badings, perhaps the most prolific contemporary Dutch composer, Rudolf Escher, Johan Cornelius Riemsdijk, Hans Henkemans, Henriette Bosmans, Piet Ketting, Jan Mul, Bernhard Meyer, Henri Zagwijn, Willem Anddriessen, Lex van Delden, and Rudolf Mengelberg, an unusually gifted composer for the voice. Jan Brands-Buys, although mainly an opera composer, wrote many songs. Marius Flothuis, one of the founders of DONEMUS, has also written some fine songs. Bernard Wagenaar migrated to the United States of America and has been active as violinist, composer, and conductor.

One unusual and very effective movement in Holland is DONEMUS, a cooperative music foundation, started in 1846, whose sole purpose is the propagation and preservation of Dutch music. The term comes from its motto: Documentatie in Nederland voor Muziek. In English: Documentation in Netherlands for Music.

Czechoslovakian songs are known mainly through notable composers Antonin Dvořák, Bedrik Smetana, and recently Leoš Janáček. There are of course other notable Czech composers, although at present securing their music is difficult, if not impossible.

Going back to the 18th century, famous composers include J. A. Planicky, Jan E. Zelenka, who was famous during the Baroque, František X. Brixi, and Leopold Koželuh. Their music was not without considerable outside influences, especially German and Russian.

Art song in Czechoslovakia became a little more established and developed in the later part of the 18th century and into the 19th with such names as Jakub Jan Ryba, Václav Tomašek, a prolific composer and perhaps the most important, and Josef Vorel. Bedřick Smetana emerged as one of the country's greatest composers, with instrumental composition as his main interest. Antonin Dvořák is internationally known, if not for his symphonies, for his "Biblical Songs." Other composers are Zdeněk Fibich, Rudolf Karel, Vitězslav Novák, and Josef B. Foerster.

To the above list may be included Vilem Petrželka, Jaroslav Kvapil, Jaroslav Křička, who composed operas and song cycles, Emil Axman, Karel B. Jirák, who wrote many song cycles, and Bohuslav Martinů. In addition, Moravian composers contributed in no small way toward the development of Czech vocal literature.

So well-known among musicians are the contributions of ancient Greece to art, literature, and music, that the artistic temperament of the country and its people is often taken for granted. With this background, Greece would have been at the head of musical developments to this day had the social and political health of the nation not been disturbed by outside conquest and internal turmoil.

Greek music only started to reawaken in the middle of the 19th

century due to the popularity of Italian opera. Among the composers of this
period were Kikolaos Manzaros, Spyridon Xyndas, and Spyros Samaras. The
songs of George Lambelet started a national movement in composition.
Others contributed to song literature: Manolis Kalomiris, Mario Varvoglis,
M. Theodorakis, Manos Hadjidakis, Georges Ponirides, and Nikos Skalkottas,
who was a pupil of Jarnach and Schoenberg.

Greek music is not as yet easily available, but it is hoped that the
few reviewed here will lend some encouragement to exploring contemporary
musical efforts of a land which first gave birth to organized music as we
know it today.

Hungary, like Czechoslovakia, is known mostly to the music world by
a few names. The country has the figures of Franz Liszt, Zoltán Kodály,
and Béla Bartók. Of the three, Liszt is the most international not only in
his music and the texts of his songs, but also in his life-style. He is often
classified as a German composer, which is not unreasonable since most of
his life and work were spent in Germany and in association with German
arts. Bartók and Kodály may be considered thoroughly Hungarian because in
their entire careers there was no relaxing from their Hungarian background,
heritage, and interest in developing the country's music. Their work on the
collection, preservation, and use of Hungarian folk songs, a monumental
study recognized internationally, is perhaps the life-blood of the ideas in
their work and their being.

Bartók died in New York City on September 26, 1945, in complete
poverty, ill health, and most shameful neglect by his musical associates,
publishers, and institutions that personally knew him and recognized his genius. The sudden loss is rendered even more tragic by Bartók's deathbed
words: "The trouble is that I have to go with so much still to say." Kodály
carried his Hungarian background and respect for the folk songs of his country over into his musical teaching, for which he also became famous.

Looking further back in the centuries, in the late Middle Ages min-
strels supplied the music at the courts as well as at informal gatherings.
Traveling singers with the kobuz, a type of lute, in the 16th century sang
not only the short folk songs but also epics of some length based on Biblical
or historical subjects. One of the best-known of these singers was Sebastian
Tinódi.

Choral music and solo songs were used to a greater extent in the 17th
century with the growing popularity of the harpsichord. Secular songs were
given more emphasis, and in the 18th century new innovations in Hungarian
folk songs and dances appeared. Nationalistic operas such as those by Ferenc
Erkel started to appear in the 19th century.

Among those who wrote songs and operas were Jenő Hubay, Ernő
Dohnányi, and László Lajtha. These three men wrote only a few songs, but
like Bartók and Kodály used features of the folk song in their works. Among
the younger composers who followed those just mentioned are: Pál Járdányi,
Pál Kadosa, Ferenc Szabó, and György Ranki.

The Bible gives many accounts of ancient Jewish music: musical instruments, cantillation, dances, and rituals. Although most of the original
songs have not been preserved, we have an idea of how they were used
through what was handed down of sacred chants, some of which were adopted
and modified by the Christian church.

There is a great wealth of music in the Jewish culture, and this has been internationalized through the migrations of Jews to many lands. The Petrograd Jewish Folk-Song Society, for example, has gathered about 3,000 folk songs of different types.

Much of the more original and mature composing is done mainly for synagogue services. A Jewish national movement in music, started around 1915, received greater backing and emphasis after World War II and the establishment of the state of Israel.

Among the great and lesser composers of music today are several Jews who migrated to other lands. To make a complete listing of Jewish song writers and composers of Jewish extraction would involve most chapters of this work. Therefore, the small list here is confined to those closely associated with or living in the motherland.

Among the great song and opera composers with Jewish background are the following: Giacomo Meyerbeer, Jacques Helévy, Felix Mendelssohn, Jacques Offenbach, Gustav Mahler, Arnold Schoenberg, Ernest Bloch, Darius Milhaud, George Gershwin, and Aaron Copland.

The music of Japan is not as old as that of China, but it can claim precedence in antiquity to that of any European nation. Interest in Japanese music by westerners became more pronounced after World War II, especially with the increased activities in ethnomusicology in American universities.

The vocal music reviewed in this work may be representative of the overall production of modern Japanese composers. Most of it is in the modern idiom with western aspects thrown in. Many of the major Japanese composers are western-trained, having studied with famous teachers in Europe. Among the best-known Japanese composers are Ikuma Dan, Mareo Ishiketa, Koichi Kishi, Saburo Takata, Sadao Bekku, and Yoshinao Nakada.

The Japanese have shown great interest in western music. In many compositions of recent years there are western elements as well as elements of Japanese folk music. They have also learned some of the Russian approach to the treatment of folk songs through the use of pentatonic scales. Widespread performing of western music has increased in the country and instead of the one pre-war symphony, Japan now has several, in addition to increased music activity in its schools.

Philippine music, for the greater part of the population, is not what it ought to be. The Spanish-type popular ballad is the type heard almost exclusively. Eighteenth- and 19th century Spanish life-style was emulated, copied, and practiced. The arts followed the path of the fiesta-loving and frivolous life aristocratic Spaniards seemed to love in the Philippine setting. Any indigenous characteristics in the music were completely replaced. Sentimental Spanish-type popular ballads emerged in the form of the kundiman of Tagalog-speaking sections and the balitaw of Visayan areas.

Right after World War II, interest in the collection, preservation, and use of Philippine indigenous arts slowly emerged. As in Japan, this happened through ethnomusicological research. In spite of increased collecting of Philippine traditional music, there is still very little result in the use of basic Philippine elements in the art song. The two song cycles reviewed here represent rare exceptions. The first, "Songs of the Pagan," is an example of the non-western type; the second, "Seashore," is a balanced wedding of

Philippine and western musical styles. It is hoped that more of this type
of writing will help add interest and refreshing vitality to recital programs.

Early-known secular Polish songs are folk songs, as in most cultures.
Church music dominated much of the earliest formal vocal song making and
performing. In the 17th and 18th centuries, composers for the voice
emerged. Among them were Mikolaj Zieleński, Marcin Mielczewski, Stanislaw Szarzyński (a monk), and Damian (a monk, full name unknown). Most
of their work was centered on solos for use in church.

During the last part of the 18th century the operas and songs of
Maciej Kamieński, Jan Stefani, Józef Elsner, and French works were quite
popular. Józef Nowakowski emerged as an important song composer during
the first part of the 19th century. Frederic Chopin wrote only 19 songs, all
of which are considered among the best examples of Polish art songs.
Other names at this time are those of Stanislaw Moniuszko, Wladyslaw Zeleń-
ski, Zygmunt Noskowski, Stanislaw Niewiadomski, and Eugeniusz Pankiewicz.
Much of what was produced during the 19th century belongs to the sentimental and melancholy type of song, in keeping with the mood of the Polish people at that time.

The 20th century brought to Poland some important composers who
attained international reputation. The following wrote some very fine songs
for the solo voice: Karol Szymanowski, Mieczyslaw Karlowicz, Feliks Nowo-
wiejski, Ludomi Rózycki, Józef Szulc, Tadeusz Szeligowski, Andrzej Panufnik,
Witold Lutoslawski, and Kazimierz Serocki. The name of Lady Dean Paul,
who used Poldowski as a pseudonym, must not be forgotten for she produced
fine songs to French and English texts that made her quite popular with recitalists.

Many songs by Polish composers are in the German Lied and French
art song tradition. German and other foreign poets have been the sources of
song texts. It is not yet easy, however, to secure Polish music, because of
the absence of favorable cultural exchange between Poland and nations outside
of the communist bloc. However, a limited number of songs and cycles may
be obtained from dealers in the United States and Great Britain.

Switzerland, a very small country bounded by large powers and influ-
ential cultures, has developed some vocal literature of its own, but under-
standably it is influenced by her neighbors. Its composers wrote mostly to
German and French texts.

One of the best-known musicians in Europe in the 16th century was
Ludwig Senfl who wrote a good number of solo songs with accompaniment.
In the 17th and 18th centuries other song composers entered the limelight.
They were Johann Ludwig Steiner, Johann Caspar Bachofen, Johannes Schmid-
lin, Franz J. L. Meyer von Schauensee, Johann Heinrich Egli, and Johann
Jakob Walder.

In the 19th century the names of Hans Georg Nägeli, Louis Nieder-
meyer, Karl Attenhofer, Wilhelm Baumgartner, and Thomas Fröhlich were
prominent. Pierre Maurice, Rudolf Ganz (who later lived in the United
States), and Gustave Ferrari are counted among the early 20th century Swiss
composers.

Othmar Schoeck has become one of the most important Swiss composers of the 20th century.   He gave a great amount of attention to song writing, and his solo works are available through Universal Edition.   Frank Martin, another significant composer, did not write many songs, but the few credited to him are among the best contemporary works for the voice.   Other names may also be mentioned: Willi Burkhard, Albert Moeschinger, Conrad Beck, and Heinrich Sutermeister.   One should also mention the name of Ernest Bloch, who became an American citizen, and of Arthur Honegger, whose parentage is Swiss.

A. BELGIUM

FRANCIS DE BOURGUIGNON, 1890-1961

6885. Mandoline   Soprano
Poet: Paul Verlaine. f3-b4(d5) a3-g4 Animated in moderate slow
tempo. Starts with "la, la, la" section after an extended prelude.
Generally light. Best for coloratura or high lyric soprano. Showy
piece. See the settings by Fauré, Debussy, Dupont, Szulc, and
"Fêtes galantes" by Hahn. Poldowsky also wrote a setting. Acc: 4
(S)CeBeDeM-Centre Belge de Documentation Musicale

GUILLAUME LEKEU, 1870-1894

6886. Sur une tombe   Men
Poet: Anon. d3-g4 f3-d4 Sustained in slow tempo. Has some in-
tense, climactic passages. Subdued, slower ending. Has passages
in quasi-recitative style. Acc: 3 AMF (Ch. V-B)

FLOR PEETERS

6887. Ivory Tower. Op. 47. Six sacred songs (6 Marienlieder) to poems
by Albe (Flemish poet). English version by Hugh Ross. High voices
and piano. All songs are short. The vocal line does not offer any
technical or vocal difficulties. Mostly sustained, with an overall
range of eb3-a4. Frankfurt & New York: C. F. Peters. Titles:
   (1) Ivory tower   (4) Hidden wonder
   (2) The elected   (5) Bride and mother
   (3) The blessed   (6) Maria

Note: See the author's Vocal Solos for Protestant Services for other sacred
songs by Flor Peeters.

B. CANADA

OLIVE ATKEY

6888. Young shepherd's song   Tenor or Baritone
Poet: Olive Atkey. c3-f4 f3-c4 Animated in rapid tempo. Re-
quires rapid and fluent enunciation. Joyous. A light novelty-style
song. Fine as teaching and performing material for young voices.
Acc: 3-4 (S)BI

JOHN BECKWITH

Five Lyrics of the T'ang Dynasty. A set for high voice and piano. Chinese
poems translated by Witter Bynner. (SC)BI

6889.   (1) The staircase of jade   High Voices
        Poet: Li Po, 699-762. e3-a4 a3-d# 4 Sustained vocal part in fast
        tempo. Requires lightness. High tessitura. Climactic high ending
        with long-held final note. Constantly pulsating accompaniment, all
        on treble range. Acc: 3-4

6890.   (2) The limpid river   High Voices
        Poet: Wang Wei, 699-759. e3-g# 4 g3-e4 Sustained in moderate
        tempo. Generally subdued and unhurried. Generally high tessitura.
        Requires fine P. Very subdued ending. Transparent accompaniment.
        Acc: 3

6891.   (3) The inlaid harp   High Voices
        Poet: Li Shang-Yin, 813-858.   d3-gb 4   g3-eb 4 Sustained in moder-
        ate slow tempo. Starts and ends gently. Has some dramatic high
        climaxes. Middle section has plucked-strings effect. Descriptive
        texts. Acc: 3-4

6892.   (4) On a rainy night   High Voices
        Poet: Li Shang-Yin, 813-858.   d3-g4 g3-d4 Sustained in slow tem-
        po. Generally on MF level. Generally gentle. Text has suggestions
        of nostalgia. Acc: 3

6893.   (5) Parting at a wine-shop   High Voices
        Poet: Li Po, 699-762. e3-g4 g3-e4 Sustained vocal part in mod-
        erately fast tempo. Requires some fluent enunciation. Has some
        climactic passages and a climactic high ending. Agitated and unsus-
        tained accompaniment. Acc: 4

GENA BRANSCOMBE

6894.   Old woman rain   All Voices
        Poet: Louise Driscoll. e# 3-g# 4 g# 3-c# 4 Sustained in moderate
        slow tempo. Has slower middle section. Generally on MF level.
        Has some climactic passages. Agitated accompaniment. Descriptive
        text. Acc: 4 CON

JEAN COULTHARD

6895.   Ecstasy   Medium Voices
        Poet: Duncan Campbell Scott.   c# 3-f# 4   f# 3-d# 4 Animated in lively
        tempo. Brilliant and exultant. Has climactic passages and a climac-
        tic high ending. A climactic song--effective as ending piece in a re-
        cital group. Very agitated, sonorous and difficult accompaniment.
        See the setting by Walter Rummel. Acc: 4-5 (S)BI

MAURICE DELA

6896.   La lettre   High Voices
        Poet: Henri Barbusse. db 3-a4 f3-db 4 Sustained in slow tempo.
        Tranquil, generally on MF level. Requires fine P and PP. Starts
        very gently. Very subdued ending. In romantic style, with impres-
        sionistic touches. Acc: 3-4 (S)BI

6897.   Ronde   High Voices

Poet: Victor Hugo. d3-g4 g3-d4 Animated in moderate lively tempo. Generally on MF level. Requires some fluent enunciation. Incisive rhythm. 6 verses. Acc: 3-4 (S)BI

6898. Spleen   Medium Voices
Poet: Paul Verlaine. e3-f♯4 f♯3-d4 Sustained in moderate tempo. Starts gently. Generally on MF level. Subdued ending. Agitated accompaniment in the middle section. In romantic style, with impressionistic touches. French text. See the setting by Claude Debussy. Acc: 3-4 (S)BI

MARVIN DUCHOW

6899. For a rose's sake   Medium Voices
Poet: Anon. Medieval French ballad, translation by Andrew Lang. c♯3-e4 e3-d4 Animated in moderate lively tempo. Has one climactic section. The vocal part requires movement, but with grace. Low ending. Acc: 3 (S)BI

WILLIAM FRANCE

6900. Drop, drop, slow tears   Medium Voices
Poet: Phineas Fletcher, 1582-1650. c3-e♭4 g3-c4 Sustained in slow tempo. Generally on MF level. Has one short climactic passage and some frequent meter changes. Long-held high ending. Quasi-sacred text by a medieval poet. Acc: 3 (S)BI

PATRICIA BLOMFIELD HOLT

6901. Solitaire   High Voices
Poet: Amy Lowell. f3-a4 g3-f4 Third and final song in "Three Songs of Contemplation." Sustained in moderate slow tempo. Generally tranquil. Has some climactic passages. Subdued ending. Fine for high, light voices. Acc: 4 (SC)BL

GEORGE HURST

6902. Alone at the door   High Voices
Poet: Wei Chung, translation by Teresa Li. b2-g4 a♭3-e4 Sustained in slow tempo. Subdued throughout. Requires fine P and PP. Has passages in gentle declamatory style. Very subdued ending. First in the set: "Two Chinese Love Songs," available separately. Acc: 3-4 (S)BI

6903. Among the bamboos   High Voices
Poet: Tu Fu, translation by Gertrude L. Joerissen. c3-a♭4 a3-f4 Sustained in slow tempo. Requires fine P and PP. Has climactic passages. Very subdued ending line, marked from PP to PPPP. Second in the set: "Two Chinese Love Songs," available separately. Acc: 3 (S)BI

6904. Music when soft voices die   High Voices
Poet: Percy Bysshe Shelley. f♯3-a4 a3-e4 Sustained in moderate slow tempo. Starts gently. Has one dramatic high passage. Very

subdued ending section with a high ending.   See the settings by Henry
Ley and Udo Kasemets.   Acc: 3   (S)BI

RICHARD JOHNSTON

6905. Bruce County ballad   Medium Voices
Poet: Mentie Du Val.   c3-e4   e3-d4   Slightly animated in moderate
tempo.   Generally on MF level.   Subdued, low ending.   In the style
of a folk song.   Acc: 3   (S)BI

UDO KASEMETS

Three Miniatures.   Poems by Percy Bysshe Shelley.   High voice and piano.
    (SC)BI

6906. (1) To the moon   High Voices
d3-f4   g3-d4   Sustained in moderate slow tempo.   Starts very subduedly.   Generally subdued.   Acc: 3

6907. (2) A widow bird sate mourning   High Voices
c#3-gb4   g3-d#4   Sustained vocal part in moderate lively tempo.
Graceful, generally on MF level.   Has one climactic high passage.
Acc: 3-4

6908. (3) Music, when soft voices die   High Voices
f3-f#4   f#3-d4   Sustained in slow tempo.   Somewhat grave.   Generally subdued.   Requires fine P and PP.   Very subdued, low ending.
See the settings by George Hurst and Henry Ley.   Acc: 3

WALTER MacNUTT

Two Songs of William Blake.   From the poet's Songs of Innocence.   High
    voice and piano.   (SC)BI

6909. (1) The lamb   High Voices
d3-f4   f3-d4   Sustained in moderate slow tempo.   Requires simplicity.
Generally on MF level.   Very subdued ending.   See the settings by
Ernest Bacon and Theodore Chanler.   Acc: 3

6910. (2) Spring   High Voices
e3-g4   g3-e4   Animated in lively tempo.   Requires fluent enunciation.
Starts and ends strongly.   Climactic final note.   Joyful and bright.
Acc: 3-4

WELFORD RUSSELL

6911. Blow, blow, thou winter wind   High, Medium Voices
Poet: William Shakespeare, from his As You Like It.   c3-f4   f3-d4
Has sustained and slow sections contrasting with animated and lively
sections.   Has climactic high passages.   Climactic high ending.   See
the settings by Thomas Arne and Roger Quilter.   Acc: 3-4   (S)BI

6912. Come away, come away death   Tenor
Poet: William Shakespeare, from his Twelfth Night.   d#3-f#4   e3-e4

Sustained in moderate tempo. Generally on MF level. Has some
slightly climactic passages. Requires simplicity. See the settings
by Gerald Finzi, Roger Quilter, John Koch, Mario Castelnuovo-
Tedesco, and Jean Sibelius. Acc: 3 (S)BI

6913. Have you seen but a bright lily grow?   High Voices
Poet: Ben Jonson. c3-g4 g3-eb4 Sustained in moderate tempo.
Generally light and on MF level. Subdued ending. Fine for light
voices. See the settings by Anonymous English Composer and Robert
Johnson. Acc: 3 (S)BI

6914. I gave her cakes, and I gave her ale   Tenor
Poet: Anon. d3-g4 d3-f4 Animated in fast tempo. Requires rapid
enunciation. Bright, joyful, and outgoing. Has climactic passages.
Strong last phrase with a falling ending. Acc: 3-4 (S)BI

6915. My true love hath my heart   Soprano
Poet: Philip Sidney, 1554-1586. f3-f4 f3-d4 Sustained in moderate
tempo. Has frequent meter changes. Generally on MF level. Subdued ending. See the setting by John Ireland. Acc: 3 (S)BI

SOEUR SAINT-JEAN-DU-SACRÉ-COEUR, C. N. D.

6916. Lorsque je mourrai   Medium Voices
Poet: Rina Lasnier. f3-e4 g3-d4 Sustained in slow tempo. Generally on MF level. Generally gentle. Impressionistic style. Acc:
3 (S)BI

HARRY SOMERS

6917. A bunch of rowan   Medium, Low Voices
Poet: Diana Skala. a2-c4 d3-b3 Sustained in slow tempo. Gentle
and subdued beginning and ending sections. Strong middle section.
In impressionistic style. Acc: 3-4 (S)BI

ALAN THOMPSON

6918. Night   Medium Voices
Poet: H. T. J. Coleman. db3-eb4 db3-db4 Very sustained in
slow tempo. Gentle and subdued throughout. Arpeggiated accompaniment. In romantic style. Acc: 3 (S)BI

6919. Reverie of a soldier   Tenor or Baritone
Poet: Mentie Du Val. db3-f4 f3-db4 Sustained in slow tempo.
Requires fine P and PP. Has some climactic passages. Very subdued low ending. In romantic, pseudo-impressionistic style. Acc:
3-4 (S)BI

6920. The oxen   High Voices
Poet: Thomas Hardy. d3-g4 e3-e4 Generally sustained in varied
tempi. Starts in quasi-parlando style, and subdued. Has climactic
high passages. Climactic high ending. A song for high voice rather
than the indicated medium voice. In romantic style. Acc: 3-4
(S)BI

6921. Where he sleeps   Soprano
       Poet: Mentie Du Val.   e3-g4 g3-eb4 Sustained in moderate tempo.
       Marked "simply and tenderly." Has climactic high passages. Sub-
       dued and slow ending. In romantic style. Acc: 3-4 (S)BI

C. CZECHOSLOVAKIA

ANTONÍN DVOŘÁK, 1841-1904

Dvořák's best-known songs are his set of ten Biblical Songs, very popular
now in Great Britain and the United States. They are also the most useful
for they are frequently featured in church services and on the recital stage.
Although the English version of the edition published by Simrock does not follow the notation of the original Czech texts closely, it is still the best in
prosody for singing. For this reason, it is the edition reviewed for this
work. The Simrock English version was approved by Dvořák himself.

Dvořák's songs are most German in style, and are all very finely written for
the voice. Like Brahms, Dvořák used characteristics of folk music, and for
this reason, his songs offer no serious vocal and musical difficulties. He
uses some subtle shadings and illustrative figures to interpret textual meanings. The emotional range of his songs stays mostly on the moderate plane
and is never exaggerated. His use of dramatic styles is always just right
for the needs of the text. Gypsy Songs is a very fine cycle. Its fourth
piece is the ever well-known "Songs my mother taught me."

FFS   Four Favorite Songs. Selected from the Biblical Songs. High, low.
       New York: R. D. Row Music Co.

FSD   Vier Lieder. Four Songs. Op. 82. Antonín Dvořák. Original Ger-
       man text by O. Malybrok-Stieler. Czech version by N. J. Novotný.
       Unidentified English version. Prague: Artia. (Note: This collection
       is considered by some as the composer's best writing.)

I. Secular Works

Gypsy Songs. A cycle of seven songs, Op. 55. Antonín Dvořák. Texts by
       Adolf Heyduk. High, low. German texts; English version by Humph-
       rey Procter-Gregg. For all voices. Edition reviewed: International
       Music Co.

6922. (1) My song of love   All Voices
       d3-g4 a3-f4 Sustained in moderate tempo. Generally strong and
       energetic. Has some climactic passages and a climactic ending. Re-
       quires very fine high P and PP. Slightly extended piano prelude and
       postlude. Generally agitated accompaniment. Acc: 3-4

6923. (2) Ei! Triangle be chiming   All Voices
       g3-a4 g3-f4 Animated in lively tempo. Strong and energetic. Re-
       quires fine high P. Agitated accompaniment. Acc: 4

6924. (3) Here in the wood   All Voices
       d3-g4 f#3-eb4 Sustained in moderate tempo. Generally subdued,

requires fine P and PP. Very subdued high ending. Acc: 3

6925. (4) Songs as mother sang them   All Voices
f♯1-g4 a3-g4 Sustained in moderate slow tempo. Generally subdued. The vocal part moves in 2/4 while the accompaniment is
played in 6/8. Best for soprano. Descending ending. There are
many editions of this song, mostly under the title: Songs my mother
taught me. Acc: 4 (S)GS-English & German. 56S, 50M

6926. (5) Set the fiddles scraping   All Voices
a3-a4 a3-f4 Animated in moderate lively tempo. Has faster sections. Generally strong. Climactic ending. Agitated accomapniment.
Acc: 4

6927. (6) Flowing sleeve and trouser   All Voices
e3-g4 a3-e4 Animated in lively tempo. Strong, climactic, and accented. Rhythmic, agitated accompaniment. Acc: 4

6928. (7) The cliffs of Tatra   All Voices
f3-g4(bb4) g3-f4 Animated in lively tempo. Strong, climactic.
Dramatic high ending. Very strong piano prelude. Agitated accompaniment. Acc: 4-5

Love Songs. Op. 83. Czech title: Pisňe milostné, 1888. A set of eight
songs, not a cycle. Texts in Czech, with German and English versions. High voice and piano. May be performed separately. Poems
by Gustav Pfleger-Moravský. Hamburg: N. Simrock.

6929. (1) Never will love lead us   High Voices
c♯3-a4 a3-e4 Sustained in moderate slow tempo. Has some climactic passages. Climactic ending. Agitated accompaniment. Acc:
3-4

6930. (2) Death reigns in many a human breast   High Voices
c♯3-g4 g3-e4 Sustained in moderate tempo. Requires fine P and
PP. Has two climactic passages. Subdued ending note. Acc: 3-4

6931. (3) I wander oft past yonder house   High Voices
e3-g4 e3-e4 Animated in moderate lively tempo. Has climactic
high passages. Climactic ending. Acc: 3

6932. (4) I know, that on my love   High Voices
db3-gb4 f3-db4 Sustained in moderate tempo. Starts gently. Has
climactic passages. Climactic ending. Acc: 3-4

6933. (5) Nature lies peaceful in slumber   High Voices
eb3-ab4 f3-eb4 Animated in moderate lively tempo. Graceful.
Requires fine P and PP. Climactic ending. Gently agitated accompaniment. Acc: 3-4

6934. (6) In deepest forest glade I stand   High Voices
b2-g4 f♯3-d♯4 Sustained in moderate slow tempo. Has dramatic
high passages. Very subdued, "falling" ending. Not for light, high
voices. Generally agitated accompaniment. Acc: 3-4

6935. (7) When thy sweet glances on me fall   High Voices
d3-g4 g3-d4 Sustained in moderate slow tempo. Has climactic high
passages. Requires fine P to PPP. Very subdued low ending. Acc: 3-4

6936. (8) Thou only dear one   High Voices
       e3-f♯4   e3-e4 Sustained in moderate slow tempo. Starts gently.
       Has climactic passages. Subdued ending. Arpeggiated accompani-
       ment, requiring considerable control. Acc: 3-4

Single Songs and an Excerpt

6937. Am Bache   Medium, Low Voices
       Poet: Ottilie Malybrok-Stieler. First line: Leise rinnt der Bach
       und klaget. English title: At the brook. a2-d♭4 d3-b♭3 Animated
       in quite rapid tempo. Has contrasts of gentle and strong passages.
       Climactic ending. Agitated accompaniment reminds one of Schubert's
       "Wohin." Acc: 4 FSD

6938. Die Stickerin   Baritone, Bass
       Poet: Ottilie Malybrok-Stieler. English title: Over her embroidery.
       b2-e4 f♯3-d4 Sustained in slow tempo. Has climactic passages.
       Requires fine P and PP. Descending, subdued ending line. Agitated
       accompaniment. Acc: 3-4 FSD

6939. Frühling   Medium, Low Voices
       Poet: Ottilie Malybrok-Stieler. English title: Spring-tide. a♭2-e♭4
       e♭3-c4 Sustained in moderate tempo. Has contrasting strong and
       gentle passages. Tranquil ending section. Descending ending line in
       more than 1-1/2 octaves. Agitated accompaniment. Acc: 3-4 FSD

6940. Give ear, ye people!   Bass
       Work: ST. LUDMILLA, an oratorio, 1886, libretto by Jaroslav
       Vrchlický. g1-f♭3 e♭2-d♭3 Sustained in moderate slow tempo.
       Dramatic and vigorous. Subdued ending after high, dramatic climax.
       Full-sounding, sometimes agitated accompaniment. Acc: 4 ASS-B

6941. Lasst mich allein   Medium, Low Voices
       Poet: Ottilie Malybrok-Stieler. English title: Leave me alone.
       a♯2-d♯4 c♯3-c♯4 Sustained in moderate slow tempo. Has a few
       short climactic passages. Requires fine P to PPP. Very subdued
       low ending. Agitated accompaniment. Considered Dvořák's most
       beautiful song. Highly recommended. Acc: 4 FSD

6942. The lark   Women
       Poet: Wenceslaus Hanka. e3-f4 g♯3-e4 Gently animated in moder-
       ate lively tempo. Generally light. Has some climactic passages.
       Gently agitated accompaniment. English version: Willis Wager. Not
       recommended for contralto. Acc: 4 50A

II. Sacred Works

Biblical Songs. Op. 99. Antonín Dvořák. A set of ten songs with texts
       from the Book of Psalms. Considered the best sacred solo composi-
       tions of Dvořák. Texts in Czech, with German and English versions.
       High, low. Hamburg: N. Simrock--published in two books. Other
       editions: International Music Co.

6943. (1) Clouds and darkness   All Voices
       Text: Psalm 97:2-6. d♯3-f♯4 g♯3-d♯4 Sustained in generally mod-
       erate slow tempo. Dramatic and declamatory. Has some agitated
       accompaniment. Subdued ending. Acc: 3-4

6944.   (2) Lord, thou art my refuge   All Voices
        Text: Psalm 119:114, 115, 117, 120.   a3-e4   g♯3-e4   Sustained in
        moderate slow tempo. Has some slightly climactic passages.   Sub-
        dued ending. Acc: 3-4

6945.   (3) Hear my prayer, O Lord   All Voices
        Text: Psalm 55:1-8.   e♭3-a4   g3-e♭4   Sustained in generally slow
        tempo. Has some dramatic passages.   Strong ending in descending
        line. Acc: 3-4

6946.   (4) God is my shepherd   All Voices
        Text: Psalm 23.   e3-f♯4   f♯3-e4   Very sustained in moderate slow
        tempo. Subdued, gentle, requires fine P and PP. Descending end-
        ing line. Acc: 3 FFS

6947.   (5) I will sing new songs of gladness   All Voices
        Text: Psalm 144:9; 145:1-6.   g3-g4   g3-e4   Animated in moderate
        tempo.   Majestic, with some dramatic climaxes.   Has impressive and
        climactic ending. Bright, exultant song of praise.   Acc: 3-4   FFS

6948.   (6) Hear my prayer, O Lord   All Voices
        Text: Psalm 61:1, 3-4; 63:1, 4.   e3-g4   g3-e4   Sustained in moder-
        ate slow tempo. Starts very gently. Has some climactic passages.
        Requires fine PP and PPP. Descending ending line. Acc: 3

6949.   (7) By the waters of Babylon   All Voices
        Text: Psalm 137:1-5.   d3-g4   g3-e4   Sustained in moderate slow
        tempo. Starts gently. Has some slightly dramatic passages and agi-
        tated accompaniment. Subdued ending. Acc: 4 FFS

6950.   (8) Turn Thee to me and have mercy   All Voices
        Text: Psalm 25:16-18, 20.   f3-f4   g3-c4   Sustained in moderate slow
        tempo. Has some dramatic passages. Grave and intense. Subdued
        ending phrase. Acc: 3

6951.   (9) I will lift mine eyes   All Voices
        Text: Psalm 121:1-4.   f♯3-g4   a3-e4   Sustained in moderate tempo.
        Declamatory, generally subdued. Requires fine P and PP. Gentle.
        Acc: 3 FFS

6952.   (10) Sing ye a joyful song   All Voices
        Text: Psalm 98:1, 7-8; 96:12.   f3-g4   b♭3-f4   Animated in moderate
        lively tempo. Joyous and bright. Has some dramatic passages. Cli-
        mactic and strong ending. Agitated accompaniment abounds in triplet
        figures. Acc: 4

Sacred Excerpt

6953.   Inflammatus et accensus   Contralto
        Work: STABAT MATER, choral work, Latin text.   a2-e4   c3-d4
        Sustained in moderate slow tempo. Majestic, has climactic passages.
        Requires some flexibility. Subdued ending. English version: James
        A. Jenkins. Acc: 3 (VS)OD

LEOŠ JANÁČEK, 1854-1928

6954.   The Diary of One Who Vanished. Czech title: Zápisník zmizelého.

A cycle of 22 movements for tenor (18 songs), contralto, three female voices, and piano. One movement is for piano alone. English
translations by Bernard Keeffe. Poems by an anonymous author.
Prague: Artia. Note: Most of the songs are short. This famous
cycle is Janáček's most important and significant work.

BOLESLAV VOMACKA

<u>1914.</u> Op. 11. Boleslav Vomacka. A cycle of five movements for high
and orchestra; piano reduction is available. Texts by Rudolfa Medka,
Frani Šramka, Stanislava Hanusě, Otakara Lheera. Czech texts,
with French and German (reviewed here) versions. Prague: Hudebni
Matice Umělecké Besedy, c/o J. & W. Chester, London, and Max
Eschig, Paris. Note: All songs are interpretatively difficult. A
beautiful cycle.

6955. (1) 1914   High Voices
First Czech line: V krvavé vřavě dusi se svět. First German line:
Blutiges Grauen liegt auf der Welt. g♭2-b♭4 b♭3-g♭4 Sustained in
slow tempo. Majestic. Starts gently on high tessitura. Has dramatic high passages, and a dramatic high ending. Intense. Not for
light voices. Acc: 3-4

6956. (2) Der Soldat im Felde   High Voices
First Czech line: Voják v poli. c3-b♭4 f3-f4 Sustained in varied
tempi. Starts in moderate tempo. Requires fine P and PP. Has
climactic high passages. Very subdued, high ending marked PP.
Agitated accompaniment. Acc: 4

6957. (3) Der Verwundete   High Voices
First Czech line: Raněnij. f3-a♭4 a♭3-g♭4 Sustained in slow tempo. Generally subdued, requires fine P and PP. Sad texts. Very
subdued ending line. Acc: 3

6958. (4) Gevatter Tod   High Voices
First Czech line: Kmotra smrt. b2-c♭5 f3-e♭4 Sustained in moderate slow tempo. Requires very fine P and PP. The c♭5 is a
staccato note marked PP. Requires flexibility. Intense. Subdued
ending. Acc: 3-4

6959. (5) Den Toten   High Voices
First Czech line: Za mrtvými. e♭3-a♭4 a♭3-f4 Sustained in mod-
erate slow tempo. Subdued throughout. Requires very fine P and
PP. Gentle. Very subdued and contemplative ending. Acc: 3

Note on Other Czech Composers

The following three composers wrote in the pseudo-German style, with
infusion of Czech folk idioms. Accompaniments are in the style of
Beethoven or Mozart tradition.
    Jan Ladislav Dusík, 1760-1812
    Josef Rösler, 1773-1813
    Jan Václav Hugo Voříšeks, 1791-1825
These composers used poems with German and Italian texts: Hölty,
Goethe, and Muchler. This author has examined two collections, but
because copies are presently not conveniently available, none of the
music is reviewed here.

D. GREECE

GLA   Griechische Lieder. Edited by Fivos Anoyanakis. Twenty-seven
       Greek art songs.   Greek texts, with German and French translations.
       Vienna: Universal Edition. (Entries are listed here in the German
       version.)

A. EVANGELATOS

6960. Wiegenlied   High Voices
       Poet: Aeotikho. f3-g4 g3-d4 Sustained in moderate slow tempo.
       Very subdued and gentle. Requires simplicity. Has some sudden
       changes of meter. Acc: 3 GLA

MANOLIS KALOMIRIS, 1883-1962

6961. Der tempel   Medium Voices
       Poet: K. Palames. b♭2-f4 f3-e♭4 Sustained in slow tempo. Mod-
       erately grave. Requires fine PP. Chordal accompaniment through-
       out. Acc: 3 GLA

THEODORE KARYOTAKIS

6962. Anastasia   Men
       Poet: S. Skhipes. g3-a♭4 g3-d4 Sustained in moderate slow tem-
       po. Generally in recitative style. Generally strong and has some
       intensity. Acc: 3 GLA

G. B. KASASSOGLU

6963. O Erde!   High Voices
       Poet: S. Morkhes. c3-g4 g3-e♭4 Sustained in moderate slow tem-
       po. Requires fine P and PP. Ends with subdued cadenza. Extended
       piano prelude. Acc: 3-4 GLA

GEORGE LAMBELET, 1875-1945

6964. Die Blumenbekränzte   High Voices
       Poet: M. Malakhasi. f3-a4 g3-g4 Gently animated in slow tempo.
       Has florid, vocalized "ah" passage. Requires flexibility. Subdued
       high ending on g4. Generally agitated accompaniment. Acc: 3-4
       GLA

ANDREAS NEZERITIS

6965. Der König und die Schone Maid   High Voices
       Poet: Aeotikho. b♭2-g4 e3-e4 Generally animated in varied tem-
       po. Dramatic, best for the heavier voices. Interpretatively not
       easy. Dramatic high ending. Full-sounding accompaniment. Acc:
       3-4 GLA

MENELAOS PALLANTIOS

6966. Zigeuner   High Voices
       Poet: Theokharis. g3-bb4 a3-a4 Animated in lively tempo.
       Rhythmic and dancelike. Has florid figures vocalized on "ah." Cli-
       mactic high ending on a4. Best for coloratura soprano or high lyric
       soprano. Acc: 3-4 GLA

GEORGE PONIRIDIS

6967. Notre dame von Sparta   All Voices
       Poet: Sikhelianas. f3-f4 g3-d4 Generally sustained in slow tempo.
       In recitative style throughout. Climactic ending. Acc: 3 GLA

EMIL RIADES, 1890-1935

6968. Ging ein Mädchen zu der Quelle   High Voices
       Poet: Emil Riadis. d3-ab4 a3-f4 Animated in moderate lively
       tempo. Has quasi-recitative passages. Climactic ending. Best for
       high, light voices. Acc: 3 GLA

St. VALTETZIOTIS

6969. Lingos   Men
       Poet: Aemotikho. a3-f#4 a3-e4 Generally animated in varied tem-
       pi. Starts in quite lively movement. Requires some flexibility. Cli-
       mactic ending. Acc: 3 GLA

MARIO VARVOGLIS

6970. Euricome   High Voices
       Poet: A. Solomas. e3-g4 ab3-f4 Sustained vocal part in moderate
       lively tempo. Has dramatic climaxes and a climactic ending. Slower
       ending section. Agitated, rather intense accompaniment. Acc: 4
       GLA

LEONIDAS ZORAS

6971. Die Schalmei   All Voices
       Poet: Anon. db3-e4 g3-c4 Sustained in slow tempo. Generally
       subdued, gentle, and pastoral with interludes for a "flute" melody.
       Acc: 3 GLA

                          E. HUNGARY

BELÁ BARTÓK, 1881-1945

Bartók's art songs grew out of his interest in Hungarian folk songs. His
first compositions are in the style of the peasant music which he loved. All

of his songs are very well written for the voice. Unfortunately only a few
are available in editions with suitable English translations. Bartók's use of
dissonances is done with economy and always tastefully rendered. His original compositions have been greatly overshadowed in popularity by his folksong arrangements and the results of his researches on Hungarian music.

DJB   Der Junge Bartók. Edited by D. Dille. Hungarian texts, with Ger-
      man versions. Vienna: B. Schott's Söhne.

FLB   Fünf Lieder. Bela Bartók. Anonymous texts, possibly by the com-
      poser. German version by Endre Ady. Hungarian texts, with Ger-
      man version. Vienna: Universal Edition.

FSB   Five Songs. Op. 16. Belá Bartók. English and German versions.
      London: Boosey & Hawkes.

6972. Abend   Medium Voices
       Poet: Harsányi Kálmán. German version: Imre Ormay. bb 2-f4
       eb 3-eb 4 Sustained in slow tempo. Has one climactic passage. Acc:
       5 DJB

6973. Diese Rose pflück ich hier   High Voices
       Poet: Friedrich Rückert. bb 2-bb 4 eb 3-f4 Sustained in moderate
       tempo. Requires simplicity. Acc: 4 DJB

6974. Herbstgeräusche   Medium, High Voices
       Poet: Belá Bartók (?). Hungarian title: Az öszi lárma. Also
       listed under the German title: Herbst. db 3-f4 gb 3-eb 4 Sustained
       in slow tempo. Descending ending line. Not for light voices. Has
       very agitated, fast-moving accompaniment. Acc: 5 FLB, FSB

6975. Herbsttränen   Medium Voices
       Poet: Belá Bartók (?). Hungarian title: Három öszi konnycsepp.
       c3-f4 f3-d4 Sustained in moderate slow tempo. Generally tranquil
       and subdued. Acc: 3 FLB, FSB, 50A

6976. Ich fühle deinen odem   High, Medium Voices
       Poet: Friedrich Rückert. f3-f4 f3-eb 4 Sustained in moderate tem-
       po. Requires simplicity. Subdued ending. Not for very heavy
       voices. Acc: 3-4 DJB

6977. Ich kann nicht zu dir   Medium Voices
       Poet: Belá Bartók (?). Hungarian title: Nem mehetek hozzád. c3-
       f# 4 f3-d4 Sustained in moderate slow tempo. Has some gentle re-
       citative style as well as climactic passages. Subdued, low ending.
       Acc: 3-4 FLB, FSB

6978. Im Tale   Baritone, Bass
       Poet: Anon. db 2-eb 3 e2-c3 Sustained in moderate slow tempo.
       Generally gentle, requires fine P. Has one climactic passage. In
       quasi-recitative style. Extended piano postlude. Text in Hungarian,
       with German and English versions. Acc: 4 DZL-4

6979. Mein Bett ruft   Medium Voices
       Poet: Belá Bartók (?). Hungarian title: Az ágyam hivogat. c3-f# 4
       eb 3-d4 Generally sustained in varied tempi. Requires fine P and
       PP. Has climactic passages and those in quasi-recitative style.
       Acc: 4 FLB, FSB

6980.   Mit dem Meere allein   Men
Poet: Bela Bartók (?). Hungarian title: Egyedül a tenerrel. b#2-
f#4 d#3-d#4 Sustained in moderate slow tempo. Starts and ends
in recitative style. Extended piano postlude. Agitated accompaniment in the middle section and requiring very fine control. Acc: 4
FLB, FSB

6981.   Wiegenlied   Women
Poet: Anon. f3-eb4 f3-eb4 Sustained in moderate slow tempo.
Tranquil and subdued. In gentle recitative style. Requires simplicity.
Texts in three languages and English translation. Acc: 3 DZL-2

ZOLTÁN KODÁLY, 1882-1967

Kodály, like his fellow-countryman Bartók, spent much of his career in the
interest of Hungarian folksong research and collection. Also like Bartók,
the start of his art song composing came from his exposure to folk music.
Kodály's songs, while retaining facets of Hungarian peasant music, were also
injected with some French and German influences, especially in the treatment of accompaniments. Many of his piano accompaniments are in the purely art song style and out of the bounds of ethnic music. His melodies may
retain part of the ethnic feeling and contour. His rhythms have vitality, and
it is in the lively and rhythmic vibrance that Kodály seems to be at his best.

FSK   Five Songs. Öt Dal, Op. 9. Zoltán Kodály. Hungarian texts, with
German versions. London: Boosey & Hawkes, Ltd.

TSK   Three Songs. Op. 14. Zoltán Kodály. Hungarian texts, with German and English versions. London: Boosey & Hawkes, Ltd.

6982.   Énekszó. Other title: Dalok Népi Versekre (Song Album). Zoltán
Kodály. Op. 1. A set of 16 miniatures or short songs to Hungarian
texts. For various voices. Budapest: Zeneműkiadó Vállalat, 1954
(c/o Boosey & Hawkes). Overall range: g2-g4 Printed in small
booklet form, 5 x 7 inches, instead of the regular music sheet size.

6983.   Adam, wo bist du?   Baritone
Poet: Endre Ady. Hungarian title: Ádám, hol vagy? g1-e3 c#2-
c#3 Sustained in moderate tempo. Majestic; has some dramatic passages. Requires fine P. Subdued ending on high tessitura. Accompaniment is mostly with chords. Acc: 3-4 FSK

6984.   Blume, du holde   Medium Voices
Poet: Béla Balázs. Hungarian title: Kicsi virágom. a2-g#4 c3-d4
Animated in moderate lively tempo. Slower middle section. Has
dramatic high passages with agitated accompaniment. Requires fine
high P. Subdued low ending with b2 as last note. Acc: 4 FSK

6985.   Der Wald   Low Voices
Poet: Béla Balázs. Hungarian title: Az erdő. f2-eb4 bb2-a3
Sustained in slow tempo. Generally subdued, with some strong, climactic phrases. Requires fine P and PP. Low tessitura. Low ending on bb2. Acc: 3 FSK

6986.   Exile   Men
Poet: Béla Balázs. Hungarian title: Siralmas nékem. German
title: Gesang des Verbannten. a2-g4 d3-d4 Sustained in varied

892 Solo Voice Repertoire

slow tempi. Has sections in quasi-recitative style. Requires some
fine P and PP. Starts strongly. Intense, sad text. If transposed,
may be sung by lower voices. Acc: 3 TSK

6987. Heart on fire — Men
Poet: Anon. 17th century poet. Hungarian title: Imhol nyitva én
kebelem. German title: Gleich dem Feuer. d3-g4 g3-e4 Sustained in generally moderate tempo. In varied moods. Starts strongly. Has dramatic climaxes and quasi-recitative passages. May be
transposed for lower voices. Original key: C minor. Acc: 3
TSK

6988. Nachts — Medium Voices
Poet: Béla Balázs. Hungarian title: Éjjel. b2-f4 e3-c4 Sustained
first section in varied slow tempi. Sustained vocal part in the second section which is in lively tempo. Has climactic passages. Subdued, descending ending line. Agitated, strong accompaniment toward
the end. Acc: 4 FSK

6989. Sapphos Liebesgesang — Medium, Low Voices
Poet: Endre Ady. Hungarian title: Sappho szerelmes éneke. cb3-
eb4 eb3-db4 Sustained in moderate slow tempo. Starts very subdued. Has climactic passages. Strong middle section with arpeggiated accompaniment. Very subdued, falling ending after long climactic crescendo. Acc: 4 FSK

6990. Stay, sweet bird — Tenor
Poet: Anon. 17th century poet. Hungarian title: Várj meg mada-
ram. e3-b4 a3-f#4 Animated in quite lively tempo. Requires
fluent enunciation and flexibility. Generally strong and climactic.
Also requires fine P. Dramatic high ending on b4. Generally agitated accompaniment. Acc: 4 TSK

JOSEPH KOSMA

DCK D'Autres Chanson de Jacques Prévert et Joseph Kosma. Twenty-five
songs. Paris: Enoch & Cie.

21C 21 Chansons de Jacques Prévert et Joseph Kosma. French text only.
Paris: Enoch & Cie.

6991. Fête foraine — High Voices
Poet: Jacques Prévert. c3-g4 f3-e4 Animated in very rapid tem-
po. Requires some fluent enunciation. Has climactic passages.
Somewhat subdued ending after climax. Acc: 3-4 21C

6992. Le cancre — High Voices
Poet: Jacques Prévert. d3-a4 g3-d4 Animated in moderate lively
tempo. Requires fluent enunciation. Slightly slower ending section
with climactic last two notes (a4 & g4). Acc: 3 DCK

6993. Le gardien du phare aime beaucoup trop les oiseaux — All Voices
Poet: Jacques Prévert. d#3-e4 a3-e4 Sustained in moderate slow
tempo. Tranquil, in quasi-recitative. Generally subdued, with climactic passages. Acc: 3 21C

6994. Les oiseaux du souci							High, Medium Voices
Poet: Jacques Prévert. d3-f4 g3-d4 Sustained in slow tempo.
Has sections in recitative style. Generally subdued, requires fine P
and PP. Very subdued, high ending. Acc: 3 DCK

FERENCZ (FRANZ) LISZT, 1811-1886

Liszt is best known as a virtuoso pianist and composer of orchestral and
keyboard music. One generally does not identify him as a notable composer
of songs, but the truth is that Liszt ranks with the greatest writers of 19th-
century Lieder. The first songs he wrote date from 1839. He produced
more than 70 pieces to poems in French, German, Italian, Hungarian, and
English. Most outstanding are his settings of Goethe, Heine, and Hugo. A
close examination of his songs reveals a craftsman still relatively unknown
in the field of solo song. Liszt wrote many fine songs for the middle and
lower voices, which is not true of most composers. His style is varied,
and he wrote with ease and facility the lyric, dramatic, and recitative types.
It is time now that singers and teachers of singing pay some attention to the
songs of Liszt, for in him we have a forgotten master of the Lied.

FLM   Franz Liszts Musikalische Werke. Complete works published by
      Breitkopf & Härtel, Leipzig, republished by Gregg Press, Ltd.,
      Hants, England. (Note: Vol. VII: Lieder und Gesänge, bound in
      three separate books. Beautifully printed in vocal score size. Ex-
      pensive, but available. FLM-1 means Vol. VII, part I.)

TSL   Twelve Songs. Franz Liszt. High, low. German text, with English
      version by Theodore Baker. New York: G. Schirmer, Inc.

20L   20 Ausgewählte Lieder. Selected Songs. Franz Liszt. High, medi-
      um, low. Edited by Eugen D'Albert. German text with French and
      English versions. Breitkopf & Härtel (C. F. Kahnt, Leipzig).

Drei Sonette von Petrarca. A set of Italian texts by Francesco Petrarca.
      The first and third are indicated for Baritone or Mezzo-Soprano, the
      third for Baritone alone. German version by Peter Cornelius.
      FLM-3

6995. (1) Sonett XXXIX: Benedetto sia il giorno	Baritone, Mezzo-Soprano
c3-e4 eb3-c#4(db4) Sustained in moderate tempo. Starts gently.
Generally on MF level, with some high climactic passages. First
section requires some gentle, fluent enunciation. Subdued final phrase,
with falling ending. Acc: 3

6996. (2) Sonett XC: Pace non trovo							Baritone
d2-d3 e2-c#3 Generally sustained in varied tempi. Starts in moderate slow tempo. Middle section has dramatic, intense high passages, with agitated accompaniment. Has one unaccompanied passage.
Subdued high ending. Acc: 3-4

6997. (3) Sonett CV: I' vidi in terra angelici
          costumi					Baritone, Mezzo-Soprano
d3-f4 f3-d4 Sustained in very slow tempo. Marked: Molto lento e
placido. Slightly faster middle section. Has one unaccompanied passage. Generally subdued, with two short climactic passages. Requires fine P and PP. Very subdued ending phrases marked PP.
Tranquil piano postlude. Acc: 3-4

894   Solo Voice Repertoire

Single Song in Italian

6998. La perla   Mezzo-Soprano, Contralto
Poet: Princess Therese von Hohenlohe. b♯2-e♯4 e3-c♯4 Sustained in moderate lively tempo. Generally on MF level. Has some
climactic passages. Subdued, low ending. Acc: 3 FLM-3

Single Song in English

6999. Go not, happy day   Tenor, Baritone
Poet: Alfred Tennyson. d♯3-e4 f♯3-c♯4 English is the original
text, not the translation. Generally sustained in moderate lively tempo. Beginning and ending sections have only occasional chords in the
accompaniment. Ending phrase is unaccompanied. Acc: 3 FLM-3

Single Songs in French

7000. Comment, disaient-ils   High Voices
Poet: Victor Hugo. d3-a4(c5) g♯3(a♭3)-e4 Animated in moderate
lively tempo. Starts gently in declamatory style. Has dramatic high
passages, an ossia section with high tessitura, and an ad libitum descending cadenza at the end. Acc: 3-4 FLM-1

7001. Enfant, si j'etais roi   High Voices
Poet: Victor Hugo. c3-a4 e♭3-e♭4 Sustained in moderate slow
tempo. Dramatic high passages over agitated accompaniment. Requires vocal energy and flexibility. Exultant and bright. Slightly subdued ending with extended piano postlude. German version by Peter
Cornelius. Acc: 4 FLM-1

7002. Gastibelza, Bolero   Bass
Poet: Victor Hugo. f1-e3 d2-d3 Animated in lively tempo, with
variations. An extended song of 16 pages, and best for basso can-
tante. Requires considerable flexibility. Generally strong and energetic. Requires fluent enunciation. Climactic ending. Acc: 5
FLM-1

7003. Il m'aimait tant!   Soprano, Mezzo-Soprano
Poet: Frau E. von Girardin. d♯3-a♭4 f3-f4 Sustained in varied
tempi. Starts in moderate slow tempo; ends with animated section in
moderate lively tempo. Ending section has dramatic passages and a
more agitated accompaniment. Subdued ending after high climax.
Acc: 3-4 FLM-1

7004. J'ai perdu ma force et ma vie   Baritone, Contralto
Poet: Alfred de Musset. c3-e♭4 e3-c4 Sustained in slow tempo.
Unaccompanied starting phrases. Generally subdued. Requires fine
P. Has some agitated accompaniment in the second half. Sparce ac-
companiment in ending section. Acc: 3 FLM-3

7005. Jeanne d'Arc au bûcher   Mezzo-Soprano
Poet: Alexander Dumas. c3-g♯4(a4) e3-d♯4 A dramatic scene, 12
pages. Subdued beginning vocal line. Has dramatic and intense passages. Also requires fine P. Subdued high ending. Acc: 4 FLM-3

7006. La tombe et la rose   Medium, Low Voices
Poet: Victor Hugo. a2-e4 e♭3-d4 Sustained in slow tempo. Generally subdued and dark. Has some declamatory phrases and agitated
accompaniment. Acc: 3-4 FLM-1

7007.   Le vieux vagabond   Bass
        Poet: Pierre Jean de Béranger. e1-f3 b1-c3 Sustained vocal part
        in moderate lively tempo. Dramatic, energetic, has a wide range.
        Requires flexibility. Has marked "declamando" phrases. Strong de-
        scending ending. e1 is the last note, sustained for 9 beats and
        marked FF. Acc: 4 FLM-1

7008.   Oh, quand je dors   Men
        Poet: Victor Hugo. d♯3-a4 f♯3-g♯4 Sustained in moderate slow
        tempo. Has dramatic climaxes. Requires fine high P and PP.
        Ends on sustained, very subdued g♯4. Best for tenor or high bari-
        tone. Acc: 3 TSL, 20L, 40F (Ch. V), FLM-1

7009.   S'il est un charmant gazon   All Voices
        Poet: Victor Hugo. d♭3-e♭4 f3-d♭4 Sustained in moderate fast
        tempo. Graceful; requires fine P. Acc: 4 TSL, FLM-1

Single Songs in German

7010.   An Edlitam   Tenor, Baritone
        Poet: Friedrich von Bodenstedt. f3-e♭4 f3-d4 Sustained in mod-
        erate tempo, followed by fast and brilliant section. Generally on
        MF level with some climactic passages. Subdued high ending. Acc:
        3 FLM-3

7011.   Bist du!   All Voices
        Poet: Elim Metschersky. d3-f4(a4) e3-e4 Sustained in moderate
        slow tempo. Requires fine P. Has some climactic passages. Sub-
        dued ending section. Original key. Acc: 4 20L, FLM-3

7012.   Das Veilchen   All Voices
        Poet: Joseph Müller. f3-g♭4 g♭3-e♭4 Sustained in moderate slow
        tempo. Requires simplicity and a straightforward treatment. Re-
        quires fine P and PP. Generally subdued. Text is sacred (Roman
        Catholic) oriented. Acc: 3 20L, FLM-2

7013.   Der du von dem Himmel bist   All Voices
        Poet: Johann Wolfgang von Goethe. e♭3-g4 b♭3-f4 Sustained in
        slow tempo. Has dramatic passages. Requires fine high P. Sub-
        dued low ending. Accompaniment is mostly in sustained chords. See
        "Wanderers Nachtlied" by Schubert and Pfitzner. Acc: 3 20L,
        FLM-1, DLL-transposed, (Ch. VI)

7014.   Der Fischerknabe   All Voices
        Poet: Friedrich von Schiller. d3-a♭4 g♯3-e4 Original key. Sus-
        tained in moderate lively tempo. Requires fine P. Very subdued
        ending with sustained a4 as the last note. Acc: 5 20L, FLM-1

7015.   Des Tages laute Stimmen schweigen   Low Voices
        Poet: Ferdinand von Saar. b2-d♯3 e3-c♯4 Very sustained in
        varied slow tempi. Subdued, requires fine P and PP. Very subdued,
        unaccompanied, descending ending line. Mainly chordal accompani-
        ment. Acc: 3 FLM-3

7016.   Die drei Zigeuner   High, Medium Voices
        Poet: Nikolaus Lenau. Original key. b2-g4 d3-e4 Mostly in reci-
        tative style. In varying moods and tempi. Climactic ending. Narra-
        tive text. Acc: 5 TSL, 20L, FLM-3

7017.   Die Loreley   High Voices
        Poet: Heinrich Heine.   b2-g4(bb4) f3-f4 Sustained in varied tempi,
        but generally moderate. Has climactic high passages. Requires fine
        high P and PP. Very subdued, sustained high ending with g4 as final
        note. Acc: 4 FLM-2, TSL, 20L, 50M

7018.   Die Macht der Musik   High Voices
        Poet: Helene d'Orléans. d#3-a4(b4) f#3-f#4 Generally sustained in
        varied tempi and moods. Starts in moderate slow tempo. Has faster
        middle section with agitated accompaniment. Has dramatic high pas-
        sages and some short quasi-recitative passages, and a strong and de-
        scending ending. Not for light, high voices. Acc: 4 FLM-1

7019.   Die Schlüsselblumen   High, Medium Voices
        Poet: Joseph Müller. Original key. d#3-f#4 eb3-eb4 Animated
        in moderate tempo. Light, in mezzo voce. Requires fluent enuncia-
        tion and flexibility. Ends in slower tempo. Acc: 3 TSL, 20L,
        FLM-2

7020.   Die stille Wasserrose   Mezzo-Soprano or Tenor
        Poet: Emanuel Geibel. c#3-gb4 f#3-e4 Sustained in moderate
        slow tempo. Has some climactic high passages. Requires fine P
        and PP. Slow, subdued ending. Acc: 3 FLM-3

7021.   Die tote Nachtigall   High Voices
        Poet: Philipp Kaufmann. b2-a4 f#3-f#4 Generally sustained in
        moderate tempo. Requires flexibility. Has some florid figures,
        trills and climactic passages. Ends with a cadenza. The first set-
        ting. Acc: 3 FLM-1

7022.   Die Vätergruft   Baritone, Bass
        Poet: Ludwig Uhland. g1(f1)-e3 db2-c3 Sustained in slow tempo.
        Middle section is majestic, in moderate tempo, dramatic, with inten-
        sity, and high tessitura. Very subdued and slow ending section.
        Acc: 3-4 FLM-2

7023.   Du bist wie eine Blume   All Voices
        Poet: Heinrich Heine. c#3-e4 f#3-d#4 Sustained in slow tempo.
        Gentle, one of Liszt's appealing songs. See the settings by Schumann,
        Wolf, Rubinstein, and Chadwick's "Thou art so like a flower." Acc:
        3 TSL, 20L, FLM-2

7024.   Ein Fichtenbaum steht einsam   All Voices
        Poet: Heinrich Heine. First of two settings. b2(g2)-d4 f#3-c4
        Sustained in slow tempo. Generally subdued, requires fine P and PP.
        First part has element of gentle declamation. Slower ending section.
        Strong final chords in accompaniment. Acc: 3 FLM-2, 20L-three
        steps lower

7025.   Es muss ein Wunderbares sein   All Voices
        Poet: Oscar von Redwitz. c3-eb4 f3-db4 Very sustained in mod-
        erate slow tempo. Gentle. Subdued ending. Requires simplicity.
        Original key. Acc: 2-3 POS-1, TSL, 20L, FLM-2

7026.   Es rauschen die Winde   Medium, High Voices
        Poet: Ludwig Rellstab. e3-f#4 g3-e4 Last setting. Animated in
        moderate lively tempo. Slow and sustained middle section. Has
        some short, unaccompanied or sparsely accompanied passages, and

climactic passages. Requires fine high P and PP. Subdued ending on eb4. Acc: 4 FLM-2

7027. Es war ein König in Thule   All Voices
Poet: Johann Wolfgang von Goethe, from his Faust. Original key. g# 2-f4 eb 3-db 4 Animated in moderate tempo. Has dramatic climaxes. Best for the heavier voices. See the following settings: "Aus Goethe's 'Faust'" by Beethoven, "Der König von Thule" by Zelter, "Il élait un Roi de Thule" in Gounod's FAUST. Acc: 3 TSL, 50M, FLM-2

7028. Freudvoll und leidvoll   Medium, High Voices
Poet: Johann Wolfgang von Goethe. Original key. b2-f# 4 d# 3-d# 4 Sustained in moderate slow tempo. Short. See the setting by Beethoven. Acc: 3 TSL, 20L, FLM-1

7029. Gebet   Mezzo-Soprano, Contralto
Poet: Friedrich von Bodenstedt, after Lermontof. First line: In Stunden der Entmutigung. b# 2-eb 4 d# 3-b3 Sustained in slow tempo. Subdued, requires fine P. Subdued, descending ending line. Acc: 3 FLM-3

7030. Hohe Liebe   Tenor
Poet: Ludwig Uhland. f3-a4 ab 3-eb 4 Sustained in moderate slow tempo. Generally on MF level, with some slightly climactic passages. Descending ending line in diminuendo. May be transposed for lower voices. Acc: 3 FLM-2

7031. Ich liebe dich   All Voices
Poet: Friedrich Rückert. Original key. db 3-f4(ab 4) f3-eb 4 Sustained in slow tempo. Requires fine P. Has climactic passages. Subdued, ascending ending. Acc: 3 20L, FLM-3

7032. Ich möchte hingehn   All Voices
Poet: Georg Herwegh. e3-g# 3(a4) f# 3-f# 4 Generally sustained in varied tempi and moods. Requires fine P. Has dramatic passages and a climactic ending marked FF. Interpretatively difficult. Acc: 4 20L, FLM-2

7033. Im Rhein, im schönen Strome   Tenor
Poet: Heinrich Heine. e3-f# 4(g# 4) e3-e4 Second setting, 1856. Sustained in moderate tempo in flowing style. Has climactic high passages. Requires fine P and PP. Climactic ending. Agitated accompaniment. May be transposed for baritone. See the settings by Robert Franz and Robert Schumann. Acc: 4 FLM-2, 20L

7034. In Liebeslust   High, Medium Voices
Poet: Hoffmann von Fallersleben. db 3-f4 f3-db 4 Animated in lively tempo. Joyful and bright. Has dramatic climaxes and a subdued ending. Acc: 4 TSL, 20L, FLM-2

7035. Kling leise, mein Kind   Tenor
Poet: Johannes Nordmann. Other title: Ständchen. First setting, 1848. e3-g# 4 f# 3-f# 4 Sustained vocal line in moderate lively tempo, with variations. Subdued, requires very fine P and PP. Gentle, smooth flowing, and lyric. May be transposed for baritone. Acc: 4 FLM-1

7036. Kling leise, mein Kind   Tenor
       Poet: Johannes Nordmann. Other title: Ständchen. Second setting.
       e3-g#4 f#3-f#4 Sustained vocal part in moderate fast tempo. Starts
       very subdued. Generally subdued with some sweeping lines. Re-
       quires fine P and PP, and flexibility. Very subdued ending on f#4.
       Generally agitated accompaniment. May be transposed for baritone.
       Acc: 4 FLM-2, TSL-one step lower, 20L

7037. Mignon's Lied   Women
       Poet: Johann Wolfgang von Goethe. First line: Kennst du das Land.
       g2-eb4 eb3-eb4 Sustained in slow tempo. Has some intensity and
       gentle passages in recitative style. See the settings: "Mignon" by
       Beethoven and Wolf, "Mignon's Lied" by Tchaikovsky, "Mignon's
       Gesang" by Schubert, and "Kennst du das Land" by Zelter and Schu-
       mann. Acc: 4 TSL, 20L, FLM-2

7038. Morgens steh ich auf und frage   Tenor, Baritone
       Poet: Heinrich Heine. e#3-eb4 f#3-d4 Gently animated in moder-
       ate lively tempo. Generally on MF level. Slow ending phrase on
       high notes. Acc: 3 FLM-2

7039. O lieb   High Voices
       Poet: Ferdinand Freiligrath. eb3-a4 f#3-e4 Sustained vocal part
       in lively tempo. Agitated, dramatic, and intense middle section with
       high tessitura. Has recitado phrases. Subdued ending. The melo-
       dy of this song (c. 1845) is the same as that of his well-known piano
       solo entitled "Liebesträume" (c. 1850). Acc: 3-4 FLM-2

7040. Sei still   Medium, Low Voices
       Poet: Henriette von Schorn. c3-d4 e3-a4 Sustained in slow tempo.
       Generally on MF level. In quasi-recitative style. Has unaccompanied
       passages. Subdued and very sustained ending section. Contemplative.
       Acc: 3 FLM-3

7041. Über allen Gipfeln ist Ruh   All Voices
       Poet: Johann Wolfgang von Goethe. d3-g4 a3-e4 Sustained in slow
       tempo. Very tranquil and subdued. Has some climactic passages.
       Very subdued, "falling" ending. Listed in 50M and 20L as "Wander-
       ers Nachtlied." See "Wanderers Nachtlied" by Schubert, "Nachtlied"
       by Schumann, "Ruhe" by Zelter, and "Ilmenau" by Ives. Acc: 3
       FLM-2, 50M, 20L

7042. Und sprich   Mezzo-Soprano, Contralto
       Poet: Rüdiger von Biegeleben. db3-eb4 f3-c4 Very sustained in
       slow tempo. Generally subdued, requires fine P and PP. Generally
       in gentle declamatory style. Accompaniment consists mainly of sus-
       tained chords. Acc: 3 FLM-3

7043. Vergiftet sind meine Lieder   Tenor, Baritone
       Poet: Heinrich Heine. f#3-f4 g#3-e4 Generally sustained, in dec-
       lamatory style, in moderate tempo. Starts strongly. Has mostly
       dramatic passages. Climactic ending. Short. Acc: 3 FLM-2

7044. Weimars Toten   Bass, Bass-Baritone
       Poet: Franz von Schober. ab1(f#1)-f3 c2-eb3 Sustained in moder-
       ate tempo. Dramatic, energetic, and intense. Requires flexibility
       and fine command of high notes. Also requires fine high P. Has
       declamatory passages. Dramatic ending. Acc: 4 FLM-1

7045. Wer nie sein Brod mit Tränen ass   Mezzo-Soprano
      Poet: Johann Wolfgang von Goethe.   First of two settings.   b2-f4(g4)
      d3-d4 Sustained in moderate slow tempo.   Has climactic passages,
      and passages requiring fine high PP.   Subdued, descending ending
      line.   Generally agitated accompaniment.   Acc: 3-4   FLM-2

7046. Wer nie sein Brod mit Tränen ass   Low Voices
      Poet: Johann Wolfgang von Goethe.   Second of two settings.   a2-f4
      d3-c4 Sustained in slow tempo.   Has dramatic passages.   Starts and
      ends in quasi-declamatory style.   Slow, descending ending after strong,
      high climax.   Also set to music by Robert Schumann, Franz Schubert,
      and Hugo Wolf.   Acc: 3   FLM-3

7047. Wider möcht ich dir begegnen   All Voices
      Poet: Peter Cornelius.   e3-gb4(bb4)   ab3-gb4 Sustained in moder-
      ate tempo.   Has dramatic climaxes.   Requires fine P.   Climactic
      ending.   Acc: 3-4   20L, FLM-3

7048. Wie singt die Lerche schön   High Voices
      Poet: Heinrich Hoffmann von Fallersleben.   f#3-f#4 a3-e4 Ani-
      mated in lively tempo, with some slower passages.   Generally on
      MF level, mainly lyric in style.   Subdued high ending.   Generally agi-
      tated accompaniment.   May be transposed for medium voices.   Acc:
      3-4   FLM-2

Note: See also the set entitled: Drei Lieder aus Schillers 'Wilhelm Tell'
      for high voice and piano. FLM-2 Titles:
         1. Der Fischerknabe
         2. Der Hirt
         3. Der Alpenjäger

                              F.   ISRAEL

FSI   Famous Songs of Israel.   Edited by Issachar Miron.   Hebrew texts,
       with English translations.   New York: Mills Music Inc.

GSI   Great Songs of Israel.   Edited by Issachar Miron.   Hebrew texts,
       with English translations.   New York: Mills Music Inc.

                            ─────────

PAUL (originally FRANKENBURGER) BEN-HAIM

7049. Psalm XXIII   Medium Voices
      Poet: Psalm 23.   g2-d4(g4)   d3-c4 Sustained in moderate tempo.
      Generally tranquil, on MF level.   Has some climactic passages.
      Strong and climactic ending.   Extended piano prelude and postlude.
      Hebrew text, with English translation.   Acc: 3-4   (S)IS

NIRA CHEN

7050. Iti milvanon   Medium, Low Voices
      Poet: Song of Songs, Solomon.   English title: Come with me.   b2-
      c4 e3-b3 Sustained in moderate slow tempo.   Has strong passages.
      Descending ending line.   Acc: 3   FSI

900 Solo Voice Repertoire

MARC LAVRY

7051. Yeshan mahmadi   All Voices
       Poet: Yaakov Cohen. English title: Come sleep, little dear. d3-
       c♯4 f♯3-b3 Sustained in slow tempo. Gentle, calm, and subdued.
       Best for women. Acc: 3 GSI

SARAH LEVI-TANAI

7052. Hanoded   All Voices
       Poet: Sarah Levi-Tanai. English title: Song of the wanderer. d3-
       e4 g3-d4 Animated in lively tempo. Cheerful, and generally on
       MF level. Acc: 3 FSI

ISSACHAR MIRON

7053. Halleluiah   All Voices
       Poet: Only the word "halleluiah. " d3-e4 f3-d4 Animated in very
       fast tempo. Requires some flexibility. Joyful, and generally strong.
       Climactic ending. Acc: 3 GSI

7054. Metzi'ah   All Voices
       Poet: Lea Goldberg. English title: A puddle-full of heaven. c3-d4
       e3-c4 Animated in moderate tempo. Spirited and joyful. Generally
       on MF level. Descending ending line. 3 verses. Acc: 3 GSI

7055. Shiru Li   All Voices
       Poet: Emanuel Zamir. English title: Someone who vanished. c3-
       c4 d3-a3 Animated in lively tempo. Cheerful, requires some fluent
       enunciation. Generally on MF level. Acc: 3 GSI

AMITAI NEEMAN

7056. Lu   All Voices
       Poet: Amitai Neeman. English title: If. c3-d4 f3-c4 Animated
       in moderate lively tempo. Spirited and hearty. Generally on MF
       level. Descending ending. Acc: 3 GSI

SHLOMO SHARON

7057. Tanim bidmi leil   All Voices
       Poet: Tamar Friedland. English title: Silently, silently. g3-e4
       a3-d4 Animated in moderate tempo. Spirited, but generally subdued.
       Descriptive text telling about jackals in the moonlight. Acc: 3 GSI

LAZAR WEINER

FJA   Five Jewish Art Songs. Lazar Weiner. Yiddish texts, with English
       translations. Bryn Mawr: Mercury Music Corp. , c/o Theodore
       Presser.

———————

7058. Der Yid mitn fidl   All Voices

Poet: A. Lutzky. c3(a2)-f4 e3-d4 Generally sustained in varied
tempi. Has recitative passages. Climactic ending. Humorous. A
conversation between a shiftless husband and a nagging wife. Acc:
3-4 FJA

7059. Di reid funem novi   High Voices
Poet: Magister. English title: The words of the prophet. g3-b♭4
a♭3-f♯4 Generally sustained in varied tempi. Starts majestically.
Has passages in recitative style. Generally a dramatic song on texts
of prophecy. Dramatic ending. Not for light voices. Acc: 4 FJA

7060. Dos gold fun daine oign   High Voices
Poet: S. I. Imber. English title: The gold of your eyes. f♯3-g♯4
g♯3-e4 Sustained in moderate then moderate slow tempo. Has dramatic passage toward the end. Acc: 4 FJA

7061. Gebet   High Voices
Poet: A. Berger. f♯3-a♭4 g♯3-f4 Sustained in slow tempo. Generally subdued. Requires some flexibility. Subdued ending. Religious text. Acc: 3-4 FJA

7062. Vig-lid   Soprano
Poet: Peretz Markish. English title: Slumber song. d3-g4 f3-d4
Sustained in varied tempi. Subdued. Rather thick accompaniment,
requiring gentleness and considerable control. Acc: 4 FJA

MOSHE WILENSKY

7063. Haya hu afor   Low Voices
Poet: Oded Avisar. English title: Just a glance. g2-c4 a2-a3
Sustained in moderate slow tempo. Calm. Low tessitura, has sev-
eral a2's. 2 verses. Acc: 2-3 FSI

G. JAPAN

JLC-2 Japanese Lied Collection. Japanese script, phonetic translation and
English title. Tokyo: Kawai-Gakufu Co.

JLC   Japanese Lied Collection. Edited by Tamotsu Kinoshita. With Japanese script, phonetic transcription, and English titles. Tokyo: Kawai-
Gakufu Co.

SADAO BEKKU

Studied with Darius Milhaud, Olivièr Messiaen, and Jean Rivièr. His style
shows very strong western influences.

CSB   A Collection of Songs composed by Sadao Bekku. Provided with Japanese script and a phonetic text. Tokyo: Ongaku-no-Tomo Sha, Inc.

7064. A glowworm   High Voices

Poet: Ōki. Japanese title: Hotaru. e♭3-f4 f3-e♭4 Animated in moderate lively tempo. Generally delicate, with one climactic passage. Best for men. Acc: 3 CSB

7065. A shower of rain   Men
Poet: Ōki. Japanese title: Ryō-u. d♯3-f4 g3-f4 Animated in quite fast tempo. Requires fluent enunciation. Has some strong passages. Strong entrance. Acc: 3-4 CSB

7066. Alone in the woods   All Voices
Poet: Michizo Tachihara. Japanese title: Hitori hayashi de. c3-a♭4 g3-g4 Sustained in moderate lively tempo. Requires very fine P. Has some climactic passages. Rather delicate accompaniment. Subdued ending. Best for light, high voices. Acc: 3-4 CSB

7067. Cherry blossoms lane   Men
Poet: Shuichi Katō. Japanese title: Sakura yoko-cho. e♭3-g4 g3-e♭4 Gently animated vocal part in varied tempi. Starts adagio. Requires fluent enunciation and flexibility. Has some short parlando passages and florid figures. Acc: 3 CSB

7068. The sea bird   Men
Poet: Sōtarō Hagiwara. Japanese title: Umi-dori. b♭2-g♯4 e3-e4 Generally sustained in moderate slow tempo. In the style of a gentle recitative. Requires fine PP. Has climactic passages and a subdued ending. Acc: 3 CSB

IKUMA DAN

Dan is the author of the first successful Japanese opera, YUZURU. His writing style reveals a strong western influence.

IDS   Ikuma Dan Collected Songs. Fifty songs with English translations and notes by Dorothy Guyver. Tokyo: Ongaku-no-Tomo.

————————

Three Ko-uta. A cycle of three songs for medium voice and piano. Best for men's voices. Poems by Hakushu Kitahara. IDS

7069. (1) Bird of spring   Medium Voices
c3-f4 f3-d4 Sustained in moderate tempo. Generally gentle. Requires some flexibility. Subdued ending. Acc: 3

7070. (2) Dianthus   Medium Voices
b2-d♯4(f♯4) e3-d♯4 Sustained in moderate slow tempo. Has several b2's. Generally subdued. Subdued low ending. Acc: 3

7071. (3) Spider lily   Medium Voices
b2-f4 b2-d4 Animated in lively tempo. Has recitative-like passages and dramatic passages. Uses several vocal portamenti. Ends very subdued in the low register, with sustained b2's in ending passages. Text of the song is best for men's voices. Acc: 3-4

Single Songs

7072. A cicada   Men
Poet: Toichiro Kitayama. Japanese title: Higurashi. First line:

Higure higurashi. e3-g4 ab3-f4 Sustained in moderate slow tempo. Generally subdued, requires very fine P and PP. Very subdued ending. Acc: 3 JLC

7073. Alley children   High Voices
Poet: Minoru Ohki. d3-g4 g3-g4 Animated in moderate lively tempo. Generally light with some gentle recitative-like passages. Subdued ending. Extended piano postlude. Has some "authentic" Japanese rhythms. Best for light voices. Acc: 3 IDS

7074. Cicadas   High Voices
Poet: Fuyuichiro Kitayama. e3-g4 ab3-f4 Sustained in moderate slow tempo. Generally subdued. Requires very fine P. Very subdued ending. Has some "authentic" Japanese rhythms. Acc: 3 IDS

7075. Shells   High Voices
Poet: Sakutaro Hagiwara. eb3-g4 a3-f♯4 Sustained in moderate slow tempo. Subdued, requires very fine P. Marked "misterioso." Subdued ending. Generally light and agitated accompaniment. Acc: 3-4 IDS

7076. Sparrow's dance   High, Medium Voices
Poet: Hakushu Kitahara. eb3-f4 g3-eb4 Animated in lively tempo. Generally light. Climactic ending on descending line. Has some traditional Japanese rhythms. 4 verses. Best for light high voices. Acc: 3-4 IDS

7077. Spring   High, Medium Voices
Poet: Shuntaro Tanikawa. db3-f4 ab3-eb4 Animated in moderate tempo. Graceful, bright, and exultant. Subdued ending. Acc: 3 IDS

7078. The leg   High Voices
Poet: Hakushu Kitahara. d3-g♯4 g♯3-f4 Animated in moderate lively tempo. Has some strong passages and a climactic ending. Starts gently. Narrative text. Said to be more Japanese in style than western. Acc: 3-4 IDS

7079. The snow maiden   Medium, Low Voices
Poet: Hakushu Kitahara. a2-d4 e3-bb3 Sustained in slow tempo. Gentle, subdued throughout. Subdued, descending ending. Acc: 3 IDS

MAREO ISHIKETA

Professor of Music at The Tokyo University of Arts. Composer of one opera.

CSI   A Collection of Songs composed by Mareo Ishiketa. Tokyo: Ongaku-no-Tomo. (Note: Original Japanese script and a phonetic pronunciation. English titles provided, but no text translations.)

7080. A dove and a boy   Men
Poet: Kazuhiko Natori. Japanese title: Hato to Shōnen. db3-gb4 f3-e4 Sustained in varied tempi. Requires fine P. Has a few somewhat climactic passages. Subdued, and melodically fragmentary ending section. First line: Syōnen wa hato. Acc: 3 CSI

7081. Burning sunset   Women
       Poet: Jūkichi Yagi. Japanese title: Yūyake. f3-g#4 bb3-f4 Sus-
       tained in slow tempo. Generally subdued; high ending. First line:
       Yūyake o abi. Acc: 3 CSI

7082. Requiem   Men
       Poet: Yoshiki Hattori. Japanese title: Chinkon-shi. First line:
       Tada somerarete. c3-ab4 f3-f4 An extended song in varied moods
       and tempi. Has some dramatic passages. Interpretatively difficult.
       Subdued ending. Eighteen pages, with extended piano prelude. One
       of the composer's latest songs. Acc: 3-4 CSI

7083. Serene flames   All Voices
       Poet: Jūkichi Yagi. Japanese title: Shizuka na hono-o. First line:
       Hitotsu no ki ni. f#3-f4 g3-d4 Sustained in slow tempo. Grave
       and subdued. Requires very fine P. Short. Acc: 3 SCI

7084. The foxes   Men
       Poet: Kōtarō Jimbo. Japanese title: Kitsune. First line: Ogitsune
       da. bb2-e4 eb3-db4 Animated vocal part in moderate tempo. Gen-
       erally somewhat subdued. Abounds in repeated notes. Requires
       some fluent enunciation. Dramatic high ending. One of the compos-
       er's latest songs. Acc: 3 CSI

KOICHI KISHI

JLK   Japanische Lieder. Koichi Kishi. Four original art songs and two
       folk song arrangements. Berlin: Richard Birnbach. (Note: Songs
       by a Japanese composer on Japanese texts, but written in the western
       style. Japanese texts, with German versions by Lore Kornell.)

       ─────────────

7085. Akai kanzachi   Soprano
       Poet: Koichi Kishi. German title: Mein korallenroter kamm. c3-b4
       e3-f4 Sustained in moderate tempo. Has faster middle section and
       climactic high passages. Slightly climactic ending. Acc: 3 JLK

7086. Amanohara   High Voices
       Poet: Abeno Nakamaro. German title: Ewig gleicher Mond. eb3-
       ab4 eb3-eb4 Sustained in moderate slow tempo. Generally strong,
       with a dramatic high climax. Subdued high ending. Dramatic, ex-
       tended piano prelude. Acc: 4 JLK

7087. Kago kaki   High Voices
       Poet: Koichi Kishi. German title: Sänftenträger. e3-a4 g3-e4
       Animated in lively tempo. Starts with highest notes in the song. Re-
       quires fluent enunciation. Short. Acc: 4 JLK

7088. Kamome   High Voices
       Poet: Koichi Kishi. German title: Möwe. b2-gb4 e3-e4 Animated
       in lively tempo. Very tranquil, slower middle section. Starts with
       an imitation of a seagull's cry. Requires fluent enunciation. Climac-
       tic high ending. Agitated accompaniment. Acc: 4 JLK

7089. Yaezakura   High Voices
       Poet: Kino Tsuraynki. German title: Kirschblüte. c3-g4(b4) g3-
       g4 Sustained in moderate slow tempo. Has vocalized passage.

Generally gentle; best for light voices.   Extended piano prelude.   Acc: 3 JLK

YASUJI KIYOSE

7090. Softly   High Voices
Poet: Ishikawa Takuboku.   First line: Yawaraka ni.   g3-f4 a3-d4
Sustained in moderate slow tempo.   Subdued, short, and delicate.
Chordal accompaniment.   Acc: 2-3 JLC

YOSHINAO NAKADA

Nakada's compositions show strong western influences.

CSN   A Collection of Songs composed by Yoshinao Nakada.   Tokyo: Kawai
Gakufu.

7091. At another time   All Voices
Poet: Tatsuji Miyoshi.   Japanese title: Mata aru toki wa.   d3-eb4
g3-d4 Gently animated vocal part in moderate tempo.   In the style
of a gentle recitative.   Slightly climactic ending.   Acc: 2-3 CSN

7092. Ballad   Men
Poet: Sakihito Tatsuno.   b2-f♯4 e3-e4 Sustained in moderate tempo.
Requires some flexibility.   Has dramatic passages.   Subdued low end-
ing.   Generally agitated accompaniment.   Not for light, high voices.
Acc: 3-4 CSN

7093. Children in the wind   All Voices
Poet: Yumeji Takehisa.   Japanese title: Kaze no kodomo.   First
line: Kaze no kodomo ga.   f3-ab4 f3-db4 Sustained in moderate
slow tempo.   Requires simplicity and very fine high P and PP.   Subdued, delicate, and gentle.   Acc: 2 JLC

7094. Gate to the unknown world   Women
Poet: Masakiyo Miyamoto.   db3-f4 gb3-db4 Animated in moderate
tempo.   Requires very fine P and PP.   Generally subdued, with a
subdued ending.   Gently agitated accompaniment.   Acc: 3 CSN

7095. Maidens in broad daylight   Men
Poet: From "Matinée Poétique," translated into Japanese by Shin-
ichirō Nakamura.   Japanese title: Mahiro ni otometachi.   e3-f♯4
g♯3-e4 Animated in moderate slow tempo.   Requires fine P and PP.
Has climactic passages.   Slightly climactic ending.   Agitated accompaniment.   Acc: 4 CSN

7096. On the sand   Men
Poet: Tatsuji Miyoshi.   Japanese title: Sajō.   c3-db4 eb3-c4 Sustained vocal part in moderate tempo.   Generally subdued with a few
climactic passages.   Requires very fine P and PP.   Agitated accompaniment throughout.   Extended postlude in the piano part.   Acc: 4
CSN

7097. Paulownia flowers   All Voices
Poet: Tatsuji Miyoshi.   Japanese title: Kiri no hana.   eb3-a4

a♭3-e4 Gently animated vocal part in moderate slow tempo. Requires very fine P and PP. Has one climactic high passage. Subdued ending. Acc: 3 CSN

7098. Song of Spring   All Voices
       Poet: Ryōsuke Hatanaka. Japanese title: Haru no uta. First song
       in the set of four entitled "Songs of the Four Seasons." e♭3-g♭4
       f3-e4 Gently animated in moderate slow tempo. Abounds in triplet
       figures. Requires very fine P and PP. Subdued high ending. Acc:
       3-4 CSN

7099. Song of Winter   All Voices
       Poet: Ryōsuke Hatanaka. Japanese title: Fuyu no uta. Fourth song
       in the set of four entitled "Songs of the Four Seasons." d3-a♭4 g3-
       f4 Animated in lively tempo. Slower middle section. Has dramatic
       passages. Requires fine P and PP. Climactic ending. A fine ending piece for any Oriental group. Acc: 4 CSN

7100. The lullaby   Women
       Poet: Sumako Fukao. Japanese title: Komori uta. First line:
       Minasan otagaini. b2-e4 c3-c4 Sustained in moderate slow tempo.
       Subdued and gentle. Requires some flexibility. Very subdued low
       ending on hummed passage. Acc: 2 JLC-2

MINAO SHIBATA

7101. The fire mountain   Men
       Poet: Shinpei Kusano. Japanese title: Kaji no yama no. First line:
       Hi no yama no. a2-e♭4 e3-d4 Animated in quite lively tempo.
       Energetic, with some dramatic sections. Has quasi-recitative passages. Subdued parlando ending section. Acc: 3-4 JLC-2

OSAMU SHIMIZU

7102. The snake   Men
       Poet: Saisei Muro-o. Japanese title: Hebi. First line: Hebi o
       nagamuru kokoro. d♯3-g♯4 f♯3-f♯4 Animated in lively tempo. Requires fluent enunciation and flexibility. Has energetic and dramatic
       sections. Climactic high ending on g♯4. Generally agitated accompaniment. Acc: 3-4 JLC-2

SABURO TAKATA

President of the Japanese Society for Contemporary Music. His songs show
a very strong Western influence.

STS   Saburo Takata 50 Songs. Japanese script and the phonetic equivalent.
       Tokyo: Ongaku-no-Tomo Sha Corp.

────────────

7103. Basha   Men
       Poet: Tatsuji Miyoshi. English title: Horse carriage. f3-g♭4 a♭3-
       f4 Gently animated vocal part in moderate slow tempo. Gently agitated accompaniment. Subdued, requires very fine P and PP. Acc:
       3-4 STS

7104. Ichi no hanaya   Women
      Poet: Sumako Fukao.   English title: Flower market.   c#3-f#4 f#3-
      e4 Animated vocal part in generally moderate slow tempo. Has pas-
      sages in quasi-recitative style. Climactic ending. Acc: 3 STS

7105. Semi   Men
      Poet: Tatsuji Miyoshi.   English title: Cicada.   d3-f#4 f#3-d4 Sus-
      tained in moderate slow tempo.   Generally gentle, requires fine P
      and PP. Has one strong passage. Very subdued ending. Acc: 3
      STS

7106. Uriko   Men
      Poet: Sumako Fukao.   English title: Shop-boy.   c3-f4 f3-e4 Ani-
      mated in lively tempo.   Has some strong passages and a climactic
      ending. Requires fluent enunciation. Arpeggiated accompaniment.
      Acc: 3-4 STS

7107. Zassō   Men
      Poet: Fuyuhiko Kitagawa.   English title: Grass.   c3-f4 e3-c4 Ani-
      mated in moderate lively tempo.   In quasi-recitative style. Starts
      gently. Climactic, strong ending. Acc: 3 STS

H.   THE NETHERLANDS

I.   Compositions until 1830

WILLEM DE FESCH, 1687-1761

In England he was known as William Defesch.

7108. Canzonetta   High Voices
      Poet: Anon.   First line: Tu fai la superbetta.   e3-g4 g3-d4 Ani-
      mated in lively tempo.   Bright, 7 verses.   Italian text.   Acc: 2-3
      SSO

7109. Daphne   All Voices
      Poet: J. Lyly.   d3-e4 e3-d4 Sustained in moderate tempo.   Grace-
      ful. Has ritornello. Acc: 3 RES-2

FRANÇOIS JOSEPH GOSSEC, 1734-1829

7110. Dors mon enfant   Mezzo-Soprano, Contralto
      Work: ROSINE or L'ÉPOUSE ABANDONÉE, opera 1786, libretto by
      N. Gersin.   Part of Rosine.   c#3-f#4 e3-d4 Very sustained in
      quite slow tempo.   Requires very fine P and PP. Has two climactic
      passages. Very subdued descending ending. Acc: 3 PBA-MC
      (Ch. V)

7111. Doux repos, innocente paix   Dramatic Soprano
      Work: THÉSÉE, opera 1782, libretto by Étienne Morel de Chefdeville,
      after Quinault.   Part of Médée.   eb3-bb4 g3-g4 Sustained, first in
      moderate slow tempo, then faster, more animated. Has recitative

sections. Dramatic, with a climactic ending. Acc: 4 CCF (Ch. V)

7112. R: Ah! faut--il me venger
       A: Ma rivale triomphe   Dramatic Soprano
       Work: THÉSÉE, opera 1782, libretto by Étienne Morel de Chefdeville,
       after Quinault. Part of Médée. f♯3-a4 g3-g4 Strong recitative and
       animated aria in moderate lively tempo. Strong, dramatic. Has
       frequent long-held notes and a climactic ending. Agitated accompani-
       ment. Acc: 4 CCF (Ch. V)

7113. R: Le valeureux Thésée
       A: Ne verrais-je point paraitre   Dramatic Soprano
       Work: THÉSÉE, opera 1782, libretto by Étienne Morel de Chefdeville,
       after Quinault. Part of Églé. f3-bb4 g3-g4 Strong recitative and a
       sustained aria in moderate tempo. Has dramatic passages, climactic
       ending, and agitated accompaniment. Acc: 3-4 CCF (Ch. V)

7114. R: Aux douceurs du sommeil
       A: Rempli de cette noire image   Lyric Bass
       Work: SABINUS, opera 1773, libretto by Michel Paul Guy de Cha-
       banon de Maugris. Part of Sabinus. a1-f♯3(g3) e2-d3 Animated in
       fast tempo. Has dramatic passages and a climactic ending. Acc:
       3-4 CCF (Ch. V)

7115. R: Thésée a triomphé
       A: Un tendre engagement va plus loin   Dramatic Soprano
       Work: THÉSÉE, opera 1782, libretto by Étienne Morel de Chefdeville,
       after Quinault. Part of Médée. f3-ab4(bb4) f3-f4 Strong recitative
       and generally sustained aria in moderate, then lively tempo. Dramat-
       ic. Climactic ending. Agitated accompaniment in the final section.
       Acc: 4 CCF (Ch. V)

CONSTANTIN (CONSTANTIJN) HUYGENS, 1596-1687

PSP   Pathodia Sacra et Profana. Thirty-nine sacred and secular songs by
       Constantine Huygens. Edited by Fritz Noske. Amsterdam: North-
       Holland Publishing Co. , 1957.

                         I. Secular Works

7116. Air   High Voices
       Poet: Constantin Huygens. c♯3-a4 g3-f4 Sustained in moderate
       tempo. Has some slightly climactic passages. Climactic ending.
       Continuo accompaniment. Acc: 3 PSP

7117. Quel neo, quel vago neo   All Voices
       Poet: Giambattista Marino. Other title: Aria. e3-e4 e3-e4 Sus-
       tained in moderate tempo. In gentle recitative style. Slightly cli-
       mactic ending. The modern setting is much too measured for the
       style of this period. Acc: 2-3 SSO

7118. Sérénade   All Voices
       Poet: Constantin Huygens. d3-f4 f3-d4 Sustained in moderate tem-
       po. Generally on MF level. Continuo accompaniment. Best for
       men's voices. First line: Ne crains le serein. Acc: 3 PSP

II.   Sacred Works

7119.   Domine, ne in furore tuo arguas me   High, Medium Voices
        Poet: Psalm 6:2-4.   a2-f#4   f#3-d4 Sustained in moderate tempo.
        Has florid passages and a climactic ending.   Continuo accompaniment.
        Latin text. Acc: 3 PSP

7120.   Erravi Domine   All Voices
        Poet: Psalm 119:176.   e3-e4 g3-d4 Sustained in moderate tempo.
        Has one long florid passage.   Generally on MF level.   Latin text.
        Continuo accompaniment. Acc: 3 PSP

ROLAND DE LASSUS, 1532-1594

7121.   Mon coeur se recommande à vous   All Voices
        Poet: Anon.   The song is dated 1560.   e3-f4 g3-d4 Sustained in
        moderate tempo.   Generally subdued.   Requires fine P and PP.   Acc:
        2-3 ETP-1

II.   Compositions after 1830

HENDRIK ANDRIESSEN

7122.   Fiat Domine   High, Medium Voices
        Poet: Thomas A. Kempis.   e3-g4 g3-d4 Sustained in moderate
        tempo.   Generally subdued, requires fine P and PP.   Subdued ending.
        Constantly moving accompaniment, ending with syncopated rhythms.
        Sacred text.   Scored for voice and piano or organ. Acc: 3 (S) Wed.
        J. R. Roseum, Utrecht

HENK (HENDRIK HERMAN) BADINGS

DLB   Drei Liederen.   Henk Badings.   Amsterdam: Broekman & Van Pop-
        pel.

8SB   8 Songs.   Henk Badings.   Poems by e. e. cummings.   Medium voice
        and piano.   A published manuscript, difficult to read.   Amsterdam:
        DONEMUS.

———

Chanson Orientales.   Henk Badings.   A set of four songs for medium voice
        and piano.   The texts are French translations of different Chinese
        poems.   Amsterdam: DONEMUS.

7123.   (1) L'Indifférente   Medium Voices
        Poet: Wan-Tai.   d3-f4 f3-d4 Somewhat animated vocal part in slow
        tempo.   Requires some fluent enunciation.   Generally on MF level.
        Has some quasi-recitative phrases.   Acc: 3

7124.   (2) La jeune fille nue   Medium Voices
        Poet: Li-Chuang-Kia.   d3-e4 f#3-d4 Animated in very fast tempo.
        Generally light, with some strong passages.   Requires fluent enuncia-
        tion.   Climactic high ending on d4.   Agitated accompaniment, mostly
        in treble range.   Acc: 4

7125.   (3) Derniere promenade   Medium Voices
        Poet: Chang-Wou-Kien.   e3-e4   f♯3-c4   Slightly animated vocal part
        in slow tempo.   Subdued.   Short, one page.   Accompaniment consists
        mostly of sustained chords.   Acc: 3

7126.   (4) Sur les bords Jo-Yeh   Medium Voices
        Poet: Li Tai Po.   f3-f4   f3-d4   Animated in lively tempo.   Has
        some slightly strong passages.   Requires fine P and lightness.   Has
        a few florid passages.   Very agitated, mostly arpeggiated accompani-
        ment.   Slightly climactic ending.   Acc: 5

Liederen van den Dood.   Henk Badings.   Texts by different poets.   A set of
        three songs for baritone and piano.   Amsterdam: DONEMUS.

7127.   (1) Edigius, waer bestu bleven   Baritone
        Poet: Anon.   a♯1-e3   c♯2-c3   Sustained in slow tempo.   Requires
        fine P.   Has some slightly strong passages.   Subdued, descending
        ending.   Acc: 3

7128.   (2) O, als ik dood zal zijn   Baritone
        Poet: J. H. Leopold.   c♯2-d3   d2-a2   Sustained in moderate slow
        tempo.   Generally subdued and short.   Requires fine P and PP.
        Generally gentle.   Acc: 3

7129.   (3) Triomf van den dood   Baritone
        Poet: J. Werumeus Buning.   c♯2-f3   e2-d3   Animated in march tem-
        po.   Strong, climactic, and triumphal.   Has dramatic high passages
        and dotted rhythms.   Dramatic ending.   Accompaniment mostly on
        full chords.   Acc: 3

Single Songs

7130.   All in green went my love riding   Mezzo-Soprano
        Poet: e. e. cummings.   c3-g♭4   e3-d♭4   Animated in moderate tem-
        po.   Requires some flexibility.   Generally strong, with F and FF
        markings.   Descending ending line after high climax.   Acc: 3   8SB

7131.   Burying friends   Medium Voices
        Poet: Kenneth Slessor.   c3-f♯4   e3-e♭4   Generally sustained in slow,
        grave tempo.   Has passages in quasi-recitative style.   Climactic pas-
        sages.   Descending ending line.   Extended piano prelude and postlude.
        Acc: 3-4   (S)DO

7132.   Coplas   High, Medium Voices
        Poet: Hendrik de Vries.   b2-g♯4   d3-d4   Sustained in varied tempi.
        Starts slowly and very subdued.   Requires fine P and PP.   Has dra-
        matic passages.   Rapid ending section.   Descending ending line after
        high climax.   Accompaniment has agitated sections.   Acc: 4-5
        (S)BP

7133.   If I have made, my lady, intricate   Baritone
        Poet: e(dward) e(stlin) cummings.   b2-g♭4   e3-d♭4   Animated vocal
        part in moderate tempo.   Requires flexibility.   Generally gentle, on
        MF level.   Has dotted rhythms.   Acc: 3   8SB

7134.   Petrus Weenende   Medium, High Voices
        Poet: Heiman Dullaart.   c3-g4   e3-e4   Sustained in generally moder-
        ate slow tempo.   Has some variations in tempi, with some slightly

animated vocal parts. Requires some fine P to PPP. Very subdued
high ending on d#4. Acc: 3 DLB

HENRIETTA (HILDA) BOSMANS, 1895-1952

DMB   Dix Melodies. Medium voice and piano. Henrietta Bosmans. Ten
songs, with texts by different poets. Amsterdam: Broekmans & Van
Poppel.

7135. Die heil'gen drei Kön'ge aus Morgenland   High, Medium Voices
Poet: Heinrich Heine. b2-g4 e3-e♭4 Animated in lively tempo.
Has climactic passages. Climactic high ending. Has recitative pas-
sages. Starts gently. Acc: 3 (S)BP

7136. Een Lied voor Spanje   Medium Voices
Poet: J. Werumeus Buning. b2-e3 e3-d4 Animated in lively tempo, with variations. Has strong and dramatic sections. Also requires fine P. Has passages in quasi-recitative style. Climactic
ending. Acc: 4 In: Samenklank, Vol. 2, BP

7137. Im Mondenglanze ruht das Meer   Medium Voices
Poet: Heinrich Heine. c3-e4 d3-c4 Sustained in moderate slow
tempo. Starts and ends subdued. Has climactic passages. Very
subdued low ending. Has some quasi-recitative passages. Acc: 3
(S)BP

7138. L'anneau   Medium, Low Voices
Poet: Fernand Mazade. c3-e♭4 f3-c4 Sustained in moderate tempo,
with variations. Has climactic passages. Requires fine P. Very
subdued low ending. Agitated accompaniment. Acc: 3 DMB

7139. Le naufrage   Medium Voices
Poet: André Verdet. b♭2(a♭2)-f#4 e3-e4 Sustained in moderate
tempo, with variations. Has climactic passages. Requires fine P.
Very subdued low ending. Agitated accompaniment. Acc: 3 DMB

ALPHONS DIEPENBROCK, 1862-1921

7140. Les chats   Medium, Low Voices
Poet: Charles Baudelaire. b2(g#2)-e4 d#3-b3 Sustained in slow
tempo. Gentle. Requires some fine P and PP. Subdued throughout,
in quasi-recitative style. Very subdued low ending. Acc: 3
(S)C. V. de Nieuwe Musiekhandel, Amsterdam

MARIUS (M. HENDRIKUS) FLOTHUIS

7141. Lied   Medium, Low Voices
Poet: J. H. Leopold. d3-c4 f3-a♭4 Sustained in moderate tempo.
Short. Generally on MF level. No strong passages or contrasts.
Acc: 3 In: Samenklank, Vol. 2, BP

JAAP GERAEDTS

7142. The world   Baritone
       Poet: Henry Vaughan. c♯2-e4 e♭2-b2 Sustained in moderate tem-
       po. Has dramatic passages. In quasi-recitative style. Starts strong-
       ly. Ends with subdued, long-held note. Acc: 3 (S)DO

7143. Tortelduve   Mezzo-Soprano
       Poet: Hoffmann von Fallersleben. d3-f4 e3-d4 Sustained in mod-
       erate slow tempo. Generally on MF level. Short, gentle. Very
       subdued low ending. Acc: 3 (S)DO

PIET KETTING

Three Sonnets. Piet Ketting. A set of songs for medium voice and piano.
       Texts by William Shakespeare. The original English texts, with a
       Dutch version by Balthazar Verhagen. Amsterdam: DONEMUS.

7144. (1) Since I left you   Medium Voices
       Poem: Sonnet CXIII. c♯3(a♯2)-e4 c♯3-c♯4 Sustained in moderate
       tempo. Has some climactic passages. Starts and ends subdued.
       Subdued low ending. Acc: 3

7145. (2) The little love-god   Medium Voices
       Poem: Sonnet CLIV. b♭2-f4 f3-d♭4 Sustained in slow tempo. Has
       two florid passages. In quasi-recitative style. Starts and ends gen-
       tly. Requires fine P and PP. Acc: 3

7146. (3) Music to hear   Medium Voices
       Poem: Sonnet VIII. c♯3-f♯4 f♯3-c♯4 Animated in very rapid tem-
       po. Starts and ends strongly. Subdued middle section. Requires
       some fluent enunciation. Has dramatic passages. Climactic ending
       on d♯4. Agitated accompaniment. Acc: 4

(KURT) RUDOLF MENGELBERG, 1892-1959

HVV   Hart van Vlaanderen. Rudolf Mengelberg. Nine songs. Amsterdam:
      Broekmans & Van Poppel.

                          _____

Chamber Music. Rudolf Mengelberg. Poems from Chamber Music, by
       James Joyce. A cycle of nine songs for medium voice and piano.
       Amsterdam: Broekmans & Van Poppel. (A fine cycle. Well recom-
       mended.)

7147. (1) Strings in the earth and air   Medium Voices
       d♭3-e4 g3-c4 Animated in moderate lively tempo. Generally sub-
       dued. Short. Generally gentle. Has repeated notes. Acc: 3

7148. (2) Lean out of the window   Medium Voices
       d3-e4 e3-d4 Sustained vocal part in moderate lively tempo. Grace-
       ful. Generally subdued; requires fine P and PP. Very subdued, high
       ending. Acc: 3

7149. (3) Winds of May   Medium Voices
       b♭2-f4 f3-d4 Sustained vocal part in rapid tempo. Has dramatic

passages.   Subdued, low ending section.   Agitated accompaniment.
Acc: 4

7150.   (4) My dove, my beautiful one   Medium Voices
ab 2-f♯ 4   f♯ 3-e4   Sustained vocal part in moderate lively tempo.
Has some climactic passages.   Requires fine P and PP.   Ends on
long-held eb 4 marked PP.   Acc: 3

7151.   (5) Because your voice was at my side   Medium Voices
db 3-eb 4   f3-db 4   Sustained in moderate slow tempo.   Generally subdued, with two slightly climactic passages.   Subdued low ending.
Acc: 3

7152.   (6) O, it was out by Donnycarney   Medium Voices
d3-gb 4   f3-eb 4   Animated in lively tempo.   Has one climactic passage.   Subdued first part.   Descending, subdued ending line.   Acc:
3

7153.   (7) Rain has fallen all the day   Medium Voices
eb 3-e♯ 4   g♯ 3-c♯ 4   Sustained in moderate slow tempo.   Subdued
throughout, requires fine P and PP.   See the settings by Samuel
Barber, Ernest Moeran, and Robert Ward.   Acc: 3

7154.   (8) Sleep now, O sleep now   Medium Voices
e3-f4   f3-db 4   Sustained in moderate tempo.   Generally subdued, with
a couple of short climactic phrases.   Requires fine P and PP.   Subdued, low ending.   See the settings by Sergius Kagen and Samuel
Barber.   Acc: 3

7155.   (9) I hear an army   Medium Voices
bb 2-f4   c3-d♯ 4   Animated in march tempo.   Accented, with dramatic
passages.   Intense.   Subdued ending section with very subdued descending ending line.   Generally agitated accompaniment.   See the
setting by Samuel Barber.   Acc: 4

Single Songs

7156.   Het klokgebed   All Voices
Poet: Guido Gezelle.   d3-e4   e3-c4   Sustained in moderate tempo.
Requires fluent enunciation.   Has climactic passages and a subdued
ending.   Acc: 3 HVV

7157.   Hosannah   Medium Voices
Poet: Guido Gezelle.   bb 2-e4 (f♯ 4)   g3-e4   Animated in lively tempo.
Strong, exultant, and climactic.   Has slightly florid figures.   Climac-
tic high ending.   Not for light voices.   Acc: 3-4 HVV

Note: See also Suid-Afrikaanse Liedere.   Nine songs for medium voice and
piano.   Amsterdam: Broekmans & Van Poppel.

BERNHARD VAN SIGTENHORST MEYER, 1888-1953

VGL   Vijf Geestelijke Liederen.   Op. 21.   Bernhard Meyer.   Five sacred
songs with texts in Dutch, German, and English.   Amsterdam: G.
Alsbach & Co.

7158. De nare schaduw is aan't breeken   High Voices
       Poet: Jan Luyken. f3-a4 g3-e4 Sustained in moderate tempo. Has
       climactic high passages. Slightly extended piano postlude. English
       first line: The somber shadows are dispersing. Acc: 3 VGL

7159. Ick meenden oock de Godheyt woonde verre   High, Medium Voices
       Poet: Jan Luyken. f3-f♯4 g3-d4 Sustained vocal part in moderate
       lively tempo. Generally subdued; no contrasts in dynamics. English
       first line: I once believed the God-head dwelt serenely on a high
       throne. Acc: 3 VGL

JAN (JOHAN) MUL

Van Langendonck Liederen. Jan Mul. A set of four songs for medium
       voice and piano. Texts by Prosper van Langendonck. Amsterdam:
       Broekmans & Van Poppel.

7160. (1) Frisse, blonde Kinderjaren   Medium Voices
       c♯3-d♯4 f♯3-c♯4 Gently animated vocal part in moderate slow tem-
       po. Generally subdued. Subdued low ending. Acc: 3

7161. (2) Ik weet niet waar ik ga   Medium Voices
       a2-e♭4 e3-c4 Animated in moderate lively tempo. Has slower mid-
       dle section. Requires some fluent enunciation. Starts and ends
       strongly. In quasi-recitative style. Acc: 3-4

7162. (3) O pure nacht, zo zoel   Medium Voices
       c♯3-d♯4 d♯3-c♯4 Sustained in slow tempo. Requires some fluent
       enunciation. Subdued low ending. Generally agitated accompaniment.
       Acc: 3-4

7163. (4) De bomen staan van bloesems vol   Medium Voices
       d3-e4 e3-c♯4 Animated in moderate slow tempo. Generally on MF
       level. Subdued, quasi-recitative, descending ending line. Agitated
       accompaniment. Acc: 5

JAN NIELAND

7164. Old-English cradle-song   All Voices
       Poet: Anon. c3-f4 f3-d4 Sustained in moderate tempo. Gentle,
       generally subdued, graceful. A Christmas song. Acc: 3 (S)BP

HANS SCHOUMAN

ONS   Oud-Nederlandsche Liedern. Hans Schouman. Utrecht: J. A. H.
       Wagenaar.

       ———————————

7165. De boeren   Medium Voices
       Poet: Anon. g3-d4 g3-d4 Gently animated in moderate lively tem-
       po. Generally on MF level. Light and agitated accompaniment.
       Acc: 3 ONS

7166. Het hemelsch Jerusalem   Medium Voices
       Poet: Anon. d♭3-e♭4 e♭3-c4 Sustained in moderate slow tempo.

Slightly faster middle section.   Subdued ending.   Generally on MF
level.   Acc: 3 ONS

MAX VREDENBURG

<u>Au Pays des Vendanges</u>.   Max Vredenburg.   A set of three songs for bari-
tone or mezzo-soprano and piano.   Best for baritone.   Poems by
Ronsard, Molière, and Basselin.   English title: In the Wine Country.
Three drinking songs.   Amsterdam: DONEMUS.

7167.   (1) Odelette   Baritone, Mezzo-Soprano
Poet: Pierre de Ronsard.   English title: Little ode.   d3-e4 f3-c4
Animated in moderate lively tempo.   Bright, has florid passages.
Requires some flexibility.   Has vigorous passages.   Acc: 3

7168.   (2) Chanson a boire   Baritone, Mezzo-Soprano
Poet: Jean Baptiste Poquelin Molière.   English title: Drinking song.
e3-g4 a3-e4 Animated in moderate lively tempo.   Bold, joyous, in
3/4 time.   Climactic high ending.   2 verses.   Acc: 3

7169.   (3) Bon vin donne vigueur!   Baritone, Mezzo-Soprano
Poet: Basselin.   English title: Good wine gives strength.   eb3-f4
f3-db4 Animated in moderate lively tempo.   Bold, joyous, 2 verses.
Semi-climactic ending.   Acc: 3

I. PHILIPPINES

NONI ESPINA (Full name: A[NGEL] BEAUNONI ESPINA)

<u>Baybayon</u>.   English title: Seashore.   Music and texts in Cebuano (Philippine)
and English by the composer.   A song cycle of eight movements for
high voice and piano.   Dayton, Oh: Capella Music c/o Lorenz, Inc.,
1969.   (Includes a guide for Cebuano diction, and English for performance.   The music is a wedding of Far Eastern and Western styles.)

7170.   (1) Balay daplin sa baybayon   High Voices
English: House by the seashore.   e3-g4 g3-e4 Sustained in moder-
ate slow tempo.   Has climactic high passages.   Requires fine P.
Gently agitated accompaniment.   Subdued high ending.   Acc: 3-4

7171.   (2) Kinhason   High Voices
English: Seashells.   eb3-g4 g3-e4 Gently animated in moderate
tempo.   Light, delicate, gently joyous.   Requires some fluent enunciation and flexibility.   Unmeasured, free.   Ends with descending, vocalized passage.   Requires light accompaniment.   Acc: 3-4

7172.   (3) Manga pukot   High Voices
English: Fishnets.   c3-g4 g3-c4 Sustained in moderate slow tempo.
Generally gentle, requires simplicity.   Descriptive; some rubato re-
quired.   Descending ending line.   Acc: 3

7173.   (4) Laylay   High Voices
English: Lullaby.   d3-d#4 d3-c4 "Laylay" is the compound syllable

used in singing lullabies. Lullaby is sung by man or woman. Very
sustained and delicate in slow tempo. Subdued throughout, requires
very fine P and PP. Requires simplicity and gentle freedom. Acc:
3

7174.   (5) Habagat   High Voices
English: Monsoon. f3-ab4 ab3-ab4 Sustained vocal part in moderate tempo. Strong, with dramatic climaxes. Majestic, broad, descriptive. Dramatic high ending, from ab4-f4, last note sustained.
Very agitated accompaniment. Acc: 4-5

7175.   (6) Harana   High Voices
English: Serenade. e3-a4 g3-e4 Recollection of a serenade, not
the serenade itself. Very sustained in moderate slow tempo. Has
frequent meter changes and flowing lines. Tranquil, generally subdued, very reflective. Subdued high ending, from g4 to e4. Acc:
3-4

7176.   (7) Tabun ug owak   High Voices
English: Heron and crow. d3-f#4 f3-d4 First section: bright in
moderate slow tempo; inwardly joyous. Second section: dark in slow
tempo; grave, subdued, somewhat foreboding, with funereal march in
the accompaniment. Interpretatively not easy. Acc: 3-4

7177.   (8) Bonbon   High Voices
English: Sand. c3-g4 a3-e4 Sustained in moderate tempo. Majestic, broad, generally marked. Descriptive first part. Dramatic,
powerful, with a high ending section; ends on a long-held g4. Full-
sounding piano accompaniment with heavy, full chord clusters. Acc:
4

Manga Awit sa Magdiwata. English: Songs of the Pagan. The music, most
Philippine texts, and all English by the composer. A cycle of five
movements for medium voice (or all voices), piano, with optional
flute, ten-inch gong, and drum; or piano alone. May be sung with
any combination of instruments indicated. Includes diction guide to
Philippine texts. Dumaguete, Phil. : Silliman Music Foundation, Inc. ,
1968. (The cycle has been performed with success by high voices.)
(SC)VD

7178.   (1) Gayumko gimanggaman   Medium, or All Voices
English: My sacrificial spear. d3-d#4 eb3-c4 Animated in moderate lively tempo. Rhythmic; requires flexibility. Has strong contrasts in dynamics. The brisk second half requires fluent enunciation. Subdued and nonritarded ending. Acc: 4

7179.   (2) Bulak sa kabuntagon   Medium, or All Voices
English: Flower of morning. c3-d4 d3-c4 Very sustained in slow
tempo. Tranquil, subdued, reflective, delicate. Recitative-style
middle section. Subdued ending. Delicate piano part throughout.
Acc: 3

7180.   (3) Salangi, salangi yanut   Medium, or All Voices
English: Pledge of loyalty. With flute. e3-b3 e3-a3 The voice
part is sustained in moderate tempo, is short, and supplements the
flute. Subdued throughout. Acc: 3

7181.   (4) Bankaw ug taming   Medium, or All Voices

English: Spear and shield. With gong and drum parts. e♭3-e4 f3-
c4 Animated in lively tempo. Accented, strong, bold, rhythmic.
Performance intended without finesse, but without exaggeration. A
war chant by priest or priestess in ancient times. Acc: 3-4

7182. (5) Ililang   Medium, or All Voices
English: A lover's lament. With flute. d3-e4 e3-d4 Very sustained in slow tempo. Subdued and sad throughout. Has some intervalic complexities. Very subdued ending with a spoken sigh. "Ililang"
is the name of the loved one for whom the lament is sung. Acc: 3

Single Song

7183. Shepherd's psalm   High Voices
Text: Psalm 23. e♭3-g♯4 f3-f4 Sustained in moderate tempo, with
variations. Subdued beginning and ending. Has climactic high passages and some florid figures. Requires flexibility. Chromatic, with
some rhythmic complexities. Scored for voice, flute, and piano;
also for voice and piano. Acc: 4 (S)VD

J. POLAND

FRYDERYK FRANCISZEK (FRÉDÉRIC FRANÇOIS) CHOPIN, 1810-1849

Chopin wrote only 19 songs. Some of them are from an early period in his
composing career. Although the songs are not in any way near the high
quality of his piano music, they are at least better than the average Polish
song compositions of his time. In some of them one finds infusions of the
Polish folk song style and suggestions of Polish dance rhythms, such as the
mazurka. All of Chopin's vocal music is published in the collected complete
works by The Fryderyk Chopin Institute of Warsaw.

CCW Chopin Complete Works. Vol. XVII: Songs. Edited by Ignacy J.
     Paderewski. Original Polish texts, with English versions. Warsaw:
     The Fryderyk Chopin Institute through Polish Music Publications
     (Polskie Wydawnictwo Muzyczne), 1962.

SPS Seventeen Polish Songs. Frederick Chopin. Original keys. Polish
     texts, with English versions. Edited by Jan Sliwinski. London:
     Paterson's Publications. (Note: Has very fine notes on the com-
     poser.)

SSC Seventeen Songs. Frederick Chopin. German and English versions
     only. High, low. New York: G. Schirmer, Inc.

Note: Opus 74 is only an arbitrary number. The English titles used in this
      work are based on CCW.

7184. A drinking song   Men
Poet: Stephan Witwicki. Polish title: Hulanka. German: Bacchanal.
Op. 74, No. 4. First Polish line: Szynkareczko boj, sil Boga. d3-
f4 f3-c4 Animated in very lively tempo. A mazurka, outgoing, joyous, and generally strong. 4 verses. Original key: three steps

lower.   Acc: 3 CCW, SSC, SPS

7185. A girl's desire   All Voices
Poet: Stephan Witwicki. Polish title: Gdzie lubi. German: Was
ein junges Mädchen liebt. Op. 74, No. 5. First Polish line:
Strumyk lubi. d♯3-e4 f♯3-c4 Animated in lively tempo. Requires
some flexibility. Generally light, graceful. Original key. Acc: 3
CCW, SSC, SPS

7186. A Lithuanian song   Women
Poet: Ludwik Osinski. Polish title: Piosnka Litewska. German:
Lithauisches Lied. Op. 74, No. 16. First Polish line: Bardzo
raniuchno. e3-e4 f3-c4 Gently animated vocal part in moderate
tempo. Requires some characterization. The short interlude is a
mazurka. Original key: one step lower. Acc: 3 CCW, SSC, SPS

7187. A maiden's wish   All Voices
Poet: Stephan Witwicki. Polish title: Zyczenie. German: Mädchens
Wunsch. Op. 74, No. 1. First Polish line: Gdybym ja byla. c♯3-
e4 f♯3-d4 Animated in lively tempo. A mazurka. Graceful, gentle, and generally on MF level. Best for men's voices. Original key:
one step lower. Acc: 3 CCW, SSC, SPS, SVR-2

7188. A melody   All Voices
Poet: Zygmunt Krasinski. Polish title: Melodya. German: Eine
Melodie. Op. 74, No. 9. First Polish line: Z gor, gdzie. d♯3-
g4 f♯3-d4 Sustained in moderate slow tempo. Has climactic passages and a low, subdued ending. Sad text, rather intense. Written
in the style of an arioso. Original key. Chopin's last song. Acc:
3 CCW, SSC, SPS

7189. Death's divisions   All Voices
Poet: Bohdan Zaleski. Polish title: Dwojaki koniec. German:
Zwei Leichen. Op. 74, No. 11. First Polish line: Rok sic kochali.
e3-f4 f3-e♭4 Sustained in moderate lively tempo. Generally on MF
level. Best for medium or low voices. Narrative text. Original
key: three steps lower. Acc: 3 CCW, 50M, SSC, SPS

7190. Faded and vanished   All Voices
Poet: Bohdan Zaleski. Polish title: Neima czego trzeba. German:
Melancholie. Op. 74, No. 13. First Polish line: Mgta mi do oczu.
e3-f4 f3-d4 Sustained in slow tempo. Climactic ending. 4 verses.
Original key. Acc: 2-3 CCW, SSC, SPS

7191. Leaves are falling   Medium, Low Voices
Poet: Wincent Pol. Polish title: Spiew grobowy. German: Polens
Grabgesang. Op. 74, No. 17. First Polish line: Leci liście z
drzewa. b♭2-f4 e♭3-c4 A nationalistic song, with texts perhaps by
Chopin himself grieving on the unhappy fate of Poland in strife. Sustained, first in moderate, then slow tempo. Generally subdued, requires fine P and PP. Original key. Acc: 3 CCW, SSC, SPS

7192. My sweetheart   High, Medium Voices
Poet: Adam Mickiewicz. Polish title: Moja pieszczotka. German:
Meine Freuden. Op. 74, No. 12. First Polish line: Moja pieszc-
zotka. d♭3-a♭4 f3-e♭4 Gently animated in moderate lively tempo.
Graceful. Descending ending after strong climax. Original key.
Acc: 3 CCW, 50M, SSC, SPS

7193. Out of my sight!   All Voices
Poet: Adam Mickiewicz. Polish title: Precz z moich oczu! German: Mir aus den Blicken! First Polish line: Precz z moich. Op. 74, No. 6. e3-f4 f3-d4 Sustained in moderate tempo. Has clear-cut contrasts in dynamics. First part is a slow mazurka. First verse in 3/4; second and third verses in 2/4 meter. Original key: three steps lower. Acc: 3 CCW, SSC, SPS

7194. Sad river   All Voices
Poet: Stephan Witwicki. Polish title: Smutna rzeka. German: Trübe Wellen. Op. 74, No. 3. First Polish line: Rzeko z cudzo-ziemców. c#3-d#4 f#3-d4 Sustained in moderate slow tempo. Generally subdued. Narrative and somber texts. Best for the darker voices. Original key. Acc: 3 CCW, SSC, SPS

7195. Spring   Men
Poet: Stephan Witwicki. Polish title: Wiosna. German: Der Frühling. Op. 74, No. 2. First Polish line: Blyszcza krople. g3-g4 a3-d4 Gracefully animated in moderate slow tempo. Requires fine high PP. Generally on MF level. Original key. Acc: 3 CCW, SSC, SPS

7196. The bridegroom   All Voices
Poet: Stephan Witwicki. Polish title: Narzeczony. German: Die Heimkehr. Op. 74, No. 15. First Polish line: Wiatr zaszumiat. d#3-e4 f#3-e4 Animated in very fast tempo. Requires fluent enunciation. Extended piano prelude and postlude in fast-moving chromatic scale figures. 4 verses. Original key: three steps lower. Acc: 3-4 CCW, SSC, SPS

7197. The handsome lad   Women
Poet: Bohdan Zaleski. Polish title: Sliczny chlopiec. German: Mein Geliebter. Op. 74, No. 8. First Polish line: Wzniosty, smukty. c#3-f#4 f#3-d4 Animated in moderate lively tempo. In folk song style, requires simplicity. Descending ending line. 3 verses and refrain. Original key. Acc: 3 CCW, SSC, SPS

7198. The messenger   Men
Poet: Stephan Witwicki. Polish title: Posel. German: Der Bote. Op. 74, No. 7. First Polish line: Rosnie trawka. First line in SPS: Blysto ranne ziotko. e3-f4 f3-d4 Sustained in moderate slow tempo. Requires simplicity. 3 verses. Original key: three steps lower. Acc: 3 CCW, SSC, SPS

7199. The ring   Men
Poet: Stephan Witwicki. Polish title: Pierścień. German: Das Ringlein. Op. 74, No. 14. First Polish line: Smutno nianki ci. eb3-d4 g3-c4 Sustained in moderate tempo. Generally on MF level. Simple melody, 2 verses. Original key. Acc: 2 CCW, SSC, SPS

7200. The warrior   Men
Poet: Stephan Witwicki. Polish title: Wojak. German: Der Reiters-mann von der Schlacht. Op. 74, No. 10. First Polish line: Rzy moj gniady. f3-f4 ab3-db4 Animated in lively tempo. Requires simplicity. Rhythmic. 3 verses. Original key. Acc: 3 CCW, SSC, SPS

WITOLD LUTOSLAWSKI

FSL   Five Songs. Witold Lutoslawski. A set of five songs for women's
        voices and piano. Texts by Kaziniera Illakowicz. English version by
        Ann and Adam Czerniawski. Celle: Hermann Moeck Verlag, 1963.

_____

7201. Church bells   Soprano, Mezzo-Soprano
       Poet: Kazimiera Illakowicz. Polish title: Dzwony cerkiewne. c3-f4
       e3-c4 Sustained in moderate tempo. Starts gently. Strong, dramatic
       second half with some wide intervalic skips. Acc: 3 FSL

7202. Knights   Contralto
       Poet: Kazimiera Illakowicz. bb 2-c4 d3-c4 Polish title: Rycerze.
       Animated in very rapid tempo. Requires flexibility. Starts strongly.
       Subdued ending section. In quasi-recitative style. Very subdued end-
       ing. Acc: 4 FSL

7203. The sea   Soprano, Mezzo-Soprano
       Poet: Kazimiera Illakowicz. Polish title: Morze. db 3-f4 f3-e4
       Sustained in moderate tempo. Starts very gently. Subdued throughout.
       Requires very fine P and PP. Detached, delicate accompaniment
       throughout. Acc: 3 FSL

7204. The wind   Soprano, Mezzo-Soprano
       Poet: Kazimiera Illakowicz. Polish title: Wiatr. c3-g# 4 e3-e4
       Generally animated in fast tempo. Vigorous, energetic, and mostly
       marked F and FF. Has long-held notes and agitated accompaniment.
       Dramatic, descending ending line. Not for light voices. Acc: 4
       FSL

7205. Winter   Mezzo-Soprano, Contralto
       Poet: Kazimiera Illakowicz. Polish title: Zima. a2-e4 d3-c4
       Sustained in moderate slow tempo. Starts very gently. Very subdued
       throughout. Requires very fine PP. Dark, descriptive. Descending
       ending line. Acc: 3 FSL

MICHAL KLEOFAS OGIŃSKI, 1765-1833

RMO   Romanse. Michal Kleofas Ogiński. Seventeen songs with Polish texts
       and French versions. Krakow: Polskie Wydawnictwo Muzyczne,
       c/o A. Broude.

_____

7206. Dafni   Medium Voices
       Poet: Giovanni Battista Perucchini. Polish title: Do Dafnisa. c# 3-
       f4 f# 3-e4 Sustained in moderate slow tempo. Graceful. Generally
       on MF level. Has some florid figures and a few climactic passages.
       Climactic ending. Acc: 3 RMO

7207. Doux souvenir   High Voices
       Poet: Anon. Polish title: Wspomnienia. f3-ab 4 ab 3-f4 Sustained
       in moderate slow tempo. Generally on MF level. Has one florid
       figure. 3 verses. Acc: 3 RMO

7208. Polonese   High Voices
       Poet: Anon. Polish title: Polonez. f3-a4 f3-f4 The song is in

two parts, namely Polonese I and Polonese II. Both are semi-animated in moderate tempo. Has some florid passages and climactic passages. Requires flexibility. Climactic ending. Agitated accompaniment in dance style. Acc: 3-4 RMO

IGNACY (JAN) PADEREWSKI, 1860-1941

7209. Ach! Die Qualen   All Voices
       Poet: Adam Mickiewicz.   f♯ 3-f♯ 4   g♯ 3-f♯ 4 Sustained in moderate
       lively tempo. Light. Requires fine P and PP. Very subdued ending.
       Acc: 3 50M

ANDRZEJ PANUFNIK (Now a British citizen)

7210. Hommage à Chopin   Soprano
       Five vocalises for soprano and piano. e♭ 3-a♭ 4 g3-g4 May be per-
       formed as one work or separately. Singer is given full liberty in the
       use of vowels and breathing marks. The first and last songs may be
       transposed a minor third. All require flexibility and a good command
       of high notes. The musical themes of this suite are based on Polish
       folk melodies. Duration: 15 minutes. Acc: 3-4 London: Boosey
       & Hawkes.

POLDOWSKI (LADY DEAN PAUL, born Irene Regine Wieniawska), 1880-1932

7211. Brume   High, Medium Voices
       Poet: Paul Verlaine. d3-f4 f3-c4 Sustained in slow tempo. Tran-
       quil, rather somber. Has some climactic high passages. Subdued
       ending. Not for light, high voices. Acc: 3 (S)HO

7212. Dansons la gigue   Men
       Poet: Paul Verlaine. d3-g4 g3-g4 Quite animated in very fast tem-
       po. Outgoing and strong. Starts in quasi-recitative style. Climactic
       and very strong ending on g4. May be transposed for the lower
       voices, but not suitable for bass. See the setting by Carpenter. Acc:
       4 40F-2 (Ch. V), (S)CH

7213. L'Heure exquise   All Voices
       Poet: Paul Verlaine. d♭ 3-a♭ 4 d♭ 3-d♭ 4 Sustained in slow tempo.
       Starts and ends calmly. Dramatic middle section. Very subdued
       ending. See the settings by Szulc & Hahn, "Apaisement" by Chausson,
       "La lune blanche" by Fauré and Delius, "La bonne chanson" by Stra-
       vinsky. Acc: 3 40F (Ch. V), (S)AD, CH

KAZIMIERZ SEROCKI

Eyes of Air. Polish title: Oczy Powietrza. Kazimierz Serocki. A song
       cycle in five movements for soprano and piano. Words by Julian
       Przyboś. English by Ann and Adam Czerniawski. Text in Polish,
       with English and German versions. Cracow: Polskie Wydawnictwo
       Muzyczne.

7214. (1) Meeting   Soprano
       Polish title: Spotkanie. c3-a4 f3-d4 Sustained in slow tempo. In

quasi-recitative. Generally subdued, requires fine P and PP. Has
spoken ending marked "misterioso." Acc: 3

7215. (2) Lilac   Soprano
Polish title: Bez.   d♯3-b♭4   g3-e4 Sustained in moderate tempo.
Has energetic, dramatic high passages. Also requires very fine high
P. Has frequent meter changes. Subdued, descending ending line
with the last word spoken. Acc: 3-4

7216. (3) A passing moment   Soprano
Polish title: Chwila.   d♭3(a♯2)-a4   g3-e4 Sustained in slow tempo.
Subdued, requires fine P. Requires simplicity. Spoken ending on
a♯2. Acc: 3

7217. (4) The path   Soprano
Polish title: Sciezka.   c3-a4   e3-e4 Sustained in moderate slow
tempo. Starts gently. Requires very fine high PP. Has one dramatic high passage and quasi-recitative passages. Subdued low ending.
Acc: 3

7218. (5) Evening   Soprano
Polish title: Wieczór.   c3-a4   f3-e4 Sustained in slow tempo.
Starts gently. Generally subdued. Requires very fine high P. In
gentle quasi-recitative. Subdued ending phrase which ascends over
one octave and sustained a4 marked perpendosi. Acc: 3

Heart of the Night. Polish title: Serce Nocy. Kazimierz Serocki. A song
cycle in five movements for baritone and piano. Texts by Konstanty
I. Galczyński. Texts in Polish, with English version by Ann and
Adam Czerniawski and German. English version is on a separate
sheet with the melody. Cracow: Polskie Wydawnictwo Muzyczne.

7219. (1) Night   Baritone
Polish title: Noc.   g♯1-f3   c2-c♯3 Generally sustained in slow tempo. Starts in quasi-recitative style. Requires very fine high PP.
Generally on MF level. Has some frequent meter changes. Requires
fine P and PP. Very subdued ending. Acc: 4

7220. (2) Epistle to lovers   Baritone
Polish title: Epistola do zakochanych.   a♭1-e3   e♭2-c3 Sustained in
moderate tempo. Requires fine P and PP. Generally subdued. Subdued ending. Has sudden changes in meter. Acc: 3

7221. (3) Meeting with my mother   Baritone
Polish title: Spotkanie z matka.   c2-e3   e2-d3 Generally sustained
in moderate tempo. Requires very fine high P to PPP. Subdued
throughout on high tessitura. Difficult. Accompaniment is mostly on
treble range. Acc: 4

7222. (4) The sleigh   Baritone
Polish title: Sanie.   b♭1(a♭1)-f3   c2-c3 Sustained in moderate tempo. Has quasi-recitative passages. Generally on MF level. Requires fine P. Subdued ending with a final spoken phrase. The a♭1
is spoken. Acc: 3

7223. (5) The moon   Baritone
Polish title: Ksieżyc.   a1(a♭1)-e3   d3-c4 Generally in parlando
style on MF level. Requires very fine high P and PP. Has many

subdued passages.   Descending ending with a final spoken passage.
The a♭1 is spoken.   Acc: 3

JÓSEF SZULC, 1875-1935

7224.   Clair de lune   All Voices
Poet: Paul Verlaine.   d♭3-g♭4   f3-f4 Sustained in very slow tempo.
Dynamics are P and PP almost throughout.   Very subdued final sec-
tion.   Constantly moving, light accompaniment.   See the settings by
Debussy and Fauré.   Acc: 4 40F-2 (Ch. V)

7225.   Mandoline   Soprano
Poet: Paul Verlaine.   d3-a4(b4)   g3-e4 Animated in quite rapid tempo.   Requires fluent and crisp enunciation, and flexibility.   Has dramatic passages, and a dramatic high ending (e4 or b4).   Very agitated accompaniment.   See the settings by Debussy, Fauré, Dupont,
Bourguignon, and "Fetes galantes" by Hahn.   Poldowski also wrote a
setting to this same text.   Acc: 4   (S)RL

KAROL (MACIEJ) SZYMANOWSKI, 1882-1937

4SS   4 Songs.   Op. 54.   Karol Szymanowski.   Four songs for high voice
and piano.   Texts by James Joyce, from his "Chamber Music," with
Polish version by J. Iwaszkiewicz.   Cracow: Polskie Wydawnictwo
Muzyczne.

Des Hafis Liebeslieder.   Op. 24.   Karol Szymanowski.   Poems by Hafiz.
Polish texts, with German versions by Hans Bethge.   A set of six
songs for high voice and piano.   Vienna: Universal Edition.

7226.   (1) Wünsche   High Voices
Polish title: Życzenia.   c♯3-g4   f♯3-e4 Sustained in moderate slow
tempo.   Starts very gently.   Has climactic passages.   Requires fine
PP.   Descending ending line.   Agitated accompaniment.   Acc: 4

7227.   (2) Die einsige Arzenei   High Voices
Polish title: Jedyne lekarstwo.   c♯3(b2)-g4(g♯4)   g♯3-d4 Sustained
in lively tempo.   Strong entrance.   Has climactic passages.   Requires
fine P and PP.   Subdued, low ending.   Agitated accompaniment.   Acc:
4

7228.   (3) Die brennenden Tulpin   High Voices
Polish title: Płonące Tulipany.   e3-a4   g3-d4 Sustained in slow tempo.   Starts gently.   Has one dramatic high passage.   Has some intensity.   Very subdued low ending.   Agitated accompaniment.   Acc:
4

7229.   (4) Tanz   High Voices
Polish title: Taniec.   e3-g♯4(a4)   a3-e4 Animated in moderate live-
ly tempo.   Rhythmic.   Starts PP.   Requires fine high P and PP.
Agitated movement.   Acc: 3-4

7230.   (5) Der verliebte Ostwind   High Voices
Polish title: Zakochany wiatr.   f3(e3)-g4   b♭3-e4 Animated in lively
tempo.   Has climactic and intense passages.   Requires fine high P.

924   Solo Voice Repertoire

Very agitated accompaniment. Acc: 4

7231. (6) Trauriger Frühling   High Voices
Polish title: Smutna wiosna. e3-f♯4 f♯3-e4 Sustained in moderate
slow tempo. Has climactic passages. Requires fine P and PP. Subdued, descending ending. Acc: 4

Pieśni Muezzine Szalonego. English: Songs of the Crazy Muezzin. German:
Lieder des verliebten Muessine. Polish texts, with German versions
by Rudolf Stefan Hoffman. Op. 42. Six songs for high voice and
piano. Only numbers one and two are given here. Also has French
version. These songs are vocally difficult. Vienna: Universal Edition.

7232. (1) Allah, Allah, Akbar, Allah!   High Voices
Poet: Muezzina. c♯3-g♯4 g3-e4 Sustained in moderate tempo.
Vocal part is chromatic. Requires some flexibility. Has climactic
passages and florid figures. Acc: 3-4

7233. (2) O Vielgeliebte!   High Voices
Poet: Muezzina. g3-g♯4 a3-a4 Animated in moderate lively tempo.
Generally light. Requires fine high P and PP. Ends with florid,
vocalized passage on "ah" vowel. Chromatic vocal part. Agitated
accompaniment. Acc: 4

Slopiewnie. Op. 46. Karol Szymanowski. Texts by Julian Tuwim. Polish
texts, with German and French versions. A set of five songs for
high voice and piano. Numbers two and three are given here.
Vienna: Universal Edition.

7234. (2) Zielone slowa   High Voices
German title: Grüne lust. First German line: Dort im waldigen.
d3-a4 a3-f♯4 Sustained in varied tempi. Starts slowly and ends in
very rapid tempo. Requires very fine high PP. Has climactic high
passages. Climactic high ending on "Ah!". Acc: 3-4

7235. (3) Sw. Franciszek   High Voices
German title: Der heilige Franziskus. f♯3-g♯4 a3-f♯4 Sustained
in slow tempo. In quasi-recitative. Requires fine high P and PP.
Has short "alleluja" passage. Very subdued high ending. Sacred
texts. Acc: 3

Single Songs

7236. Gentle lady   High Voices
Poet: James Joyce. Polish title: Droga mjoa. e♭3-f4 f♯3-c♯4
Sustained in moderate slow tempo. Generally subdued. Requires
very fine P to PPPP. Very subdued ending. Acc: 3 4SS

7237. Lean out   High Voices
Poet: James Joyce. Polish title: Zlocisty wlos. e♭3-g4 a♭3-f4
Animated in very fast tempo. Requires fluent enunciation and some
flexibility. Has climactic passages. Ends with very subdued vocalized passage. Acc: 3-4 4SS

7238. Lied des Mädchens am Fenster   Soprano
Poet: Alfons Paquet. d♭3-a♭4 f3-e♭4 Sustained in moderate slow
tempo. Generally subdued, requires very fine high PP and PPP.

Low, subdued ending. Best for high, light voices, coloratura soprano
or high lyric soprano. Acc: 4 50A

7239. My dove   High Voices
       Poet: James Joyce. Polish title: Turkawko moja. d♯3-g♯4 a♭3-
       e♭4 Animated in lively tempo. Has dramatic high passages. De-
       scending ending with high climax. Generally a climactic song. Acc:
       4-5 4SS

7240. Sleep now   High Voices
       Poet: James Joyce. Polish title: Zaśnij. e♭3-g♭4 g♯3-d♭4 Sus-
       tained in moderate slow tempo. Has climactic passages. Requires
       fine high P and PP. Very subdued high ending. See the settings by
       Samuel Barber, Sergius Kagen, and Vincent Persichetti's "Unquiet
       heart." Acc: 3 4SS

                        K. SWITZERLAND

                  I. Compositions until 1830

JEAN-JACQUES ROUSSEAU, 1712-1778

7241. J'ai perdu tout mon bonheur   High Voices
       Work: Le Devin du Village, a pastorale 1752, libretto by the com-
       poser. c3-g4 f3-f4 Sustained in moderate tempo. Has some cli-
       mactic passages and some recitative sections. Requires fine high P.
       Descending ending line. Acc: 3 AUK

7242. Je vais revoir ma charmante   Tenor
       Work: Le Devin du Village, a pastorale 1752, libretto by the com-
       poser. Part of Colin. d3-b♭4 g3-g4 Sustained first part and ani-
       mated second part in moderate slow tempo. Requires fine high P.
       Has climactic high passages. Graceful second part, requiring flexi-
       bility. Subdued, descending ending line. Acc: 3-4 PBA-Ta (Ch. V)

7243. Le rosier   All Voices
       Poet: De Laire. g3-e4 a3-d4 Sustained in moderate slow tempo.
       Generally light and graceful. Gently agitated accompaniment. This
       simple song comes from the collection entitled Consolations des mis-
       ères de ma vie, 1781. Acc: 3 ETP-1 (Ch. V)

7244. Que le jour me dure!   All Voices
       Poet: Anon. g3-b3 g3-b3 Sustained in moderate tempo. A song
       built on just three notes. 3 verses. Acc: 2 EDF-2 (Ch. V)

7245. Romance   All Voices
       Poet: M. de Corancez. First line: Une nymphe était si tant belle.
       e3-e4 g♯3-c♯4 Gently animated in moderate tempo. Graceful,
       short melody. 8 verses, narrative text. Acc: 2-3 SSO

II.   Compositions from 1830

GUSTAVE FERRARI, 1872-1948

7246. J'ai tant de choses à vous dire   High Voices
        Poet: Lamquet. e3-g♯4 a3-e4 Animated in moderate lively tempo.
        Graceful, light, and generally subdued. Acc: 3 MFS-1

7247. Le miroir   All Voices
        Poet: Edouard Haraucourt. c♯3-d4 e3-c4 Original key. Sustained
        in very slow tempo. Gentle, tranquil, and subdued. In gentle quasi-
        recitative style. Mostly subdued chords in the accompaniment. Acc:
        2 40F-2 (Ch. V), GAS

ROBERT GERHARD

7248. Els Ballaires dins un sac   Men
        Poet: Catalan folk poem. English title: Dancing in a sack. Ger-
        man text: R. S. Hoffman, English text: J. B. Trend. a♭3-f4
        b♭3-f4 Animated in lively tempo. Generally light. Humorous narra-
        tive. May be transposed for lower voices. Acc: 4 In: Sis
        Cançons Populars de Catalunya, Universal Edition

7249. La calandria   Men
        Poet: Catalan folk poem. English title: The lark. English text:
        J. B. Trend; German text: R. S. Hoffman. g♯3-f♯4 a3-e4 Gently
        animated in slow tempo. Gentle and lyric. May be transposed for
        lower voices. Acc: 3 In: Sis Cançons Populars de Catalunya

FRANK MARTIN, 1890-1974

Martin, one of the most outstanding Swiss composers, has not written many
works for solo voice. The bulk of his compositions are in the area of instrumental music, although he also wrote an opera and some choral music.
The style in most of his works is a combination of the 12-tone technique and
chordal and homophonic styles. Thus, he built a type of modern music of
his own which is considered a contribution to the history of modern music.
Among his best solo voice compositions is the set entitled Sechs Monologe
aus Jedermann, on poems by Hugo von Hofmannsthal.

DMM Drey Minnelieder für Sopran und Klavier. Frank Martin. German
      texts by different poets. Vienna: Universal Edition.

Quatre Sonnets à Cassandre. Frank Martin. Texts by Pierre de Ronsard.
      Mezzo-Soprano, flute, viola and cello. Piano reduction available.
      Zurich: Hug & Cie.

7250. (1) Qui voudra voir comme un dieu   Mezzo-Soprano
        e3-f4 g3-d4 Sustained in generally moderate tempo, with variations.
        Requires simplicity. Generally light. Gentle, descending ending line.
        Acc: 3

7251. (2) Nature ornant la dame   Mezzo-Soprano
        b2-e4 f♯3-c♯4 Sustained in slow tempo. Generally subdued, with
        climactic passages toward the end. Subdued descending ending line.
        Acc: 3

7252. (3) Avant le temps   Mezzo-Soprano
       c3-e4 f3-c4 Animated in lively tempo. Light. Starts very gently
       and subduedly. In quasi-recitative style. Has one climactic passage
       near the end. Acc: 3-4

7253. (4) Quand je te vois   Mezzo-Soprano
       d3(a2)-d4 f3-c4 Subdued in slow tempo. Has some intensity and
       quasi-recitative passages. Very subdued, slightly extended prelude.
       Acc: 3

7254. Sechs Monologe aus Jedermann. Frank Martin. Poems by Hugo von
       Hofmannsthal. A cycle of six songs for baritone or contralto. Or-
       chestral accompaniment; piano reduction is available. The songs are
       in general in the recitative style. Has some dramatic passages.
       The ending section is sustained and somewhat subdued. The entire
       cycle is vocally demanding and interpretatively difficult. Overall
       range and tessitura: a2-f4 d3-d4 Titles:
           Ist alls zu End das Freudenmahl
           Ach Gott, wie graust mir vor dem Tod
           Ist als wenn eins gerufen hält
           So wollt ich ganz zernichtet sein
           Ja! ich glaub! solches hat er vollbracht
           O ewiger Gott! o gottliches Gesicht!
       (SC) Universal Edition

Single Songs

7255. Ach herzeliep...   Soprano
       Poet: Anon. 13th century poet. d3-g4 g3-d4 Sustained in slow
       tempo. Generally strong. Ends with slightly florid passage. The
       beginning piano part is a one-line treble melody against the vocal line.
       Acc: 3 DMM

7256. Ez stuont ein frouwe alleine...   Soprano
       Poet: Dietmar von Eist. d3-g4 a3-e4 Sustained in moderate slow
       tempo. Slightly slower ending. Has climactic passages. Low, sub-
       dued ending. Acc: 3 DMM

7257. Unter der linden   Soprano
       Poet: Walther von der Vogelweide. d3-a4 f♯3-e4 Animated in live-
       ly tempo. Vigorous. Has dramatic passages and florid figures. Re-
       quires fine P. Climactic ending. Acc: 3 DMM

OTHMAR SCHOECK, 1886-1957

Songs comprise the greatest output of Othmar Schoeck, one of Switzerland's
most important 20th-century composers. Belonging to the romantic spirit of
song writing, Schoeck composed more than 400 songs on texts by such great
poets as Mörike, Lenau, Eichendorff, Uhland, Claudius, Hafiz, Goethe, as
well as the best-known Swiss poets, Meyer, Keller, and Leuthold. He uses
varied styles in his songs, bringing out many emotional shades, colors and
expressions. Schoeck is a product of many influences, including the greatest
song composers of the past. In later years, with more experience and maturity, all these blended into a highly personal style which resulted in his
works becoming true representatives of the Swiss artistic spirit.

His songs are all very well written for the voice. They have some beautiful
and fresh sounding melodies set over some rich harmonic structures. Most

of them are published in several volumes by Hug & Cie, and Breitkopf &
Härtel.   Among those considered his best songs are "Sommerabend," "Schil-
flied," "Das bescheidene Wünschlein," "Der Hufschmied" and "Das Heiligste."

HBS   Das Holde Bescheiden.   Two volumes.   Othmar Schoeck.   Vienna:
        Universal Edition.

LGG   Lieder nach Gedichten von Goethe.   Op. 19a.   Othmar Schoeck.
        Eight songs.   Leipzig: Breitkopf & Härtel.

LGS   Ausgewählte Lieder und Gesänge.   Othmar Schoeck.   High, medium,
        low.   Three volumes of 9, 10, and 9 songs respectively.   German
        texts, with English and French versions.   Wiesbaden & Leipzig:
        Breitkopf & Härtel.

LWD   Lieder aus dem westöstlichen Divan von Goethe.   Op. 19b.   Othmar
        Schoeck.   Thirteen songs.   Leipzig: Breitkopf & Härtel.

USS   Unter Sternen.   Vols. I & II.   Othmar Schoeck.   Medium voice and
        piano.   Twenty-two songs to poems by Gottfried Keller.   Vienna:
        Universal Edition.

————

7258.   Fünf Venezianische Epigramme.   Othmar Schoeck.   A set of five
        short songs in different tempi and moods.   May also be performed
        singly.   The last song has agitated accompaniment, with a slightly
        strong ending on descending melody.   Texts by Johann Wolfgang von
        Goethe.   For high voice and piano.   Not for light voices.   Overall
        range and tessitura: bb2-a4 f3-f4   First lines:
        (1) Warum leckst du dein Mäulchen
        (2) Eine einzige Nacht
        (3) Wie sie klingeln
        (4) Seh' ich den Pilgrim
        (5) Diese Gondel vergleich'
        Acc. for all songs: 4   (SC)LWD

Nachhall.   Op. 70.   Othmar Schoeck.   Poems by Nikolaus von Lenau and
        Matthias Claudius.   A song cycle of 12 movements for medium voice
        and orchestra.   Piano reduction is available.   Vienna: Universal
        Edition.   (Duration: 30 minutes and 40 seconds.)

7259.   (1) Nachhall   Medium Voices
        a2-d4   c3-b3 Sustained in moderate slow tempo.   Tranquil.   Most
        notes lie below b3.   Acc: 4

7260.   (2) Einsamkeit   Medium Voices
        bb2-d4   c3-c4 Sustained in moderate tempo.   Tranquil and flowing.
        Has some quasi-recitative sections.   Acc: 4

7261.   (3) Mein Herz   Medium Voices
        eb3-f4   f3-db4 Sustained in moderate tempo.   Has dramatic pas-
        sages.   Acc: 4

7262.   (4) Veränderte Welt   Medium Voices
        bb2-e4   eb3-d4 Vigorous and strong.   Ends with a long diminuendo.
        Acc: 4

7263.   (5) Abendheimkehr   Medium Voices a2(g2)-e4   d3-d4 Sustained in moderate lively tempo. Has a broader, descending ending line. Acc: 4

7264. (6) Auf eine holländische Landschaft   Medium Voices
a2(g# 2)-c4 d3-b3 Sustained, with a low tessitura. Dark, subdued throughout. Acc: 4

7265. (7) Stimme des Windes   Medium Voices
b2-d4   d3-b3 Sustained, very tranquil, and subdued. Has passages in gentle recitative style. Acc: 4

7266. (8) Der falsche Freund   Medium Voices
c# 3-f4   d3-d4 Sustained with free, recitative style. Broad, strong, climactic ending. Acc: 4

7267. (9) Niagara   Medium Voices
b2-e4(f# 3)   d3-d4 Sustained in moderate tempo. Flowing. Requires very fine PPP. Acc: 4

7268. (10) Heimatklang   Medium Voices
b2-eb 4   d3-d4 Sustained and tranquil. Mostly on MF level. The extended instrumental interlude leads to the next song without break. Acc: 5

7269. (11) Der Kranich   Medium Voices
ab 2-f4   e3-e4 Sustained in moderate tempo. Has a more chromatic vocal line than the other excerpts. Acc: 4

7270. (12) O du Land   Medium Voices
Poet: Matthias Claudius. d# 3-e4   e3-c4 Very sustained in moderate tempo. Tranquil, subdued, and contemplative. Acc: 4

Single Songs

7271. Abendlied   Medium, High Voices
Poet: Gottfried Keller. d# 3-f# 4   e3-e4 Sustained in moderate tempo. Flowing. Requires very fine high P and PP. Climactic ending. Acc: 3-4 USS-1

7272. Abendlied an die Natur   Medium Voices
Poet: Gottfried Keller. b2-f4   eb 3-eb 4 Sustained in moderate slow tempo. Has some faster tempi. Subdued ending. Acc: 3 USS-1

7273. Am Walde   High, Medium Voices
Poet: Anon. c# 3-f# 4   f# 3-e4 Sustained in moderate tempo. Tranquil and subdued. Requires fine PP. Acc: 3 HBS-1 (low)

7274. Besuch in Urach   High Voices
Poet: Eduard Mörike. c3-bb 4   f3-g4 An extended song, 22 pages. In varying moods and tempi. Best for dramatic high voices. Vocally demanding. Requires fine high PP. Subdued ending. Acc: 5 HBS-2

7275. Dämmrung senkte sich von oben   Medium, Low Voices
Poet: Johann Wolfgang von Goethe. ab 2-d4   eb 3-c4 Sustained vocal part in moderate tempo. Slightly faster second half with a short return to the original tempo. Gently agitated accompaniment. Very subdued and gentle. Acc: 3 LGG, DZL-3, LGS-1

7276. Das bescheidene Wünschlein   All Voices
       Poet: Carl Spittler. eb3-gb4   eb3-eb4   Sustained in varied tempi
       and moods.   Marked "calm."   Has some climactic passages.   De-
       scending ending.   Narrative.   Acc: 3-4 LGS-3

7277. Das Madchen an den Mai   Soprano
       Poet: Eduard Mörike.   d3-a4   f#3-f4   Sustained and flowing.   In
       quasi-recitative style.   Acc: 3-4 HBS-1

7278. Das Tal   Medium Voices
       Poet: Gottfried Keller.   c3-eb4   eb3-c4   Gracefully animated in
       moderate tempo.   Gentle, generally subdued.   Very subdued ending.
       Short.   Acc: 3 USS-1

7279. Der Geprüfte   High Voices
       Poet: Eduard Mörike.   c3-bb4   f3-g4   Has varied moods and tempi.
       Has strong and dramatic passages.   Requires fine high P and flexi-
       bility.   Strong and climactic ending.   Vocally demanding.   For dra-
       matic high voices.   Acc: 5 HBS-2

7280. Der Hufschmied   All Voices
       Poet: Carl Spittler.   c3-f#4   e3-e4   Animated in lively tempo.   Re-
       quires fluent enunciation and some characterization for the two char-
       acters in the song.   Rhythmic.   Has some climactic passages.   Re-
       quires some fine P.   Amusing text.   Subdued ending.   Acc: 3-4
       LGS-3

7281. Die Verklärende   Medium Voices
       Poet: Michelangelo Buonarroti, translated into German.   b2-f4   f3-
       d#4   Very sustained in moderate slow tempo.   Has climactic pas-
       sages.   Requires very fine high P.   Subdued high ending.   Short.   A
       fine song to introduce one to Schoeck's compositions.   A 1907 compo-
       sition.   Acc: 3-4 DDK-3 (Ch. VI)

7282. Frühgesicht   Medium Voices
       Poet: Gottfried Keller.   bb2(g2)-f4   d3-e4   Sustained in moderate
       tempo.   Starts and ends in recitative style.   Agitated accompaniment
       in the middle section.   Acc: 3-4 USS-2

7283. Gebet   High Voices
       Poet: Eduard Mörike.   c#3-a4   f3-f4   Sustained and strong first sec-
       tion.   Subdued and tranquil ending.   See the setting by Hugo Wolf.
       Acc: 3-4 HBS-2

7284. Gekommen ist der Mai   Contralto, Mezzo-Soprano
       Poet: Heinrich Heine.   gb2-bb3   bb2-eb3   Generally sustained in
       moderate tempo.   Delicate and subdued.   Low tessitura.   Low ending.
       Gently agitated accompaniment.   Acc: 3 DZL-2

7285. Haben sie von deinen Fehlen   Low Voices
       Poet: Johann Wolfgang von Goethe.   gb2-d#4   c3-ab3   Sustained in
       moderate slow tempo.   Has phrases in quasi-recitative style.   Gen-
       erally subdued.   Has slightly faster and calmer tempi sections.   Sub-
       dued ending.   Acc: 3 LWD

7286. Herbstgefühl   High Voices
       Poet: Johann Wolfgang von Goethe.   c3-ab4   g3-db4   Sustained in
       moderate slow tempo.   Tranquil, subdued, requires very fine high P

and PP. Slightly climactic ending. Not for light, high voices. Acc:
3 LGG, LGS-1

7287. Höre den Rat   Low Voices
Poet: Johann Wolfgang von Goethe. g# 2-c4   c3-g3 Sustained in
moderate slow tempo. Very subdued, in recitative style. Has some
low tessitura. Very subdued low ending, g# 2 the final note. Acc:
3 LWD

7288. Mailied   High Voices
Poet: Johann Wolfgang von Goethe. c# 3-a4   f# 3-g4 Generally sustained in moderate tempo. Requires some flexibility and very fine
high PP. Has climactic passages. Ends with passages marked PPP.
Acc: 3 LGG

7289. Mit einem gemalten Band   High Voices
Poet: Johann Wolfgang von Goethe. d# 3-a4   a3-e4 Animated in
moderate lively tempo. Light and delicate. Best for light, high
voices. Acc: 3 LGG, DZL-1, LGS-1

7290. Nachklang   Medium, Low Voices
Poet: Johann Wolfgang von Goethe. a# 2-d4   f# 3-c# 4 Sustained in
slow tempo. Has some low tessitura. Subdued throughout. Arpeggiated accompaniment. Not for light voices. Acc: 3 GSB (Ch. VI),
LGS-1

7291. Nur zu!   High Voices
Poet: Eduard Mörike. f3-a4   ab 3-g4 Sustained in moderate tempo.
Has some dramatic passages and high tessitura. Requires fine high
notes. Acc: 5 HBS-1

7292. Parabase   High Voices
Poet: Johann Wolfgang von Goethe. c3-gb 4   g3-g4 Sustained in
moderate slow tempo. Has climactic high passages and a climactic
ending. Has some full-sounding chords. Acc: 3 LGG

7293. Peregrina   Baritone
Poet: Eduard Mörike. bb 1-gb 3   eb 2-db 3 Sustained in slow tempo.
Has a slightly faster middle section, climactic high passages. Re-
quires fine P to PPP. Starts dramatically. Very subdued ending.
Acc: 3-4 DZL-4

7294. Rastlose Liebe   High Voices
Poet: Johann Wolfgang von Goethe. First line: Dem Schnee, dem
Regen, dem Wind. eb 3-g4   g3-eb 4 Animated in lively tempo. Agi-
tated movement. Requires fluent enunciation and flexibility. General-
ly strong, climactic. Climactic ending. Agitated accompaniment.
Acc: 4 LGG, LGS-1

7295. Selige Sehnsucht   High Voices
Poet: Johann Wolfgang von Goethe. b2-g4   e3-e4 Sustained vocal
part in moderate lively tempo. Starts gently. Has climactic passages. Somewhat dramatic final section with descending line and diminuendo. Very strong piano postlude. A climactic song, excellent
for the end of a group. Best for the heavier voices. Acc: 3-4
LWD

7296. Stille der Nacht   Medium Voices

Poet: Gottfried Keller. c3-f4 e3-e♭4 Sustained in moderate tempo and steady movement. Subdued, requires fine P and PP. Subdued descending ending line. Acc: 3 USS-1

7297. Stilleben   Medium, Low Voices
Poet: Gottfried Keller. a2-d4 a2-a3 Gently animated in generally moderate tempo. Generally subdued, with low tessitura. Low, subdued, gentle ending. Requires very legato accompaniment. Acc: 3 USS-1

7298. Suleika   High Voices
Poet: Johann Wolfgang von Goethe. a2-a4 e3-e4 Animated in lively tempo. Has climactic high passages. Descending ending line and extended piano postlude. Acc: 3-4 LWD

7299. Suleika und Hatem   High Voices
Poet: Johann Wolfgang von Goethe. c3-a4 f3-e4 A conversation between two characters. Sustained vocal part in moderate tempo. Requires very fine high P. Generally gentle, no strong dynamics. Subdued ending. Acc: 3 LWD

7300. Tod und Dichter   Medium Voices
Poet: Gottfried Keller. b♭2-f4 d♭3-d♭4 Generally sustained in recitative style. Requires characterization and some flexibility. Very subdued starting. Low ending. Acc: 3 USS-2

7301. Trost der Kreatur   Medium, Low Voices
Poet: Gottfried Keller. b2-d♯4 b2-a3 Very sustained in slow tempo. Calm, very subdued, and with a low tessitura. Extremely legato in the accompaniment. Acc: 3 USS-1

7302. Ungeduld   High Voices
Poet: Johann Wolfgang von Goethe. c3-a♭4 g3-c4 Animated in lively tempo. Has one high climactic passage. Generally on MF level. Subdued, descending ending line. Acc: 3 LGG

7303. Unmut   Low, Medium Voices
Poet: Johann Wolfgang von Goethe. a2-f4(g4) d3-a3 Sustained in moderate tempo. Requires fine PP. Has one climactic high passage. Subdued ending with bold, accented piano postlude. Starts very gently. Acc: 3 LWD

7304. Unter Sternen   Medium Voices
Poet: Gottfried Keller. c♯3-f4 f3-d4 Animated in moderate lively tempo. Climactic ending. Requires some fluent enunciation. Agitated, arpeggiated accompaniment. Acc: 4 USS-1

7305. Widmung   High Voices
Poet: Eduard Mörike. f3-a4 g3-g4 Sustained in moderate slow tempo. Tranquil, requires fine high PP. Acc: 4 HBS-1

Note: See also Ausgewählte Lieder und Gesänge by Othmar Schoeck. Three volumes of 9, 10, and 9 songs respectively, in high, medium, and low keys. German texts, with English and French versions. Leipzig: Breitkopf & Härtel.

CHAPTER XI

SOLO EXCERPTS FROM THE OPERAS

for

Coloratura Soprano	Lyric Tenor
Lyric Soprano	Dramatic Tenor
Dramatic Soprano	Baritone
Mezzo-Soprano	Bass-Baritone and
Contralto	Basso

Introduction

Solo excerpts from the operas constitute an important part of solo recital repertoire and of the entire literature for the voice. This, of course,
means that the accompaniment is mostly a reduction of the orchestral score
to be played on the piano. Many recitals, as we all know, include one or
more arias from operas, and a chapter giving information on the many possibilities and choices will, it is hoped, be helpful.

The arias given here are of operatic works from the 19th and 20th
centuries. In addition, excerpts from the operas of Mozart and Cherubini
are included because the best-known have been in steady use in the repertoire
of a good number of opera companies, and there have been revivals of some
of the less-known in recent years in opera workshops.

Entries of operatic excerpts are classified according to the following
voices: coloratura soprano, lyric soprano, dramatic soprano, mezzo-soprano,
contralto, lyric tenor, dramatic tenor, baritone, and bass-baritone and basso.

No effort has been made to drastically limit the number of operas included, because all of the arias listed are now available not only from vocal
scores, but also in sheet music and collections. Moreover, many vocal
scores are available on loan from public and institutional libraries. The material in this chapter is not aimed to serve the singer for just five years or
so, but for a long time. This is a record, perhaps historically too, of the
production of our great dramatic composers. This chapter presents what
presently exists, and its reference value cannot be outmoded. Furthermore,
the number of arias reviewed gives singers a wide choice of material for
varied capabilities, which is one of the main aims of this work. To represent the dramatic field in a recital, one does not always have to draw from
the "traditional" staples of Donizetti, Puccini, or Verdi. So much "common-
ness" in recital programs derives from the fact that many singers cleave to
the tradition of performing only what are considered "standards." Some
repertoire expectations by the general recital-going public have become pe-
destrian. When a soprano is announced as giving a recital, people automati-
cally expect that she will include "Un bel di" (MADAMA BUTTERFLY) and/
or "Mi chiamano Mimi" (LA BOHEME) in her program. When a tenor is
scheduled many expect him to do "Celeste Aida" (AIDA) and/or "Che gelida
manina" (LA BOHEME). A baritone is always expected to sing something
like "Eri tu" (UN BALLO IN MASCHERA), even if he is only nineteen years

old. When the repertoire is narrowed thus, the musical experience and
knowledge of the public is also narrowed. Many young recitalists are forced
to sing Verdi even before the full capabilities of their instruments are real-
ized. The result is damage all the way around: to vocal chords, vocal technique, and Verdi! This reference provides many available operatic arias to
choose from. The singer who uses it wisely will help dispel an unworthy
"tradition."

Accompanying arias from dramatic works has often posed serious problems for the pianist, mainly because he is faced with a score transcribed
and reduced from a work for a very large ensemble comprised of sounds
with varied timbres and colors. The accompanist generally plays what is
printed on the vocal score, assuming that the arrangements represent something like what might be expected from an orchestra.

The value of such an extremely limited outlet cannot be compensated
by a purely pianistic approach. The accompanist would do the excerpt more
justice if he refers to the full or instrumental score, and writes down on his
piano score the names of the instruments that have the most important melodic or thematic responsibility in each passage, and thus, with imagination,
help to compensate, even in this small way, for what might be missing from
a straight pianistic approach. In other words, the piano accompanist must
be able to think orchestrally. To give a specific example. The legato mo-
tion from one note to another by a trumpet is not the same as that accomplished by a violin. The trumpet defines its "legato" notes with a tap on
each note, while the violin connects its notes with greater subtleness from
finger tip to finger tip. Although the piano sound is still mainly percussive,
yet it is possible subtly to differentiate the "trumpet style" from the "violin
style" in melodic phrases assigned to either. The pianist who does not know
what instruments are involved in certain passages will naturally approach his
accompanying in a strictly blunt pianistic manner. The subtlety and sensitivity necessary in accompanying arias may not easily be applied by pianists
with only average professional experience, but it certainly has been demon-
strated time and again by great accompanists. It is something to aim for.

It is not practical nor musical for an accompanist to play all the notes
found in a transcription or heavily orchestrated passages. To do so would be
disastrous unless one were a virtuoso. Here again, reference to the orchestral score will be a most valuable help; one can decide which note to leave
out without sacrificing the structure and unity of the passage. One must not,
under some circumstances, be afraid of or apologetic in playing the almost
"bare bones" of the accompaniment when it is too thick to manage comforta-
bly. After all, the intelligent listener will not expect the piano to mimic
the operatic orchestra.

The entries in this chapter include some important facts about the
opera and its libretto, and these are given after the opera-title entry. These
facts appear only on the very first entry, if there are several arias from
one specific opera. This is done to avoid repetition. The operas included
in this chapter are entered alphabetically by the complete titles of the operas.
The excerpts under each opera title are arranged alphabetically by the first
word of each aria.

OPERAS CONSIDERED IN CHAPTER XI

Italian Composers

FRANCO ALFANO

La Risurrezione, 1904, 2 acts

VINCENZO BELLINI

I Capuletti ed i Montecchi, 1830,
 4 parts
I Puritani di Scozia, 1835, 3 acts
Il Pirata, 1827, 2 acts
La Sonnambula, 1831, 2 acts
La Straniera, 1829, 2 acts
Norma, 1831, 4 acts

ARRIGO BOITO

Mefistofele, 1868, 4 acts
Nerone, 1916, 4 acts

ALFREDO CATALANI

La Wally, 1892, 4 acts
Loreley (or Elda), 1890, 3 acts

LUIGI CHERUBINI

Les Abencèrages (or L'Etendard
 de Grenade), 1813, 3 acts
Medea, 1797, 3 acts

FRANCESCO CILÈA

Adriana Lecouvreur, 1902, 4 acts
L'Arlesiana, 1897, 3 acts

GAETANO DONIZETTI

Anna Bolena, 1830, 2 acts
Betly (or La Capanna Svizzera),
 1836, 1 act
Don Pasquale, 1843, 3 acts
Don Sebastiano, 1843, 5 acts
Il Campanello di Notte, 1836, 1 act
La Favorita, 1840, 4 acts
La Fille du Régiment, 1840, 2 acts
La Regina di Golconda, 1828,
 2 acts
L'Elisir d'Amore, 1832, 2 acts
Linda di Chamounix, 1842, 3 acts
Lucia di Lammermoor, 1835,
 3 acts
Lucrezia Borgia, 1833, 2 acts
Maria di Rohan, 1843, 3 acts

Poliuto (or I Martiri), 1840, 3 acts
Rita, 1860, 1 act

UMBERTO GIORDANO

Andrea Chénier, 1896, 4 acts
Fedora, 1898, 3 acts

RUGGIERO LEONCAVALLO

La Bohème, 1897, 4 acts
Pagliacci, 1892, 2 acts
Zazà, 1900, 4 acts

PIETRO MASCAGNI

Cavalleria Rusticana, 1889, 1 act
Iris, 1898, 3 acts
L'Amico Fritz, 1891, 3 acts

ITALO MONTEMEZZI

L'Amore dei Tre Re, 1913, 3 acts

AMILCARE PONCHIELLI

I Promessi Sposi, 1856, 4 acts
Il Figiuol Prodigo, 1880, 4 acts
La Gioconda, 1876, 4 acts

GIACOMO PUCCINI

Il Trittico, 1918:
 Il Tabarro, 1 act
 Suor Angelica, 1 act
 Gianni Schicchi, 1 act
La Bohème, 1896, 4 acts
La Fanciulla del West, 1910, 3 acts
Le Villi, 1884, 1 act (Milan);
 2 acts (Turin)
Madama Butterfly, 1904, 3 acts
Manon Lescaut, 1893, 4 acts
Tosca, 1900, 3 acts
Turandot, 1926, 3 acts

GIOACCHINO ROSSINI

Guillaume Tell, 1829, 4 acts
Il Barbiere di Siviglia, 1816, 3 acts
La Cenerentola, 1817, 2 acts
La Gazza Ladra, 1817, 2 acts
Le Siège de Corinthe, 1826, 3 acts
L'Italiana in Algeri, 1813, 2 acts
Otello (or Moro di Venezia), 1816,
 3 acts

ROSSINI (cont.)

Semiramide, 1823, 2 acts
Tancredi, 1813, 2 acts
Zelmira, 1822, 1 act

GIUSEPPE VERDI

Aida, 1871, 4 acts
Alzira, 1845, 2 acts
Aroldo (or Stiffelio), 1857, 3 acts
Attila, 1846, 3 acts
Don Carlos, 1867, 4 acts
Ernani, 1844, 4 acts
Falstaff, 1893, 3 acts
I Due Foscari, 1844, 3 acts
I Lombardi all Prima Crociata,
    1843, 4 acts
I Masnadieri, 1847, 4 acts
I Vespri Siciliani, 1856, 5 acts
Il Corsaro, 1848, 4 acts
Il Trovatore, 1853, 4 acts
La Battaglia di Legnano, 1849,
    3 acts
La Forza del Destino, 1862, 4 acts
La Traviata, 1853, 4 acts
Luisa Miller, 1849, 3 acts
Macbeth, 1847, 4 acts
Nabucco, 1842, 4 acts
Otello, 1887, 4 acts
Rigoletto, 1851, 4 acts
Simon Boccanegra, 1857, 3 acts
Un Ballo in Maschera, 1859, 5 acts

FRANCO VITTADINI

Anima Allegra, 1921, 3 acts

French Composers

ADOLPHE ADAM

Le Chalet, 1834, 1 act
Le Postillon de Longjumeau, 1836,
    3 acts
Si J'Étais Roi, 1852, 3 acts

DANIEL FRANÇOIS AUBER

Fra Diavolo (or L'Hôtellerie de
    Terrcine), 1830, 3 acts
Le Domino Noir, 1837, 3 acts
Manon Lescaut, 1856, 4 acts

HECTOR BERLIOZ

La Damnation de Faust, 1846,

4 acts
Le Troyens à Carthage, 1863, 3 acts

GEORGES BIZET

Carmen, 1875, 4 acts
Djamileh, 1871, 1 act
La Jolie Fille de Perth, 1866,
    4 acts
Les Pêcheurs de Perles, 1863, 3
    acts

ALFRED BRUNEAU

L'Attaque du Moulin, 1893, 4 acts

EMMANUEL CHABRIER

Gwendoline, 1886, 2 acts

GUSTAVE CHARPENTIER

Louise, 1900, 4 acts

FELICIEN DAVID

La Perle du Brésil, 1851, 3 acts
Lalla-Roukh, 1862, 2 acts

CLAUDE DEBUSSY

Pelléas et Mélisande, 1902, 5 acts

LÉO DELIBES

Lakmé, 1883, 3 acts

PAUL DUKAS

Ariane et Barbe-Bleue, 1907, 3
    acts

BENJAMIN GODARD

Jocelyn, 1888, 4 acts
La Vivandière, 1895, 3 acts
Le Tasse, 1878, 3 parts

CHARLES GOUNOD

Cinq-Mars, 1877, 4 acts
Faust, 1859, 5 acts
La Reine de Saba, 1861, 4 acts
Philémon et Baucis, 1859, 2 acts
Mireille, 1863, 3 acts, orig. 5
Roméo et Juliette, 1864, 5 acts
Sapho, 1850, 3 acts

JACQUES HALÉVY

Charles VI, 1843, 5 acts
La Fée aux Roses, 1847, 3 acts
La Juive, 1835, 5 acts
La Reine de Chypre, 1841, 5 acts

FERDINAND HEROLD

La Pré aux Clercs, 1832, 3 acts

ÉDOUARD LALO

Le Roi d'Ys, 1888, 3 acts

VICTOR MASSÉ

Galathée, 1852, 2 acts
Les Noces de Jeannette, 1853,
1 act

JULES MASSENET

Don César de Bazan, 1872, 4 acts
Hérodiade, 1881, 4 acts
La Navaraise, 1894, 2 acts
Manon, 1884, 5 acts
Sapho, 1897, 5 acts
Thaïs, 1894, 3 acts
Le Cid, 1885, 4 acts
Le Jongleur de Notre-Dame, 1902,
3 acts
Le Roi de Lahore, 1877, 5 acts
Thérèse, 1907, 2 acts
Werther, 1892, 4 acts

ÉTIENNE MEHUL

Joseph, 1807, 3 acts

ANDRÉ MESSAGER

Fortunio, 1907, 4 acts

PIERRE MONSIGNY

Le Déserteur, 1769, 3 acts

JACQUES OFFENBACH

Les Contes d'Hoffman, 1881, 3
acts

FRANCIS POULENC

Dialogues des Carmélites, 1957,
3 acts

MAURICE RAVEL

L'Heure Espagnole, 1907, 1 act

CAMILLE SAINT-SAËNS

Étienne Marcel, 1879, 4 acts
Henry VIII, 1883, 4 acts
Samson et Dalila, 1877, 3 acts

AMBROISE THOMAS

Hamlet, 1868, 5 acts
Le Caïd, 1849, 2 acts
Mignon, 1871, 3 acts

German Composers

LUDWIG VAN BEETHOVEN

Fidelio, 1805, 2 acts

ALBAN BERG

Lulu, 1937, 3 acts, unfinished
Wozzeck, 1925, 3 acts

PETER CORNELIUS

Der Barbier von Bagdad, 1858, 2
acts

FRIEDRICH VON FLOTOW

Martha, 1847, 4 acts

PAUL HINDEMITH

Cardillac, 1926, 3 acts
Mathis der Maler, 1938, 7 scenes

ERICH KORNGOLD

Die Tote Stadt, 1920, 3 acts

KONRADIN KREUTZER

Das Nachtlager von Granada, 1834,
2 acts

ALBERT LORTZING

Czaar und Zimmermann (or Die
Zwei Peter), 1837, 3 acts
Undine, 1845, 4 acts

HEINRICH MARSCHNER

Hans Heiling, 1833, 3 acts

GIACOMO MEYERBEER

L'Africaine, 1865, 5 acts
Le Pardon de Ploërmel (or
  Dinorah), 1859, 3 acts
Le Prophète, 1849, 5 acts
Les Huguenots, 1836, 5 acts
L'Étoile du Nord, 1854, 3 acts
Roberto il Diavolo, 1831, 5 acts

WOLFGANG AMADEUS MOZART

Ascanio in Alba, 1771, 2 acts
Così fan Tutte (or La Scuola degli
  Amanti), 1790, 2 acts
Der Schauspieldirektor, 1786, 1 act
Die Entführung aus dem Serail,
  1782, 3 acts
Die Zauberflöte, 1791, 2 acts
Don Giovanni (or Il Dissoluto
  Punito), 1787, 2 acts
Idomeneo, Re di Creta, 1781, 3
  acts
Il Re Pastore, 1775, 2 acts
La Clemenza di Tito, 1791, 2 acts
La Finta Giardiniera, 1775, 3 acts
La Finta Semplice, 1868, 3 acts
Le Nozze di Figaro, 1786, 4 acts
Lucio Silla, 1772, 3 acts
Mitridate, Rè di Ponto, 1770, 3
  acts
Zaide (or Das Serail), 1779, 2 acts,
  unfinished

VICTOR NESSLER

Der Trompeter von Säkkingen,
  1884, 4 acts

OTTO NICOLAI

Die Lustigen Weiber von Windsor,
  1849, 3 acts

ARNOLD SCHÖNBERG

Moses und Aron, 1954, 2 acts,
  unfinished

FRANZ SCHUBERT

Fierrabras, 1826, 3 acts

ROBERT SCHUMANN

Genoveva, 1850, 4 acts

LOUIS SPOHR

Faust, 1816, 3 acts
Jessonda, 1823, 3 acts
Zemire und Azor, 1819, 4 acts

JOHANN STRAUSS

Die Fledermaus, 1874, 3 acts
Zigeunerbaron, 1885, 3 acts

RICHARD STRAUSS

Ariadne auf Naxos, 1912, 1 act
Der Rosenkavalier, 1911, 3 acts
Die Frau Ohne Schatten, 1919, 3
  acts
Elektra, 1909, 1 act
Salome, 1905, 1 act

RICHARD WAGNER

Das Liebesverbot, 1836, 2 acts
Der Fliegende Holländer, 1843, 3
  acts
Der Ring des Nibelungen:
  Das Rheingold, 1869, 1 act
  Die Walküre (1), 1870, 3 acts
  Siegfried (2), 1876, 3 acts
  Götterdämmerung (3), 1874, 3
    acts
Die Feen, 1834, 3 acts
Die Meistersinger von Nürnberg,
  1867, 3 acts
Lohengrin, 1850, 3 acts
Parsifal, 1882, 3 acts
Rienzi, der Letzte der Tribunen,
  1842, 5 acts
Tannhäuser und der Sängerkrieg auf
  der Wartburg, 1845, 3 acts
Tristan und Isolde, 1865, 3 acts

American Composers

DAVID AMRAM

Twelfth Night, 1969, 2 acts

SAMUEL BARBER

Antony and Cleopatra, 1966, 3 acts
Vanessa, 1958, 4 acts

JACK BEESON

Lizzie Borden, 1965, 3 acts

AARON COPLAND

The Tender Land, 1954, 2 acts

CARLISLE FLOYD

Susannah, 1955, 2 acts
Wuthering Heights, 1958, 3 acts

GEORGE GERSHWIN

Porgy and Bess, 1935, 3 acts

VICTOR HERBERT

Natoma, 1911, 3 acts

GIAN-CARLO MENOTTI

Amahl and the Night Visitors,
1951, 1 act
Amelia Goes to the Ball, 1937,
1 act
The Consul, 1950, 3 acts
The Medium, 1946, 2 acts
The Old Maid and the Thief, 1937,
1 act
The Saint of Bleeker Street, 1954,
3 acts
The Telephone, 1947, 1 act

DOUGLAS MOORE

The Ballad of Baby Doe, 1956,
2 acts
The Devil and Daniel Webster,
1938, 1 act
The Wings of the Dove, 1961, 1 act

KURT WEILL

Street Scene, 1947, 2 acts

British Composers

MICHAEL BALFE

The Bohemian Girl, 1843, 3 acts

BENJAMIN BRITTEN

A Midsummer Night's Dream,
1960, 3 acts

Albert Herring, 1947, 3 acts
Billy Budd, 1951, 4 acts
Gloriana of Essex, 1953, 3 acts
Peter Grimes, 1945, 3 acts
The Beggar's Opera, 1948, 3 acts
The Rape of Lucretia, 1946, 2 acts
The Turn of the Screw, 1953, 2
acts

ARTHUR THOMAS

Nadesha, 1885, 4 acts

RALPH VAUGHAN WILLIAMS

Hugh the Drover (or Love in the
Stocks), 1924, 2 acts

Russian Composers

ALEXANDER BORODIN

Prince Igor, 1890, 4 acts

MODEST MUSSORGSKY

Boris Godunov, 1874, 3 acts
Khovanschina, 1886, 5 acts

NIKOLAI RIMSKY-KORSAKOF

Le Coq d'Or, 1909, 3 acts
Pskovityanka, 1892, 4 acts
Sadko, 1898, 7 scenes
Snégourotchka, 1882, 4 acts

DIMITRY SHOSTAKOVICH

Lady Macbeth of the Mtsensk District, 1934, 4 acts

IGOR STRAVINSKY

The Rake's Progress, 1951, 3 acts

PETER TCHAIKOVSKY

Eugene Onégin, 1879, 3 acts
Jeanne d'Arc, 1879, 4 acts
Pique Dame, 1890, 3 acts

Czechoslovakian Composers

ANTONÍN DVOŘÁK

Rusalka, 1900, 3 acts

LEOŠ JANÁČEK

Jenůfa, 1904, 3 acts

BEDŘICH SMETANA

The Bartered Bride (Prodaná
Nevěsta), 1866, 3 acts

Spanish Composer

ENRIQUE GRANADOS

Goyescas, 1916, 3 scenes

Argentine Composer

ALBERTO GINASTERA

Don Rodrigo, 1964, 3 acts

1. COLORATURA SOPRANO

Bibliography

CAO-S   Celebri Aria D'Opera: Soprano. Original languages. Second of six volumes for all voices. Milan: G. Ricordi.

CAO-SL   Celebri Aria D'Opera: Soprano Leggero. Original languages. First of six volumes for all voices. Milan: G. Ricordi.

KAS   Koloratur Album. Soprano. Twenty-two arias and songs. Edited by Mathilde de Castrone Marchesi. Frankfurt: C. F. Peters.

MAO   Mozart Arias from Operas for Soprano. Four volumes. Original languages, with English translations. Edited by S. Kagen. New York: International Music Co.

MFL   Master Lessons on Fifty Opera Arias. Vol. II: The Music. Edited by Weldon Whitlock. Soprano: 27; Mezzo-Soprano: 4; Tenor: 12; Baritone: 8. Milwaukee: Pro Musica Press.

MSO   The Modern Soprano Operatic Album. Thirty-two arias. Original texts and English versions. New York: Franco Colombo.

OAR   Opern-Arien. Operatic arias in six volumes (two vols. for soprano) in original languages and German versions. Soprano: 36 & 44 arias; Mezzo-Soprano & Contralto: 34 arias; Tenor: 47 arias; Baritone: 30 arias; Basso: 34 arias. Nos. 4231A & B to 4235 in the catalog. Frankfurt: Edition Peters. (Note: OAR-S1 refers to the first volume for soprano.)

OAS   Opern-Arien für Sopran. G. Verdi arias, two volumes. Edited by Kurt Soldan. Italian texts, with German versions. Frankfurt: Edition Peters.

OGS   Opern-Gesänge für Sopran. Richard Wagner arias. German texts. Edited by Kurt Soldan. Frankfurt: C. F. Peters.

OPA-1   Operatic Anthology. Vol. 1: Soprano. Edited by Kurt Adler. New York: G. Schirmer, Inc. (Note: The older edition is edited by Kurt Schindler. Some entries here appear also in Vol. 2 for Mezzo-Soprano.)

OPR   Operatic Repertoire. Twenty-five soprano arias and 15 soprano and tenor duets. Edited by Fausto Cleva. Cincinnati: The Willis Music Co.

ORC   Operatic Repertoire for Coloratura Soprano. Edited by Wilfred Pelletier. Original texts, with English versions. Bryn Mawr: Theodore Presser Co.

ORS   Opera Repertoire for Soprano. Twenty-seven arias. Edited by Gregory Castleton. Original texts, with English versions. Includes synopses of opera plots. Bryn Mawr: Theodore Presser Co.

PDA   The Prima Donna's Album. Forty-two operatic arias. Newly re-
           vised and edited by Kurt Adler. Original texts, with English ver-
           sions. New York: G. Schirmer, Inc.

15A   Fifteen Arias for Coloratura Soprano. Original texts, with English
           translations. Some arias have added cadenzas by Estelle Liebling.
           New York: G. Schirmer, Inc.

A. Italian Composers

VINCENZO BELLINI, 1801-1835

7306. R: Eccomi in lieta vesta
       A: Oh! Quante volte
       Opera: I CAPULETTI ED I MONTECCHI, 1830, libretto by Felice
       Romani, based on Shakespeare's Romeo and Juliet. Part of Giulietta,
       Act I.   d3-c5 g3-g4 Extended recitative and sustained aria in mod-
       erate slow tempo. Has florid passages. Acc: 3-4 (VS)B-H, GR.
       (S)GR

7307. Ah! Son vergin vezzosa
       Opera: I PURITANI DI SCOZIA, 1835, libretto by Carlo Pepoli,
       based ultimately on Walter Scott's Old Mortality. Part of Elvira, Act
       I.   d3-b4 a3-g4 Animated in lively tempo. Brilliant, quite florid;
       requires considerable flexibility. Three other voices join, in the full
       score. Acc: 3-4 (VS)NO. KAS, CAO-SL

7308. R: O rendetemi la speme
       A: Qui la voce sua soave
       Opera: I PURITANI DI SCOZIA. Part of Elvira, Act II. eb3-ab4
       g3-eb4 Sustained in moderate slow tempo. Requires fine P and PP.
       Lyric throughout. Acc: 3 (VS)NO. ORC, KAS. (S)GR

7309. Sai come arde in petto mio
       Opera: I PURITANI DI SCOZIA. Part of Elvira, Act I. e3-b4 g3-
       g4 Animated in lively tempo. Florid, requires flexibility. The aria
       ends before Sir George's entrance. Acc: 3-4 (VS)NO

7310. Vien, diletto, è in ciel la luna
       Opera: I PURITANI DI SCOZIA. Part of Elvira, Act II. eb3-
       db5(eb5) ab3-ab4 Sustained in moderate lively tempo. Very florid,
       requires much flexibility. Has sustained high notes. Extended post-
       lude. Acc: 3-4 (VS)NO. ORC

7311. R: Oh! se una volta sola
       A: Ah! non credea mirarti...Ah, non giunge
       Opera: LA SONNAMBULA, 1831, libretto by Felice Romani, based
       on a vaudeville by Eugène Scribe. Part of Amina, Act II. eb3-eb5
       g3-a4 First part is sustained in moderate slow tempo. Second and
       third parts are faster and more climactic. The excerpt ends the op-
       era with ensemble. In the full score, the excerpt includes the part
       of Elvino. Acc: 4 (VS)GR, GS. OPR, ORC, 15A, PDA, KAS,
       CAO-SL. (S)GR

7312. R: Care compagne
       A: Come per me sereno.... Sovra il sen
       Opera: LA SONNAMBULA. Part of Amina, Act I. d3-d♭5 g3-b♭4
       Sustained in moderate tempo, with a quite rapid ending section. Very
       florid, requires considerable flexibility. Has descending chromatic
       passages. In the full score, has choral background. Difficult. Acc:
       4 (VS)GR, GS. KAS, CAO-SL. (S)GR

7313. De' lieti auguri a voi son grata
       Opera: LA SONNAMBULA. Part of Lisa, Act II. f3-c5 a3-b♭4
       Animated vocal part in moderate slow tempo. Has florid passages,
       generally in descending lines. Climactic ending. In the score the
       excerpt has a solo voice (Alexis) singing the duet and a chorus back-
       ground. Acc: 3-4 (VS)GR, GS.

7314. Tutto è gioia, tutto è festa
       Opera: LA SONNAMBULA. Part of Lisa, Act I. e♭3-c5 g3-a♭4
       Gently animated in moderate lively tempo. Requires flexibility. Has
       some florid figures. Mainly lyric. Acc: 3-4 (VS)GR, GS.

7315. Qual suon! Ah! Sventurato il cor
       Opera: LA STRANIERA, 1829, libretto by Felice Romani. Part of
       Alaide, Act I. f3-b♭4(c5) b♭3-g4 Sustained in moderate slow tem-
       po. c5 is part of an introductory cadenza and its performance is
       optional. Acc: 3-4 (VS)GR

LUIGI CHERUBINI, 1760-1842

7316. R: Io cedo alla buona
       A: O amore, vieni a me
       Opera: MEDEA, 1797, libretto by François Benoit Hoffman. Origi-
       nal in French. Part of Glauce, Act I. f3-c5 g3-g4 Animated aria
       in lively tempo. Has frequent high notes and an extended, florid ca-
       denza toward the climactic ending. Extended postlude which may be
       shortened or omitted. Accompaniment of this realization is overelab-
       orate. Acc: 4 (VS)GR

GAETANO DONIZETTI, 1797-1848

7317. R: Quel guardo il cavaliere
       A: So anch'io la virtù magica
       Opera: DON PASQUALE, 1843, libretto by the composer, Michele
       Accursi (Giacomo Ruffini), based on Angelo Anelli's novel. Part of
       Norma, Act I. d3-d♭5 g3-a4 Sustained recitative in moderate slow
       tempo and animated aria in moderate lively tempo. Florid; requires
       flexibility. Has several b♭4's and c5's. Acc: 4 (VS)GR. ORC,
       PDA, KAS, CAO-SL. (S)GR

7318. Prendi, per me sei libero
       Opera: L'ELISIR D'AMORE, 1832, libretto by Felice Romani, based
       on Eugène Scribe. Part of Adina, Act II. c3-a4(c5) a3-g4 Sus-
       tained in moderate tempo. Florid, requires flexibility. Has cadenzas.
       Acc: 3-4 (VS)GR, GS

7319. R: Ah, tardai troppo
       A: O luce di quest' anima

Opera: LINDA DI CHAMOUNIX, 1842, libretto by Gaetano Rossi.
Part of Linda, Act I. c3-c5 g3-g4 Recitative and aria in moderate
lively tempo. Requires flexibility. Has florid figures and grace
notes. Climactic ending. Acc: 3-4 (VS)GR. ORC, OPR, PDA

7320. Chacun le sait
Opera: LA FILLE DU RÉGIMENT, 1840, libretto by Vernoy de Saint-
Georges and Jean François Bayard. Part of Marie, Act I. c3-a4(c5)
f3-f4 Animated in lively tempo. Has martial and dramatic sections.
Climactic high ending. Joyful. Donizetti's first French opera. Acc:
3-4 ORC. Italian texts: (VS)NO, GR. PDA

7321. Il faut partir
Opera: LA FILLE DU RÉGIMENT. Part of Marie, Act I. e3-a4
ab3-f4 Slightly animated vocal part in moderate tempo. Requires
flexibility. Has climactic passages and a subdued ending. Acc: 3-4
ORC. Italian texts: (VS)NO, GR

7322. R: C'en est donc fait
A: Par le rang et par l'opulence
Opera: LA FILLE RÉGIMENT. Part of Marie, Act II. c3-bb4(eb5)
ab3-g4 Generally sustained in moderate tempo. Has faster sections,
florid passages, and dramatic passages. Has martial enthusiasm.
Climactic high ending. Acc: 3-4 ORC, OAR-S2. Italian texts:
(VS)NO, GR

7323. Il dolce suono mi colpi di sua voce
Opera: LUCIA DI LAMMERMOOR, 1835, libretto by Salvatore Cammarano, after Sir Walter Scott's The Bride of Lammermoor. Part
of Lucia, Act III. Popular title of the aria: The mad scene.
d3(bb2)-bb4(eb5) g3-g4 Sustained in moderate slow tempo. Very
florid, usually performed with many additional cadenzas and flourishes,
making it a show stopper. Interpretatively and musically difficult.
See the cadenzas introduced by Estelle Liebling and Mathilde Marchesi.
Acc: 4 (VS)GR, GS. 15A, CAO-SL, OAR-S2

7324. Regnava nel silenzio
Opera: LUCIA DI LAMMERMOOR. Part of Lucia, Act I. c3-c5
f#3-g4 Sustained in slow tempo. Slightly faster ending section.
Quite florid, requires flexibility. Requires fine high P and PP. Dif-
ficult. Climactic ending. Acc: 4 (VS)GR, GS. ORC, PDA, KAS,
CAO-SL, OAR-S2. (S)GR

7325. R: Havvi un Dio
A: Benigno il cielo arridere
Opera: MARIA DI ROHAN, 1843, libretto by Salvatore Cammarano.
Part of Maria, Act III. c3-c5 g3-g4 Sustained recitative in slow
tempo. Sustained aria in moderate slow tempo. Quite florid, requires
flexibility. Climactic ending. Acc: 3-4 (VS)GR

7326. Di quaiso a vi lagrime
Opera: POLIUTO or I MARTIRI, 1840, libretto by Eugène Scribe,
after Pierre Corneille. Original in French. Part of Paolina, Act I.
c3-bb4 g3-g4 Sustained in moderate slow tempo. Florid, requires
flexibility. Subdued low ending. Acc: 3 (VS)SR

UMBERTO GIORDANO, 1867-1948

7327. R: Evvia! Eccone un altro
       A: Il Parigino è come il vino
       Opera: FEDORA, 1898, libretto by Arturo Colautti, after the drama
       by Victorien Sardou. Part of Olga Sukarew, Act II. c♯3-a4 g3-g4
       Animated in lively tempo. Generally light. On MF level. Has pas-
       sages with high tessitura. Very fast ending section, with g4 as final
       note. Acc: 3-4 (VS)CS

GIACOMO PUCCINI, 1858-1924

7328. Quando men vo
       Opera: LA BOHÈME, 1896, libretto by Giuseppe Giacosa and Luigi
       Illica. Part of Musetta, Act II. Common title: Musetta's waltz.
       e3-b4 f♯3-f♯4 Sustained in graceful and elegant waltz. Climactic
       ending. Acc: 3-4 ORS, MSO, PDA. (VS)GR, GS. (S)GR-2 keys

7329. L'ora, o Tirsi
       Opera: MANON LESCAUT, 1893, libretto by Marco Praga, Domenico
       Oliva, and Luigi Illica, after a novel by Prévost. Part of Manon,
       Act II. d3-a4(c5) f3-g4 Animated in moderate tempo. Joyous; re-
       quires flexibility; has some short florid figures. Generally on the
       light, lyric side. Climactic and dramatic ending. Acc: 3 MSO. (S)GR

GIOACCHINO (ANTONIO) ROSSINI, 1792-1868

7330. Pour notre amour (It.: Ah! se privo di speme è l'amore)
       Opera: GUILLAUME TELL, 1829, libretto by Étienne de Jouy and
       Hippolyte Bis, after Schiller's drama. Original text: French. Part
       of Mathilde, Act III. d3-b4(c5) g3-g4 Animated in moderate lively
       tempo. Has florid passages requiring flexibility. Generally agitated.
       Has climactic high passages and a climactic ending with a florid ca-
       denza. Acc: 4-5 (VS) Troupenas-French; GR-Italian; B-H-Italian &
       English

7331. R: Ils s'éloignent enfin (It.: Ei mi segula)
       A: Sombre forêt désert triste (It.: Selva opaca deserta brughiera)
       Opera: GUILLAUME TELL. Part of Mathilde, Act II. e♭3(d3)-
       a♭4(b♭4) g3-f4 Slightly extended recitative and sustained aria in
       moderate slow tempo. Requires flexibility. Has some wide intervalic
       skips. Full-sounding, more climactic ending section. Acc: 3-4
       OPR, CAO-S (Italian only). (VS) Troupenas-French; GR-Italian; B-H-
       Italian & English

7332. Una voce poco fa
       Opera: IL BARBIERE DI SIVIGLIA, 1816, libretto by Cesare Sterbini,
       after Beaumarchais' comedy. Part of Rosina, Act I. A transcription
       for mezzo-soprano. g♯2-g♯4(b4) c♯3-f♯4 Sustained in moderate
       slow tempo. Florid, requires flexibility. Has some recitative-like
       passages. Traditional version by Estelle Liebling, GS. Acc: 3-4
       (VS)GS, GR. OPA-2, OPR, ORC, 15A, KAS, CAO-SL, OAR-S2.
       (SC)EE-Variations

7333. Sventurata! mi credea
       Opera: LA CENERENTOLA, 1817, libretto by Jacopo Ferretti, after

Perrault. Part of Clorinda, Act II. bb2-bb4 f3-g4 Sustained in
moderate slow tempo. Florid, requires considerable flexibility. Has
many wide and quick intervalic skips and several bb4's. Climactic,
florid ending. Acc: 3-4 (VS)FC

7334. Assisa a piè d'un salice
Opera: OTELLO or MORO DI VENEZIA, 1816, libretto by Francesco
Berio, after William Shakespeare's drama. Part of Desdemona, Act
III. c3-g4 f3-f4 Generally sustained in moderate slow tempo. Has
florid passages; requires considerable flexibility. Generally on MF
level. Gentle. Acc: 3-4 (VS)GR. KAS. (S)GR

GIUSEPPE (FORTUNINO FRANCESCO) VERDI, 1813-1901

7335. R: Santo di patria
A: Allor che i forti corono
Opera: ATTILA, 1846, libretto by Temistocle Solera. Part of Oda-
bella, in the Prologue. bb2-c5 g3-g4 Sustained in moderate slow
to moderate tempo. Requires flexibility. Has dramatic and florid
passages. Has several scale passages that move in full two-octave
phrases or more. Climactic ending. With a choral background in
the full score. Acc: 3-4 (VS)GR. OAS-1

7336. R: Liberamente or piangi
A: Oh! nel fuggente nuvolo
Opera: ATTILA, 1846, libretto by Temistocle Solera. Part of Oda-
bella, Act I. d3-c5 g3-g4 Recitative and generally sustained aria
in moderate tempo. Has florid passages; requires flexibility. Requires fine P. Agitated accompaniment. Acc: 4 ORC, OAS-1.
(VS)GR

7337. Sul fil d'un soffio etesio
Opera: FALSTAFF, 1893, libretto by Arrigo Boito, after Shakespeare's The Merry Wives of Windsor. Part of Nannetta, Act III.
d#3-a4 g#3-a4 Sustained in slow tempo. Slightly faster last section.
Has some recitative-like passages. Requires very fine high P, especially for the sustained a4 at the end. Acc: 3-4 MSO. (S)GR.
(VS)GS, GR

7338. O madre, dal cielo
Opera: I LOMBARDI ALL PRIMA CROCIATA, 1843, libretto by
Temistocle Solera, based on a romance by Tommaso Grossi. Part
of Giselda, Act II. d3-db5 ab3-ab4 Sustained in moderate tempo.
Has some very florid passages. In some sections the tessitura stays
high. Acc: 4 (VS)GR. OAS-1

7339. R: Venerabile, o padre
A: Lo squardo avea degli angeli
Opera: I MASNADIERI, 1847, libretto by Andrea Maffei, based on
Schiller's drama. Part of Amalia, Act I. d3(c#3)-c5 f#3-g4 Sus-
tained in moderate tempo. Generally light, requires flexibility. Re-
quires very fine high P and PP. Has florid passages. Acc: 3-4
(VS)GR

7340. Tu del mio Carlo al seno
Opera: I MASNADIERI. Part of Amalia, Act II. f3-c5 g3-g4 Sustained in slow tempo. Requires simplicity. Mainly lyric. Has florid

passages.   Requires flexibility.   Acc: 3-4   (VS)GR

7341. Mercè, dilette amiche
       Opera: I VESPRI SICILIANI, 1856, libretto by E. Caime, after
       Eugène Scribe and Charles Duveyrier.   Part of Elena, Act V.   a2-
       c♯5 g♯3-g♯4   Animated in lively tempo.   Florid, requires flexibility.
       Requires fluent enunciation.   Climactic high ending.   With choral part
       in the score.   Acc: 4 (VS)GR, CP.   OAS-2.   (S)GR

7342. Tacea la notte placida
       Opera: IL TROVATORE, 1853, libretto by Salvatore Cammarano,
       after Antonio Gutiérrez's play.   Part of Leonora, Act I.   ab2-c5
       eb3-g4 Sustained in moderate slow tempo, with variations.   Florid,
       has cadenzas with more than two-octave descending scale passages.
       Requires flexibility.   Climactic ending on ab4.   Difficult.   Acc: 4
       (VS)GR, GS, B-H.   MSO, OPA-1, OAS-2, PDA, CAO-S.   (S)GR

7343. Tu vedrai che amore in terra
       Opera: IL TROVATORE.   Part of Leonora, Act IV.   c3-c5 f3-a4
       Animated in lively tempo.   Exultant and joyous.   Requires flexibility.
       Has a few florid passages.   Climactic ending with sustained c5.
       Acc: 4 (VS)GR, GS, B-H

7344. R: Attendo nè a me giungon mai
       A: Addio del passato
       Opera: LA TRAVIATA, 1853, libretto by Francesco Maria Piave,
       based on a play by the younger Dumas.   Part of Violetta, Act III.
       e3-a4 a3-a4 Sustained in moderate tempo.   A generally subdued
       song with PP and PPP markings.   Has some short florid figures.
       Requires very fine high P and PP, and flexibility.   Ends on subdued
       a4.   Acc: 3-4 (VS)GR, GS, B-H.   OAS-2, CAO-S.   (S)GR

7345. R: È strano!
       A: Ah, forse è lui
       Opera: LA TRAVIATA.   Part of Violetta, Act I.   c3-c5(db5) f3-c5
       Generally sustained in varied tempi and moods.   Florid, has cadenzas
       and several c5's.   Extended, difficult, and vocally demanding.   Cli-
       mactic ending.   Acc: 4 (VS)GR, GS, B-H.   MSO, ORS, OAS-2,
       15A, PDA.   (S)GR

7346. Lo vidi, e'l primo palpito
       Opera: LUISA MILLER, 1849, libretto by Salvatore Cammarano,
       based on Schiller's tragedy.   Part of Luisa, Act I.   f♯3-c5 g3-g4
       Animated vocal part in moderate tempo.   Requires very fine high P
       and PP.   Has florid passages.   Climactic ending.   Acc: 3 (VS)GR.
       OAS-1

7347. R: Gualtier Maldè
       A: Caro nome
       Opera: RIGOLETTO, 1851, libretto by Francesco Maria Piave, after
       Victor Hugo's play.   Part of Gilda, Act I.   c♯3(b2)-c5(c♯5) f3-a4
       Sustained in moderate tempo.   Florid; requires considerable flexibility.
       Has cadenzas.   Generally light.   Subdued ending on trilled e4.   Acc:
       4 (VS)GS, GR.   ORC, OAS-1, MSA (no recitative), 15A, PDA, CAO-
       SL.   (S)GR

7348. Tutte le feste al tempio
       Opera: RIGOLETTO.   Part of Gilda, Act II.   The first part of the

Gilda and Rigoletto duet.   e3-a4   g3-f♯4   Sustained in moderate slow
tempo. Has florid passages and figures. Has one cadenza at the
end of the solo part. Requires some flexibility. Acc: 3-4 OAS-1.
(VS)GS, GR.   (S)GR

7349. Saper vorreste si che si veste
       Opera: UN BALLO IN MASCHERA, 1859, libretto by Antonio Somma,
       after Scribe's libretto. Part of Oscar, Act III. d3-b4 a3-f♯4 Ani-
       mated in moderate lively tempo. Generally light, graceful. Requires
       some flexibility. The verses are interspersed with "tra la la" pas-
       sages. Acc: 3-4 (VS)GS, GR. ORC, OAS-2, PDA, CAO-SL.
       (S)GR

7350. Volta la terra
       Opera: UN BALLO IN MASCHERA. Oscar's aria, Act I. d3-b♭4(c5)
       f3-g4 Animated in lively tempo. Requires flexibility and fluent enun-
       ciation. Generally light. Abounds in staccati phrases. Climactic,
       high ending on b♭4. Acc: 4 (VS)GS, GR. OAS-2, PDA, CAO-SL.
       (S)GR

B. French Composers

ADOLPHE (CHARLES) ADAM, 1803-1856

7351. Je vais donc le revoir
       Opera: LE POSTILLON DE LONGJUMEAU, 1836, libretto by Adolph
       de Leuvon and Leon Brunswick. Part of Mme. Latour, Act II. d3-
       c♯5 g3-g4 Recitative and sustained aria in slightly slow tempo, with
       moderate tempo in the middle section. Has florid passages, and a
       climactic ending. Requires flexibility. Agitated accompaniment to-
       ward the end. Acc: 3-4 (VS)BR

7352. Mon petit mari
       Opera: LE POSTILLON DE LONGJUMEAU. Part of Madeleine, Act
       I. d3-b♭4 g3-e♭4 Animated in moderate fast tempo. Has florid
       figures. Graceful, generally light. Slightly agitated accompaniment.
       Acc: 3-4 (VS)BR

DANIEL FRANÇOIS ESPRIT AUBER, 1782-1871

7353. R: Ne craignez rien, Milord
       A: Quel bonheur, je respire
       Opera: FRA DIAVOLO or L'HÔTELLERIE DE TERRCINE, 1830,
       libretto by Eugène Scribe. Part of Zerlina, Act II. d3-b4(c5) g3-
       f♯4 Rapid parlando recitative and an animated aria in moderate lively
       tempo. Has some florid passages. Requires flexibility. Ends with
       descending cadenza. Acc: 3-4 (VS)NO, BR

7354. R: Je suis sauvée enfin
       A: Flamme vengeresse
       Opera: LE DOMINO NOIR, 1837, libretto by Eugène Scribe. Part of
       Angèle, Act III. b2-b4 e3-e4 Animated recitative requiring fluent,
       rapid enunciation. Animated aria in lively tempo. Requires flexibil-
       ity. Florid ending section. Climactic ending. Acc: 3-4 (VS)BR

7355. C'est l'histoire amoureuse

Opera: MANON LESCAUT, 1856, libretto by Eugène Scribe, after
Abbé Prévost's novel. Part of Manon, Act I. d3-d5 a3-g4 Common title: The laughing song. Animated in fast tempo. Generally
light. Climactic ending. Acc: 3 (VS)BO

GEORGES BIZET, 1838-1875

7356. R: Me voila seule dans la nuit
A: Comme autrefois
Opera: LES PÊCHEURS DE PERLES, 1862-1863, libretto by Michel
Carré and Eugène Cormon. Part of Léila, Act II. c3-c5 f3-f4
Sustained aria in moderate slow tempo. Has also some animated sec-
tions. Generally subdued, requires fine P. Acc: 3-4 (VS)EC

7357. O Dieu Brahma!
Opera: LES PÊCHEURS DE PERLES. Part of Léila, Act I. b2(d3)-
c5 g3-g4 Starts in slow tempo, then moves into moderate and florid
section. Requires flexibility and fine high P. Has choral ensemble
in the full score. Acc: 3-4 (VS)EC

(ALEXIS) EMMANUEL CHABRIER, 1841-1894

7358. Blonde aux yeux de pervenche
Opera: GWENDOLINE, 1886, libretto by Catulle Mendèz. Part of
Gwendoline, Act I. c♯3-a4 a3-e4 Sustained in moderate slow tempo. Slightly faster second section. Gentle, generally subdued. Gently agitated accompaniment. Acc: 3-4 (VS)EN

FÉLICIEN (CÉSAR) DAVID, 1810-1876

7359. Charmant oiseau qui sous l'ombrage
Opera: LA PERLE DU BRÉSIL, 1851, libretto by J. Gabriel and
Sylvain Saint-Étienne. Part of Zora, Act III. d3-b4 g3-g4 Sus-
tained in first moderate, then slower tempi. Has florid passages.
Requires flexibility and fine P and PP. Acc: 3-4 (VS)HC. ORC

7360. Si vous ne savez plus charmer
Opera: LALLA-ROUKH, 1862, libretto by Michel Carré and Hippolyte Lucas, after Thomas Moore. Part of Mirza, Act I. e3-c5 g3-
f4 Animated in moderate-lively and lively tempo. Has some florid
figures. Acc: 3-4 (VS)EG

(CLEMENT PHILIBERT) LÉO DÉLIBES, 1836-1891

7361. Où va la jeune Indoue
Opera: LAKMÉ, 1883, libretto by Edmond Gondinet and Philippe
Gille. Part of Lakmé, Act II. Common title: Indian bell song. e3-
c♯5(e5) b3-b4 Animated vocal part in moderate slow to fast tempi.
Climactic ending. Florid, requires considerable flexibility. Acc: 3
(VS)HC, IM. ORC, 15A

7362. R: Les fleurs me paraissent plus belles
A: Pourquoi dans les grands bois
Opera: LAKMÉ. Part of Lakmé, Act I. e3-ab4 g3-f4 Gentle

recitative and sustained aria in moderate slow tempo. Requires fine
P. Has climactic passages. Subdued ending. Acc: 4 (VS)HC, IM.
ORC

7363.   Sous le ciel tout étoilé
        Opera: LAKMÉ. Part of Lakme, Act III. Common title: Berceuse.
        g3-g4(c5) bb3-g4 Sustained in moderate tempo. Tranquil, subdued,
        and gentle. Requires fine P. A lullaby. Acc: 3 (VS)HC, IM.
        ORC

CHARLES (FRANÇOIS) GOUNOD, 1818-1893

POG   Popular Operatic Songs. Charles Gounod. Edited by Albert Visetti.
       Most arias have the original texts, and English and Italian versions.
       London: Augener, Ltd.

7364.   Heureux petit berger!
        Opera: MIREILLE, 1863, libretto by Michel Carré, after Frédéric
        Mistral. Part of Mireille, Act IV. g3-a4 a3-g4 Sustained in mod-
        erate tempo. Requires simplicity, grace, very fine P. Generally
        gentle. Subdued ending. Acc: 3 (VS)EC

7365.   Le jour se lève
        Opera: MIREILLE. Part of Andreloun, Act IV. d3-g4 g3-e4 Sus-
        tained in moderate slow tempo. Generally gentle and subdued. Vo-
        calized ending with sustained last note (g4) on P to PP. Acc: 3
        (VS)EC

7366.   R: Trahir Vincent!
        A: Mon coeur ne peut changer
        Opera: MIREILLE. Part of Mireille, Act II. d3-db5 g3-g4 Sus-
        tained aria in slow tempo. Requires fine P and PP. Has dramatic
        passages. Requires flexibility. Florid toward the ending. Climactic
        ending. Acc: 3-4 (VS)EC

7367.   O légères hirondelle
        Opera: MIREILLE. Part of Mireille, Act I. f#3-d5(e5) a3-a4 A
        supplementary air, especially written for Mme. Miolan-Carvalho. A
        showy piece in waltz time. Florid and bright. Requires flexibility.
        Has climactic ending. Acc: 3 (VS)EC. ORC, POG

7368.   R: Il a perdu ma trace
        A: Ô riante nature
        Opera: PHILÉMON ET BAUCIS, 1859, libretto by Jules Barbier and
        Michel Carré. Part of Baucis, Act II. d3-c#5(d5) g#3-g#4 Sus-
        tained in slightly slow tempo. Has a lively, animated section. Florid,
        requires flexibility. Has some dramatic passages. Vocally demand-
        ing and difficult. Acc: 3-4 (VS)EC. POG

7369.   Philémon m'aimerait encore
        Opera: PHILÉMON ET BAUCIS. Part of Baucis, Act II. e3-b4 a3-
        a4 Sustained in moderate tempo. Has dramatic passages, sustained
        high notes, recitative sections, and a climactic ending. Acc: 3-4
        (VS)EC

7370.   Ah! Je veux vivre dans le reve

Opera: ROMÉO ET JULIETTE, 1864, libretto by Jules Barbier and
Michel Carré, after Shakespeare. Part of Juliette, Act I. Common
title: Juliet's waltz song. e3(c3)-d5 g3-a4 Animated in waltz tempo. Joyous, rhythmic, and graceful. Requires flexibility. Has
florid passages and cadenzas. Climactic high ending. Acc: 3-4
(VS)GS. ORC, 15A, PDA, POG

7371. R: Dieu! Quel frisson court dans mes veines?
       A: Amour, ranime mon courage
       Opera: ROMÉO ET JULIETTE. Part of Juliette. Act IV. d3-c5
       f3-a4 Aria is usually omitted in the production. Sustained in moder-
       ate tempo. Has recitatives between song sections. Uses a good num-
       ber of sustained high notes and trills. Climactic high ending on bb4.
       Acc: 4 (VS)GS

7372. R: Depuis hier je cherche en vain mon maître
       A: Que fais-tu blanche tourterelle
       Opera: ROMÉO ET JULIETTE. Part of Stephano, Act III. f3-c5
       f3-g4 Animated in moderate tempo. Moderately light. Has two
       florid, descending passages. Climactic ending. Acc: 4 (VS)GS.
       POG

(JACQUES FRANÇOIS) FROMENTAL (ÉLIAS) HALÉVY, 1799-1862

7373. R: Des roses, partout des roses
       A: O suave et douce
       Opera: LA FÉE AUX ROSES, 1847, libretto by Eugène Scribe and
       J. H. Vernoy de Saint-Georges. Part of Nérilha, Act II. bb2-c5
       g3-g4 Recitative and sustained air: first in moderate slow tempo,
       then animated in lively tempo. Florid, requires flexibility. Acc:
       3-4 (VS)HL

7374. Près de toi je crois
       Opera: LA FÉE AUX ROSES. Part of Nérilha, Act I. d3(bb2)-
       ab4(c5) g3-eb4 Sustained in moderate slow tempo. Has two ca-
       denzas. Requires flexibility. Acc: 3-4 (VS)HL

(LOUIS JOSEPH) FERDINAND HÉROLD, 1791-1833

7375. À la fleur du bel âge
       Opera: LE PRÉ AUX CLERCS, 1832, libretto by François Antoine
       Eugène de Planard. Part of Nicette, Act III. e3-a4 e3-e4 Ani-
       mated in moderate tempo. Graceful. Air ends with "oui toujours."
       With choral ensemble in the score. Acc: 3-4 (VS)BR

7376. Jours de mon enfance
       Opera: LE PRÉ AUX CLERCS. Part of Isabelle, Act II. b2-b4
       e3-e4 Animated vocal part in moderate tempo. Has florid passages,
       climactic ending. Air precedes "Oui Marguerite en qui j'espère."
       Acc: 3-4 (VS)BR

VICTOR (FÉLIX MARIE) MASSÉ, 1822-1884

7377. R: Que dis-tu? Je t'écoute
       A: Fleur parfumée

Opera: GALATHÉE, 1852, libretto by Jules Barbier and Michel Carré. Part of Galathée, Act I. d3(c♯3)-b4(d5) e3-e4 Recitative and
sustained, gracefully animated aria in moderate slow tempo. Has
some very florid sections and cadenzas. Climactic high ending. Acc:
3-4 (VS) Cendrier, c/o Léon Grus

7378. Sa couleur est blonde
Opera: GALATHÉE. Part of Galathée, Act II. c3-c5 f3-f4 Animated in moderate tempo. Rhythmic. Has florid passages, and a
climactic ending. Requires fine high P. Acc: 3-4 (VS) Cendrier,
c/o Léon Grus

7379. Au bord du chemin
Opera: LES NOCES DE JEANNETTE, 1853, libretto by Jules Barbier
and Michel Carré. Part of Rossignol, one-act opera. d♯3-c5(d♭5)
a♭3-g4 Animated in generally moderate tempo. Has long, extremely
florid cadenzas. Requires considerable flexibility. Climactic high
ending. Acc: 4 (VS)LG

JULES (ÉMILE FRÉDÉRIC) MASSENET, 1842-1912

7380. Je suis encor tout étourdie
Opera: MANON, 1884, libretto by Henri Meilhac and Philippe Gille,
after Prévost's novel. Part of Manon, Act I. d3-b♭4 f3-g4 In
varied tempi and moods. Generally sustained. Has dramatic passages. The suggested cadenzas go as high as e5. Interpretatively
difficult. Acc: 3-4 (VS)GS

7381. R: Est-ce vrai?
A: Obéissons quand leur voix appelle
Opera: MANON. Common title: Gavotte. e3-c5(d5) a3-a4 Dramatic, showy recitative and animated, lighter aria. Requires flexibility. Bright. Acc: 3 OPA-1. (VS)GS

7382. Oui dans les bois et dans la plaine
Opera: MANON. Part of Manon, Act III. Sometimes sung in place
of the Gavotte in Act III. d3-d5 g3-a4 Animated in lively tempo.
Jovial. Slower middle section. Requires very fine high PPP, and
flexibility for the florid passages. With choral background in the full
score. In the Appendix of the GS score. Acc: 3-4 (VS)GS

7383. Voyons, Manon. plus de chimères
Opera: MANON. Part of Manon, Act I. f♯3-a4 f♯3-f♯4 Sustained
in somewhat slow tempo. Has some quasi-recitative passages, climactic passages, and subdued ending. Acc: 3 (VS)GS

JACQUES OFFENBACH, 1819-1880

7384. Les oiseaux dans la charmille
Opera: LES CONTES D'HOFFMAN, 1881, libretto by Jules Barbier
and Michel Carré, after E. T. A. Hoffmann. Part of Olympia, Act
II. e♭3-b♭4(e5) g3-b♭4 Gently animated in moderate tempo. Very
florid, has several extended cadenzas. Requires fine high P and PP,
and flexibility. Difficult. Climactic high ending. Has choral background in the score. Acc: 3-4 (VS)GS. ORC, PDA

(CHARLES LOUIS) AMBROISE THOMAS, 1811-1896

7385. R: Sa main depuis hier na pas touché ma main!
       A: Les serments ont des ailes!
       Opera: HAMLET, 1868, libretto by Jules Barbier and Michel Carré,
       after William Shakespeare. Part of Ophélie, Act II. c♯3-b4(c♯5)
       g♯3-a4 Extended recitative and sustained aria in moderate lively tem-
       po. Has climactic, quasi-dramatic passages. Climactic ending.
       Acc: 4 (VS)HL

7386. R: A vos jeux, mes amis
       A: Pâle et blonde
       Opera: HAMLET. Part of Ophélie, Act IV. d3-c♯5(e5) g♯3-a4
       Extended scena and aria in varied tempi and moods. Very florid, re-
       quires considerable flexibility. Climactic, florid ending. Difficult.
       Acc: 4 (VS)HL

7387. R: À merveille
       A: Alerte, alerte
       Opera: MIGNON, 1871, libretto by Jules Barbier and Michel Carré.
       Part of Filina, Act II. An interpolation written for and sung by Mme.
       Volpini at the London performance. d3-c5(d5) g3-g4 A short,
       strong recitative and an animated aria in moderate lively tempo. Has
       a short, slower section, short and florid figures, and some cadenzas.
       Requires flexibility and fluent enunciation. Acc: 3-4 (VS)GS

7388. Je connais un pauvre enfant
       Opera: MIGNON. Part of Mignon, Act II. d3(c3)-b4(d5) f♯3-g4
       Common title: Styrienne. Key of d minor in the score; at times
       transposed one tone higher. In varying tempi. Starts moderately.
       Sustained, with florid passages. Requires considerable flexibility.
       Difficult. Although wide in range and has a high tessitura, the char-
       acter calls for a mezzo-soprano. Acc: 3-4 (VS)GS

7389. R: Oui, pour ce soir
       A: Je suis Titania
       Opera: MIGNON. Part of Filina, Act II. c3-c5(e♭5) g3-a4 Com-
       mon title: Polonaise. Animated in moderate tempo, polonaise style.
       Quite florid, with several difficult cadenzas. Requires considerable
       flexibility. Climactic ending. Acc: 3-4 (VS)GS. ORC, 15A, PDA

C.   German Composers

LUDWIG VAN BEETHOVEN, 1770-1827

7390. O wär ich schon mit der vereint
       Opera: FIDELIO, c. 1803-1805, libretto by Joseph Sonnleithner and
       George Frederick Treitschke. Part of Marcelline, Act I. g3-a4
       g3-g4 Animated in alternating moderate and lively tempi. Requires
       flexibility, especially with the faster ending section. Generally agi-
       tated accompaniment. Acc: 4-5 (VS)GS, B-H. OAR-S1

FRIEDRICH (FREIHERR) VON FLOTOW, 1812-1883

7391. R: Zum treuen Freunde geh'
       A: Den Theuren zu versöhnen

Opera: MARTHA, 1847, libretto by W. Friedrich (Friedrich Wilhelm
Riese).   Part of Lady Harriet, Act IV.   b♭2-d5 f3-a♭4 Sustained
aria in moderate tempo. Has florid cadenzas and passages with high
tessitura.   Climactic ending.   Acc: 3-4 (VS)GS

GIACOMO MEYERBEER, 1791-1864

7392. R: Adieu, mon doux rivage
       A: Pour celle dui m'est chère
       Opera: L'AFRICAINE, 1865, libretto by Eugène Scribe.   Part of Inèz,
       Act I.   f♯3(c♯3)-a4(c5) g3-f♯4 Sustained aria in moderate slow tem-
       po. Has free cadenza at the end. Agitated accompaniment. Acc:
       3-4   (VS)BR

7393. R: Bellah! ma chèvre chèrie!
       A: Dors petite, dors tranquille
       Opera: LE PARDON DE PLOËRMEL, 1859, libretto by Michel Carré
       and Jules Barbier. Part of Dinorah, Act I.   d3-b4 a3-f4 Other
       title: Berceuse. Sustained in moderate slow tempo. Graceful, gen-
       tle, and light. Requires very fine P and PP. Agitated, but very
       light accompaniment. Acc: 4 (VS)BR

7394. R: La nuit est froide et sombre!
       A: Ombre légère qui suis mes pas
       Opera: LE PARDON DE PLOËRMEL, or DINORAH.   Part of Dinorah,
       Act II.   d♭3-d5 g♭3-g4 Animated aria in tempi varying from mod-
       erato to allegro. Extremely florid; a showy piece. Requires con-
       siderable flexibility. Difficult. Ends with extended cadenza. Acc:
       4 ORC, KAS.   (VS)BR

7395. Sombre destinée
       Opera: LE PARDON DE PLOËRMEL, or DINORAH.   Part of Dinorah,
       Act II.   e♭3-g4 g♭3-e♭4 Sustained in moderate tempo. Generally
       light. Agitated accompaniment. Acc: 3-4 (VS)BR

7396. Mon coeur s'élance et palpite
       Opera: LE PROPHÈTE, 1849, libretto by Eugène Scribe.   Part of
       Berthe, Act I.   b♭2-c5 f3-f4 Animated in lively tempo. Slightly
       slower middle section. Brilliant and florid. Requires flexibility.
       Has an extended cadenza at the end. Climactic ending. Acc: 3-4
       (VS)BR, B-H, Benoit

7397. R: Nobles seigneurs, salut
       A: Une dame noble et sage
       Opera: LES HUGUENOTS, 1836, libretto by Eugène Scribe and Emile
       Deschamps. Part of Urbain, Act I.   d3-b♭4(c5) g3-g4 Majestic
       recitative in moderate tempo. Aria is sustained in moderate slow
       tempo. Florid, requires flexibility. Ends with cadenza. Acc: 3
       (VS)BR. ORS

7398. Ah! que j'ai peur
       Opera: L'ÉTOILE DU NORD, 1854, libretto by Eugène Scribe.   Part
       of Prascovia, Act I.   c3-c5 a♭3-f4 Animated in lively tempo.
       Spirited and bright. Has one florid cadenza at the end. With ensem-
       ble of three other characters. Acc: 3-4 (VS)MT

7399. Nel lasciar la Normandia

Opera: ROBERTO IL DIAVOLO, 1831, libretto by Eugène Scribe. Originally in French; the Italian version is reviewed here. Part of Alice, Act III. d3-a4(c5) g3-f4 Animated in lively tempo. Also has a recitative and slower passages. Has cadenzas and a climactic ending. Acc: 3-4 (VS)BR. PDA

7400. Roberto, o tu che adoro
Opera: ROBERTO IL DIAVOLO. Part of Isabella, Act IV. c3-c5 f3-g4 Sustained in moderate tempo. Has florid passages; requires flexibility. Has dramatic passages and a climactic ending. Acc: 4 (VS)BR. PDA

WOLFGANG AMADEUS MOZART, 1756-1791

10C   10 Arias from Operas for Coloratura Soprano. Wolfgang Amadeus Mozart. Original texts, with separate English translations. New York: International Music Co.

7401. Dal tuo gentil sembiante
Opera: ASCANIO IN ALBA, 1771 (K. 111), libretto by Giuseppe Parini. Part of Fauno, Act II. eb3-eb5 a3-g4 Slightly animated vocal part in moderate lively tempo. Has florid passages. Requires flexibility. Agitated accompaniment. Acc: 3-4 10C

7402. Bester Jüngling, mit Entzükken
Opera: DER SCHAUSPIELDIREKTOR, 1786 (K. 486), libretto by Gottlieb Stephanie, II. Part of Mlle. Warblewell, one-act opera. eb3-bb4 g3-g4 First part is sustained in moderate slow tempo. Second part is animated in moderate lively tempo. Has one florid cadenza. Climactic ending. Acc: 3-4 10C

7403. Da schlägt die Abschiedsstunde
Opera: DER SCHAUSPIELDIREKTOR. Part of Mme. Heartmelt, one-act opera. f#3-d5 g3-g4 Sustained in moderate slow tempo. Has two florid passages toward the end. Slightly subdued ending. Acc: 3-4 10C

7404. Ach ich liebte, war so glücklich
Opera: DIE ENTFÜHRUNG AUS DEM SERAIL, 1782 (K. 384), libretto by Gottlieb Stephanie II, after C. F. Bretzner's play. f3-d5 a3-a4 Part of Constanza, Act I. Sustained in moderate slow tempo. Florid, requires flexibility. Most florid passages have a tessitura between g4-c5. Acc: 3-4 10C, PDA, OAR-S1. (VS)CP

7405. Durch Zärtlichkeit und Schmeicheln
Opera: DIE ENTFÜHRUNG AUS DEM SERAIL. Part of Blonde, Act II. e3-e5 a3-g4 Gently animated in moderate slow tempo. Graceful. Has florid passages. Requires some flexibility. Somewhat subdued ending. Acc: 3-4 10C, PDA, OAR-S1. (VS)CP

7406. Martern aller Arten
Opera: DIE ENTFÜHRUNG AUS DEM SERAIL. Part of Constanza, Act II. b2-d5 a3-a4 Animated in lively tempo. Florid, requires flexibility and fluent enunciation. Has passages with long, sustained c5's. Energetic, with some strong passages. Difficult vocally. Acc: 4 10C, KAS, OAR-S1. (VS)CP

7407. R: Welcher Wechsel Seele
       A: Traurigkeit ward mir zum Lose
       Opera: DIE ENTFÜHRUNG AUS DEM SERAIL.   Part of Constanza,
       Act II.   f♯3-b4 a3-g4 Subdued recitative and sustained aria in mod-
       erate tempo.   Generally subdued.   Has some florid figures.   Sad
       text.   Acc: 3-4 10C, (VS)CP

7408. Welche Wonne
       Opera: DIE ENTFÜHRUNG AUS DEM SERAIL.   Part of Blonde, Act
       II.   d3-a4 g3-g4 Animated in lively tempo.   Requires fluent enun-
       ciation.   Climactic ending.   Acc: 3-4 (VS)CP.   MAO-2, OAR-S1

7409. Ach, ich fuhl's
       Opera: DIE ZAUBERFLÖTE, 1791 (K. 620), libretto by Emanuel
       Schikaneder and Johann Georg Giesecke.   Part of Pamina, Act II.
       c♯3-b♭4 f♯3-g4 Animated, somewhat florid, in moderate slow tem-
       po.   Generally light.   Requires fluent enunciation.   Acc: 3-4 (VS)GS,
       CP.   OPA-1, MAO-1, PDA, OAR-S1.   (S)GS

7410. Der Hölle Rache
       Opera: DIE ZAUBERFLÖTE.   Part of the Queen of the Night, Act III.
       Common titles: "Vengeance aria" or "Revenge aria. "   f3-f5 a3-a4
       Animated in lively tempo.   Florid, with very high tessitura in pas-
       sages.   Requires considerable flexibility.   Difficult.   Sometimes sung
       in too tame a manner.   Acc: 3-4 (VS)GS, CP.   10C, ORC, 15A,
       KAS, OAR-S1.   (S)GS

7411. R: O zittre nicht, mein lieber Sohn!
       A: Zum Leiden bin ich auserkoren
       Opera: DIE ZAUBERFLÖTE.   Part of the Queen of the Night, Act I.
       d3-f5 a3-a4 Majestic recitative and sustained aria, first in moder-
       ate slow tempo, then in moderate lively tempo.   Has one extended
       cadenza in the last section.   Climactic ending.   Acc: 3-4 10C,
       KAS, OAR-S1.   (VS)GS, CP

7412. Se il padre perdei
       Opera: IDOMENEO, RE DI CRETA, 1781 (K. 366), libretto by Giam-
       battista Varesco.   Part of Ilia, Act II.   e♭3-b♭4 b♭3-g4 Sustained
       in moderate slow tempo.   Has florid figures; requires flexibility.
       Generally on MF level.   Climactic ending.   Acc: 3-4 (VS)IM, CP

7413. S'altro che lagrime
       Opera: LA CLEMENZA DI TITO, 1791 (K. 621), libretto by Caterino
       Mazzolà, after Pietro Metastasio.   Part of Servilia, Act II.   f♯3-a4
       g3-g4 Sustained in minuet tempo.   Short, with a climactic ending.
       Acc: 3 (VS)CP.   MAO-2

7414. Geme la tortorella
       Opera: LA FINTA GIARDINIERA, 1775 (K. 196), libretto by Ranieri
       da Calzabigi (?).   Part of Sandrina, Act I.   f♯3-c5 a3-a4 Animated
       vocal part in moderate slow tempo.   Florid, requires flexibility.   Cli-
       mactic ending.   Acc: 4 MAO-2

7415. R: In un istante
       A: Parto, m'affretto
       Opera: LUCIO SILLA, 1772 (K. 135), libretto by Giovanni di Gamerra.
       Part of Giunia, Act II.   f♯3-d5 a3-g4 Moderate slow, then lively
       recitative, and animated aria in lively tempo.   Has florid passages,

mostly in triplet figures. Requires flexibility. Climactic ending.
Acc: 3-4 10C

7416. Trostlos schluchzet Philomele
Opera: ZAIDE or DAS SERAIL, 1779 unfinished, (K. 344), libretto
by Johann Andreas Schachtner. Part of Zaide, Act II. e3-a4 a3-a4
Sustained in moderate slow tempo. Florid, requires flexibility. Climactic ending. Acc: 3-4 MAO-2

LOUIS SPOHR, 1784-1859

7417. Hohe Götter! Schauet nieder
Opera: JESSONDA, 1823, libretto by Eduard Heinrich Gehe, after
Antoine Lemierre. Part of Jessonda, Act III. e3-bb4 a3-g4 Sustained in moderate slow tempo. Strong entrance. Has florid passages, requires flexibility. Climactic ending. Acc: 3-4 In: Soprano Arias, CP

7418. Rose, wie bist du reizend und mild!
Opera: ZEMIRE UND AZOR, 1819, libretto by Johann Jakob Ihlée,
after Marmontel's libretto. Part of Zemire, Act L e3-f#4 f#3-e4
Sustained in moderate slow tempo. Generally gentle, requires fine
P. Has a florid passage near the end. Acc: 3 (VS)AC

JOHANN STRAUSS, 1825-1899

7419. Klänge der Heimat
Opera: DIE FLEDERMAUS, 1874, libretto by Carl Haffner and
Richard Genée, after Meilhac and Halévy's vaudeville. Part of Rosa-
linda, Act II. Common title: Czárdás. c#3-d5 f#3-a4 Animated
vocal part in slow tempo. Has florid passages. Requires flexibility.
Climactic, high ending on "la la la" syllables. Acc: 3 OPA-1,
(VS)GS

7420. Mein Herr Marquis
Opera: DIE FLEDERMAUS. Adele, Act II. d3-d5 g3-g4 Common
title: Laughing song. Animated, graceful, and coquetish. 2 verses,
ending with laughter (pitched) and a final cadenza. Acc: 3-4 OPA-1,
(VS)GS. (S)GS

RICHARD STRAUSS, 1864-1949

7421. Kommt der neue Gott gegangen
Opera: ARIADNE AUF NAXOS, 1911-1912, libretto by Hugo von Hofmannsthal. Part of Zerbinetta, one-act opera. d3-d5 a3-a4 Sustained in moderate tempo. Has florid passages and a climactic ending. With ensemble in the score. Acc: 3-4 (VS)AF, B-H

7422. R: Grossmächtige Prinzessin
A: Noch glaub' ich dem einen ganz mich gehörend
Opera: ARIADNE AUF NAXOS. Part of Zerbinetta, one-act opera.
bb2-f#5 a3-b4 Generally sustained in varied tempi and moods. Has
florid passages, and extended cadenzas. Has passages with very high
tessitura. Ends with cadenza on sustained e5. Very difficult and vocally demanding. A real "tour de force." Acc: 4-5 (VS)AF, B-H

CARL MARIA (FRIEDRICH ERNST) VON WEBER, 1786-1826

7423. Kommt ein Schlanker Bursch
      Opera: DER FREISCHÜTZ, 1821, libretto by Friedrich Kind, after
      the Gespensterbuch. Part of Annie, Act II. c3-a4(b4) g3-g4 Ani-
      mated in moderate lively tempo. Requires some flexibility and fluent
      enunciation. Climactic ending. Acc: 4 (VS)GS, CP. OAR-S2

7424. R: Einst träumte meiner del'gen Base
      A: Trübe Augen, Liebchen, taugen
      Opera: DER FREISCHÜTZ. Part of Annie, Act III. d3-bb4 g3-g4
      Animated in lively tempo. Has florid passages. Requires flexibility.
      Has several bb4's. Climactic ending. Acc: 3-4 (VS)CP, GS.
      OAR-S2

D. American Composer

VICTOR HERBERT, 1859-1924

7425. I list the trill in golden throat
      Opera: NATOMA, 1911, libretto by Joseph D. Redding. Part of
      Barbara, Act II. db3-c5 a3-a4 Sustained in moderate tempo. Re-
      quires fine P. Has climactic and a dramatic ending section. Agi-
      tated accompaniment, with some arpeggiated sections. One step low-
      er in MLF. Acc: 4 (VS)GS. MLF

E. British Composer

MICHAEL WILLIAM BALFE, 1808-1870

7426. I dreamt that I dwelt in marble halls
      Opera: THE BOHEMIAN GIRL, 1843, libretto by Alfred Bunn. Part
      of Arline, Act II. eb3-g4 g3-f4 Sustained in moderate slow tempo.
      Graceful, gentle, and melodious. Requires some fine P. Gently cli-
      mactic ending. Acc: 3 (VS)GS. (S)GS

F. Russian Composer

NIKOLAI RIMSKY-KORSAKOF, 1844-1908

7427. Salut a toi, soleil de flamme!
      Opera: LE COQ D'OR, 1906-1907, libretto by Vladimir Bielsky,
      based on Pushkin. Part of Queen of Shemakha, Act II. f#3-a4(d5)
      a3-g4 Animated in moderate lively tempo. Has florid cadenzas; re-
      quires flexibility. Requires fine P and flexibility. Has dramatic pas-
      sages, and a very subdued, descending ending. In exotic style.
      Mostly performed in the English version: Hymn to the sun. Acc:
      3-4 MLF, ORC

2. LYRIC SOPRANO

Bibliography for Lyric Soprano and Dramatic Soprano

CAO-M   Celebri Aria D'Opera: Mezzo-Soprano & Contralto. Third of six volumes for all voices. Milan: G. Ricordi.

CAO-S   Celebri Aria D'Opera: Soprano. Second of six volumes for all voices. Milan: G. Ricordi.

CAO-SL   Celebri Aria D'Opera: Soprano Leggero. First of six volumes for all voices. Milan: G. Ricordi.

KAS   Koloratur Album. Soprano. Twenty-two arias and songs. Edited by Mathilde de Castrone Marchesi. Frankfurt: C. F. Peters.

MAO   Mozart Arias from Operas for Soprano. Four volumes. Edited by S. Kagen. New York: International Music Co.

MLF   Master Lessons on Fifty Opera Arias. Vol. II: The Music. Twenty-seven for soprano, 4 for mezzo-soprano, 12 for tenor, 8 for baritone. Edited by Weldon Whitlock. Milwaukee: Pro Musica Press.

MSO   The Modern Soprano Operatic Album. Thirty-two arias. Original texts and English versions. New York: Franco Colombo.

OAM   Opern-Arien für Mezzo-Soprano (Alt). Giuseppe Verdi. Edited by Kurt Soldan. Frankfurt: C. F. Peters.

OAR   Opern-Arien. Operatic arias in 6 volumes (2 for soprano) in original languages and German versions. Soprano: 36 & 44; Mezzo-Soprano & Contralto: 34; Tenor: 47; Baritone: 30; Basso: 34. Nos. 4231A & B to 4235 in the catalog. Frankfurt: Edition Peters. (Note: OAR-S1 refers to the first volume for soprano.)

OAS   Opern-Arien für Sopran. Giuseppe Verdi arias. Two volumes. Edited by Kurt Soldan. Italian texts, with German versions. Frankfurt: C. F. Peters.

OGS   Opern-Gesänge für Sopran. Richard Wagner. German texts. Edited by Kurt Soldan. Frankfurt: C. F. Peters.

OPA-1   Operatic Anthology. Vol. 1: Soprano. Edited by Kurt Adler. New York: G. Schirmer, Inc. (The older edition is by Kurt Schindler. Some entries in the soprano section of RSV are found in Vol. 2 for Mezzo-Soprano.)

OPA-2   Operatic Anthology. Vol. 2: Mezzo-Soprano and Contralto. Edited by Kurt Adler. New York: G. Schirmer, Inc. (The older edition is by Kurt Schindler.)

OPR   Operatic Repertoire. Twenty-five soprano arias and 15 soprano and tenor duets. Edited by Fausto Cleva. Original text, with English versions. Cincinnati: The Willis Music Co.

ORC   Operatic Repertoire for Coloratura Soprano. Edited by Wilfred Pelletier. Original texts, with English versions. Bryn Mawr: Theodore Presser Co.

ORS   Opera Repertoire for Soprano. Twenty-seven arias. Edited by Gregory Castleton. Original texts, with English versions. Includes synopses of opera plots. Bryn Mawr: Theodore Presser Co.

PDA   The Prima Donna's Album. Forty-two operatic arias. Original keys. Original texts, with English versions. Newly revised and edited by Kurt Adler. New York: G. Schirmer, Inc.

15A   Fifteen Arias for Coloratura Soprano. Original texts, with English versions. Some arias have added cadenzas by Estelle Liebling. New York: G. Schirmer, Inc.

A. Italian Composers

FRANCO ALFANO, 1876-1954

7428. Dio pietoso
       Opera: LA RISURREZIONE, 1904, libretto by Cesare Hanau, after Leo Tolstoi's tragedy. Katucha's aria, Act II. c3(b2)-g4(b4) g3-g4 Sustained in slow tempo. Grave. Has faster middle section. Generally strong, with dramatic ending passages. Requires fine P.
       Acc: 3 MLF

VINCENZO BELLINI, 1801-1835

7429. Ascolta: se Romeo t'uccise un figlio
       Opera: I CAPULETI ED I MONTECCHI, 1830, libretto by Felice Romani, based on Shakespeare's Romeo and Juliet. Part of Romeo, Act I. In the opera, sung by mezzo-soprano or high contralto; separately, may be sung by soprano. g2-g4 g3-f#4 Sustained in slow tempo. Graceful. Has florid passages. Acc: 3-4 (VS)BH, GR

7430. R: Eccomi in lieta vesta
       A: Oh! Quante volte
       Opera: I CAPULETTI ED I MONTECCHI. Giulietta's recitative and aria, Act I. d3-c5 g3-g4 Extended recitative and sustained aria in moderate slow tempo. Has florid passages. Acc: 3-4 (VS)BH, GR. (S)GR

7431. Ah! Son vergin vezzosa
       Opera: I PURITANI DI SCOZIA, 1835, libretto by Carlo Pepoli, based ultimately on Walter Scott's Old Mortality. Elvira's aria, Act I. d3-b4 a3-g4 Animated in lively tempo. Brilliant, quite florid. Requires considerable flexibility. In the original score, this aria is joined by three other voices. Acc: 3-4 (VS)NO. KAS, CAO-SL. (S)GR

7432. R: O rendetemi la speme
       A: Qui la voce sua soave
       Opera: I PURITANI DI SCOZIA. Elvira's recitative and aria, Act II.
       e♭3-a♭4 g3-e♭4 Sustained in moderate slow tempo. Requires fine
       P and PP. Lyric throughout. Acc: 3 (VS)NO. ORC, KAS. (S)GR

7433. Sai come arde in petto mio
       Opera: I PURITANI DI SCOZIA. Elvira's aria, Act I. e3-b4 g3-g4
       Animated in lively tempo. Florid, requires flexibility. Aria ends
       before the entrance of Sir George. Acc: 3-4 (VS)NO

7434. Vien, diletto è in ciel la luna
       Opera: I PURITANI DI SCOZIA. Elvira's aria, Act II. e♭3-d♭5(e♭5)
       a♭3-a♭4 Sustained in moderate lively tempo. Very florid, requires
       considerable flexibility. Has sustained high notes. Extended postlude.
       Acc: 3-4 (VS)NO. ORC

7435. Col sorriso d'innocenza
       Opera: IL PIRATA, 1827, libretto by Felice Romani. Part of Imo-
       gene, Act II. e3-a4 g3-g4 Sustained in moderate slow tempo.
       Quite florid, requires flexibility. Descending ending after high climax.
       Acc: 3-4 (VS)GR

7436. Lo sognai ferito
       Opera: IL PIRATA. Part of Imogene, Act I. c♯3-b♭4 a3-g4 Sus-
       tained in moderate tempo. Quite florid; requires flexibility. Descend-
       ing ending after climactic high note. With other characters in the
       score. Acc: 3 (VS)GR

7437. Quando al padre
       Opera: IL PIRATA. Part of the Imogene-Ernesto duet; air by Imo-
       gene, Act II. c♯3-c♯5 g♯3-g♯4 Sustained in moderate tempo.
       Florid toward the ending of this excerpt. Requires flexibility. Acc:
       3 (VS)GR

7438. R: Oh! se una volta sola
       A: Ah! non credea mirarti.... Ah, non giunge
       Opera: LA SONNAMBULA, 1831, libretto by Felice Romani, based
       on a vaudeville by Eugène Scribe. Common title of the aria: The
       sleepwalking scene. Part of Amina, Act II. e♭3-e♭5 g3-a4 First
       part is sustained in moderate slow tempo. Second and third parts are
       faster and more climactic. With the ensemble this ends the opera in
       a dramatic finale. Acc: 4 (VS)GS, GR. OPR, ORC, 15A, PDA,
       KAS, CAO-SL. (S)GR

7439. R: Care compagne
       A: Come per me sereno ... sovra il sen
       Opera: LA SONNAMBULA. Part of Amina, Act I. d3-d♭5 g3-b♭4
       Sustained in moderate tempo. Quite rapid ending section. Very florid,
       requires considerable flexibility. Has descending chromatic scale pas-
       sages. In the score, this is sung with choral background. Difficult.
       Acc: 4 (VS)GS, GR. KAS, CAO-SL. (S)GR

7440. De' lieti auguri a voi son grata
       Opera: LA SONNAMBULA. Part of Lisa, Act II. f3-c5 a3-b♭4
       Animated vocal part in moderate slow tempo. Has florid passages.
       The melody is in generally descending lines. Climactic ending. In
       the full score, other characters sing in this excerpt. Acc: 3-4
       (VS)GS, GR

7441. Tutto è gioia, tutto è festa
Opera: LA SONNAMBULA. Part of Lisa, Act I. e♭3-c5 g3-a♭4
Gently animated in moderate lively tempo. Requires flexibility. Has
some florid passages. Mainly lyric in style. Acc: 3 (VS)GS, GR.
OAR-S2

7442. R: Sono all'ara
A: Ciel piètoso
Opera: LA STRANIERA, 1829, libretto by Felice Romani, based on
a novel by C. V. P. d'Arlincourt. Part of Alaide, Act II. c3-c5
g3-f4 Slightly dramatic recitative and sustained aria in slow tempo.
Requires some maestoso treatment. One cadenza toward the end.
Acc: 3-4 (VS)GR

7443. Qual suon! Ah! Sventurato il cor
Opera: LA STRANIERA. Part of Alaide, Act I. f3-b♭4(c5) b♭3-
g4 Sustained in moderate slow tempo. c5 is part of an introductory
cadenza and its performance is optional. Acc: 3 (VS)GR

7444. Casta diva
Opera: NORMA, 1831, libretto by Felice Romani, based on a tragedy
by Louis Alexandre Soumet. Part of Norma, Act I. e3-c5 g3-a4
Very sustained in moderate slow tempo. Tempo varies with faster,
brilliant movement starting in the middle section. Quite florid in
passages. Requires flexibility. Musically and vocally difficult. With
vocal ensemble in the full score. Acc: 4 (VS)GS, GR. OPR,
PDA, KAS, OAR-S2. (S)GR

7445. E tu pure
Opera: NORMA. Part of Adalgisa, Act I. c3-a♭4 a♭3-g4 Sustained in moderate tempo. Climactic ending. Somewhat florid. Gently agitated accompaniment. Part of a duet. Acc: 3-4 (VS)GS, GR

7446. Oh non tremare
Opera: NORMA. Part of Norma, Act I. c3-c5 g3-a4 First part
is sustained in moderate tempo. Second part is marked in moderate
slow tempo. Florid, rather strong, dramatic. This solo is part of
the finale terzetto. Acc: 3-4 (VS)GS, GR

ARRIGO BOITO, 1842-1918

7447. L'altra notte in fondo al mare
Opera: MEFISTOFELE, 1868, libretto by the composer. Part of
Margherita, Act III. d3-b4 f♯3-g4 Sustained in slow tempo. Dra-
matic, dark, and florid. Has two extended cadenzas. Requires flex-
ibility. Descending ending after a climactic a4. Acc: 3-4 (VS)GR.
OPR, MSO, ORS, CAO-S. (S)IM, GR

ALFREDO CATALANI, 1854-1893

7448. Ebben? Ne andrò lontana
Opera: LA WALLY, 1892, libretto by Luigi Illica, based on Wilhelmine von Hillern's novel. Part of Wally, Act I. e3-b4 g♯3-g4
Sustained in moderate slow tempo. Generally gentle, subdued, with
some dramatic climaxes. Requires fine P and PP. Low, strong
ending. Acc: 3-4 (VS)GR. MSO, CAO-S. (S)GR

7449. Nè mai dunque avrò pace?
Opera: LA WALLY. Part of Wally, Act III. d3-bb4 a3-g4 Sustained in moderate, then moderate-slow tempo. Requires very fine
P and PP. Has dramatic high passages. Ends with medium low
recitative. Acc: 3-4 (VS)GR. (S)GR

7450. O neve, o figlia candida del cielo
Opera: LA WALLY. Part of Wally, Act IV. f3-bb4(c5) a3-f4 Sustained in moderate tempo. Generally lyric in style. Climactic ending. Acc: 3 (VS)GR

7451. Un dì, verso il Murzoll
Opera: LA WALLY. Part of Walter, Act I. d3-b4 g3-g4 Animated
in moderate lively tempo with variations. Has dramatic passages and
florid passages. Requires flexibility. Climactic ending. Acc: 3-4
(VS)GR

7452. Amor, celeste ebbrezza
Opera: LORELEY, 1890, libretto by Carlo D'Ormeville and Angelo
Zanardini. Part of Anna, Act II. d3-c5 g3-f#4 Sustained in moderate tempo. Requires fine high P and PP. Requires some flexibility. Climactic high ending on trilled g4. Acc: 3-4 (VS)GR. (S)GR

7453. Da chè tutta mi son data
Opera: LORELEY, 1890, libretto by Carlo D'Ormeville and Angelo
Zanardini. Part of Loreley, Act I. d3-bb4 g3-f4 Animated in lively tempo. Has climactic passages. The aria ends before the section
which starts with "l'april, l'april." Acc: 3-4 (VS)GR

7454. R: Dove son? d'onde vengo
A: Ma ... forse è un orrido sogno
Opera: LORELEY. Part of Loreley, Act I. d3-c5 g3-g4 Secco
recitative and an aria in varied tempi, with choral interpolations in
the score. Requires flexibility. Has some florid passages and a climactic ending. Acc: 3-4 (VS)GR

7455. O forze recondite
Opera: LORELEY. Part of Loreley, Act I. d3-c5 g3-g4 Animated
in lively tempo. Has some sustained passages and sustained high
notes. Climactic high ending. Acc: 3-4 (VS)GR

LUIGI CHERUBINI, 1760-1842

7456. Dei tuoi figli la madre
Opera: MEDEA, 1797, libretto by François Benoit Hoffman. Original in French. Part of Medea, Act I. f3-bb4 a3-g4 Sustained in
moderate slow tempo. Dramatic and intense. Climactic vocal ending.
Acc: 4 (VS)GR

7457. Del fiero duol che il cor
Opera: MEDEA. Part of Medea, Act III. bb2-bb4 f3-g4 Generally sustained in slow tempo. In varied moods. Dramatic and vocally
demanding. Climactic ending. Interpretatively difficult. Acc: 4
(VS)GR

7458. R: Io cedo alla buona
A: O amore, vieni a me

Opera: MEDEA. Part of Glauce, Act I. f3-c5 g3-g4 Animated
aria in lively tempo. Has considerable use of high notes. Has extended, florid cadenza toward the end. Extended postlude in the instrumental part may be omitted. Climactic ending. Acc: 4 (VS)GR

FRANCESCO CILÈA, 1866-1950

7459. Acerba volutta
Opera: ADRIANA LECOUVREUR, 1902, libretto by Arturo Colautti,
after Eugène Scribe. Part of the Princess, Act II. c3-a4 f3-f4
Originally for mezzo-soprano. A dramatic aria, first in fast tempo,
then closes with sustained section in moderate slow tempo. Has climactic passages. Acc: 4 (VS)CS

7460. R: Troppo signori
A: Io son l'umile ancella
Opera: ADRIANA LECOUVREUR. Part of Adriana, Act I. c3-ab4
g3-f4 Sustained in moderate slow tempo. Tranquil, requires simplicity, and fine PP. Has dramatic passages. Strong, climactic,
high ending. Acc: 3-4 (VS)CS. OPR. (S)IM

7461. Poveri fiori, gemme de' prati
Opera: ADRIANA LECOUVREUR. Part of Adriana, Act IV. d3-a4
g3-g4 Sustained in moderate slow tempo. Requires very fine P and
PP. Generally gentle. Climactic passage toward the end. Subdued
ending phrase. Acc: 3-4 (VS)CS. OPR. (S)IM

GAETANO DONIZETTI, 1797-1848

7462. Al dolce guidami
Opera: ANNA BOLENA, 1830, libretto by Felice Romani. Part of
Anna, Act II. e3(bb2)-a4(bb4) g3-g4 Sustained in moderate slow
tempo. Florid, requires flexibility. Acc: 3-4 (VS)GR

7463. R: Quel guardo il cavaliere
A: So anch'io la virtù magica
Opera: DON PASQUALE, 1843, libretto by the composer and Michele
Accursi (Giacomo Ruffini), based on Angelo Anelli's novel. Part of
Norina, Act I. d3-db5 g3-a4 Sustained recitative in moderate slow
tempo and animated aria in moderate lively tempo. Florid, requires
flexibility. Has several bb4's and c5's. Climactic ending. Acc: 4
(VS)GR. ORC, PDA, KAS, CAO-SL, OAR-S2. (S)GR

7464. Da me lungi ancor vivendo
Opera: IL CAMPANELLO DI NOTTE, 1836, libretto by the composer,
based on a vaudeville by Leon Brunswick. Part of Serafina, one-act
opera. d#3-a4 g#3-f#4 Part of the Finale. Sustained in moderate
slow tempo. Has some florid figures. A fine air for young sopranos.
Acc: 3 (VS)IM, GR

7465. Non morrete
Opera: IL CAMPANELLO DI NOTTE. Part of Serafina, one-act
opera. Second part of the duet. e3(d#3)-f#4 f#3-e4 Slightly animated in moderate lively tempo. Has short, florid figures. Ends
with cadenza. A fine air for young sopranos. Acc: 3-4 (VS)IM,
GR

7466. R: Fia dunque vero
A: O mio Fernando!
Opera: LA FAVORITA, 1840, libretto by Alphonse Royer, Gustave
Vaëz, and Eugène Scribe. Part of Leonora, Act III. b2(a2)-g#4
e3-f4 Dramatic recitative. Aria starts gently and sustained, then
becomes dramatic. Acc: 3-4 (VS)GR. OPA-2. (S)GR

7467. Chacun le sait
Opera: LA FILLE DU RÉGIMENT, 1840, libretto by Jules Vernoy de
Saint-Georges and Jean François Bayard. Donizetti's first French
opera. Part of Marie, Act I. c3-a4(c5) f3-f4 Animated in lively
tempo. Has martial and dramatic sections. Climactic high ending.
Joyful. Acc: 3-4 ORC. Italian version: (VS)NO, GR. PDA

7468. Il faut partir
Opera: LA FILLE DU RÉGIMENT. Part of Marie, Act I. e3-a4
ab3-f4 Slightly animated vocal part in moderate tempo. Requires
flexibility. Has climactic passages and a subdued ending. Acc: 3-4
ORC. Italian texts: (VS)NO, GR

7469. R: C'en est donc fait
A: Par le rang et par l'opulence
Opera: LA FILLE DU RÉGIMENT. Part of Maria, Act II. c3-bb4
(eb5) ab3-g4 Generally sustained in moderate tempo. Has faster
passages, florid passages, and dramatic passages. Martial enthusiasm. Climactic high ending. Acc: 3-4 ORC, OAR-S1. Italian
versions, (VS)NO, GR

7470. Che val ricchezza e trono
Opera: LA REGINA DI GOLCONDA, 1828, libretto by Felice Romani.
Part of Alina, Act I. c3-c5 g3-f4 Sustained in moderate slow tempo. Has florid passages, and some slightly animated sections. Requires flexibility. Climactic ending. Acc: 3-4 (VS)GR

7471. Prendi, per me sei libero
Opera: L'ELISIR D'AMORE, 1832, libretto by Felice Romani, based
on Eugène Scribe. Part of Adina, Act II. c3-a4(c5) a3-g4 Sustained in moderate tempo. Florid, requires flexibility. Has cadenzas.
Acc: 3-4 (VS)GS, GR

7472. R: Ah, tardai troppo
A: O luce di quest' anima
Opera: LINDA DI CHAMOUNIX, 1842, libretto by Gaetano Rossi.
Part of Linda, Act I. c3-c5 g3-g4 Recitative and animated aria in
moderate lively tempo. Requires flexibility. Has florid figures and
grace notes. Climactic ending. Acc: 3-4 (VS)GR. ORC, OPR,
PDA. (S)GR

7473. Il dolce suono mi colpi di sua voce
Opera: LUCIA DI LAMMERMOOR, 1835, libretto by Salvatore Cammarano, after Sir Walter Scott's novel The Bride of Lammermoor.
Part of Lucia, Act III. Common title: The mad scene. d3(bb2)-
bb4(eb5) g3-g4 Sustained in moderate slow tempo. Very florid,
usually performed with many added cadenzas and flourishes, making
it a show stopper. Interpretatively and musically difficult. See the
cadenzas introduced by Estelle Liebling and Mathilde Marchesi. Acc:
4 (VS)GS, GR. 15A, CAO-SL, OAR-S2

7474. Regnava nel silenzio
       Opera: LUCIA DI LAMMERMOOR. Part of Lucia, Act I. c3-c5
       f♯3-g4 Sustained in slow tempo. Slightly faster ending section.
       Quite florid, requires flexibility. Requires fine high P and PP. Dif-
       ficult. Climactic ending. Acc: 4 ORC, PDA, KAS, CAO-SL, OAR-
       S1. (VS)GS, GR. (S)GR

7475. Com' è bello quale in canto
       Opera: LUCREZIA BORGIA, 1833, libretto by Felice Romani, based
       on Victor Hugo's play. Part of Lucrezia, in the Prologue. d3-ab4
       g3-f4 Sustained in moderate slow tempo. Requires flexibility. Gen-
       erally gentle. Acc: 3 (VS)B-H, GR. KAS

7476. M'odi, ah! m'odi io non t'imploro
       Opera: LUCREZIA BORGIA. Part of Lucrezia, Act II. d♯3-a4
       g♯3-g♯4 Gently animated vocal part in slow tempo. Florid, requires
       flexibility. Low ending. Acc: 3-4 (VS)B-H, GR

7477. R: Havvi un Dio
       A: Benigno il cielo arridere
       Opera: MARIA DI ROHAN, 1843, libretto by Salvatore Cammarano.
       Part of Maria, Act III. c3-c5 g3-g4 Sustained recitative in slow
       tempo. Sustained aria in moderate slow tempo. Quite florid, re-
       quires flexibility. Climactic ending. Acc: 3-4 (VS)GR

7478. Di quaiso a vi lagrime
       Opera: POLIUTO or I MARTIRI, 1840, libretto by Eugène Scribe,
       after Thomas Corneille. Original in French. Part of Paolina, Act I.
       c3-bb4 g3-g4 Sustained in moderate slow tempo. Florid; requires
       flexibility. Subdued low ending. Acc: 3 (VS)SR

7479. R: È lindo e civettin
       A: Van la casa e l'albergo
       Opera: RITA, 1860, libretto by Gustave Vaëz. Part of Rita, one-act
       opera. e3(c♯3)-b4 f♯3-f♯4 Short recitative and animated aria in
       moderate lively tempo. Faster ending section. Has some florid pas-
       sages. Requires fluent enunciation. Climactic high ending. Acc:
       3-4 (VS)GR

UMBERTO GIORDANO, 1867-1948

7480. La mamma morta
       Opera: ANDREA CHÉNIER, 1896, libretto by Luigi Illica. Part of
       Maddalena, Act III. c♯3-b4 e3-g4 Subdued first section in recita-
       tive style, then without break, moves on to more sustained section in
       moderate slow tempo. Has dramatic passages before the subdued,
       quasi-recitative ending. Acc: 3-4 (VS)CS, IM. OPR, MLF

7481. Dio di giustizia
       Opera: FEDORA, 1898, libretto by Arturo Colautti, after Victorien
       Sardou's drama. Part of Fedora, Act III. c3-a4 f3-f4 Sustained in
       moderate tempo. Has dramatic climaxes. Subdued, low ending after
       high climax. Acc: 3-4 (VS)CS

7482. Il Parigino e come il vino
       Opera: FEDORA. Part of Olga Sukarew, Act II. c♯3-a4 a3-g4
       Animated in lively tempo. Generally light, requires flexibility. Acc:
       4 (VS)CS

7483. R: Rigida è assai la sera
       A: O grandi occhi lucenti
       Opera: FEDORA. Part of Fedora, Act I. e3-a4 g♯3-f♯4 Sustained
       in moderate slow tempo. Generally subdued and gentle. Subdued end-
       ing. Acc: 3-4 (VS)CS. OPR

7484. R: Ascoltami! Se fosse pentita
       A: Se quell' infelice
       Opera: FEDORA. Part of Fedora, Act III. d3-a4 a3-f4 Animated
       aria in lively tempo. Slower ending section. Has dramatic and cli-
       mactic passages. Agitated accompaniment. Acc: 3-4 (VS)CS

RUGGIERO LEONCAVALLO, 1858-1919

7485. Ed ora, conoscetela
       Opera: LA BOHÈME, 1897, libretto by Giuseppe Giacosa and Luigi
       Illica, after Henri Murger's novel. Part of Mimi, Act I. d3-a4
       a3-f4 Sustained in moderate tempo. Has passages requiring fluent
       enunciation. Climactic high ending. Acc: 3-4 (VS)CS

7486. R: Qual fiamma avea
       A: Stridono lassù
       Opera: PAGLIACCI, 1892, libretto by the composer. Part of Nedda,
       Act I. Common title: Ballatella. c♯3-a4(b4) f♯3-g♯4 Animated in
       fast tempo. Requires fluent enunciation. Climactic, subdued ending.
       Acc: 4 OPA-1, OPR, MLF. (VS)GS

7487. Ah! Oh, che quadretto!
       Opera: ZAZÀ, 1900, libretto by the composer, after a play by
       Pierre Berton and Charles Simon. Part of Zazà, Act II. Animated
       in lively tempo. Climactic ending in staccati. Common title: Zazà's
       laughing song. Acc: 3 (VS)CS

7488. Dir che ci sono al mondo
       Opera: ZAZÀ. Part of Zazà, Act III. c3-a4 f3-f4 Sustained in
       moderate slow tempo. Has dramatic high climaxes. Intense, in sev-
       eral places marked. Subdued ending. Acc: 3-4 (VS)CS

7489. S'io l'avessi, Toto
       Opera: ZAZÀ. Part of Zazà, Act III. d♯3-g♯4 g3-f♯4 Generally
       sustained in varied tempi. Has dramatic passages and recitative pas-
       sages. Somewhat intense. Climactic ending on "nessun...ti strap-
       perà." The excerpt may proceed to include "Dir che ci sono al mon-
       do," omitting intervening part. Acc: 3-4 (VS)CS

7490. Via, non mi torturare!
       Opera: ZAZÀ. Part of Zazà, Act I. d3-a4 g3-f♯4 Sustained in
       moderate slow tempo. Has climactic passages. Subdued, slow ending.
       Acc: 3 (VS)CS

PIETRO MASCAGNI, 1863-1945

7491. R: Ho fatto un triste
       A: S'era malata la mia amica
       Opera: IRIS, 1898, libretto by Luigi Illica. Part of Iris, Act I.
       d3-b♭4 f♯3-f♯4 Subdued and contemplative recitative. The aria
       starts with a recitative-like passage, is quite subdued, then moves

gradually into a dramatic, agitated section. Subdued ending. Acc:
3-4 (VS)GR

7492. Un dì ero piccina
       Opera: IRIS, 1898, libretto by Luigi Illica. Part of Iris, Act II.
       d3-a4 e3-f♯4 Sustained in moderate tempo. Requires fine P. Cli-
       mactic and dramatic ending. Acc: 3 MSO

7493. Son pochi fiori
       Opera: L'AMICO FRITZ, 1891, libretto by P. Suardon, after Erck-
       mann-Chatrian's novel. Part of Suzel, Act I. d3-g4 g3-f4 Sus-
       tained in moderate slow tempo. First part is in recitative style.
       Generally on the gentle, subdued side. Acc: 3 (VS)CS

GIACOMO (ANTONIO DOMENICO) PUCCINI, 1858-1924

7494. O mio babbino caro
       Opera: GIANNI SCHICCHI, 1918, libretto by Giovacchino Forzano.
       Third opera in the Trittico. Part of Lauretta, one-act opera. e♭3-
       a♭4 f3-f4 Sustained in moderate slow tempo. Requires fine high
       PP. Very lyric. Subdued ending. Acc: 3-4 (VS)GR. MSO, (S)GR

7495. Donde lieta usci
       Opera: LA BOHÈME, 1896, libretto by Giuseppe Giacosa and Luigi
       Illica, based on Murger's novel. Part of Mimi, Act III. d♭3-b♭4
       f3-f4 Sustained in slow tempo. Generally gentle, with sad texts.
       Has some climactic passages. Subdued ending after a dramatic cli-
       max. Acc: 3-4 (VS)GS, GR. MSO, OPR, MLF, PDA. (S)GR

7496. Quando men vo
       Opera: LA BOHÈME. Part of Musetta, Act II. Common title:
       Musetta's waltz. e3-b4 f♯3-f♯4 Sustained, graceful and elegant
       waltz. Completely lyric in style, with climactic passages. Climac-
       tic ending. Acc: 3 (VS)GS, GR. ORS, MSO, PDA. (S)GR

7497. Mi chiamano Mimi
       Opera: LA BOHÈME. Part of Mimi, Act I. d3-a4 f♯3-f♯4 Sus-
       tained in generally slow tempo. Generally gentle. Ends in recitative
       passage over sustained chord. Acc: 3-4 (VS)GS, GR. MSO, OPA-
       1, ORS, MLF, CAO-S. (S)GS, GR

7498. Oh, se sapeste
       Opera: LA FANCIULLA DEL WEST, 1910, libretto by Guelfo Civinini
       and Carlo Zangarini, based on David Belasco's play. Part of Minnie,
       Act II. English title: The Girl of the Golden West. c♯3-b4 f♯3-
       g4 Sustained, joyous, and climactic. Sustained high ending on b4.
       Acc: 3 MSO, (VS)GR. (S)GR

7499. Se come voi piccina io fossi
       Opera: LE VILLI, 1884, libretto by Ferdinando Fontana. Part of
       Anna, Act I (revised version in two acts; original is in one act). d3-
       a4 f♯3-f♯4 Sustained in moderate slow tempo. Has dramatic pas-
       sages. Requires fine PP and PPP, and flexibility. Slightly climactic
       ending. Acc: 4 (VS)GR

7500. Ancora un passo.... Spira sul mare
       Opera: MADAMA BUTTERFLY, 1904, libretto by Giuseppe Giacosa

and Luigi Illica, after Belasco's drama of John Long's story. Common title: Entrata di Butterfly. Part of Butterfly, Act I. f3-bb4
(db 5) gb 3-gb 4 Sustained in slow tempo. Requires fine P. In quasi-recitative in several passages. Rather subdued high ending with optional final note. Acc: 4 (VS)GS, GR. MSO. (S)GR

7501. Che tua madre dovrà prenderti in braccio
Opera: MADAMA BUTTERFLY. Part of Butterfly, Act II. db 3-ab 4(bb 4) eb 3-gb 4 Sustained in moderate tempo which varies slightly toward the second half. Climactic, dramatic ending section. Acc: 3 (VS)GS, GR. MSO. (S)GR

7502. Tu tu, piccolo Iddio!
Opera: MADAMA BUTTERFLY. Part of Butterfly, Act III. Other title: Butterfly's farewell aria. d3-a4 g3-f♯4 Sustained in moderate slow tempo. Starts in recitative style. Has climactic passages, but gently lyric in style. Descending ending after high climax. Acc: 3 (VS)GR. (S)GR

7503. Un bel dì, vedremo
Opera: MADAMA BUTTERFLY. Part of Butterfly, Act II. db 3-bb 4 f3-gb 4 Sustained in slow tempo. Generally calm, mostly subdued except for the dramatic and climactic high ending. Has quasi-recitative passages. Traditionally bb 4 is sung on the last syllable of "l'aspetto" at the end, instead of the original bb 3. Acc: 3-4 (VS)GS, GR. MSO, MLF. (S)GS-high, medium, low; GR; IM

7504. In quelle trine morbide
Opera: MANON LESCAUT, 1893, libretto by Marco Praga, Domenico Oliva, and Luigi Illica, based on Prévost's novel. Part of Manon, Act II. eb 3-bb 4 f3-gb 4 Sustained but moving vocal part in moderate tempo. Requires fine P. Has dramatic climaxes and a subdued ending. Short. Acc: 3 MSO, OPA-1, ORS, PDA. (VS)GR. (S)GS, GR, IM

7505. L'ora, o Tirsi
Opera: MANON LESCAUT. Part of Manon, Act II. d3-a4(c5) f3-f4 Animated in moderate tempo. Joyous, requires flexibility. Has some short florid figures. Generally light. Climactic, dramatic ending. Acc: 3 MSO. (VS)GR; (S)GR

7506. Sola, perduta, abbandonata
Opera: MANON LESCAUT. Part of Manon, Act IV. c3-bb 4 ab 3-g4 Sustained in slow tempo. Has dramatic passages. Requires fine high P. Intense. Acc: 4 (VS)IM, GR. OPR. (S)GR, IM

7507. Senza mamma, o bimbo, tu sei morto!
Opera: SUOR ANGELICA, 1918, libretto by Giovacchino Forzano. Part of Suor Angelica, one-act opera, second in the Trittico. d3-a4 e3-g4 Sustained in moderate slow tempo. Generally subdued and gentle. Very subdued ending on sustained a4. Requires very fine P and PP. Acc: 3-4 (VS)GR. (S)GR

7508. Io de' sospiri
Opera: TOSCA, 1900, libretto by Giuseppe Giacosa and Luigi Illica, based on Sardou's drama. Part of the Young Shepherd, Act III. b2-e4 e3-c♯4 Sustained in moderate slow tempo. Generally subdued. Subdued, descending ending. Acc: 3 (VS)GS, GR

7509. Non la sospiri la nostra casetta
      Opera: TOSCA. Part of Tosca, Act I. f3-bb4 ab3-ab4 Sustained
      in moderate lively tempo. Dramatic. Requires fine P. Very sub-
      dued ending. Acc: 3-4 (VS)GS, GR. MSO, ORS. (S)GR

7510. Vissi d'arte, vissi d'amore
      Opera: TOSCA. Part of Tosca, Act II. eb3-bb4 gb3-gb4 Sus-
      tained in slow tempo. Generally subdued, tranquil and requires fine
      P. In quasi-recitative style. Has climactic passages. Acc: 3
      (VS)GS, GR. MSO, ORS, MLF, PDA, CAO-S. (S)GS, GR

7511. Del primo pianto
      Opera: TURANDOT, 1926, unfinished, completed by Franco Alfano;
      libretto by Giuseppe Adami and Renato Simoni, based on Carlo Goz-
      zi's play. Part of Turandot, Act III. eb3-a4 a3-f#4 Sustained in
      moderate tempo. Starts gently and in subdued tones. Has dramatic
      high climaxes. Also requires fine P. Dramatic high ending. Acc:
      4 (VS)GR. (S)GR

7512. In questa reggia
      Opera: TURANDOT. Part of Turandot, Act II. c#3-c5 f3-g4 Sus-
      tained in generally slow tempo, varying according to mood. Requires
      fine P. Has strong, dramatic sections. Climactic, strong ending on
      high tessitura. Acc: 3-4 (VS)GR. MSO. (S)GR

7513. Signore, ascolta!
      Opera: TURANDOT. Part of Liù, Act I. db3-bb4 gb3-ab4 Sus-
      tained in slow tempo. Subdued ending on sustained ab4 to bb4. Re-
      quires fine P and PP. Has some climactic high passages. Acc:
      3-4 MSO (VS)GR. (S)GR

7514. Tanto amore segreto
      Opera: TURANDOT. Part of Liù, Act III. f3-bb4 a3-g4 Sus-
      tained in slow tempo. Starts gently on high notes. Intense. Has
      dramatic climaxes. Subdued high ending passage. Acc: 3-4 (VS)
      GR. (S)GR

7515. Tu che di gel sei cinta
      Opera: TURANDOT. Part of Liù, Act III. eb3-bb4 gb3-gb4 Sus-
      tained in moderate slow tempo. Requires fine high P. Climactic and
      dramatic ending. Acc: 3 MSO, CAO-S, (VS)GR. (S)GR

GIOACCHINO (ANTONIO) ROSSINI, 1792-1868

7516. Pour notre amour (It.: Ah! se privo di speme è l'amore)
      Opera: GUILLAUME TELL, 1829, libretto by Étienne de Jouy and
      Hippolyte Bis, after Schiller's drama. Original text: French. Part
      of Mathilde, Act III. d3-b4(c5) g3-g4 Animated in moderate lively
      tempo. Has florid passages requiring flexibility. Generally agitated.
      Has climactic high passages and a climactic ending with a florid ca-
      denza. Acc: 4-5 (VS) Troupenas-French; GR-Italian; B-H-Italian &
      English

7517. R: Ils s'éloignent enfin (It.: Ei mi seguìa)
      A: Sombre forêt désert triste (It.: Selva opaca deserta brughiera)
      Opera: GUILLAUME TELL. Part of Mathilde, Act II. eb3(d3)-ab4
      (bb4) g3-f4 Slightly extended recitative and sustained aria in

moderate slow tempo. Requires flexibility. Has some wide intervalic skips. Full-sounding, more climactic ending section. Acc: 3-4 OPR, CAO-S (Italian only).   (VS) Troupenas-French; GR-Italian; B-H-Italian & English

7518. Una voce poco fa
Opera: IL BARBIERE DI SIVIGLIA, 1816, libretto by Cesare Sterbini, after Beaumarchais' comedy. Part of Rosina, Act I. A transposition from mezzo-soprano. g#2-g#4(b4) c#3-f#4 Sustained in moderate slow tempo. Florid, requires flexibility. Has some recitative-like passages. Traditional version by Estelle Liebling, GS. Composer's variations for this aria, "Varianten zur Cavatine der Rosina 'Una voce poco fa'," Edition Eulenburg (1973). Acc: 3-4 (VS)GS, GR. OPA-2, OPR, 15A, PDA, KAS, CAO-SL, (SC)EE-Variations

7519. Sventurata! mi credea
Opera: LA CENERENTOLA, 1817, libretto by Jacopo Ferretti, after Charles Perrault. Part of Clorinda, Act II. bb2-bb4 f3-g4 Sustained in moderate slow tempo. Florid, requires considerable flexibility. Has many wide and quick intervalic skips, and several bb4's. Climactic, florid ending. Acc: 3-4 (VS)FC

7520. Di piacer mi balza il cor
Opera: LA GAZZA LADRA, 1817, libretto by Giovanni Gherardini, after a comedy by d'Aubigny and Caigniez. Part of Ninetta, Act I. b2-a4 e3-f#4 Animated vocal part, first in moderate then faster tempi. Quite florid, requires flexibility. Has dramatic passages and climactic ending. Acc: 3-4 (VS)EG. PDA, KAS. (S)GR

7521. R: Cielo! che diverrò?
A: Dal soggiorno degli estinti
Opera: L'ASSEDIO DI CORINTO, 1826, libretto by Luigi Balocchi and Alexandre Soumet. Part of Pamira, Act II. c3-bb4 f3-f4 Slightly extended recitative and sustained aria in moderate slow tempo. Florid, requires flexibility. Climactic ending. Original is French. Acc: 3-4 (VS)GR

7522. Assisa a' piè d'un salice
Opera: OTELLO or MORO DI VENEZIA, 1816, libretto by Francesco Berio, after William Shakespeare's drama. Part of Desdemona, Act III. c3-g4 f3-f4 Generally sustained in moderate slow tempo. Has florid passages. Requires considerable flexibility. Generally on MF level. Gentle. Acc: 3-4 (VS)GR. KAS. (S)GR

7523. R: Bel raggio lusinghier
A: Dolce pensiero
Opera: SEMIRAMIDE, 1823, libretto by Gaetano Rossi, after Voltaire's tragedy. Part of Semiramide, Act I. c#3-a4 g#3-f#4 Sustained in moderate slow tempo. Quite florid, requires flexibility. With choral background in the full score. Acc: 4 (VS)B-H. PDA, KAS.

7524. R: Eccolo, a voi l'affido
A: Ciel pietoso, ciel clemente
Opera: ZELMIRA, 1822, libretto by Andrea Leone Tottola. Part of Emma, Act II. c3-bb4 f3-e4 Slightly florid recitative and sustained aria in moderate slow tempo. Has florid passages in the aria. Climactic ending. Acc: 3-4 (VS)MR. PDA

GIUSEPPE (FORTUNINO FRANCESCO) VERDI, 1813-1901

7525. R: Qui Radamès verrà
       A: O cieli azzurri
       Opera: AIDA, 1871, libretto by Antonio Ghislanzoni, after Bey's
       story. Part of Aida, Act III. b2-c5 e3-g4 Sustained in moderate
       tempo. Aria is generally subdued; requires very fine high P and PP.
       Very subdued ending on a4. Has some climactic passages. Very
       agitated accompaniment in the middle section. In some editions, this
       excerpt is listed under "Oh patria mia" which is the Andante mosso
       part of the recitative. Acc: 4 (VS)GS, GR. MSO, OPA-1, ORS,
       OPR, OAS-2, MLF. (S)GS, GR

7526. Ritorna vincitor!
       Opera: AIDA. Part of Aida, Act I. db3(c3)-bb4 eb3-g4 Sustained
       in varied tempi. Dramatic quasi-recitative entrance. A dramatic
       aria; also requires very fine high P and PP in the final section.
       Very subdued ending. Acc: 3-4 (VS)GS, GR. MSO, OPA-1, ORS,
       OAS-2, MLF, CAO-5   (S)GR

7527. R: Oh cielo! dove son io!
       A: Ah! dagli scanni eterei
       Opera: AROLDO, 1857, libretto by Francesco Maria Piave. b2-b4
       a#3-f#4 Part of Mina, Act II. A dramatic scena and a slow, lyric
       aria which ends with cadenza. Has climactic high passages. See
       "Ah dal sen di quella tomba," which is actually a continuation of this
       excerpt, with a duet interpolation. Acc: 4 (VS)GR

7528. Ah dal sen di quella tomba
       Opera: AROLDO. Part of Mina, Act II. bb2-c5 g3-g4 Sustained
       vocal part in moderate lively tempo. Faster middle section. Has
       florid passages. Requires flexibility. Climactic ending with a two-
       measure sustained bb4. See "Ah, dagli scanni eterei," which is the
       first part of this excerpt. Acc: 3-4 (VS)GR. OAS-1

7529. R: Santo di patria
       A: Allor che i forti corono
       Opera: ATTILA, 1846, libretto by Temistocle Solera. Part of Oda-
       bella, in the Prologue. bb2-c5 g3-g4 Sustained in moderate slow
       to moderate tempo. Requires flexibility. Has dramatic and florid
       passages. Has several scale passages that move in full two-octave
       phrases or more. Climactic ending. With choral background in the
       full score. Acc: 3-4 (VS)GR. OAS-1

7530. Nei giardin del bello saracin ostello
       Opera: DON CARLOS, 1867, libretto by Francois Joseph Méry and
       Camille du Locle, after Friedrich von Schiller. Part of Eboli, Act
       II. d#3-a4 g#3-e4 Animated in lively tempo. Florid, graceful.
       Has cadenza at the end of each verse or section. With women's
       chorus in the score. Acc: 4 (VS)GR

7531. R: Sorta è la notte
       A: Ernani, involami
       Opera: ERNANI, 1844, libretto by Francesco Maria Piave. Part of
       Elvira, Act I. bb2-c5 eb3-bb4 Aria is first sustained in moderate
       slow tempo, then goes into a much faster, animated section. Dramat-
       ic and florid, requires considerable flexibility. Vocalized, climactic
       ending. Requires a very fine command of high notes, has several
       c5's. Acc: 4 OPA-1, OAS-1 (VS)GR. (S)GR

7532. Sul fil d'un soffio etesio
       Opera: FALSTAFF, 1893, libretto by Arrigo Boito, after Shake-
       speare's The Merry Wives of Windsor. Part of Nannetta, Act III.
       d♯3-a4 g♯3-a4 Sustained in slow tempo. Slightly faster last sec-
       tion. Has some recitative-style passages. Requires very fine high
       P, especially for the sustained a4 at the end. Acc: 3-4 MSO.
       (VS)GR, GS

7533. R: No, mi lasciate
       A: Tu al ciu sguardo onnipossente
       Opera: I DUE FOSCARI, 1844, libretto by Francesco Maria Piave,
       based on Byron's drama. Part of Lucrezia, Act I. b2-c5 a2-a4
       Agitated recitative and sustained aria in moderate tempo. Florid, re-
       quires flexibility. Requires the majestic approach in some passages.
       Has dramatic passages and a climactic ending. With choral part in
       the score. Acc: 3-4 (VS)GR

7534. O madre, dal cielo
       Opera: I LOMBARDI ALLA PRIMA CROCIATA, 1843, libretto by
       Temistocle Solera, based on a romance by Tommaso Grossi. Part
       of Giselda, Act II. d3-db5 ab3-ab4 Sustained in moderate tempo.
       Has some very florid passages. In some sections the tessitura stays
       rather high. Acc: 4 (VS)GR. OAS-1

7535. Te, Vergin santa, invoco! Salve Maria!
       Opera: I LOMBARDI ALLA PRIMA CROCIATA. Part of Giselda,
       Act I. c♯3-bb4 f♯3-f♯4 Common title: Preghiera. Sustained in
       moderate tempo. Dramatic, also requires fine high P. Climactic
       ending. Agitated accompaniment. Acc: 4 (VS)GR. OAS-1

7536. R: Venerabile, o padre
       A: Lo squardo avea degli angeli
       Opera: I MASNADIERI, 1847, libretto by Andrea Maffei, based on
       Schiller's drama. Part of Amalia, Act I. d3(c♯3)-c5 f♯3-g4 Sus-
       tained in moderate tempo. Generally light, requires flexibility. Re-
       quires very fine high P and PP. Has florid passages. Acc: 3-4
       (VS)GR

7537. Tu del mio Carlo al seno
       Opera: I MASNADIERI. Part of Amalia, Act II. f3-c5 g3-g4 Sus-
       tained in slow tempo. Requires simplicity and flexibility. Mainly
       lyric. Has florid passages. Acc: 3-4 (VS)GR

7538. Mercè, dilette amiche
       Opera: I VESPRI SICILIANI, 1856, libretto by E. Caime, after
       Eugène Scribe and Charles Duveyrier. Part of Elena, Act V. a2-
       c♯5 g♯3-g♯4 Animated in lively tempo. Florid, requires flexibility.
       Requires fluent enunciation. Climactic high ending. With choral part
       in the score. Acc: 4 (VS)GR, CP. OAS-2

7539. R: Egli non riede ancora!
       A: Non so le tetre immagini
       Opera: IL CORSARO, 1848, libretto by Francesco Maria Piave, based
       on Byron's drama. Part of Medora, Act I. c3(b2)-c5 g3-g4 Sus-
       tained aria in moderate slow tempo. Graceful. Requires fine high P
       to PPP. Ends with short cadenza. Acc: 3-4 (VS)GR. OAS-1

7540. R: Timor di me
       A: D'amor sull' ali rosee

Opera: IL TROVATORE, 1853, libretto by Salvatore Cammarano, after Antonio Gutierrez's play. Part of Leonora, Act IV. c3-bb4 (db5) f3-g4 Recitative and aria in slow tempo. Has some florid figures and cadenzas. Requires fine P and PP. Aria starts very subdued. Acc: 3-4 (VS)GS, GR, B-H. MSO, OPA-1, ORS, OPR, OAS-2. (S)GR

7541. Tacea la notte placida
Opera: IL TROVATORE. Part of Leonora, Act I. ab2-c5 eb3-g4 Sustained in moderate slow tempo, with some variations. Florid, has cadenzas with more than two-octave descending scales. Requires flexibility. Climactic ending on ab4. Difficult. Acc: 4 (VS)GS, GR, B-H. MSO, OPA-1, OAS-2, PDA, CAO-S

7542. Tu vedrai che amore in terra
Opera: IL TROVATORE. Part of Leonora, Act IV. c3-c5 f3-a4 Animated in lively tempo. Exultant and joyous. Requires flexibility. Has a few florid passages. Climactic ending with sustained c5. Acc: 4 (VS)GS, GR, B-H.

7543. R: Voi lo diceste
A: Quante volte come in dono
Opera: LA BATTAGLIA DI LEGNANO, 1849, libretto by Salvatore Cammarano. Part of Lida, Act I. d3-c5 g3-g4 Generally strong recitative and sustained aria in moderate slow tempo. Florid, requires flexibility. Climactic ending. Aria is generally in lyric style. Acc: 3-4 (VS)GR

7544. R: Son giunta!
A: Madre, pietosa Vergine
Opera: LA FORZA DEL DESTINO, 1862, libretto by Francesco Maria Piave, after Duke of Rivas' play. Part of Leonora, Act II. b2-b4 e3-g#4 Common title: Leonora's prayer. Dramatic recitative and sustained aria in moderate tempo. Subdued ending. Aria has a recitative section in the middle. Acc: 4 (VS)GR, CP, IM, B-H (Italian & English). OPA-1, OAS-2. (S)GR

7545. Pace, pace, mio Dio
Opera: LA FORZA DEL DESTINO. Part of Leonora, Act III. c#3-bb4 f3-g4 Sustained in moderate slow tempo. Requires fine high P as well as dramatic energy. Fast, climactic ending section, with sustained bb4 as the last note. Acc: 4 (VS)GR, CP, IM, B-H (Italian & English). OPA-1, ORS, OAS-2, MLF, CAO-S. (S)GS, GR

7546. R: Attendo nè a me giungon mai
A: Addio del passato
Opera: LA TRAVIATA, 1853, libretto by Francesco Maria Piave, based on a play by the younger Dumas. Part of Violetta, Act III. e3-a4 a3-a4 Sustained in moderate tempo. A generally subdued aria with PP and PPP markings. Requires flexibility. Has some short florid figures. Requires very fine high P and PP. Ends subdued on a4. Acc: 3-4 (VS)GS, GR, B-H. OAS-2, CAO-S

7547. R: È strano!
A: Ah, forse è lui
Opera: LA TRAVIATA. Part of Violetta, Act I. c3-c5(db5) f3-c5 Generally sustained in various tempi and moods. Florid, has cadenzas and several c5's. Extended, difficult, vocally demanding. Climactic

ending. Acc: 4 (VS)GS, GR, B-H. MSO, ORS, OAS-2, 15A, PDA.
(S)GR

7548. Lo vidi, e'l primo palpito
Opera: LUISA MILLER, 1849, libretto by Salvatore Cammarano,
based on Schiller's tragedy. Part of Luisa, Act I. f#3-c5 g3-g4
Animated vocal part in moderate tempo. Requires very fine high P
and PP. Has florid passages. Climactic ending. Acc: 3 (VS)GR.
OAS-1

7549. Tu puniscimi, o signore
Opera: LUISA MILLER. Part of Luisa, Act II. c#3-b4 g#3-f#4
Animated in moderate tempo. Requires flexibility. Has florid passages, and a subdued, descending ending line. Agitated accompaniment. Acc: 3-4 (VS)GR. OAS-1

7550. La luce langue
Opera: MACBETH, 1847, libretto by Francesco Maria Piave, after
Shakespeare. Part of Lady Macbeth, Act II. b2-b4 f#3-f#4 Sus-
tained vocal part in moderate lively tempo. Dramatic and generally
strong. Climactic ending, with generally agitated accompaniment.
Interpretatively not easy. Acc: 4 (VS)GR. OAS-1

7551. Si colmi il calice di vino
Opera: MACBETH. Part of Lady Macbeth, Act II. Common title:
Brindisi (Drinking song). d3-c5 g3-g4 Animated in moderate lively
tempo. Requires flexibility. Joyous, has staccati passages, and a
climactic high ending on bb4. Acc: 3-4 (VS)GR. OAS-1. (S)GR

7552. Una macchia.... è qui tuttora
Opera: MACBETH. Part of Lady Macbeth, Act IV. Common title:
The mad scene. cb3-d5 f3-gb4 Sustained in moderate slow tempo.
Dramatic, interpretatively difficult. Requires fine PP. Very sub-
dued ending. Acc: 4 (VS)GR. OPR, OAS-1

7553. R: Ambrizioso spirto
A: Vieni! t'affretta!
Opera: MACBETH. Part of Lady Macbeth, Act I. b2-b4(c5) f#3-
g#4 Generally sustained in moderate slow tempo, then fairly lively
tempo. Has dramatic and strong passages. Requires flexibility. Interpretatively difficult. Climactic ending. Acc: 3-4 (VS)GR. OPR,
OAS-1

7554. R: Ben io t'invenni
A: Anch'io dischiuso un giorno
Opera: NABUCCO, 1842, libretto by Temistocle Solera. Part of
Abigaille, Part II. c3-c5 f#3-g4 Extended, dramatic recitative end-
ing in a phrase with a two-octave skip downward. Lyric, graceful
aria with several florid passages. Cadenza at the end with c5, marked
PP. Acc: 4 (VS)GR. OAS-1, OPR

7555. Oh dischiuso è il firmamento!
Opera: NABUCCO. Part of Fenena, Part IV. c3-a4 f3-e4 Sus-
tained, lyric in moderate slow tempo. Gentle and short. Acc: 3
(VS)GR

7556. Ao: Salce! Salce!
A: Ave Maria

Opera: OTELLO, 1887, libretto by Arrigo Boito, after Shakespeare.
Part of Desdemona, Act IV.   eb3-ab4   eb3-eb4   The arioso, "Salce!
Salce!" (Canzone del salice or Willow song), is followed immediately
by the aria, "Ave Maria." The arioso is sustained in slow tempo
and mostly very subdued, with very gentle recitative-style passages.
The aria is sustained in moderate slow tempo, starting with recitative-
style section on one note: eb3.   Generally gentle, subdued, and in
prayer style.   Requires very fine high P.   Both arioso and aria are
available together or separately from GR.   Acc: 3 (VS)GR.   MSO,
OPA-1, ORS, PDA.   (S)GR

7557. R: Mi parea
       A: Piangea cantando
       Opera: OTELLO. Part of Desdemona, Act IV. Common title:
       "Salce, salce" or "The willow song." b2-a#4   e3-f#4   Sustained aria
       in moderate tempo. Generally subdued, requires fine P and PP. In
       concert performance of the single excerpt, it is sometimes sung un-
       interrupted and goes directly into the "Ave Maria" which follows it.
       Acc: 3-4 (VS)GR. OAS-1, MSO, MLF

7558. R: Gualtier Maldè
       A: Caro nome
       Opera: RIGOLETTO, 1851, libretto by Francesco Maria Piave, after
       Victor Hugo's play. Part of Gilda, Act I. c#3(b2)-c5(c#5) f3-a4
       Sustained in moderate tempo. Florid; requires considerable flexibility.
       Has cadenzas. Generally light. Subdued ending on trilled e4. Acc:
       4 (VS)GS, GR. ORC, OAS-1, MSO (no recitative), 15A, PDA, CAO-
       SL. (S)GS, GR

7559. Tutte le feste al tempio
       Opera: RIGOLETTO. Part of Gilda, Act II--the first part of the
       Gilda-Rigoletto duet. e3-a4 g3-f#4 Sustained in moderate slow tem-
       po. Has florid figures and one florid cadenza at the end of the solo
       part. Requires some flexibility. Acc: 3-4 (VS)GS, GR. OAS-1.
       (S)GR

7560. Come in quest' ora bruna
       Opera: SIMON BOCCANEGRA, 1857, libretto by Francesco Maria
       Piave, after Gutierrez. Revised by Arrigo Boito. Part of Amelia,
       Act I. db3-bb4 f3-g4 Sustained in slow tempo. Generally gentle,
       requires fine P. Accompaniment requires considerable control. Acc:
       4 OPA-1 (VS)GR

7561. R: Ecco l'orrido campo
       A: Ma dall' arido stelo divulsa
       Opera: UN BALLO IN MASCHERA, 1859, libretto by Antonio Somma,
       after Scribe's libretto. Part of Amelia, Act II. b2(a2)-c5 f3-ab4
       Dramatic recitative and dramatic, sustained aria. Intense. Climactic
       ending with a short cadenza. Acc: 4 (VS)GS, GR. OPR, OAS-2.
       (S)GR

7562. Morrò, ma prima in grazia
       Opera: UN BALLO IN MASCHERA. Part of Amelia, Act III. a2-
       cb5 f3-gb4 Sustained in moderate slow tempo. Starts very gently
       and very subduedly. Climactic ending with short cadenza. Acc: 3-4
       (VS)GS, GR. OPR, OAS-2, PDA. (S)GR

7563. Saper vorreste di che si veste

Opera: UN BALLO IN MASCHERA. Part of Oscar, Act III. d3-b4
a3-f#4 Animated in moderate lively tempo. Generally light, requires flexibility. Graceful. Verses are interspersed with "tra la
la" passages. Acc: 3-4 (VS)GS, GR. ORC, MSO, OAS-2, CAO-
SL. (S)GR

7564. Volta la terra
Opera: UN BALLO IN MASCHERA. Part of Oscar, Act I. d3-bb4
(c5) f3-g4 Animated in lively tempo. Requires flexibility and fluent
enunciation. Generally light. Abounds in staccati phrases. Climactic high ending on bb4. Acc: 4 (VS)GS, GR. OAS-2, PDA, CAO-
SL. (S)GR

B. French Composers

ADOLPHE (CHARLES) ADAM, 1803-1856

7565. R: De vos nobles ayeux
A: Des souverains du rivage
Opera: SI J'ÉTAIS ROI, 1852, libretto by Adolphe Philippe d'Ennery
and Jules Brésil. Part of Néméa, Act II. c#3(a2)-b4 g#3-f#4
Generally subdued and florid recitative and an animated aria in lively
tempo. Graceful. Has florid passages and an extended vocalized
passage toward the climactic ending. Acc: 3-4 (VS)AL

7566. R: C'est moi qui chaque jour
A: Entends-tu sous les bambous
Opera: SI J'ÉTAIS ROI. Part of Zélida, Act III. eb3-bb4 f3-f4
Common title: Air Indien. Subdued recitative in moderate tempo.
Sustained aria in moderate tempo. Two verses with extended, florid,
vocalise after each verse. Acc: 3-4 (VS)AL

7567. Je vais donc le revoir
Opera: LE POSTILLON DE LONGJUMEAU, 1836, libretto by Adolphe
de Leuvon and Leon Brunswick. Part of Mme. Latour, Act II. d3-
c#5 g3-g4 Recitative and sustained aria in slightly slow tempo, with
moderate tempo in the middle section. Has florid passages, and a
climactic ending. Requires flexibility. Agitated accompaniment toward the end. Acc: 3-4 (VS)BR

7568. Mon petit mari
Opera: LE POSTILLON DE LONGJUMEAU. Part of Madeleine, Act
I. d3-bb4 g3-eb4 Animated in moderately fast tempo. Has florid
figures. Graceful and generally light. Slightly agitated accompaniment. Acc: 3-4 (VS)BR

DANIEL FRANÇOIS ESPRIT AUBER, 1782-1871

7569. R: Ne craignez rien, Milord
A: Quel bonheur, je respire
Opera: FRA DIAVOLO or L'HÔTELLERIE DE TERRCINE, 1830,
libretto by Eugène Scribe. Part of Zerlina, Act II. d3-b4(c5) g3-f#4
Rapid parlando recitative and an animated aria in moderate lively tempo. Has some florid passages. Requires flexibility. Ends with descending cadenza. Acc: 3-4 (VS)NO, BR. OAR-S2

7570. Voyez sur cette roche
Opera: FRA DIAVOLO or L'HÔTELLERIE DE TERRCINE.   Part of
Zerlina, Act I.   d3-g4   g3-d4   Animated in moderate lively tempo.
Graceful; a part of the Marquis may be excluded in a solo perform-
ance of the aria.   Acc: 3-4   (VS)BR.   OAR-S2

7571. R: Je suis sauvée enfin
A: Flamme vengeresse
Opera: LE DOMINO NOIR, 1837, libretto by Eugène Scribe.   Part of
Angèle, Act III.   b2-b4   e3-e4   Animated recitative requiring fluent
and rapid enunciation.   Animated aria in lively tempo.   Requires
flexibility.   Florid ending section.   Climactic ending.   Acc: 3-4
(VS)BR

7572. La belle Inèz fait florès
Opera: LE DOMINO NOIR.   Part of Angèle, Act II.   db3-ab4   f3-
eb4   Common title: Aragonaise.   Animated in moderate tempo.
Dancelike and graceful.   Acc: 3-4   (VS)BR

7573. C'est l'histoire amoureuse
Opera: MANON LESCAUT, 1856, libretto by Eugène Scribe, after
Abbé Prévost's novel.   Part of Manon, Act I.   d3-d5   a3-g4   Common title: The laughing song.   Animated in fast tempo.   Generally
light.   Climactic ending.   Acc: 3   (VS)BO

HECTOR BERLIOZ, 1803-1869

7574. Autrefois un roi de Thulé
Opera: LA DAMNATION DE FAUST, 1846, libretto by the composer,
after Goethe's drama.   A concert opera.   Part of Marguerite, Act
IV.   c3-f4   f3-d4   Gently animated vocal part in moderate tempo.
Generally light and graceful.   Subdued, low ending.   Acc: 3   (VS)CT,
BH

7575. D'amour l'ardente flamme
Opera: LA DAMNATION DE FAUST.   Part of Marguerite, Act V.
c3-a4   g3-g4   Sustained in slow tempo.   Slightly faster middle section.   Generally gentle; requires fine P and some flexibility.   Acc:
3-4   (VS)CT, BH

GEORGES BIZET, 1838-1875

7576. R: C'est des contrebandiers
A: Je dis, que rien ne m'épouvante
Opera: CARMEN, 1873-1874, libretto by Henri Meilhac and Ludovic
Halévy, based on Merimée's story.   Part of Micaëla, Act III.   d3-b4
f3-g4   Faster middle section.   Dramatic, with several climactic high
notes.   Acc: 4   (VS)GS.   OPA-1, ORS, OPR

7577. R: Me voilà seule dans le nuit
A: Comme autrefois
Opera: LES PÊCHEURS DE PERLES, 1862-1863, libretto by Michel
Carré and Eugène Cormon.   Part of Léila, Act II.   c3-c5   f3-f4
Sustained aria in moderate slow tempo.   Has also some animated sec-
tions.   Generally subdued, requires fine P.   Acc: 3-4   (VS)EC.
OPR

7578. O Dieu Brahma!
Opera: LES PÊCHEURS DE PERLES. Part of Leila, Act I. b2(d3)-
c5 g3-g4 Starts in slow tempo, then moves into a moderate lively
and florid section. Requires flexibility and fine high P. Has choral
ensemble in the full score. Acc: 3-4 (VS)EC

ALEXIS EMMANUEL CHABRIER, 1841-1894

7579. Blonde aux yeux de pervenche
Opera: GWENDOLINE, 1886, libretto by Catulle Mendèz. Part of
Gwendoline, Act I. c#3-a4 a3-e4 Sustained in moderate slow tem-
po. Slightly faster second section. Gentle and generally subdued.
Gently agitated accompaniment. Acc: 3-4 (VS)EN

GUSTAVE CHARPENTIER, 1860-1956

7580. Depuis le jour
Opera: LOUISE, 1900, libretto by the composer. Part of Louise,
Act III. d3-b4 g3-a4 In varied tempi. Starts very sustained and
tranquil. Requires very fine high PP on held b4. With a rather in-
tense inward joy. Abounds in long-held high notes. Acc: 4 (VS)GS.
(S)HL, IM. MLF

FÉLICIEN (CÉSAR) DAVID, 1810-1876

7581. Charmant oiseau qui sous l'ombrage
Opera: LA PERLE DU BRÉSIL, 1851, libretto by J. Gabriel and
Sylvain Saint-Étienne. Part of Zora, Act III. d3-b4 g3-g4 Sus-
tained in first moderate, then slower tempi. Has florid passages.
Requires flexibility and fine P and PP. Acc: 3-4 (VS)HL. ORC

7582. Si vous ne savez plus charmer
Opera: LALLA-ROUKH, 1862, libretto by Michel Carré and Hippolyte
Lucas, after Thomas Moore. Part of Mirza, Act I. e3-c5 g3-f4
Animated in moderate lively and lively tempi. Has some florid fig-
ures. Acc: 3-4 (VS)EG

(CLÉMENT PHILIBERT) LÉO DÉLIBES, 1836-1891

7583. R: Les fleurs me paraissent plus belles
A: Pourquoi dans les grands bois
Opera: LAKMÉ, 1883, libretto by Edmond Gondinet and Philippe
Gille. Part of Lakme, Act I. Common title: Indian bell song. e3-
ab4 g3-f4 Gently animated recitative and sustained aria in moderate
slow tempo. Requires fine P. Has climactic passages. Generally
subdued. Acc: 4 (VS)HL, IM. (S)GS

7584. Sous le ciel tout étoilé
Opera: LAKMÉ. Part of Lakme, Act III. Common title: Berceuse.
g3-g4(c5) bb2-g4 Sustained in moderate tempo. Tranquil, subdued,
and gentle. Requires fine P. A lullaby. Acc: 3 (VS)HL, IM.
ORC

PAUL DUKAS, 1865-1935

7585.   O, mes clairs diamants!
        Opera: ARIANE ET BARBE-BLEUE, 1907, libretto by Maurice
        Maeterlinck.   Part of Ariana, Act I.   f♯3-a♯4   g♯3-f♯4   Sustained
        in moderate tempo.   Has faster sections and dramatic passages.   Cli-
        mactic ending.   A dramatic monologue.   Agitated accompaniment.
        Acc: 4-5   (VS)AD

BENJAMIN (LOUIS PAUL) GODARD, 1849-1895

7586.   Viens avec nous petit
        Opera: LA VIVANDIÈRE, 1895, libretto by Henri Cain.   Part of
        Marion, Act I.   c3-f4   f3-d4   Animated in moderate tempo.   March
        rhythm.   Acc: 3   (VS)EC

7587.   Il m'est doux de revoir la place
        Opera: LE TASSE, 1878, libretto by Charles Grandmougin.   Part of
        Leonora, Act III.   e♭3-b♭4   f3-f4   Sustained in slow tempo.   Slightly
        faster middle section.   Climactic high ending on g♭4.   Agitated ac-
        companiment.   Acc: 4   (VS)GH.   (S)IM, HL

CHARLES (FRANÇOIS) GOUNOD, 1818-1893

POG   Popular Operatic Songs.   Charles Gounod.   Edited by Albert Visetti.
      Most arias have the original texts, and English and Italian versions.
      London: Augener, Ltd.

      ─────────────

7588.   R: Allons, n'y pensons plus!
        A: Ah! Je ris de me voir si belle
        Opera: FAUST, 1852-1859, libretto by Jules Barbier and Michel
        Carré, after Goethe.   Part of Marguerite, Act III.   b2-b4   e3-g♯4
        Common titles: "The jewel song" or "Bijou song."   Sustained in mod-
        erate lively tempo.   Graceful and bright.   Usually sung with the pre-
        ceding "Il etait un Roi de Thule" (The king of Thule).   Acc: 3-4
        OPA-1, 15A, PDA.   (VS)GS

7589.   R: Je voudrais bien savoir
        A: Il était un Roi de Thule
        Opera: FAUST, 1852-1859, libretto by Jules Barbier and Michel
        Carré.   Part of Marguerite, Act III.   e3-f4   e3-e4   Gently animated
        in moderate tempo.   Generally gentle.   Usually sung, without inter-
        ruption, with the succeeding "Ah! Je ris de me voir" (The jewel
        song).   Other settings: "Aus Goethe's 'Faust'" by Beethoven, "Der
        König von Thule" by Zelter, "Es war ein König in Thule" by Liszt.
        Acc: 3-4   (VS)GS.   OPA-1, ORS, PDA

7590.   R: Elles se cachaient!
        A: Il ne revient pas
        Opera: FAUST.   Part of Marguerite, Act IV.   d♯3-a♯4(b4)   g3-f♯4
        Common title: Spinning-wheel song.   Sustained in moderate slow tem-
        po.   Subdued, contemplative ending after climax.   Very agitated ac-
        companiment.   Acc: 4-5   (VS)GS

7591.   Comme la naissante aurore

Opera: LA REINE DE SABA, 1861, libretto by Jules Barbier and
Michel Carré. Part of Benoni, Act I. e♭3-b♭4 g3-e♭4 Sustained
in moderate slow tempo. Starts gently. Generally lyric, with some
slightly climactic passages. Climactic high ending with an upward
scale run. Acc: 3 (VS)EC. POG

7592. R: Me voilà seule enfin!
A: Plus grand, dans son obscurite
Opera: LA REINE DE SABA. Part of Balkis, Act III. c3(a2)-b4
f♯3-f♯4 Recitative and sustained aria in moderate slow tempo. Has
faster middle section. Climactic ending. Has dramatic passages.
Acc: 4 (VS)EC. ORS, POG

7593. Heureux petit berger!
Opera: MIREILLE, 1863, libretto by Michel Carré, after Frédéric
Mistral. Part of Mireille, Act IV. g3-a4 a3-g4 Sustained in moderate tempo. Requires simplicity, grace, and very fine P. Generally gentle, with a subdued ending. Acc: 3 (VS)EC

7594. Le jour se lève
Opera: MIREILLE. Part of Andreloun, Act IV. d3-g4 g3-e4 Sustained in moderate slow tempo. Generally gentle and subdued. Vocalized ending with sustained last note (g4) on P and PP. Acc: 3
(VS)EC

7595. R: Trahir Vincent!
A: Mon coeur ne peut changer
Opera: MIREILLE. Part of Mireille, Act II. d3-d♭5 g3-g4 Sustained aria in slow tempo. Requires fine P and PP. Has dramatic
passages. Requires flexibility. Florid toward the end. Climactic
ending. Acc: 3-4 (VS)EC

7596. O legères hirondelle
Opera: MIREILLE. Part of Mireille, Act I. f♯3-d5(e5) a3-a4 A
supplementary air, specially written for Mme. Miolan-Carvalho. A
showy piece in waltz tempo. Florid and bright. Has climactic ending. Acc: 3 (VS)EC. ORC, POG

7597. Ah! Si je redevenais belle
Opera: PHILÉMON ET BAUCIS, 1859, libretto by Jules Barbier and
Michel Carré. Part of Baucis, Act I. e3-a4 g3-f4 Sustained in
moderate slow tempo. Has recitative-like section. Subdued ending.
Acc: 3-4 (VS)EC. POG

7598. Philémon m'aimerait encore
Opera: PHILÉMON ET BAUCIS. Part of Baucis, Act II. e3-b4
a3-a4 Sustained in moderate tempo. Has dramatic passages, and
sustained high notes, recitative sections, and a climactic ending.
Acc: 3-4 (VS)EC

7599. Ah! Je veux vivre dans le rêve
Opera: ROMÉO ET JULIETTE, 1864, libretto by Jules Barbier and
Michel Carré, after Shakespeare. Part of Juliette, Act I. Common
title: Juliet's waltz song. e3(c3)-d5 g3-a4 Animated in waltz tempo. Joyous, rhythmic, and graceful. Requires flexibility. Has
florid passages and cadenzas. Climactic high ending. Acc: 3-4
(VS)GS. ORC, 15A, PDA, POG

7600. R: Dieu! Quel frisson court dans mes veines?
       A: Amour ranime mon courage
       Opera: ROMÉO ET JULIETTE. Part of Juliette, Act IV. d3-c5
       f3-a4 Aria is usually omitted in the production. Sustained in moder-
       ate tempo. Has recitatives between the song sections. Uses a good
       number of sustained high notes and trills. Requires flexibility. Cli-
       mactic high ending on bb4. Acc: 4 (VS)GS

7601. R: Depuis hier je cherche en vain mon maître
       A: Que fais-tu, blanche tourterelle
       Opera: ROMÉO ET JULIETTE. Part of Stephano, Act III. f3-c5
       f3-g4 Animated in moderate tempo. Moderately light. Has two
       florid, descending ending passages. Climactic ending. Acc: 4
       (VS)GS. POG

(JACQUES FRANÇOIS) FROMENTAL (ÉLIAS) HALÉVY, 1799-1862

7602. R: Des roses, partout des roses
       A: O suave et douce
       Opera: LA FÉE AUX ROSES, 1847, libretto by Eugène Scribe and
       J. H. Vernoy de Saint-Georges. Part of Nerilha, Act II. bb2-c5
       g3-g4 Recitative and sustained air, first in moderate slow tempo,
       then animated in lively tempo. Florid, requires flexibility. Acc:
       3-4 (VS)HL

7603. Près de toi je crois
       Opera: LA FÉE AUX ROSES. Part of Nerilha, Act I. d3(bb2)-ab4
       (c5) g3-eb4 Sustained in moderate slow tempo. Has two cadenzas.
       Requires flexibility. Acc: 3-4 (VS)HL

7604. Il va venir!
       Opera: LA JUIVE, 1835, libretto by Eugène Scribe. Part of Rachel,
       Act II. c3-cb5 f3-f4 Sustained in moderate slow tempo. Climactic
       ending on descending line, close to two octaves. Acc: 3-4 (VS)HL

7605. Je l'ai revu
       Opera: LA JUIVE. Part of Eudoxie, Act III. c3-bb4 g3-g4 Ani-
       mated in lively tempo. Requires flexibility. Has florid passages.
       Ends with cadenza. Acc: 3-4 (VS)HL

7606. Mon dous seigneur et maître
       Opera: LA JUIVE. Part of Eudoxie, Act III. e3-b4 g3-g4 Com-
       mon title: Bolero. Animated in moderate lively tempo. Dancelike
       and bright. Climactic ending. Acc: 3-4 (VS)HL

(LOUIS JOSEPH) FERDINAND HÉROLD, 1791-1833

7607. À la fleur de bel âge
       Opera: LE PRÉ AUX CLERCS, 1832, libretto by François Antoine
       Eugène de Planard. Part of Nicette, Act III. e3-a4 e3-e4 Ani-
       mated in moderate tempo. Graceful. Air ends with "oui toujours."
       With choral ensemble in the score. Acc: 3-4 (VS)BR

7608. Jours de mon enfance
       Opera: LE PRÉ AUX CLERCS. Part of Isabelle, Act II. b2-b4 e3-
       e4 Animated vocal part in moderate tempo. Has florid passages,

climactic ending. This air precedes "Oui Marguerite en qui j'espère."
Acc: 3-4 (VS)BR

7609. Oui Marguerite en qui j'espère
Opera: LE PRÉ AUX CLERCS. Part of Isabelle, Act II. b2-b4
g#3-g#4 Animated in moderate lively tempo. Has florid passages
and climactic passages. Faster ending section. Requires fine high
PP. Climactic ending. Acc: 4 (VS)BR

7610. Souvenir de jeune âge
Opera: LE PRÉ AUX CLERCS. Part of Isabelle, Act I. eb3-ab4
ab3-eb4 Animated in moderate lively tempo. Graceful, 2 verses.
Acc: 3-4 (VS)BR

(VICTOR ANTOINE) ÉDOUARD LALO, 1823-1892

7611. R: De tous côtés j'aperçois dans la plaine
A: Lorsque je t'ai vu soudain
Opera: LE ROI D'YS, 1888, libretto by Edouard Blau. Part of
Margared, Act II. eb3-g4 g3-f4 Dramatic recitative and animated
aria in fast tempo. Has some sustained vocal passages, dramatic
passages, and climactic ending. Acc: 3-4 (VS)HL

7612. Vainement j'ai parlé de l'absence éternelle
Opera: LE ROI D'YS. Part of Rosenn, Act I. d3-b4 g3-e4 Sus-
tained in varied tempi. Starts moderately. Requires fine P and PP.
Climactic ending. Acc: 3 (VS)HL

VICTOR (FÉLIX MARIE) MASSÉ, 1822-1884

7613. R: Que dis-tu? Je t'ecoute
A: Fleur parfumée
Opera: GALATHÉE, 1852, libretto by Jules Barbier and Michel Carré. Part of Galathée, Act I. d3(c#3)-b4(d5) e3-e4 Recitative, and
gracefully animated aria in moderate slow tempo. Has some very
florid passages and cadenzas. Climactic high ending. Acc: 3-4
(VS)CR, LS

7614. Sa couleur est blonde
Opera: GALATHÉE. Part of Galathée, Act II. c3-c5 f3-f4 Animated in moderate tempo. Rhythmic. Has florid passages. Requires fine high P. Climactic ending. Acc: 3-4 (VS)CR, LS

7615. Au bord du chemin
Opera: LES NOCES DE JEANNETTE, 1853, libretto by Jules Barbier
and Michel Carré. Part of Rossignol, one-act opera. d#3-c5(db5)
ab3-g4 Animated in generally moderate tempo. Has long, extremely
florid cadenzas. Requires considerable flexibility. Climactic high
ending. Acc: 4 (VS)LS

JULES (ÉMILE FRÉDÉRIC) MASSENET, 1842-1912

7616. R: Te quitter! moi?
A: Ami, la mort n'est pas cruelle
Opera: HÉRODIADE, 1881, libretto by Paul Milliet and Henri

Grémont (Georges Hartmann), after a story by Flaubert. Part of
Salome, Act IV. b2-a4 f3-f4 Sustained aria in moderate slow tempo. Requires fine P and PP. Has dramatic passages. Aria ends
with "ne me reveille pas!" Acc: 3 (VS)HL

7617.   Charme des jours passes
        Opera: HÉRODIADE. Part of Salome, Act III. d3-c5 g#3-g#4
        Sustained in moderate slow tempo. Has faster tempi in the middle
        section. Dramatic, strong, and intense second half of the aria. Cli-
        mactic ending. c5 is sustained. Acc: 4 (VS)HL

7618.   R: Celui dont la parole
        A: Il est doux, il est bon
        Opera: HÉRODIADE. Part of Salome, Act I. eb3-bb4 f3-g4 Sus-
        tained aria in moderate slow tempo. Dramatic, with a climactic and
        strong ending section. Acc: 3-4 (VS)HL. OPA-1, ORS, MLF

7619.   R: De cet affreux combat
        A: Pleurez, pleurez, mes yeaux
        Opera: LE CID, 1885, libretto by Adolphe Philippe D'Ennery, Louis
        Gallet, and Edouard Blau, after Pierre Corneille. Part of Chimene,
        Act III. c#3-b4 f#3-g4 Sustained in slow tempo. Slightly faster
        middle section. Requires fine P. Dramatic passages. Subdued, de-
        scending ending. Acc: 3-4 OPA-1 (VS)HL

7620.   Plus de tourments
        Opera: LE CID. Part of L'Infante, Act II. f3-bb4 g3-f4 Sustained
        in moderate tempo. Generally subdued, requires fine high P. Strong,
        high ending. Has gently moving florid passages. Acc: 3-4 (VS)HL.
        ORS

7621.   Allons! Il le faut! .... Adieu, notre petite table
        Opera: MANON, 1884, libretto by Henri Meilhac and Philippe Gille.
        Part of Manon, Act II. d3-bb4 g3-f4 First part is animated in
        lively tempo. Agitated accompaniment, strong and climactic. Second
        part is sustained, gentle, in moderate slow tempo, and quite subdued.
        Requires fine P and PP. Acc: 3-4 (VS)HS, GS. (S)HL, IM

7622.   Je suis encore tout étourdie
        Opera: MANON. Part of Manon, Act I. d3-bb4 f3-g4 In varied
        tempi and moods. Generally sustained. Has dramatic passages.
        The suggested cadenzas go as high as e5. Interpretatively difficult.
        Acc: 3 (VS)GS, HS

7623.   R: Est-ce vrai?
        A: Obéissons quand leur voix appelle
        Opera: MANON. Part of Manon, Act III. Common title: Gavotte.
        e3-c5(d5) a3-a4 Dramatic, showy recitative and an animated and
        lighter aria. Requires flexibility. Bright. Acc: 3-4 OPA-1.
        (VS)GS, HS

7624.   Oui dans les bois et dans la plaine
        Opera: MANON. Part of Manon, Act III. Sometimes sung in place
        of the Gavotte in Act III. d3-d5 g3-a4 Animated in lively tempo.
        Jovial. Slower middle section. Requires very fine high PPP, and
        flexibility for the florid passages. With choral background in the
        score. In the Appendix of the GS score. Acc: 3-4 (VS)GS, HS

7625. Voyons, Manon, plus de chimères
Opera: MANON. Part of Manon, Act I. f♯3-a4 f♯3-f♯4 Sustained
in slightly slow tempo. Has some quasi-recitative passages, climactic passages, and a subdued ending. Acc: 3 (VS)GS, HS

7626. R: Ces gens que je connais
A: Pendant en an je fus ta femme
Opera: SAPHO, 1897, libretto by Henri Cain and Arthur Bernède,
after Daudet. Part of Fanny, Act IV. f♯3-b♭4 a3-a4 Slightly ani-
mated vocal part in moderate tempo. Has slower and faster sections.
Requires very fine high P and PP. Acc: 3 (VS)HL

7627. R: Ah! je suis seule
A: Dis-moi que je suis belle
Opera: THAÏS, 1894, libretto by Louis Gallet, after Anatole France.
Part of Thaïs, Act II. d3-b4(d5) f3-g4 Generally in recitative style
in varied tempi and moods. Interpretatively difficult. Has dramatic
passages. Also requires fine P. Climactic high ending. Acc: 3-4
(VS)HL, IM. MLF

7628. R: Je ne veux rien garder
A: L'amour est une vertu rare
Opera: THAÏS. Part of Thaïs, Act II. c3-b♭4 f3-e4 Subdued, con-
templative recitative, and a sustained aria in moderate slow tempo.
Requires very fine P and PP. Has some climactic passages. Acc:
3-4 (VS)HL, IM

7629. Du gai soleil plein de flamme
Opera: WERTHER, 1892, libretto by Edouard Blau, Paul Milliet, and
Georges Hartmann, after Goethe. Part of Sophie, Act II. e3-a4
g♯3-e4 Sustained in moderate tempo. Graceful. Generally on MF
level. Climactic high ending. Acc: 3 (VS)HL

ANDRÉ (CHARLES PROSPER) MESSAGER, 1853-1929

7630. Hélas! rien qu'un mot!
Opera: FORTUNIO, 1907, libretto by G. A. de Caillavet and Robert
de Flers, after Alfred de Musset. Part of Jacqueline, Act II. f3-g4
g3-f4 Sustained in moderate slow tempo. Has climactic passages.
Subdued ending. Acc: 3 (VS)EC

JACQUES OFFENBACH, 1819-1880

7631. Elle a fui, la tourterelle!
Opera: LES CONTES D'HOFFMANN, 1881, libretto by Jules Barbier
and Michel Carré, after Hoffmann. Part of Antonia, Act III. d3-a4
f3-f♯4 Sustained aria in moderate slow tempo. Requires fine PP.
Has dramatic passages and a subdued ending. Acc: 3 OPA-1
(VS)GS

FRANCIS POULENC, 1899-1963

7632. Mes chères filles
Opera: DIALOGUES DES CARMÉLITES, 1957, libretto by Georges
Bernanos, after Gertrude von le Fort. Part of the New Prioress,

Act II.   d3-b♭4   f3-f4   Sustained in moderate slow tempo.   Requires
fine P. Has strong, dramatic sections.   Subdued ending before the
part of Mother Marie.   Acc: 3 (VS)FC

7633. Mes filles, voilà que d'achève notre première nuit
Opera: LES DIALOGUES DES CARMÉLITES.   Part of the Prioress,
Act III.   e3-b♭4   g3-f4   Sustained in slow tempo.   Calm and gentle.
Has dramatic passages. Requires fine PP. Has recitative-like pas-
sages. Acc: 3-4 (VS)FC

(JOSEPH) MAURICE RAVEL, 1875-1937

7634. Oh! La pitoyable aventure!
Opera: L'HEURE ESPAGNOLE, 1907, libretto by Franc-Nohain
(Maurice Legrand).   Part of Concepcion, Scene 17.   c♯3-a4   f3-f4
Generally sustained in varied tempi. Dramatic. Requires flexibility.
Climactic ending. Acc: 4 (VS)AD

(CHARLES) CAMILLE SAINT-SAËNS, 1835-1921

7635. O beaux reves evanouis!
Opera: ETIENNE MARCEL, 1879, libretto by Louis Gallet.   Part of
Béatrix, Act II.   c3-a♭4   g3-f4   Sustained in moderate slow tempo.
Lyric, generally on MF level. Has recitative-like passages. Sub-
dued ending. Acc: 3-4 (VS)AD

(CHARLES LOUIS) AMBROISE THOMAS, 1811-1896

7636. R: Sa main depuis hier n'a pas touché ma main!
A: Les serments ont des ailes!
Opera: HAMLET, 1868, libretto by Jules Barbier and Michel Carré,
after William Shakespeare.   Part of Ophélie, Act II.   c♯3-b4(c♯5)
g♯3-a4   Extended recitative and sustained aria in moderate lively tempo. Has climactic passages and quasi-dramatic passages. Climactic
ending. Acc: 4 (VS)HL

7637. Je connais un pauvre enfant
Opera: MIGNON, 1871, libretto by Jules Barbier and Michel Carré.
Part of Mignon, Act II.   Common title: Styrienne.   d3(c3)-b4(d5)
f♯3-g4   In varying tempi, starts in moderate tempo. Sustained,
florid, has coloratura passages. Difficult. Requires considerable
flexibility. Although the excerpt has a wide range and maintains a
high tessitura, the character calls for a mezzo-soprano voice. Key
of D minor in the score, at times transposed one tone higher. Acc:
3-4 (VS)GS

C.   German and Austrian Composers

LUDWIG VAN BEETHOVEN, 1770-1827

7638. O wär ich schon mit dir vereint
Opera: FIDELIO, c. 1803-1805, libretto by Joseph Sonnleithner and
Georg Frederick Treitschke.   Part of Marcelline, Act I.   g3-a4   g3-
g4 Animated in alternating moderate and lively tempi. Requires

flexibility. Faster ending section. Generally agitated accompaniment.
Acc: 4-5 (VS)GS, B-H. OAR-S1

ALBAN BERG, 1885-1935

7639. Auf einmal springt er auf....
Opera: LULU, finished posthumously in 1937, libretto by the composer, after Frank Wedekind. Part of Lulu, Act I. Common title: Canzonetta. eb 3-g4(bb 4) a3-e4 Sustained in moderate slow tempo. Graceful and gentle. Subdued, falling ending. Acc: 3-4 (VS)UE

7640. Du kannst mich nicht dem Gericht ausliefern!
Opera: LULU. Part of Lulu, Act II. e3-c#5 f#3-f#4 Common title: Arietta. Sustained in moderate lively tempo. Has dramatic high passages. Climactic ending. Requires sensitivity to pitch. Acc: 4 (VS)UE

7641. Wenn sich die Menschen
Opera: LULU. Part of Lulu, Act II. Common title: Lulu's Lied. c3-c5(d5) g3-g4 Sustained in moderate tempo. Has dramatic high climaxes. Requires very fine high P. Has florid passages. Requires flexibility and sensitivity to pitch. Descending ending line. Acc: 4 (VS)UE. (S)UE

7642. Was die Leute wollen!
Opera: WOZZECK, 1925, libretto by the composer, after Georg Büchner. Part of Marie, Act I. c#3-bb4 f3-f4 Sustained in slow tempo. Slower middle section. Requires very fine high PP. Generally subdued and gentle. Requires flexibility and pitch sensitivity. Acc: 4 (VS)UE

7643. Was die Steine glänzen?
Opera: WOZZECK. Part of Marie, Act II. a2(e3)-b4 g3-g4 Sustained in varied tempi. Starts lively and bright. Requires flexibility and sensitivity to pitch. Acc: 4 (VS)UE

FRIEDRICH (FREIHERR) VON FLOTOW, 1812-1883

7644. R: Zum treuen Freunde geh'
A: Den Theuren zu versöhnen
Opera: MARTHA, 1847, libretto by W. Friedrich (Friedrich Wilhelm Riese). Part of Lady Harriet, Act IV. bb2-d5 f3-ab4 Sustained aria in moderate tempo. Has florid cadenzas and passages with high tessitura. Climactic ending. Acc: 3-4 (VS)GS

7645. Letzte Rose, wie magst du
Opera: MARTHA. Part of Lady Harriet, Act II. Common title: Ballad. f3-f4 f3-f4 This is the old Irish air, popularly known as "The last rose of summer," translated from Thomas Moore and used in the opera. Sustained in slow tempo. Gentle. Acc: 3 (VS)GS. OAR-S2

PAUL HINDEMITH, 1895-1963

7646. Mein Geliebter kommt

Opera: CARDILLAC, 1926, libretto by Ferdinand Lion. Part of the
Daughter, Act II. d3-a4 b3-f4 Sustained in moderate tempo. Re-
quires fine P. Has climactic passages and slightly florid passages.
Acc: 4 (VS)SC

7647. Das ist der Kreuzweg
Opera: MATHIS DER MALER, 1938, libretto by the composer. Part
of Ursula, Part 7. d♯3-a4 g♯3-f4 Sustained in moderate slow tempo. Requires fine P. Has climactic passages. Faster middle section. Subdued ending on "ist es des Lebens wert?" Acc: 3-4
(VS)SC

ERICH (WOLFGANG) KORNGOLD, 1897-1957

7648. Glück, das mir verblied
Opera: DIE TOTE STADT, 1920, libretto by Paul Schott, after
Georges Rodenbach. Part of Marietta, Act I. f3-bb4 a3-f4 Sus-
tained in generally slow tempo. Has some slightly faster tempi.
Generally subdued, requires very fine high P and PP. Has gently agi-
tated accompaniment and extended instrumental postlude. Acc: 3-4
MLF, (VS)SC

KONRADIN KREUTZER, 1780-1849

7649. Leise wehet, leise wallet rings der Thau
Opera: DAS NACHTLAGER VON GRANADA, 1834, libretto by Karl
Johann Braun. Part of Gabriele, Act II. c♯3-a4 e3-e4 Gracefully
animated in moderate lively tempo. Extended postlude. 2 verses.
Acc: 3 (VS)CP

7650. R: Da mir alles nun entrissen
A: Seine fromme Liebesgabe
Opera: DAS NACHTLAGER VON GRANADA. Part of Gabriele, Act
I. d3-bb4 g3-g4 Recitative and sustained aria, first in moderately
slow, then lively tempo. Graceful allegro section. Requires some
flexibility. Has dramatic passages and a climactic ending. Acc:
3-4 (VS)CP. OAR-S2

(GUSTAV) ALBERT LORTZING, 1801-1851

7651. Die Eifersuchtist eine Plage
Opera: CZAAR UND ZIMMERMANN or DIE ZWEI PETER, 1837,
libretto by the composer, after J. T. Merle's play. Part of Marie,
Act I. c3-g4 g3-e4 Animated in moderate slow tempo. Requires
fluent and rapid enunciation, and flexibility. Mainly a diction song.
Acc: 3-4 (VS)CP. OAR-S2

7652. R: So wisse, dass in allen Elementen
A: Doch kann auf Erden
Opera: UNDINE, 1845, libretto by the composer, after a story by
Friedrich de La Motte Fouque. Part of Undine, Act II. e3-b4 g♯3-
f♯4 Extended recitative and sustained vocal part in moderate tempo.
Has dramatic passages and some slightly florid passages. Climactic
ending. Acc: 3-4 (VS)CP. OAR-S2

HEINRICH AUGUST MARSCHNER, 1795-1861

7653. R: Wehe mir! Wohin
       A: Einst war so tiefer Friede
       Opera: HANS HEILING, 1833, libretto by Eduard Devrient. Part of
       Anna, Act II. e3-a4 g3-f4 Recitative and sustained aria in moder-
       ate slow tempo. Has some florid figures. Climactic high ending.
       Acc: 3-4 (VS)CP. OAR-S1

GIACOMO MEYERBEER, 1791-1864

7654. D'ici je vois la mer immense
       Opera: L'AFRICAINE, 1865, libretto by Eugène Scribe. Part of
       Sélica, Act V. c3-bb4(b4) f3-f4 Has recitative and some passages
       in various tempi. Agitated accompaniment in the andante section.
       Interpretatively difficult. Aria may end with the andante section, on
       "il mereçoit aux cieux." Acc: 4 (VS)BR, BH

7655. R: Adieu, mon doux rivage
       A: Pour celle qui m'est chère
       Opera: L'AFRICAINE. Part of Ine, Act I. f♯3(c♯3)-a4(c5) g3-f♯4
       Sustained aria in moderate slow tempo. Has free cadenza at the end.
       Agitated accompaniment. Acc: 3-4 (VS)BR, BH

7656. Sur mes genoux fils du soleil
       Opera: L'AFRICAINE. Part of Sélica, Act II. b2-b4 g3-f♯4 Sus-
       tained in varied tempi. Requires grace. Florid; requires flexibility.
       Has dramatic sections. Interpretatively difficult. This aria is in the
       Italian version in OPR. Acc: 4 (VS)BR, BH. OPR

7657. R: Bellah! ma chèvre chèrie!
       A: Dors petite, dors tranquille
       Opera: LE PARDON DE PLOËRMEL or DINORAH, 1859, libretto by
       Michel Carré and Jules Barbier. Part of Dinorah, Act I. d3-b4
       a3-f4 Other title: Berceuse. Sustained in moderate slow tempo.
       Graceful, light accompaniment. Acc: 4 (VS)BR

7658. R: Me voici! Hoël
       A: Le vieux sorcier de la montague
       Opera: LE PARDON DE PLOËRMEL or DINORAH. Part of Dinorah,
       Act II. d♯3-g4 g3-e4 Gently animated air in moderate tempo.
       Graceful and light. Requires fine P and PP. Acc: 3 (VS)BR

7659. R: La nuit est froide et sombre!
       A: Ombre légère qui suis mes pas
       Opera: LE PARDON DE PLOËRMEL or DINORAH. Part of Dinorah,
       Act II. db3-d5 gb3-g4 Animated aria in tempi varying from mod-
       erate to allegro. A showy piece, extremely florid. Requires con-
       siderable flexibility. Difficult. Ends with extended cadenza. Acc:
       4 ORC, KAS. (VS)BR

7660. Sombre destinée
       Opera: LE PARDON DE PLOËRMEL or DINORAH. Part of Dinorah,
       Act II. eb3-g4 gb3-eb4 Sustained in moderate tempo. Generally
       light. Agitated accompaniment. Acc: 3-4 (VS)BR

7661. Ainsi je te verrai périn?

Opera: LES HUGUENOTS, 1836, libretto by Eugène Scribe and Emile Deschamps. Part of Valentine, Act V.   c3-a4(c5) g3-ab4 Animated in lively tempo. Requires fluent enunciation. Dramatic and strong. Climactic ending on descending cadenza, a full two octaves. Acc: 3-4 (VS)BR

7662. O beau pays de la Touraine
Opera: LES HUGUENOTS. Part of Marguerite, Act II.   d3(c3)-b4 g3-g4 Sustained in moderate tempo. Very florid, requires considerable flexibility. Requires very fine high P and PP. Has cadenza and many sustained high notes. Vocally demanding and difficult musically. Climactic ending. Acc: 4 (VS)BR

7663. R: Je suis seule chez moi!
A: Parmiles pleur mon rêve se ranime
Opera: LES HUGUENOTS. Part of Valentine, Act IV.   c3(b♯2)-bb4 (c5) g3-g4 Dramatic recitative and sustained aria in moderate slow tempo. Has dramatic and energetic passages. Has climactic ending with cadenza. Acc: 4 (VS)BR. OPA-1 (aria only)

7664. R: Nobles seigneurs, salut
A: Une dame noble et sage
Opera: LES HUGUENOTS. Part of Urbain, Act I.   d3-bb4(c5) g3-g4 Majestic recitative in moderate tempo. Aria is sustained in moderate slow tempo. Florid, requires flexibility. Ends with a cadenza. Acc: 3-4 (VS)BR, B-H. ORS

7665. Ah! que je peur
Opera: L'ÉTOILE DU NORD, 1854, libretto by Eugène Scribe. Part of Prascovia, Act I.   c3-c5 ab3-f4 Animated in lively tempo. Spirited and bright. Has one florid cadenza at the end. With ensemble of three other characters. Acc: 3-4 (VS)MT

7666. Nel lasciar la Normandia
Opera: ROBERTO IL DIAVOLO, 1831, libretto by Eugène Scribe. Original in French. Part of Alice, Act III. Italian version used here. d3-a4(c5) g3-f4 Animated in lively tempo. Also has a recitative and slower passages. Has cadenzas and a climactic ending. Acc: 3-4 (VS)BR. PDA

7667. Roberto, o tu che adoro
Opera: ROBERTO IL DIAVOLO. Original in French; Italian version used here. Part of Isabella, Act IV.   c3-c5 f3-g4 Sustained in moderate tempo. Has florid passages. Requires flexibility. Has dramatic passages and a climactic ending. Acc: 4 (VS)BR. PDA

WOLFGANG AMADEUS MOZART, 1756-1791

7668. L'ombra de' rami tuoi
Opera: ASCANIO IN ALBA, 1771 (K. 111), libretto by Giuseppe Parini. Part of Venus (Venere), Part I.   d3-g4 g3-g4 Animated in lively tempo. Florid; requires flexibility and fluent enunciation. Acc: 3-4 MAO-2

7669. R: Temerari
A: Come scoglio
Opera: COSÌ FAN TUTTE or LA SCUOLA DEGLI AMANTI, 1790

(K. 588), libretto by Lorenzo da Ponte. Part of Fiordiligi, Act I.
a2-c5 d3-a4 Dramatic recitative and sustained aria in moderate
slow tempo. Majestic. Has florid figures and some wide intervalic
skips. Requires flexibility. Extremely wide range, and vocally demanding. In IMC, starts with the aria. Acc: 4 OPA-1, MAO-3,
OAR-S1. (VS)GS

7670. È amore un ladroncello
Opera buffa: COSÌ FAN TUTTE or LA SCUOLA DEGLI AMANTI.
Part of Dorabella, Act II. e3-g4 f3-g4 Animated in quite lively
tempo. Requires flexibility and fluent enunciation. Climactic ending.
Generally light. Acc: 3-4 (VS)GS, GR

7671. R: Ei parte... senti
A: Per pietà, ben mio
Opera buffa: COSÌ FAN TUTTE or LA SCUOLA DEGLI AMANTI.
Part of Fiordiligi, Act II. a2-b4 c♯3-g♯4 An adagio-allegro aria
(rondo). Has wide range and florid passages. Climactic and florid
ending. Not easy. With horn obbligato in the full score. Acc: 4
(VS)GS. MAO-3, OAR-S1

7672. Una donna a quindici anni
Opera buffa: COSÌ FAN TUTTE or LA SCUOLA DEGLI AMANTI.
Part of Despina, Act II. d3-b4 g3-g4 Animated vocal part in moderate slow tempo. Requires flexibility and fluent enunciation. Generally light. Acc: 3-4 (VS)GS. MAO-2, OAR-S1

7673. Welche Wonne
Opera: DIE ENTFÜHRUNG AUS DEM SERAIL, 1782 (K. 384), libretto
by Gottlieb Stephanie II. Part of Blonde, Act II. d3-a4 g3-g4 Animated in lively tempo. Requires fluent enunciation. Climactic ending. Acc: 3-4 (VS)CP. MAO-2, OAR-S1

7674. Ach, ich fühl's
Opera: DIE ZAUBERFLÖTE, 1791 (K. 620), libretto by Emanuel
Schikaneder and Johann Georg Giesecke. Part of Pamina, Act II.
c♯3-b♭4 f♯3-g4 Animated, slightly florid part, in moderate slow
tempo. Generally light. Requires fluent enunciation. Acc: 3-4
(VS)GS, CP. OPA-1, MAO-1, OAR-S1

7675. Ah, fuggi il traditor!
Opera: DON GIOVANNI or IL DISSOLUTO PUNITO, 1787 (K. 527),
libretto by Lorenzo da Ponte. Part of Donna Elvira, Act I. f♯3-a4
g3-g4 Animated in lively tempo. Has florid passages. Climactic
ending. Acc: 3-4 (VS)GS, CP. MAO-4

7676. Batti, batti, o bel Masetto
Opera: DON GIOVANNI or IL DISSOLUTO PUNITO. Part of Zerlina,
Act I. c3-b♭4 f3-g4 Animated in moderate slow tempo. Graceful
and light. Requires flexibility. Has some florid figures. Acc: 4
(VS)GS, CP. MAO-1, OAR-S1. (S)GR

7677. R: In quali eccessi
A: Mi tradì quell' alma ingrata
Opera: DON GIOVANNI. Part of Donna Elvira, Act II. d3-b♭4 f3-
a♭4 Dramatic recitative, and an animated aria in moderate lively
tempo. Has florid passages. Acc: 3-4 (VS)GS, CP. MAO-4, OPR

7678. R: Crudele?
A: Non mi dir
Opera: DON GIOVANNI. Part of Donna Anna, Act II. e3-bb4 a3-
a4 Sustained aria, first in rather slow, then livelier tempo. The
vocal lines are gently animated. Requires flexibility. High tessitura.
The last section has one long coloratura cadenza. Acc: 4 (VS)GS,
CP. OPA-1, MAO-4, OPR, OAR-S1. (S)GR

7679. R: Don Ottavio, son morta!
A: Or sai chi l'onore
Opera: DON GIOVANNI. Part of Donna Anna, Act I. eb3-a4 g3-
a4 Extended recitative in varied moods. A sustained dramatic aria
in moderate slow tempo. Climactic ending. Agitated accompaniment
almost throughout the aria. Acc: 3-4 (VS)GS, CP. MAO-4

7680. Vedrai, carino
Opera: DON GIOVANNI. Part of Zerlina, Act II. g3-g4 g3-e4
Sustained in moderate slow tempo. Graceful and light. Has some
slightly animated vocal passages. Slightly climactic ending. Acc:
3-4 (VS)GS, CP. CPS, MAO-1, OAR-S1. (S)GR

7681. R: Oh, smania! oh furie!
A: D'Oreste, d'Ajace
Opera: IDOMENEO, RE DI CRETA, 1781 (K. 366), libretto by Giambattista Varesco, after Danchet. Part of Elektra, Act III. eb3-c5
ab3-ab4 Dramatic recitative and animated aria in very fast tempo.
Tessitura of the aria is quite high, with ab4 sung often. Florid toward the climactic ending. Requires considerable flexibility and
fluent enunciation. Acc: 4 (VS)IM, CP. MAO-4

7682. R: Parto, e l'unico oggetto
A: Idol mio, se ritroso
Opera: IDOMENEO, RE DI CRETA. Part of Elektra, Act II. f3-a4
a3-g4 Recitative and a sustained aria in moderate slow tempo.
Starts gently on MF level. Has climactic passages and two florid
passages. Descending ending line. MAO-4 has only the aria. Acc:
3-4 (VS)IM, CP. MAO-4

7683. R: Ah qual gelido orror
A: Il padre adorato ritrovo
Opera: IDOMENEO, RE DI CRETA. Part of Idamante, Act I. e3-
g4 a3-f4 Dramatic recitative, mostly with very agitated accompani-
ment. Animated aria in lively tempo. Has some climactic passages.
Generally agitated accompaniment. Subdued ending. Acc: 3-4
(VS)IM, CP

7684. No, la morta io non pavento
Opera: IDOMENEO, RE DI CRETA. Part of Idamante, Act III. e3-
g4 a3-g4 Animated in lively tempo, with a slow middle section.
Has dramatic passages and a climactic ending. Excerpt ends with
"il bella seren. " Generally agitated accompaniment. Acc: 4
(VS)IM, CP

7685. Non ho colpa
Opera: IDOMENEO, RE DI CRETA. Part of Idamante, Act I. e3-
a4 a3-f4 Sustained in varied tempi. Starts slowly, and majestically.
Has passages with high tessitura. Requires some flexibility. Lively
ending section. Requires fluent enunciation. Acc: 4 (VS)IM, CP

7686. Padre, germani, addio!
Opera: IDOMENEO, RE DI CRETA. Part of Ilia, Act I. f3-a4 a3-
g4 Animated vocal part in moderate tempo. Has fragmentary melodies and florid passages. Requires some flexibility. Has climactic
passages. Excerpt ends with short recitative. Quite high tessitura.
Acc: 3-4 (VS)IM, CP

7687. Se il padre perdei
Opera: IDOMENEO, RE DI CRETA. Part of Ilia, Act II. eb3-bb4
bb3-g4 Animated vocal part in moderate slow tempo. Has florid
figures. Requires flexibility. Climactic ending. Generally on MF
level. Acc: 3-4 (VS)IM, CP

7688. R: Solitudini amiche
A: Zeffiretti lusinghieri
Opera: IDOMENEO, RE DI CRETA. Part of Ilia, Act III. e#3-a4
g#3-f#4 Subdued recitative and a sustained, graceful aria in moderate tempo. Has florid passages and some wide intervalic skips. Requires some flexibility. Subdued high ending. MAO-1 has only the
air. Acc: 3-4 (VS)IM, CP. MAO-1, OAR-S1

7689. L'amerò, sarò costante
Opera: IL RE PASTORE, 1775 (K. 208), libretto by Pietro Metastas-
io. Part of Aminta, Act II. eb3-b4 g3-ab4 Sustained in moderate
slow tempo. Has florid passages. The long cadenza inserted is by
Johann Lauterbach. Requires flexibility. Acc: 3-4 (VS)WR.
MAO-2

7690. Deh, per questo istante
Opera: LA CLEMENZA DI TITO, 1791 (K. 621), libretto by Caterino
Mazzolà, after Metastasio. Part of Sesto, Act II. c#3-g#4 e3-f#4
Sustained adagio and in animated allegro. Has some slightly florid
passages. Climactic ending. Acc: 3-4 (VS)CP, IM. MAO-3

7691. Deh, se piacer mi vuoi
Opera: LA CLEMENZA DI TITO. Part of Vitellia, Act I. b2-b4
d3-g4 First in slow, then lively tempo. Sustained first part, animated second. Has florid passages and a climactic ending. Acc: 3
(VS)CP, IM. MAO-3, OAR-S1

7692. Non più di fiori
Opera: LA CLEMENZA DI TITO. Part of Vitellia, Act II. g2-a4 c3-
g4 A short, somewhat sustained larghetto section and a longer, animated allegro. Has some sustained, dramatic passages. Explores
the low register a few times from g2 to bb2. Climactic ending. Agitated accompaniment. Acc: 4 (VS)CP, IM. MAO-4, MLF, OAR-S1

7693. S'altro che lagrime
Opera: LA CLEMENZA DI TITO. Part of Servilia, Act II. f#3-a4
g3-g4 Sustained in minuet tempo. Climactic ending. Short. Acc:
3 (VS)CP, IM. MAO-2

7694. Crudeli, fermate
Opera: LA FINTA GIARDINIERA, 1775 (K. 196), libretto by Ranieri
Calzabigi (?). Part of Sandrina, Act II. eb3-ab4 ab3-g4 Animated
in fast, agitated tempo. Requires fluent enunciation. Dramatic, requires flexibility. Acc: 4 MAO-3

7695. Geme la tortorella
      Opera: LA FINTA GIARDINIERA. Part of Sandrina, Act I. f#3-c5
      a3-a4 Animated vocal part in moderate slow tempo. Florid, requires
      flexibility. Climactic ending. Acc: 4 MAO-2

7696. Noi donne poverine
      Opera: LA FINTA GIARDINIERA. Part of Sandrina, Act I. e3-bb4
      f3-g4 Animated in moderate, then lively tempo. Graceful, requires
      flexibility. Has some short florid figures. Slightly climactic ending.
      Acc: 3 MAO-1

7697. Senti l'eco ove t'aggiri
      Opera: LA FINTA SEMPLICE, 1768 (K. 51), libretto by Carlo Gol-
      doni, arranged by Marco Coltellini. Part of Rosina, Act I. eb3-a4
      g3-g4 Sustained in moderate slow tempo, alternating with animated
      and graceful, slightly faster tempi. Has florid passages and some
      wide intervalic skips. Requires flexibility. Climactic ending. Acc:
      3-4 (VS)GR. MAO-2

7698. Un marito, donne care
      Opera buffa: LA FINTA SEMPLICE. Part of Ninetta, Act II. d3-a4
      g3-g4 Animated in slow tempo. Requires some flexibility and fluent
      enunciation. Acc: 3-4 (VS)GR. MAO-1

7699. R: Giunse al fin il momento
      A: Deh vieni, non tardar
      Opera: LE NOZZE DI FIGARO, 1786 (K. 492), libretto by Lorenzo
      da Ponte, after Beaumarchais. Part of Susanna, Act IV. c3(a2)-a4
      f3-f4 Gentle, sustained recitative and sustained aria in moderate
      slow tempo. Graceful and gently rhythmic. Acc: 3 (VS)GS. OPA-
      1, MAO-1, ORS, OAR-S1. (S)GR

7700. R: E Susanna non vien!
      A: Dove sono i bei momenti
      Opera: LE NOZZE DI FIGARO. Part of the Countess, Act III. d3-
      a4 g3-g4 Sustained aria, first in moderate slow tempo, followed by
      lively tempo. Requires some flexibility. Climactic ending. Acc:
      3-4 (VS)GS. MAO-3, OAR-S1

7701. Il capro e la capretta
      Opera: LE NOZZE DI FIGARO. Part of Marcellina, Act IV. f#3-
      b4 g3-g4 This aria has a tessitura which is more for the soprano
      voice than the assigned mezzo-soprano. Animated: starts in minuet
      tempo, the second half in allegro. Has some extended florid pas-
      sages; requires flexibility and fluent enunciation. Climactic ending.
      Amusing text. Acc: 3-4 (VS)GS, GR

7702. Non so più cosa son, cosa faccio
      Opera: LE NOZZE DI FIGARO. Part of Cherubino, Act I. eb3-g4
      g3-f4 Animated in rapid tempo. Requires some fluent enunciation.
      Bright and slightly outgoing. Has climactic passages. Generally on
      MF level. Acc: 3-4 (VS)GS. CAO-S, OAR-S1. (S)GR

7703. Porgi, amor, qualche ristoro
      Opera: LE NOZZE DI FIGARO. Part of the Countess, Act II. Com-
      mon title: Cavatina. d3-ab4 g3-f4 Sustained in slow tempo. Gen-
      tle throughout, with underlying emotional intensity. Acc: 3-4
      (VS)GS. OPA-1, MAO-3, OAR-S1. (S)GR

7704. Un moto di gioia
Opera: LE NOZZE DI FIGARO.   Part of Susanna, an optional air.
b2-g4   g3-g4   Animated in moderate lively tempo.   Slightly florid.
Generally gentle.   Acc: 3-4   (VS)GS.   MAO-2

7705. Venite, inginocchiatevi
Opera: LE NOZZE DI FIGARO.   Part of Susanna, Act II.   d3-g4
a3-e4   Animated in moderate lively tempo.   In quasi-declamatory
style.   Fragmentary phrases due to the character of the text.   Generally on MF level.   Interpretatively not easy.   Acc: 3-4   (VS)GS,
GR

7706. Voi, che sapete
Opera: LE NOZZE DI FIGARO.   Part of Cherubino, Act II.   c3-f4
f3-f4   Sustained in moderate tempo.   Rhythmic.   Requires simplicity
and a lyric approach.   Acc: 3-4   (VS)GS, GR.   OPA-2.   (S)GR

7707. Frà i pensier
Opera seria: LUCIO SILLA, 1772 (K. 135), libretto by Giovanni di
Gamerra, edited by Metastasio.   Part of Giunia, Act III.   eb3-ab4
g3-ab4   A sustained andante and an animated allegro.   Quite high
tessitura in the last 20 measures.   Mostly agitated accompaniment.
Acc: 4   MAO-4

7708. Pupille amate
Opera seria: LUCIO SILLA.   Part of Cecilio, Act III.   e3-a4   g3-
f#4   Gently animated in minuet tempo.   Graceful and light.   Requires
some flexibility.   Acc: 3   MAO-1

7709. Parto: nel gran cimento
Opera seria: MITRIDATE, RÈ DI PONTO, 1770 (K. 87), libretto by
Vittorio Amadeo Cigna-Santi, after Racine.   Part of Sifare, Act I.
e3-b4   g#3-g#4   Animated vocal part, with alternating andante and
allegro sections.   Allegro sections are florid, and require flexibility.
Acc: 4   MAO-3

7710. Tu sai per chi m'accese
Opera seria: MITRIDATE, RÈ DI PONTO.   Part of Ismene, Act III.
e3-b4   g3-a4   Animated in moderate lively tempo.   Has florid passages, requires flexibility and some fine P.   Has some wide intervalic skips.   Acc: 3-4   MAO-4

7711. Ruhe sanft, mein holdes Leben
Opera: ZAIDE or DAS SERAIL, 1779 unfinished (K. 344), libretto by
Johann Andreas Schachtner.   Part of Zaide, Act I.   g3-b4   a3-a4
Gracefully animated in minuet tempo.   Slightly slower middle section.
Extended, florid lines toward the end.   Plot of this unfinished opera
is similar to DIE ENTFÜHRUNG AUS DEM SERAIL.   Acc: 3-4
MAO-1, AUK

7712. Trostlos schluchzet Philomele
Opera: ZAIDE or DAS SERAIL.   Part of Zaide, Act II.   e3-a4   a3-
a4   Sustained in moderate slow tempo.   Florid, requires flexibility.
Climactic ending.   Acc: 3-4   MAO-2

VICTOR NESSLER, 1841-1890

7713. Verlorene Liebe
Opera: DER TROMPETER VON SÄKKINGEN, 1884, libretto by Victor
von Scheffel. Part of Maria, Act III. d♯3-b4 f♯3-f♯4 Animated in
lively tempo. Slower middle section. Requires flexibility. Climactic high ending on b4. Acc: 3 (VS)JS

(CARL) OTTO (EHRENFRIED) NICOLAI, 1810-1849

7714. R: Wohl denn! gefasst ist der Entschluss
A: So schweb ich Dir Geliebter zu
Opera: DIE LUSTIGEN WEIBER VON WINDSOR, 1849, libretto by
Hermann Salomon Mosenthal, after Shakespeare. Part of Anna, Act
III. d3-b4 g♯3-g♯4 Recitative in varied tempi and moods, and a
slow to fast aria. Climactic ending. Agitated accompaniment in the
fast section. Acc: 4 (VS)CP, BH. OAR-S2

7715. R: Nun eilt herbei, Witz, heitre
A: Verführer! Warum stellt
Opera: DIE LUSTIGEN WEIBER VON WINDSOR. Part of Fluth, Act
I. c3-b♭4 g3-f4 Recitative and animated aria in slow to medium-
fast tempo. Florid, requires flexibility. Climactic high ending.
Acc: 3-4 (VS)CP, BH. OAR-S2

ROBERT SCHUMANN, 1810-1856

7716. R: Dort schleichen über'n Hof sie sacht
A: O du der über Alle wacht
Opera: GENOVEVA, 1847-1850, libretto by Robert Reinick, altered
by the composer, after Ludwig Tieck and Friedrich Hebbel. Part of
Genoveva, Act II. e♭3-g4 g3-e♭4 Subdued recitative and sustained
aria in slow tempo. Has climactic passages. Subdued ending. Acc:
3-4 (VS)BH

LOUIS SPOHR, 1784-1859

7717. Dürft ich mich nennen sein eigen
Opera: FAUST, 1816, libretto by Pierre Joseph Bernard, after the
traditional legend. Part of Rosa, Act II. f3-g4 g3-e♭4 Sustained
in moderate slow tempo. Generally gentle and slightly subdued. Subdued ending. Acc: 3 (VS)B-H

7718. R: Die stille Nacht
A: Ja, ich fühl' es
Opera: FAUST. Part of Cunegunda, Act I. c♯3(a2)-b♭4 g3-g4
An extended and difficult scena. Aria is first sustained in moderate
slow tempo, then animated in lively tempo, with florid and dramatic
passages. Climactic ending. Interpretatively difficult. Acc: 4
(VS)B-H

7719. Welch ein Wahn hat mich verblendet
Opera: FAUST. Part of Cunegunda, Act II. e♭3-a♭4 g3-g4 First
part is sustained in moderate slow tempo. Second part is animated
and lively. Has florid passages. Dramatic, especially toward the
end. Acc: 4 (VS)B-H

7720. R: Als in mitternächt'ger Stunde
       A: Die ihr Fühlende betrübet
       Opera: JESSONDA, 1823, libretto by Eduard Heinrich Gehe, after
       Antoine Lemierre. Part of Jessonda, Act I. eb3-bb4 a3-g4 Sus-
       tained in moderate slow tempo. Has climactic passages. Slower
       final section. Has florid passages. Acc: 3-4 CP, Soprano arias

7721. Hohe Götter! Schauet nieder
       Opera: JESSONDA. Part of Jessonda, Act III. e3-bb4 a3-g4 Sus-
       tained in moderate slow tempo. Strong entrance. Has florid pas-
       sages and a climactic ending. Requires flexibility. Acc: 3-4 CP,
       Soprano arias

7722. Rose, wie bist du reizend und mild!
       Opera: ZEMIRE UND AZOR, 1819, libretto by Johann Jakob Ihlee,
       after Marmontel's libretto. Part of Zemire, Act I. e3-f♯4 f♯3-e4
       Sustained in moderate slow tempo. Generally gentle, requires fine
       P. Has a florid passage near the end. Acc: 3 (VS)AC

JOHANN STRAUSS, 1825-1899

7723. Klänge der Heimat
       Opera: DIE FLEDERMAUS, 1874, libretto by Carl Haffner and
       Richard Genée, after Meilhac and Halévy's vaudeville.   Part of Rosa-
       linda, Act II. Common title: Czardas. c♯3-d5 f♯3-a4 Animated
       vocal part in slow tempo. Has florid passages. Requires flexibility.
       Climactic, high ending on "la la la" syllables. Acc: 3-4 OPA-1,
       (VS)GS

7724. Mein Herr Marquis
       Opera: DIE FLEDERMAUS. Part of Adele, Act II. d3-d5 g3-g4
       Common title: Laughing song. Animated, graceful, joyous, coquetish.
       2 verses, ending with laughter (pitched) and a final cadenza. Acc:
       3-4 (VS)GS. OPA-1

7725. Ein Mädchen hat es gar nicht gut
       Operetta: ZIGEUNERBARON, 1885, libretto by Ignaz Schnitzer, after
       Mor Jokai's libretto. Part of Arsena, Act III. d3-a4 g3-e4 Ani-
       mated in lively tempo. Requires some flexibility. Climactic ending.
       Acc: 3-4 (VS)AC

7726. So elend und so treu
       Operetta: ZIGEUNERBARON. Part of Soffi, Act I. c♯3-b4 g3-a4
       Sustained in moderate tempo. Faster ending section. Requires fine
       high P and PP. Has passages with high tessitura. Climactic ending.
       Acc: 3 (VS)AC

RICHARD STRAUSS, 1864-1949

7727. Ein Schönes war: heiss Theseus-Ariadne
       Opera: ARIADNE AUF NAXOS, 1911-1912, libretto by Hugo von Hof-
       mannsthal. Part of Ariadne, one-act opera. eb3-bb4 ab3-eb4
       Sustained in moderate slow tempo. Has faster sections. Requires
       very fine high P and PP. Subdued ending. Acc: 3-4 (VS)AF, B-H

7728. Es gibt ein Reich
       Opera: ARIADNE AUF NAXOS. Part of Ariadne, one-act opera.

ab 2-bb 4   g3-f4   Sustained in moderate tempo.   Has slower sections.
Starts quietly and calmly.   Has dramatic passages.   Subdued ending.
Acc: 3-4   (VS)AF, B-H

7729.   Kommt der neue Gott gegangen
        Opera: ARIADNE AUF NAXOS.   Part of Zerbinetta, one-act opera.
        d3-c5   a3-a4   Sustained in moderate tempo.   Has florid passages.
        Climactic high ending.   With ensemble in the score.   Acc: 3-4
        (VS)AF

7730.   R: Grossmächtige Prinzessin
        A: Noch glaub' ich dem einen ganz mich gehörend
        Opera: ARIADNE AUF NAXOS.   Part of Zerbinetta, one-act opera.
        bb 2-f# 5   a3-b4   Generally sustained in varied tempi and moods.   Has
        florid passages and extended cadenzas.   Has passages with very high
        tessitura.   Very difficult, vocally demanding, a real "tour de force."
        Ends with a cadenza with a sustained e5.   Acc: 4-5   (VS)AF, B-H

7731.   Die Fremden standen an der Wand
        Opera: ELEKTRA, 1909, libretto by Hugo von Hofmannsthal.   Part
        of Chrysothemis, one-act opera.   d3-cb 4   g# 3-g# 4   Sustained in fast
        moving tempo.   Has high climaxes and dramatic passages.   Climactic
        high ending on sustained cb 5.   Requires a lyric voice that is on the
        heavy side.   Acc: 3-4   (VS)B-H

7732.   Wie stark du bist!
        Opera: ELEKTRA.   Part of Elektra, one-act opera.   d# 3-b4   g3-g4
        Sustained vocal part in fast tempo.   Dramatic, strong, has high cli-
        maxes.   Climactic ending on "an der Reife Tag."   Acc: 3-4   (VS)B-H,
        AF

RICHARD WAGNER, 1813-1883

7733.   Welch wunderbar Erwarten
        Opera: DAS LIEBESVERBOT, 1836, libretto by the composer, after
        Shakespeare's Measure for Measure.   Part of Mariana, Act II.   eb 3-
        ab 4   ab 3-f4   Sustained in moderate slow tempo.   Generally subdued,
        requires fine P and PP.   Ends with its only florid passage.   Wagner's
        first performed opera.   Acc: 3-4   OGS

7734.   Wie muss ich doch beklagen
        Opera: DIE FEEN, 1834, libretto by the composer, after Carlo Goz-
        zi's comedy.   Part of Ada, Act I.   e3(d# 3)-a4   a3-e4   Sustained in
        somewhat slow tempo.   Has climactic passages and a few florid fig-
        ures.   Subdued, descending ending line.   Generally agitated accompani-
        ment.   From Wagner's first opera.   Acc: 3-4   OGS

7735.   Mein Erbe nun nehm' ich zu eigen
        Music Drama: GÖTTERDÄMMERUNG, 1874, libretto by the composer.
        Part of Brünnhilde, Act III.   A continuation of "Starke scheite," but
        may also be performed separately.   Strong, energetic, fast, and dra-
        matic.   Uses much of the higher notes in full voice.   Climactic end-
        ing.   Both this and its preceding excerpt appear in OGS.   Acc: 5
        (VS)GS.   OGS

7736.   Einsam in trüben Tagen
        Opera: LOHENGRIN, 1850, libretto by the composer.   Part of Elsa,

Act I, Scene 2. Common title: Elsa's dream. e♭3-a♭4 f3-g♭4 Sustained in slow tempo. Dramatic. Has some octave intervalic skips. In recitative style, with extended instrumental postlude. Full-sounding accompaniment. Acc: 4 (VS)GS, UE. MSO, OPA-1, ORS, OPR, OGS

7737. Euch Lüften, die mein Klagen
Opera: LOHENGRIN. Part of Elsa, Act II, Scene 2. e3-f4 a3-f4 Sustained in moderate slow tempo. Generally subdued. Very subdued ending. Short, fairly simple melody. Acc: 3 (VS)GS, UE. OPA-1, OGS

7738. Allmächt'ge Jungfrau
Opera: TANNHÄUSER (complete title: TANNHÄUSER UND DER SÄNGERKRIEG AUF DER WARTBURG), 1845, libretto by the composer. Common title: Elizabeth's prayer. Part of Elizabeth, Act III, Scene 1. d♭3-g♭4 g♭3-g♭4 Very sustained in slow tempo. Slightly faster middle section. Requires fine P and PP. Has dramatic passages. Low ending. Acc: 3-4 (VS)GS. OPA-1, ORS, OGS

7739. Dich, theure Halle
Opera: TANNHÄUSER. Part of Elizabeth, Act II, Scene 1. d♯3-a4(b4) g3-g4 Common title: Elizabeth's greeting. Sustained in lively tempo. Majestic in passages. Climactic ending. Acc: 3-4 (VS)GS. OPA-1, ORS, OGS

CARL MARIA VON WEBER, 1786-1826

7740. Hier liegt, welch' matervolles Loos!
Opera: ABU HASSAN, 1811, libretto by Franz Karl Hiemer, after a tale from the Arabian Nights. Part of Fatime, one-act opera. a♭2-a♭4 f3-g4 Sustained in moderate slow tempo. Ends with a short cadenza. Acc: 3-4 (VS)CP

7741. Wird Philomele trauern
Opera: ABU HASSAN. Part of Fatime, one-act opera. d3-a4 g3-f4 Animated in first moderate lively tempo, then lively tempo. Florid, requires some flexibility. Climactic ending. Acc: 3-4 (VS)CP

7742. Kommt ein schlanker Bursch
Opera: DER FREISCHÜTZ, 1821, libretto by Friedrich Kind, after the Gespensterbuch. Part of Annie, Act II. c3-a4(b4) g3-g4 Animated in moderate lively tempo. Requires flexibility and some fluent enunciation. Climactic ending. Acc: 4 (VS)GS. OAR-S2

7743. Scene: Wie nahte mir der Schlummer
A: Leise, leise, fromme Weise
Opera: DER FREISCHÜTZ. Part of Agatha (Agnes), Act II. b2-b4 f♯3-f♯4 Scena with recitative and short song sections, and an animated, fast, energetic air. Requires fluent enunciation. Dramatic final section. Acc: 4 OPA-1, OAR-S2

7744. R: Einst träumte meiner sel'gen Base
A: Trübe Augen, Liebchen, taugen
Opera: DER FREISCHÜTZ. Part of Annie, Act III. d3-b♭4 g3-g4 Animated in lively tempo. Has florid passages and several b♭4's. Requires flexibility. Climactic ending. Acc: 3-4 (VS)GS, CP. OAR-S2

7745.   Und ob die Wolke
        Opera: DER FREISCHÜTZ.   Part of Agatha (Agnes), Act III.   Com-
        mon title: Cavatina.   eb3-ab4   eb3-f4   Gently animated vocal part
        in slow tempo.   Requires fine high P.   Subdued throughout.   Acc: 3
        (VS)GS, CP.   OPA-1, OAR-S2

7746.   Glöcklein im Thale!
        Opera: EURYANTHE, 1823, libretto by Wilhelmine Helmine von
        Chézy.   Part of Euryanthe, Act I.   e3-g4   g3-e4   Gently animated
        vocal part in moderate slow tempo.   Generally gentle.   Acc: 3
        (VS)NO, CO.   OAR-S2

7747.   R: So bin ich nun verlassen
        A: Hier dicht am Quell
        Opera: EURYANTHE.   Part of Euryanthe, Act III.   c3-f#4   g3-e4
        Slow recitative, and gently animated vocal part in slow tempo.   Gen-
        erally subdued.   Acc: 3   (VS)NO, CP

7748.   R: Eil' edler Held!
        A: Ja, o Herr, mein Heil, mein Leben
        Opera: OBERON, 1826, libretto by James Robinson Planché, after
        Wieland's story.   Part of Reiza, Act I.   e3-b4   g3-g4   Animated in
        fast tempo.   Generally strong and dramatic.   Climactic ending.   Acc:
        3-4   (VS)CP.   OAR-S2

7749.   Ozean! Du Ungeheuer!
        Opera: OBERON.   Part of Reiza, Act II.   c3(bb2)-c5   f3-ab4   In
        varied tempi and moods.   Dramatic, highly energetic.   Vocally de-
        manding and difficult.   Last part has many extremely high notes.
        Acc: 4   OPA-1, OAR-S2.   (VS)CP

7750.   Traure, mein Herz
        Opera: OBERON.   Part of Reiza, Act III.   b2-f4   f3-db4   Sustained
        in moderate slow tempo.   Lyric, and generally on MF level.   Subdued
        ending.   Acc: 3-4   (VS)CP

D.   American Composers

SAMUEL BARBER

MSB   Music for Soprano and Orchestra.   Samuel Barber.   Operatic and
        Concert Scenes.   Reduction for Voice and Piano.   New York: G.
        Schirmer, Inc.

7751.   Give me my robe, put on my crown
        Opera: ANTONY AND CLEOPATRA, 1966, texts by William Shake-
        speare.   Part of Cleopatra, Act III.   Other title: Death of Cleopatra.
        db3-bb4   f3-g4   Sustained in varied tempi.   Faster and animated mid-
        dle section.   Dramatic, has some high climaxes.   Requires fine P.
        Dramatic high ending (bb4).   Agitated accompaniment.   Acc: 5
        (VS)GS.   MSB

7752.   Give me some music
        Opera: ANTONY AND CLEOPATRA.   Part of Cleopatra, Act I.   c3-
        bb4   f3-g4   Generally sustained in moderate slow tempo.   Has faster
        sections.   Starts gently.   In quasi-recitative, with dramatic passages.
        Subdued high ending.   Acc: 5   (VS)GS.   MSB

7753. Do not utter a word
       Opera: VANESSA, 1958, libretto by Gian-Carlo Menotti. Part of
       Vanessa, Act I. d3-bb♭4 f♯3-f4 First part is sustained in moder-
       ate tempo; second part is animated in fast tempo, with agitated accom-
       paniment. Has dramatic high passages. Second part is rather in-
       tense. Dramatic high ending. Acc: 3-4 (VS)GS. MSB, (S)GS

7754. Must the winter come so soon
       Opera: VANESSA. Part of Erika, Act I. eb3-f4 g3-eb4 Sus-
       tained in moderate slow tempo. Tranquil, generally subdued. Re-
       quires fine P. Acc: 3 (VS)GS. MSB, (S)GS

7755. Under the willow tree
       Opera: VANESSA. Part of Vanessa, Act I. b2-a4 e3-e4 Sustained
       in graceful waltz tempo. Requires some flexibility. Cadenza at end-
       ing, marked F to FF on a4. Acc: 3-4 (VS)GS. MSB, 20C, (S)GS

JACK HAMILTON BEESON

7756. L'Hirondelle, swallows circle in the sky
       Opera: LIZZIE BORDEN, 1965, libretto by Kenward Elmslie, after a
       scenario by Richard Plant. Part of Abbie, Act II. Other title:
       Abbie's bird song. c♯3-c♯5 e3-g♯4 Sustained in moderate tempo.
       Generally subdued and gentle. Has some climactic high passages.
       Has one florid passage. Requires flexibility. High, sustained ending.
       Generally agitated accompaniment. Acc: 4 (VS)B-H, (S)B-H

AARON COPLAND

7757. Once I thought I'd never grow tall
       Opera: THE TENDER LAND, 1954, libretto by Horace Everett. Part
       of Laurie, Act I. c3-g4 d3-e4 Sustained in moderate slow tempo.
       Slightly varied tempo in the middle. Gentle. Subdued high ending on
       g4. Acc: 4 (VS)B-H

7758. Thank you, thank you all
       Opera: THE TENDER LAND. Part of Laurie, Act II. c3-bb4 g3-
       f4 Sustained in quite slow tempo. Requires fine P. Has some cli-
       mactic passages. Subdued ending. Acc: 3-4 (VS)B-H

CARLISLE FLOYD

7759. Ain't it a pretty night
       Opera: SUSANNAH, 1955, libretto by the composer. Part of Susan-
       nah, Act I. bb2-bb4 eb3-f♯4 Sustained in slow tempo. Generally
       gentle, with quasi-recitative passages. Has dramatic climaxes. Sub-
       dued low ending. Acc: 3-4 (VS)B-H

7760. The trees on the mountains are cold
       Opera: SUSANNAH. Part of Susannah, Act II. db3-bb4 g3-g4
       Sustained in moderate slow tempo. Uses many high notes, frequent
       bb4's. Has some wide intervalic skips. Subdued high ending. Acc:
       3-4 (VS)B-H

7761. Oh, Nelly, I've fallen in love
       Opera: WUTHERING HEIGHTS, 1958, libretto by the composer, after

1002   Solo Voice Repertoire

Emily Brontë's novel.   Part of Isabella, Act II.   eb3-a#4   g3-f#4
Gently animated in moderate tempo.   Requires fine high P.   Has dramatic passages and a subdued ending.   Acc: 3-4   (VS)B-H

7762.   R: Heathcliff, don't! I can bear what I feel
        A: Look at me, Heathcliff
        Opera: WUTHERING HEIGHTS.   Part of Cathy, in The Prologue.
        e3-a4(c5)   a3-a4   Dramatic recitative and sustained aria in moderate
        tempo.   Has dramatic and climactic passages.   Requires very fine
        high PP on a4.   Acc: 3-4   (VS)B-H

7763.   I've dreamt in my life dreams
        Opera: WUTHERING HEIGHTS.   Part of Cathy, Act II.   bb2-b4   g3-
        ab4 Generally sustained in varied moods and tempi.   Has dramatic
        passages and climactic ending on gb4.   Starts gently.   Requires fine
        P.   Acc: 4-5   (VS)B-H

GEORGE GERSHWIN, 1898-1937

7764.   Summer time
        Opera: PORGY AND BESS, 1935, libretto by Du Bose Heyward and
        Ira Gershwin (the composer's brother).   Part of Clara, Act I.   f#3-
        f#4   a3-f#4   A lullaby.   Sustained in moderate tempo.   Subdued,
        rather plaintive.   Acc: 3   (VS) Gershwin Publishing Co.

7765.   My man's gone now
        Opera: PORGY AND BESS.   Part of Serena, Act I.   e3-b4   g3-g4
        Sustained in moderate lively tempo.   Rhythmic.   Climactic ending.
        Acc: 3-4   (VS) Gershwin Publishing Co.

VICTOR HERBERT, 1859-1924

7766.   I list the trill in golden throat
        Opera: NATOMA, 1911, libretto by Joseph D. Redding.   Part of
        Barbara, Act II.   db3-c5   a3-a4   Sustained in moderate tempo.   Re-
        quires fine P.   Has climactic passages and a dramatic ending section.
        Agitated accompaniment, has arpeggiated sections.   One step lower in
        MLF.   Acc: 4   (VS)GS.   MLF

GIAN-CARLO MENOTTI

Italian by birth; American by training and musical expression.

7767.   While I waste these precious hours
        Opera: AMELIA GOES TO THE BALL, 1937, libretto by the com-
        poser.   Original text in Italian.   Part of Amelia, one-act opera.   d3-
        bb4   g3-g4   Sustained in slow tempo.   Starts subdued.   Has dramatic
        passages.   Very subdued high ending (f#4 or a4).   Acc: 3-4   (VS)GR

7768.   To this we've come
        Opera: THE CONSUL, 1950, libretto by the composer.   Part of Mag-
        da, Act II.   b2-bb4   f3-f4   Sustained in slow tempo.   Has dramatic
        climaxes.   Has some frequent changes in meter.   Acc: 3   (VS)GS,
        (S)GS

7769.   The black swan
        Opera: THE MEDIUM, 1946, libretto by the composer.   Part of
        Monica, one-act opera.   d3-g4   f3-e♭4   Sustained in moving allegretto.
        Requires simplicity.   Generally on MF level.   Ending on g4.   Acc: 3
        (VS)GS, (S)GS.   20C

7770.   Steal me, sweet thief
        Opera: THE OLD MAID AND THE THIEF, 1937, libretto by the com-
        poser.   Part of Laetitia, Scene VI, one-act opera.   c3-b4   g3-f4
        Sustained in moderate slow tempo.   Has climactic passages.   Re-
        quires fine P and PP.   Subdued, slower ending after climax.   Acc:
        3-4   (VS)GR

7771.   O, sweet Jesus, spare me this agony
        Opera: THE SAINT OF BLEEKER STREET, 1954, libretto by the
        composer.   Part of Annina, Act I.   d3-c5   f3-f4   Sustained in moder-
        ate tempo.   Has recitative and song styles, dramatic passages, and
        intense passages.   Generally full-sounding accompaniment.   Interpreta-
        tively difficult.   Acc: 3-4   (VS)GS

7772.   Hello! Hello?   Oh, Margaret, it's you
        Comic opera: THE TELEPHONE, 1947, libretto by the composer.
        Part of Lucy, one-act opera for two characters.   d3-d5   e3-f4   Ani-
        mated in lively tempo.   Has vocalized passages.   Requires flexibility.
        Interpretatively not easy.   Acc: 3-4   (VS)GS

DOUGLAS STUART MOORE, 1893-1969

7773.   Ah, willow, where we met together
        Opera: THE BALLAD OF BABY DOE, 1956, libretto by John La-
        touche.   Part of Baby Doe, Act I.   Common title: Willow song.   f3-
        d5   g3-g4   Sustained in moderate slow tempo.   Gentle, subdued, and
        requires very fine high P and PP.   Starts and ends with vocalized
        passages.   Acc: 3-4   (VS)CC

7774.   Always through the changing of sun and shadow
        Opera: THE BALLAD OF BABY DOE.   Part of Baby Doe, Act II.
        Common title: Farewell song.   d♯3-b4   f♯3-f♯4   Sustained in mod-
        erate slow tempo.   Tranquil, subdued, requires very fine P and PP.
        Subdued, sustained high ending.   This excerpt ends the opera.   Acc:
        3-4   (VS)CC

7775.   Dearest Mama, I am writing
        Opera: THE BALLAD OF BABY DOE.   Part of Baby Doe, Act I.
        Other title: Letter song.   e3-c♯5   f♯3-f♯4   Sustained in moderate
        lively tempo.   Slower middle section.   Generally moves in gentle rec-
        itative style.   Climactic ending.   Acc: 3-4   (VS)CC

7776.   Gold is a fine thing
        Opera: THE BALLAD OF BABY DOE.   Part of Baby Doe, Act I.
        Common title: Silver song.   e3-c♯5   g♯3-g♯4   Sustained in moderate
        tempo.   Requires fine P.   Has climactic passages.   Subdued ending
        after climax on c♯5.   Acc: 3-4   (VS)CC

7777.   Now may there be a blessing
        Opera: THE DEVIL AND DANIEL WEBSTER, 1938, libretto by
        Stephen Vincent Benét.   Part of Mary, one-act folk opera.   c3-f4

f3-d4 Sustained in moderate tempo. Generally in gentle recitative style, and generally subdued. Ends with "Amen." Text is a paraphrase of a Biblical passage. Acc: 3 (VS)B-H

7778. Ev'rything is likely looking
Opera: THE WINGS OF THE DOVE, 1961, libretto by Ethan Ayer. Part of Milly, Scene III. f#3-a4 g#3-f#4 Animated in moderate lively tempo. Dramatic passages at the end. Climactic ending. Gently agitated accompaniment. Acc: 3-4 (VS)GS

7779. When all is fair and still
Opera: THE WINGS OF THE DOVE. Part of Milly, Scene II. d#3-a4 g#3-f#4 Sustained in moderate tempo. Has some climactic passages. Requires some fine P. Generally gentle. Ends with descending portamenti. Gracefully animated accompaniment. Acc: 3-4 (VS)GS

KURT WEILL, 1900-1950

German by birth, American opera.

7780. Somehow I never could believe
Opera: STREET SCENE, 1947, libretto by Langston Hughes and Elmer Rice. Part of Anna Maurrant, Act I. d3-a4 f3-f4 Sustained in moderate slow tempo. Has dramatic and forceful passages. Requires fine P. Has slight variations in tempi. Climactic high ending. Interpretatively not easy. Acc: 3-4 (VS)CC

E. British Composers

MICHAEL WILLIAM BALFE, 1808-1870

7781. I dreamt that I dwelt in marble halls
Opera: THE BOHEMIAN GIRL, 1843, libretto by Alfred Bunn. Part of Arline, Act II. eb3-g4 g3-f4 Sustained in moderate slow tempo. Graceful, gentle, and melodious. Requires some fine P. Gently climactic ending. Acc: 3 (VS)GS, (S)GS

BENJAMIN BRITTEN

7782. May Queen! May Queen!
Opera: ALBERT HERRING, 1947, libretto by Eric Crozier, after Guy de Maupassant. Part of Lady Billows, Act I. a#2-ab4 g3-f4 Animated in lively tempo. A scena, generally in recitative style. Has dramatic climaxes; also requires fine P and PP. Interpretatively not easy. The excerpt ends on "I'm waiting! First?" Acc: 3-4 (VS)B-H

7783. My heart leaps up with joy
Opera: ALBERT HERRING. Part of Miss Wordsworth, Act II. db3-bb4 ab3-g4 Sustained in moderate slow tempo. Dramatic; has high tessitura. Agitated, scalewise accompaniment. The excerpt ends with the dramatic "Albert! Albert!" or the short recitative after it. Acc: 4 (VS)B-H

7784. Child, you're not too young to know

Opera: PETER GRIMES, 1945, libretto by Montagu Slater, after a
poem by George Crabbe. Part of Ellen, Act II. a♯2-a♯4 f♯3-f♯4
Starts gently, simply, and unaccompanied. Sustained in moderate
tempo. Has dramatic passages toward the end. Very subdued low
ending (a♯2) after descending line. Acc: 3-4 (VS)B-H

7785. Embroidery in childhood
Opera: PETER GRIMES. Part of Ellen, Act III. Other title: Em-
broidery aria. b2-b♭4 d3-f♯4 Gently animated vocal part in mod-
erate tempo. Subdued and tranquil. Requires very fine high PP and
PPP. Subdued descending ending. Requires flexibility. Acc: 3-4
(VS)B-H

7786. I'm like a skiff on the ocean tossed
Opera: THE BEGGAR'S OPERA, 1948, libretto by John Gay, adapted
by Tyrone Guthrie. Part of Lucy, Act III. e♭3-a♭4 a♭3-g4 Animated in very lively tempo. Strong and marked. Descending ending
after high climax. A new setting of original airs. Acc: 3-4
(VS)B-H

7787. Lost in my labyrinth
Opera: THE TURN OF THE SCREW, 1953, libretto by Myfanwy
Piper, after a story by Henry James. Part of the Governess, Act II.
c♯3-g♯4 g♯3-e4 Animated in very fast tempo. Requires fluent
enunciation and fine PP. Has climactic passages. Agitated, scalewise accompaniment. Acc: 4 (VS)B-H

RALPH VAUGHAN WILLIAMS, 1872-1958

7788. Here on my throne
Opera: HUGH THE DROVER or LOVE IN THE STOCKS, 1924, libretto by Harold Child. Part of Mary, Act II. e3-g4 a3-e4 Sustained
in slow tempo. Generally lyric. Acc: 3-4 (VS)JC

F. Russian Composers

ALEXANDER PORFIREVICH BORODIN, 1833-1887

7789. Ihr, Thränen, fliesst
Opera: PRINCE IGOR, 1869-1887, libretto by Vladimir V. Stassof.
Unfinished opera, completed by Rimsky-Korsakov and Glazunof. Part
of Jaroslavna, Act IV. c♯3-b4 g3-f♯4 Other title: Jaroslavna's
complaint. Starts with chantlike figures. Requires flexibility, some
fluent enunciation, and fine P and PP. Subdued ending on sustained
b4. A scena. Acc: 3-4 (VS)MB, (S)MB

7790. Seit langer Zeit ist schon
Opera: PRINCE IGOR. Part of Jaroslavna, Act I. d3-a4 g♯3-f♯4
In varied tempi, moods, and styles. Has quasi-recitative passages
and climactic passages. Requires fine P. Ends with high P. Acc:
4 (VS)MB, (S)MB

NIKOLAI ANDREYEVICH RIMSKY-KORSAKOV, 1844-1908

7791. Byelo, baby, hush my little fawn

Opera: PSKOVITYANKA (The Maid of Pskov), 1892, libretto by the
composer, after L. A. Mey's play. A cradle song. e♭3-f4 f3-f4
Sustained in moderate tempo. A lullaby, subdued throughout, and
requires fine P and PP. Tranquil. English version by Robert H.
Hamilton. Acc: 3 MRS-2

7792. Said the thunder to the cloud
Opera: SNÉGOUROTCHKA (Snow Maiden), 1880-1881, libretto by the
composer, after a play by Nikolai A. Ostrovsky. Part of Shepherd
Lehl, Act III. e♭3-f4 f3-e♭4 Gently animated in moderate lively
tempo. Graceful. Has alternating gently declamatory passages with
short song section. Light and pastoral. English version by Frederick H. Martens. Acc: 3-4 MRS-2

DIMITRY SHOSTAKOVICH, 1906-1975

7793. I can't sleep again! But I will try!
Opera: LADY MACBETH OF THE MTSENSK DISTRICT (LADY MAC-
BETH MTSENSKOGO UYEZDA), 1934, libretto by the composer and
A. Preis, after Nikolai Leskov. Part of Katerina, Act I. c3(b2)-
a♭4(b♭4) e3-f4 Sustained in moderate slow tempo. Starts gently.
Has dramatic high passages. Also requires very fine high P and PP.
Subdued ending phrase. Acc: 3-4 (S)SM

IGOR FEODOROVICH STRAVINSKY, 1882-1971

7794. R: My father! Can I desert him
A: I go, I go to him
Opera: THE RAKE'S PROGRESS, 1951, libretto by W(ystan) H(ugh)
Auden and Chester Kallman, after the paintings by Hogarth. Part of
Anne, Act I. e♭3-c5 g3-g4 Recitative and sustained aria in moder-
ate lively tempo. Has climactic passages and florid figures. Climac-
tic ending on sustained c5. Acc: 3-4 (VS)B-H

7795. R: How strange!
A: O heart, be stronger
Opera: THE RAKE'S PROGRESS. Part of Anne, Act II. c♯3-g4
g3-f♯4 Sustained in moderate tempo. Has a few florid figures. Subdued low ending. Acc: 3-4 (VS)B-H

7796. R: No word from Tom
A: Quietly, night, O find him
Opera: THE RAKE'S PROGRESS. Part of Anne, Act I. b2-b4 b3-
f♯4 Sustained aria in moderate slow tempo. Requires some flexi-
bility, and some very fine high P and PP. Low, subdued ending.
Acc: 3-4 (VS)B-H

PETER (PIOTR) ILYICH TCHAIKOVSKY, 1840-1893

7797. Though I should die for it
Opera: EUGENE ONÉGIN, 1877-1878, libretto by the composer and
Konstantin S. Shilovsky, after Pushkin. Part of Tatiana, Act I. Common title: Tatiana's letter scene. d♭3-b♭4 f3-f4 In varied moods
and tempi. Starts animated in fairly lively tempo. An extended and
dramatic scena. Has some extended instrumental interludes. Cli-

mactic ending. Best for the heavier voices. Acc: 4 OPA-1
(VS)GS

7798. R: Oui, Dieu le vent!
A: Adieu, forêts
Opera: JEANNE D'ARC, 1878-1882, libretto by the composer, after
Schiller. Part of Joan, Act I. db3-a4 g3-f4 A dramatic recitative
and a sustained aria in varied moods and tempi. Requires fine P.
Climactic ending. Acc: 3-4 ORS, OPA-2, MLF

G. Czechoslovakian Composers

ANTONÍN DVOŘÁK, 1841-1904

7799. In vain it is
Opera: RUSALKA, 1900, libretto by Jaroslav Kvapil. Part of Rusalka, Act II. d3-bb4(b4) g3-g4 Animated in lively tempo. Requires
fluent enunciation. Has dramatic passages. Dramatic, intense high
ending. Acc: 3-4 (VS)AR-in Czech, German, and English

7800. R: Unfeeling cruel waters' might
A, Robbed of my youth
Opera: RUSALKA. Part of Rusalka, Act III. c3-a4 f3-f4 Sustained in slow tempo. Generally subdued, also has climactic passages. Climactic ending. Acc: 3-4 (VS)AR

7801. Song to the moon
Opera: RUSALKA. Part of Rusalka, Act I. db3-bb4 gb3-gb4
Sustained in slow tempo. Requires very fine PP. Graceful. Has
some climactic passages. Climactic ending with agitated accompaniment. Acc: 3-4 MLF. (VS)AR

LEOŠ JANÁČEK, 1854-1928

7802. Mutter, mir ist mein Kopf schwer
Opera: JENUFA (Jeji pastorkyna), 1894-1903, libretto by the composer, after Preissova's drama. Part of Jenufa, Act II. c#3-bb4
ab3-gb4 Generally sustained in varied tempi and moods. Has dramatic climaxes. Requires fine high P. Interpretatively difficult. A
dramatic scena. Text of vocal score: Czech and German. Acc: 4
(VS)UE

BEDŘICH SMETANA, 1824-1884

7803. How can I live
Opera: THE BARTERED BRIDE (PRODANÁ NEVĚSTA), 1863-1866,
libretto by Karel Sabina. Part of Marie, Act III. Other title:
Marenka's aria. c3-ab4 f3-g4 In recitative style before the mod-
erato assai section. Sustained in varied tempi, but mostly moderate.
Acc: 3-4 OPA-1, (VS)GS

H. Spanish Composer

ENRIQUE GRANADOS, 1867-1916

7804. ¡Es un sueno!
Opera: GOYESCAS, 1916, libretto by Fernando Periquet y Zuaznabar.
Part of Rosario, Tableau III. bb 2-b4 g3-g4 A final scene and tab-
leau. Sustained in varied tempi and moods. Has dramatic passages.
Intense, also requires very fine PP. Has interpolations by Fernando's
part. Extended and difficult. Low ending after climactic high note.
Acc: 4 (VS)GS-Spanish & English

7805. La maja si es que ha de ser
Opera: GOYESCAS. Part of a solo voice, man or woman, in the
Finale of Tableau II. With chorus in the score. g3-f4 bb 3-eb 4
Animated in lively tempo. Has florid figures. Acc: 3 (VS)GS

7806. Porqué entre sombras et ruiseñor
Opera: GOYESCAS. Part of Rosario, Tableau III. Common title:
La maja y el ruiseñor. b♯ 2-a4 f♯ 3-f♯ 4 Sustained in moderate slow
tempo. Melancholic, subdued, and tranquil. Has florid figures.
Acc: 3-4 (VS)GS

I. Argentine Composer

ALBERTO GINASTERA

7807. A la sombra de la oliva
Opera: DON RODRIGO, 1964, libretto by Alejandro Casona. Part of
Florinda, Act II. b2-g4 f3-e4 Sustained in moderate slow tempo.
Lyric in style. Chromatic, and rhythmically complex. Requires con-
siderable flexibility. Generally on MF level. Subdued, long-held end-
ing. Assigned to dramatic soprano in the score. Acc: 4 (VS)B-H

7808. Alla en las verdes Asturias
Opera: DON RODRIGO. Part of Florinda, Act III. Other title:
Romance. c♯ 3(ab 2)-g♯ 4 g3-f4 Sustained in slow tempo. Rhyth-
mically complex. Requires flexibility. Has strong passages. Sub-
dued ending. Assigned to dramatic soprano in the score. Acc: 4
(VS)B-H

7809. ¡Noche, estrella da noche!
Opera: DON RODRIGO. Part of Florinda, Act II. Other title: Aria.
b2-a4 e3-e4 Generally sustained style. Requires fluent and rapid
enunciation and very fine high P. Rhythmically complex. Subdued
ending. Assigned to dramatic soprano in the score. Acc: 4
(VS)B-H

3. DRAMATIC SOPRANO

See the Bibliography at the beginning of the Lyric Soprano Section

A. Italian Composers

VINCENZO BELLINI, 1801-1835

7810. Ascolta: se Romeo t'uccise un figlio
Opera: I CAPULETTI ED I MONTECCHI, 1830, libretto by Felice
Romani, based on Shakespeare's Romeo and Juliet. Romeo's aria,
Act I. In the opera, for mezzo-soprano or high contralto; separately,
may be sung by soprano. g2-g4 g3-f#4 Sustained in slow tempo.
Graceful, has florid figures. Acc: 3 (VS)B-H, GR

7811. Casta diva
Opera: NORMA, 1831, libretto by Felice Romani, based on a tragedy
by Louis Alexander Soumet. Part of Norma, Act I. e3-c5 g3-a4
Very sustained in moderate slow tempo, with variations starting in
the middle section. Has florid passages. Requires flexibility. Musically and vocally difficult. With vocal ensemble in the full score.
Acc: 4 (VS)GS, GR. OAR-S2, OPR, (S)GS, GR

7812. R: Sgombra è la sacra selva
A: Deh! proteggimi, o Dio!
Opera: NORMA. Part of Adalgisa, Act I. bb2-gb4 eb3-eb4 Ex-
tended recitative and sustained short aria in slow tempo. Slightly
florid. Requires flexibility. Generally subdued. Acc: 3 (VS)GS,
GR

7813. E tu pure
Opera: NORMA. Part of Adalgisa, Act I. c3-ab4 ab3-g4 Sustained in moderate tempo. Climactic ending. Slightly florid. Gently
agitated accompaniment. Part of a duet. Acc: 3-4 (VS)GS, GR

7814. Oh non tremare
Opera: NORMA. Part of Norma, Act I. c3-c5 g3-a4 First part
is sustained in moderate tempo. Second part is marked in moderate
slow tempo. Florid, rather strong, and dramatic. This excerpt is
part of the final terzetto. Acc: 3-4 (VS)GS, GR

ARRIGO BOITO, 1842-1918

7815. L'altra notte in fondo al mare
Opera: MEFISTOFELE, 1868, libretto by the composer. Part of
Margherita, Act III. d3-b4 f#3-g4 Sustained in slow tempo. Dra-
matic, dark, and florid. Has two extended cadenzas. Requires flexi-
bility. Descending ending after climactic a4. Acc: 3-4 (VS)GR.
OPR, MSO, ORS, CAO-S. (S)IM, GR

7816. A notte cupa
Opera: NERONE, 1916, libretto by the composer. Part of Asteria,

Act I. c♯3-b♭4 f3-g4 Sustained in moderate tempo. Dramatic,
and interpretatively difficult. In varied moods. Has some agitated
passages. Acc: 4 MSO

7817. Invan mi danni!
Opera: NERONE. Part of Asteria, Act II. b2-c5 g3-g4 Sustained
in moderate slow tempo. Dramatic. Sustained c5 requires full voice,
followed by gradually descending vocal line at the end. Acc: 3-4
MSO

ALFREDO CATALANI, 1854-1893

7818. Ebben? Ne andrò lontana
Opera: LA WALLY, 1892, libretto by Luigi Illica, based on Wilhelmine von Hillern's novel. Part of Wally, Act I. e3-b4 g♯3-g4
Sustained in moderate slow tempo. Generally gentle, subdued, with
some dramatic climaxes. Requires fine P and PP. Low, strong ending. Acc: 3-4 (VS)GR. MSO. (S)GR

7819. Nè mai dunque avrò pace?
Opera: LA WALLY. Part of Wally, Act III. d3-b♭4 a3-g4 Sustained in moderate, then moderate-slow tempo. Requires very fine
P and PP. Has dramatic high passages. Ends with medium low
recitative. Acc: 3-4 (VS)GR. (S)GR

7820. Da chè tutta mi son data
Opera: LORELEY, 1890, libretto by Carlo D'Ormeville and Angelo
Zanardini. Part of Loreley, Act I. d3-b♭4 g3-f4 Animated in lively tempo. Has climactic passages. Aria ends before the section
which starts with "l'april, l'april." Acc: 3-4 (VS)GR

7821. R: Dove son? d'onde vengo
A: Ma..... forse è un orrido sogno
Opera: LORELEY. Part of Loreley, Act I. d3-c5 g3-g4 Secco
recitative and an aria in varied tempi, with choral interpolations in
the full score. Requires flexibility; has some florid passages. Climactic ending. Acc: 3-4 (VS)GR

7822. O forze recondite
Opera: LORELEY. Part of Loreley, Act I. d3-c5 g3-g4 Animated
in lively tempo. Has some sustained passages and sustained high
single notes. Climactic high ending. Acc: 3-4 (VS)GR

LUIGI CHERUBINI, 1760-1842

7823. Dei tuoi figli la madre
Opera: MEDEA, 1797, libretto by François Benoit Hoffman. Original
in French. Part of Medea, Act I. f3-b♭4 a3-g4 Sustained in moderate slow tempo. Dramatic and intense. Climactic vocal ending.
Acc: 4 (VS)GR

7824. Del fiero duol che il cor
Opera: MEDEA. Part of Medea, Act III. b♭2-b♭4 f3-g4 Generally
sustained in slow tempo. In varied moods. Dramatic, vocally demanding. Climactic ending. Interpretatively difficult. Acc: 4
(VS)GR

7825. Solo un pianto
       Opera: MEDEA. Part of Neri, Act II. d3-g4 g3-eb4 Sustained in
       moderate slow tempo. Has slightly animated passages and a climac-
       tic ending. Acc: 4 (VS)GR

FRANCESCO CILÈA, 1866-1950

7826. Acerba volutta
       Opera: ADRIANA LECOUVREUR, 1902, libretto by Arturo Colautti,
       after Eugène Scribe. Part of the Princess, Act II. c3-a4 f3-f4
       Originally for mezzo-soprano. A dramatic aria, first in fast tempo,
       then closes with sustained section in moderate slow tempo. Has cli-
       mactic passages. Acc: 4 (VS)CS

7827. R: Troppo, signori
       A: Io son l'umile ancella
       Opera: ADRIANA LECOUVREUR. Part of Adriana, Act I. c3-ab4
       g3-f4 Sustained in moderate slow tempo. Tranquil, requires simplic-
       ity and some fine PP. Has dramatic passages. Strong, climactic,
       high ending. Acc: 3-4 (VS)CS. OPR, (S)IM

7828. Poveri fiori, gemme de' prati
       Opera: ADRIANA LECOUVREUR. Part of Adriana, Act IV. d3-a4
       g3-g4 Sustained in moderate slow tempo. Requires very fine P and
       PP. Generally gentle. Has climactic passages toward the end. Sub-
       dued ending phrases. Acc: 3 (VS)CS. OPR, (S)IM

7829. Esser madre e un inferno
       Opera: L'ARLESIANA, 1897, libretto by Leopoldo Marenco, based on
       Alphonse Daudet's play. Part of Rosa, Act III. d3(c3)-a4 f3-f4
       Sustained in slow tempo. After the recitative section, a sustained
       adagio with some climactic passages. Slower ending section, going
       back some into the recitative style. Very subdued high ending on f4.
       Acc: 3-4 MLF

GAETANO DONIZETTI, 1797-1848

7830. R: Fia dunque vero
       A: O mio Fernando!
       Opera: LA FAVORITA, 1840, libretto by Alphonse Royer, Gustave
       Vaëz, and Eugène Scribe. Part of Leonora, Act III. b2(a2)-g#4
       e3-f4 Dramatic recitative. Aria starts gently and sustained, then
       becomes dramatic. Acc: 3-4 (VS)GR. OPA-2. (S)GR

7831. Che val ricchezza e trono
       Opera: LA REGINA DI GOLCONDA, 1828, libretto by Felice Romani.
       Part of Alina, Act I. c3-c5 g3-f4 Sustained in moderate slow tem-
       po. Has florid passages; requires flexibility. Has slightly animated
       sections. Climactic ending. Acc: 3-4 (VS)GR

UMBERTO GIORDANO, 1867-1948

7832. La mamma morta
       Opera: ANDREA CHÉNIER, 1896, libretto by Luigi Illica. Part of
       Maddalena, Act III. c#3-b4 e3-g4 Subdued first section in recitative

style, then without break, moves on to more sustained section in moderate slow tempo. Has dramatic passages before the subdued, quasi-recitative ending. Acc: 3-4 (VS)CS, IM

7833. Temer? Perche?
Opera: ANDREA CHÉNIER. Part of Bersi, Act II. f3-g4 f3-f4
Starts in recitative style. Animated in lively tempo. Dramatic, with a climactic high ending. Acc: 4 (VS)CS, IM

7834. Dio di giustizia
Opera: FEDORA, 1898, libretto by Arturo Colautti, after Victorien Sardou's drama. Part of Fedora, Act III. c3-a4 f3-f4 Sustained in moderate tempo. Has dramatic climaxes. Subdued, with a low ending after high climax. Acc: 3-4 (VS)CS

PIETRO MASCAGNI, 1863-1945

7835. Voi lo sapete, O mamma
Opera: CAVALLERIA RUSTICANA, 1889, libretto by Giovanni Targione-Tozzetti and Guido Menasci, after Verga's story. Part of Santuzza, one-act opera. b2-a4 f♯3-f♯4 Sustained in slow tempo. Generally with short vocal phrases. Dramatic. Also requires fine P. First part is in quasi-recitative style. Acc: 3-4 (VS)GS.
OAR-S2, OPA-1, ORS. (S)GS, GR

7836. Un dì, ero piccina
Opera: IRIS, 1898, libretto by Luigi Illica. Part of Iris, Act II. d3-a4 e3-f♯4 Sustained in moderate tempo. Requires fine P. Climactic and dramatic ending. Acc: 3 MSO. (S)GR

7837. Son pochi fiori
Opera: L'AMICO FRITZ, 1891, libretto by P. Suardon, after Erckmann-Chatrian's novel. Part of Suzel, Act I. d3-g4 g3-f4 Sustained in moderate slow tempo. First part is in recitative style. Generally on the gentle, subdued side. Acc: 3-4 (VS)CS

AMILCARE PONCHIELLI, 1834-1886

7838. Suicidio!
Opera: LA GIOCONDA, 1876, libretto by Arrigo Boito, after Victor Hugo. Part of Gioconda, Act IV. c♯3-b4 e3-g♯4 Sustained in moderate slow tempo. Dramatic. Has some wide intervalic skips. Also requires fine P. Subdued and gradually descending ending phrase.
Acc: 4 MSO, ORS. (VS)GS, GR. (S)GR

GIACOMO (ANTONIO DOMENICO) PUCCINI, 1858-1924

7839. Donde lieta usci
Opera: LA BOHÈME, 1896, libretto by Giuseppe Giacosa and Luigi Illica, based on Murger's novel. Part of Mimi, Act III. d♭3-b♭4 f3-f4 Sustained in slow tempo. Generally gentle, with sad texts. Has some climactic passages. Subdued ending after dramatic climax. Acc: 3-4 (VS)GS, GR. MSO, OPR. (S)GR

7840. Mi chiamano Mimi

Opera: LA BOHÈME.   Part of Mimi, Act I.   d3-a4   f♯3-f♯4   Sustained in generally slow tempo.   Generally gentle.   Ends in recitative passage over sustained chord.   Acc: 3-4 (VS)GS, GR.   MSO, OPA-1, ORS.   (S)GS, GR

7841.   Se come voi piccina io fossi
Opera: LE VILLI, 1884, libretto by Ferdinando Fontana.   Part of Anna, Act I (revised version in two acts; original in one act).   d3-a4 f♯3-f♯4 Sustained in moderate slow tempo.   Has dramatic passages. Requires fine PP and PPP, and flexibility.   Slightly climactic ending. Acc: 4 (VS)GR

7842.   Ancora un passo.... Spira sul mare
Opera.   MADAMA BUTTERFLY, 1904, libretto by Giuseppe Giacosa and Luigi Illica, after Belasco's drama on John L. Long's story. Common title: Entrata di Butterfly.   Part of Butterfly, Act I.   f3-b♭4(d♭5) g♭3-g♭4 Sustained in slow tempo.   Requires fine P.   In quasi-recitative in several passages.   Rather subdued high ending with optional final note.   Acc: 4 (VS)GS, GR.   MSO.   (S)GR

7843.   Che tua madre dovrà prenderti in braccio
Opera: MADAMA BUTTERFLY.   Part of Butterfly, Act II.   d♭3-a♭4(b♭4) e♭3-g♭4 Sustained in moderate tempo, which varies slightly toward the second half.   Climactic, dramatic ending section.   Acc: 3 (VS)GR, GS.   MSO.   (S)GR

7844.   Tu, tu, piccolo Iddio!
Opera: MADAMA BUTTERFLY.   Part of Butterfly, Act III.   Other title: Butterfly's farewell aria.   d3-a4   g3-f♯4 Sustained in moderate slow tempo.   Starts in recitative style.   Has climactic passages, but gently lyric in style.   Descending ending after high climax.   Acc: 3 (VS)GR, GS.   (S)GR

7845.   Un bel dì, vedremo
Opera: MADAMA BUTTERFLY.   Part of Butterfly, Act II.   d♭3-b♭4 f3-g♭4 Sustained in slow tempo.   Generally calm, mostly subdued. Dramatic, climactic ending.   Has quasi-recitative passages.   Traditionally the b♭4 is sung on the last syllable of "l'aspetto" instead of an octave below as in the original score.   Acc: 3 (VS)GS, GR. MSO.   (S)GS, GR

7846.   In quelle trine morbide
Opera: MANON LESCAUT, 1893, libretto by Marco Praga, Domenico Oliva, and Luigi Illica, based on Abbé Prèvost's novel.   Part of Manon, Act II.   e♭3-b♭4   f3-g♭4 Sustained but moving vocal part in moderate tempo.   Requires fine P.   Has dramatic climaxes and a subdued ending.   Short.   Acc: 3 MSO, OPA-1, ORS.   (S)GR

7847.   Sola, perduta, abbandonata
Opera: MANON LESCAUT.   Part of Manon, Act IV.   c3-b♭4   a♭3-g4 Sustained in slow tempo.   Has dramatic passages.   Requires fine high P.   Intense.   Acc: 4 (VS)IM, GR.   OPR.   (S)GR

7848.   Non la sospiri la nostra casetta
Opera: TOSCA, 1900, libretto by Giuseppe Giacosa and Luigi Illica. Part of Tosca, Act I.   f3-b♭4   a♭3-a♭4 Sustained in moderate lively tempo.   Dramatic.   Also requires fine P.   Very subdued ending. Acc: 3-4 (VS)GS, GR.   MSO, ORS.   (S)GR

7849. Vissi d'arte, vissi d'amore
Opera: TOSCA. Part of Tosca, Act II. e♭3-b♭4 g♭3-g♭4 Sustained in slow tempo. Generally subdued, tranquil, and requires fine P. In quasi-recitative style. Has climactic passages. Acc: 3-4 (VS)GS, GR. MSO, ORS. (S)GS, GR

7850. Del primo pianto
Opera: TURANDOT, 1926, unfinished, completed by Franco Alfano; libretto by Giuseppe Adami and Renato Simoni, based on Carlo Gozzi's play. Part of Turandot, Act III. e♭3-a4 a3-f♯4 Sustained in moderate tempo. Starts gently and in subdued tones. Has dramatic high climaxes. Also requires fine P. Dramatic high ending. Acc: 4 (VS)GR. (S)GR

7851. In questa reggia
Opera: TURANDOT. Part of Turandot, Act II. c♭3-c5 f3-g4 Sustained in generally slow tempo, varying according to mood. Requires fine P. Has strong and dramatic sections. Climactic, strong ending on high tessitura. Acc: 3-4 (VS)GR. (S)GR

7852. Signore, ascolta!
Opera: TURANDOT. Part of Liu, Act I. d♭3-b♭4 g♭3-a♭4 Sustained in slow tempo. Subdued ending on sustained a♭4-b♭4. Requires fine P. and PP. Has some climactic high passages. Acc: 3-4 (VS)GR. MSO. (S)GR

7853. Tanto amore segreto
Opera: TURANDOT. Part of Liu, Act III. f3-b♭4 a3-g4 Sustained in slow tempo. Starts gently on high notes. Intense. Has dramatic climaxes. Subdued high ending passage. Acc: 3-4 (VS)GR. (S)GR

7854. Tu che di gel sei cinta
Opera: TURANDOT. Part of Liu, Act III. e♭3-b♭4 g♭3-g♭4 Sustained in moderate slow tempo. Requires fine high P. Climactic, dramatic ending. Acc: 3 (VS)GR. MSO. (S)GR

GIUSEPPE (FORTUNINO FRANCESCO) VERDI, 1813-1901

7855. R: Qui Radamès verrà!
A: O cieli azzurri
Opera: AIDA, 1871, libretto by Antonio Ghislanzoni, after Bey's story. Part of Aida, Act III. b2-c5 e3-g4 Sustained in moderate tempo. Aria is generally subdued, requires very fine high P and PP. Very subdued high ending on a4. Has some climactic passages. Very agitated accompaniment in the middle section. In some editions this excerpt is listed under "Oh patria mia" which is the Andante mosso part of the recitative. Acc: 4 (VS)GS, GR. MSO, OPA-1, ORS, OPR, OAS-2. (S)GS, GR

7856. Ritorna vincitor!
Opera: AIDA. Part of Aida, Act I. d♭3-b♭4 e♭3-g4 Sustained in varied tempi. Dramatic quasi-recitative entrance. A dramatic aria. Also requires very fine high P and PP in the final section. Very subdued ending. Acc: 3-4 (VS)GS, GR. MSO, OPA-1, ORS, OAS-2. (S)GS, GR

7857. Non pianger, mia compagna

Opera: DON CARLOS, 1867, libretto by François Joseph Méry and Camille du Locle, after Friedrich von Schiller. Part of Elisabetta, Act II. b2-bb4 g3-f4 Sustained in moderate tempo. Has climactic passages. Requires some flexibility. With chorus in the full score. Acc: 4 (VS)GR. (S)GR

7858. O don fatale
Opera: DON CARLOS. Part of Eboli, Act IV. cb3-cb5 eb3-ab4 Sustained in moderate tempo. Faster, more agitated and dramatic final section. Requires fine PP. Dramatic high ending. Acc: 4 (VS)GR. OPA-2, ORS. (S)GR

7859. Tu che le vanità
Opera: DON CARLOS. Part of Elisabetta, Act IV. a#2-a#4 d#3-g#4 In varied moods and tempi. Requires fine P to PPP. Has dramatic, climactic sections. Ending section is marked PPP. Agitated accompaniment toward the end. Scena and aria. Acc: 4 (VS)GR. OPA-1. (S)GR

7860. R: Sorta è la notte
A: Ernani, involami
Opera: ERNANI, 1844, libretto by Francesco Maria Piave. Part of Elvira, Act I. db2-c5 eb3-bb4 Aria is first sustained in moderate slow tempo; then goes into a much faster, and animated section. Dramatic and florid; requires considerable flexibility. Vocalized, climactic ending. Has many high notes, with several c5's. Acc: 4 (VS)GR. OPA-1, OAS-1. (S)GR

7861. R: No, mi lasciate
A: Tu al ciu sguardo onnipossente
Opera: I DUE FOSCARI, 1844, libretto by Francesco Maria Piave, based on Byron's drama. Part of Lucrezia, Act I. b2-c5 a3-a4 Agitated recitative and sustained aria in moderate tempo. Florid, requires flexibility. Requires some majestic approach in some passages. Has dramatic passages and a climactic ending. With choral part in the full score. Acc: 3-4 (VS)GR

7862. Te, Vergin santa, invoco! Salve Maria!
Opera: I LOMBARDI ALLA PRIMA CROCIATA, 1843, libretto by Temistocle Solera, based on a romance by Tommaso Grossi. Part of Giselda, Act I. c#3-bb4 f#3-f#4 Common title: Preghiera. Sustained in moderate tempo. Dramatic, also requires fine high PP. Climactic ending. Agitated accompaniment. Acc: 4 (VS)GR. OAS-1

7863. R: Timor di me
A: D'amor sull' ali rosee
Opera: IL TROVATORE, 1853, libretto by Salvatore Cammarano, after Antonio Gutierrez's play. Part of Leonora, Act IV. c3-bb4 (db5) f3-g4 Recitative and aria in slow tempo. Has some florid figures and cadenzas. Requires fine P and PP. Aria starts very subdued. Acc: 3-4 (VS)GS, GR. MSO, OPA-1, ORS, OPR, OAS-2. (S)GR

7864. Tacea la notte placida
Opera: IL TROVATORE. Part of Leonora, Act I. ab2-c5 eb3-g4 Sustained in moderate slow tempo, with some variations. Florid, has cadenzas with more than two-octave descending scales. Requires

flexibility. Climactic ending on a♭4. Difficult. Acc: 4 (VS)GS,
GR. MSO, OPA-1, OAS-2. (S)GR

7865. Tu vedrai che amore in terra
Opera: IL TROVATORE. Part of Leonora, Act IV. c3-c5 f3-a4
Animated in lively tempo. Exultant and joyous. Requires flexibility.
Has a few florid passages. Climactic ending with sustained c5.
Acc: 4 (VS)GS, GR

7866. R: Son giunta!
A: Madre, pietosa Vergine
Opera: LA FORZA DEL DESTINO, 1862, libretto by Francesco Maria
Piave, after Duke of Rivas' play. Part of Leonora, Act II. b2-b4
e3-g♯4 Common title: Leonora's prayer. Dramatic recitative and
sustained aria in moderate tempo. Subdued ending. Aria has a reci-
tative section in the middle. Acc: 4 (VS)GR, CP, IM, B-H (Italian
& English). OPA-1, OAS-2. (S)GR

7867. Me pellegrina ed orfana
Opera: LA FORZA DEL DESTINO. Part of Leonora, Act I. c3-b♭4
f3-f4 Sustained in moderate slow tempo. Generally subdued, requires fine high P and PP, and flexibility. Intense. Low, subdued
ending. Acc: 3-4 (VS)GR, CP, IM, B-H (Italian & English).
OAS-2. (S)GR

7868. Pace, pace, mio Dio
Opera: LA FORZA DEL DESTINO. Part of Leonora, Act III. c♯3-
b♭4 f3-g4 Sustained in moderate slow tempo. Requires fine high
P as well as dramatic energy. Fast, climactic ending section with
sustained b♭4 as the last note. Acc: 3-4 (VS)GS, CP, IM, B-H
(Italian & English). OPA-1, ORS, OAS-2. (S)GR, GS

7869. Tu puniscimi, o signore
Opera: LUISA MILLER, 1849, libretto by Salvatore Cammarano,
based on Schiller's tragedy. Part of Luisa, Act II. c♯3-b4 g♯3-
f♯4 Animated in moderate tempo. Requires flexibility. Has florid
passages, and a subdued, descending ending line. Agitated accompaniment. Acc: 3-4 (VS)GR. OAS-1

7870. La luce langue
Opera: MACBETH, 1847, libretto by Francesco Maria Piave, after
Shakespeare. Part of Lady Macbeth, Act II. b2-b4 f♯3-f♯4 Sus-
tained vocal part in moderate lively tempo. Dramatic and generally
strong. Climactic ending, with generally agitated accompaniment.
Interpretatively not easy. Acc: 4 (VS)GR. OAS-1

7871. Si colmi il calice di vino
Opera: MACBETH. Part of Lady Macbeth, Act II. Common title:
Brindisi (Drinking song). d3-c5 g3-g4 Animated in moderate lively
tempo. Requires flexibility. Has staccati passages. Joyous, with a
climactic ending on b♭4. Acc: 3-4 (VS)GR. OAS-1. (S)GR

7872. Una macchia... a qui tuttora
Opera: MACBETH. Part of Lady Macbeth, Act IV. Common title:
The mad scene. c♭3-d5 f3-g♭4 Sustained in moderate slow tempo.
Dramatic, interpretatively difficult. Requires fine PP. Very subdued
ending. Acc: 4 (VS)GR. OPR, OAS-1

7873. R: Ambizioso spirto
       A: Vieni! t'affretta!
       Opera: MACBETH. Part of Lady Macbeth, Act I. b2-b4(c5) f#3-
       g#4 Generally sustained in moderate slow, then fairly lively tempo.
       Has dramatic and strong passages. Requires flexibility. Interpreta-
       tively difficult. Climactic ending. Acc: 3-4 (VS)GR. OPR, OAS-1

7874. Ave Maria
       Opera: OTELLO, 1887, libretto by Arrigo Boito, after Shakespeare.
       Part of Desdemona, Act IV. eb3-ab4 eb3-eb4 Sustained in moder-
       ate slow tempo. Starts with recitative section on one note: eb3.
       Generally gentle, subdued, in prayer style. Requires fine high P.
       Acc: 3-4 (VS)GR. MSO, OPA-1, ORS. (S)GR

7875. R: Mi parea
       A: Piangea cantando
       Opera: OTELLO. Part of Desdemona, Act IV. Common title:
       "Salce, salce" or "The willow song." b2-a#4 e3-f#4 Sustained aria
       in moderate tempo. Generally subdued, requires fine P and PP. In
       concert performance of the excerpt, it is sometimes sung uninterrupt-
       ed and goes directly into the "Ave Maria" which follows it. Acc:
       3-4 (VS)GR. OPA-1, MSO

7876. Come in quest' ora bruna
       Opera: SIMON BOCCANEGRA, 1857, libretto by Francesco Maria
       Piave, after Gutierrez. Revised by Arrigo Boito. Part of Amelia,
       Act I. db3-bb4 f3-g4 Sustained in slow tempo. Generally gentle,
       requires fine P. Accompaniment requires considerable control. Acc:
       4 OPA-1. (VS)GR

7877. R: Ecco l'orrido campo
       A: Ma dall' arido stelo divulsa
       Opera: UN BALLO IN MASCHERA, 1859, libretto by Antonio Somma,
       after Scribe's libretto. Part of Amelia, Act II. b2(a2)-c5 f3-ab4
       Dramatic ending, with short cadenza. Acc: 4 (VS)GS, GR. (S)GR.
       OPR, OAS-2

7878. Morrò, ma prima in grazia
       Opera: UN BALLO IN MASCHERA. Part of Amelia, Act III. a2-
       cb5 f3-gb4 Sustained in moderate slow tempo. Starts very gently
       and very subduedly. Climactic ending, with short cadenza. Acc:
       3-4 (VS)GS, GR. OPR, OAS-2. (S)GR

B. French Composers

HECTOR BERLIOZ, 1803-1869

7879. D'amour l'ardente flamme
       Opera: LA DAMNATION DE FAUST, 1846, libretto by the composer,
       after Goethe's drama. A concert opera. Part of Marguerite, Act V.
       c3-a4 g3-g4 Sustained in slow tempo. Slightly faster middle section.
       Generally gentle, requires fine P and some flexibility. Acc: 3-4
       (VS)CT, BH

GEORGES BIZET, 1838-1875

7880. R: C'est des contrebandiers

A: Je dis, que rien ne m'épouvante
Opera: CARMEN, 1873-1874, libretto by Henri Meilhac and Ludovic
Halévy, based on Mérimée's story.   Part of Michaëla, Act III.   d3-
b4 f3-g4 Sustained in moderate tempo. Gently moving, animated
lines.   Faster middle section.   Dramatic, with several climactic high
notes. Acc: 4 (VS)GS. OPA-1, ORS, OPR.   (S)GS

GUSTAVE CHARPENTIER, 1860-1956

7881. Depuis le jour
Opera: LOUISE, 1900, libretto by the composer.   Part of Louise,
Act III.   d3-b4 g3-a4 In varied tempi. Starts very sustained, tranquil.   Requires very fine high PP on held b4. With a rather intense
joy. Abounds in long-held high notes. Acc: 4 (VS)GS.   (S)HL, IM

PAUL DUKAS, 1865-1935

7882. O, mes claire diamants!
Opera: ARIANE ET BARBE-BLEUE, 1907, libretto by Maurice
Maeterlinck. Part of Ariane, Act I.   f♯3-a♯4 g♯3-f♯4 Sustained in
moderate tempo. Has faster sections and dramatic passages. Climactic ending. Agitated accompaniment throughout. A dramatic monologue. Acc: 4-5 (VS)AD

BENJAMIN (LOUIS PAUL) GODARD, 1849-1895

7883. Il m'est doux de revoir la place
Opera: LE TASSE, 1878, libretto by Charles Grandmougin.   Part of
Leonora, Act III.   e♭3-b♭4 f3-f4 Sustained in slow tempo.   Slightly
faster middle section. Climactic high ending on g♭4. Agitated accompaniment. Acc: 4 (VS)GH.   (S)IM, HL

CHARLES (FRANÇOIS) GOUNOD, 1818-1893

7884. R: Allons, n'y pensons plus!
A: Ah! Je ris de me voir si belle
Opera: FAUST, 1852-1859, libretto by Jules Barbier and Michel Carré, after Goethe. Part of Marguerite, Act III.   b2-b4 e3-g♯4 Common titles: "The jewel song" and "Bijou song." Sustained in moderate lively tempo. Graceful and bright. Usually sung with the preceding "Il etait un Roi de Thule" (The king of Thule). Acc: 3-4
(VS)GS. OPA-1.   (S)GS

7885. R: Elles se cachaient!
A: Il ne revient pas
Opera: FAUST. Part of Marguerite, Act IV.   d♯3-a♯4(b4) g3-f♯4
Common title: Spinning-wheel song. Sustained in moderate slow tem-
po. Subdued, contemplative ending after climax. Very agitated ac-
companiment. Acc: 4-5 (VS)GS

7886. R: Me voilà seule enfin!
A: Plus grand, dans son obscurite
Opera: LA REINE DE SABA, 1861, libretto by Jules Barbier and
Michel Carré, after Gerard de Nerval.   Part of Balkis, Act III.

c3(a2)-b4 f♯3-f♯4 Recitative and sustained aria in moderate slow tempo. Has faster middle section. Climactic ending. Has dramatic passages. Acc: 4 (VS)EC. ORS

7887. Ah! Si je redevenais belle
Opera: PHILÉMON ET BAUCIS, 1859, libretto by Jules Barbier and Michel Carré. Part of Baucis, Act I. e3-a4 g3-f4 Sustained in moderate slow tempo. Has recitative-like section. Subdued ending. Acc: 3 (VS)EC

(JACQUES FRANÇOIS) FROMENTAL (ELIAS) HALÉVY, 1799-1862

7888. Il va venir!
Opera: LA JUIVE, 1835, libretto by Eugène Scribe. Part of Rachel, Act II. d3-c♭5 f3-f4 Sustained in moderate slow tempo. Climactic ending on descending line, close to two octaves. Acc: 3-4 (VS)HL

(VICTOR ANTOINE) ÉDOUARD LALO, 1823-1892

7889. R: De tous côtés j'aperçois dans la plaine
A: Lorsque je t'ai vu soudain
Opera: LE ROI D'YS, 1888, libretto by Edouard Blau. Part of Margared, Act II. e♭3-g4 g3-f4 Dramatic recitative and animated aria in fast tempo. Has some sustained vocal passages, dramatic passages, and climactic ending. Acc: 3-4 (VS)HL

7890. Vainement j'ai parlé de l'absence eternelle
Opera: LE ROI D'YS. Part of Rozenn, Act I. d3-b4 g3-e4 Sustained in varied tempi. Starts in moderate tempo. Requires fine P and PP. Climactic ending. Acc: 3 (VS)HL

JULES (EMILE FREDERIC) MASSENET, 1842-1912

7891. Charme des jours passés
Opera: HÉRODIADE, 1881, libretto by Paul Milliet and Henri Grémont. Part of Salome, Act III. d3-c5 g♯3-g♯4 Sustained in moderate slow tempo. Has faster tempi in the middle section. Dramatic, strong, intense second half of the aria. Climactic ending. c5 is sustained. Acc: 4 (VS)HL

7892. R: Celui dont la parole
A: Il est doux, il est bon
Opera: HÉRODIADE. Part of Salome, Act I. e♭3-b♭4 f3-g4 Sustained aria in moderate slow tempo. Dramatic, with a climactic and strong ending section. Acc: 3-4 (VS)HL. OPA-1, ORS. (S)GS

7893. R: Une dot! Et combien?
A: Ah! Mariez donc son coeur
Opera: LA NAVARAISE, 1894, libretto by Jules Claretie and Henri Cain. Part of Anita, Act I. c♯3-a♯4 a♯3-f♯4 Sustained aria in moderate slow tempo. Has climactic passages. Requires fine P. Dramatic high ending on a♯4. Acc: 4 (VS)HL

7894. R: De cet affreux combat
A: Pleurez, pleurez, mes yeaux

Opera: LE CID, 1885, libretto by Adolphe Philippe D'Ennery, Louis Gallet and Edouard Blau, after Corneille. Part of Chimène, Act III. c#3-b4 f#3-g4 Sustained in slow tempo. Slightly faster middle section. Requires fine P. Dramatic passages. Subdued descending ending. Acc: 3-4 OPA-1. (VS)HL

7895. Plus de tourments
Opera: LE CID. Part of L'Infante, Act II. f3-b♭4 g3-f4 Sustained in moderate tempo. Generally subdued, requires fine high P. Strong, high ending. Has gently-moving florid passages. Acc: 3-4 (VS)HL. ORS

7896. R: Ces gens que je connais
A: Pendant un an je fus ta femme
Opera: SAPHO, 1897, libretto by Henri Cain and Arthur Bernède, after Daudet. Part of Fanny, Act IV. f#3-b♭4 a3-a4 Slightly animated vocal part in moderate tempo. Has slower and faster sections. Requires very fine high P and PP. Acc: 3 (VS)HL

7897. R: Ah! je suis seule
A: Dis-moi que je suis belle
Opera: THAÏS, 1894, libretto by Louis Gallet, after Anatole France. Part of Thaïs, Act II. d3-b4(d5) f3-g4 Generally in recitative style in varied tempi and moods. Interpretatively difficult. Has dramatic passages. Also requires fine P. Climactic high ending. Acc: 3-4 (VS)HL, IM

7898. R: Je ne veux rien garder
A; L'amour est une vertu rare
Opera: THAÏS. Part of Thaïs, Act II. c3-b♭4 f3-e4 Subdued, contemplative recitative and sustained aria in moderate slow tempo. Requires very fine P and PP. Has some climactic passages. Acc: 3-4 (VS)HL

JACQUES OFFENBACH, 1819-1880

7899. Elle a fui, la tourterelle!
Opera: LES CONTES D'HOFFMAN, 1881, libretto by Jules Barbier and Michel Carré, after Hoffmann. Part of Antonia, Act III. d3-a4 f3-f#4 Sustained aria in moderate slow tempo. Requires fine PP. Has dramatic passages and a subdued ending. Acc: 3-4 OPA-1

(JOSEPH) MAURICE RAVEL, 1875-1937

7900. Oh! La pitoyable aventure!
Opera: L'HEURE ESPAGNOLE, 1907, libretto by Franc-Nohain (Maurice Legrand). Part of Concepcion, Scene 17. c#3-a4 f3-f4 Generally sustained in varied tempi. Dramatic. Requires flexibility. Climactic ending. Acc: 4 (VS)AD

C.   German and Austrian Composers

LUDWIG VAN BEETHOVEN, 1770-1827

7901. R: Abscheulicher!
A: Komm, Hoffnung

Opera: FIDELIO, c. 1803-1805, libretto by Joseph Sonnleithner and
Georg Frederick Treitschke. Part of Leonore, Act I. b2-b4 f#3-
g#4 Dramatic recitative and an animated aria. Requires flexibility.
Has florid passages, and a dramatic, climactic final section. Acc:
4 OPA-1, OAR-S1. (VS)CP

ALBAN BERG, 1885-1935

7902. Auf einmal springt er auf....
       Opera: LULU, unfinished, first performed in 1937, libretto by the
       composer, after Frank Wedekind. Part of Lulu, Act I. Common
       title: Canzonetta. eb3-g4(bb4) a3-e4 Sustained in moderate slow
       tempo. Graceful and gentle. Subdued, falling ending. Acc: 3-4
       (VS)UE

7903. Du kannst mich nicht dem Gericht ausliefern!
       Opera: LULU. Part of Lulu, Act II. e3-c#4 a3-a4 Common title:
       Arietta. Sustained in moderate lively tempo. Has dramatic high pas-
       sages. Climactic ending. Requires sensitivity to pitch. Acc: 4
       (VS)UE

7904. Wenn sich die Menschen
       Opera: LULU. Part of Lulu, Act II. Common title: Lulu's Lied.
       c3-c4(d4) g3-a4 Sustained in moderate tempo. Has dramatic high
       climaxes. Requires very fine high P. Has florid passages. Re-
       quires flexibility and sensitivity to pitch. Descending ending line.
       Acc: 4 (VS)UE

7905. Was die Leute wollen!
       Opera: WOZZECK, 1925, libretto by the composer, after Georg
       Büchner. Part of Marie, Act I. c#3-bb4 f3-f4 Sustained in slow
       tempo. Slower middle section. Requires very fine high PP. Gen-
       erally subdued and gentle. Requires flexibility and sensitivity to pitch.
       Acc: 4 (VS)UE

7906. Was die Steine glanzen?
       Opera: WOZZECK. Part of Marie, Act II. a2(e3)-b4 g3-g4 Sus-
       tained in varied tempi. Starts lively and bright. Requires flexibility
       and sensitivity to pitch. Acc: 4 (VS)UE

ERICH (WOLFGANG) KORNGOLD, 1897-1957

7907. Gluck, das mir verlieb
       Opera: DIE TOTE STADT, 1920, libretto by Paul Schott, after
       Georges Rodenbach. Part of Marietta, Act I. f3-bb4 a3-f4 Sus-
       tained in generally slow tempo. Has some slightly faster sections.
       Generally subdued, requires very fine high P and PP. Has gently
       agitated accompaniment and extended instrumental postlude. Acc:
       3-4 MLF, (VS)SC

KONRADIN KREUTZER, 1780-1849

7908. Leise wehet, leise wallet rings der Thau
       Opera: DAS NACHTLAGER VON GRANADA, 1834, libretto by Karl
       Johann Braun. Part of Gabriele, Act II. c#3-a4 e3-e4 Gracefully
       animated in moderate lively tempo. Extended postlude. 2 verses.

Acc: 3 (VS)CP. OAR-S2

7909. R: Da mir alles nun entrissen
       A: Seine fromme Liebesgabe
       Opera: DAS NACHTLAGER VON GRANADA. Part of Gabriele, Act I.
       d3-b♭4 g3-g4 Recitative and sustained aria, first moderately slow,
       then lively tempo. Graceful allegro section. Requires some flexibil-
       ity. Has dramatic passages and a climactic ending. Acc: 3-4
       (VS)CP. OAR-S2

GIACOMO MEYERBEER, 1791-1864

7910. D'ici je vois la mer immense
       Opera: L'AFRICAINE, 1865, libretto by Eugène Scribe. Part of
       Sélica, Act V. c3-b♭4(b4) f3-f4 Has recitative and song passages
       in various tempi. Agitated accompaniment in the andante section.
       Interpretatively difficult. Aria may end with the andante section, on
       "il merecoit aux cieux." Acc: 4 (VS)BR, BH

7911. Sur mes genoux fils du soleil
       Opera: L'AFRICAINE. Part of Sélica, Act II. b2-b4 g3-f♯4 Sus-
       tained in varied tempi. Requires grace. Florid, requires flexibility.
       Has dramatic passages. Interpretatively difficult. This aria is in
       the Italian version in OPR. Acc: 4 (VS)BR, BH. OPR

7912. O beau pays de la Touraine
       Opera: LES HUGUENOTS, 1836, libretto by Eugène Scribe and Emile
       Deschamps. Part of Marguerite, Act II. d3(c3)-b4 g3-g4 Sustained
       in moderate tempo. Very florid, requires considerable flexibility.
       Requires very fine high P and PP. Has cadenzas and many sustained
       high notes. Vocally demanding and difficult musically. Climactic end-
       ing. Acc: 4 (VS)BR

WOLFGANG AMADEUS MOZART, 1756-1791

7913. R: Temerari
       A: Come scoglio
       Opera: COSÌ FAN TUTTE or LA SCUOLA DEGLI AMANTI, 1790
       (K. 588), libretto by Lorenzo da Ponte. Part of Fiordiligi, Act I.
       a2-c5 d3-a4 Dramatic recitative and sustained aria in moderate
       slow tempo. Majestic, has florid figures. Requires flexibility. Has
       some wide intervalic skips, and an extremely wide range. Vocally
       demanding. IMC does not have the recitative. Acc: 4 (VS)GS.
       OPA-1, MAO-3, OAR-S1

7914. R: Ei parte....senti
       A: Per pieta, ben mio
       Opera: COSÌ FAN TUTTE or LA SCUOLA DEGLI AMANTI. Part of
       Fiordiligi, Act II. a2-b4 c♯3-g♯4 Climactic, florid ending. Not
       easy. With horn obbligato in the score. Acc: 4 (VS)GS. MAO-3,
       OAR-S1

7915. Ah, fuggi il traditor!
       Opera: DON GIOVANNI or IL DISSOLUTO PUNITO, 1787 (K. 527),
       libretto by Lorenzo da Ponte. Part of Donna Elvira, Act I. f♯3-a4
       g3-g4 Animated in lively tempo. Has florid passages. Climactic
       ending. Acc: 3-4 (VS)GS, CP, GR. MAO-4

7916. R: In quali eccessi
       A: Mi tradì quell' alma ingrata
       Opera: DON GIOVANNI. Part of Donna Elvira, Act II. d3-b♭4 f3-
       a♭4 Dramatic recitative, and an animated aria in moderate lively
       tempo. Has florid passages. Acc: 3-4 (VS)GS, CP, GR. MAO-4,
       OPR

7917. R: Don Ottavio, son morta!
       A: Or sai chi l'onore
       Opera: DON GIOVANNI. Part of Donna Anna, Act I. e♭3-a4 g3-a4
       Extended recitative in varied moods. A sustained, dramatic aria in
       moderate slow tempo. Climactic ending. Agitated accompaniment al-
       most throughout the aria. Acc: 3-4 (VS)GS, CP, GR. MAO-4

7918. R: Crudele?
       A: Non mi dir
       Opera: DON GIOVANNI. Part of Donna Anna, Act II. e3-b♭4 a3-
       a4 Sustained aria, first in rather slow, then livelier tempi. The
       vocal lines are gently animated. Requires flexibility. High tessitura.
       The last section has one long coloratura cadenza. Acc: 4 (VS)GS,
       CP, GR. OPA-1, MAO-4, OPR, OAR-S1. (S)GR

7919. Vedrai, carino
       Opera: DON GIOVANNI. Part of Zerlina, Act II. g3-g4 g3-e4
       Sustained in moderate slow tempo. Graceful and light. Has some
       slightly animated vocal passages. Slightly climactic ending. Acc:
       3-4 (VS)CP, GR, GS. CPS, MAO-1, OAR-S1. (S)GR

7920. R: Oh smania! oh furie!
       A: D'Oreste, d'Ajace
       Opera: IDOMENEO, RE DI CRETA, 1781 (K. 366), libretto by Giam-
       battista Varesco. Part of Elektra, Act III. e♭3-c5 g3-g4 A dra-
       matic recitative and a dramatic aria in very quick tempo. Energetic
       and strong. Has some high soaring lines. The two c5's are part of
       a florid run. Vocally demanding. Dramatic high ending. Acc: 4-5
       (VS)IM, CP

7921. R: Parto, e l'unico oggetto
       A: Idol mio, se ritroso
       Opera: IDOMENEO, RE DI CRETA. Part of Elektra, Act II. f3-a4
       a3-g4 Recitative and a sustained aria in moderate slow tempo.
       Starts gently on MF level. Has climactic passages and two florid
       passages. Descending ending line. Acc: 3-4 (VS)IM, CP

7922. Tutte nel cor vi sento
       Opera: IDOMENEO, RE DI CRETA. Part of Elektra, Act I. d3-a4
       f3-f4 Animated in lively tempo. Dramatic, requires energy and flex-
       ibility. Has some wide intervalic skips. Dramatic ending. Agitated
       accompaniment. Acc: 4-5 (VS)IM, CP

7923. Deh, se piacer mi vuoi
       Opera: LA CLEMENZA DI TITO, 1791 (K. 621), libretto by Caterino
       Mazzolà, after Metastasio. Part of Vitellia, Act I. b2-b4 d3-g4
       First in slow, then lively tempo. Sustained first part; animated sec-
       ond part. Has florid passages. Climactic ending. Acc: 3-4
       (VS)CP. MAO-3, OAR-S1

7924. Non più di fiori
       Opera: LA CLEMENZA DI TITO. Part of Vitellia, Act II. g2-a4

c3-g4   A short, somewhat sustained larghetto section and a longer
animated allegro. Has some sustained, dramatic passages. Explores
the low register a few times from g2 to bb2. Climactic ending. Agitated accompaniment. Acc: 4 (VS)CP. MAO-4, OAR-S1

7925. Al desio di chi t'adora
       Opera: LE NOZZE DI FIGARO, 1786 (K.492), libretto by Lorenzo
       da Ponte, after Beaumarchais. Optional aria for the Countess. b2-
       a4 e3-g4 Sustained, starts in slow tempo; then becomes lively and
       agitated. Florid, requires flexibility. Climactic ending. Acc: 4
       MAO-3. (VS)GS, GR

7926. R: E Susanna non vien!
       A: Dove sono i bei momenti
       Opera: LE NOZZE DI FIGARO. Part of the Countess, Act III. d3-
       a4 g3-g4 Sustained aria, first in moderate slow tempo, followed by
       lively tempo. Requires some flexibility. Climactic ending. Acc: 3
       (VS)GS, GR. (S)GS. MAO-3, OAR-S1

7927. Non so più cosa son, cosa faccio
       Opera: LE NOZZE DI FIGARO. Part of Cherubino, Act I. eb3-g4
       g3-f4 Animated in rapid tempo. Requires some fluent enunciation.
       Bright, somewhat gently outgoing. Has climactic passages. General-
       ly on MF level. Acc: 3-4 (VS)GS, GR. OAR-S1, CAO-S. (S)GS,
       GR

7928. Porgi, amor, qualche ristoro
       Opera: LE NOZZE DI FIGARO. Part of the Countess, Act II. Com-
       mon title: Cavatina. d3-ab4 g3-f4 Sustained in slow tempo. Gen-
       tle throughout, with underlying emotional intensity. Acc: 3 (VS)GS,
       GR. OAR-S1, OPA-1, MAO-3. (S)GS, GR

7929. Parto: nel gran cimento
       Opera seria: MITRIDATE, RÈ DI PONTO, 1770 (K.87), libretto by
       Vittorio Amadeo Cigna-Santi, after Racine. Part of Sifare, Act I.
       e3-b4 g#3-g#4 Animated vocal part with alternating andante and
       allegro sections. Allegro sections are florid, requiring flexibility.
       Acc: 4 MAO-3

7930. Tiger! wetze nur die Klauen
       Opera: ZAIDE or DAS SERAIL, 1779, unfinished (K.344), libretto by
       Johann Andreas Schachtner. Part of Zaide, Act II. d3-a4 g3-g4
       Animated in very fast tempo. Slower middle section. Strong and
       dramatic. Accented in some passages. Climactic ending. The plot
       of this opera is similar to DIE ENTFÜHRUNG AUS DEM SERAIL.
       Acc: 4 MAO-4, (S)IM

(CARL) OTTO (EHRENFRIED) NICOLAI, 1810-1849

7931. R: Wohl denn! gefasst ist der Entschluss
       A: So schweb ich Dir Geliebter zu
       Opera: DIE LUSTIGEN WEIBER VON WINDSOR, 1849, libretto by
       Hermann Salomon Mosenthal, after Shakespeare. Part of Anna, Act
       III. d3-b4 g#3-g#4 Recitative in varied tempi and moods, and a
       slow-to-fast aria. Climactic ending. Agitated accompaniment in the
       fast section. Acc: 4 (VS)CP, BH. OAR-S2

7932. R: Nun eilt herbei, Witz, heitre
A: Verführer! Warum stellt
Opera: DIE LUSTIGEN WEIBER VON WINDSOR. Part of Fluth, Act
I. c3-bb4 g3-f4 Recitative and animated aria in slow to medium-
fast tempo. Florid, requires flexibility. Climactic high ending.
Acc: 3-4 (VS)CP, BH. OAR-S2

FRANZ SCHUBERT, 1797-1828

7933. Die Brust gebeugt von Sorgen
Opera: FIERRABRAS, 1826, libretto by Joseph Kupelwieser, after
Calderon. Part of Florinda, Act II. f♯3-g4 a♯3-f♯4 Vigorous,
animated in very lively tempo. Has dramatic passages. Generally
strong. Climactic ending. Acc: 4 BH, Arias for Soprano

ROBERT SCHUMANN, 1810-1856

7934. R: Dort schleichen über'n Hof sie sacht
A: O du der über Alle wacht
Opera: GENOVEVA, 1847-1850, libretto by Robert Reinick, altered
by the composer, after Ludwig Tieck and Friedrich Hebbel. Part of
Genoveva, Act II. eb3-g4 g3-eb4 Subdued recitative and sustained
aria in slow tempo. Has climactic passages. Subdued ending. Acc:
3-4 (VS)BH

LOUIS SPOHR, 1784-1859

7935. R: Als in mitternächt'ger Stund
A: Die ihr Fühlende betrübet
Opera: JESSONDA, 1823, libretto by Eduard Heinrich Gehe, after
Antoine Lemierre. Part of Jessonda, Act I. eb3-bb4 a3-g4 Sus-
tained in moderate slow tempo. Has climactic passages. Slower
final section. Has florid passages. Acc: 3-4 CP, Soprano Arias

RICHARD STRAUSS, 1864-1949

7936. Es gibt ein Reich
Opera: ARIADNE AUF NAXOS, 1911-1912, libretto by Hugo von Hofmannsthal. Part of Ariadne, one-act opera. ab2-bb4 g3-f4 Sustained in moderate tempo. Has slower sections. Starts quietly and
calmly. Has dramatic passages. Subdued ending. Acc: 3-4 (VS)
AF, B-H

7937. Da geht er hin, der aufgeblasne schlechte Kerl
Opera: DER ROSENKAVALIER, 1909-1910, libretto by Hugo von Hofmannsthal. Part of the Marschallin, Act I. Common title: Marschallin's monologue. c3-g4 f3-d4 In recitative style and in varied
tempi and moods. Subdued ending. Interpretatively difficult. Acc:
3-4 (VS)B-H

7938. Aus unsern Taten steigt ein Gericht!
Opera: DIE FRAU OHNE SCHATTEN, 1914-1917, libretto by Hugo
von Hofmannsthal. Part of the Kaiserin, Act III. b2-bb4 g3-a4
Sustained in moderate slow tempo. Has dramatic passages. Slightly

subdued ending.   Acc: 3-4   (VS)B-H

7939.   Barak! Ich hab es nicht gethan!
        Opera: DIE FRAU OHNE SCHATTEN.   Part of the Frau, Act II.
        g♭3-b♭4   a♭3-a♭4   Very sustained vocal part in moderate lively tem-
        po. Has many long-held high notes.   Dramatic, with a climactic end-
        ing.   Acc: 3-4 (VS)B-H

7940.   Ist mein Liebster dahin
        Opera: DIE FRAU OHNE SCHATTEN.   Part of the Kaiserin, Act I.
        d♯3-d5   g3-g4   Moderately animated in moderate tempo.   Requires
        some grace. Has dramatic passages, often using a high tessitura.
        Vocally not easy.   Acc: 4 (VS)B-H

7941.   Allein! Weh, ganz allein
        Opera: ELEKTRA, 1906-1908, libretto by Hugo von Hofmannsthal.
        Part of Elektra, one-act opera.   c3-b♭4   g3-g4   An extended and dra-
        matic scena in different tempi and moods. Starts majestically, and
        ends in a broad dramatic climax.   Interpretatively difficult.   Acc: 4
        (VS)B-H, AF

7942.   Orest! Es ruhrt sich niemand
        Opera: ELEKTRA.   Part of Elektra, one-act opera. a♭2-b♭4   g3-g4
        Sustained vocal part in varied tempi. Dramatic, has high climaxes.
        Strong. Requires very fine high P. Subdued ending on "Du zitterst
        ja am ganzen Leib?" Acc: 4 (VS)B-H, AF

7943.   Wie stark du bist!
        Opera: ELEKTRA.   Part of Elektra, one-act opera.   d♯3-b4   g3-g4
        Sustained vocal part in fast tempo. Dramatic, strong, has high cli-
        maxes.   Climactic ending on "an der Reife Tag." Acc: 3-4 (VS)
        B-H, AF

7944.   Ah! Du wolltest mich nicht deinen Mund
        Opera: SALOME, 1905, libretto by Oscar Wilde, translated by Hed-
        wig Lachmann. Part of Salome, one-act opera. b♭2-b♭4   g♯3-g♯4
        In varied styles and tempi. Dramatic, vocally demanding and difficult.
        Aria ends with "das Geheimnis des Todes" on g♭2.   Acc: 5 (VS)
        B-H

7945.   Dein Haar ist grässlich!
        Opera: SALOME.   Part of Salome, one-act opera.   d♯3-b4   g♯3-a4
        Sustained in lively tempo. Dramatic and intense. Very subdued, sus-
        tained ending on f4.   Acc: 4 (VS)B-H

7946.   Ich will nicht bleiben
        Opera: SALOME.   Part of Salome, one-act opera. b2-a♭4   f♯3-f♯4
        Sustained vocal part in varied tempi. Requires fine P. Has dramatic
        passages.   Subdued ending on "die rein geblieben ist." Acc: 4
        (VS)B-H

RICHARD WAGNER, 1813-1883

7947.   R: Jo-ho-hoe! Jo-ho-hoe!
        A: Traft ihr das Schiff?
        Opera: DER FLIEGENDE HOLLÄNDER, 1843, libretto by the com-
        poser. Part of Senta, Act II, No. 7. Other title: Ballad. b♭2-g4

f3-g4 In varied moods and tempi. Narrative, interpretatively difficult. Requires fine PP. Very subdued ending section. Senta's story
of the legend of The Flying Dutchman. Acc: 4 (VS)GS, CP. OGS,
OPA-1

7948. Mein Erbe nun nehm' ich zu eigen
Music Drama: GÖTTERDÄMMERUNG, third day of the festival drama,
DER RING DES NIBELUNGEN, 1874, libretto by the composer. Part
of Brünnhilde, Act III. A continuation of "Starke scheite," but may
be performed separately. Strong, energetic, fast, and dramatic.
Uses much of the higher notes in full voice. Climactic ending. Both
this excerpt and its preceding section appear in OGS. Acc: 5
(VS)GS, CP. OGS

7949. Starke scheite schichtet mir dort
Music Drama: GÖTTERDÄMMERUNG. Part of Brünnhilde, Act III,
Scene 3. a♯2-a4 e3-g4 Majestic and marked. Has sustained pas-
sages as well as dramatic passages. The excerpt may end with "ruhe,
du Gott" or continue and finish the entire scena. Acc: 5 (VS)GS,
CP. OGS

7950. Zu neuen Thaten, theurer Helde
Music Drama: GÖTTERDÄMMERUNG. Part of Brünnhilde, in The
Prologue. c3-g4 f3-f4 Sustained in moderate tempo. Tranquil and
generally subdued. Acc: 3-4 (VS)GS, CP

7951. R: Schläfst du Gast?
Scena: Der Männer Sippe
Music Drama: DIE WALKÜRE, first day of the festival drama, DER
RING DES NIBELUNGEN, 1870, libretto by the composer. Part of
Sieglinde, Act I, Scene 3. b2-a4 f♯3-g4 In varied moods and tem-
pi. Has sustained passages. Dramatic final section. Climactic end-
ing. Acc: 4 (VS)GS-German & English; CP-German. OPA-1, OGS

7952. Du bist der Lenz
Music Drama: DIE WALKÜRE. Part of Sieglinde, Act I, Scene 3.
c3-a♭4 g3-f4 Sustained in moderate tempo. Has dramatic climaxes.
Climactic ending. Exultant. Acc: 4-5 (VS)GS-German & English;
CP-German

7953. Hojoto-ho!
Music Drama: DIE WALKÜRE. Part of Brünnhilde, Act II, Scene 1.
d♭3-c5 g3-b4 Strong, energetic, and dramatic. Requires flexibility.
Has octave intervalic skips. Vocally demanding; uses several very
high notes. Acc: 4-5 (VS)GS-German & English; CP-German. OGS

7954. So ist es denn
Music Drama: DIE WALKÜRE. Part of Fricka, Act II, Scene 1.
c×3-g♯4 e3-e4 Sustained in moderate lively tempo. Dramatic, intense coda. Excerpt ends with the climactic "lass' auch zertreten!"
Acc: 4-5 (VS)GS-German & English; CP-German

7955. War es so schmählich, was ich verbrach
Music Drama: DIE WALKÜRE. Part of Brünnhilde, Act III, Scene 3.
a2-g4 f♯3-f♯4 Starts in low, subdued recitative. Sustained in slow
tempo. Generally subdued. Acc: 3-4 (VS)GS-German & English;
CP-German

7956.   Einsam in trüben Tagen
        Opera: LOHENGRIN, 1850, libretto by the composer.   Part of Elsa,
        Act I, Scene 2.   Common title: Elsa's dream.   eb3-ab4   f3-gb4
        Sustained in slow tempo.   Dramatic.   Has some octave intervalic
        skips.   In recitative style, with extended instrumental postlude.   Full-
        sounding accompaniment.   Acc: 4   (VS)GS-German & English; CP-
        German.   MSO, OPA-1, ORS, OPR, OGS

7957.   Entweihte Götter!
        Opera: LOHENGRIN.   Part of Ortrud, Act II, Scene 2.   f#3-a#4
        g#3-f#4   Common title: Ortrud's curse.   Sustained vocal part in
        fast tempo.   Dramatic, climactic, strong throughout.   Acc: 3   (VS)
        GS-German & English; CP-German.   OPA-2

7958.   Euch Lüften, die mein Klagen
        Opera: LOHENGRIN.   Part of Elsa, Act II, Scene 2.   e3-f4   a3-f4
        Sustained in moderate slow tempo.   Generally subdued.   Short.   Very
        subdued ending.   Acc: 3   (VS)GS-German & English; CP-German.
        OPA-1, OGS

7959.   Ich sah das Kind
        Music Drama: PARSIFAL, 1882, libretto by the composer.   Part of
        Kundry, Act II.   Common title: Kundry's Erzählung.   c3-a#4   e3-
        f#4   Sustained in very moderate tempo.   Generally gentle and subdued.
        Has some dramatic passages.   Subdued ending.   Acc: 4   (VS)GS-
        German & English; CP-German.   OGS

7960.   Ich sah die Städte
        Opera: RIENZI, DER LETZTE DER TRIBUNEN, 1842, libretto by the
        composer, after Mary Mitford's drama.   Part of Friedensbote (Mes-
        senger), Act II.   bb2-a4   a3-f#4   Sustained in moderate tempo.   Re-
        quires some flexibility.   Has some florid figures.   With chorus in the
        full score.   Acc: 3-4   (VS)SC

7961.   Ewig war ich, ewig bin ich
        Music Drama: SIEGFRIED, second day of the festival drama, DER
        RING DES NIBELUNGEN, 1876, libretto by the composer.   Part of
        Brünnhilde, Act III, Scene 3.   e3-c5   f#3-g4   Sustained in moderate
        tempo.   Generally calm, with dramatic crescendi in some passages.
        Acc: 4   (VS)GS-German & English; CP-German.   OGA

7962.   Dich, theure Halle
        Opera: TANNHÄUSER UND DER SÄNGERKRIEG AUF DER WART-
        BURG, 1845, libretto by the composer.   Part of Elizabeth, Act II,
        Scene 1.   d#3-a4(b4)   g3-g4   Common title: Elizabeth's greeting.
        Sustained in lively tempo.   Has majestic passages.   Climactic ending.
        Acc: 3-4   (VS)GS-German & English; CP-German.   OPA-1, ORS,
        OGS

7963.   Allmächt'ge Jungfrau
        Opera: TANNHÄUSER UND DER SÄNGERKRIEG AUF DER WART-
        BURG.   Part of Elizabeth, Act III.   Scene 1.   Common title: Eliza-
        beth's prayer.   db3-gb4   gb3-gb4   Very sustained in slow tempo.
        Slightly faster middle section.   Requires fine P and PP.   Has dramat-
        ic passages.   Low ending.   Acc: 3-4   (VS)GS-German & English;
        CP-German.   OPA-1, ORS, OGS

7964.   Geliebter, komm'!   Sieh' dort die Grotte

Opera: TANNHÄUSER UND DER SÄNGERKRIEG AUF DER WART-
BURG. Part of Venus, Act I, Scene 2. f♯3-a4 g♯3-f♯4 Sustained
in moderate tempo. Requires fine P. Gentle and tranquil throughout.
Acc: 4-5 (VS)GS-German & English; CP-German

7965. Mild und leise
Opera: TRISTAN UND ISOLDE, 1865, libretto by the composer. Part
of Isolde, Act III, Scene 3. Common title: Isolde's Liebestod. d♯3-
a♭4 f♯3-g♯4 First sustained in moderate tempo; then slightly animated and more musically complex. Dramatic. Subdued ending.
Full-sounding accompaniment. Acc: 5 (VS)GS-German & English;
CP-German. OPΛ-1, ORS, OGS

CARL MARIA VON WEBER, 1786-1826

7966. Scene: Wie nahte mir der Schlummer
A: Leise, leise, fromme Weise
Opera: DER FREISCHÜTZ, 1821, libretto by Friedrich Kind. Part
of Agatha (Agnes), Act II. b2-b4 f♯3-f♯4 Scena with recitative and
short song sections. Animated, fast, and energetic aria. Requires
fluent enunciation. Dramatic final section. Acc: 4 OPA-1, OAR-
S2, (VS)CP-German

7967. Und ob die Wolke
Opera: DER FREISCHÜTZ. Part of Agatha (Agnes), Act III. Common title: Cavatina. e♭3-a♭4 e♭3-f4 Gently animated vocal part
in slow tempo. Requires fine high P. Subdued throughout. Acc:
3-4 OPA-1, OAR-S2, (VS)CP-German

7968. Bethörte! die an meine Liebe glaubt
Opera: EURYANTHE, 1823, libretto by Wilhelmine Helmine von
Chézy. Part of Eglantine, Act I. a♯2-c5 g♯3-g♯4 Generally in
fast tempo. Has dramatic passages, florid passages, and a climactic ending. Requires flexibility. Acc: 4 (VS)NO, CP. OAR-M

7969. O mein Leid ist unermessen
Opera: EURYANTHE. Part of Eglantine, Act I. d♯3-g4 g3-e4
Animated in fast tempo. Has climactic passages. Subdued, low end-
ing. Acc: 3-4 (VS)NO, CP. OAR-M

7970. R: Eil' edler Held!
A: Ja, o Herr, mein Heil, mein Leben
Opera: OBERON, 1826, libretto by James Robinson Planché, after
Wieland's story. Part of Reiza, Act I. e3-b4 g3-g4 Animated in
fast tempo. Generally strong and dramatic. Climactic ending. Acc:
3-4 (VS)CP-German. OAR-S2

7971. Ozean! Du Ungeheuer!
Opera: OBERON. Part of Reiza, Act II. c3(b♭2)-c5 f3-a♭4 In
varied tempi and moods. Dramatic and highly energetic. Vocally demanding and difficult. Last part has many extremely high notes.
Acc: 4 OPA-1, OAR-S2. (VS)CP-German

7972. Traure, mein Herz
Opera: OBERON. Part of Reiza, Act III. b2-f4 f3-d♭4 Sustained
in moderate slow tempo. Lyric, generally on MF level. Subdued
ending. Acc: 3-4 (VS)CP-German

D.   American Composer

AARON COPLAND

7973. But ends don't end
Opera: THE TENDER LAND, 1954, libretto by Horace Everett. Part
of Ma Moss, Act III. d♭3-g♭4 g3-e♭4 Sustained in slow tempo.
Generally strong and climactic. Subdued ending. The last song in
the opera. Acc: 3-4 (VS)B-H

E.   Russian Composer

PETER (PIOTR) ILYICH TCHAIKOVSKY, 1840-1893

7974. Though I should die for it
Opera: EUGENE ONÉGIN, 1877-1878, libretto by the composer and
Konstantin S. Shilovsky, after Pushkin. Part of Tatiana, Act I.
Common title: Tatiana's letter scene. d♭3-b♭4 f3-f4 In varied
moods and tempi. Starts animated in fairly lively tempo. An extend-
ed and dramatic scena. Has some extended instrumental interludes.
Climactic ending. Best for the heavier voices. Acc: 4 OPA-1

F.   Czechoslovakian Composers

ANTONÍN DVOŘÁK, 1841-1904

7975. In vain it is
Opera: RUSALKA, 1900, libretto by Jaroslav Kvapil. Part of Rusalka, Act II. d3-b♭4(b4) g3-g4 Animated in lively tempo. Requires
fluent enunciation. Has dramatic passages. Dramatic, intense high
ending. Acc: 3-4 (VS)AR

LEOŠ JANÁČEK, 1854-1928

7976. Mutter, mir ist Kopf schwer
Opera: JENUFA (Její pastorkyna), 1894-1903, libretto by the composer, after Preissova's drama. Part of Jenufa, Act II. c♯3-b♭4
a♭3-g♭4 Generally sustained in varied tempi and moods. Has dramatic climaxes. Requires fine high P. Interpretatively difficult. A
dramatic scena. Text of the vocal score is in Czech and German.
Acc: 4 (VS)UE

G.   Spanish Composer

ENRIQUE GRANADOS, 1867-1916

7977. ¡Es un sueño!
Opera: GOYESCAS, 1916, libretto by Fernando Periquet y Zuaznabar.
Part of Rosario, Tableau III. b♭2-b4 g3-g4 A final scene and
tableau. Sustained in varied tempi and moods. Has dramatic passages. Intense; also requires very fine PP. Has interpolations by
Fernando's part. Extended and difficult. Low ending after climactic
high note. Acc: 4 (VS)GS-Spanish & English

H.   Argentine Composer

ALBERTO GINASTERA

7978. A la sombra de la oliva
Opera: DON RODRIGO, 1964, libretto by Alejandro Casona. Part of
Florinda, Act II. b2-g4 f3-e4 Sustained in moderate slow tempo.
Lyric in style. Chromatically and rhythmically complex. Requires
considerable flexibility. Generally on MF level. Subdued, long-held
ending. Acc: 4 (VS)B-H

7979. Alla en las verdes Asturias
Opera: DON RODRIGO. Part of Florinda, Act III. Other title: Romance. c#3(ab2)-g#4 g3-f4 Sustained in slow tempo. Rhythmically
complex. Requires flexibility. Has strong passages. Subdued ending. Acc: 4 (VS)B-H

7980. ¡Noche, estrella da noche!
Opera: DON RODRIGO. Part of Florinda, Act II. Other title:
Aria. b2-a4 e3-e4 Generally sustained style. Requires fluent and
rapid enunciation and very fine high P. Rhythmically complex. Subdued ending. Acc: 4 (VS)B-H

4. MEZZO-SOPRANO

Bibliography for Mezzo-Soprano and Contralto

CAO-M   Celebri Aria D'Opera. Mezzo-Soprano and Contralto. Third of 6 volumes for all voices. Milan: G. Ricordi.

MLF   Master Lessons on Fifty Opera Arias. Vol. II: The Music. 27 for soprano; 4 for mezzo-soprano; 12 for tenor; 8 for baritone. Edited by Weldon Whitlock. Milwaukee: Pro Musica Press.

MRS-2   Modern Russian Songs. Vol. II. High, Low. Edited by Ernest Newman. Bryn Mawr: Oliver Ditson. (The spelling of Russian names in this edition is not consistent.)

OAM   Opern-Arien für Mezzo-Sopran (Alt). Giuseppe Verdi. Edited by Kurt Soldan. Leipzig: Edition Peters.

OAR   Opern-Arien. Operatic arias in 6 volumes (2 for soprano) in original languages and German versions. Thirty-four arias for Mezzo-Soprano and Contralto, No. 4232 in the catalog. Frankfurt: Edition Peters.

OPA-1   Operatic Anthology. Vol. 1: Soprano. Edited by Kurt Adler. New York: G. Schirmer, Inc. (The older edition is edited by Kurt Schindler.)

OPA-2   Operatic Anthology. Vol. 2: Mezzo-Soprano and Contralto. Edited by Kurt Adler. New York: G. Schirmer, Inc. (The older edition is edited by Kurt Schindler.)

ORS   Opera Repertoire for Soprano. Twenty-seven arias. Edited by Gregory Castleton. Original text, with English versions. Includes synopses of opera plots. Bryn Mawr: Theodore Presser Co.

PDA   The Prima Donna's Album. Forty-two operatic arias. Original texts, with English versions. Newly revised and edited by Kurt Adler. New York: G. Schirmer, Inc.

A. Italian Composers

VINCENZO BELLINI, 1801-1835

7981. Ascolta: se Romeo t'uccise un figlio
     Opera: I CAPULETTI ED I MONTECCHI, 1830, libretto by Felice Romani, based on Shakespeare's Romeo and Juliet. Part of Romeo, Act I. Originally for mezzo-soprano or high contralto. g2-g4 g3-f♯4 Sustained in slow tempo. Graceful; has florid figures. Acc: 3-4 (VS)B-H, GR

7982. Deh! tu, bell'anima
Opera: I CAPULETTI ED I MONTECCHI. Part of Romeo, Act II.
e3-g4 g3-f4 Sustained in moderate slow tempo. Fine for young
voices. Requires some flexibility. Generally on MF level. Short,
simpler than most arias. Acc: 3 CAO-M, OAR-M. (VS)B-H, GR

7983. Ah! se non m'ami più
Opera: LA STRANIERA, 1829, libretto by Felice Romani, based on
a novel by d'Arlincourt. Part of Isoletta, Act II. e3-e4 g3-d4
Sustained in moderate slow tempo. Agitated accompaniment. Acc:
4 (VS)GR

7984. R: Sgombra e la sacra selva
A: Deh! proteggimi, o Dio!
Opera: NORMA, 1831, libretto by Felice Romani. Part of Adalgisa,
Act I. b♭2-g♭4 e♭3-e♭4 Extended recitative and sustained short
aria in slow tempo. Slightly florid and generally subdued. Requires
flexibility. Acc: 3-4 (VS)GS, GR

7985. E tu pure
Opera: NORMA. Part of Adalgisa, Act I. c3-a♭4 a♭3-g4 Sustained in moderate tempo. Slightly florid. Gently agitated accompaniment. Climactic ending for the solo part. Part of a duet. Acc:
3-4 (VS)GS, GR

ARRIGO BOITO, 1842-1918

7986. Fanuel.... moriro?
Opera: NERONE, 1916, libretto by the composer. Part of Rubria,
Act IV. c3-e♭4 e3-c4 Sustained in slow tempo. In gentle recita-
tive style, with frequent repeated notes. Subdued ending. Acc: 3-4
(VS)GR

7987. Padre nostro che sei ne' cieli
Opera: NERONE. Part of Rubria, Act I. c3-e♭4 c3-e♭4 Sustained in moderate slow tempo. Most passages are in recitative
style, in monotone. Acc: 3-4 (VS)GR

LUIGI CHERUBINI, 1760-1842

7988. Solo un pianto
Opera: MEDEA, 1797, libretto by François Benoit Hoffman. Original in French. Part of Neris, Act II. d3-g4 g3-e♭4 Sustained in
moderate slow tempo. Has slightly animated vocal passages. Climactic ending. Acc: 4 (VS)GR

FRANCESCO CILÈA, 1866-1950

7989. Acerba volutta
Opera: ADRIANA LECOUVREUR, 1902, libretto by Arturo Colautti,
after Eugène Scribe. Part of the Princess, Act II. c3-a4 f3-f4
Originally for mezzo-soprano. A dramatic aria, first in fast tempo,
then ends with sustained section in moderate slow tempo. Has climactic passages. Acc: 4 (VS)CS

7990. R: Esser madre e un inferno
A: Sai che gli ho dato
Opera: L'ARLESIANA, 1897, libretto by Leopoldo Marenco, based on
Alphonse Daudet's play. Part of Rosa, Act III. d3(c3)-a4 f3-f4
Sustained in slow tempo. After the recitative section, a sustained
adagio with some climactic passages. Slower ending section, going
back into the recitative style. Very subdued high ending on f4. Acc:
3-4 MLF (VS)CS

GAETANO DONIZETTI, 1797-1848

7991. R: E sgombro il loco
A: Ah! parea che per incanto
Opera: ANNA BOLENA, 1830, libretto by Felice Romani. Part of
Smeton, Act I. ab2-g4 db3-eb4 Recitative in varied moods and a
sustained aria in moderate tempo. Florid, requires considerable
flexibility. Acc: 3-4 (VS)GR

7992. Al dolce guidami
Opera: ANNA BOLENA. Part of Anna, Act II. e3(bb2)-a4(bb4) g3-
g4 Sustained in moderate slow tempo. Florid, requires flexibility.
Acc: 3-4 (VS)GR

7993. Deh! non voler costringere
Opera: ANNA BOLENA. Part of Smeton, Act I. g2-g4 bb2-eb4
Sustained in moderate slow tempo. Has florid passages. Requires
flexibility. Acc: 3-4 (VS)GR

7994. R: Ove celare, oh Dio!
A: Terra adorata de' padri miei
Opera: DON SEBASTIANO, 1843, libretto by Eugène Scribe. Original in French. Part of Zaida, Act II. b2-g4 e3-e4 Sustained in
moderate slow tempo. Requires some flexibility. Descending ending
line. Acc: 3-4 (VS)GR, EO. (S)GR

7995. R: Fia dunque vero...
A: O mio Fernando!
Opera: LA FAVORITA, 1840, libretto by Alphonse Royer, Gustave
Vaëz and Eugène Scribe. Part of Leonora, Act III. b2(a2)-g#4 e3-
f4 Dramatic recitative. Aria starts gently and sustained, then be-
comes dramatic. Acc: 3-4 (VS)GR. OPA-2. (S)GR

7996. Cari luoghi ov'io passai
Opera: LINDA DI CHAMOUNIX, 1842, libretto by Gaetano Rossi.
Part of Peirotto, Act I. c3-f4 d3-c4 Sustained in moderate tempo.
Graceful. Acc: 3-4 (VS)GR

7997. Il segreto per esse felice
Opera: LUCREZIA BORGIA, 1833, libretto by Felice Romani, based
on Victor Hugo's play. Part of Orsini, Act II. c3-f4 e3-d4 Animated in lively tempo. Requires some flexibility. 2 verses with
choral section between. Acc: 3-4 (VS)B-H

7998. Per non istare in ozio
Opera: MARIA DI ROHAN, 1843, libretto by Salvatore Cammarano.
Part of Gondi, Act I. g2-g4 e3-c4 Sustained in moderate tempo.
Has dramatic climaxes and a climactic ending. Acc: 3-4 (VS)GR

UMBERTO GIORDANO, 1867-1948

7999. Temer? Perche?
       Opera: ANDREA CHÉNIER, 1896, libretto by Luigi Illica. Part of
       Bersi, Act II. f3-g4 f3-f4 Starts in recitative style. Animated in
       lively tempo. Dramatic, with climactic high ending. Acc: 4 (VS)
       CS, IM

RUGGIERO LEONCAVALLO, 1858-1919

8000. Da quel suon soavemente
       Opera: LA BOHÈME, 1897, libretto by Giuseppe Giacosa and Luigi
       Illica, after Henri Murger's novel. Part of Musetta, Act II. a2-a4
       e3-f♯4 Gracefully animated in waltz time. Wide range. Very sub-
       dued ending. Acc: 3 (VS)CS

PIETRO MASCAGNI, 1863-1945

8001. Voi lo sapete, O Mamma
       Opera: CAVALLERIA RUSTICANA, 1889, libretto by Giovanni Targi-
       one-Tozzetti and Guido Menasci, after Verga's story. Part of San-
       tuzza, one-act opera. b2-a4 f♯3-f♯4 Sustained in slow tempo.
       Generally short vocal phrases. Dramatic, requires fine P. The first
       part is in quasi-recitative style. Acc: 3-4 (VS)GS. OPA-1, ORS.
       (S)GS

8002. R: Povero amico
       A: O pallida, che un giorno mi guardasti
       Opera: L'AMICO FRITZ, 1891, libretto by P. Suardon, after Erck-
       mann-Chatrian's novel. Part of Beppe, Act III. d3-g4 g3-d4 Sus-
       tained aria in moderate slow tempo. Requires fine P. Has dramatic
       passages. Acc: 3-4 (VS)GR, CS

AMILCARE PONCHIELLI, 1834-1886

8003. Ah! E questo della misera
       Opera: I PROMESSI SPOSI, 1856, libretto adapted from Alessandro
       Manzoni. Part of Signora di Monza, Act III. c3-f4 e3-eb4 Sus-
       tained in moderate tempo. More animated, slightly faster ending sec-
       tion. Has climactic passages and a climactic ending. Acc: 3-4
       (VS)GR

8004. R: In questo loco solitario e mesto
       A: Involontaria vittima
       Opera: I PROMESSI SPOSI. Part of Signora di Monza, Act III. c3-
       g4 f3-f4 Extended recitative and sustained aria in moderate tempo.
       Has climactic passages. Descending ending line. Acc: 3-4 (VS)GR

8005. Scena: Ho il cor
       A: Stella del marinar!
       Opera: LA GIOCONDA, 1876, libretto by Arrigo Boito, after Victor
       Hugo. Part of Laura, Act II. a♯2-a4 e3-f4 Animated aria in mod-
       erate tempo. Has slightly slower section. Subdued high ending.
       Acc: 3-4 OPA-2. (VS)GS, GR. (S)GR

1036   Solo Voice Repertoire

8006. Voce di donna
       Opera: LA GIOCONDA. Part of La Cieca, Act I. b♭2-g4 e♭3-e♭4
       Sustained in moderate slow tempo. Lyric, and generally subdued.
       Acc: 3-4 OPA-2. (VS)GS, GR. (S)GR, GS

GIACOMO (ANTONIO DOMENICO) PUCCINI, 1858-1924

8007. Sulla vetta tu del monte
       Opera: MANON LESCAUT, 1893, libretto by Marco Praga, Domenico
       Oliva and Luigi Illica, based on Prévost's novel. Part of the Voice,
       Act II. b♭2-e♭4 g3-d4 Sustained in moderate slow tempo. Gener-
       ally subdued, with background women's chorus in the full score. Low,
       declamatory-style ending. Acc: 3 (VS)GR. (S)GR

8008. Io de' sospiri
       Opera: TOSCA, 1900, libretto by Giuseppe Giacosa and Luigi Illica.
       Part of the Young Shepherd, Act III. b2-e4 e3-c♯4 Sustained in
       moderate slow tempo. Generally subdued. Subdued, descending end-
       ing. Acc: 3-4 (VS)GS, GR

GIOACCHINO (ANTONIO) ROSSINI, 1792-1868

8009. R: Che vecchio sospettoso!
       A: Il vecchiotto cerca moglie
       Opera: IL BARBIERE DI SIVIGLIA, 1816, libretto by Cesare Sterbini,
       after Beaumarchais' comedy. Part of Bertha, Act II. c♯3-a4 e3-
       f♯4 Animated in lively tempo. Slightly faster ending section. Re-
       quires fluent enunciation. Climactic ending. Acc: 3-4 (VS)GS, GR.
       OAR-M. (S)GR

8010. Una voce poco fa
       Opera: IL BARBIERE DI SIVIGLIA. Part of Rosina, Act I. g♯2-
       g♯4(b4) c♯3-f♯4 Sustained in moderate slow tempo. Florid, re-
       quires flexibility. Has some recitative-style passages. Often trans-
       posed for soprano. Composer's variations for this aria, "Varianten
       zur Cavatine der Rosina 'Una voce poco fa'," Edition Eulenburg (1973).
       Acc: 3-4 (VS)GS, GR. OPA-2. (S)GS, GR. (SC)EE-Variations

8011. Non più mesta
       Opera: LA CENERENTOLA, 1817, libretto by Jacopo Ferretti, after
       Perrault. Part of Cenerentola (Cinderella), Act I. g♯2-b4 c♯3-a4
       Common title: Cavatina. Animated vocal part in moderate slow tem-
       po. Very florid, has high tessitura in some passages. Has a wide
       range. Vocally demanding and difficult. Requires considerable flexi-
       bility. A coloratura-mezzo aria. Acc: 3-4 (VS)MR. OPA-2,
       OAR-M

8012. Sventurata mi credea
       Opera: LA CENERENTOLA. Part of Clorinda, Act II. b♭2-b♭4
       f3-g4 Very florid aria, first in slow, then in lively tempo. Requires
       flexibility. Has some wide intervalic skips. Climactic ending. Acc:
       3-4 (VS)MR

8013. Una volta c'era un re
       Opera: LA CENERENTOLA. Part of Cenerentola, Act II. c3-d4
       e3-c4 Sustained in moderate slow tempo. Generally on MF level.

Generally simple and short.   Has a few short florid figures.   Acc:
3 (VS)FC, MS

8014. Di piacer me balza il cor
Opera: LA GAZZA LADRA, 1817, libretto by Giovanni Gherardini,
after a comedy by d'Aubigny and Caigniez.   Part of Ninetta, Act I.
b2-a4 e3-f♯4 Animated vocal part in moderate tempo, followed by
faster tempo.   Quite florid, requires flexibility.   Has dramatic passages and a climactic ending.   Acc: 3-4 (VS)EG, GR. PDA. (S)GR

8015. R: Amici, in ogni evento
A: Pensa alla patria
Opera: L'ITALIANA IN ALGERI, 1813, libretto by Angelo Anelli.
Part of Isabella, Act II. a2-b4 e3-d♯4 Extended recitative and sus-
tained aria in moderate slow tempo.   Very florid excerpt, requires
considerable flexibility.   An operatic "show piece," a "tour de force."
Difficult and vocally demanding.   With men's chorus in the score.
Acc: 3-4 (VS)GR

8016. Per lui che adoro
Opera: L'ITALIANA IN ALGERI.   Part of Isabella, Act II. c3-d4
e3-b♭4 Sustained in moderate slow tempo.   Florid, requires flexibility. Generally light. Acc: 3 (VS)GR

8017. Cruda sorte! amor tiranno!
Opera: L'ITALIANA IN ALGERI. Part of Isabella, Act I. b2-f4
d3-c4 Sustained in moderate tempo.   Majestic; has some florid passages.   Requires flexibility.   Strong ending.   Has short choral interpolation. Acc: 3-4 (VS)GR

8018. R: Eccomi alfine
A: Ah! quel giorno ognor
Opera: SEMIRAMIDE, 1823, libretto by Gaetano Rossi, after Voltaire's tragedy.   Part of Arsace, Act I. g2-g♯4 d♯3-e4 Extended
recitative and sustained aria in moderate slow tempo.   Very florid,
requires flexibility. Acc: 3-4 (VS)B-H, GR

8019. R: Bel raggio lusinghier
A: Dolce pensiero
Opera: SEMIRAMIDE.   Part of Semiramide, Act I.   c♯3-a4 g♯3-
f♯4 Sustained in moderate slow tempo.   Quite florid, requires flexi-
bility.   With choral background in the score.   Acc: 4 (VS)B-H, GR.
PDA.   (S)GR

8020. In sì barbara
Opera: SEMIRAMIDE.   Part of Arsace, Act II. g2-g4 c3-d4 Starts
animated in moderate tempo, then moves faster.   Florid, requires
flexibility and fluent enunciation.   Acc: 3-4 (VS)B-H, GR. OPA-2

8021. R: Dove son io
A: Ah che scordar non so
Opera: TANCREDI, 1813, libretto by Gaetano Rossi.   Part of Tancredi, Act II. b2-d4 e♭3-c4 Recitative and sustained aria in moderate slow tempo.   Has some florid figures.   Low ending.   Acc:
3-4 (VS)SR, GR

8022. R: O patria dolce
A: Di tanti palpiti e tanto pene

Opera: TANCREDI. Part of Tancredi, Act I. c♯3-g4 f♯3-e4 Extended recitative and sustained aria in moderate tempo. Has florid figures and passages. Requires some flexibility. Agitated accompaniment. Acc: 3-4 (VS)GR, SR

8023. Tu chei mi seri conforti
Opera: TANCREDI, Part of Isaura, Act II. g2-e♭4 e♭3-c4 Sustained in slightly slow tempo. Has slightly florid figures, and passages with low tessitura. Requires flexibility. Acc: 3-4 (VS)GR, SR

8024. R: Eccolo, a voi l'affido
A: Ciel pietoso, ciel clemente
Opera: ZELMIRA, 1822, libretto by Andrea Leone Tottola. Part of Emma, Act II. c3-b♭4 f3-e4 Slightly florid recitative and sustained aria in moderate slow tempo. Has florid passages. Climactic ending. Acc: 3-4 (VS)GS, MR. PDA

GIUSEPPE (FORTUNINO FRANCESCO) VERDI, 1813-1901

8025. Nei giardin del bello saracin ostello
Opera: DON CARLOS, 1867, libretto by François Joseph Méry and Camille du Locle, after Friedrich von Schiller. Part of Eboli, Act II. d♯3-a4 g♯3-e4 Animated in lively tempo. Florid and graceful. Has cadenza at the end of each verse or section. With women's chorus in the full score. Acc: 4 (VS)GR, CP. OAM. (S)GR

8026. O don fatale
Opera: DON CARLOS. Part of Eboli, Act IV. c♭3-c♭5 e♭3-a♭4 Sustained in moderate tempo. Faster, more agitated, dramatic last section. Requires fine PP. Climactic ending. Acc: 3-4 (VS)GR, CP. OPA-2, OAM. (S)GS, GR

8027. Condotta ell'era in ceppi
Opera: IL TROVATORE, 1853, libretto by Salvatore Cammarano, after Gutierrez's play. Part of Azucena, Act II. a2-b♭4 e3-e4 Sustained in moderate slow tempo, then faster and more agitated section. Has dramatic passages, and those marked with PPP over an agitated accompaniment. Subdued, low ending after climactic passage. Acc: 4 (VS)GS, GR. OPA-2, OAM. (S)GR

8028. Stride la vampa
Opera: IL TROVATORE. Part of Azucena, Act II. b2-g4 e3-e4 Common title: Azucena's narrative. Animated in moderate lively tempo. Has some short, florid figures. Requires flexibility. Rhythmic. Climactic ending. Acc: 3-4 (VS)GS, GR. OPA-2, OAM. (S)GR, GS

8029. Al suon del tamburo
Opera: LA FORZA DEL DESTINO, 1862, libretto by Francesco Maria Piave, after Duke of Rivas' play. Part of Preziosilla, Act II. b2-b4 f♯3-f♯4 Animated in lively tempo. Requires flexibility. Has dramatic climaxes and climactic high ending on b4. Generally a non-legato accompaniment. Acc: 3-4 (VS)GR, B-H (Italian & English), IM. OAM. (S)GR

8030. Venite all' indovina

Opera: LA FORZA DEL DESTINO. Part of Preziosilla, Act III.
d♯3-a4(c5) f♯3-e4 Animated in quite fast tempo. Requires flexibility and fluent enunciation. Outgoing, with many strong and brilliant
passages. Ends with climactic and florid passage. Has choral background. Part of the choral scena. Acc: 3-4 OAM. (VS)GR, B-H
(Italian & English), IM (Italian & English)

8031. È lui! Ne' palpiti come risento adesso
Opera: UN BALLO IN MASCHERA, 1859, libretto by Antonio Somma,
after Scribe's libretto. Part of Ulrica, Act I. g2-ab4 f♯3-g4 Sustained in moderate lively tempo. Starts in declamatory style, later
becoming dramatic. Has some very subdued passages with an ele-
ment of mystery. Low ending, very subdued. Acc: 4 (VS)GS, GR

8032. Re dell' abisso, affrettati
Opera: UN BALLO IN MASCHERA. Part of Ulrica, Act I. Common title: Invocation aria. g2-ab4 d3-g4 Sustained in moderate
slow tempo. Starts very subdued, then becomes dramatic after the
first half. Low, very subdued ending. Acc: 4   (VS)GS, GR.
(S)GR. OPA-2, OAM

B. French Composers

DANIEL FRANÇOIS ESPRIT AUBER, 1782-1871

8033. Voyez sur cette roche
Opera: FRA DIAVOLO or L'HOTELLERIE DE TERRCINE, 1830,
libretto by Eugène Scribe. Part of Zerlina, Act II. d3-g4 g3-d4
Animated in moderate lively tempo. Graceful. Has also the part of
the Marquis in the full score. Acc: 3-4 (VS)NO, BR

8034. La belle Inès fait florès
Opera: LE DOMINO NOIR, 1837, libretto by Eugène Scribe. Part
of Angèle, Act II. db3-ab4 f3-eb4 Common title: Aragonaise.
Animated in moderate tempo. Dancelike and graceful. Acc: 3-4
(VS)BR

HECTOR BERLIOZ, 1803-1869

8035. Autrefois un roi de Thulè
Opera: LA DAMNATION DE FAUST, 1846, libretto by the composer,
after Goethe's drama. A concert opera. Part of Marguerite, Act
IV. c3-f4 f3-d4 Gently animated vocal part in moderate tempo.
Generally light and graceful. Subdued, low ending. Acc: 3-4 (VS)
CT

8036. R: Ah! Je vais mourir
A: Adieu fière cité
Opera: LES TROYENS À CARTHAGE, second part of a two-part
opera, LES TROYENS, 1856-1859, libretto by the composer, based
on the story by Virgil. Part of Didon (Dido) Act V. Common title:
Didon's monologue. d3-f4 f3-eb4 In varied moods and tempi. Generally in recitative style. Solemn, requires fine P and PP. Last
part is sustained in slow tempo. Acc: 3-4 (VS)EC

8037. Errante sur les mers

Opera: LES TROYENS À CARTHAGE. Part of Didon, Act I. c3-f4
g3-d4 Sustained in moderate tempo. Descending, subdued ending.
Generally on MF level. Generally agitated accompaniment. Acc:
3-4 (VS)EC

8038. Il m'aime! non! son coeur
Opera: LES TROYENS À CARTHAGE. Part of Didon, Act IV. e3-
g4 a3-f4 Sustained in moderate slow tempo. Has climactic passages. Acc: 3-4 (VS)EC

GEORGES BIZET, 1838-1875

8039. R: Voyons, que j'essaie
A: En vain pour éviter
Opera: CARMEN, 1873-1874, libretto by Henri Meilhac and Ludovic
Halévy, based on Merimée's story. Part of Carmen, Act III. Com-
mon title: Card scene. b2-f4 c3-e♭4 Aria starts subdued and
builds to a dramatic and intense climax. Acc: 3-4 (VS)GS. OPA-2

8040. L'amour est un oiseau rebelle
Opera: CARMEN. Part of Carmen, Act I. Common title: Habanera. d3-f♯4 d3-d4 Animated in moderate tempo. Rhythmic,
with some climactic passages. Climactic ending. Choral background
in the score. The melody is by Sebastian Yradier. Acc: 3-4 (VS)
GS. OPA-2, (S)GS

8041. Près des remparts de Séville
Opera: CARMEN. Part of Carmen, Act I. Common title: Seguidilla. b2-f♯4(b4) d3-e4 Animated in moderate lively tempo. Graceful and rhythmic. Ends with "tra la la" passage. Has some climactic passages. Acc: 3-4 (VS)GS. OPA-2

8042. Nour-Eddim, roi de Lahore
Opera Comique: DJAMILEH, 1871, libretto by Louis Gallet. Part of
Djamileh, one-act opera. c3-g4 e3-e4 Animated vocal part in moderate slow tempo. Rhythmic and dance-like. Requires some flexibility. Acc: 3-4 (VS)EC

8043. Sans doute l'heure est prochaine
Opera Comique: DJAMILEH. Common title: Lamento. Part of
Djamileh, one-act opera. e3-f4 f♯3-d4 Sustained in slow tempo.
Requires fine P and PP. Subdued ending. Acc: 3-4 (VS)EC

ALFRED BRUNEAU, 1857-1934

8044. Françoise, ah! vous allez la voir
Opera: L'ATTAQUE DU MOULIN, 1893, libretto by Louis Gallet,
after Emile Zola. Part of Marcelline, Act I. c3-g4 g3-d4 Sustained in moderate tempo. Has climactic passages. Subdued ending.
Acc: 3-4 (VS)EC

(ACHILLE) CLAUDE DEBUSSY, 1862-1918

8045. Voici ce qu'il écrit à son frère Pelléas
Opera: PELLÉAS ET MELISANDE, 1892-1902, libretto by Maurice

Maeterlinck. Part of Genevieve, Act I. a2-d4 d3-a3 In gentle
recitative style throughout, in moderate tempo. Requires fine enunciation. Subdued. Acc: 2-3 (VS)AD, IM

BENJAMIN (LOUIS PAUL) GODARD, 1849-1895

8046. Viens avec nous petit
Opera: LA VIVANDIÈRE, 1895, libretto by Henri Cain. Part of
Marion, Act I. c3-f4 f3-d4 Animated in moderate tempo. March
rhythm. Acc: 3-4 (VS)EC

CHARLES (FRANÇOIS) GOUNOD, 1818-1893

8047. R: Par quel trouble profond
A: Nuit resplendissante
Opera: CINQ-MARS, 1876-1877, libretto by Louis Gallet and Paul
Poirson, after Alfred de Vigny's novel. Part of Marie, Act I. d#3-
g4 f#3-f#4 Secco recitative and sustained aria in slow tempo.
Tranquil, with very gently agitated accompaniment. Acc: 3-4 (VS)
LS

8048. Si le bonheur à sourire t'invite
Opera: FAUST, 1852-1859, libretto by Jules Barbier and Michel Carré, after Goethe. Part of Siebel, Act IV. Common title: Romance.
c#3-e4 f#3-e4 Gently animated in moderate slow tempo. Generally
gentle. Acc: 3-4 (VS)GS

8049. Faites-lui mes aveux
Opera: FAUST. Part of Siebel, Act III. d3-g4 e3-f4 Animated in
lively tempo. Graceful, with a climactic ending. Has recitative in
the middle. Acc: 3-4 (VS)GS. OPA-2. (S)GS

8050. Le jour se lève
Opera: MIREILLE, 1863, libretto by Michel Carré, after Frédéric
Mistral. Part of Andreloun, Act IV. d3-g4 g3-e4 Sustained in
moderate slow tempo. Generally gentle and subdued. Vocalized ending with sustained last note (g4) on P to PP. Acc: 3-4 (VS)EC

8051. Voici la saison mignonne
Opera: MIREILLE. Part of Taven, Act II. c3-e4 eb3-d4 Animated in moderate lively tempo. Graceful and generally light. Acc:
3-4 (VS)EC

8052. R: Depuis hier je cherche en vain mon maitre
A: Que fais-tu, blanche tourterelle
Opera: ROMÉO ET JULIETTE, 1864, libretto by Jules Barbier and
Michel Carré. Part of Stephano, Act III. f3-c5 f3-g4 Animated in
moderate tempo. Moderately light. Has two florid, descending pas-
sages. Climactic ending. Acc: 4 (VS)GS. OPA-2

8053. R: Où suis-je?
A: O ma lyre immortelle
Opera: SAPHO, 1850, libretto by Émile Augier. Part of Sapho, Act
III. c3-bb4 f3-f4 Sustained aria in moderate slow tempo. Slow,
climactic high ending with a sustained bb4. Arpeggiated accompani-
ment. Opera ends with this aria. Acc: 4 (VS)EC

(JACQUES FRANÇOIS) FROMENTAL (ÉLIAS) HALÉVY, 1799-1862

8054. R: Sous leur sceptre de fer
       A: Humble fille des champs
       Opera: CHARLES VI, 1843, libretto by Germain and Casimir Dela-
       vigne. Part of Edette, Act IV. b♭2(f♯2)-g♯4 e3-e4 Extended reci-
       tative and sustained aria in moderate slow tempo. Has climactic pas-
       sages. Climactic ending. Acc: 3-4 (VS)BR

8055. Le gondolier dans sa pauvre nacelle
       Opera: LE REINE DE CHYPRE, 1841, libretto by Vernoy de Saint-
       Georges. Part of Catarina, Act II. a♭2-a♭4 e♭3-e♭4 In varied
       tempi and moods. Has recitative sections. Dramatic ending section
       with agitated accompaniment. Climactic ending. Acc: 4 (VS)MR

(VICTOR ANTOINE) ÉDOUARD LALO, 1823-1892

8056. R: De tous côtes j'aperçois dans la plaine
       A: Lorsque je t'ai vu soudain
       Opera: LE ROI D'YS, 1888, libretto by Édouard Blau. Part of Mar-
       gared, Act II. e♭3-g4 g3-f4 Dramatic recitative and animated aria
       in fast tempo. Has some sustained vocal passages, dramatic pas-
       sages, and climactic ending. Acc: 3-4 (VS)HC

VICTOR (FÉLIX MARIE) MASSÉ, 1822-1884

8057. Sa couleur est blonde
       Opera: GALATHÉE, 1852, libretto by Jules Barbier and Michel Carré.
       Part of Galathee, Act II. c3-c5 f3-f4 Animated in moderate tempo.
       Rhythmic. Has florid passages. Requires fine high P. Climactic
       ending. Acc: 3-4 (VS)CR, LS

8058. Tristes amours!
       Opera: GALATHÉE. Part of Pygmalion, Act I. g2-e♭4 e♭3-c4
       Sustained in moderate tempo. Faster, animated ending section. Cli-
       mactic ending. This excerpt is sung by either bass or mezzo-soprano
       in their respective transposed editions. Acc: 3-4 (VS)CR, LS

JULES (ÉMILE FRÉDÉRIC) MASSENET, 1842-1912

8059. Dors, ami, dors et que les songes
       Opera: DON CÉSAR DE BAZAN, 1872, libretto by Adolphe Philippe
       d'Ennery and Jules Chantepie, after d'Ennery and Dumanoir. Part of
       Lazarille, Act II. Common title: Berceuse. b2-g♯4 e3-d♯4 Sus-
       tained in moderate slow tempo. Subdued and gentle. Slightly faster
       middle section. Very subdued ending. Acc: 3 (VS)GS, HC

8060. Hérode! Hérode! Ne me refuse pas!
       Opera: HÉRODIADE, 1881, libretto by Paul Milliet and Henri Gré-
       mont (Georges Hartmann), after a story by Flaubert. Part of Hérodi-
       ade, Act I. b♭2-a4 e♭3-f4 Sustained in moderate slow tempo.
       Starts gently then becomes dramatic and emphatic. Subdued ending.
       Acc: 3-4 (VS)HC, IM

8061. R: Vengemoi d'une suprême offense!
       A: J'allais ce matin au désert

Opera: HÉRODIADE. Part of Hérodiade, Act L. bb 2(a2)-a4 f3-f4
Generally sustained in generally moderate tempo. Has fast and agi-
tated sections. Dramatic. Subdued ending after dramatic climax.
Aria ends with "Rappeletoi!" Acc: 3-4 (VS)HC

8062.   R: Repose, ô belle amoureuse
        A: Ferme les yeux, ô belle maîtresse
        Opera: LE ROI DE LAHORE, 1877, libretto by Louis Gallet. Part
        of Kaled, Act II. A supplementary aria especially composed for Mlle.
        Fouquet and sung after No. 7. b2-a4(bb 4) f3-f4 Subdued recitative
        and sustained aria in moderate slow tempo. Faster middle section.
        Climactic ending. Acc: 3-4 (VS)HC

8063.   Oui, mon coeur étouffe mon coeur
        Opera: THÉRÈSE, 1907, libretto by Jules Claretie. Part of Thérèse,
        Act II. a2-g4 eb 3-eb 4 Sustained, generally in moderate lively tem-
        po. Generally strong, broad ending. Dramatic ending on sustained
        g4. Agitated accompaniment. Acc: 4 (VS)HC

8064.   Va! laisse couler mes larmes
        Opera: WERTHER, 1892, libretto by Edouard Blau, Paul Milliet and
        Georges Hartmann, after Goethe. Part of Charlotte, Act III. c3-f4
        e3-e4 Sustained in slow tempo. Has some dramatic passages as
        well as those requiring PP. Short. Subdued ending. Acc: 3-4
        OPA-2. (VS)HC, IM

8065.   Werther! Qui m'aurait dit la place que dans mon coeur
        Opera: WERTHER. Part of Charlotte, Act III. c3-g4 f3-e4 Com-
        mon title: Letter aria. Sustained in mainly moderate tempo. Has
        slower and faster sections. Has dramatic passages. Low and very
        subdued ending after climax. Acc: 3-4 (VS)HC, IM

FRANCIS POULENC, 1899-1963

8066.   Mes chères filles, j'ai encore
        Opera: DIALOGUES DES CARMÉLITES, 1957, libretto by Georges
        Bernanos, after Gertrude von le Fort. Part of the second Prioress,
        Act II. eb 3-bb 4 f3-f4 Sustained in moderate slow tempo. General-
        ly subdued. Requires fine P. Has dramatic passages. Subdued end-
        ing. Acc: 3-4 (VS)FC

(CHARLES) CAMILLE SAINT-SAËNS, 1835-1921

8067.   R: Samson recherchant ma présence
        A: Amour, viens aider
        Opera: SAMSON ET DALILA, 1877, libretto by Ferdinand Lemaire.
        Part of Dalila, Act II. ab 2-g4 eb 3-eb 4 Sustained in moderate tem-
        po. Has some dramatic passages. Low, subdued ending. Acc: 3
        (VS)GS. OPA-2. (S)GS

8068.   Mon coeur s'ouvre a ta voix
        Opera: SAMSON ET DALILA. Part of Dalila, Act II. bb 2-gb 4
        eb 3-eb 4 Sustained in moderate slow tempo. Slower middle section.
        Has some climactic passages. Subdued, agitated accompaniment in
        the middle section. Acc: 4 (VS)GS. OPA-2

8069.   Printemps qui commence

Opera: SAMSON ET DALILA.   Part of Dalila, Act II.   b2-e4   e3-e4
Sustained in moderate slow tempo.   Requires fine P.   Has some gentle recitative.   Subdued ending.   Acc: 3   (VS)GS.   OPA-2

(CHARLES LOUIS) AMBROISE THOMAS, 1811-1896

8070.   R: Toi, partir!   Non!   Il t'aime
A: Dans son regard plus sombre
Opera: HAMLET, 1868, libretto by Jules Barbier and Michel Carré,
after William Shakespeare.   Part of Queen Gertrude, Act II.   c3-ab4
f3-f4   Sustained aria in moderate slow tempo.   Requires fine P.
Has dramatic passages.   Climactic ending.   Acc: 4   (VS)HC

8071.   Connais-tu le pays
Opera: MIGNON, 1871, libretto by Jules Barbier and Michel Carré.
Part of Mignon, Act I.   c3-f4   eb3-eb4   Sustained in moderate tem-
po.   Requires fine P and PP.   Has some passages in recitative style.
Has dramatic passages.   Acc: 3-4   (VS)GS.   OPA-2

8072.   Je connais un pauvre enfant
Opera: MIGNON.   Part of Mignon, Act II.   Common title: Styrienne.
d3(c3)-b4(d5)   f♯3-g4   In varying tempo, starts moderately.   Sustained,
florid, and difficult.   Requires considerable flexibility.   Acc: 3-4
(VS)GS

8073.   R: C'est moi
A: Me voici dans son boudoir
Opera: MIGNON.   Part of Frederick, Act II.   bb2-f4   eb3-eb4
Common title: Rondo-Gavotte, arranged from the Entr'acte.   Ani-
mated aria with staccati passages.   An interpolation.   Acc: 3-4
(VS)GS.   OPA-2

C.   German and Austrian Composers

FRIEDRICH (FREIHERR) VON FLOTOW, 1812-1883

8074.   Jägerin, schlau im Sinn
Opera: MARTHA, 1847, libretto by W. Friedrich (Friedrich Wilhelm
Riese).   Part of Nancy, Act III.   c3-a4   e3-d4   Animated in lively
tempo.   2 verses.   See "Esse mesto il mio cor non sapria," for use
of this air in a more elaborate version.   Acc: 3   (VS)GS.   OAR-M

8075.   Esser mesto il mio cor
Opera: MARTHA.   Part of Nancy, Act III.   A supplementary air
written for Mme.   Nantier-Didiée and used in place of the original
"Jägerin, schlau im Sinn."   This is a more elaborate version, in
Italian text.   a♯2(g♯2)-b4   d3-f♯4   Animated in lively tempo.   Florid
third part, ending in a showy cadenza.   Acc: 3-4   (VS)GS

GIACOMO MEYERBEER, 1791-1864

8076.   Ah! mon fils, sois béni!
Opera: LE PROPHÈTE, 1849, libretto by Eugène Scribe.   Part of
Fidès, Act II.   b2-a♯4   f♯3-d♯4   Sustained in moderate slow tempo.
Animated middle section.   Ends with cadenza.   Acc: 3-4   (VS)BT,
BR.   OPA-2, OAR-M

8077. R: Il va venir!
       A: Comme un éclair précipité
       Opera: LE PROPHÈTE. Part of Fidès, Act V. a♭2-b♭4(c5) f3-f4
       Dramatic recitative and animated aria in moderate lively tempo.
       Florid, requires flexibility and fluent enunciation. Faster tempo in
       ending section. Ends with cadenza. Vocally demanding. Acc: 4
       (VS)BT, BR

8078. Donnez, donnez
       Opera: LE PROPHÈTE. Part of Fidès, Act IV. b2-g4 e3-e4 Gen-
       erally sustained vocal part in moderate tempo. Intense in some pas-
       sages. Sad text. Subdued ending. Acc: 3-4 (VS)BT, BR. OPA-
       2, OAR-M

8079. R: Qui je suis? Moi!
       A: Je suis, hélas! la pauvres
       Opera: LE PROPHÈTE. Part of Fidès, Act IV. a♭2(b♭2)-a♭4 g3-
       e♭4 Subdued recitative and sustained aria in moderate tempo. Has
       dramatic passages. Ends with descending cadenza. Acc: 3-4 (VS)
       BT, BR

8080. R: O pretres de Baal
       A: O toi qui m'abandonnes
       Opera: LE PROPHÈTE. Part of Fidès, Act V. a♭2-a♭4(b♭4) e♭3-
       d♭4 Sustained in moderate slow tempo. Slightly animated vocal part
       in the middle of the excerpt. Has optional cadenza at the end. Acc:
       3-4 (VS)BT, BR

8081. Non, non, vous n'avez jamais
       Opera: LES HUGUENOTS, 1836, libretto by Eugène Scribe and Emile
       Deschamps. Part of the Page, Act I. A supplementary aria written
       for Mlle. Alboni, and perhaps performed in place of the Cavatine in
       Act I. b2(f2)-g4(b♭4) e♭3-g4 Animated in moderate lively tempo.
       Requires fluent enunciation. Florid. Climactic ending with cadenza.
       With women's chorus in the full score. Acc: 4 (VS)BR

8082. Vanne, disse, al figlio mio
       Opera: ROBERTO IL DIAVOLO, 1831, libretto by Eugène Scribe.
       Part of Alice, Act I. e3(d♯3)-b4 g♯3-e4 Sustained in moderate
       slow tempo. Florid, requires flexibility. Requires fine P and PP.
       Has dramatic passages. Acc: 3-4 (VS)BR

WOLFGANG AMADEUS MOZART, 1756-1791

7AM   7 Arias for Mezzo-Soprano. Wolfgang Amadeus Mozart. Edited by
      Sergius Kagen. Original texts, with separate English translations.
      New York: International Music Co.

8083. Deh, per questo istante
       Opera: LA CLEMENZA DI TITO, 1791 (K. 621), libretto by Caterino
       Mazzolà, after Metastasio. Part of Sesto, Act II. c♯3-g♯4 e3-f♯4
       Sustained adagio and an animated allegro. Has some slightly florid
       figures. Climactic ending. Acc: 3-4 (VS)CP. MAO-3, OAR-M

8084. Deh, se piacer mi vuoi
       Opera: LA CLEMENZA DI TITO. Part of Vitellia, Act I. b2-b4
       d3-g4 First slow, then lively tempo. Sustained first part, and

animated second part. Has florid passages and a climactic ending.
Acc: 3-4 (VS)CP. MAO-3, OAR-S1

8085. R: Ecco il punto
A: Non più di fiori
Opera: LA CLEMENZA DI TITO. Part of Vitellia, Act II. a2(g2)-
a4 f3-f4 Dramatic recitative and sustained larghetto-allegro aria.
Requires some flexibility. Climactic ending. Acc: 3-4 (VS)CP.
OPA-2, OAR-S1

8086. Parto, parto
Opera: LA CLEMENZA DI TITO. Part of Sextus, Act I. c3-b♭4
f3-f4 Sustained vocal part in moderate slow tempo, followed by an
animated section. Has florid passages, and a climactic ending.
Acc: 3-4 (VS)CP. OPA-2, OAR-M

8087. Al desio di chi t'adora
Opera: LE NOZZE DI FIGARO, 1786 (K. 492). Libretto by Lorenzo
da Ponte, after Beaumarchais. Optional aria for the Countess. b2-
a4 e3-g4 Sustained, starts in slow tempo, then becomes lively and
agitated. Florid, requires flexibility. Climactic ending. Acc: 4
(VS)GS, GR. OPA-3

8088. Il capro e la capretta
Opera: LE NOZZE DI FIGARO. Part of Marcellina, Act IV. f♯3-
b4 g3-g4 This aria has too high a tessitura for mezzo-soprano; in
many performances the part is sung by a soprano. Animated: starts
in minuet tempo and the second half in allegro. Has some extended
florid passages; requires flexibility and fluent enunciation. Climactic
ending. Amusing text. Acc: 3-4 (VS)GS, GR

8089. Non so più cosa son, cosa faccio
Opera: LE NOZZE DI FIGARO. Part of Cherubino, Act I. e♭3-g4
g3-f4 Animated in rapid tempo. Requires some fluent enunciation.
Bright, somewhat gently outgoing. Has climactic passages. Generally on MF level. Acc: 3-4 (VS)GS, GR. CAO-S. (S)GR

8090. Voi, che sapete
Opera: LE NOZZE DI FIGARO. Part of Cherubino, Act II. c3-f4
f3-f4 Sustained in moderate tempo. Rhythmic. Requires simplicity
and a lyric approach. Acc: 3-4 (VS)GS, GR. OPA-2. (S)GR

JOHANN STRAUSS, 1825-1899

8091. Chacun à son goût
Opera: DIE FLEDERMAUS, 1874, libretto by Carl Haffner and Rich-
ard Genée, after Meilhac and Halévy's vaudeville. Part of Prince
Orlofsky, Act II. c3-a♭4 e♭3-e♭4 Animated in lively tempo. Re-
quires simplicity. 2 verses. French text edition. Acc: 3-4
OPA-2

RICHARD STRAUSS, 1864-1949

8092. Ein Tag bricht an
Opera: DIE FRAU OHNE SCHATTEN, 1914-1917, libretto by Hugo
von Hofmannsthal. Part of the Nurse (Amme), Act I. a♭2-a♭4

g3-g4 Animated in moderate lively tempo. Generally strong and dramatic. Climactic ending. In the duet with Kaiserin. Acc: 4
(VS)B-H

8093. Ja, du! Denn du bist klug
Opera: ELEKTRA, 1906-1908, libretto by Hugo von Hofmannsthal.
Part of Klytämnestra, one-act opera. a♯2-g4 c3-e4 A dramatic ex-
cerpt in varied moods and tempi. Generally in recitative style.
Has some high climaxes. Also requires a fine command of the low
range. Very subdued ending on "ich will nicht länger träumen."
Acc: 4 (VS)B-H

RICHARD WAGNER, 1813-1883

8094. Weiche Wotan! weiche!
Music Drama: DAS RHEINGOLD, 1853-1854, libretto by the com-
poser, in the Prologue of the festival drama, DER RING DES NIBE-
LUNGEN. Part of Erda, Scene 4. b♯2-e4 e3-e4 Sustained in slow
tempo. Generally subdued. Subdued high ending. Acc: 3 (VS)GS,
CP

8095. R: Jo-ho-hoe! Jo-ho-hoe!
A: Traft ihr das Schiff?
Opera: DER FLIEGENDE HOLLÄNDER, 1843, libretto by the composer. Part of Senta, Act II, No. 7. Other title: Ballad. b♭2-g4
f3-g4 In varied moods and tempi. Narrative, interpretatively difficult. Requires fine PP. Very subdued ending section. Senta's story
of the legend of The Flying Dutchman. Acc: 4 (VS)GS, CP. OGS,
OPA-1

8096. So ist es denn
Music Drama: DIE WALKÜRE, 1870, first day of the festival drama,
DER RING DES NIBELUNGEN, libretto by the composer. Part of
Fricka, Act II, Scene 1. c✕3-g♯4 e3-e4 Sustained in moderate live-
ly tempo. Dramatic and intense scena. Excerpt ends with the cli-
mactic "lass' auch zertreten." Acc: 4-5 (VS)GS, CP

8097. Wo in Bergen du dich birgst
Music Drama: DIE WALKÜRE. Part of Fricka, Act II, Scene 1.
c3-g♯4 e3-e4 A dramatic scena in moving, agitated tempo. Re-
quires fluent enunciation. Strong, with climactic ending. Cutting out
Wotan's part, the excerpt continues through "So ist es denn aus mit."
Acc: 4 (VS)GS, CP. OPA-2

8098. Höre mit Sinn
Music Drama: GÖTTERDÄMMERUNG, third day of the festival drama,
DER RING DES NIBELUNGEN, 1874, libretto by the composer. Part
of Waltraute, Act I, Scene 3. g2-g4 c3-e4 Sustained in varied
tempi and moods. Generally subdued, and in recitative style. A
dramatic narrative. Acc: 4 (VS)GS, CP. OPA-2

8099. Entweihte Götter!
Opera: LOHENGRIN, 1850, libretto by the composer. Part of Ortrud, Act II, Scene 2. f♯3-a♯4 g♯3-f♯4 Common title: Ortrud's
curse. Sustained vocal part in fast tempo. Dramatic, climactic,
and strong throughout. Acc: 3-4 (VS)GS, CP. OPA-2

8100.   Ich sah das Kind
        Music Drama: PARSIFAL, 1882, libretto by the composer.   Part of
        Kundry, Act II.   Common title: Kundry's Erzählung.   c3-a♯4   e3-
        f♯4   Sustained in very moderate tempo.   Generally gentle and subdued.
        Has some dramatic passages.   Subdued ending.   Acc: 4   (VS)GS,
        CP.   OGS

8101.   R: Gerechter Gott!   So ist's entschieden schon!
        A: In seiner Blüthe bleicht mein Leben
        Opera: RIENZI, DER LETZTE DER TRIBUNEN, 1842, libretto by
        the composer, after Mary Mitford's drama.   Part of Adriano, Act III.
        c♯3-a4   a3-g4   A dramatic scena and an andante-allegro-vivace air.
        Has florid passages and dramatic passages.   Uses many high notes.
        Climactic ending.   Extended instrumental postlude.   Acc: 4   (VS)SC.
        OPA-2

8102.   Geliebter, komm'!   Sieh' dort die Grotte
        Opera: TANNHÄUSER UND DER SÄNGERKRIEG AUF DER WART-
        BURG, 1845, libretto by the composer.   Part of Venus, Act I, Scene
        2.   f♯3-a4   g♯3-f♯4   Sustained in moderate tempo.   Requires fine P.
        Gentle, tranquil throughout.   Acc: 4-5   (VS)GS, CP

8103.   Einsam wachend in der Nacht
        Opera: TRISTAN UND ISOLDE, 1865, libretto by the composer.
        Part of Brangäna, Act II, Scene 2.   f♯3-f♯4   a3-e4   Sustained in
        moderate slow tempo.   Requires fine P.   Tranquil, with gently agi-
        tated accompaniment.   Acc: 4-5   (VS)GS, CP

CARL MARIA VON WEBER, 1786-1826

8104.   Bethörte!   die an meine Liebe glaubt
        Opera: EURYANTHE, 1823, libretto by Wilhelmine Helmine von Chézy.
        Part of Eglantine, Act I.   a♯2-c5   g♯3-g♯4   Generally in fast tempo.
        Has dramatic passages, florid passages, and a climactic ending.   Re-
        quires flexibility.   Acc: 4   (VS)NO, CP.   OAR-M

8105.   R: So bin ich nun verlassen
        A: Hier dicht am Quell
        Opera: EURYANTHE.   Part of Euryanthe, Act III.   c3-f♯4   g3-e4
        Slow recitative and gently animated aria in slow tempo.   Generally
        subdued.   Acc: 3   (VS)NO, CP

8106.   Arabien, mein Heimatland
        Opera: OBERON, 1826, libretto by James Robinson Planché, after
        Wieland's story.   Part of Fatime, Act III.   a3-e♭4   f♯3-d4   Sustained
        first half, and animated, lively and dance-like second half.   Acc:
        3-4   (VS)CP.   OAR-M

8107.   Arabiens einsam Kind
        Opera: OBERON.   Part of Fatime, Act II.   d♯3-e4   f♯3-d♯4   Gently
        animated vocal part in moderate tempo.   Requires some flexibility.
        Acc: 3-4   (VS)CP.   OAR-M

8108.   Traure, mein Herz
        Opera: OBERON, Part of Reiza, Act III.   b2-f4   f3-d♭4   Sustained
        in moderate slow tempo.   Lyric, and generally on MF level.   Sub-
        dued ending.   Originally for soprano.   Acc: 3-4   (VS)CP

D. American Composers

SAMUEL BARBER

MSB   Music for Soprano and Orchestra. High, low. Samuel Barber. Re-
      duction for piano. New York: G. Schirmer, Inc.

8109. Do not utter a word
       Opera: VANESSA, 1958, libretto by Gian-Carlo Menotti. Part of
       Vanessa, Act I.   d3-bb♭4   f♯3-f4   First part is sustained in moder-
       ate tempo; second part is animated in fast tempo with agitated accom-
       paniment. Has dramatic high passages. Second part is rather in-
       tense. Dramatic high ending. Acc: 3-4 (VS)GS. MSB. (S)GS

8110. Must the winter come so soon
       Opera: VANESSA. Part of Erika, Act I.   e♭3-f4 g3-e♭4 Sustained
       in moderate slow tempo. Tranquil, and generally subdued. Requires
       fine P. Acc: 3 (VS)GS. MSB. (S)GS

8111. Under the willow tree
       Opera: VANESSA. Part of Vanessa, Act I. b2-a4 e3-e4 Sustained
       in graceful waltz tempo. Requires some flexibility. Cadenza at the
       end, marked from F to PP on a4. (S) is an arrangement from the
       full score, the melody being a part of the ensemble. Acc: 3-4 (VS)
       GS. MSB, 20C. (S)GS

JACK BEESON

8112. In the garden the flowers wither and die
       Opera: LIZZIE BORDEN, 1965, libretto by Kenward Elmslie, after
       a scenario by Richard Plant. Part of Margret, Act I. d3-a4 f♯3-
       f♯4 Title on sheet music: Margret's garden aria. Words of this
       aria are by the composer. Gently animated vocal part in varied tem-
       pi. Has climactic passages. Requires fine high P. Very subdued
       high ending. Acc: 4 (VS)B-H, (S)B-H

AARON COPLAND

8113. But ends don't end
       Opera: THE TENDER LAND, 1954, libretto by Horace Everett. Part
       of Ma Moss, Act III. d♭3-g♭4 g3-e♭4 Sustained in slow tempo.
       Generally strong and climactic. Subdued ending. The last song in
       the opera. Acc: 3-4 (VS)B-H

CARLISLE FLOYD

8114. Take off that frown and lift your brows
       Opera: WUTHERING HEIGHTS, 1958, libretto by the composer, after
       Emily Brontë. Part of Nelly, Act I. c♭3-g4 d3-e4 Sustained in
       moderate slow tempo. Has some climactic passages. Acc: 3 (VS)
       B-H

GIAN-CARLO MENOTTI

Italian by birth.   American opera.

8115.   All that gold!
        Opera: AMAHL AND THE NIGHT VISITORS, 1951, libretto by the
        composer. Part of the Mother, one-act opera. bb2-g4 eb3-f4
        Sustained in moderate slow tempo. Starts gently and subdued. Has
        climactic passages. Ends in very subdued, parlando style. Acc: 3
        (VS)GS

8116.   I shall find for you shells and stars
        Opera: THE CONSUL, 1950, libretto by the composer. Part of the
        Mother, Act II. Common title: Lullaby. f2(a2)-eb4 c3-db4 Sus-
        tained in moderate slow tempo. Subdued and gentle. Low, subdued
        ending. Acc: 3-4 (VS)GS

8117.   I'm not crying for him
        Opera: THE CONSUL. Part of the Mother, Act II. a2-f#4 d3-d4
        Sustained in slow tempo. Generally subdued. Has climactic crescen-
        do toward the end. Has intense passages. Acc: 3-4 (VS)GS

8118.   Shall we ever see the end of all this
        Opera: THE CONSUL. Part of the Mother, Act I. b2-f4 e3-c4
        Sustained in slow tempo. Has dramatic climax in the middle of the
        aria. Subdued ending. Acc: 3-4 (VS)GS

8119.   The black swan
        Opera: THE MEDIUM, 1946, libretto by the composer. Part of
        Monica, one-act opera. d3-g4 f3-eb4 Sustained in a moving alle-
        gretto. Requires simplicity. Generally on MF level. Ends on g4.
        Acc: 3-4 (VS)GS. 20C

DOUGLAS MOORE, 1893-1969

8120.   Now may there be a blessing
        Opera: THE DEVIL AND DANIEL WEBSTER, 1939, libretto by the
        composer, after Stephen Vincent Benét. Part of Mary, one-act folk
        opera. c2-f4 f3-d4 Sustained in moderate tempo. Generally in
        gentle recitative style. Generally subdued. Ends with the word
        "Amen. " Text is a paraphrase of Biblical passage. Acc: 2-3 (VS)
        B-H

8121.   To write this letter is my painful duty
        Opera: THE WINGS OF THE DOVE, libretto by Ethan Ayer after
        Henry James. Part of Kate, one-act opera. c#3-g#4 f#3-e4 Rec-
        itative style in different tempi and moods. Interpretatively not easy.
        Subdued ending. Acc: 3-4 (VS)GS

KURT WEILL, 1900-1950

German by birth.   American opera.

8122.   Somehow I never could believe
        Opera: STREET SCENE, 1947, libretto by Langston Hughes and El-
        mer Rice. Part of Anna Maurrant, Act I. d3-a4 f3-f4 Sustained

in moderate slow tempo. Has dramatic and forceful passages. Requires fine P. Has slight variations in tempo. Climactic high ending. Interpretatively not easy. Acc: 3-4 (VS)CC

E. British Composers

BENJAMIN BRITTEN

8123. One lifetime, one brain
Opera: ALBERT HERRING, 1947, libretto by Eric Crozier, after Guy de Maupassant. Part of Florence, Act I. b2-e4 e3-e4 Sustained vocal part in fast tempo. Dramatic and accented. Climactic ending. Acc: 4 (VS)B-H

8124. Thus when the swallow
Opera: THE BEGGAR'S OPERA, 1948, libretto by John Gay, adapted by Tyrone Guthrie. Part of Polly, Act II. c3-c4 eb3-bb3 Sustained in moderate slow tempo. Requires simplicity. Short. A new setting of the original air. Acc: 3 (VS)B-H

8125. Flowers bring to every year
Opera: THE RAPE OF LUCRETIA, 1946, libretto by Ronald Duncan, after André Obey's play. Part of Lucretia, Act II. Common title: Flower song. a2-e4 f3-d4 Sustained in slow tempo. Requires very fine P and PP. Gentle. Acc: 3 (VS)B-H

8126. She sleeps as a rose
Opera: THE RAPE OF LUCRETIA. Part of the Female Chorus of one voice, Act II. a2-f#4 e3-e4 Very sustained in moderate tempo. Very subdued and gentle. Requires fine PP. Acc: 3 (VS)B-H

ARTHUR GORING THOMAS, 1850-1892

8127. R: Was schreibt er mir?
A: Schwer liegt auf dem Herzen
Opera: NADESHA, 1885, libretto by Julian R. Sturgis. Original in English; German version is the one performed many times. g#2-ab4 db3-db4 Starts gently, then gradually increases intensity. Strong and dramatic ending section. Generally agitated accompaniment. Acc: 3-4 MLF

RALPH VAUGHAN WILLIAMS, 1872-1958

8128. Here on my throne
Opera: HUGH THE DROVER or LOVE IN THE STOCKS, 1924, libretto by Harold Child. Part of Mary, Act II. e3-g4 a3-e4 Sustained in slow tempo. Generally lyric. Acc: 3-4 (VS)JC

8129. Life must be full of care
Opera: HUGH THE DROVER or LOVE IN THE STOCKS. Part of Aunt Jane, Act I. c3-d4 f3-c4 Sustained in moderate slow tempo. Subdued ending. Short. Acc: 3-4 (VS)JC

F. Russian Composers

ALEXANDER PORFIREVICH BORODIN, 1833-1887

8130. Tageslicht erlischt
       Opera: PRINCE IGOR, 1869-1887, unfinished, completed by Rimsky-
       Korsakof and Glasunof, libretto by Vladimir V. Stassof. Part of
       Kontschakovna, Act II. ab 2-f4 f3-eb 4 Sustained in slow tempo.
       Has florid passages, and requires some flexibility. Subdued, low
       ending: ab 2 and bb 2. Acc: 4 (VS)MB, (S)MB

MODEST PETROVICH MUSSORGSKY, 1839-1881

8131. Ah, poor Marina!
       Opera: BORIS GODUNOV, 1868-1872, libretto by the composer,
       adapted from Pushkin's play and Karamsin's history of Russia. Part
       of Marina, Act III. b2(a2)-f# 4(g# 4) e3-e4 In varied tempi, but
       mostly animated and in mazurka style. Has some slower sections.
       Ends with laughter (pitched and unpitched). Acc: 3-4 (VS)WB, EK.
       OPA-2

8132. Once I had a duck
       Opera: BORIS GODUNOV. Part of the Hostess, Act I. c# 3-e4 f3-
       d4 Gently animated vocal part in moderate slow tempo. Strong end-
       ing. Simple melody in the folk style. Acc: 3-4 (VS)WB, EK

8133. Our little parrot Popinka
       Opera: BORIS GODUNOV. Part of Feodor, Act II. Common title:
       The parrot song. c3-eb 4 e3-c4 Animated in moderate slow tempo.
       Requires some fluent enunciation. Narrative text. Acc: 3 (VS)WB,
       EK. MRS-2

8134. Midge to woodland once did go
       Opera: BORIS GODUNOV. Part of the Nurse, Act II. Common title:
       The song of the midge and the flea. bb 2-f4 f3-c4 Animated in live-
       ly tempo. Requires fluent enunciation. Narrative and humorous.
       Acc: 3-4 (VS)WB, EK

8135. Ah, recall our first hour of radiant love
       Opera: KHOVANSCHINA, 1872-1880, unfinished, libretto by the com-
       poser, after Vladimir V. Stassof. Part of Martha, Act V. g2-ab 4
       eb 3-eb 4 Generally sustained in several slow tempi. Starts slowly.
       Requires very fine high P and PP. Generally in recitative style.
       Ends with low tessitura. Acc: 3-4 (VS)WB

8136. In her youth went the maiden forth
       Opera: KHOVANSCHINA. Part of Martha (Marfa), Act III. d3-f4
       f3-d4 Sustained in moderate slow tempo. Requires sensitive narra-
       tion. English version in MRS is by Constance Purdy. Acc: 3-4
       MRS-2. (VS)WB

NIKOLAI ANDREYEVICH RIMSKY-KORSAKOV, 1844-1908

8137. Byelo, baby, hush my little fawn
       Opera: PSKOVITYANKA (The Maid of Pskov), 1892, libretto by the
       composer, after L. A. Mey's play. A cradle song. eb 3-f4 f3-f4

Sustained in moderate tempo. Subdued throughout. Requires fine P
and PP. Tranquil. English translation by Robert H. Hamilton.
Acc: 3 MRS-2

IGOR FEODOROVICH STRAVINSKY, 1882-1971

8138. As I was saying
Opera: THE RAKE'S PROGRESS, 1951, libretto by W(ystan) H(ugh)
Auden and Chester Kallman, after Hogarth. Part of Baba, Act II.
c3-d4 d3-bb3 Animated vocal part in moderate slow tempo. Re-
quires fluent enunciation. A "diction" song. Agitated accompaniment.
Acc: 4 (VS)B-H

8139. Scorned! Abused!
Opera: THE RAKE'S PROGRESS. Part of Baba, Act II. a2-a4 d3-
eb4 Animated in moderate lively tempo. Has wide intervalic skips
and dramatic passages. Has florid passages; requires flexibility.
Acc: 3-4 (VS)B-H

PETER (PIOTR) ILYICH TCHAIKOVSKY, 1840-1893

8140. Though I should die for it
Opera: EUGENE ONÉGIN, 1877-1878, libretto by the composer and
Konstantin S. Shilovsky, after Pushkin. Part of Tatiana, Act I.
Common title: Tatiana's letter scene. db2-bb4 f3-f4 In varied
moods and tempi. Starts animated in fairly lively tempo. An ex-
tended, dramatic scena. Has some extended instrumental interludes.
Climactic ending. Best for the heavier voices. Acc: 4 OPA-1

8141. R: Oui, Dieu le vent!
A: Adieu, forêts
Opera: JEANNE D'ARC, 1878-1882, libretto by the composer, after
Schiller. Part of Joan, Act I. db3-a4 g3-f4 A dramatic recitative
and sustained aria in varied moods and tempi. Requires fine P.
Climactic ending. Acc: 3-4 ORS, OPA-2, MLF

8142. Ah! now I know!
Opera: PIQUE DAME (THE QUEEN OF SPADES), 1890, libretto by
Modest Ilyich Tchaikovsky (composer's brother) and the composer,
after Pushkin. Part of Pauline, Act I. a2-ab4 eb3-eb4 Sustained
vocal part in moderate tempo. Has dramatic climaxes. Low, subdued ending. Chordal, detached accompaniment. Acc: 3-4 (VS)GS.
OPA-2

5. CONTRALTO

See the Bibliography at the beginning of the Mezzo-Soprano Section.

<u>A. Italian Composers</u>

VINCENZO BELLINI, 1801-1835

8143. Ascolta: se Romeo t'uccise un figlio
Opera: I CAPULETTI ED I MONTECCHI, 1830, libretto by Felice
Romani, based on Shakespeare's Romeo and Juliet. Part of Romeo,
Act I. Originally for mezzo-soprano or high contralto. g2-g4 g3-
f♯4 Sustained in slow tempo. Graceful, has florid figures. Acc:
3-4 (VS)B-H, GR

8144. R: Sgombra è la sacre selva
A: Deh! proteggimi, o Dio!
Opera: NORMA, 1831, libretto by Felice Romani. Part of Adalgisa,
Act I. b♭2-g♭4 e♭3-e♭4 Extended recitative and sustained short
aria in slow tempo. Slightly florid, requires flexibility. Generally
subdued. Acc: 3-4 (VS)GS, GR

ARRIGO BOITO, 1842-1918

8145. Fanuèl.... morirò?
Opera: NERONE, 1916, libretto by the composer. Part of Rubria,
Act IV. c3-e♭4 e3-c4 Sustained in slow tempo. In gentle recita-
tive style, with frequent repeated notes. Subdued ending. Acc: 3-4
(VS)GR

8146. Padre nostro che sai ne' cieli
Opera: NERONE. Part of Rubria, Act I. c3-a♭4 c3-e♭4 Sustained in moderate slow tempo. Most passages are in recitative
monotone. Acc: 3-4 (VS)GR

GAETANO DONIZETTI, 1797-1848

8147. R: È sgombro il loco
A: Ah! parea che per incanto
Opera: ANNA BOLENA, 1830, libretto by Felice Romani. Part of
Smeton, Act I. a♭2-g4 d♭3-e♭4 Recitative in varied moods and a
sustained aria in moderate tempo. Florid, requires considerable
flexibility. Acc: 3-4 (VS)GR

8148. Deh! non voler costringere
Opera: ANNA BOLENA. Part of Smeton, Act I. g2-g4 b♭2-e♭4
Sustained in moderate slow tempo. Has florid passages. Requires
flexibility. Acc: 3-4 (VS)GR

8149. R: Ove celare, oh Dio!
A: Terra adorata de' padri miei

Opera: DON SEBASTIANO, 1843, libretto by Eugène Scribe. Original in French. Part of Zaida, Act II. b2-g4 e3-e4 Sustained in
moderate slow tempo. Requires some flexibility. Descending ending
line. Acc: 3-4 (VS)GR, EO. (S)GR

8150. R: Fia dunque vero....
       A: O mio Fernando!
       Opera: LA FAVORITA, 1840, libretto by Alphonse Royer, Gustave
       Vaëz, and Eugène Scribe. Part of Leonora, Act III. b2(a2)-g# 4
       e3-f4 Dramatic recitative. Aria starts gently and sustained, then
       becomes dramatic. Acc: 3-4 (VS)GR. OPA-2. (S)GR

8151. Cari luoghi ov'io passai
       Opera: LINDA DI CHAMOUNIX, 1842, libretto by Gaetano Rossi.
       Part of Pierotto, Act I. c3-f4 d3-c4 Sustained in moderate tempo.
       Graceful. Acc: 3-4 (VS)GR

8152. Il segreto per esser felice
       Opera: LUCREZIA BORGIA, 1833, libretto by Felice Romani, based
       on Victor Hugo's play. Part of Orsini, Act II. c3-f4 e3-d4 Ani-
       mated in lively tempo. Requires some flexibility. 2 verses with
       choral section between. Acc: 3-4 (VS)B-H

8153. Per non istare in ozio
       Opera: MARIA DI ROHAN, 1843, libretto by Salvatore Cammarano.
       Part of Gondi, Act I. g2-g4 e3-c4 Sustained in moderate tempo.
       Has dramatic climaxes and a climactic ending. Acc: 3-4 (VS)GR

UMBERTO GIORDANO, 1867-1948

8154. Temer? Perchè?
       Opera: ANDREA CHÉNIER, 1896, libretto by Luigi Illica. Part of
       Bersi, Act II. f3-g4 f3-f4 Starts in recitative style. Animated in
       lively tempo. Dramatic; has climactic high ending. Acc: 4 (VS)
       CS, IM

AMILCARE PONCHIELLI, 1834-1886

8155. Voce di donna
       Opera: LA GIOCONDA, 1876, libretto by Arrigo Boito. Part of La
       Cieca, Act I. bb 2-g4 eb 3-eb 4 Sustained in moderate slow tempo.
       Lyric, and generally subdued. Acc: 3-4 OPA-2. (VS)GR, GS.
       (S)GR, GS

GIOACCHINO (ANTONIO) ROSSINI, 1792-1868

8156. R: Che vecchio sospettoso!
       A: Il vecchiotto cerca moglie
       Opera: IL BARBIERE DI SIVIGLIA, 1816, libretto by Cesare Sterbini,
       after Beaumarchais' comedy. Part of Bertha, Act II. c# 3-a4 e3-
       f# 4 Animated in lively tempo. Slightly faster ending section. Re-
       quires fluent enunciation. Climactic ending. Acc: 3-4 (VS)GS.
       (S)GR

8157. Non più mesta

Opera: LA CENERENTOLA, 1817, libretto by Jacopo Ferretti, after Perrault. Part of Cenerentola (Cinderella), Act I. g♯2-b4 c♯3-a4 Common title: Cavatina. Animated vocal part in moderate slow tempo. Very florid, has high tessitura in some passages, and a wide range. Vocally demanding. Requires considerable flexibility. Difficult. A coloratura-mezzo aria. Acc: 3-4 (VS)MR. OPA-2

8158. Una volta c'era un re
Opera: LA CENERENTOLA. Part of Cenerentola, Act II. c3-d4 e3-c4 Sustained in moderate slow tempo. Generally on MF level. Generally simple and short. Has short, florid figures. Acc: 3-4 (VS)FC, MR

8159. R: Amici, in ogni evento
A: Pensa alla patria
Opera: L'ITALIANA IN ALGERI, 1813, libretto by Angelo Anelli. Part of Isabella, Act II. a2-b4 e3-d♯4 Extended recitative and sustained aria in moderate slow tempo. Very florid excerpt, requires considerable flexibility. An operatic "show piece" or "tour de force." Difficult and vocally demanding. With men's chorus in the full score. Acc: 3-4 (VS)GR

8160. Per lui che adoro
Opera: L'ITALIANA IN ALGERI. Part of Isabella, Act II. c3-d4 e3-b♭4 Sustained in moderate slow tempo. Florid, and requires flexibility. Generally light. Acc: 3-4 (VS)GR

8161. Cruda sorte! amor tiranno!
Opera: L'ITALIANA IN ALGERI. Part of Isabella, Act I. b2-f4 d3-c4 Sustained in moderate tempo. Majestic; has some florid passages. Requires flexibility. Strong ending. Has short choral interpolation. Acc: 3-4 (VS)GR

8162. R: Eccomi alfine
A: Ah! quel giorno ognor
Opera: SEMIRAMIDE, 1823, libretto by Gaetano Rossi, after Voltaire's tragedy. Part of Arsace, Act I. g2-g♯4 d♯3-e4 Extended recitative and sustained aria in moderate slow tempo. Very florid, requires flexibility. Acc: 3-4 (VS)B-H, GR

8163. In sì barbara
Opera: SEMIRAMIDE. Part of Arsace, Act II. g2-g4 c3-d4 Starts animated in moderate tempo, then moves faster. Florid, requires flexibility and fluent enunciation. Acc: 3-4 (VS)B-H. OPA-2

8164. R: Dove son io
A: Ah che scordar non so
Opera: TANCREDI, 1813, libretto by Gaetano Rossi. Part of Tancredi, Act II. b2-d4 e♭3-c4 Recitative and sustained aria in moderate slow tempo. Has some florid figures. Low ending. Acc: 3-4 (VS)SR, GR

8165. R: O patria dolce
A: Di tanti palpiti e tanto pene
Opera: TANCREDI. Part of Tancredi, Act I. c♯3-g4 f♯3-e4 Extended recitative and sustained aria in moderate tempo. Has florid figures and passages. Requires some flexibility. Agitated accompaniment. Acc: 3-4 (VS)GS, SR

8166. Tu chei mi seri conforti
       Opera: TANCREDI. Part of Isaura, Act II. g2-e♭4 e♭3-c4 Sus-
       tained in slightly slow tempo. Has slightly florid figures, and pas-
       sages with low tessitura. Requires flexibility. Acc: 3-4 (VS)GR,
       SR

GIUSEPPE (FORTUNINO FRANCESCO) VERDI, 1813-1901

8167. Condotta ell'era in ceppi
       Opera: IL TROVATORE, 1853, libretto by Salvatore Cammarano,
       after Antonio Gutierrez's play. Part of Azucena, Act II. a2-b♭4
       e3-e4 Sustained in moderate slow tempo, then faster agitated section.
       Has dramatic passages, also those marked with PPP over agitated
       accompaniment. Subdued, low ending after climactic passage. Acc:
       4 (VS)GS, GR. (S)GR. OPA-2, OAM

8168. Stride la vampa
       Opera: IL TROVATORE. Part of Azucena, Act II. b2-g4 e3-e4
       Common title: Azucena's narrative. Animated in moderate lively
       tempo. Has some short, florid figures. Requires flexibility. Cli-
       mactic ending. Acc: 3-4 (VS)GS, GR. OPA-2, OAM. (S)GR, GS

8169. È lui! Ne' palpiti come risento adesso
       Opera: UN BALLO IN MASCHERA, 1859, libretto by Antonio Somma,
       after Scribe's libretto. Part of Ulrica, Act I. g2-a♭4 f♯3-g4 Sus-
       tained in moderate lively tempo. Starts in declamatory style, later
       becoming dramatic. Has some very subdued passages with an ele-
       ment of mystery. Low ending, very subdued. Acc: 4 (VS)GS, GR

8170. Re dell' abisso affrettati
       Opera: UN BALLO IN MASCHERA. Common title: Invocation aria.
       Part of Ulrica, Act I. g2-a♭4 d3-g4 Sustained in moderate slow
       tempo. Starts very subdued, then becomes dramatic after the first
       half. Low, very subdued ending. Acc: 3-4 (VS)GS, GR. OPA-2,
       OAM. (S)GR

B. French Composers

HECTOR BERLIOZ, 1803-1869

8171. R: Ah! Je vais mourir
       A: Adieu fière cité
       Opera: LES TROYENS À CARTHAGE, second part of the two-part
       opera, LES TROYENS, 1856-1859, libretto by the composer, based on
       the story of Virgil. Part of Didon (Dido), Act V. Common title:
       Didon's monologue. d3-f4 f3-e♭4 In varied moods and tempi. Gen-
       erally in recitative style. Solemn, requires fine P and PP. Last
       part is sustained in slow tempo. Acc: 3-4 (VS)EC

8172. Errante sur les mers
       Opera: LES TROYENS À CARTHAGE. Part of Didon, Act I. c3-f4
       g3-d4 Sustained in moderate tempo. Descending and subdued ending.
       Generally on MF level, with generally agitated accompaniment. Acc:
       3-4 (VS)EC. OPA-2

GEORGES BIZET, 1838-1875

8173. R: Voyons, que j'essaie
       A: En vain pour éviter
       Opera: CARMEN, 1873-1874, libretto by Henri Meilhac and Ludovic
       Halévy, based on Mérimée's story. Part of Carmen, Act III. Com-
       mon title: Card scene. b2-f4 c3-eb4 Aria starts subdued and
       builds to a dramatic, intense, and heavier climax. Acc: 3-4 (VS)
       GS. OPA-2

8174. L'amour est un oiseau rebelle
       Opera: CARMEN. Part of Carmen, Act I. Common title: Habanera.
       d3-f#4 d3-d4 Animated in moderate tempo. Rhythmic, with some
       climactic passages. Climactic ending. Choral background in the
       score. The melody is by Sebastian Yradier. Acc: 3-4 (VS)GS.
       OPA-2. (S)GS

8175. Près des remparts de Séville
       Opera: CARMEN. Part of Carmen, Act I. Common title: Segui-
       dilla. b2-f#4(b4) d3-e4 Animated in moderate lively tempo. Grace-
       ful and rhythmic. Ends with "tra la la" passages. Has some climac-
       tic passages. Acc: 3-4 (VS)GS. OPA-2

8176. Nour-Eddim, roi de Lahore
       Opera: DJAMILEH, 1871, libretto by Louis Gallet. Part of Djamileh,
       one-act opera. c3-g4 e3-e4 Animated vocal part in moderate slow
       tempo. Rhythmic and dance-like. Requires some flexibility. Acc:
       3-4 (VS)EC

(ACHILLE) CLAUDE DEBUSSY, 1862-1918

8177. Voici ce qu'il écrit a son frere Pelleas
       Opera: PELLÉAS ET MÉLISANDE, 1892-1902, libretto by Maurice
       Maeterlinck. Part of Geneviève, Act I. a2-d4 d3-a3 In gentle rec-
       itative style throughout, in moderate tempo. Requires fine enuncia-
       tion. Subdued. Acc: 3 (VS)AD, IM

BENJAMIN (LOUIS PAUL) GODARD, 1849-1895

8178. Viens avec nous petit
       Opera: LA VIVANDIÈRE, 1895, libretto by Henri Cain. Part of
       Marion, Act I. c3-f4 f3-d4 Animated in moderate tempo. March
       rhythm. Acc: 3-4 (VS)EC

CHARLES (FRANÇOIS) GOUNOD, 1818-1893

8179. R: Par quel trouble profond
       A: Nuit resplendissante
       Opera: CINQ-MARS, 1876-1877, libretto by Louis Gallet and Paul
       Poirson, after Alfred de Vigny's novel. Part of Marie, Act I. d#3-
       g4 f#3-f#4 Secco recitative and sustained aria in slow tempo.
       Tranquil, with very gently agitated accompaniment. Acc: 3-4 (VS)
       LS

8180. Si le bonheur à sourire t'invite

Opera: FAUST, 1852-1859, Act IV. Libretto by Jules Barbier and Michel Carré. Common title: Romance. c#3-e4 f#3-e4 Gently animated in moderate slow tempo. Generally gentle. Acc: 3-4 (VS)GS

8181. Voici la saison mignonne
Opera: MIREILLE, 1863, libretto by Michel Carré. Part of Taven, Act II. c3-e4 eb3-d4 Animated in moderate lively tempo. Graceful and generally light. Acc: 3-4 (VS)EC

8182. R: Où suis-je?
A: O ma lyre immortelle
Opera: SAPHO, 1850, libretto by Émile Augier. Part of Sapho, Act III. c3-bb4 f3-f4 Sustained aria in moderate slow tempo. Slow, climactic high ending with a sustained bb4. Arpeggiated accompaniment. Opera ends with this aria. Acc: 4 (VS)EC

(JACQUES FRANÇOIS) FROMENTAL (ÉLIAS) HALÉVY, 1799-1862

8183. R: Sous leur sceptre de fer
A: Humble fille des champs
Opera: CHARLES VI, 1843, libretto by Germain and Casimir Delavigne. Part of Edette, Act IV. bb2(f#2)-g#4 e3-e4 Extended recitative and sustained aria in moderate slow tempo. Has climactic passages. Climactic ending. Acc: 3-4 (VS)BR

8184. Le gondolier dans sa pauvre nacelle
Opera: LE REINE DE CHYPRE, 1841, libretto by Vernoy de Saint-Georges. Part of Catarina, Act II. ab2-ab4 eb3-eb4 In varied tempi and moods. Has recitative sections. Dramatic ending section with agitated accompaniment. Climactic ending. Acc: 4 (VS)MR

VICTOR (FÉLIX MARIE) MASSÉ, 1822-1884

8185. Tristes amours!
Opera: GALATHÉE, 1852, libretto by Jules Barbier and Michel Carré. Part of Pygmalion, Act I. g2-eb4 eb3-c4 Sustained in moderate tempo. Faster, animated ending section. Climactic ending. This excerpt is sung by either bass or mezzo-soprano in their respective transposed editions. Acc: 3-4 (VS)CR, LS

JULES (ÉMILE FRÉDÉRIC) MASSENET, 1842-1912

8186. Dors, ami, dors et que les songes
Opera: DON CÉSAR DE BAZAN, 1872, libretto by Adolph Philippe d'Ennery and Jules Chantepie, after d'Ennery and Dumanoir. Part of Lazarille, Act II. Common title: Berceuse. b2-g#4 e3-d#4 Sustained in moderate slow tempo. Subdued and gentle. Slightly faster middle section. Very subdued ending. Acc: 3 (VS)GH, HC

8187. Hérode! Hérode! Ne me refuse pas!
Opera: HÉRODIADE, 1881, libretto by Paul Milliet and Henri Grémont (Georges Hartmann), after a story by Flaubert. Part of Hérodiade, Act I. bb2-a4 eb3-f4 Sustained in moderate slow tempo. Starts gently then becomes dramatic, emphatic. Subdued ending. Acc: 3 (VS)HC, IM

8188. Oui, mon coeur étouffe mon coeur
       Opera: THÉRÈSE, 1907, libretto by Jules Claretie. Part of Thérèse,
       Act II. a2-g4 eb3-eb4 Sustained, generally in moderate lively tem-
       po. Generally strong, with a broad ending. Dramatic ending on sus-
       tained g4. Agitated accompaniment. Acc: 4 (VS)HC

8189. Va! laisse couler mes larmes
       Opera: WERTHER, 1892, libretto by Edouard Blau, Paul Milliet, and
       Georges Hartmann, after Goethe. Part of Charlotte, Act III. c3-f4
       e3-e4 Sustained in slow tempo. Has some dramatic passages as
       well as those requiring PP. Short. Subdued ending. Acc: 3
       OPA-2

8190. Werther! Qui m'aurait dit la place que dans mon coeur
       Opera: WERTHER. Part of Charlotte, Act III. Common title: Let-
       ter aria. c3-g4 f3-e4 Sustained in mainly moderate tempo. Has
       slower and faster sections, and some dramatic passages. Low and
       very subdued ending after climax. Acc: 3-4 (VS)HC, IM

(CHARLES) CAMILLE SAINT-SAËNS, 1835-1921

8191. R: Samson recherchant ma présence
       A: Amour, viens aider
       Opera: SAMSON ET DALILA, 1877, libretto by Ferdinand Lemaire.
       Part of Dalila, Act II. ab2-g4 eb3-eb4 Sustained in moderate tem-
       po. Has some dramatic passages. Low and subdued ending. Acc:
       3 (VS)GS. OPA-2

8192. Mon coeur s'ouvre à ta voix
       Opera: SAMSON ET DALILA. Part of Dalila, Act II. bb2-gb4
       eb3-eb4 Sustained in moderate slow tempo. Slower middle section
       with very gently agitated accompaniment. Has some climactic pas-
       sages. Acc: 4 (VS)GS. OPA-2

8193. Printemps qui commence
       Opera: SAMSON ET DALILA. Part of Dalila, Act II. b2-e4 e3-e4
       Sustained in moderate slow tempo. Requires fine P. Has some gen-
       tle recitative passages. Subdued ending. Acc: 3 (VS)GS. OPA-2

(CHARLES LOUIS) AMBROISE THOMAS, 1811-1896

8194. R: Toi, partir! Non! Il t'aime!
       A: Dans son regard plus sombre
       Opera: HAMLET, 1868, libretto by Jules Barbier and Michel Carré,
       after William Shakespeare. Part of Queen Gertrude, Act II. c3-ab4
       f3-f4 Sustained aria in moderate slow tempo. Requires fine P. Has
       dramatic passages. Climactic ending. Acc: 4 (VS)HC

8195. R: C'est moi
       A: Me voici dans son boudoir
       Opera: MIGNON, 1871, libretto by Jules Barbier and Michel Carré.
       Part of Frederick, Act II. bb2-f4 eb3-eb4 Common title: Rondo-
       Gavotte, arranged from the Entr'acte. This is an interpolation. Ani-
       mated aria with staccati passages. Acc: 3 (VS)GS. OPA-2

C. German and Austrian Composers

FRIEDRICH (FREIHERR) VON FLOTOW, 1812-1883

8196. Jägerin, schlau im Sinn
Opera: MARTHA, 1847, libretto by W. Friedrich (Friedrich Wilhelm
Riese). Part of Nancy, Act III. c3-a4 e3-d4 Animated in lively
tempo. 2 verses. See "Esse mesto il mio cor non sapria" for use
of this air in a more elaborate version. Acc: 3-4 (VS)GS

GIACOMO MEYERBEER, 1791-1864

8197. Ah! mon fils, cois béni!
Opera: LE PROPHÈTE, 1849, libretto by Eugène Scribe. Part of
Fidès, Act II. b2-a♯4 f♯3-d♯4 Sustained in moderate slow tempo.
Animated middle section. Ends with cadenza. Acc: 3-4 (VS)BT,
BR. OPA-2, OAR-M

8198. Donnez, donnez
Opera: LE PROPHÈTE. Part of Fidès, Act IV. b2-g4 e3-e4 Generally sustained vocal part in moderate tempo. Intense in some passages, sad. Subdued ending. Acc: 3-4 (VS)BT, BR. OPA-2,
OAR-M

8199. R: Qui je suis? Moi!
A: Je suis, helas! la pauvres
Opera: LE PROPHÈTE. Part of Fidès, Act IV. a♭2(b♭2)-a♭4 g3-
e♭4 Subdued recitative and sustained aria in moderate tempo. Has
dramatic passages. Ends with descending cadenza. Acc: 3-4 (VS)
BT, BR

8200. R: O pretres de Baal
A: O toi qui m'abandonnes
Opera: LE PROPHÈTE. Part of Fidès, Act V. a♭2-a♭4(b♭4) e♭3-
d♭4 Sustained in moderate slow tempo. Slightly animated vocal part
in the middle of the excerpt. Has optional cadenza at the end. Acc:
3-4 (VS)BT, BR

WOLFGANG AMADEUS MOZART, 1756-1791

7AC   7 Arias for Contralto. Wolfgang Amadeus Mozart. Edited by Sergius
Kagen. Original texts, with separate English translations. New York:
International Music Co.

8201. R: Ecco il punto
A: Non più di fiori
Opera: LA CLEMENZA DI TITO, 1791 (K. 621), libretto by Caterino
Mazzolà. Part of Vitellia, Act II. a2(g2)-a4 f3-f4 Dramatic reci-
tative and a sustained larghetto-allegro aria. Requires some flexi-
bility. Climactic ending. Acc: 3-4 (VS)CP. OPA-2

8202. Parto, parto
Opera: LA CLEMENZA DI TITO. Part of Sextus, Act I. c3-b♭4
c3-f4 Sustained vocal part in moderate slow tempo, followed by an
animated section. Has florid passages. Climactic ending. Acc:
3-4 (VS)CP. OPA-2, OAR-M

8203. Non so più cosa son, cosa faccio
Opera: LE NOZZE DI FIGARO, 1786 (K. 492), libretto by Lorenzo da Ponte. Part of Cherubino, Act I. eb3-g4 g3-f4 Animated in rapid tempo. Requires enunciation. Bright, and somewhat gently outgoing. Has climactic passages. Generally on MF level. Acc: 3-4 (VS)GS. CAO-S. (S)GR

8204. Voi, che sapete
Opera: LE NOZZE DI FIGARO. Part of Cherubino, Act II. c3-f4 f3-f4 Sustained in moderate tempo. Rhythmic. Requires simplicity and a lyric approach. Acc: 3-4 (VS)GS. (S)GR. OPA-2

8205. Già dagli occhi il velo è tolto
Opera: MITRIDATE, RÈ DI PONTO, 1770 (K. 87), libretto by Vittorio Amadeo Cigna-Santi, after Racine. Part of Farnace, Act III. a2-d4 d3-c4 Sustained in moderate slow tempo. Lively middle section. Has florid passages and a strong, low ending. Requires flexibility. Agitated accompaniment. Acc: 4 7AC

8206. Son reo; l'error confesso
Opera: MITRIDATE, RÈ DI PONTO. Part of Farnace, Act II. a2-e4 d3-d4 Sustained and slow sections alternating with animated and lively sections. Starts majestically in full voice. Has some wide intervalic skips and climactic sections. Strong, descending ending line. Agitated accompaniment. Acc: 4 7AC

8207. Va, l'error mio palesa
Opera: MITRIDATE, RÈ DI PONTO. Part of Farnace, Act II. a2-d4(e4) d3-c4 Sustained vocal part in lively tempo. Generally strong, with florid passages. Requires flexibility. Dramatic ending. Aria is in the real contralto range. Agitated accompaniment. Acc: 3-4 7AC

8208. Venga pur, minacci e frema
Opera: MITRIDATE, RÈ DI PONTO. Part of Farnace, Act I. a2-d4 d3-d4 An extended aria in lively tempo, with moderate lively middle section. Starts gently after extended instrumental introduction. Has climactic passages and florid passages. Strong ending. Agitated accompaniment. Acc: 4 7AC

JOHANN STRAUSS, 1825-1899

8209. Chacun à son goût
Opera: DIE FLEDERMAUS, 1874, libretto by Carl Haffner and Richard Genée, after Meilhac and Halévy's vaudeville. Part of Prince Orlofsky, Act II. c3-ab4 eb3-eb4 Animated in lively tempo. Requires simplicity. 2 verses. French text edition. Acc: 3-4 OPA-2

RICHARD STRAUSS, 1864-1949

8210. Ja, du! Denn du bist klug
Opera: ELEKTRA, 1906-1908, libretto by Hugo von Hofmannsthal. Part of Klytämnestra, one-act opera. a#2-g4 c3-e4 A dramatic excerpt in varied tempi and moods. Generally in recitative style. Has some high climaxes; also requires a fine low range. Very subdued ending on "ich will nicht länger träumen." Acc: 4 (VS)B-H

RICHARD WAGNER, 1813-1883

8211. Weiche Wotan! weiche!
Music Drama: DAS RHEINGOLD, 1853-1854, libretto by the com-
poser, the Prologue of the festival drama DER RING DES NIBELUNG-
EN. Part of Erda, Scene 4.   b♯2-e4 e3-e4 Sustained in slow
tempo. Generally subdued. Subdued high ending. Acc: 3-4 (VS)
GS, CP

8212. Höre mit Sinn
Music Drama: GÖTTERDÄMMERUNG, third day of the festival drama
DER RING DES NIBELUNGEN, 1874, libretto by the composer. Part
of Waltraute, Act I, Scene 3. g2-g4 c3-e4 Sustained in varied
tempi and moods. Generally subdued, and in recitative style. A
dramatic narrative. Acc: 4 (VS)GS, CP. OPA-2

8213. So ist es denn
Music Drama: DIE WALKÜRE, 1870, first day of the festival drama
DER RING DES NIBELUNGEN, 1870, libretto by the composer. Part
of Fricka, Act II, Scene 1. c✕3-g♯4 e3-e4 Sustained in moderate
lively tempo. Dramatic and intense scena. Excerpt ends with the
climactic "lass' auch zertreten. " Acc: 4-5 (VS)GS, CP

8214. Wo in Bergen du dich birgst
Music Drama: DIE WALKÜRE. Part of Fricka, Act II, Scene 1.
c3-g♯4 e3-e4 A dramatic scena in moving and agitated tempo. Requires fluent enunciation. Strong, with a climactic ending. Cutting
out Wotan's part, the excerpt continues through "So ist es denn aus
mit. " Acc: 4 (VS)GS, CP. OPA-2

8215. R: Gerechter Gott! So ist's entschieden schon!
A: In seiner Blüthe bleicht mein Leben
Opera: RIENZI, DER LETZTE DER TRIBUNEN, 1842, libretto by
the composer, after Mary Mitford's drama. Part of Adriano, Act III.
c♯3-a4 a3-g4 A dramatic scena and an andante-allegro-vivace air.
Climactic ending. Extended instrumental postlude. Acc: 4 (VS)SC.
OPA-2

8216. Einsam wachend in der Nacht
Opera: TRISTAN UND ISOLDE, 1865, libretto by the composer. Part
of Brangäna, Act II, Scene 2. f♯3-f♯4 a3-e4 Sustained in moderate
slow tempo. Requires fine P. Tranquil, with gently agitated accompaniment. Acc: 4-5 (VS)GS, CP

CARL MARIA VON WEBER, 1786-1826

8217. R: So bin ich nun verlassen
A: Hier dicht am Quell
Opera: EURYANTHE, 1823, libretto by Wilhelmine Helmine von Chézy.
Part of Euryanthe, Act III. c3-f♯4 g3-e4 Slow recitative and gently
animated aria in slow tempo. Generally subdued. Acc: 3 (VS)NO,
CP

8218. Arabien, mein Heimatland
Opera: OBERON, 1826, libretto by James Robinson Planché, after
Wieland's story. Part of Fatime, Act III. a2-e♭4 f♯3-d4 Sustained
first half; animated, lively and dance-like second half. Acc: 3-4
(VS)CP. OAR-M

8219. Arabiens einsam Kind
       Opera: OBERON. Part of Fatime, Act II. d#3-e4 f#3-d#4 Gently
       animated vocal part in moderate tempo. Requires some flexibility.
       Acc: 3-4 (VS)CP. OAR-M

8220. Traure, mein Herz
       Opera: OBERON. Part of Reiza, Act III. b2-f4 f3-db4 Sustained
       in moderate slow tempo. Lyric, and generally on MF level. Sub-
       dued ending. Originally for soprano. Acc: 3-4 (VS)CP

                        D. American Composer

GIAN-CARLO MENOTTI

Italian by birth. American opera.

8221. All that gold!
       Opera: AMAHL AND THE NIGHT VISITORS, 1951, libretto by the
       composer. Part of the Mother, one-act opera. bb2-g4 eb3-f4
       Sustained in moderate slow tempo. Starts gently, subdued. Has cli-
       mactic passages. Ends in very subdued, parlando style. Acc: 3-4
       (VS)GS

8222. I shall find for you shells and stars
       Opera: THE CONSUL, 1950, libretto by the composer. Part of the
       Mother, Act II. Common title: Lullaby. f2(a2)-eb4 c3-db4 Sus-
       tained in moderate slow tempo. Subdued and gentle. Low, subdued
       ending. Acc: 3-4 (VS)GS

8223. I'm not crying for him
       Opera: THE CONSUL. Part of the Mother, Act II. a2-f#4 d3-d4
       Sustained in slow tempo. Generally subdued. Has climactic crescen-
       do toward the end. Has intense passages. Acc: 3 (VS)GS

8224. Shall we ever see the end of all this
       Opera: THE CONSUL. Part of the Mother, Act I. b2-f4 e3-c4
       Sustained in slow tempo. Has dramatic climax in the middle of the
       aria. Subdued ending. Acc: 3-4 (VS)GS

                        E. British Composers

BENJAMIN BRITTEN

8225. One lifetime, one brain
       Comic Opera: ALBERT HERRING, 1947, libretto by Eric Crozier,
       after Guy de Maupassant. Part of Florence, Act I. b2-e4 e3-e4
       Sustained vocal part in fast tempo. Dramatic and accented. Climac-
       tic ending. Acc: 4 (VS)B-H

8226. Flowers bring to every year
       Opera: THE RAPE OF LUCRETIA, 1946, libretto by Ronald Duncan,
       after André Obey's play. Part of Lucretia, Act II. Common title:
       Flower song. a2-e4 f3-d4 Sustained in slow tempo. Requires very
       fine P and PP. Gentle. Acc: 3-4 (VS)B-H

8227. She sleeps as a rose

Opera: THE RAPE OF LUCRETIA. Part of the Female Chorus for
One Voice, Act II. a2-f♯4 e3-e4 Very sustained in moderate tempo. Very subdued and gentle. Requires fine PP. Acc: 3 (VS)B-H

RALPH VAUGHAN WILLIAMS, 1872-1958

8228. Life must be full of care
Opera: HUGH THE DROVER or LOVE IN THE STOCKS, 1924, libretto by Harold Child. Part of Aunt Jane, Act I. c3-d4 f3-c4 Sustained in moderate slow tempo. Subdued ending. Short. Acc: 3-4
(VS)JC

F. Russian Composers

ALEXANDER PORFIREVICH BORODIN, 1833-1887

8229. Tageslicht erlischt
Opera: PRINCE IGOR, 1869-1887, unfinished, completed by Rimsky-
Korsakof and Glasunov. Libretto by Vladimir V. Stassof. Part of
Kontschakovna, Act II. a♭2-f4 f3-e♭4 Sustained in slow tempo.
Has florid passages, requires some flexibility. Subdued, low ending:
a♭2 and b♭2. Acc: 4 (VS)MB, (S)MB

MODEST PETROVICH MUSSORGSKY, 1839-1881

8230. Ah, poor Marina!
Opera: BORIS GODUNOV, 1868-1872, libretto by Vladimir V. Stassof,
adapted from Pushkin's play and Karamsin's history of Russia. Part
of Marina, Act III. b2(a2)-f♯4(g♯4) e3-e4 In varied tempi, but
mostly animated and in mazurka style. Has some slower sections.
Ends with pitched and unpitched laughter. Acc: 3-4 (VS)WB, EK.
OPA-2

8231. Our little parrot Popinka
Opera: BORIS GODUNOV. Part of Feodor, Act II. Common title:
The parrot song. c3-e♭4 e3-c4 Animated in moderate slow tempo.
Requires some fluent enunciation. Narrative text. Acc: 3 (VS)WB,
EK. MRS-2

8232. Midge to woodland once did go
Opera: BORIS GODUNOV. Part of the Nurse, Act II. b♭2-f4 f3-c4
Common title: The song of the midge and the flea. Animated in live-
ly tempo. Requires fluent enunciation. Narrative and humorous.
Acc: 3-4 (VS)WB, EK

8233. In her youth went the maiden forth
Opera: KHOVANSCHINA, 1872-1880 unfinished, libretto by the composer. Part of Martha (Marfa), Act III. d3-f4 f3-d4 Sustained in
moderate slow tempo. Requires sensitive narration. English version
in MRS is by Constance Purdy. Acc: 3 MRS-2. (VS)WB

IGOR FEODOROVICH STRAVINSKY, 1882-1971

8234. As I was saying

Opera: THE RAKE'S PROGRESS, 1951, libretto by W(ystan) H(ugh) Auden and Chester Kallman, after Hogarth. Part of Baba, Act II. c3-d4 d3-bb3 Animated vocal part in moderate slow tempo. Requires fluent enunciation. A "diction" song. Agitated accompaniment. Acc: 4 (VS)B-H

PETER (PIOTR) ILYICH TCHAIKOVSKY, 1840-1893

8235. R: Oui, Dieu le vent!
A: Adieu, forêts
Opera: JEANNE D'ARC, 1878-1882, libretto by the composer, after Schiller. Part of Joan, Act I. db3-a4 g3-f4 A dramatic recitative and sustained aria in varied moods and tempi. Requires fine P. Climactic ending. Acc: 3-4 ORS, OPA-2, MLF

8236. Ah! now I know!
Opera: PIQUE DAME (THE QUEEN OF SPADES), 1890, libretto by Modest Ilyich Tchaikovsky (composer's brother) and the composer, after Pushkin. Part of Pauline, Act I. a2-ab4 eb3-eb4 Sustained vocal part in moderate tempo. Has dramatic climaxes. Low, subdued ending. Chordal, detached accompaniment. Acc: 3-4 (VS)GS. OPA-2

6. LYRIC TENOR

Bibliography for Lyric Tenor and Dramatic Tenor

AOT   Arias from Operas for Tenor. Only volume I is published. New York: International Music Co.

CAO-T   Celebri Arie D'Opera. Tenor. Fourth of six volumes for all voices. Milan: G. Ricordi.

MLF   Master Lessons on Fifty Opera Arias. Vol. II: The Music. 27 for soprano, 4 for mezzo-soprano, 12 for tenor, and 8 for baritone. Edited by Weldon Whitlock. Milwaukee: Pro Musica Press.

MRS-2   Modern Russian Songs. High, low. Edited by Ernest Newman. Bryn Mawr: Oliver Ditson, c/o Theodore Presser. (The spelling of Russian names in this edition is not consistent.)

MTO   The Modern Tenor Operatic Album. Thirty-five arias. Original texts, with English versions. New York: Franco Colombo, Inc.

OAR-T   Opern-Arien. Operatic arias in six volumes (two volumes for soprano) in original languages and German versions. Forty-seven arias for tenor, Catalog Number 4233. Frankfurt: Edition Peters.

OAT   Opera-Arien für Tenor. Giuseppe Verdi. Edited by Kurt Soldan. Italian texts and German versions. Leipzig: C. F. Peters.

OGT   Opern-Gesänge für Tenor. Richard Wagner. German texts only. Edited by Kurt Soldan. Leipzig: C. F. Peters.

OPA-3   Operatic Anthology. Vol. III: Tenor. Edited by Kurt Adler. Original texts, with English versions. New York: G. Schirmer, Inc. (The older edition is edited by Kurt Schindler.)

ORT   Opera Repertoire for Tenor. Thirty-one arias in original texts and English versions. Edited by Gregory Castleton. Includes the synopses of the plots. Bryn Mawr: Theodore Presser Co.

All indications of range and tessitura for Lyric Tenor are based on the treble clef as printed, but sung one octave lower. Therefore, the range of c3-a4 would mean c2-a3.

A. Italian Composers

VINCENZO BELLINI, 1801-1835

8237. Ascolta; nel furor delle tempeste
     Opera: IL PIRATA, 1827, libretto by Felice Romani. Part of Gualtiero, Act I. d3-a4(d5) a3-f4 Animated in moderate lively tempo.

Has florid figures and climactic passages. Slightly agitated accompaniment. Acc: 3-4 (VS)GR

8238. R: Ebben si aduni
       A: Tu vedrai la sventurata
       Opera: IL PIRATA. Part of Gualtiero, Act II. f3-c5 g3-g4 Sustained in slow tempo. Requires some maestoso treatment. Has two florid passages. Climactic ending. Acc: 3 (VS)GR

8239. Me protegge, me difende
       Opera: NORMA, 1831, libretto by Felice Romani, based on a tragedy by Louis Alexander Soumet. Part of Pollione, Act I. eb3-ab4 (bb4) g3-g4 Animated in moderate tempo. In martial style. Has accented passages. Strong and dramatic ending. Acc: 4 (VS)GS, GR

8240. Meco all'altar di Venere
       Opera: NORMA. Part of Pollione, Act I. d3-c5 g3-g4 Sustained in moderate tempo. Has some climactic passages. Tessitura is quite high in some parts. Acc: 3-4 (VS)GS, GR. (S)GR

8241. Va, crudele, e al Dio spietato
       Opera: NORMA. Part of Pollione, Act I. c3-ab4 g3-g4 Sustained in moderate tempo. Has some climactic and florid passages. Gently agitated accompaniment. Acc: 3-4 (VS)GS, GR

ARRIGO BOITO, 1842-1918

8242. Dai campi, dai prati
       Opera: MEFISTOFELE, 1868, libretto by the composer. Part of Faust, Act I. f3-bb4 a3-f4 Sustained in slightly slow tempo. Starts subdued and gentle. Generally subdued, meditative, and calm. Acc: 3-4 (VS)GR. MTO. (S)GR

8243. Giunto sul passo estremo
       Opera: MEFISTOFELE. Part of Faust, in the Prologue. f3-ab4 ab3-f4 Sustained in moderate slow tempo. Requires fine P and PP. Has dramatic climaxes. Acc: 3-4 (VS)GR. MTO. (S)GR

ALFREDO CATALANI, 1854-1893

8244. M'hai salvato
       Opera: LA WALLY, 1892, libretto by Luigi Illica, based on Wilhelmine von Hillern's novel. Part of Hagenbach, Act IV. g3-bb4 a3-g4 Sustained in moderate tempo. Has dramatic passages. Climactic ending. Has intense passages. Acc: 3-4 (VS)GR. MTO

8245. R: Io resto e tu m'udrai
       A: In franto ogni altro vincolo
       Opera: LORELEY, 1890, libretto by Carlo D'Ormeville and Angelo Zanardini. Part of Walter, Act III. e3-b4 g#3-f#4 Recitative and sustained aria in moderate tempo. Has climactic passages. Requires some flexibility. Acc: 3-4 (VS)GR

8246. Nel verde maggio, un di dal bosco
       Opera: LORELEY. Part of Walter, Act I. e3-a4 a3-f#4 Sustained in moderate slow tempo. Generally subdued, requires very fine high

P and PP.   Faster, more animated ending section.   Acc: 3-4   (VS)
GR.   MTO.   (S)GR

LUIGI CHERUBINI, 1760-1842

8247.   R: Suspendez à ces murs mes armes
        A: J'ai vu disparaître
        Opera: LES ABENCÉRAGES or L'ETENDARD DE GRENADE, 1813,
        libretto by Victor Joseph Etienne de Jouy, after J. P. Florian's novel.
        Part of Almanzor, Act II. f♯3-a4 g3-f4 Recitative and sustained
        aria in moderate slow tempo. Dramatic ending section. Requires
        fine P. Acc: 3-4 MLF

8248.   Or che più non vedrò
        Opera: MEDEA, 1797, libretto by François Benoit Hoffman. Origi-
        nal in French. Part of Giasone, Act I. c♯3-g4 g3-e4 Sustained
        in moderate slow tempo. Slightly faster middle section. Acc: 4
        (VS)GR

FRANCESCO CILÈA, 1866-1950

8249.   La dolcissima effigie
        Opera: ADRIANA LECOUVREUR, 1902, libretto by Arturo Colautti,
        after Eugène Scribe. Part of Maurizio, Act I. f3-ab4 g3-g4 Sus-
        tained in moderate slow tempo. Generally subdued, very lyric, also
        has some climactic passages. Requires very fine high P and PP.
        Acc: 3-4 (VS)CS

8250.   L'anima ho stanca
        Opera: ADRIANA LECOUVREUR. Part of Maurizio, Act II. e♯3-a4
        b3-f♯4 Sustained in moderate slow tempo. Gentle, requires very
        fine P and PP. Short. Acc: 3-4 (VS)CS

8251.   R: È la solita storia
        A: Anch' io vorrei dormir cosi
        Opera: L'ARLESIANA, 1897, libretto by Leopoldo Marenco, based on
        Alphonse Daudet's play. Part of Federico, Act II. e3-a4 g3-f♯4
        Sustained in slow tempo. Requires very fine high P and PP. Has
        dramatic passages and a climactic ending. Acc: 4 (VS)CS, IM. (S)IM

GAETANO DONIZETTI, 1797-1848

8252.   R: Vivi tu, te non scongioro
        A: Nel veder la tua costanza
        Opera: ANNA BOLENA, 1830, libretto by Felice Romani. Part of
        Percy, Act II. e3-c5 g3-g4 Sustained aria in moderate slow tempo.
        Second part is florid, dramatic, and vocally demanding. Parts of
        other characters may be eliminated in a single and separate perform-
        ance. Acc: 3-4 (VS)GR

8253.   E fia ver?
        Opera: BETLY or LA CAPANNA SVIZZERA, 1836, libretto by the
        composer, based on Eugène Scribe's play. Part of Daniele, Act I.
        g3-bb4 bb3-g4 Sustained in moderate tempo. Has florid passages,
        passages with high tessitura, and a climactic ending. Requires flexi-
        bility. Acc: 4 (VS) Launer, Paris

8254. R: Povero Ernesto!
A: Cercherò, cercherò lontana terra
Opera: DON PASQUALE, 1843, libretto by the composer and Michele
Accursi (Giacomo Ruffini), based on Angelo Anelli's novel. Part of
Ernesto, Act II.   g3-bb4 bb3-ab4 Sustained aria in rather slow
tempo. Quite high tessitura; uses ab4's quite frequently. Requires
flexibility. Lyric, but vocally not easy. Climactic ending. Acc:
3-4 (VS)GR

8255. Com' è gentil
Opera: DON PASQUALE. Part of Ernesto, Act III.   Common title:
Ernesto's serenade.   g#3-a4 a3-a4 Sustained in moderate slow tem-
po. Graceful. Requires fine P. Climactic ending. Acc: 3 (VS)
GR. OPA-3, MTO, ORT, OAR-T. (S)GR

8256. Deserto in terra
Opera: DON SEBASTIANO, 1843, libretto by Eugène Scribe. Original in French. Part of Don Sebastiano, Act II.   f3-c5(db5) ab3-gb4
Sustained in moderate slow tempo. Has dramatic passages, sections
with high tessitura, and climactic ending. Acc: 3-4 (VS)EO

8257. R: Gran Dio! Che degno io ne divenga or vuol
A: Sì, che un tuo solo accento
Opera: LA FAVORITA, 1840, libretto by Alphonse Royer, Gustave
Vaëz, and Eugène Scribe. Part of Fernando, Act I.   e3-a4 a3-f#4
Slightly dramatic recitative in moderate slow tempo, and a marked,
animated aria in martial tempo. Has dramatic passages and climac-
tic ending. Acc: 3-4 (VS)GR, B-H

8258. Spirto gentil
Opera: LA FAVORITA. Part of Fernando, Act IV.   g3-g4(c5) b3-
g4 Sustained in slow tempo. Generally gentle, lyric, without strong
contrasts in dynamics. Sustained ending. Acc: 3-4 (VS)GR, B-H.
OPA-3, ORT.   (S)GR

8259. Una vergine, un angel di Dio
Opera: LA FAVORITA. Part of Fernando, Act I.   e3-c#5 a3-g#4
Gently animated vocal part in somewhat slow tempo. Lyric through-
out. Subdued ending. Acc: 3-4 (VS)GR, B-H.   (S)GR

8260. Amici miei che allegro giorno
Opera: LA FIGLIA DEL REGGIMENTO, 1840, libretto by Jules Vernoy de Saint-Georges and Jean François Bayard. Part of Tonio, Act
I. Italian version is reviewed here. g3-ab4(bb4) bb3-g4 Animated
in march style and tempo. Accented, with a climactic, unaccompanied ending. Extended instrumental prelude. Aria ends with "io
seguiro." Acc: 3-4 (VS)NO

8261. R: Adorata regina
A: Se valor, rispetto e fede
Opera: LA REGINA DI GOLCONDA, 1828, libretto by Felice Romani.
Part of Seide, Act I.   f3-g4(a4) g3-f4 Secco recitative and sustained
aria in maestoso delivery. Has choral ensemble in the full score,
two florid passages, and a climactic ending. Acc: 3-4 (VS)GR

8262. Quanto è bella, quanto è cara!
Opera: L'ELISIR D'AMORE, 1832, libretto by Felice Romani, based
on Eugène Scribe. Part of Nemorino, Act I.   e3-g4 g3-g4 Sustained

in somewhat slow tempo. Gentle and lyric. Faster, more graceful
ending section before the entrance of the choral part. Acc: 3-4
(VS)GS, GR. (S)GR

8263. Una furtiva lagrima
     Opera: L'ELISIR D'AMORE. Part of Nemorino, Act II. Other title:
     Romanza. f3-ab4 ab3-g4 Sustained in slow tempo. Very lyric,
     with gentleness in some passages. Requires fine P and PP. Has
     some dramatic passages. Acc: 3-4 (VS)GR, GS. (S)GR, GS.
     OPA-3, MTO, ORT, OAR-T

8264. R: Linda! Si ritirò. Povera Linda!
     A: Se tanto in ira
     Opera: LINDA DI CHAMOUNIX, 1842, libretto by Gaetano Rossi.
     Part of Carlo, Act II. f#3-ab4 a3-g4 Recitative in varied tempi
     and a sustained aria in moderate slow tempo. Climactic ending.
     Requires flexibility. Acc: 3-4 (VS)GR

8265. R: Tombe degl'avi miei
     A: Fra poco a me ricovero
     Opera: LUCIA DI LAMMERMOOR, 1835, libretto by Salvatore Cam-
     marano, after Walter Scott's novel The Bride of Lammermoor. Part
     of Edgar, Act III. f3-a4 g3-g4 Sustained aria in slow tempo.
     Mainly lyric in character. No strong contrasts in dynamics. Re-
     quires some flexibility. Acc: 3-4 (VS)GS, GR. OPA-3, OAR-T.
     (S)GR

8266. R: Nel fragor della festa
     A: Alma soave e cara
     Opera: MARIA DI ROHAN, 1843, libretto by Salvatore Cammarano.
     Part of Chalais, Act II. e3-a4 b3-f4 Recitative in varied moods
     and tempi. Sustained aria in moderate slow tempo. Has climactic
     passages and a climactic ending. Acc: 3-4 (VS)GR

8267. R: Io piego la fronte nella polve
     A: D'un alma troppo fervida
     Opera: POLIUTO or I MARTIRI, 1840, libretto by Eugène Scribe,
     after Thomas Corneille. Part of Poliuto, Act I. g3-ab4 ab3-f4
     Sustained aria in slow tempo. Requires fine P. Generally lyric and
     graceful. Acc: 3-4 (VS)SR

8268. Tra la la, allegro io son
     Opera: RITA, 1860, libretto by Gustavo Vaëz. Part of Beppe, one-
     act opera. e3-b4 g#3-g#4 Animated in lively tempo. Joyous and
     outgoing. Requires fluent enunciation and flexibility. Has several
     b4's. Climactic ending. Acc: 3-4 (VS)GR

UMBERTO GIORDANO, 1867-1948

8269. Come un bel dì di maggio
     Opera: ANDREA CHÉNIER, 1896, libretto by Luigi Illica. Part of
     Chénier, Act IV. e3-ab4 f#3-f#4 Sustained in moderate slow tem-
     po. Slightly faster second section. Dramatic and climactic last sec-
     tion. Acc: 4 (VS)CS

8270. Sì, fui soldato
     Opera: ANDREA CHÉNIER. Part of Chénier, Act IV. f3-ab4 g3-f4

1072   Solo Voice Repertoire

Sustained in moderate tempo. Declamatory style. Climactic ending
on "ma lasciami l'onor!" Acc: 3-4 (VS)CS

8271. Un dì all'azzurro spazio
      Opera: ANDREA CHÉNIER. Part of Chénier, Act I. f3-bb4 f3-f4
      Sustained in moderate slow tempo. Has quasi-recitative passages,
      dramatic passages, and a climactic ending. Acc: 3-4 (VS)CS, IM

8272. Amor ti vieta
      Opera: FEDORA, 1898, libretto by Arturo Colautti, after Victorien
      Sardou's drama. Part of Loris Ipanoff, Act II. a3-a4 c3-f4 Sus-
      tained in moderate slow tempo. Lyric throughout with climactic pas-
      sages. Arpeggiated accompaniment. Acc: 3-4 (VS)CS, IM

8273. Mia madre, la mia vecchia madre
      Opera: FEDORA. Part of Loris Ipanoff, Act II. e3-g4 a3-g4 Ani-
      mated in lively tempo, with a faster ending section. Has dramatic
      passages. Acc: 4 (VS)CS, IM

8274. Vedi io piango
      Opera: FEDORA. Part of Loris Ipanoff, Act II. g3-ab4 a3-f4
      Sustained in moderate slow tempo. Completely lyric, on the gentle,
      subdued side. Very subdued ending. Acc: 3 (VS)CS, IM

RUGGIERO LEONCAVALLO, 1858-1919

8275. Io non ho che una povera stanzetta
      Opera: LA BOHÈME, 1897, libretto by Giuseppe Giacosa and Luigi
      Illica, after Henri Murger's novel. Part of Marcello, Act II. f3-
      bb4 gb3-f4 Sustained in moderate slow tempo. Has dramatic pas-
      sages, climactic high ending. Requires fine high P and a good com-
      mand of high tessitura. Acc: 3-4 (VS)CS. MLF

8276. Testa adorata
      Opera: LA BOHÈME. Part of Marcello, Act III. f3-bb4 gb3-f4
      Sustained in slow tempo. Dramatic, and requires a fine command of
      high notes. Intense. Subdued ending. Acc: 3-4 (VS)CS

8277. Va via, fantasma del passato!
      Opera: LA BOHÈME. Part of Marcello, Act III. eb3-bb4 g3-g4
      Sustained in moderate tempo. Dramatic. Uses many high notes.
      Climactic high ending on "va via!" Agitated accompaniment. Acc:
      4 (VS)CS

8278. O, Colombina
      Opera: PAGLIACCI, 1892, libretto by the composer. Part of Peppe
      (Harlequin), Act II. e3-a4 a3-f4 Animated in moderate lively tem-
      po. A good number of phrase endings are sustained notes. Rhyth-
      mic accompaniment. Acc: 3-4 (VS)GS. (S)GS

8279. R: Recitar! Mentre preso
      A: Vesti la giubba
      Opera: PAGLIACCI. Part of Canio, Act I. e3(d3)-a4 g3-g4 Sus-
      tained aria in slow tempo. Dramatic, intense, with some passages
      in declamatory style. Climactic and dramatic ending. Acc: 3-4
      (VS)GS. OPA-3, ORT. (S)GS

8280. Ed ora.... io mi domando
Opera: ZAZÀ, 1900, libretto by the composer, after a play by P.
Berton and Ch. Simon.   Part of Milio, Act IV.   f♯3-b4 g3-f♯4 Sus-
tained in slow tempo. Has dramatic climaxes. Short. Acc: 3-4
(VS)CS

8281. O mio piccolo tavolo
Opera: ZAZÀ. Part of Milio, Act IV.   e♭3-b♭4 a♭3-a♭4 Very
sustained in moderate slow tempo. Has dramatic climaxes. Requires very fine high PP. Has some recitative passages. Subdued
ending after a dramatic climax. Agitated accompaniment. This aria
starts Act IV. Acc: 4 (VS)CS. MLF

8282. Zazà, tu mi rimproveri
Opera: ZAZÀ. Part of Milio, Act IV.   g♯3-b♭4 b♭3-a♭4 Sustained in moderate tempo. Has dramatic passages. Requires very
fine high P on a4. Climactic ending. Agitated accompaniment. Acc:
4 (VS)CS

PIETRO MASCAGNI, 1863-1945

8283. O Lola, bianca come fior di spino
Opera: CAVALLERIA RUSTICANA, 1889, libretto by Giovanni Targi-
oni-Tozzetti and Guido Menasci, after Verga's story. Common title:
Siciliana. Part of Turiddu, one-act opera. a♭3-a♭4 c4-f4 Sustained in moderate slow tempo. Graceful. Has high tessitura, climactic passages, and a subdued high ending on sustained note. The
first vocal piece in the opera, and is sung from behind the curtain,
before it opens. Acc: 3-4 (VS)GS. OPA-3, MLF, ORT

8284. Viva il vino spumeggiante
Opera: CAVALLERIA RUSTICANA. Part of Turiddu, one-act opera.
g3-g4 b3-g4 Starts gently animated in slow tempo. Stronger section
toward the end and before the return of the choral parts. Acc: 3-4
(VS)GS. OAR-T

8285. Apri la tua finestra!
Opera: IRIS, 1898, libretto by Luigi Illica. Part of Osaka, Act I.
e3-a4 a3-a4 Sustained in moderate slow tempo. Requires very fine
high P and PP. Subdued opening section. High tessitura. Has climactic passages and a subdued high ending. Acc: 3-4 (VS)GR.
MTO. (S)GR

8286. Iris, son io!
Opera: IRIS. Part of Osaka, Act III. g3-a♭4 b♭3-g4 Sustained in
moderate slow tempo. Has dramatic passages. Intense, with a climactic high ending. Agitated accompaniment. Acc: 3-4 (VS)GR

8287. Ed anche Beppe amo!
Opera: L'AMICO FRITZ, 1891, libretto by P. Suardon, after Erck-
mann-Chatrian's novel. Part of Fritz, Act II. b♭3-b♭4 a♭3-g♭4
Sustained in moderate slow tempo. Has slower and more sustained
middle section. Requires fine P. Climactic ending. Acc: 3-4
(VS)CS, GR

8288. O amore, o bella luce del core
Opera: L'AMICO FRITZ. Part of Fritz, Act III. g♭3-b♭4 a♭3-g♭4

Very sustained in slow tempo. Requires very fine high P and PP.
Starts very gently. Climactic ending section. Acc: 3-4 (VS)GR,
CS

AMILCARE PONCHIELLI, 1834-1886

8289. Cielo e mar!
Opera: LA GIOCONDA, 1876, libretto by Arrigo Boito, after Victor
Hugo. Part of Enzo, Act II. d3-bb4 g3-ab4 Sustained in moder-
ate slow tempo. Has dramatic climaxes. Subdued ending on g4 fol-
lows the dramatic passages. Acc: 4 (VS)GS, GR. OPA-3, MTO,
ORT. (S)GR

GIACOMO (ANTONIO DOMENICO) PUCCINI, 1858-1924

8290. Firenze è come un albero fiorito
Opera: GIANNI SCHICCHI, 1918, libretto by Giovacchino Forzano.
Third opera in the Trittico. Part of Rinuccio, one-act opera. f3-
bb4 a3-g4 Sustained in moderate tempo. Mainly lyric, generally
on MF level. Text extols the city of Florence as the center of culture. Acc: 3-4 (VS)GR

8291. Hai ben ragione
Opera: IL TABARRO, 1918, libretto by Giuseppe Adami. Part of
Luigi, one-act opera. First work in the Trittico. eb3-bb4 b3-g4
Starts in moderate lively tempo and ends in moderate slow tempo.
Climactic ending. Acc: 3-4 (VS)GR. MTO. (S)GR

8292. Che gelida manina
Opera: LA BOHÈME, 1896, libretto by Giuseppe Giacosa and Luigi
Illica, based on Henri Murger's novel. Part of Rodolfo, Act I. eb3-
bb4(c5) ab3-ab4 Sustained in moderate slow tempo. Very lyric in
style. Has some dramatic climaxes. Requires very fine P and PP.
Very subdued high ending. Acc: 3-4 (VS)GS, GR. OPA-3, MTO,
ORT. (S)GS, GR-three keys

8293. Ch'ella mi creda libero
Opera: LA FANCIULLA DEL WEST, 1910, libretto by Guelfo Civi-
nini and Carlo Zangarini. Part of Johnson, Act III. eb3-bb4 gb3-
gb4 Sustained in slow tempo. Has dramatic passages. Starts subdued. Acc: 3-4 (VS)GR. MTO. (S)GR

8294. Or son sei mesi
Opera: LA FANCIULLA DEL WEST. Part of Johnson, Act II. e3-
bb4 bb3-g4 Sustained in moderate slow tempo. Slower final section. Has some dramatic passages, and some intense passages.
Acc: 3-4 (VS)GR. MTO. (S)GR

8295. R: Ecco la casa
A: Torna ai felice dì
Opera: LE VILLI, 1884, libretto by Ferdinando Fontana. Part of
Roberto, Act II. f3(c3)-bb4 ab3-gb4 Dramatic recitative and sus-
tained aria in moderate slow tempo. Has dramatic passages. In-
tense. Climactic ending. Acc: 3-4 (VS)GR. MTO. (S)GR

8296. Addio, fiorito asil

Opera: MADAMA BUTTERFLY, 1904, libretto by Giuseppe Giacosa
and Luigi Illica, after Belasco's drama from John L. Long's story.
Part of Pinkerton, Act II.   f3-bb4   ab3-ab4   Sustained in slow tempo. Has dramatic passages, and a climactic ending. Intense. Acc:
3-4 (VS)GR, GS. (S)GR

8297. Amore o grillo
Opera: MADAMA BUTTERFLY. Part of Pinkerton, Act I.   f3-bb4
g3-f4 Sustained in moderate lively tempo. Has climactic passages.
Requires fine P. Acc: 3-4 (VS)GR, GS. (S)GR. MTO

8298. Ah! Manon, mi tradisce
Opera: MANON LESCAUT, 1893, libretto by Marco Praga, Domenico
Oliva, and Luigi Illica, based on Abbé Prévost's novel. Part of Des
Grieux, Act II.   e3-bb4   a3-g4 Sustained in moderate tempo. Dra-
matic. Starts gently and subduedly, then becomes intense. Subdued
ending. Acc: 3-4 (VS)IM, GR

8299. Donna non vidi mai
Opera: MANON LESCAUT. Part of Des Grieux, Act I.   e3-bb4
bb3-g4 Sustained in moderate slow tempo. Generally subdued; has
dramatic passages toward the end. Requires very fine P and PP.
Climactic ending. Acc: 3-4 (VS)IM, GR. (S)GR. OPA-3, MTO

8300. Guardate, pazzo son
Opera: MANON LESCAUT. Part of Des Grieux, Act III.   e3-b4
b3-g4 Sustained in slow tempo. Has dramatic climaxes. Descending ending line after the climax. Acc: 3-4 (VS)GR, IM. (S)GR

8301. Tra voi, belle, brune e bionde
Opera: MANON LESCAUT. Part of Des Grieux, Act I.   f3-a4   a3-
f4 Animated vocal part in moderate tempo. Climactic ending. Requires fine P. Short. Acc: 3-4 (VS)GR, IM. MTO. (S)GR

8302. E lucevan le stelle
Opera: TOSCA, 1900, libretto by Giuseppe Giacosa and Luigi Illica,
based on Sardou's drama. Part of Cavaradossi, Act III.   f#3-a4
g3-g4 Sustained in moderate slow tempo. Starts gently in declamatory style. Has dramatic passages toward the end. Acc: 3-4 (VS)
GS, GR. MTO, ORT. (S)IM, GR, GS

8303. Recondita armonia
Opera: TOSCA. Part of Cavaradossi, Act I.   f3-bb4   f3-f4 Sus-
tained in slow tempo. Generally subdued. Requires fine P and PP.
Lyric throughout. Climactic ending. Acc: 3-4 (VS)GR, GS. (S)
IM, GR-two keys, GS. OPA-3, MTO, ORT

8304. Nessun dorma!
Opera: TURANDOT, 1926, unfinished, completed by Franco Alfano,
libretto by Giuseppe Adami and Renato Simoni, based on Gozzi's play.
Part of the Prince, Act III.   d3-b4   g3-f#4 Sustained in moderate
slow tempo. Has dramatic passages. Climactic high ending. Has
high tessitura. Acc: 3-4 (VS)GR. (S)GR. MTO

8305. Non piangere, Liù!
Opera: TURANDOT. Part of the Prince, Act I.   gb3-bb4   bb3-f4
Very sustained in very slow tempo. High, soaring tessitura. Has dra-
matic passages and climactic ending. Acc: 3-4 (VS)GR. MTO. (S)GR

GIOACCHINO (ANTONIO) ROSSINI, 1792-1868

8306. R: Ne m'abandonne (It.: Non mi lasciare)
       A: Asile héréditaire (It.: O muto asil)
       Opera: GUILLAUME TELL (GUGLIELMO TELL), 1829, libretto by
       Victor Joseph Étienne de Jouy and Hippolyte Bis, after Schiller's
       drama. Original text: French. Part of Arnold, Act IV. f3-bb4(c5)
       g3-g4 Extended recitative and sustained aria in slightly slow tempo.
       Has some short florid figures. Generally high tessitura. Climactic
       ending. Acc: 4 (VS) Troupenas-French; GR-Italian; B-H-Italian &
       English

8307. Cessa di più resistere
       Opera: IL BARBIERE DI SIVIGLIA, 1816, libretto by Cesare Sterbini,
       after Beaumarchais' comedy. Part of Count Almaviva, Act II. db3-
       bb4 f3-g4 Sustained in moderate tempo. Somewhat majestic. Very
       florid, requires considerable flexibility. Difficult. Slower final sec-
       tion. Acc: 4 (VS)GS, GR

8308. Ecco ridente in cielo
       Opera: IL BARBIERE DI SIVIGLIA. Part of Count Almaviva, Act I.
       f#3-b4 g3-g4 Sustained and slow first section, then lively, animated
       main section. Florid, has chromatic scale passages. Requires flex-
       ibility. Joyful, with a climactic ending. Acc: 4 (VS)GS, GR.
       (S)GR.   OAR-T

8309. Se il mio nome
       Opera: IL BARBIERI DI SIVIGLIA. Part of Count Almaviva, Act I.
       e3-g4 a3-g4 Sustained in moderate slow tempo. Has some florid
       figures. Slightly climactic ending. Acc: 3 (VS)GS. (S)GR

8310. R: Principe più non sei
       A: Sì, ritrovarla io giuro, amor
       Opera: LA CENERENTOLA, 1817, libretto by Jacopo Ferretti, after
       Perrault. Part of Ramiro (The Prince), Act II. e3-c5 g3-g4 Strong
       recitative and animated aria in lively tempo. Quite florid, with some
       high passages and tessitura. Has two sets of c5's. Requires flexi-
       bility. Climactic ending. Acc: 4 (VS)FC

8311. Vieni! fra queste braccia
       Opera: LA GAZZA LADRA, 1817, libretto by Giovanni Gherardini,
       after a comedy by d'Aubigny and Caigniez. Part of Gianetto, Act I.
       g#3-b4 b3-g4 A sustained maestoso. Extremely florid. Has very
       high tessitura most of the time. Requires considerable flexibility.
       A coloratura-tenor required. Climactic ending. With ensemble in
       the full score. Acc: 3-4 (VS)EG, GR

8312. Ah come il cor di giubilo
       Opera: L'ITALIANA IN ALGERI, 1813, libretto by Angelo Anelli.
       Part of Lindoro, Act II. g3-b4 a3-a4 Animated in lively tempo.
       Florid, requires flexibility. Has passages with high tessitura. Cli-
       mactic ending. For high lyric tenor. Acc: 4 (VS)GR

8313. Languir per una bella
       Opera: L'ITALIANA IN ALGERI. Part of Lindoro, Act I. f3-c5
       bb3-bb4 Sustained in moderate slow tempo. Has very high tessitura.
       Difficult. Quite florid. Has a good number of bb4's, and a climactic
       ending. Requires a high, coloratura-type tenor. Acc: 3-4 (VS)GR.
       (S)GR

8314. Ah! si per voi già sento
       Opera: OTELLO or MORO DI VENEZIA, 1816, libretto by Francesco
       Berio, after William Shakespeare's drama. Part of Otello, Act I.
       a2-a4 e3-f#4 Alternating sections of animated march tempi and sus-
       tained moderate slow tempo. Florid, requires considerable flexibility.
       Has dotted figures, scale-wise passages, and some wide intervalic
       skips. Uses wide range--a2 is used four times. A cavatina. Acc:
       3-4 (VS)GR. (S)GR

8315. Ah dov'è il cimento
       Opera: SEMIRAMIDE, 1823, libretto by Gaetano Rossi, after Vol-
       taire's tragedy. Part of Idreno, Act I. c3-d5 a3-g4 Animated in
       moderate and moderate lively tempi. Extremely florid. Uses the
       high tessitura frequently. Difficult. Requires considerable flexibility.
       Requires a coloratura-type tenor. Acc: 3-4 (VS)B-H

GIUSEPPE (FORTUNINO FRANCESCO) VERDI, 1813-1901

8316. Irne lungi ancor dovrei
       Opera: ALZIRA, 1845, libretto by Salvatore Cammarano, after Vol-
       taire's play. Part of Zamoro, Act II. f3-ab4 ab3-gb4 Sustained
       in moderate slow tempo. Generally lyric with some climactic pas-
       sages. Requires some fine P and PP. Climactic ending. Agitated
       accompaniment. Acc: 4 (VS)GR. OAT

8317. Sotto il sol di Siria ardente
       Opera: AROLDO, 1857, libretto by Francesco Maria Piave. Part of
       Aroldo, Act I. d3-ab4 ab3-g4 Sustained in moderate slow tempo.
       Requires fine high PP. Generally lyric. Short. Requires flexibility.
       Ends with unaccompanied, subdued passage. Acc: 3-4 (VS)GR.
       OAT. (S)GR

8318. R: Infida! il dì che brami è questo
       A: Che non avrebbe il misero
       Opera: ATTILA, 1846, libretto by Temistocle Solera. Part of Fores-
       to, Act III. g3-a4 g3-g4 Sustained in moderate slow tempo. Has
       climactic passages. Subdued ending. Acc: 3-4 (VS)GR, CP

8319. Ella in poter del barbaro!
       Opera: ATTILA. Part of Foresto, in The Prologue. f#3(e#3)-g#4
       g#3-g#4 Sustained in moderate slow tempo. Generally lyric. Ends
       with short cadenza, subdued. Acc: 3 (VS)GR

8320. R: Fontainbleau! foresta immensa
       A: Io la vidi, e il suo sorriso
       Opera: DON CARLOS, 1867, libretto by François Joseph Méry and
       Camille du Locle, after Friedrich von Schiller. Part of Don Carlos,
       Act I. f3-b4 g3-f4 Dramatic recitative and sustained aria in mod-
       erate slow tempo. Requires fine P to PPP. The aria is generally
       subdued and gentle. Acc: 3-4 (VS)GR. OPA-3

8321. Dal labbro il canto estasiato
       Opera: FALSTAFF, 1893, libretto by Arrigo Boito, after Shake-
       speare's Merry Wives of Windsor. Part of Fenton, Act III. d#3-ab4
       ab3-f#4 Sustained in moderate slow tempo. Lyric throughout. Re-
       quires fine high P. Climactic ending. Acc: 3-4 (VS)GR, GS, IM.
       MTO. (S)GR

8322. All'infelice veglio conforta
       Opera: I DUE FOSCARI, 1844, libretto by Francesco Maria Piave,
       based on Byron's drama. Part of Jacopo, Act III. eb3-bb4 ab3-
       f4 Sustained in moderate tempo. Has one florid passage. Requires
       very fine high PP. Aria ends before Loredano's entrance. Acc:
       3-4 (VS)GR

8323. R: Brezza del suol natio
       A: Dal più remoto esiglio
       Opera: I DUE FOSCARI. Part of Jacopo, Act I. eb3-bb4 ab3-ab4
       An adagio recitative and sustained aria, first in moderate slow tempo,
       then lively tempo. Has dramatic passages, sustained high notes, and
       a climactic ending. Requires flexibility. Acc: 3-4 (VS)GR

8324. La mia letizia infondere
       Opera: I LOMBARDI ALL PRIMA CROCIATA, 1843, libretto by Te-
       mistocle Solera, based on a romance by Tommaso Grossi. Part of
       Oronte, Act III. f#3-a4 a3-f#4 Sustained in moderate slow tempo.
       Requires very fine high P and PP. Has dramatic climaxes. Very
       subdued ending on a4. Acc: 3-4 OAT. (VS)GR. (S)GR

8325. R: Come splendido e grande
       A: Di ladroni attorniato
       Opera: I MASNADIERI, 1847, libretto by Andrea Maffei, based on
       Schiller's drama. Part of Carlo, Act II. e3-ab4 g3-g4 Slightly
       dramatic recitative and sustained aria in moderate slow tempo.
       Lyric, requires very fine high P to PPP. Slightly climactic ending.
       Agitated accompaniment. Acc: 4 (VS)GR. OAT

8326. R: Son gli ebbri inverecondi
       A: O mio castel paterno
       Opera: I MASNADIERI. Part of Carlo, Act I. ab3-bb4 ab3-gb4
       Slightly subdued recitative and sustained aria in moderate slow tempo.
       Requires fine high P and PP. Mainly lyric. Slightly subdued ending.
       Acc: 3-4 (VS)GS. OAT

8327. R: È di Monforte il cenno!
       A: Giorno di pianto, di fier dolore!
       Opera: I VESPRI SICILIANI, 1856, libretto by E. Caime, after
       Eugène Scribe and Charles Duveyrier. Part of Arrigo, Act IV. eb3-
       b4 b3-g#4 Extended recitative in varied tempi and sustained aria in
       moderate slow tempo. Requires very fine high P and PP. Has dra-
       matic passages. Climactic ending. Acc: 3-4 (VS)GR. OAT

8328. Ah sì, ben mio; coll'essere
       Opera: IL TROVATORE, 1853, libretto by Salvatore Cammarano,
       after Antonio Gutierrez's play. Part of Manrico, Act III. e3-g4 g3-
       g4 Sustained in slow tempo. Has climactic passages and an unac-
       companied ending passage. OAT includes the recitative: Il presagio
       funesto. Acc: 3-4 (VS)GS, GR, CP. OPA-3, MTO, ORT, OAT.
       (S)GR

8329. Deserto sulla terra
       Opera: IL TROVATORE. Part of Manrico, Act I. bb3-ab4 bb3-g4
       Sustained in moderate slow tempo. Tessitura stays consistently high
       in this short song. Mainly lyric, on MF level. Climactic ending.
       Acc: 3-4 (VS)GS, GR, CP. (S)GR. MTO, ORT, OAT

8330. R: Or magnanima, e prima delle città
A: La pia materna mano
Opera: LA BATTAGLIA DI LEGNANO, 1849, libretto by Salvatore
Cammarano. Part of Arrigo, Act I. e3-bb4 ab3-f4 A free recita-
tive, somewhat subdued. Sustained aria in moderate slow tempo.
Has some climactic passages. Requires very fine high P and PP.
Subdued ending. Acc: 3-4 (VS)GR. OAT

8331. R: La vita è inferno
A: O, tu che in seno agli angeli
Opera: LA FORZA DEL DESTINO, 1862, libretto by Francesco
Maria Piave, after Duke of Rivas' play. Part of Don Alvaro, Act III.
db3-bb4 Extended recitative in varied tempi, and a sus-
tained aria in moderate slow tempo. Has dramatic passages, and a
climactic high ending on ab4. Acc: 3-4 (VS)GR, CP, B-H (Italian
& English), IM (Italian & English). OPA-3, ORT, OAT. (S)GR

8332. R: Lunge da lei
A: De' miei bollenti spiriti
Opera: LA TRAVIATA, 1853, libretto by Francesco Maria Piave,
based on a play by the younger Dumas. Part of Alfredo, Act II. e3-
ab4 g3-g4 Slightly extended recitative and a sustained aria in moderate slow tempo. Requires fine PPP. Gently lyric. Aria ends in
unaccompanied, quasi-recitative passage. Acc: 3-4 (VS)GS, GR,
CP. MTO, ORT, OAT. (S)GR

8333. Libiamo ne' lieti calici
Opera: LA TRAVIATA. Part of Alfredo, Act I. f3-g4 a3-eb4
Animated in moderate lively tempo. In graceful waltz, requires some
flexibility. Alfredo's part in the duet, Brindisi, or drinking song,
with Violetta. Acc: 3-4 (VS)GS, GR, CP. OAT. (S)GR

8334. R: Oh, fede negar potessi
A: Quando le sere al placido
Opera: LUISA MILLER, 1849, libretto by Salvatore Cammarano,
based on Schiller's tragedy. Part of Rodolfo, Act II. d3-ab4 ab3-
f4 Sustained in moderate slow tempo. Generally subdued, gentle,
with some climactic phrases. Ends with unaccompanied vocal line.
Acc: 3-4 (VS)GS, GR, CP. OAT. (S)GR

8335. R: O figli miei!
A: Ah, la paterna mano
Opera: MACBETH, 1847, libretto by Francesco Maria Piave, after
William Shakespeare's drama. Part of Macduff, Act IV. f3-bbb4
ab3-g4 Subdued recitative and a sustained aria in moderate tempo.
Requires very fine P and PP. Has climactic passages and ending.
Agitated accompaniment. Acc: 3-4 (VS)GR. OAT. (S)GR

8336. La donna è mobile
Opera: RIGOLETTO, 1851, libretto by Francesco Maria Piave, after
Victor Hugo. Part of the Duke of Mantua, Act III. f#3-a#4 g#3-
g#4 Energetic, graceful, and a jovial waltz. Requires some fine P.
Climactic ending. Acc: 3-4 (VS)GS, GR, CP. OPA-3, MTO, ORT,
OAT. (S)GR, GS (high & medium)

8337. R: Ella mi fu rapita!
A: Parmi veder le lagrime
Opera: RIGOLETTO. Part of the Duke of Mantua, Act II. d3-bbb4

a3-a4 Sustained aria in varied tempi. Has many high notes. Faster and climactic ending section. Mainly lyric, with some dramatic passages. Acc: 4 (VS)GS, GR, CP. OPA-3, OAT. (S)GR

8338. R: Ma dove or trovasi
A: Possente amor mi chiama
Opera: RIGOLETTO. Part of the Duke of Mantua, Act II. f♯3-a4 a3-g4 Animated in lively tempo. Has dramatic passages, passages with high tessitura, and a climactic ending. Two identical verses, with men's choral interpolation. Acc: 3-4 (VS)GS, GR, CP

8339. Questa o quella
Opera: RIGOLETTO. Part of the Duke of Mantua, Act I. e♭3-a♭4 (b♭4) a♭3-g4 Animated in moderate lively tempo. Rhythmic, joyous, and slightly outgoing. Climactic ending. Acc: 3-4 (VS)GS, GR, CP. MTO, ORT, OAT. (S)GR

8340. Di' tu se fedele il flutto
Opera: UN BALLO IN MASCHERA, 1859, libretto by Antonio Somma, after Scribe's libretto. Part of Ricardo, Act I. c3-a♭4 e♭3-g4 Animated in fast tempo. Requires fluent enunciation, fine P to PP, and some lightness on the staccati passages. Basically in 2 verses, with ensemble in the original score. Acc: 3-4 (VS)GS, GR, CP. (S)GR. OAT

8341. R: Forse la soglia attinse
A: Ma se m'è forza perderti
Opera: UN BALLO IN MASCHERA. Part of Ricardo, Act III. d3-b♭4 g3-g4 Slightly dramatic recitative and sustained aria in moderate slow tempo. Has dramatic passages. Requires fine high PP. Unaccompanied and strong ending phrase. Acc: 3-4 (VS)GS, GR, CP. OAT. (S)GR

FRANCO VITTADINI, 1884-1948

8342. È arrivata primavera as alminar!
Opera: ANIMA ALLEGRA, 1921, libretto by Giuseppe Adami and Luigi Motta, after Quintero's comedy. Part of Lucio, Act I. f3-a♭4(b♭4) a♭3-g4 Sustained in slow tempo. Has some dramatic passages, and a subdued ending. Acc: 3-4 MTO

B.   French Composers

ADOLPHE (CHARLES) ADAM, 1803-1856

8343. Elle est à moi!
Opera: LE CHALET, 1834, libretto by Eugène Scribe and Anne Honoré Melesville. Part of Daniel, one-act opera. d3-b4 g3-e4 Animated in lively tempo. Marked. Requires flexibility. Has climactic passages. Acc: 4 (VS)EC

8344. A la noblesse jem'allie
Opera: LE POSTILLON DE LONGJUMEAU, 1836, libretto by Adolphe de Leuvon and Leon Brunswick. Part of St. Phar, Act III. b2-d5 g♯3-e4 Sustained in moderate tempo. Has slower middle section. Requires flexibility. Has some florid figures. Acc: 4 (VS)BR

8345.   Elle est princesse
        Opera: SI J'ÉTAIS ROI, 1852, libretto by Adolphe Philippe d'Ennery
        and Jules Brésil. Part of Zéphoris, Act I. g♭3(f3)-c♭5 a♭3-f4
        Animated in quite rapid tempo. Slow, graceful middle section. Cli-
        mactic ending. Acc: 3-4 (VS)AL

8346.   J'ignore son nom sa naissance
        Opera: SI J'ÉTAIS ROI. Part of Zéphoris, Act I. Common title:
        Romance. f3-a♭4 a♭3-f4 Sustained in moderate slow tempo. Tes-
        situra stays high in some passages. Somewhat subdued ending. Acc:
        3-4 (VS)AL

DANIEL FRANÇOIS ESPRIT AUBER, 1782-1871

8347.   Agnès la jouvencelle
        Opera: FRA DIAVOLO or L'HOTELLERIE DE TERRCINE, 1830,
        libretto by Eugène Scribe. Part of Marquis, Act II. c♯3-a4 g♯3-
        e4 Sustained in moderate tempo. Graceful and generally light. Has
        florid passages. Requires some flexibility. Acc: 3-4 (VS)NO, BR

8348.   Pour toujours, disaitelle je suis a toi
        Opera: FRA DIAVOLO or L'HOTELLERIE DE TERRCINE. Part of
        Lorenzo, Act III. d3-a4 g3-g4 Animated in lively tempo. Has fre-
        quent dotted rhythms, climactic passages, and some passages with
        high tessitura. Acc: 3-4 (VS)NO, BR. OAR-T

8349.   Du pauvre seul ami fidèle
        Opera: LA MUETTE DE PORTICI, 1828, libretto by Eugène Scribe
        and Germaine Delavigne. Part of Masaniello, Act IV. f3(e3)-a4
        a3-f4 Slightly animated vocal part in moderate slow, but moving tem-
        po. Lyric. Subdued ending usually with short florid figures. Acc:
        3-4 OPA-3, OAR-T

HECTOR BERLIOZ, 1803-1869

8350.   Merci, doux crépuscule!
        Opera: LA DAMNATION DE FAUST, 1864, libretto by the composer,
        after Goethe's drama. A concert opera. Part of Faust, Act IV. e3-
        a♭4 g3-f4 Sustained in moderate slow tempo. Requires very fine
        high PP and PPP. Generally subdued and very lyric. Acc: 3-4
        (VS)CT

8351.   Nature immense
        Opera: LA DAMNATION DE FAUST. Part of Faust, Act V. Com-
        mon title: Invocation à la nature. f♯3-a4 a3-f4 Sustained in gen-
        erally moderate tempo. Starts majestically. Has dramatic passages.
        Agitated accompaniment. Acc: 4 (VS)CT. (S)IM

8352.   Inutiles regrets
        Opera: LES TROYENS À CARTHAGE, second part of a two-part
        opera, LES TROYENS, 1856-1859, libretto by the composer, based on
        the story of Virgil. Part of Énée, Act III. e3-b♭4(c5) g3-f4 Sus-
        tained first in lively tempo, then slower middle section. High and
        dramatic ending on b♭4 and a♭4. An extended and demanding aria,
        15 pages long. Acc: 4 (VS)EC

8353. O blonde Cérès
       Opera: LES TROYENS À CARTHAGE. Part of Iopas, Act II. e3-
       c5 g3-f4 Sustained in moderate slow tempo. Has florid figures.
       Requires flexibility. Has climactic passages, and a descending end-
       ing line. Acc: 4 (VS)EC

8354. Vallon sonore où dès l'aurore
       Opera: LES TROYENS À CARTHAGE. Part of Hylas, Act III. e♭3-
       g4 g3-f4 Quite sustained in moderate tempo. Requires fine P.
       Has climactic passages, and a very subdued, high ending. Acc: 3-4
       (VS)EC

GEORGES BIZET, 1838-1875

8355. La fleur que tu m'avais jetée
       Opera: CARMEN, 1873-1874, libretto by Henri Meilhac and Ludovic
       Halévy, based on Mérimée's story. Part of Don José, Act II. e3-
       b♭4 f3-f4 Common title: Flower song. Sustained in moderate slow
       tempo. Requires very fine P and PP. Generally subdued, and very
       lyric in style. Subdued ending. Acc: 3-4 (VS)GS. OPA-3, ORT.
       (S)GS

8356. R: Partout des cris de joie
       A: A la voix d'un amant fidèle
       Opera: LA JOLIE FILLE DE PERTH, 1866, libretto by J. H. Ver-
       noy de Saint Georges and Jules Adenis. Part of Smith, Act II. e3-
       a4 a3-g4 Subdued recitative and a sustained and subdued aria. Gen-
       tle and lyric. Requires fine P and PP. Acc: 3-4 (VS)EC

8357. De savanes et des forêts
       Opera: LES PÊCHEURS DE PERLES, 1862-1863, libretto by Michel
       Carré and Eugène Cormon. Part of Nadir, Act I. e♭3-a♭4 a♭3-g4
       Animated in lively tempo. Slower middle section. Requires fine P.
       Graceful. Has dramatic passages and a climactic ending. Acc: 3-4
       (VS)EC

8358. Je crois entendre encore
       Opera: LES PÊCHEURS DE PERLES. Part of Nadir, Act I. e3-b4
       b3-g4 Very sustained, very lyric, and in moderate tempo. General-
       ly subdued. Requires very fine high P and PP. Requires consider-
       able vocal control. Very subdued ending. Acc: 3-4 (VS)EC

ALFRED BRUNEAU, 1857-1934

8359. Lejour tombe
       Opera: L'ATTAQUE DU MOULIN, 1893, libretto by Louis Gallet,
       after Emile Zola. Part of Dominique, Act II. e♯3-a♯4 a♯3-f♯4
       Sustained in moderate tempo. Has dramatic passages. Starts sub-
       dued and gentle. Acc: 3-4 (VS)EC

GUSTAVE CHARPENTIER, 1860-1956

8360. Dans la cité lointaine
       Opera: LOUISE, 1900, libretto by the composer. Part of Julian,
       Act II. f♯3-g♯4 g♯3-e4 Sustained in moderate slow tempo. Has

some climactic passages. Ends before the full section of women's chorus. Acc: 3-4 (VS)GS, HC

FÉLICIEN (CÉSAR) DAVID, 1810-1876

8361. Zora, je cède à ta puissance
Opera: LA PERLE DU BRÉSIL, 1851, libretto by J. Gabriel and Sylvain Saint-Étienne. Part of Lorenz, Act I. f3-ab4 ab3-f4 Sustained in moderate slow tempo. Graceful. Acc: 3-4 (VS)HS

8362. Ma maîtresse a quitté la tente
Opera: LALLA-ROUKH, 1862, libretto by Michel Carré and Hippolyte Lucas, after Thomas Moore. Part of Noureddin, Act I. Common title: Romance de Noureddin. e3-a4 a3-e4 Animated in moderate tempo. Graceful. Acc: 3-4 (VS)EG

CLAUDE DEBUSSY, 1862-1918

8363. Ah! je respire enfin!
Opera: PELLÉAS ET MÉLISANDE, 1902, libretto by Maurice Maeterlinck. Part of Pelléas, Act III. d3-f#4 f3-e4 Mostly in recitative style, in varied tempi. Air ends with "une fenêtre de la tour." Acc: 4 (VS)AD

8364. Oh! Oh! qu'est-ce que c'est?
Opera: PELLÉAS ET MÉLISANDE. Part of Pelléas, Act III. c3-a4 f3-f4 In recitative style in varied tempi. Has some lyric and sustained passages. Climactic ending phrase. Interpretatively not easy. Excerpt ends with "plus m'abandonner...." Acc: 4 (VS)AD

(CLEMENT PHILIBERT) LÉO DÉLIBES, 1836-1891

8365. R: Je me souviens, sans voix
A: Ah! Viens, dans le forêt profonde
Opera: LAKMÉ, 1883, libretto by Edmond Gondinet and Philippe Gille. Part of Gerald, Act III. e3-b4 g#3-f#4 Generally gentle recitative and an animated aria in lively tempo. Has climactic passages and ending. Agitated accompaniment throughout. Acc: 4 (VS)HC, IM

8366. R: Prende le dessin
A: Fantaisie aux divins mensonges
Opera: LAKMÉ. Part of Gerald, Act I. f3-a4 g3-ab4 Slightly subdued recitative, and a sustained aria in moderate lively tempo. Generally subdued, requires very fine high P. Subdued, sustained high ending on ab4. Acc: 3-4 OPA-3, ORT

BENJAMIN (LOUIS PAUL) GODARD, 1849-1895

8367. R: Cachés dans cet asile
A: O! ne t'eveille pas encore
Opera: JOCELYN, 1888, libretto by Paul Armand Silvestre and Victor Capoul, after Alphonse de Lamartine. Common titles: "Berceuse" or "Jocelyn's lullaby." The only surviving excerpt from the opera.

Part of Jocelyn, Act II. f3-a4 a3-g4 Gentle recitative and sustained
aria in moderate slow tempo. Requires fine P and PP. Very subdued high ending. Acc: 3-4 (VS)EC. OPA-3, ORT, 56S, 20M (Godard, Ch. V). (S)GS

8368. Pleine de mon pays
       Opera: LE TASSE, 1878, libretto by Charles Grandmougin. Part of
       Tasso, Act I. f3-a4 ab3-f4 Sustained in slightly slow tempo. Has
       climactic passages. With choral ensemble near the end. Acc: 3-4
       (VS)GH

CHARLES (FRANÇOIS) GOUNOD, 1818-1893

8369. R: Quel trouble inconnu me pénètre?
       A: Salut! demeure chaste et pure
       Opera: FAUST, 1852-1859, libretto by Jules Barbier and Michel Car-
       ré, after Goethe. Part of Faust, Act II. eb3-c5 g3-f4 Sustained
       in slow tempo. Quite lyric. Generally gentle, with a subdued end-
       ing. Acc: 3-4 (VS)GS. OPA-3, MTO, ORT. (S)GS

8370. R: Mon coeur est plein d'un noir souci
       A: Anges du paradis
       Opera: MIREILLE, 1863, libretto by Michel Carré, after Frederic
       Mistral. Part of Vincent, Act V. g3-ab4 b3-g4 Sustained aria in
       moderate slow tempo. Has climactic passages. Subdued ending after
       climax. Acc: 3-4 (VS)EC

8371. R: L'amour! l'amour!
       A: Ah, lève-toi, soleil!
       Opera: ROMÉO ET JULIETTE, 1864, libretto by Jules Barbier and
       Michel Carré, after William Shakespeare. Part of Roméo, Act II.
       f3-bb4 a3-f4 Sustained in moderate slow tempo. Lyric. Has some
       climactic passages. Ending on sustained bb4. In the opera, this is
       sung below Juliette's window. Acc: 4 (VS)GS. OPA-3

8372. R: J'arrive le premier
       A: O jours heureux
       Opera: SAPHO, 1851, libretto by Émile Augier. Part of Phaon, Act
       III. eb3-bb4(db5) ab3-g4 Sustained aria in moderate slow tempo.
       Has slightly faster tempi, some dramatic climaxes, and a climactic
       ending. Acc: 4 (VS)EC

(JACQUES FRANÇOIS) FROMENTAL (ELIAS) HALÉVY, 1799-1862

8373. Ou chaque jour je viens l'attendre
       Opera: LE FÉE AUX ROSES, 1847, libretto by Eugène Scribe and
       Vernoy de Saint-Georges. Part of Prince Badel-Boudour, Act II.
       e3-b4 a3-f♯4 Sustained in moderate slow tempo. Generally subdued.
       Requires fine high P and PP. Lyric in style. Acc: 3-4 (VS)HL

8374. Dieu, que ma voix tremblante
       Opera: LA JUIVE, 1835, libretto by Eugène Scribe. Part of Éléazar,
       Act II. f3-ab4 ab3-g4 Sustained in moderate slow tempo. Has dra-
       matic passages and a climactic ending. Acc: 3-4 (VS)HL

8375. R: Va prononcer
       A: Rachel quand du Seigneur

Opera: LA JUIVE. Part of Éléazar, Act IV. e♭3-c5 g3-g4 Aria
is in varied tempi and moods. Starts sustained, in moderate slow
tempo. Has dramatic sections. Climactic ending on a♭4. An extended excerpt. Acc: 4 OPA-3

8376. Demes aveuz ombres sacrées
Opera: LA REINE DE CHYPRE, 1841, libretto by Vernoy de Saint-
Georges. Part of Gerard, Act IV. f♯3-d♭5 g3-f4 Sustained in
moderate tempo. Has dramatic passages. Subdued ending after climactic c5 and d♭5. Acc: 3-4 (VS)MR

(LOUIS JOSEPH) FERDINAND HÉROLD, 1791-1833

8377. R: Ce soir j'arrive donc
A: O ma tendre amie
Opera: LE PRÉ AUX CLERCS, 1832, libretto by François Antoine
Eugène de Planard. Part of Mergy, Act I. e3-c5 a3-g4 Recitative
and a gentle animated aria in moderate tempo. Faster middle section. Has florid passages toward the end. Graceful in some passages. Acc: 3-4 (VS)BR

(VICTOR ANTOINE) ÉDOUARD LALO, 1823-1892

8378. R: Puisqu'on ne peut fléchir
A: Vainement, ma bien-aimee
Opera: LE ROI D'YS, 1888, libretto by Edouard Blau. Part of
Mylio, Act III. e♭3-a4 a3-f♯4 Slightly animated vocal part in mod-
erate lively tempo. Requires fine high PP. Has some gentle pas-
sages. Acc: 3-4 OPA-3

JULES (EMILE FREDERIC) MASSENET, 1842-1912

8379. R: Ne pouvant réprimer
A: Adieu donc, Vains objets
Opera: HÉRODIADE, 1881, libretto by Paul Milliet and Henri Grémont (Georges Hartmann), after a story by Flaubert. Part of Jean,
Act IV. d3-b♭4 g3-g4 Aria starts in very slow tempo, then varies
as song progresses. Dramatic. Subdued high, sustained ending note:
a4 or f4. Acc: 3-4 (VS)HC

8380. Perce jusques au fond du coeur
Opera: LE CID, 1885, libretto by Adolphe Philippe D'Ennery, Louis
Gallet and Edouard Blau, after Pierre Corneille. Part of Rodrique,
Act II. f3-a4 a♭3-g4 Sustained, first in slow, then faster tempo.
Has dramatic climaxes. Acc: 3-4 (VS)HC

8381. Dans la nuit, la nuit fatale
Opera: LE ROI DE LAHORE, 1877, libretto by Louis Gallet. Part
of Alim, Act IV. g♯3-b♭4 g♯3-g♯4 Sustained in lively tempo.
Has dramatic climaxes. Requires fine high P. Acc: 3-4 (VS)HC

8382. R: Aux troupes du Sultan
A: Promesse de mon avenir
Opera: LE ROI DE LAHORE. Part of Scindia, Act IV. d♭3-g♭4
e♭3-e♭4 Dramatic recitative and a sustained to animated aria. Climactic and dramatic. Ends with a sustained g♭4. Originally for

baritone, but had been sung by heavy tenors. Acc: 3-4 (VS)HC

8383. R: Je suis seul!
       A: Ah! fuyez, douce image
       Opera: MANON, 1884, libretto by Henri Meilhac and Philippe Gille.
       Part of Des Grieux, Act III. f3-bb4 ab3-ab4 Sustained in moder-
       ate slow tempo. Has dramatic passages, and extremely wide con-
       trasts in dynamics. Very subdued ending after a dramatic climax.
       Requires very fine high PP and PPP. Acc: 3-4 OPA-3. (VS)GS

8384. R: Instant charmant
       A: En ferment les yeux
       Opera: MANON. Part of Des Grieux, Act II. Common title: Des
       Grieux's dream aria. e3-a4 a3-f#4 Gently animated vocal part in
       slow tempo. Tranquil, generally subdued, and requires fine P. Gen-
       tly agitated accompaniment. Acc: 3-4 (VS)GS. OPA-3, ORT.
       (S)GS

8385. R: Un autre est son époux
       A: J'aurais sur ma poitrine
       Opera: WERTHER, 1892, libretto by Edouard Blau, Paul Milliet and
       Georges Hartmann, after Goethe. Part of Werther, Act II. g3-bbb4
       bb3-ab4 Animated in lively tempo. Brilliant. Requires flexibility,
       fine high P and PP, and some dramatic energy. Climactic high end-
       ing on ab4. Acc: 3-4 (VS)HS, IM

8386. R: Oui! Ce qu'elle m'ordonne
       A: Lorsque l'enfant revient d'un voyage
       Opera: WERTHER. Part of Werther, Act II. f#3-g#4(b4) a3-f4
       Generally subdued recitative and sustained aria in moderate tempo.
       Generally subdued with dramatic passages at the ending section. Very
       subdued ending. Acc: 3-4 (VS)HC, IM

8387. R: Je ne sais si je veille
       A: O nature, pleine de grâce
       Opera: WERTHER. Part of Werther, Act I. f#3-a4 a3-f4 Sus-
       tained in moderate tempo. Has dramatic passages and a climactic
       high ending. Requires very fine high P and PP. Gently agitated ac-
       companiment. Acc: 3-4 (VS)HC, IM

8388. R: Traduire! Ah! bien souvent mon rêve
       A: Pourquoi me réveiller
       Opera: WERTHER. Part of Werther, Act III. f#3-a#4 a3-f#4
       Slow and rather subdued recitative. Sustained aria in moderate slow
       tempo. Requires very fine high P and PP; also requires some dra-
       matic energy. High climactic ending. Agitated accompaniment.
       Acc: 4 (VS)HC, IM

ÉTIENNE NICOLAS MÉHUL, 1763-1817

8389. R: Vainement Pharaon
       A: Champs paternels!
       Opera: JOSEPH, 1807, libretto by Alexandre Duval, based on the
       Biblical story. Part of Joseph, Act I. d#3-a4 g#3-f#4 Recitative
       and sustained aria in moderate slow tempo. Faster middle section.
       Requires fine P. Climactic ending with agitated accompaniment.
       Acc: 3-4 MLF

ANDRÉ (CHARLES PROSPER) MESSAGER, 1853-1929

8390. J'aimais la vieille maison grise
Opera: FORTUNIO, 1907, libretto by G. A. de Caillavet and Robert
de Flers, after Alfred de Musset. Part of Fortunio, Act II. e3-g4
a3-e4 Sustained in moderate slow tempo. Tranquil and generally
subdued. In gentle recitative style. Climactic ending. Acc: 3-4
(VS)EC

8391. Si vous croyez que je vais dire
Opera: FORTUNIO. Part of Fortunio, Act III. Common title:
Chanson de Fortunio. e3-a4 a3-f#4 Sustained in moderate tempo.
Requires simplicity. Slow and subdued ending section. Acc: 3-4
(VS)EC

JACQUES OFFENBACH, 1819-1880

8392. R: Allons! Courage et confiance!
A: Ah, vivre deux!
Opera: LES CONTES D'HOFFMANN, 1881, libretto by Jules Barbier
and Michel Carré, after Hoffmann. Part of Hoffmann, Act II. e3-
g4 a3-f4 Animated vocal part in moderate slow tempo. Requires
some fluent enunciation and fine P and PP. Generally subdued.
Acc: 3-4 (VS)GS

(CHARLES LOUIS) AMBROISE THOMAS, 1811-1896

8393. Pour mon pays
Opera: HAMLET, 1868, libretto by Jules Barbier and Michel Carré,
after William Shakespeare. Part of Laërte, Act I. f3-ab4(bb4)
ab3-gb4 Sustained in moderate tempo. Has dramatic passages and
a climactic ending. Has passages which require some fluent enunciation. Acc: 3-4 (VS)HC

8394. Adieu, Mignon!
Opera: MIGNON, 1871, libretto by Jules Barbier and Michel Carré.
Part of Wilhelm Meister, Act II. f3-a4 a3-g4 Sustained in moder-
ate tempo. Requires fine P and PP. Has some dramatic climaxes.
Subdued ending. Acc: 3-4 OPA-3. (VS)GS

8395. Elle ne croyait pas
Opera: MIGNON. Part of Wilhelm Meister, Act III. g3-a4 a3-g4
Sustained in moderate slow tempo. Graceful. Requires fine P.
Fairly simple melody. Climactic ending. Acc: 3-4 (VS)GS. OPA-
3, ORT

8396. Oui, je veux par le monde
Opera: MIGNON. Part of Wilhelm Meister, Act I. e3-bb4(c5) g3-
g4 Animated in lively tempo. Slightly slower middle section. Graceful in some passages. Has some short, florid passages, and some
dramatic passages. Requires flexibility. Graceful in some sections.
This excerpt is usually omitted at the Grand Opera, Paris. Acc: 4
(VS)GS

C.   German and Austrian Composers

LUDWIG VAN BEETHOVEN, 1770-1827

8397. R: Gott! welch Dunkel hier!
A: In des Lebens Frühlingstagen
Opera: FIDELIO, c. 1803-1805, libretto by Joseph Sonnleithner and
Georg Frederick Treitschke. Part of Florestan, Act II.   eb3-bb4
a3-a4   Recitative in varied tempi, and an aria in sustained and slow
tempo, followed by an animated movement in lively tempo. Has passages with high tessitura. Dramatic, and vocally demanding. Climactic ending. Acc: 4 (VS)GS, CP. OAR-T

ALBAN BERG, 1885-1935

8398. Ich möchte tauschen mit Dir
Opera: LULU, 1937, libretto by the composer, after Frank Wedekind. Part of Der Maler (the painter), Act I.   eb3-b4   g3-f4   Common title: Arioso.   Gently animated vocal part in moderate lively
tempo. Requires flexibility and sensitivity to pitch. Subdued high
ending. Acc: 4 (VS)UE

8399. Würden Sie es für möglich halten
Opera: LULU. Part of the Prince, Act I.   eb3-ab4   g3-fb4 Sustained in moderate tempo. Generally on MF level. Gentle, with a
subdued ending. Requires sensitivity to pitch. Acc: 4 (VS)UE

PETER CORNELIUS, 1824-1874

8400. Ach das Leid hab ich getragen
Opera: DER BARBIER VON BAGDAD, 1858, libretto by the composer,
based on "Arabian Nights." Part of Nureddin, Act I.   f#3-a4   b3-
f#4   Animated in very fast tempo. Dramatic. Has quite high tessitura. Acc: 4 (VS)CK, BH

8401. R: So leb' ich noch!
A: Vor deinem Fenster die Blumen
Opera: DER BARBIER VON BAGDAD. Part of Nureddin, Act I.   e3-
a4   a3-g4   Animated and fast recitative and a sustained aria in slower tempo. Requires fine P. Has dramatic passages and a climactic
high ending. Acc: 4 (VS)CK, BH. OAR-T

FRIEDRICH (FREIHERR) VON FLOTOW, 1812-1883

8402. Ach, so fromm (It.: M'appari tutt' amor)
Opera: MARTHA, 1847, libretto by W. Friedrich (Friedrich Wilhelm
Riese). Part of Lionel, Act III.   g3-bb4   a3-g4   Fairly simple vocal
part. Sustained in moderate lively tempo. Climactic ending. The
Italian version is the better-known text, due to the popularity of great
Italian tenors who sang it. Acc: 3-4 (VS)GS. OPA-3, MTO (Ital-
ian), ORT (Italian). (S)GS-Italian, French, English. OAR-T (Ger-
man)

PAUL HINDEMITH, 1895-1963

8403. Wagschalen dieser Welt!
       Opera: CARDILLAC, 1926, libretto by the composer, after Ferdinand
       Lion. Part of Kavalier, Act I. eb3-bb4 a3-f#4 Sustained in live-
       ly tempo. Starts quite strongly. Generally energetic. Climactic end-
       ing. Acc: 4 (VS)SC

GIACOMO MEYERBEER, 1791-1864

8404. R: Pays merveilleux
       A: O paradis sorti de l'onde
       Opera: L'AFRICAINE, 1865, libretto by Eugène Scribe. Part of
       Vasco da Gama, Act IV. eb3-bb4 gb3-gb4 Generally sustained in
       varied tempi and moods. More agitated middle section. Requires
       fine high P, as well as some dramatic energy. Climactic ending.
       The Italian version, "O paradiso!" is the better-known text, due to
       the popularity of great Italian tenors who sang it. Acc: 4 OPA-3
       (French), MTO (Italian), ORT (French)

8405. R: Aux armes, mes amis
       A: A la lueur de leurs torches funèbres
       Opera: LES HUGUENOTS, 1836, libretto by Eugène Scribe and Emile
       Deschamps. Part of Raoul, Act V. e3-c5 g3-g4 Sustained in very
       moderate tempo. Requires very fine high P and PP, as well as en-
       ergetic and dramatic passages. Vocally difficult. Climactic ending.
       Has choral ensemble in the score. Acc: 4 (VS)BR, BH

8406. R: Ah! Quel spectacle enchanteur
       A: Plus blanche que la blanche hermine
       Opera: LES HUGUENOTS. Part of Raoul, Act I. e3-a#4(b4) g#3-
       g#4 Sustained in moderate slow tempo. Graceful. Requires fine
       high P and PP. Florid. Ends with cadenza. Acc: 3-4 (VS)BR

8407. Achetez! voici, voici!
       Opera: L'ÉTOILE DU NORD, 1854, libretto by Eugène Scribe. Part
       of Danilowitz, Act I. db3-bb4(cb5) g3-g4 Animated in lively tempo.
       Bright, requires fluent enunciation. Slower ending section. Climac-
       tic ending with cadenza. Acc: 3-4 (VS)MT

WOLFGANG AMADEUS MOZART, 1756-1791

8408. R: Non sperarlo
       A: Ah! lo veggio quell' anima bella
       Opera: COSÌ FAN TUTTE or LA SCUOLA DEGLI AMANTI, 1790
       (K. 588), libretto by Lorenzo da Ponte. Part of Ferrando, Act II.
       f3-bb4 a3-g4 Short recitative and animated aria in moderate lively
       tempo. Livelier ending section. Requires some fluent enunciation
       and flexibility. Has some passages with high tessitura and climactic
       figures. Climactic ending. Acc: 4 (VS)GS, CP

8409. R: In qual fiero contrasto
       A: Tradito, schernito dal perfido cor
       Opera: COSÌ FAN TUTTE or LA SCUOLA DEGLI AMANTI. Part of
       Ferrando, Act II. f3-a4 g3-g4 Strong, accented recitative and an
       animated aria in lively tempo. Strong, bold, has dramatic passages.

Has passages with high tessitura. Requires fine command of high
notes, and flexibility. Acc: 4 (VS)GS, CP

8410. Un' aura amorosa
Opera: COSÌ FAN TUTTE or LA SCUOLA DEGLI AMANTI. Part of
Ferrando, Act I. d3-a4 a3-a4 Gently animated. Abounds with
short florid figures. Requires flexibility. Generally light. Acc:
3-4 (VS)GS, CP. OPA-3, AOT, OAR-T. (S)GR

8411. Frisch zum Kampfe, frisch zum Streite!
Opera: DIE ENTFÜHRUNG AUS DEM SERAIL, 1782 (K. 384), libretto
by Gottlieb Stephani II, after Christoph F. Bretzner's play. Part of
Pedrillo, Act II. d3-b4 f♯3-a4 Animated in very lively tempo.
Spirited, requires some flexibility. Has dramatic climaxes, some
wide intervalic skips, and a climactic ending. Agitated accompaniment. Acc: 4 (VS)B-H, CP. OAR-T

8412. Hier soll ich dich denn sehen
Opera: DIE ENTFÜHRUNG AUS DEM SERAIL. Part of Belmonte,
Act I. g3-a4 g3-g4 Animated in moderate slow tempo. Has dramatic high climaxes, and a climactic ending. This short aria immediately follows the overture. Acc: 3-4 (VS)B-H, CP. OAR-T

8413. Ich baue ganz
Opera: DIE ENTFÜHRUNG AUS DEM SERAIL. Part of Belmonte,
Act II. e♭3-b♭4 g3-g4 Sustained in moderate slow tempo. Has
extended florid passages. Requires flexibility. Climactic ending.
Acc: 3-4 AOT. (VS)B-H, CP

8414. Im Mohrenland gefangen war
Opera: DIE ENTFÜHRUNG AUS DEM SERAIL. Part of Pedrillo, Act
III. Other title: Romance. e♯3-d4 f♯3-d4 Sustained in moderate
tempo. Graceful, and generally on MF level. Descending ending
line. Acc: 3-4 (VS)B-H, CP

8415. R: Constanze!
A: O wie ängstlich
Opera: DIE ENTFÜHRUNG AUS DEM SERAIL, 1782 (K. 384), libretto
by Gottlieb Stephani II. Part of Belmonte, Act I. e3-a4 f♯3-f♯4
Animated aria in moderate slow tempo. Has florid figures. Requires
flexibility and fluent enunciation. Generally on MF level. Acc: 3-4
(VS)CP, B-H. OPA-3

8416. Wenn der Freude Thränen fliessen
Opera: DIE ENTFÜHRUNG AUS DEM SERAIL. Part of Belmonte,
Act II. c3-a♭4 a3-g4 Sustained section in slow tempo, followed by
animated section in moderate lively tempo. Has one short florid passage. Slightly climactic ending. Acc: 3-4 (VS)B-H, CP. OAR-T

8417. Alles fühlt der Liebe Freuden
Opera: DIE ZAUBERFLÖTE, 1791 (K. 620), libretto by Emanuel
Schikaneder and Johann Georg Gieseke. Part of Monostatos, Act II.
d3-e4 g3-d4 Animated in fast tempo. Requires quite fluent enuncia-
tion and fine P. A buffo air in 2 verses. Acc: 3-4 (VS)GS, CP.
OAR-T

8418. Dies Bildniss ist bezaubernd schön
Opera: DIE ZAUBERFLÖTE. Part of Tamino, Act I. g3-a♭4

bb 3-g4 Sustained in slow tempo. Has gently animated sections; somewhat florid. Generally lyric with some dramatic passages. Acc: 3-4 (VS)GS, CP. OPA-3, ORT, AOT, OAR-T

8419. Dalla sua pace
Opera: DON GIOVANNI or IL DISSOLUTO PUNITO, 1787 (K. 527), libretto by Lorenzo da Ponte. Part of Don Ottavio, Act I. d3-g4 g3-g4 Sustained in moderate tempo. Requires some flexibility and fine P. Acc: 3-4 (VS)GS, CP, GR, B-H. (S)GR. OPA-3, AOT, OAR-T

8420. Il mio tesoro intanto
Opera: DON GIOVANNI or IL DISSOLUTO PUNITO. Part of Don Ottavio, Act II. d3-a4 f3-g4 Sustained in moderate slow tempo. Slightly agitated middle section, and a more energetic, dramatic, ending section. Has florid figures. Acc: 4 (VS)GS, CP, GR. OPA-3, ORT, AOT, OAR-T. (S)GS, GR

8421. R: Qual mi conturbai
A: Fuor del mar ho un mar in seno
Opera: IDOMENEO, RE DI CRETA, 1781 (K. 366), libretto by Giambattista Varesco, after Danchet. Part of Idomeneo, Act II. d3-g4 g3-f# 4 Slightly extended recitative, and an animated aria in moderate lively tempo. Quite florid. Requires considerable flexibility. Has some long-held notes and dramatic passages. Climactic ending. See the Appendix in IM for another version of this excerpt. Acc: 4 (VS)IM, CP

8422. R: Sventurata Sidon!
A: Se colà ne fati è scritto
Opera: IDOMENEO, RE DI CRETA. Part of Arbace, Act III. e3-a4 g# 3-f# 4 Extended dramatic recitative and a sustained aria in moderate slow tempo. Graceful. Has some slightly florid figures and florid passages. Requires some flexibility. Slightly climactic ending. Acc: 4 (VS)IM, CP

8423. Se il tuo duol
Opera: IDOMENEO, RE DI CRETA. Part of Arbace, Act II. d3-a4 g3-g4 Animated in lively tempo. Has florid passages. Requires flexibility, fluent enunciation, and a good command of high notes. Has some intervalic skips of over an octave. Generally strong. Climactic ending with a trill. Acc: 4-5 (VS)IM, CP

8424. Scena: Popoli! a voi l'ultima legge impone Idomeneo
A: Torna la pace al core
Opera: IDOMENEO, RE DI CRETA. Part of Idomeneo, Act III. f3-g4(a4) g3-f4 Dramatic scena and a sustained aria in slow tempo, with a faster middle section. Has florid passages and climactic passages. Slightly climactic ending. Acc: 4 (VS)IM, CP

8425. Vedrommi intorno
Opera: IDOMENEO, RE DI CRETA. Part of Idomeneo, Act I. e3-g4 g3-f4 Sustained in moderate slow tempo. Has some dramatic passages, slightly florid figures, and one florid passage. Dramatic ending. Acc: 3-4 (VS)IM, CP. OAR-T

8426. Del più sublime soglio
Opera: LA CLEMENZA DI TITO, 1791 (K. 621), libretto by Caterino

Mazzolà, after Metastasio. Part of Tito, Act I. e3-a4 g3-f#4
Sustained in moderate slow tempo. Generally on MF level. Some-
what climactic ending. Generally lyric. Acc: 3-4 AOT. (VS)IM-
Italian & English; CP-German & English

8427. Che beltà, che leggiadrià
       Opera: LA FINTA GIARDINIERA, 1775 (K. 196), libretto by Ranieri
       Calzabigi (?). Part of Count Belfiore, Act I. eb3-g4 g3-f4 Gen-
       erally sustained vocal part in moderate slow tempo. Majestic. Has
       two slightly extended florid passages. Slightly climactic ending.
       Acc: 3-4 AOT

8428. In quegli anni
       Opera: LE NOZZE DI FIGARO, 1786 (K. 492), libretto by Lorenzo
       da Ponte, after Beaumarchais. Part of Basilio, Act IV. eb3-g4
       a3-f4 Sustained in moderate slow tempo. Animated, lively, and
       stronger ending section. Generally lyric, with some climactic pas-
       sages. Climactic ending with agitated accompaniment. Acc: 3-4
       (VS)GS, CP. OAR-T

8429. Guerrier, che d'un acciaro
       Opera: LUCIO SILLA, 1772 (K. 135), libretto by Giovanni di Gamerra,
       edited by Metastasio. Part of Aufidio, Act II. d3-a4 g3-g4 Ani-
       mated vocal part in lively tempo. Has florid passages. Requires
       flexibility. Slightly climactic ending. Extended instrumental prelude
       and postlude. Acc: 3-4 AOT

8430. Herr und Dreund
       Opera: ZAIDE or DAS SERAIL, 1779 unfinished (K. 344), libretto by
       Johann Andreas Schachtner. Part of Gomatz, Act I. f#3-g4 a3-g4
       Animated in moderate lively tempo. Generally on MF level. Some-
       what climactic ending. Has passages requiring fluent enunciation.
       Acc: 3-4 AOT-1

(CARL) OTTO (EHRENFRIED) NICOLAI, 1810-1849

8431. Horch, die Lerche singt im Hain
       Opera: DIE LUSTIGEN WEIBER VON WINDSOR, 1849, libretto by
       Hermann Salomon Mosenthal, after William Shakespeare. Part of
       Fenton, Act II. g3-g#4 b3-f#4 Sustained in moderate slow tempo.
       Joyful, ecstatic, and short. Acc: 4 (VS)CP. OAR-T

ARNOLD SCHÖNBERG, 1874-1951

8432. Gedankenhoch waren wir rehöht
       Opera: MOSES UND ARON, 1954 uncompleted, libretto by the com-
       poser, after Exodus III, The Bible. Part of the Youth, Act II. g3-
       b4 b3-a4 Sustained in moderate lively tempo. Dramatic and strong.
       Quite high tessitura. Climactic ending. Acc: 4 (VS)SC

RICHARD STRAUSS, 1864-1949

8433. Circe, Circe, kannst du mich hören?
       Opera: ARIADNE AUF NAXOS, 1917, libretto by Hugo von Hofmanns-
       thal. Part of Bacchus, one-act opera. g#3-a4 b3-f#4 Sustained in

moderate tempo. Generally calm and subdued. Requires very fine high P, especially the sustained ending. Acc: 3-4 (VS)AF

8434. Wenn das Herz aus Kristall zerbricht
Opera: DIE FRAU OHNE SCHATTEN, 1919, libretto by Hugo von Hofmannsthal. Part of the Kaiser, Act III. e3-bb4 a3-g#4 Sustained in moderate tempo. Slightly climactic ending. Generally calm, mainly lyric in style. Acc: 3-4 (VS)B-H

8435. Ah! Du willst nicht auf mich hören
Opera: SALOME, 1905, libretto by Hedwig Lachmann, a translation of Oscar Wilde's play. Part of Herod, one-act opera. d#3-a4 g3-g4 Sustained in varied tempi, but generally on the fast side. Interpretatively not easy. Broad, climactic ending on the phrase: "des Allerheiligsten geben." Acc: 4 (VS)B-H

RICHARD WAGNER, 1813-1883

8436. Am stillen Herd
Opera: DIE MEISTERSINGER VON NÜRNBERG, 1867, libretto by the composer. Part of Walther, Act I, Scene 3. d3-g4 f#3-f#4 Sustained in moderate tempo. Has dramatic passages. Climactic ending. Acc: 3-4 (VS)GS, CP. OPA-3, OGT

8437. Fanget an! So rief der Lenz
Opera: DIE MEISTERSINGER VON NÜRNBERG. Part of Walther, Act I, Scene 3. f3-a4 g3-a4 Sustained in moderate tempo, but moving along. Mainly lyric, with some dramatic passages. Uses high notes quite often. Ends with "das hehre Liebeslied." Climactic ending. Acc: 3-4 (VS)GS, CP. OGT

8438. Morgenlich leuchtend im rosigen Schein
Opera: DIE MEISTERSINGER VON NÜRNBERG. Part of Walther, Act III, Scene 5. e3-a4 a3-a4 Common title: Prize-song. Sustained in moderate tempo. Has broad lines and climactic passages. Quite lyric in style. Strong and climactic ending. Acc: 4 (VS)GS, CP. OPA-3, ORT, OGT

8439. Atmest du nicht mit mir die süssen
Opera: LOHENGRIN, 1850, libretto by the composer. Part of Lohengrin, Act III, Scene 2. g3-ab4 g3-g4 Sustained in very moderate tempo. Generally tranquil and subdued. Subdued ending. Acc: 3-4 (VS)GS, CP. OGT

8440. Höchstes Vertraun hast du mir schon zu danken
Opera: LOHENGRIN. Part of Lohengrin, Act III, Scene 2. f3-a4 g#3-f#4 A sustained scena in slow tempo. Has some dramatic passages. Generally in broad recitative style. Acc: 3-4 (VS)GS, CP. OGT

8441. In fernem Land
Opera: LOHENGRIN. Part of Lohengrin, Act III, Scene 3. e3-a4 f#3-f#4 Lohengrin's narration. Sustained, starts gently, then becomes dramatic. Dramatic, climactic ending. Acc: 3-4 (VS)GS, CP. OPA-3, ORT, OGT

8442. R: Schon sendet nach dem Säumigen der Gral!

A: Mein Lieber Schwan
Opera: LOHENGRIN. Part of Lohengrin, Act III, Scene 3. e3-a4
g3-g4 Sustained in moderate slow tempo. Generally gentle and subdued. Requires fine high P. Very strong, dramatic ending on "Leb'
wohl!" Acc: 3-4 (VS)GS. OGT

CARL MARIA VON WEBER, 1786-1826

8443. R: Was nun nachen
A: Ich gebe Gastereien
Opera: ABU HASSAN, 1811, libretto by Franz Karl Hiemer, after a
tale from the Arabian Nights. Part of Abu Hassan, one-act opera.
c3(a2)-g4 f3-e4 A recitative and a quite fast, animated aria. Has
a slower middle section. Requires flexibility. Climactic ending.
Acc: 3-4 (VS)CP

8444. R: Nein, länger trag' ich
A: Durch die Wälder
Opera: DER FREISCHÜTZ, 1821, libretto by Friedrich Kind, after
the Gespensterbuch. Part of Max, Act I. d3(c3)-a4 f3-g4 A scena
and a sustained aria which starts in moderate tempo. Fast, quite
energetic, and dramatic last section. Dramatic, climactic ending.
Acc: 4 (VS)CP. OPA-3, OAR-T

8445. Unter blüh'nden Mandelbäumen
Opera: EURYANTHE, 1823, libretto by Wilhelmine Helmine von
Chézy. Part of Adolar, Act I. f3-a4(bb4) bb3-g4 Sustained in
moderate tempo. Mainly lyric in style. Climactic ending. Agitated
accompaniment in the final section. Acc: 4 (VS)NO. OAR-T

8446. Wehen mir Lüfte Ruh'
Opera: EURYANTHE. Part of Adolar, Act II. eb3-ab4 g3-g4
First section is sustained in moderate slow tempo. Second section is
animated in lively tempo. Climactic ending on ab4. Acc: 3-4 (VS)
NO, CP. OAR-T

8447. Ich jub'le in Glück und Hoffnung neu!
Opera: OBERON, 1826, libretto by James Robinson Planché, after
Wieland's story. Part of Hüon, Act III. c3-g4(bb4) g3-g4 Animated
in quite fast tempo. Requires fluent enunciation and flexibility.
Strong and dramatic. Climactic ending. Not easy. Acc: 4 (VS)CP

8448. R: Ja selbst die Liebe
A: Klag' du Tochter des Morgenlands
Opera: OBERON. Part of Hüon, Act III. d#3-a4 g3-f#4 Extended
recitative in generally lively tempo, and an andante-allegro aria.
Dramatic, not for light voices. Climactic ending. Requires a heavy
lyric tenor voice, if not sung by a dramatic tenor. This excerpt ends
the opera. Acc: 4 (VS)CP

8449. Vater! hör' mich fleh'n zu dir
Opera: OBERON. Part of Hüon, Act II. e3-g4 g3-e4 Common
title: Prayer. Sustained in slow tempo. Short and generally subdued. Acc: 3-4 (VS)CP. OAR-T

8450. Von Jugend auf in dem Kampfgefild'
Opera: OBERON. Part of Hüon, Act I. d3-g4 g#3-g#4 Animated

in fast tempo. Slower middle section. Generally strong and dramatic. Vocally demanding; not for light voices. Climactic ending. Extended instrumental postlude. Acc: 4 (VS)CP

D.   American Composers

DAVID AMRAM

8451. O mistress mine
Opera: TWELFTH NIGHT, in two acts, 1969, text by William Shakespeare. Part of Feste, Act I. e3-a4 a3-e4 Sustained in moderate
tempo. Generally on MF level. Simple, graceful, and gentle. Acc:
3 (VS)CP

8452. Sigh no more ladies
Opera: TWELFTH NIGHT, text inserted from William Shakespeare's
Much Ado About Nothing. Part of Feste, Act I. f#3-g#4 g#3-f#4
Sustained in moderate tempo. Lyric and generally on MF level.
Short. Acc: 3 (VS)CP

8453. When that I was and a little tiny boy
Opera: TWELFTH NIGHT. Part of Feste, Act II, The Epilogue.
e3-g4 g3-e4 Sustained in moderate slow tempo. Starts gently.
Generally on MF level. Has two climactic passages, and a subdued,
long-held ending marked PPP. Acc: 3 (VS)CP

AARON COPLAND

8454. Daybreak will come
Opera: THE TENDER LAND, 1954, libretto by Horace Everett.
Part of Martin, Act III. d3-f#4 f#3-db4 Sustained in quite slow
tempo. Gentle; has a gentle, high ending (f#4). Acc: 3-4 (VS)B-H

8455. I'm gettin' tired of travellin'
Opera: THE TENDER LAND. Part of Martin, Act II. db3-b4 g3-
f#4 Sustained in slow tempo. Requires fine high P. Has dramatic
passages. Subdued ending. Acc: 3-4 (VS)B-H

CARLISLE FLOYD

8456. It must make the good Lord sad
Opera: SUSANNAH, 1958, libretto by the composer. Part of Sam,
Act I. e3-a4 f#3-f#4 First line: It's about the way the people is
made. Sustained in slow tempo. Very gentle and subdued. Acc:
3-4 (VS)B-H

8457. Can't you see what the gypsy has done?
Opera: WUTHERING HEIGHTS, 1958, libretto by the composer, after
Emily Brontë. Part of Hindley, in The Prologue. e3-bb4 a3-bb4
Sustained in moderate tempo. Dramatic, strong, agitated, and ac-
cented. Climactic, energetic high ending. Acc: 3-4 (VS)B-H

8458. I love you, Cathy! Then marry me, Cathy
Opera: WUTHERING HEIGHTS. Part of Edgar, Act II. e3-b4 e3-g4
Sustained in moderate slow tempo. Has some dramatic passages.

       After the climax, a subdued ending in slower tempo. Acc: 3-4
       (VS)B-H

VICTOR HERBERT, 1859-1924

8459. Gentle maiden, tell me
       Opera: NATOMA, 1911, libretto by Joseph D. Redding. Part of
       Paul, Act I. db3-ab4 f3-f4 Sustained in moderate tempo. Has
       climactic passages. Ends in quasi-recitative style. Acc: 3-4 (VS)
       GS

GIAN-CARLO MENOTTI

Italian born; American opera.

8460. 'Twas at midnight in a dream
       Opera: AMELIA GOES TO THE BALL, 1937, libretto by the com-
       poser, original text in Italian. Part of the Lover, one-act opera.
       eb3-a4 f3-f#4 Sustained in moderate slow tempo. Lyric. Climac-
       tic ending on a4. Acc: 3-4 (VS)GR

8461. I know that you all hate me
       Opera: THE SAINT OF BLEECKER STREET, 1954, libretto by the
       composer. Part of Michele, Act II. d3-c5 g3-e4 Animated vocal
       part in slow tempo. Animated second section. Has dramatic pas-
       sages. Climactic ending. Acc: 4 (VS)GS

DOUGLAS MOORE, 1893-1969

8462. I summon the jury
       Opera: THE DEVIL AND DANIEL WEBSTER, 1938, libretto by
       Stephen Vincent Benét. Part of Scratch, one-act folk opera. eb3-
       ab4 a3-f4 Animated vocal part. Has dramatic passages. Requires
       fine P. Subdued high ending. Acc: 3-4 (VS)B-H

8463. In ancient times there was a god
       Opera: THE WINGS OF THE DOVE, 1961, libretto by Ethan Ayer,
       after Henry James. Part of the Minstrel, one-act opera. eb3-ab4
       ab3-f4 Animated in moderate lively tempo. Has climactic passages
       and a subdued ending. Narrative text, in quasi-recitative style.
       Acc: 3-4 (VS)GS

KURT WEILL, 1900-1950

German born; American opera.

8464. R: At night when ev'rything is quiet
       A: Lonely house
       Opera: STREET SCENE, 1947, libretto by Langston Hughes and El-
       mer Rice. Part of Sam Kaplan, Act I. f3-bb4 g3-f4 Sustained in
       moderate slow tempo. Requires fine P and PP. Has a couple of cli-
       mactic passages. Subdued high ending. Acc: 3-4 (VS)CC

E. British Composers

MICHAEL WILLIAM BALFE, 1808-1870

8465. Then you'll remember me
Opera: THE BOHEMIAN GIRL, 1843, libretto by Alfred Bunn. Part
of Thaddeus, Act III. g3-ab4 ab3-gb4 Sustained in moderate slow
tempo. A cavatina. Generally on MF level. Has climactic high
passages in each of the 2 verses. Gently climactic ending. Acc: 3
(VS)GS. 56S. (S)GS

BENJAMIN BRITTEN

8466. Albert the Good! Long may he reign
Comic Opera: ALBERT HERRING, 1947, libretto by Eric Crozier,
after Guy de Maupassant. Part of Albert Herring, Act II. c3-bb4
g3-g4 An extended scena with dramatic as well as gentle passages.
Interpretatively complex and vocally demanding. Excerpt ends with
"lose my nerve and fly!" Acc: 4 (VS)B-H

8467. "Heaven helps those who help themselves"
Comic Opera: ALBERT HERRING. Part of Albert, Act II. e3-bb4
g3-f4 In different tempi and moods. Has dramatic passages. Requires fine high P. Interpretatively difficult. Mostly in recitative
style. Acc: 4 (VS)B-H

8468. O go, go! Go away!
Opera: ALBERT HERRING. Part of Albert Herring, Act II. e3-bb4
a3-g4 Animated in lively tempo. Dramatic, with high climaxes.
Heavy, intense, somewhat bitter. Interpretatively not easy. Has
florid passages and agitated accompaniment. Acc: 3-4 (VS)B-H

8469. I am an old man
Opera: BILLY BUDD, 1951, libretto by E. M. Forster and Eric
Crozier, after Hermann Melville. Part of Captain Vere, in The Pro-
logue. eb3-a4 f#3-g4 Sustained in moderate slow tempo. Narra-
tive, in recitative style. Has dramatic passages. Unaccompanied.
Acc: 3-4 (VS)B-H

8470. We committed his body to the deep
Opera: BILLY BUDD. Part of Captain Vere, in The Epilogue. d3-
ab4 a3-f4 Sustained in slow tempo. Has some dramatic passages.
Generally in recitative style. Tranquil, contemplative, generally subdued ending section. Low ending, unaccompanied. Acc: 4 (VS)B-H

8471. In dreams I've built myself
Opera: PETER GRIMES, 1945, libretto by Montagu Slater, after a
poem by George Crabbe. Part of Peter, Act II. d3-b4 f#3-f#4
Sustained in slow tempo. Generally subdued, requires very fine high
P. Florid. Dramatic high ending, a full two lines mostly on g4.
Acc: 3-4 (VS)B-H

8472. Picture what that day was like
Opera: PETER GRIMES. Part of Peter, Act I. d3-a4 e3-f4 Sustained in moderate tempo. Has dramatic passages. Requires fine
high P and PP. Very subdued ending. Narrative text. Acc: 4
(VS)B-H

8473.   In the heart of a man is depressed
        Opera: THE BEGGAR'S OPERA, 1948, libretto by John Gay, adapted
        by Tyrone Guthrie.   Part of Macheath, Act I.   d3-f♯4 a3-e4 Sus-
        tained in moderate slow tempo.   Generally on MF level.   Climactic
        ending.   A new setting of original airs.   Acc: 3   (VS)B-H

8474.   The first time at the looking glass
        Opera: THE BEGGAR'S OPERA.   Part of Macheath, Act II.   e3-e4
        a3-e4 Sustained in moderate lively tempo.   Graceful, and has a sub-
        dued ending.   Sustained chordal accompaniment throughout.   A new
        setting of original airs.   Acc: 3   (VS)B-H

8475.   The second lute song of the Earl of Essex
        Opera: GLORIANA OF ESSEX, 1953, libretto by W. Plomer.   Part
        of Robert Devereux, Earl of Essex.   c3-g4 f3-f4 Sustained in very
        slow tempo.   To be sung freely.   Has florid passages and some fine
        P and PP.   Requires some flexibility.   Generally subdued.   Ends
        with subdued, descending, florid line.   Acc: 3   (S)B-H, (VS)B-H

8476.   Tarquinius does not wait
        Opera: THE RAPE OF LUCRETIA, 1946, libretto by Ronald Duncan,
        after Andre Obey.   Part of the Male Chorus (solo voice), Act I.
        Common title: The ride.   eb3-bb4 f♯3-f4 Animated in very rapid
        tempo.   Energetic.   Has a few short florid passages.   Slower, quite
        subdued ending section.   Not for light voices.   Acc: 4   (VS)B-H

RALPH VAUGHAN WILLIAMS, 1872-1958

8477.   Alone and friendless
        Opera: HUGH THE DROVER or LOVE IN THE STOCKS, 1924, libret-
        to by Harold Child.   Part of Hugh, Act I.   d3-ab4 f3-f4 Sustained
        in slow tempo.   Starts slowly, has climactic passage toward the end.
        Acc: 3-4   (VS)JC

                        F.   Russian Composers

ALEXANDER PORFIREVICH BORODIN, 1833-1887

8478.   R: Tageslicht langsam erlischt
        A: Ah, wo bist du?
        Opera: PRINCE IGOR, 1869-1887 unfinished, completed by Rimsky-
        Korsakof and Glazunof.   Libretto by Vladimir V. Stassof.   Part of
        Wladimir Igorewitsch, Act II.   eb3-bb4 g3-e4 Recitative and sus-
        tained air in moderate slow tempo.   Has dramatic high passages.
        Requires very fine high P.   Ends with ab4 marked P.   Acc: 3-4
        (VS)MB.   (S)MB

NIKOLAI ANDREYEVICH RIMSKY-KORSAKOV, 1844-1908

8479.   A song of India
        Opera: SADKO, 1898, libretto by the composer and Vladimir Ivano-
        vich Bielsky.   Part of the Hindu merchant, Act II, or Scene IV.
        First line: Unnumbered diamonds lie within the caverns.   d3-g4 g3-
        e4 Sustained in moderate slow tempo.   Has slightly florid lines.
        Generally subdued.   Requires gentle lyricism, flexibility, and fine P

and PP. Descriptive and slightly atmospheric. Very subdued ending.
English and French versions in MRS are by Constance Purdy. Acc:
3-4 MRS-2, 56S, ATS (Ch. IX)

IGOR FEODOROVICH STRAVINSKY, 1882-1971

8480.   Love, too frequently betrayed
        Opera: THE RAKE'S PROGRESS, 1951, libretto by W(ystan) H(ugh)
        Auden and Chester Kallman, after Hogarth. Part of Tom, Act I.
        f♯3-g♯4 g♯3-f♯4 Sustained in moderate tempo. Requires some
        flexibility. Generally on MF level. Subdued ending. Acc: 3-4
        (VS)B-H

8481.   Prepare yourselves, heroic shades
        Opera: THE RAKE'S PROGRESS. Part of Tom, Act III. g3-a4 b3-
        f♯4 Sustained in slow tempo. Has climactic passages. Short.
        Acc: 3-4 (VS)B-H

8482.   R: Here I stand
        A: Since it is not by merit
        Opera: THE RAKE'S PROGRESS. Part of Tom, Act I. e3-a4 g3-
        f4 Extended recitative and a sustained aria in moderate tempo. Cli-
        mactic ending on sustained high note. Acc: 3-4 (VS)B-H

PETER (PIOTR) ILYICH TCHAIKOVSKY, 1840-1893

8483.   How far, how far
        Opera: EUGENE ONÉGIN, 1877-1878, libretto by the composer and
        Konstantin S. Shilovsky, after Pushkin. Part of Lenski, Act II. d3-
        a♭4 f♯3-g4 Sustained in moderate slow tempo. Has some slightly
        faster sections and dramatic passages. Starts reflectively. Subdued
        ending. Title in IM score: O where, O where. Acc: 3-4 (VS)GS,
        IM. OPA-3

                    G.   Czechoslovakian Composers

ANTONÍN DVOŘÁK, 1841-1904

8484.   A week you've followed by my side
        Opera: RUSALKA, 1900, libretto by Jaroslav Kvapil. Part of the
        Prince, Act II. e♭3-a♭4 g3-f4 Sustained first in moderate slow
        tempo, then becomes animated and faster. Has climactic passages.
        Dramatic ending on a♭4. Acc: 3-4 (VS)AR

8485.   Gentle snowwhite doe!
        Opera: RUSALKA. Part of the Prince, Act III. f3-a♭4 a3-f4 Ani-
        mated in lively tempo. Agitated and slightly intense. Has climactic
        passages. The vocal score indicated is in Czech, with German and
        English versions. Acc: 3-4 (VS)AR

8486.   You are a vision that will vanish
        Opera: RUSALKA. Part of the Prince, Act II. e♭3-b♭b4 a♭3-a♭4
        Sustained in moderate slow tempo. Has dramatic climaxes and a high
        dramatic ending. Agitated accompaniment. Acc: 4 (VS)AR

BEDŘICH SMETANA, 1824-1884

8487. R: You are caught
       A: Soon now, my dearest
       Opera: THE BARTERED BRIDE (PRODANA NEVESTA), 1863-1866,
       libretto by Karel Sabina. Part of Jenik, Act II. e3-a4 g3-g4 Dra-
       matic recitative and sustained aria in moderate slow tempo. Re-
       quires fine P and PP. Has dramatic passages. Dramatic and cli-
       mactic ending. Acc: 3-4 (VS)GS. OPA-3

                        H.   Spanish Composer

ENRIQUE GRANADOS, 1867-1916

8488. La maja si es que ha de ser
       Opera: GOYESCAS, 1916, libretto by Fernando Periquet y Zuaznabar.
       Part of a Solo Voice, man or woman, with chorus. Finale of Tab-
       leau II. g3-f4 bb3-eb4 Animated in lively tempo. Has florid fig-
       ures. Vocal score is in Spanish and English. Acc: 3-4 (VS)GS

                        I.   Argentine Composer

ALBERTO GINASTERA

8489. España toma mi anillo
       Opera: DON RODRIGO, 1964, libretto by Alejandro Casona. Part of
       Don Rodrigo, Act I. Other title: Cavatina. e3-a4 g3-g4 Sustained
       in slow tempo. Has one dramatic passage. Generally lyric. Sub-
       dued high ending on long-sustained a4. Assigned to dramatic tenor
       in the score. Acc: 4 (VS)B-H

7. DRAMATIC TENOR

All indications of range and tessitura for Dramatic Tenor are based on the treble clef as printed, but sung one octave lower. Therefore, the range of c3-a4 would mean c2-a3. Dramatic Tenor Bibliography: see the bibliography at the beginning of the Lyric Tenor section.

A. Italian Composers

VINCENZO BELLINI, 1801-1835

8490. Meco all'altar di Venere
Opera: NORMA, 1831, libretto by Felice Romani, based on a tragedy by Louis Alexander Soumet. Part of Pollione, Act I. d3-c5 g3-g4 Sustained in moderate tempo. Has some climactic passages. Tessitura is quite high in some passages. Acc: 3-4 (VS)GS, GR. (S)GR

ARRIGO BOITO, 1842-1918

8491. Giunto sul passo estremo
Opera: MEFISTOFELE, 1868, libretto by Felice Romani. Part of Faust, in the Prologue. f3-ab4 ab3-f4 Sustained in moderate slow tempo. Requires fine P and PP. Has dramatic climaxes. Acc: 3-4 (VS)GR. MTO. (S)GR

UMBERTO GIORDANO, 1867-1948

8492. Come un bel dì di maggio
Opera: ANDREA CHÉNIER, 1896, libretto by Luigi Illica. Part of Chénier, Act IV. e3-ab4 f#3-f#4 Sustained in moderate slow tempo. Slightly faster second section. Dramatic, climactic last section. Acc: 4 (VS)CS, IM

8493. Un dì all'azzurro spazio
Opera: ANDREA CHÉNIER. Part of Chénier, Act I. f3-bb4 f3-f4 Sustained in moderate slow tempo. Has quasi-recitative passages, dramatic passages, and a climactic ending. Acc: 3-4 (VS)CS, IM

RUGGIERO LEONCAVALLO, 1858-1919

8494. Testa adorata
Opera: LA BOHÈME, 1897, libretto by Giuseppe Giacosa and Luigi Illica. Part of Marcello, Act III. f3-bb4 gb3-f4 Sustained in slow tempo. Dramatic, requires very fine high notes. Intense. Subdued ending. Acc: 3-4 (VS)CS

8495. Va via, fantasma del passato!
Opera: LA BOHÈME. Part of Marcello, Act III. eb3-bb4 g3-g4 Sustained in moderate tempo. Dramatic; uses many high notes.

1102   Solo Voice Repertoire

Climactic high ending on "va via!" Agitated accompaniment. Acc:
4 (VS)CS

8496. R: Recitar! Mentre preso
       A: Vesti la giubba
       Opera: PAGLIACCI, 1892, libretto by the composer. Part of Canio,
       Act I. e3(d3)-a4 g3-g4 Sustained aria in slow tempo. Dramatic,
       intense, has some passages in declamatory style. Climactic and dra-
       matic ending. Acc: 3 (VS)GS. OPA-3, ORT

PIETRO MASCAGNI, 1863-1945

8497. Mamma, quel vino è generoso
       Opera: CAVALLERIA RUSTICANA, 1890, libretto by Giovanni Targi-
       oni-Tozzetti and Guido Menasci, after Giovanni Verga. Part of Turid-
       du, one-act opera. eb3-bb4 bb3-ab4 Sustained. Starts in lively
       tempo, then moves into moderate tempo. Has dramatic climaxes.
       Tessitura stays high in some passages. Climactic ending. Acc: 4
       (VS)GS

AMILCARE PONCHIELLI, 1834-1886

8498. Cielo e mar!
       Opera: LA GIOCONDA, 1876, libretto by Arrigo Boito, after Victor
       Hugo. Part of Enzo, Act II. d3-ab4 g3-ab4 Sustained in moderate
       slow tempo. Has dramatic climaxes. Subdued ending on g4, follow-
       ing the dramatic passage. Acc: 4 (VS)GS, CP, GR. OPA-3, MTO,
       ORT. (S)GR

GIACOMO (ANTONIO DOMENICO) PUCCINI, 1858-1924

8499. Recondita armonia
       Opera: TOSCA, 1900, libretto by Giuseppe Giacosa and Luigi Illica.
       Part of Cavaradossi, Act I. f3-bb4 f3-f4 Sustained in slow tempo.
       Generally subdued, requires fine P and PP. Lyric throughout. Cli-
       mactic ending. Acc: 3-4 (VS)GR, GS. OPA-3, MTO, ORT.
       (S)GS, IM, GR-two keys

GIUSEPPE (FORTUNINO FRANCESCO) VERDI, 1813-1901

8500. R: Se quel guerrier io fossi
       A: Celeste Aida
       Opera: AIDA, 1871, libretto by Antonio Ghislanzoni. Part of Ra-
       dames, Act I. d3-bb4 f3-g4 Sustained and lyric in moderate tempo.
       Requires very fine high P to PPPP. Also has passages requiring
       dramatic energy. Very subdued, high ending on bb4. Acc: 4
       (VS)GS, GR. OPA-3, MTO, ORT, OAT. (S)GR, GS

8501. R: Mercè, diletti amici
       A: Come ruggiada al cespite
       Opera: ERNANI, 1844, libretto by Francesco Maria Piave. Part of
       Ernani, Act I. g3-a4 bb3-g4 Sustained, first in moderate, then in
       fast tempo. Requires some flexibility. Has dramatic passages, and
       choral interpolations in the score. Slightly climactic ending. Acc:
       3-4 (VS)GR, CP. OAT. (S)GR

8502. R: Notte! Perpetua notte
       A: Non maledirmi, o prode
       Opera: I DUE FOSCARI, 1844, libretto by Francesco Maria Piave.
       Part of Jacopo, Act II. e3-b♭4 b3-g4 Recitative in varied tempi
       and moods, and an animated aria in moderate tempo. Has sustained
       passages in the middle of the aria. Climactic ending on a4. Agi-
       tated accompaniment. Acc: 4 (VS)GR. OAT

8503. R: È di Monforte il cenno!
       A: Giorno di pianto, di fier dolore!
       Opera: I VESPRI SICILIANI, 1856, libretto by E. Caime, after the
       original in French by Eugène Scribe and Charles Duveyrier. Part of
       Arrigo, Act IV. e♭3-b4 b3-g♯4 Extended recitative in varied tem-
       pi and a sustained aria in moderate slow tempo. Requires very fine
       high P and PP. Has dramatic passages. Climactic ending. Acc:
       3-4 (VS)GR. OAT

8504. Ah! che la morte ognora
       Opera: IL TROVATORE, 1853, libretto by Salvatore Cammarano,
       after Antonio Gutierrez's play. Part of Manrico, Act IV. g3-ab♭4
       c3-ab♭4 Sustained in moderate tempo. High tessitura. Climactic
       ending on ab♭4. This excerpt is a part of a duet with choral back-
       ground. Acc: 3-4 (VS)GS, GR. MTO, ORT

8505. Ah sì, ben mio; coll'essere
       Opera: IL TROVATORE. Part of Manrico, Act III. e3-g4 g3-g4
       Sustained in slow tempo. Has climactic passages and an unaccom-
       panied ending passage. OAT includes the recitative: Il presagio
       funesto. Acc: 3-4 (VS)GS, GR, CP. OPA-3, MTO, ORT, OAT.
       (S)GR

8506. Di quella pira l'orrendo foco
       Opera: IL TROVATORE. Part of Manrico, Act III. g3-a4 g3-g4
       Animated in lively tempo. Faster ending. Requires fine P. Has
       some strong and dramatic passages. Acc: 4 (VS)GS, GR, CP.
       OAT. (S)GR

8507. R: La vita è inferno
       A: O, tu che in seno agli angeli
       Opera: LA FORZA DEL DESTINO, 1862, libretto by Francesco Maria
       Piave, after Duke of Rivas' play. Part of Don Alvaro, Act III. d♭3-
       b♭4 g3-ab♭4 Extended recitative in varied tempi, and a sustained
       aria in moderate slow tempo. Has dramatic passages, and a climac-
       tic high ending on ab♭4. Acc: 3-4 (VS)GR, CP, B-H (Italian & Eng-
       lish), IM (Italian & English). OPA-3, ORT, OAT. (S)GR

8508. Dio! Mi potevi scagliar tutti i mali
       Opera: OTELLO, 1887, libretto by Arrigo Boito, after William Shake-
       speare. Part of Otello, Act III. e♭3-b♭4 ab♭3-g4 Starts very sub-
       dued in broken recitative, then becomes more sustained. Has climac-
       tic passages. Ends as in the first mood. Acc: 4 (VS)GS, GR.
       MTO. (S)GR

8509. R: Tu? Indietro! Fuggi!
       A: Ora e per sempre addio
       Opera: OTELLO. Part of Otello, Act II. e3-b♭4 g3-g4 Animated
       in lively tempo. Dramatic and strong. Vocally demanding, and in-
       terpretatively difficult. Acc: 5 (VS)GS, GR. MTO, ORT. (S)GR

8510. R: O inferno! Amelia qui!
       A: Sento avvampar nell'anima
       Opera: SIMON BOCCANEGRA, 1881 libretto by Francesco Maria
       Piave, after Antonio Gutierrez's play. Part of Gabriele, Act II. e3-
       a4 a3-g♯4 Sustained in moderate tempo. Generally strong and cli-
       mactic first section. Slower second section. Climactic and unaccom-
       panied ending. Acc: 3-4 (VS)GR

                              B.   French Composers

HECTOR BERLIOZ, 1803-1869

8511. Inutiles regrets
       Opera: LES TROYENS À CARTHAGE, second part of a two-part
       opera, LES TROYENS, 1856-1859, libretto by the composer, based
       on the story of Virgil. Part of Énée, Act III. e3-b♭4(c5) g3-f4
       Sustained, first in lively tempo, then slower middle section. High,
       dramatic ending on b♭4 and a♭4. An extended and demanding aria,
       15 pages long. Acc: 4 (VS)EC

GEORGES BIZET, 1838-1875

8512. La fleur que tu m'avais jetée
       Opera: CARMEN, 1873-1874, libretto by Henri Meilhac and Ludovic
       Halévy, based on Mérimée's story. Part of Don José, Act II. e3-
       b♭4 f3-f4 Common title: Flower song. Sustained in moderate slow
       tempo. Requires very fine P and PP. Generally subdued. Subdued
       ending. Acc: 3-4 (VS)GS. OPA-3, ORT

CHARLES (FRANÇOIS) GOUNOD, 1818-1893

8513. R: Faiblesse de la race humaine!
       A: Inspirez-moi, race divine!
       Opera: LA REINE DE SABA, 1861, libretto by Jules Barbier and
       Michel Carré, after Gerard de Nérval. Part of Adoniram, Act II.
       f3-a4 g3-g4 Dramatic and extended scena and sustained aria in mod-
       erate slow tempo. Has dramatic passages and a climactic ending.
       Agitated and full-sounding accompaniment. Acc: 4-5 (VS)EC

8514. R: L'amour! l'amour!
       A: Ah, lève-toi, soleil!
       Opera: ROMÉO ET JULIETTE, 1864, libretto by Jules Barbier and
       Michel Carré, after William Shakespeare. Part of Roméo, Act II.
       f3-b♭4 a3-f4 Sustained in moderate slow tempo. Lyric, with some
       climactic passages. Ending on sustained b♭4. In the opera, this ex-
       cerpt is sung below Juliette's window. Acc: 4 (VS)GS. OPA-3

JULES (ÉMILE FRÉDÉRIC) MASSENET, 1842-1912

8515. R: Aux troupes du Sultan
       A: Promesse de mon avenir
       Opera: LE ROI DE LAHORE, 1877, libretto by Louis Gallet. Part
       of Scindia, Act IV. d♭3-g♭4 e♭3-e♭4 Dramatic recitative and a
       sustained to animated aria. Climactic, dramatic, ending with a

sustained g♭4. Originally for baritone, but had been sung by the heavier tenor voices. Acc: 3-4 (VS)HC

8516. R: Un autre est son époux
A: J'aurais sur ma poitrine
Opera: WERTHER, 1892, libretto by Edouard Blau, Paul Milliet, and Georges Hartmann, after Goethe. Part of Werther, Act II. g3-b♭♭4 b♭3-a♭4 Animated in lively tempo. Brilliant, requires flexibility. Requires fine P and PP, and some dramatic energy. Climactic high ending on a♭4. Acc: 3-4 (VS)HC

ANDRÉ (CHARLES PROSPER) MESSAGER, 1853-1929

8517. J'aimais la vieille maison grise
Opera: FORTUNIO, 1907, libretto by G. A. de Caillavet and Robert de Flers, after Alfred de Musset. Part of Fortunio, Act II. e3-g4 a3-e4 Sustained in moderate slow tempo. Tranquil and generally subdued. In gentle recitative style. Climactic ending. Acc: 3-4 (VS)EC

GIACOMO MEYERBEER, 1791-1864

8518. R: Ah! Quel spectacle enchanteur
A: Plus blanche que la blanche hermine
Opera: LES HUGUENOTS, 1836, libretto by Eugène Scribe and Emile Deschamps. Part of Raoul, Act I. e3-a♯4(b4) g♯3-g♯4 Sustained in moderate slow tempo. Graceful. Requires fine high P and PP. Florid. Ends with a cadenza. Acc: 3-4 (VS)BR

8519. R: Aux armes, mes amis
A: A la lueur de leurs torches funebres
Opera: LES HUGUENOTS. Part of Raoul, Act V. e3-c5 g3-g4 Sustained in very moderate tempo. Requires very fine high P and PP. Has energetic and dramatic passages. Vocally difficult. Climactic ending. With choral ensemble in the score. Acc: 4 (VS) BR, BH

C. German and Austrian Composers

LUDWIG VAN BEETHOVEN, 1770-1827

8520. R: Gott! welch Dunkel hier!
A: In des Lebens Frühlingstagen
Opera: FIDELIO, c. 1803-1805, libretto by Joseph Sonnleithner and Georg Frederick Treitschke. Part of Florestan, Act II. e♭3-b♭4 a3-a4 Recitative in varied tempi, and an aria in sustained and slow tempo, followed by an animated movement in lively tempo. Has passages with high tessitura. Dramatic and vocally demanding. Climactic ending. Acc: 4 (VS)GS. OAR-T

WOLFGANG AMADEUS MOZART, 1756-1791

8521. R: Qual mi conturbai
A: Fuor del mar ho un mar in seno

Opera: IDOMENEO, RE DI CRETA, 1781 (K. 366), libretto by Giambattista Varesco, after Danchet. Part of Idomeneo, Act II. d3-g4 g3-f♯4 Slightly extended recitative, and an animated aria in moderate lively tempo. Quite florid. Requires considerable flexibility. Has some long-held notes, and dramatic passages. Climactic ending. See the Appendix in IM for another version of this excerpt. Acc: 4 (VS)IM, CP

8522. Scena: Popoli! a voi l'ultima legge impone Idomeneo
A: Torna la pace al core
Opera: IDOMENEO, RE DI CRETA. Part of Idomeneo, Act III. f3-g4(a4) g3-f4 Dramatic scena and a sustained aria in slow tempo, with a faster middle section. Has florid passages and climactic passages. Slightly climactic ending. Acc: 4 (VS)IM, CP

8523. Vedrommi intorno
Opera: IDOMENEO, RE DI CRETA. Part of Idomeneo, Act I. e3-g4 g3-f4 Sustained in moderate slow tempo. Has some dramatic passages, slightly florid figures, and one florid passage. Dramatic ending. Acc: 3-4 (VS)IM, CP. OAR-T

RICHARD STRAUSS, 1864-1949

8524. Bleib und wache
Opera: DIE FRAU OHNE SCHATTEN, 1919, libretto by Hugo von Hofmannsthal. Part of the Kaiser, Act I. b2-bb4 g♯3-g♯4 Generally sustained vocal part in generally fast tempo. Dramatic; has strong, high climaxes. Climactic and imposing ending. Vocally demanding. Acc: 4 (VS)B-H

8525. O weh, Falke, o weh!
Opera: DIE FRAU OHNE SCHATTEN. Part of the Kaiser, Act II. c3-bb4 g3-g4 Sustained in moderate tempo. Uses a good number of sustained high notes. Dramatic, with a climactic ending. Vocally demanding. Acc: 4 (VS)B-H

8526. Wenn da Herz aus Kristall zerbricht
Opera: DIE FRAU OHNE SCHATTEN. Part of the Kaiser, Act III. e3-bb4 a3-g♯4 Sustained in moderate tempo. Slightly climactic ending. Generally calm, mainly lyric in style. Acc: 3-4 (VS)B-H

RICHARD WAGNER, 1813-1883

8527. Immer ist Undank Loges Lohn!
Music Drama: DAS RHEINGOLD, 1853-1854, libretto by the composer, the Prologue of the festival drama, DER RING DES NIBELUNGEN. Part of Loge, one-act Prologue, Scene 2. d3-g4 a3-f♯4 Sustained vocal part in lively tempo. Has some climactic passages. Slightly subdued ending. Acc: 3-4 (VS)GS, CP. OGT

8528. Willst jenes Tag's
Opera: DER FLIEGENDE HOLLÄNDER, 1843, libretto by the composer. Part of Erik, Act III, Number 15. Other title: Cavatina. f3-bb4 g3-g4 Sustained in moderate slow tempo. Slightly subdued, with generally simple melody. Lyric. Subdued, descending ending line. Acc: 3-4 (VS)GS, CP. OGT

8529. Am stillen Herd
       Opera: DIE MEISTERSINGER VON NÜRNBERG, 1867, libretto by the
       composer. Part of Walther, Act I, Scene 3. d3-g4 f♯3-f♯4 Sus-
       tained in moderate tempo. Has dramatic passages. Climactic end-
       ing. Acc: 3-4 (VS)GS, CP. OPA-3, OGT

8530. Fanget an! So rief der Lenz
       Opera: DIE MEISTERSINGER VON NÜRNBERG. Part of Walther,
       Act I, Scene 3. f3-a4 g3-a4 Sustained in moderate tempo, but
       moves along. Mainly lyric, with some dramatic passages. Uses
       high notes quite often. Ends with "das hehre Liebeslied." Climactic
       ending. Acc: 3-4 (VS)GS, CP. OGT

8531. Morgenlich leuchtend im rosigen Schein
       Opera: DIE MEISTERSINGER VON NÜRNBERG. Part of Walther,
       Act III, Scene 5. e3-a4 a3-a4 Common title: Prize song. Sus-
       tained in moderate tempo. Has broad lines and climactic passages.
       Quite lyric in style. Strong, climactic ending. Acc: 4 (VS)GS, CP.
       OPA-3, ORT, OGT

8532. Ein Schwert verhiess mir der Vater
       Music Drama: DIE WALKÜRE, 1870, libretto by the composer, first
       day of the festival drama, DER RING DES NIBELUNGEN. Part of
       Siegmund, Act I, Scene 3. c3-g4 f3-f4 Generally sustained in mod-
       erate slow tempo. Has some octave intervalic skips. Generally sub-
       dued. Also has some dramatic passages. Acc: 3-4 (VS)GS, CP.
       OGT

8533. Siegmund heiss ich und Siegmund bin ich!
       Music Drama: DIE WALKÜRE. Part of Siegmund, Act I, Scene 3.
       e3-g4 g3-e4 Sustained vocal part in very fast tempo. Dramatic.
       Slightly subdued ending. Agitated accompaniment. Acc: 4 (VS)GS,
       CP. OGT

8534. Winterstürme wichen dem Wonnemond
       Music Drama: DIE WALKÜRE. Part of Siegmund, Act I, Scene 3.
       c3-g4 f3-f4 Common title: Siegmund's love song. Sustained in
       moderate tempo. Starts gently, then moves on to more energetic,
       dramatic passages. Climactic ending. Agitated accompaniment.
       Acc: 4 (VS)GS, CP. OPA-3, ORT, OGT

8535. Brünnhilde! Heilige Braut!
       Music Drama: GÖTTERDÄMMERUNG, third day of the festival drama,
       DER RING DES NIBELUNGEN, 1874, libretto by the composer. Part
       of Siegfried, Act III, Scene 2. b♭2-a4 g3-e4 Sustained in very slow
       tempo. Generally subdued. Siegfried's death song. Acc: 4 (VS)
       GS, CP. OGT

8536. Atmest du nicht mir die süssen
       Opera: LOHENGRIN, 1850, libretto by the composer. Part of Lohen-
       grin, Act III, Scene 2. g3-ab4 g3-g4 Sustained in very moderate
       tempo. Generally tranquil and subdued. Subdued ending. Acc: 3-4
       (VS)GS, CP. OGT

8537. Höchstes Vertraun hast du mir schon zu danken
       Opera: LOHENGRIN. Part of Lohengrin, Act III, Scene 2. f3-a4
       g♯3-f♯4 A sustained scena in slow tempo. Has some dramatic pas-
       sages. Generally in broad recitative style. Acc: 3-4 (VS)GS, CP.
       OGT

8538. In fernem Land
       Opera: LOHENGRIN. Part of Lohengrin, Act III, Scene 3. e3-a4
       f♯3-f♯4 Lohengrin's narration. Starts gently in sustained style, then
       becomes dramatic. Dramatic and climactic ending. Acc: 3-4 (VS)
       GS, CP. OPA-3, ORT, OGT

8539. R: Schon sendet nach dem Säumigen der Gral!
       A: Mein Lieber Schwan
       Opera: LOHENGRIN. Part of Lohengrin, Act III, Scene 3. e3-a4
       g3-g4 Sustained in moderate slow tempo. Generally gentle and sub-
       dued. Requires fine high P. Very strong and dramatic ending on
       "Leb' wohl!" Acc: 3-4 (VS)GS, CP. OGT

8540. Amfortas! Die Wunde!
       Music Drama: PARSIFAL, 1882, libretto by the composer. Part of
       Parsifal, Act II, Scene 2. d3-a4 f3-f4 Generally sustained vocal
       part, first in fast, then slow tempo. Has dramatic climaxes. Also
       requires fine P. Generally agitated accompaniment. Acc: 4 (VS)
       GS, CP. OGT

8541. Nur eine Waffe taugt
       Music Drama: PARSIFAL. Part of Parsifal, Act III, Scene 2. d3-
       g4 a3-e4 Sustained in slow tempo. Has some climactic and majes-
       tic passages. Climactic ending. Generally agitated accompaniment.
       Parsifal's final scene. Acc: 4 (VS)GS, CP. OGT

8542. Allmächt'ger Vater, blick herab!
       Opera: RIENZI, DER LETZTE DER TRIBUNEN, 1842, libretto by
       the composer, after Mary Mitford's drama. Part of Rienzi, Act V.
       Common title: Rienzi's prayer. f3-ab4 g3-f4 Sustained in slow
       tempo. Somewhat majestic. Subdued ending. Acc: 3-4 (VS)SC.
       OGT

8543. Ich liebte glühend meine hohe Braut
       Opera: RIENZI, DER LETZTE DER TRIBUNEN. Part of Rienzi,
       Act V. e3-a4 a3-f♯4 Sustained in moderate tempo. Majestic. Re-
       quires some flexibility. Climactic ending. Acc: 3-4 (VS)SC

8544. Ihr nicht bei'm Feste?
       Opera: RIENZI, DER LETZTE DER TRIBUNEN. Part of Rienzi,
       Act IV. e3-ab4 g3-f4 Sustained in slow tempo. Quite melodic,
       lyric in style. Acc: 3-4 (VS)SC

8545. Ho-ho! Schmiede mein Hammar
       Music Drama: SIEGFRIED, 1876, second day of the festival drama,
       DER RING DES NIBELUNGEN, libretto by the composer. Part of
       Siegfried, Act I, Scene 3. g3-a4 a3-a4 Energetic, strong, in mod-
       erate lively tempo. Dramatic. Has wide intervalic skips. Marked,
       vocally demanding. Climactic ending. Acc: 4 (VS)GS, CP. OGT

8546. Nothung! Nothung! Neidliches Schwert
       Music Drama: SIEGFRIED. Part of Siegfried, Act I, Scene 3. d3-
       a4 a3-a4 Spirited, strong, in moderate lively tempo. Dramatic,
       rhythmic, with a climactic ending. Marked. Vocally demanding.
       Acc: 4 (VS)GS, CP. OGT

8547. Dir töne Lob! Die Wunder sei'n gepriesen
       Opera: TANNHÄUSER UND DER SÄNGERKRIEG AUF DER WARTBURG,

1845, libretto by the composer.   Part of Tannhäuser, Act I, Scene 2.
e3-g♭4   a3-f♯4   Slightly sustained vocal part in lively tempo.   Slightly slower middle section.   Generally strong and energetic.   Climactic
ending.   Acc: 3-4   (VS)GS, CP

8548.   Stets soll nur dir
Opera: TANNHÄUSER UND DER SÄNGERKRIEG AUF DER WARTBURG.
Part of Tannhäuser, Act I, Scene 2.   f♯3-a♭4   g3-g4   Sustained in
lively tempo.   A lyric setting, with some dramatic passages.   Pizzi-
catto accompaniment as of lyre.   Climactic ending.   Accompaniment
at the end does not resolve, and therefore, this beautiful excerpt is
hardly sung separately.   If preferred, the accompaniment at the end
may use the chord of E♭-major on the singer's e♭4 note.   Acc:
3-4   (VS)GS, CP

8549.   Inbrust im Herzen
Opera: TANNHÄUSER UND DER SÄNGERKRIEG AUF DER WARTBURG.
Part of Tannhäuser, Act III, Scene 3.   d♯3-a4   a♭4-f4   Generally
sustained in different tempi and moods.   Starts moderately slow.
Generally in recitative style.   Has dramatic climaxes, and a dramat-
ic ending section.   Rather extended.   Acc: 4   (VS)GS, CP.   OGT

8550.   R: Und drauf Isolde
A: Wie sie selig, hehr und milde
Opera: TRISTAN UND ISOLDE, 1865, libretto by the composer.
Part of Tristan, Act III, Scene I.   e3-g4   a3-e4   Sustained in moder-
ate tempo.   Very tranquil, lyric, and gentle.   Excerpt ends with
"Wie schön bist du!"   Acc: 3-4   (VS)GS, CP

CARL MARIA VON WEBER, 1786-1826

8551.   R: Nein, länger trag' ich
A: Durch die Wälder
Opera: DER FREISCHÜTZ, 1821, libretto by Friedrich Kind, after
the Gespensterbuch.   Part of Max, Act I.   d3(c3)-a4   f3-g4   A scena
and a sustained aria which starts in moderate tempo.   Fast, quite
energetic, dramatic last section.   Dramatic and climactic ending.
Acc: 4   OPA-3, OAR-T,   (VS)CP

8552.   Unter blüh'nden Mandelbäumen
Opera: EURYANTHE, 1821, libretto by Wilhelmine Helmine von Chézy.
Part of Adolar, Act I.   f3-a4(b♭4)   b♭3-g4   Sustained in moderate
tempo.   Mainly lyric in treatment.   Climactic ending.   Agitated accompaniment in the final section.   Acc: 4   (VS)NO.   OAR-T

8553.   Ich jub'le in Glück und Hoffnung neu!
Opera: OBERON, 1826, libretto by James Robinson Planché, after
Wieland's story.   Part of Hüon, Act III.   c3-g4(b♭4)   g3-g4   Ani-
mated in quite fast tempo.   Requires fluent enunciation and flexibility.
Strong and dramatic.   Climactic ending.   Not easy.   Acc: 4   (VS)
CP

8554.   R: Ja selbst die Liebe
A: Klag' du Tochter des Morgenlands
Opera: OBERON.   Part of Hüon, Act III.   d♯3-a4   g3-f♯4   Extended
recitative in generally lively tempo, and an andante-allegretto aria.
Dramatic, not for light voices.   Climactic ending.   This excerpt ends
the opera.   Acc: 4   (VS)CP

8555.   Schreckensschwur!
        Opera: OBERON. Part of Oberon, Act I. d3(c3)-g4 g3-e♭4 Ani-
        mated in quite fast tempo. Requires fluent enunciation and flexibility.
        Strong and dramatic. Not for light voices. Acc: 3-4 (VS)CP

8556.   Von Jugend auf in dem Kampfgefild'
        Opera: OBERON. Part of Hüon, Act I. d3-b4 g♯3-g♯4 Animated
        in fast tempo. Slower middle section. Generally strong and dramat-
        ic. Vocally demanding, with climactic ending. Extended instrumental
        postlude. Acc: 4 (VS)CP

D. American Composer

CARLISLE FLOYD

8557.   Can't you see what the gypsy has done?
        Opera: WUTHERING HEIGHTS, 1958, libretto by the composer, after
        Emily Brontë. Part of Hindley, in The Prologue. e3-b♭4 a2-b♭4
        Sustained in moderate tempo. Dramatic, strong, agitated, and ac-
        cented. Climactic, energetic high ending. Acc: 3-4 (VS)B-H

E. British Composer

BENJAMIN BRITTEN

8558.   Albert the Good! Long may he reign
        Comic Opera: ALBERT HERRING, 1947, libretto by Eric Crozier,
        after Guy de Maupassant. Part of Albert Herring, Act II. c3-b♭4
        g3-g4 An extended scena with dramatic as well as gentle passages.
        Interpretatively complex and vocally demanding. Excerpt ends with
        "lose my nerve and fly!" Acc: 4 (VS)B-H

8559.   "Heaven helps those who help themselves"
        Comic Opera: ALBERT HERRING. Part of Albert, Act II. e3-b♭4
        g3-f4 In different tempi and moods. Has dramatic passages. Re-
        quires fine high P. Interpretatively difficult. Mostly in recitative
        style. Acc: 4 (VS)B-H

8560.   O go, go! Go away!
        Comic Opera: ALBERT HERRING. Part of Albert, Act II. e3-b♭4
        a3-g4 Animated in lively tempo. Dramatic, with high climaxes.
        Heavy, intense, somewhat bitter. Interpretatively not easy. Has
        florid passages and agitated accompaniment. Acc: 3-4 (VS)B-H

8561.   In dreams I've built myself
        Opera: PETER GRIMES, 1945, libretto by Montagu Slater, after a
        poem by George Crabbe. Part of Peter, Act II. d3-b4 f♯3-f♯4
        Sustained in slow tempo. Generally subdued, requires very fine high
        P. Florid. Dramatic high ending, a full two lines mostly on g4.
        Acc: 3-4 (VS)B-H

8562.   Tarquinius does not wait
        Opera: THE RAPE OF LUCRETIA, 1946, libretto by Ronald Duncan,
        after Andre Obey. Part of the Male Chorus (solo voice), Act I.
        Common title: The ride. e♭3-b♭4 f♯3-f4 Animated in very rapid
        tempo. Energetic. Has a few short, florid passages. Slower, quite
        subdued ending section. Not for light voices. Acc: 4 (VS)B-H

F.   Argentine Composer

ALBERTO GINASTERA

8563. España toma mi anillo
Opera: DON RODRIGO, 1964, libretto by Alejandro Casona.   Part of
Don Rodrigo, Act I. Other title: Cavatina.   e3-a4 g3-g4 Sustained
in slow tempo.   Has one dramatic passage.   Generally lyric.   Subdued high ending on long-sustained a4.   Acc: 4   (VS)B-H

8564. Señor del perdón
Opera: DON RODRIGO.   Part of Don Rodrigo, Act III.   Other title:
Aria da Chiesa.   d#3-a4 g3-g4 Sustained in moderate tempo.
Marked "lamentoso."   Intense, grave, with some dramatic passages.
Requires considerable flexibility.   Rhythmically complex.   Subdued,
high ending.   Acc: 4-5   (VS)B-H

8. BARITONE

Bibliography

AAB   Aria Album for Baritone and Bass.   Fifty-four arias from cantatas, oratorios, and operas.   Original texts and German versions. Frankfurt & New York: C. F. Peters.

CAO-Br   Celebri Aria D'Opera.   Baritone.   Fifth of six volumes for all voices.   Milan: G. Ricordi.

OAB   Opern-Arien für Baritone.   Giuseppe Verdi.   Italian texts and German versions.   Edited by Kurt Soldan.   Frankfurt: C. F. Peters.

OAR-Br   Opern-Arien.   Operatic arias in six volumes (two for soprano) in original texts and German versions.   Thirty arias for baritone, catalog number 4234.   Frankfurt: Edition Peters.

OGB   Opern-Gesänge für Bariton.   Richard Wagner.   German texts only. Edited by Kurt Soldan.   Frankfurt: C. F. Peters.

OPA-4   Operatic Anthology.   Vol. IV: Baritone.   Edited by Kurt Adler. Original texts, with English versions.   New York: G. Schirmer, Inc.   (The older edition is edited by Kurt Schindler.)

A. Italian Composers

VINCENZO BELLINI, 1801-1835

8565.   Sì, vincemmo, e il pregio io sento
     Opera: IL PIRATA, 1827, libretto by Felice Romani.   Part of Ernesto, Act I.   b♭1-f3   g2-d3   Sustained in moderate slow tempo. Florid, requires flexibility.   Acc: 3-4   (VS)GR

8566.   Tu m'apristi in cor ferita
     Opera: IL PIRATA.   Part of Ernesto, Act II.   b1-f♯3   e2-d3   Sustained in moderate tempo.   Florid, requires flexibility.   Has dramatic passages.   Excerpt is part of the Imogene-Ernesto duet.   Acc: 3-4   (VS)GR

ARRIGO BOITO, 1842-1918

8567.   Ave Signor.   Perdona se il mio gergo
     Opera: MEFISTOFELE, 1868, libretto by the composer.   Part of Mefistofele, in The Prologue.   b♭1-e♭3(f3)   d3-c4   Animated in moderately lively tempo.   Generally detached.   Requires some flexibility. Has a graceful section.   Acc: 3-4   (VS)GR

ALFREDO CATALANI, 1854-1893

8568. L'Hagenbach qui?
Opera: LA WALLY, 1892, libretto by Luigi Illica, based on Wilhel-
mine von Hillern's novel. Part of Gellner, Act III. f♯2-f♯3 g♯2-
f♯3 Animated in lively tempo. Dramatic, with quite high tessitura.
High, dramatic ending on f♯3. Agitated accompaniment. Acc: 4
(VS)GR

8569. Schiavo de' tuoi begli occhi
Opera: LA WALLY. Part of Gellner, Act II. c2-f3 g♭2-e3 Sustained in moderate slow tempo. Generally strong, dramatic, and with
a high tessitura. Dramatic high ending on the words "Wally! Wally!"
Acc: 3-4 (VS)GR

FRANCESCO CILÉA, 1866-1950

8570. R: E a te nè un bacio mai
A: Come due tizzi accesi
Opera: L'ARLESIANA, 1897, libretto by Leopoldo Marenco, based on
Alphonse Daudet's play. Part of Baldassare, Act I. b1-g♯3 f♯2-
c♯3 Recitative consisting mostly of repeated notes. Sustained aria
in moderate slow tempo, with gentle grace. Has slightly faster section. Subdued high ending. Acc: 4 (VS)CS

GAETANO DONIZETTI, 1797-1848

8571. Bella siccome un angelo
Opera: DON PASQUALE, 1843, libretto by the composer and Michele
Accursi (Giacomo Ruffini), based on Angelo Anelli's novel. Part of
Dr. Malatesta, Act I. c2(ab1)-eb3(f3) eb2-eb3 Sustained in mod-
erate slow tempo. Lyric in quality. An aria with a slightly comic
sense rather than a serious emotional approach. The cadenzas are
sometimes omitted in performance. Acc: 3-4 (VS)GR. OAR-Br,
OPA-4 (Spicker; Adler), (S)GR

8572. R: Sente il cielo
A: O Lisbona, alfin ti miro
Opera: DON SEBASTIANO, 1843, libretto by Eugène Scribe. Original in French. Part of Camoen, Act III. d2-f3 f2-eb3 Gentle recitative and a sustained aria in moderate slow tempo. Lyric, with
some dramatic phrases. In the Otos edition, the recitative starts
with "Gioco di rea fortuna. " Acc: 3 (VS)EO. OPA-4 (Spicker),
(S)GR

8573. Non fuggir, t'arresta
Opera: IL CAMPANELLO DI NOTTE, 1836, libretto by the composer,
based on Brunswick, Troin and Lhèrie's vaudeville. Part of Enrico,
one-act opera. e2(d♯2)-d3(e3) f♯2-c♯3 Sustained in moderate lively
tempo. Has some slightly climactic passages. Ends with a cadenza.
The first part of the duet. A fine air for young baritones. Acc:
3-4 (VS)IM

8574. R: Alcun gli fea
A: Vien, Leonora
Opera: LA FAVORITA, 1840, libretto by Alphonse Royer, Gustave

Vaëz, and Eugène Scribe.   Part of Alfonso, Act II.   c2-f3   e2-d3
Sustained in slow tempo.   Has dramatic passages, passages with high
tessitura, and a climactic ending.   Requires flexibility.   Acc: 3-4
(VS)GR, B-H.   (S)GR

8575. R: Che vegg'io?
       A: Sei pur tu che ancor rivedo?
       Opera: LA REGINA DI GOLCONDA, 1828, libretto by Felice Romani.
       Part of Volmar, Act II.   b1-e3   f♯2-d♯3   A recitative and an ani-
       mated aria.   High tessitura; generally strong.   An excerpt from a
       duet.   Acc: 3-4   (VS)GR

8576. Ambo nati in questa valle
       Opera: LINDA DI CHAMOUNIX, 1842, libretto by Gaetano Rossi.
       Part of Antonio, Act I.   d2-e3   g2-d3   Sustained in moderate tempo.
       Has climactic passages.   High tessitura.   Climactic ending.   Acc:
       3-4   (VS)GR

8577. Cruda, funesta smania
       Opera: LUCIA DI LAMMERMOOR, 1835, libretto by Salvatore Cam-
       marano, after Walter Scott's novel, The Bride of Lammermoor.   Part
       of Enrico (Henry), Act I.   c♯2-f3(g3)   e2-e3   Generally sustained in
       varied tempi and moods.   Has strong, dramatic sections and a cli-
       mactic ending.   Tessitura stays high in some sections.   Acc: 4
       (VS)GR, GS.   OPA-4 (Spicker; Adler).   (S)GR

8578. Voce fatal di morte
       Opera: MARIA DI ROHAN, 1843, libretto by Salvatore Cammarano.
       Part of Chevreuse, Act III.   f2-f3   g2-e♭3   Sustained in moderate
       slow tempo.   Has quite high tessitura.   Best for high baritone.   May
       also be sung singly by heavy tenor.   Strong and dramatic.   Vocally
       demanding.   Climactic ending.   Acc: 3-4   (VS)GR

8579. R: Decio, signor del Mondo
       A: Di tua beltade immagine
       Opera: POLIUTO or I MARTIRI, 1840, libretto by Eugène Scribe,
       after Pierre Corneille.   Part of Severo, Act I.   c2-e♭3   e♭2-d♭3
       Recitative and a sustained aria in moderate slow tempo.   Lyric in
       style.   Slightly climactic ending.   Acc: 3-4   (VS)SR

8580. La mia casa per modello
       Opera: RITA, 1840, libretto by Gustave Vaëz.   Part of Gasparo, one-
       act opera.   c2-e3   d2-d3   Animated in moderate lively tempo.   Has
       recitative passages.   Requires fluent enunciation.   Climactic high end-
       ing.   Humorous text.   Acc: 3-4   (VS)GR

UMBERTO GIORDANO, 1867-1948

8581. Nemico della patria?
       Opera: ANDREA CHÉNIER, 1896, libretto by Luigi Illica.   Part of
       Gerard, Act III.   c♯2-f♯3   f♯2-d3   Generally in recitative style in
       moderate slow tempo.   Song style starts in the middle of the excerpt.
       Has some dramatic passages.   Subdued, falling ending after the main
       climax.   Acc: 3-4   (VS)CS, IM

8582. Compiacente a' colloquii
       Opera: ANDREA CHÉNIER.   Part of Gerard, Act I.   c♯2-f♯3

f# 2-d3 Sustained in moderate tempo in the first section; animated and fast second section. The second section is dramatic and strong. Climactic high ending on f# 3. This aria opens the opera. Acc: 4 (VS)CS, IM

8583. La donna russa
       Opera: FEDORA, 1898, libretto by Arturo Colautti, after Victorien Sardou's drama. Part of De Siriex, Act II. eb 2-f3 g2-eb 3 Animated in lively tempo. Has faster sections. Generally strong and outgoing. Dramatic and emphatic ending. Acc: 3-4 (VS)CS

RUGGIERO LEONCAVALLO, 1858-1919

8584. Alza l'occhio celeste
       Opera: LA BOHEME, 1897, libretto by Giuseppe Giacosa and Luigi Illica, after Henri Murger's novel. Part of Schaunard, Act II. b1-e3 e2-d3 Sustained in moderate tempo. Very florid, requires flexibility. A comic aria. Acc: 3-4 (VS)CS

8585. L'immenso tesoro
       Opera: LA BOHEME. Part of Rodolfo, Act II. c2-f3 f3-e4 Sustained in moderate tempo. Has dramatic energy and high tessitura. Acc: 3-4 (VS)CS

8586. Scuoti, o vento
       Opera: LA BOHEME. Part of Rodolfo, Act IV. c# 2-g3 e2-e3 Sustained in moderate tempo. Dramatic and vocally demanding. Tessitura stays high in some sections. Climactic ending. Acc: 4 (VS)CS

8587. Si può? Si può?
       Opera: PAGLIACCI, 1892, libretto by the composer. Part of Tonio, in The Prologue. b1-f3 e2-e3 Sustained in generally moderate slow tempo that varies in certain passages. Has some sweeping lines. Climactic. Some singers sing an ab 3 on the word "voi," 8 measures from the end of the vocal part, and g3 at the end, on the third syllable of "incominciate!" These are only traditional additions by singers rather than the intentions of the composer. Transposed editions are available. Acc: 3-4 (VS)GS. OPA-4 (Spicker; Adler). (S)GS-two keys

8588. Buona Zazà del mio buon tempo
       Opera: ZAZÀ, 1900, libretto by the composer, after a play by Pierre Berton and Charles Simon. Part of Cascart, Act II. c2-f3 f2-eb 3 Sustained in moderate slow tempo. Has climactic high passages. Very subdued ending after climax. Acc: 3-4 (VS)CS

8589. Zazà, piccola zingara
       Opera: ZAZÀ. Part of Cascart, Act IV. f2-gb 3(ab 3) gb 2-f3 Sustained in slow tempo. Quite high tessitura. Very lyric in style. Has dramatic passages and a climactic high ending. Acc: 3-4 (VS) CS. (S)IM

PIETRO MASCAGNI, 1863-1945

8590. Il cavallo scalpita

Opera: CAVALLERIA RUSTICANA, 1889, libretto by Giovanni Targi-
oni-Tozzetti and Guido Menasci, after Verga's story. Part of Alfio,
one-act opera. eb 2-f# 3   f# 2-f# 3 Animated vocal part with a sustained ending note. Accented, dramatic, and energetic. Quite high
tessitura with long-held f# 3's. Acc: 3-4 (VS)GS. OPA-4 (Spicker),
OAR-Br

8591. R: Vediam! Così stai bene!
A: Or ti conviene
Opera: IRIS, 1898, libretto by Luigi Illica. Part of Kyoto, Act II.
eb 2-f3 f# 2-d3 Sustained aria in moderate slow tempo. Starts gently. Has climactic passages. Spoken ending phrase after dramatic
climax. Acc: 3-4 (VS)GR

8592. Per voi ghiottoni inutili
Opera: L'AMICO FRITZ, 1891, libretto by R. Suardon, after Erckmann-Chatrian's novel. Part of David, Act I. Common title: Song
of the rabbi. d2-f3 g2-eb 3 Sustained in moderate tempo. Has
slower tempi. Generally strong and broad. Tessitura stays high
most of the time. Acc: 3-4 (VS)CS

ITALO MONTEMEZZI, 1875-1952

8593. Italia, è tutto il mio ricordo!
Opera: L'AMORE DEI TRE RE, 1913, libretto by the composer, after
Sem Benelli's tragedy. Part of Archibaldo, Act I. a1-f3 d2-d3
Animated in generally lively tempo. Has dramatic passages, sections
with high tessitura, and a climactic ending. Acc: 3-4 (VS)GR

AMILCARE PONCHIELLI, 1834-1886

8594. R: La vision spariva!
A: Raccogli e calma
Opera: IL FIGIUOL PRODIGO, 1880, libretto by Angelo Zanardini.
Part of Amenofi, Act III. c2-f3 e2-e3 Subdued scena and a sus-
tained aria in moderate slow tempo. Has dramatic passages. Also
requires very fine high P. Dramatic high ending on sustained f3.
Acc: 3-4 CAO-Br

8595. O monumento!
Opera: LA GIOCONDA, 1876, libretto by Arrigo Boito, after Victor
Hugo. Part of Barnaba, Act I. Common title: Barnaba's monologue.
d2-g3 f2-f3 In varied tempi. Starts in moderate tempo, then moves
on to faster sections. Dramatic and strong in some passages. Climactic ending. Acc: 3-4 (VS)GS, GR. (S)GR

8596. Ah! Pescator, affonda l'esca
Opera: LA GIOCONDA. Part of Barnaba, Act II. eb 2-f3 f2-eb 3
Animated in fast, spirited tempo. Outgoing, joyous. Requires fluent
enunciation and flexibility. Climactic ending. Other title: Canzone-
Barcarola. Acc: 4 OPA-4 (Spicker; Adler). (VS)GS, GR. (S)GR

GIACOMO (ANTONIO DOMENICO) PUCCINI, 1858-1924

8597. Scorri, fiume eterno!

Opera: IL TABARRO, 1918, libretto by Giuseppe Adami. Part of
Michele, one-act opera. b♭1-g3 e♭2-e♭3 Sustained in slow tempo.
Starts gravely. Has dramatic passages, and a climactic high ending.
Agitated accompaniment in the last section. Acc: 4 (VS)GR

8598. Minnie, dalla mia casa son partito
Opera: LA FANCIULLA DEL WEST, 1910, libretto by Guelfo Civini-
ni and Carlo Zangarini. Part of Rance, Act I. b1-f♯3 e2-d♯3
Sustained in moderate slow tempo. Starts gently. Has climactic
passages and a dramatic high ending. Also requires some fine P.
Short. Acc: 3-4 (VS)GR. CAO-Br

8599. Se la giurata fede
Opera: TOSCA, 1900, libretto by Giuseppe Giacosa and Luigi Illica.
Part of Scarpia, Act II. d♭2-g♭3 g♭2-e♭3 Sustained in moderate
slow tempo. Dramatic, with some high tessitura. Part of a scena
with Tosca. Acc: 3-4 (VS)GS, GR. (S)GR

8600. R: No! possibil non è
A: Anima santa della figlia mia
Opera: LE VILLI, 1884, libretto by Ferdinando Fontana. Part of
Guglielmo, Act II. b♭1-f3(g3) g2-e♭3 Dramatic scena and a sus-
tained aria in moderate slow tempo. Has passages with high tessi-
tura. Dramatic. Acc: 3-4 (VS)GR. (S)GR

GIOACCHINO (ANTONIO) ROSSINI, 1792-1868

8601. Sois immobile (It.: Resta immobile)
Opera: GUILLAUME TELL (It.: GUGLIELMO TELL), 1829, libretto
by Victor Joseph Étienne de Jouy and Hippolyte Bis, after Schiller's
drama. Original text: French. Part of William Tell, Act III. c2-
f3 f2-d♭3 Sustained in moderate slow tempo. In lyric style. Has
passages with high tessitura. Agitated accompaniment. Acc: 3-4
(VS) Troupenas-French; GR-Italian; B-H-Italian & English. OPA-4
(Spicker-Italian)

8602. Largo al factotum della cita
Opera: IL BARBIERE DI SIVIGLIA, 1816, libretto by Cesare Sterbini,
after Beaumarchais' comedy. Part of Figaro, Act I. d2-g3 g2-e3
Animated in fast tempo. Outgoing, narrative, requires very fluent
enunciation which is sometimes rapid. Rhythmic, with some high
tessitura. Vocally demanding. Usually the g3 is sung, although the
lower octave is also used. Acc: 4 (VS)GS, GR. OPA-4 (Spicker;
Adler), OAR-Br. (S)GR, GS-two keys

8603. R: Miei rampolli femminini
A: Mi sognai fra il fosco e il chiaro
Opera: LA CENERENTOLA, 1817, libretto by Jacopo Ferretti, after
Perrault. Part of Magnifico, Act I. a1-f♯3 d2-d3 Extended recita-
tive and an animated aria in moderate lively tempo. Requires fluent
enunciation. Some passages require flexibility. Climactic ending.
Acc: 3-4 (VS)MR, GR

8604. R: Eterni Dei! che sento!
A: Oh colpo impensato
Opera: LA GAZZA LADRA, 1817, libretto by Giovanni Gherardini,
after a comedy by d'Aubigny and Caigniez. Part of Fernando, Act II.

c2-f3   f2-db3   Animated aria in moderate lively tempo.   Florid, with
triplet figures.   Requires flexibility.   Climactic ending.   Agitated accompaniment.   Acc: 3-4   (VS)EG, GR

8605.   R: Qu'à ma voix la victoire s'arrête!
        A: La gloire et la fortune
        Opera: LE SIÈGE DE CORINTHE, 1826, libretto by Alexandre Sou-
        met and Luigi Balocchi.   Part of Mahomet, No. 3.   bb1-f3   d2-e3
        Dramatic recitative and a maestoso aria.   Generally strong, in some
        sections pompous.   Has florid figures and a climactic ending.   Re-
        quires some flexibility.   Acc: 4   (VS)NS.   OPA-4 (Spicker)

8606.   R: Con tutta la sua boria
        A: La femmine d'Italian
        Opera: L'ITALIANA IN ALGERI, 1813, libretto by Angelo Anelli.
        Part of Haly, Act II.   c2-d3(e3)   g2-c3   Animated in moderate lively
        tempo.   High tessitura and climactic ending.   Slightly agitated accom-
        paniment.   Acc: 3-4   (VS)GR

8607.   Ho un gran peso
        Opera: L'ITALIANA IN ALGERI.   Part of Taddeo, Act II.   d2-e3
        f#2-d3   Animated in lively tempo.   Has passages which require fluent
        enunciation.   Climactic ending.   Acc: 4   (VS)GR

8608.   Già d'insolito ardore
        Opera: L'ITALIANA IN ALGERI.   Part of Mustafà, Act I.   bb1-f3
        eb2-eb3   Animated in lively tempo.   Florid, requires considerable
        flexibility.   High tessitura in some passages.   Climactic, descending
        ending line.   A basso-cantante piece.   Acc: 4   (VS)GR

GIUSEPPE (FORTUNINO FRANCESCO) VERDI, 1813-1901

8609.   R: Ei fugge, e con tal foglio
        A: Mina, pensai che un angelo
        Opera: AROLDO, 1857, libretto by Francesco Maria Piave.   Part of
        Egberto, Act III.   c2-gb3   eb2-eb3   Scena in different tempi and
        moods, and a sustained aria in slow tempo.   Has some climactic pas-
        sages, and a descending ending line.   Acc: 3-4   (VS)GR.   OAB

8610.   R: Tregua è cogl'unni
        A: Dagl' immortali vertici
        Opera: ATTILA, 1846, libretto by Temistocle Solera.   Part of Ezio,
        Act II.   c2-g3   f2-f3   Sustained in moderate slow tempo.   Dramatic
        and strong.   Has some sections with high tessitura.   Climactic end-
        ing.   Acc: 3-4   (VS)GR.   OAB, OPA-4 (Spicker)

8611.   R: Son io, mio Carlo
        A: Per me giunto
        Opera: DON CARLOS, 1867, libretto by François Joseph Méry and
        Camille du Locle, after Friedrich von Schiller.   Part of Rodrigo, Act
        IV.   c2-gb3   e2-e3   A sustained aria in varied tempi and moods.
        Requires fine high P and PP.   Has dramatic passages and emotionally
        intense sections.   Climactic ending.   Acc: 3-4   (VS)GS, GR.
        OPA-4 (Spicker; Adler).   (S)GR, GS

8612.   Lo vedremo, veglio audace
        Opera: ERNANI, 1844, libretto by Francesco Maria Piave.   Part of

Don Carlos, Act II. d2-f#3 f#2-e3 Sustained in moderate tempo.
Has dramatic passages and agitated accompaniment. Acc: 3-4 (VS)
GR. OPA-4 (Spicker; Adler). (S)GR

8613. R: Gran Dio!
A: Oh de' verd' anni miei
Opera: ERNANI. Part of Don Carlos, Act III. c2-gb3 g2-db3 A
dramatic recitative and a sustained aria in moderate tempo. Has
some florid figures. Tessitura stays high most of the time. Has
dramatic passages and a climactic ending. Best for high baritone.
Acc: 3-4 (VS)GR. OAB, (S)GR

8614. È sogno? o realtà....
Opera: FALSTAFF, 1893, libretto by Arrigo Boito, after Shakespeare's Merry Wives of Windsor. Part of Ford, Act II. bb1-g3
eb2-f3 Generally sustained in varied moods and tempi. Interpretatively difficult. Dramatic and vocally demanding. Sustained and very
subdued ending. Acc: 4 (VS)GS, GR, IM. OPA-4 (Spicker; Adler).
(S)GS, GR

8615. R: Ehi! paggio!
A: L'onore! Ladri!
Opera: FALSTAFF. Part of Falstaff, Act I. ab1-g3 e2-e3 Fairly
fast recitative, and a sustained allegro aria. Requires fine P and
PP. Has several g3's and dramatic passages. Climactic ending.
Musically and vocally not easy. Acc: 3-4 (VS)GS, GR, IM.
OPA-4 (Spicker; Adler)

8616. R: Eccomi solo al fine
A: O vecchio cor che batti
Opera: I DUE FOSCARI, 1844, libretto by Francesco Maria Piave,
based on Byron's drama. Part of Doge, Act I. c2-f3 f2-d3 Recitative and a sustained aria in moderate slow tempo. Has florid figures and dramatic passages. Requires some flexibility. Climactic
ending. Acc: 3-4 (VS)GR. OAB

8617. R: Vecchio, spiccai da te quell' odiato
A: La sua lampada vitale
Opera: I MASNADIERI, 1847, libretto by Andrea Maffei, based on
Schiller's drama. Part of Francesco, Act I. d2-f3 eb2-e3 A
scena and a sustained aria in moderate slow tempo. Has dramatic
passages. Requires fine P and PP. Climactic ending. Acc: 3-4
(VS)GR. OAB

8618. R: Tradimento! Risorgono i defunti!
A: Pareami che sorto da lauto convito
Opera: I MASNADIERI. Part of Francesco, Act IV. c2-f3 f2-d3
Slightly dramatic scena and a sustained aria in moderate tempo. Re-
quires fine PP as well as some dramatic energy. Requires flexibil-
ity. Acc: 4 (VS)GR. OAB

8619. In braccio alle dovizie
Opera: I VESPRI SICILIANI, 1856, libretto by E. Caime, after the
original French by Eugène Scribe and Charles Duveyrier. Part of
Monforte, Act III. c#2-f#3 f#2-d#3 Animated in lively tempo.
Has slower sections. Requires flexibility and fine high P and PP.
Has passages requiring some dramatic energy. Generally subdued.
Acc: 4 (VS)GR. OAB

8620.   R: Tutto e deserto
        A: Il balen del suo sorriso
        Opera: IL TROVATORE, 1853, libretto by Salvatore Cammarano,
        after Antonio Gutierrez's play.   Part of Conti di Luna, Act II.   a1-
        f3 f2-f3 Recitative in moderate tempo, and a slow, sustained aria.
        Climactic ending with cadenza.   Acc: 3-4 (VS)GS, GR, CP.   OPA-
        4 (Spicker; Adler), OAB.   (S)GR

8621.   R: Spento tra le fiamme
        A: Ah! m'abbraccia d'esultanza
        Opera: LA BATTAGLIA DI LEGNANO, 1849, libretto by Salvatore
        Cammarano.   Part of Rolando, Act I.   d2-f3 f2-d3 Animated in
        moderate lively tempo.   Slightly slower middle section.   Has pas-
        sages with high tessitura.   Climactic ending.   Acc: 3-4 (VS)GR

8622.   R: Sui lombardi campi
        A: Se al nuovo di pugnando
        Opera: LA BATTAGLIA DI LEGNANO.   Part of Rolando, Act III.
        c2-f3(g3) f2-d3 A scena and a sustained aria in moderate slow tem-
        po.   Requires fine PP.   Mainly lyric in style.   Acc: 3-4 (VS)GR

8623.   Son Pereda, son ricco d'onore
        Opera: LA FORZA DEL DESTINO, 1862, libretto by Francesco Ma-
        ria Piave.   Part of Don Carlo, Act II.   c#2-f#3 e2-d3 Animated
        in moderate lively tempo.   Has dramatic passages and dotted rhyth-
        mic figures.   Slightly faster ending phrase.   Acc: 3-4 (VS)GS, IM,
        CP.   OAB.   (S)GR

8624.   Toh, toh! Poffare il mondo
        Opera: LA FORZA DEL DESTINO.   Part of Fra Melitone, Act III.
        a1-gb3 e2-d3 Animated in moderate lively tempo.   In recitative style.
        Has climactic passages and a climactic ending.   Requires fluent enun-
        ciation.   Has passages with high tessitura.   Acc: 3-4 (VS)GR, IM,
        CP.   OAB

8625.   R: Morir! Tremenda cosa!
        A: Urna fatale
        Opera: LA FORZA DEL DESTINO.   Part of Don Carlo, Act II.   b1-
        f#3 e2-e3 A dramatic scena in varied tempi and moods.   Has sev-
        eral dramatic passages.   Climactic ending, with cadenza.   Acc: 4
        (VS)GR, IM, CP.   OPA-4 (Spicker; Adler), OAB.   (S)GR

8626.   Di provenza il mar
        Opera: LA TRAVIATA, 1853, libretto by Francesco Maria Piave,
        after a play by the younger Dumas.   Part of Germont, Act II.   db2-
        gb3 f2-f3 Sustained in moderate tempo.   Graceful.   Has dramatic
        passages at the ending part of the two verses.   Acc: 3 (VS)GS, GR,
        CP.   OPA-4 (Spicker; Adler), OAB.   (S)GS, GR

8627.   Il mio sangue, la vita darei
        Opera: LUISA MILLER, 1849, libretto by Salvatore Cammarano,
        based on Schiller's tragedy.   Part of Walter, Act I.   bb1-gb3 eb2-
        d3 Sustained in moderate slow tempo.   Has dramatic climaxes.   Cli-
        matic ending with a cadenza.   Acc: 3-4 (VS)GR.   (S)GR

8628.   Sacra la scelta è d'un consorte
        Opera: LUISA MILLER.   Part of Miller, Act I.   d2-gb3 f2-f3 Sus-
        tained in moderate slow tempo.   Majestic, best for high baritone.

Tessitura stays high. Climactic high ending. Acc: 4 (VS)GR.
OAB. (S)GR

8629. Mi si affaccia un pugnal?
Opera: MACBETH, 1847, libretto by Francesco Maria Piave, after
William Shakespeare. Part of Macbeth, Act I. c♯2-f3 e♭2-c3 In
different tempi and moods. Has some dramatic passages and a climactic ending. Acc: 3-4 (VS)GR. OAB

8630. R: Perfidi!
A: Pietà, rispetto, onore
Opera: MACBETH. Part of Macbeth, Act IV. c2-f3 f2-e♭3 A
dramatic scena and a sustained aria in moderate slow tempo. Has
some climactic passages. Requires fine P and PP. Acc: 3-4 (VS)
GR. OPA-4 (Spicker; Adler), OAB. (S)GR

8631. Chi mi toglie il regio scettro?
Opera: NABUCCO, 1842, libretto by Temistocle Solera. Part of
Nabucco, Act II, in the Finale. c2-f3 a♭2-e♭3 Sustained vocal part
in lively tempo. Has slower section. High tessitura throughout, dra-
matic passages, and a climactic ending. Acc: 3-4 (VS)GR. OAB,
(S)GR

8632. R: Vanne; la tua meta gia vedo
A: Credo in un Dio
Opera: OTELLO, 1887, libretto by Arrigo Boito, based on William
Shakespeare's play. Part of Iago, Act II. a♯1-f♯3 f2-e♭3 A reci-
tative and aria generally in recitative style and moving in moderate
tempo. Dramatic and strong. Also requires fine PP. Climactic
ending on sustained f3. Acc: 3-4 (VS)GR, GS, IM. OPA-4 (Spicker;
Adler). (S)GR, GS

8633. R: Si, la mia figlia
A: Cortigiani, vil razza
Opera: RIGOLETTO, 1851, libretto by Francesco Maria Piave, after
Victor Hugo. Part of Rigoletto, Act II. c2-g♭3 f2-e♭3 Sustained
aria in moderate tempo, with slight variations. Dramatic, and deeply
intense. Climactic and difficult. Dramatic ending. Agitated accompaniment. CP edition starts the recitative earlier, with "Ah, ella e
qui dunque." Acc: 4 (VS)GS, GR, CP. OPA-4 (Spicker; Adler),
OAB. (S)GR

8634. Pari siamo
Opera: RIGOLETTO. Part of Rigoletto, Act I. c2-f3 f2-e3 In
varied moods and tempi. Dramatic, generally in recitative style. Interpretatively difficult. Climactic ending. Acc: 3-4 (VS)GR, GS,
CP. OPA-4 (Spicker; Adler), OAB. (S)GR

8635. Fratricidi! Plebe! patrizi!
Opera: SIMON BOCCANEGRA, 1857, libretto by Francesco Maria
Piave, after a drama by Antonio Garcia Gutierrez, and revised by
Arrigo Boito in 1881. Part of the Doge, Act I. e♭2-f♯3 e♭2-c♯3
Generally sustained in moderate tempo. Slightly slower second sec-
tion. Has dramatic passages. Acc: 3-4 (VS)GR

8636. Alla vita che t'arride
Opera: UN BALLO IN MASCHERA, 1859, libretto by Antonio Somma,
after Scribe's libretto. Part of Renato, Act I. c2-g3 f2-d3

Sustained in moderate slow tempo. Has dramatic passages, and
staccati phrases. Climactic ending. Acc: 3-4 (VS)GS, GR, CP.
OAB. (S)GR

8637.   R: Alzatti! la tuo figlio
        A: Eri tu che macchiavi
        Opera: UN BALLO IN MASCHERA. Part of Renato, Act III. a1-g3
        e2-f3 Slightly dramatic recitative and a sustained aria in moderate
        slow tempo. Requires fine P. Has some strong and dramatic pas-
        sages. Climactic ending. Acc: 3-4 (VS)GS, GR, CP. OPA-4
        (Spicker; Adler), OAB. (S)GR, GS

B.   French Composers

ADOLPHE (CHARLES) ADAM, 1803-1856

8638.   Oui des choristes
        Opera: LE POSTILLON DE LONGJUMEAU, 1836, libretto by Adolphe
        de Leuvon and Leon Brunswick. Part of Alcindor, Act II. a1-e3(f3)
        c2-c3 Animated in lively tempo. Has climactic passages. Requires
        fine P. Outgoing. Acc: 3-4 (VS)BR

8639.   Dans le sommeil l'amour
        Opera: SI J'ÉTAIS ROI, 1852, libretto by Adolphe Philippe d'Ennery
        and Jules Brésil. Part of the King of Goa, Act I. eb2-ab3 ab2-
        eb3 Sustained in somewhat slow tempo. High tessitura; best for
        high baritone or heavy tenor. Lyric in style, with some climactic
        passages. Climactic ending. Acc: 3-4 (VS)AL

8640.   La fleur boit la rosée
        Opera: SI J'ÉTAIS ROI. Part of the King of Goa, Act II. g2-f3
        bb2-eb3 Sustained in moderate tempo. Strong ending on high tessi-
        tura. With choral part in the full score. Acc: 3-4 (VS)AL

HECTOR BERLIOZ, 1803-1869

8641.   R: Maintenant, chantons a cette belle
        A: Devant la maison
        Opera: LA DAMNATION DE FAUST, 1846, libretto by the composer,
        after Goethe's drama. b1-f♯3 e2-c♯3 Common title: Mephisto's
        serenade. Part of Mephistophele, Act IV. Animated aria in waltz
        tempo and rhythm. Requires fine P. Has strong passages. With
        choral part in the full score. Acc: 3-4 (VS)CT

8642.   Une puce gentile
        Opera: LA DAMNATION DE FAUST. Part of Mephistophele, Act II.
        Common title: Chanson de la Puce. d2-f3 f2-d3 Animated in mod-
        erate lively tempo. Generally on MF level. Climactic high ending.
        Acc: 3 (VS)CT. (S)IM

8643.   Voici des roses
        Opera: LA DAMNATION DE FAUST. Part of Mephistophele, Act III.
        c♯2-e3 e2-c♯3 Sustained in moderate slow tempo. Graceful and
        gentle throughout. Acc: 3-4 (VS)CT

GEORGES BIZET, 1838-1875

8644. Votre toast, je peux vous le rendre
Opera: CARMEN, 1873-1874, libretto by Henri Meilhac and Ludovic
Halévy, based on Mérimée's story. Part of Escamillo, Act II. bb1-
f3 d2-eb3 Common title: Toreador's song. Animated in moderate
lively tempo. Very rhythmic, accented, generally strong, and outgoing. Dramatic high ending. Acc: 3-4 (VS)GS, CP. (S)GS

8645. R: L'orage s'est calmé
A: O Nadir, tendre ami
Opera: LES PÊCHEURS DE PERLES, 1862-1863, libretto by Michel
Carré and Eugène Cormon. Part of Zurga, Act III. b1-f#3 d2-d3
Sustained aria in moderate slow tempo. Starts gently. Requires fine
high P. Has climactic passages. Agitated accompaniment in certain
sections. Acc: 3-4 (VS)EC

GUSTAVE CHARPENTIER, 1860-1956

8646. R: Les pauvres gens
A: Voir naitre un enfant
Opera: LOUISE, 1900, libretto by the composer. Part of the Father,
Act IV. a#1-f3(g3) e2-e3 A dramatic scena in varied tempi. In-
terpretatively difficult and vocally demanding. Has climactic pas-
sages; also requires very fine P and PP. Acc: 4 (VS)GS, HC

FÉLICIEN (CÉSAR) DAVID, 1810-1876

8647. Jusqu'a ce jour
Opera: LA PERLE DU BRÉSIL, 1851, libretto by J. Gabriel and
Sylvain Saint-Étienne. Part of Salvador, Act I. g1-e3(f3) c2-c3
Sustained in moderate tempo. Has slower middle section. Climactic
ending. Agitated accompaniment. Acc: 4 (VS)HC

BENJAMIN (LOUIS PAUL) GODARD, 1849-1895

8648. Nous montions a l'assaut
Opera: LA VIVANDIÈRE, 1895, libretto by Henri Cain. Part of
Balafre, Act II. d2-g3 g2-d3 Animated in march tempo. Strong
and outgoing. High tessitura; climactic ending. Acc: 3 (VS)EC

8649. Je veux, en ce beau jour
Opera: LE TASSE, 1878, libretto by Charles Grandmougin. Part of
Duke D'Este, Act III. Common title: Serenade. c#2-f#3 f#2-e3
Sustained in moderate tempo. Lyric in style, with some climactic
passages. Requires fine P and PP. Climactic ending. Acc: 3-4
(VS)GH

CHARLES (FRANÇOIS) GOUNOD, 1818-1893

8650. Écoute-moi bien, Marguerite
Opera: FAUST, 1852-1859, libretto by Jules Barbier and Michel
Carré, after Goethe. Part of Valentine, Act IV. Common title: The
death of Valentine. c2-f3 f2-d3 Sustained in moderate slow tempo.

Starts in declamatory style.   Has some dramatic passages.   Subdued
ending.   Acc: 3-4   (VS)GS, CP

8651.   Avant de quitter ces lieux
        Opera: FAUST.   Part of Valentine, Act II.   c2-g3 f2-f3 Sustained
        in moderate slow tempo.   Middle section is slightly animated, with
        martial slow tempo.   Often sung one step lower in db-major, for a
        warmer tone.   Acc: 3-4   (VS)GS, CP.   OPA-4 (Spicker; Adler, both
        in db-major).   (S)GS-two keys

8652.   R: Oui, despuis quatre jours
        A: Sous les pieds d'une femme
        Opera: LA REINE DE SABA, 1861, libretto by Jules Barbier and
        Michel Carré, after Gérard de Nerval.   Part of Soliman, Act IV.
        c2(f1)-eb3 e2-d3 Sustained in slow tempo.   Has dramatic passages
        and a climactic ending.   Requires fine P and PP.   A transposed edi-
        tion for baritone in the Appendix of the vocal score.   Acc: 3-4
        (VS)EC

8653.   Si les filles d'Arles
        Opera: MIREILLE, 1863, libretto by Michel Carré, after Frédérick
        Mistral.   Part of Ourrias, Act II.   c2-f3 e2-d3 Animated in mod-
        erate lively tempo.   Graceful and outgoing.   Subdued ending.   De-
        tached accompaniment.   Acc: 4   (VS)EC

8654.   Mab, la reine des Mensonges
        Opera: ROMÉO ET JULIETTE, 1864, libretto by Jules Barbier and
        Michel Carré, after William Shakespeare.   Part of Mercutio, Act I.
        Common title: Ballade of Queen Mab.   d2-f#3 f#2-e3 Animated in
        lively tempo.   Tessitura stays consistently high.   Climactic ending.
        Acc: 4   (VS)GS, CP

(JACQUES FRANÇOIS) FROMENTAL (ELIAS) HALÉVY, 1799-1862

8655.   C'est grand pitie que ce roi
        Opera: CHARLES VI, 1843, libretto by Germain and Casimir Dela-
        vigne.   Part of the King, Act II.   e2-f3 g2-d3 Sustained in moder-
        ate tempo.   Mainly lyric.   Acc: 3-4   (VS)BR

8656.   Non, non, ne crois pas
        Opera: LA FÉE AUX ROSES, 1847, libretto by Eugène Scribe and
        Vernoy de Saint-Georges.   Part of Atalmuc, Act III.   ab1-eb3 c2-
        db3 First animated in lively tempo, then sustained in moderate slow
        tempo.   Requires some flexibility.   Climactic high ending.   Acc: 3-4
        (VS)HL

VICTOR (FÉLIX MARIE) MASSÉ, 1822-1884

8657.   R: Enfin, me voila seul
        A: Qu'un autre se marie
        Opera: LES NOCES DE JEANNETTE, 1853, libretto by Jules Barbier
        and Michel Carré.   Part of Jean, one-act opera.   bb1-f3 f2-eb3
        Animated aria in fast tempo.   Requires flexibility.   Tessitura stays
        high most of the time.   Has dramatic passages and a climactic end-
        ing.   Acc: 4   (VS)LS

JULES (ÉMILE FRÉDÉRIC) MASSENET, 1842-1912

8658. R: Dors, o cité perverse
        A: Astres étincilante
        Opera: HÉRODIADE, 1881, libretto by Paul Milliet and Henri Gré-
        mont (George Hartmann), after a story by Flaubert. Part of Phanuel,
        Act III. b1-eb3(f3) d2-d3 Generally sustained, in varied moods and
        tempi. Starts slowly. Has dramatic passages and a climactic end-
        ing. Generally in recitative style. Has some agitated accompani-
        ment. Acc: 3-4 (VS)HC

8659. Salomé! Salomé!
        Opera: HÉRODIADE. Part of Herod, Act I. c2-f3 eb2-f3 Sus-
        tained in varied tempi and moods. Has andante and allegro passages.
        Requires fine P. Has dramatic passages. Starts in recitative style.
        First line: Elle e fui le palais. Acc: 3-4 (VS)HC. OPA-4
        (Spicker; Adler)

8660. R: Ce breuvage pourrait
        A: Vision fugitive
        Opera: HÉRODIADE. Part of Herod, Act II. c2-gb3 eb2-f3 Sus-
        tained aria in moderate slow tempo. Has dramatic passages and a
        good number of sustained high notes: f3 and gb3. Acc: 3-4 (VS)
        HC. OPA-4 (Spicker; Adler). (S)GS

8661. Marie avec l'Enfant Jesus
        Opera: LE JONGLEUR DE NOTRE-DAME, 1902, libretto by Maurice
        Léna. Part of Boniface, Act II. Common title: Légende de la
        Sauge. c2-f3 eb2-d3 Sustained in moderate slow tempo. In the
        style of a gentle recitative. Has dramatic passages. Requires some
        fine P. Excerpt ends with "outes les fleurs." Acc: 3-4 (VS)HC

8662. R: Aux troupes de Sultan
        A: Promesse de mon avenir
        Opera: LE ROI DE LAHORE, 1877, libretto by Louis Gallet. Part
        of Scindia, Act IV. db2-gb3 eb2-eb3 A dramatic recitative and a
        sustained-animated aria. Climactic, dramatic ending with sustained
        final gb3. Acc: 3-4 (VS)HC. OPA-4 (Spicker)

8663. Voila donc la terrible cité
        Opera: THAÏS, 1894, libretto by Louis Gallet, after a novel by Ana-
        tole France. Part of Anathaël, Act I. b1-f3 e2-c#3 Sustained
        vocal part in moderate lively tempo. With majesty. Middle part is
        faster and more dramatic. Climactic high ending. Agitated accom-
        paniment. Acc: 4 (VS)HC

8664. Tu songes a l'ami
        Opera: THÉRÈSE, 1907, libretto by Jules Claretie. Part of Andre,
        Act II. c2-eb3 e2-c3 Sustained in moderate tempo. Starts in gen-
        tle recitative style. Climactic ending. Acc: 3-4 (VS)HC

8665. Quelle prière de reconnaissance et d'amour
        Opera: WERTHER, 1892, libretto by Edouard Blau, Paul Milliet and
        Georges Hartmann. Part of Albert, Act I. c2-eb3 eb2-db3 Sus-
        tained in moderate slow tempo. Tessitura stays high most of the
        time. Generally subdued. Acc: 3-4 (VS)HC

PIERRE ALEXANDRE MONSIGNY, 1729-1817

8666. Adieu, chere Louise
       Opera: LE DÉSERTEUR, 1769, libretto by Jean Michel Sedaine.
       Part of Alexis, Act III. d2-f3 eb2-eb3 Sustained in slow tempo.
       Requires fine PP. Lyric and generally tranquil. Has a short reci-
       tative before the ending section. Very subdued ending. Acc: 3-4
       (VS)EN. OPA-4 (Spicker)

8667. Ah! je respire
       Opera: LE DÉSERTEUR. Part of Alexis, Act I. a1-f♯3 f♯2-d3
       Sustained vocal part: first in moderate lively tempo, then in lively
       tempo. Majestic. Has dramatic passages. Climactic ending. Acc:
       3-4 (VS)EN

JACQUES OFFENBACH, 1819-1880

8668. R: Allez! Pour te livrer combat
       A: Scintille, diamant
       Opera: LES CONTES D'HOFFMANN, 1881, libretto by Jules Barbier
       and Michel Carré, after E. T. A. Hoffmann. Part of Dappertutto.
       bb1-f♯3(g♯3) e2-e3 Strong recitative and a sustained aria which
       starts gently and then moves into a dramatic section. Climactic end-
       ing. Acc: 3-4 (VS)GS. OPA-4 (Spicker; Adler)

(CHARLES) CAMILLE SAINT-SAËNS, 1835-1921

8669. Qui donc commande quand il aime!
       Opera: HENRY VIII, 1883, libretto by Léonce Détroyat and Paul
       Armand Silvestre. Part of Henry, Act I. d2-f♯3 f♯2-f♯3 General-
       ly sustained with consistently high tessitura. Has dramatic and strong
       passages. Requires fine PP. Climactic ending. Acc: 3-4 (VS)AD.
       OPA-4 (Spicker)

(CHARLES LOUIS) AMBROISE THOMAS, 1811-1896

8670. R: La fatigue alourdit mes pas
       A: Comme une pale fleur
       Opera: HAMLET, 1868, libretto by Jules Barbier and Michel Carré,
       after William Shakespeare's tragedy. Part of Hamlet, Act V. bb1-
       f♯3 d2-d3 Sustained recitative, and a sustained gentle aria in mod-
       erate slow tempo. Dramatic ending. Acc: 3-4 (VS)HC

8671. R: J'ai pu frapper le misérable
       A: Etre ou ne pas etre!
       Opera: HAMLET. Part of Hamlet, Act III. Text is based on "To
       be or not to be." Common title: Hamlet's monologue. c♯2-d♯3
       e2-c♯3 Strong recitative and a sustained adagio section. Requires
       fine PP. Has dramatic passages. Contemplative text. Acc: 3-4
       (VS)HC

8672. O vin, dissipe la tristesse
       Opera: HAMLET. Part of Hamlet, Act II. Common title: Drinking
       song. c♯2-f3(g3) f2-f3 A drinking song of the introspective, more
       sustained type rather than the rousing, jovial style. Moderate tempo.

Has a climactic and dramatic ending. Acc: 3-4 (VS)HC. OPA-4
(Spicker; Adler)

C.   German and Austrian Composers

LUDWIG VAN BEETHOVEN, 1770-1827

8673. Ha! welch' ein Augenlick!
Opera: FIDELIO, c. 1803-1805, libretto by Joseph Sonnleithner and
Georg Frederick Treitschke. Part of Pizarro, Act I. ab1-e3 d2-
d3 Sustained vocal part over an agitated accompaniment. Strong
and dramatic. Climactic ending. Acc: 3-4 (VS)GS, CP. OAR-Br

PAUL HINDEMITH, 1895-1963

8674. Auf denn zum letzten Stück
Opera: MATHIS DER MALER, 1938, libretto by the composer, inspired by Matthias Grünewald's painting. Part of Mathis, 7th Scene
(not divided into "acts"). c#2-d3 f2-c3 Sustained in very slow tempo. Generally subdued; requires fine high P. In recitative style.
Subdued ending. This aria ends the opera. Acc: 3-4 (VS)SC

KONRADIN KREUTZER, 1780-1849

8675. Ein Schütz bin ich
Opera: DAS NACHTLAGER VON GRANADA, 1834, libretto by Karl
Johann Braun, after Friedrich Kind. Part of Jäger, Act I. c2-f3
e2-d3 Animated in lively tempo. Outgoing and majestic. Climactic
ending. 2 verses. Acc: 3-4 (VS)CP

8676. Fürwahr, fürwahr es ist ein Abenteuer
Opera: DAS NACHTLAGER VON GRANADA. Part of the Jäger, Act
II. b1-f3 e1-e3 Animated in varied tempi, from adagio to allegro.
Tessitura stays high in several sections. Requires fine P and PP.
Very subdued ending. Acc: 4 (VS)CP

(GUSTAV) ALBERT LORTZING, 1801-1851

8677. Sonst spielt' ich mit Scepter
Opera: CZAAR UND ZIMMERMANN, 1837, libretto by the composer,
after J. T. Merle's play. Part of Zar, Act III. eb2-f3 g2-eb3
Sustained in moderate slow tempo. Tessitura stays high. 3 verses.
Acc: 3 (VS)CP

8678. Es wohnt am Seegestade
Opera: UNDINE, 1845, libretto by the composer, based on a story
by Friedrich de La Motte Fouqué. Part of Kühleborn, Act II, in the
Finale. a1-e3 e2-c3 Animated in moderate lively tempo. Graceful
and short. Acc: 3-4 (VS)CP. AAB

HEINRICH (AUGUST) MARSCHNER, 1795-1861

8679. An jenem Tag

Opera: HANS HEILING, 1833, libretto by Eduard Devrient. Part of Hans Heiling, Act I. d# 2-f# 3 e2-e3 In varied tempi and moods. Dramatic, requires flexibility. Has passages with high tessitura. Climactic ending. Acc: 3-4 (VS)CP. OPA-4 (Spicker), OAR-Br

(JAKOB LUDWIG) FELIX MENDELSSOHN (BARTHOLDY), 1809-1847

8680. Ich bin ein vielgereister Mann
Opera: DIE HEIMKEHR AUS DER FREMDE, 1829, libretto by Karl Klingemann. Part of Kauz, No. 4. g1-f# 3 e2-e3 Animated in very fast tempo. Slower middle section. Requires flexibility. High tessitura in some sections. Descending, climactic ending line. Best for high baritone. Acc: 3-4 (VS)BH

GIACOMO MEYERBEER, 1791-1864

8681. Adamastor, roi des vagues profondes
Opera: L'AFRICAINE, 1865, libretto by Eugène Scribe. Part of Nelusko, Act III. a# 2-e3(f# 3) e2-e3 In varied tempi and moods. Mostly energetic and dramatic. Very fast last section. Climactic high ending. Acc: 3-4 (VS)BR. OPA-4 (Spicker)

8682. Fille des rois, a toi l'hommage
Opera: L'AFRICAINE. Part of Nelusko, Act II. c2-g3 f2-f3 In varied tempi and moods. Tessitura stays high in certain passages. Last section is animated, marked, and dramatic. Climactic ending. Acc: 3-4 (VS)BR. OPA-4 (Spicker)

8683. R: Erase moi tonnerre
A: L'avoir tant adorée
Opera: L'AFRICAINE. Part of Nelusko, Act IV. d# 2-e3(f# 3) f# 2-c# 3 Sustained in moderate tempo. Has climactic passages. Climactic high ending. With ensemble in the full score. Acc: 3-4 (VS) BR

8684. Ah! mon remords te venge
Opera: LE PARDON DE PLOËRMEL or DINORAH, 1859, libretto by Jules Barbier and Michel Carré. Part of Hoël, Act III. db 2-gb 3 f2-gb 3 Sustained in moderate slow tempo. In lyric style. Has several gb 3's. Generally high tessitura. Requires fine PP. Climactic ending passage. Best for high baritone. Acc: 3-4 (VS)BR. OPA-4 (Spicker)

8685. O puissante magie
Opera: LE PARDON DE PLOËRMEL or DINORAH. Part of Hoël, Act I. Animated in lively tempo. Spirited and energetic. Requires fluent enunciation and flexibility. Has faster sections. Ends with florid passage. Agitated accompaniment. Acc: 4 (VS)BR

8686. Io t'ingannai, colpevol sono
Opera: ROBERTO IL DIAVOLO, 1831, libretto by Eugène Scribe. Italian version reviewed here. Part of Bertram, Act V. a1-e3 e2-c# 3 Animated in very lively tempo. Requires fine P. Has dramatic passages. Agitated movement. Acc: 4 (VS)BR

WOLFGANG AMADEUS MOZART, 1756-1791

20M   20 Arias from Operas for Bass and Baritone. Wolfgang Amadeus
Mozart. Two volumes. Edited by Sergius Kagen. Original texts,
with separate English translations. New York: International Music
Co.

8687. Donne mie le fate a tanti
Opera: COSÌ FAN TUTTE or LA SCUOLA DEGLI AMANTI, 1790
(K. 588), libretto by Lorenzo da Ponte. Part of Guglielmo, Act II.
b1-e3   d2-d3   Animated in moderate lively tempo.   Requires fluent
enunciation.   Slightly climactic ending.   Has touch of humor.   Acc:
4   (VS)GS, CP, IM.   20M-1, OAR-Br

8688. R: Le nostre pene
A: Non siate ritrosi
Opera: COSÌ FAN TUTTE or LA SCUOLA DEGLI AMANTI.   Part of
Guglielmo, Act I.   d2-e3   f♯2-d3   Sustained and gentle aria.   Has no
strong contrasts in dynamics.   Humorous.   Acc: 3-4   (VS)GS, CP,
IM.   OPA-4 (Spicker; Adler), OAR-Br

8689. Der Vögelfanger bin ich ja
Opera: DIE ZAUBERFLÖTE, 1791 (K. 620), libretto by Emanuel
Schikaneder and Johann Georg Giesecke.   Part of Papageno, Act I.
d2-e3   e3-d4   Animated in moderate slow tempo.   Generally light.
3 verses with some whistling.   Acc: 3-4   (VS)GS, CP.   OPA-4
(Spicker; Adler), 20M-2, OAR-Br

8690. Ein Mädchen oder Weibchen
Opera: DIE ZAUBERFLÖTE.   Part of Papageno, Act II.   b1-d3   d2-
d3   Alternating andante and allegro sections.   Gently animated vocal
part.   Requires some flexibility.   Acc: 3   (VS)GS, CP.   OPA-4
(Spicker; Adler), 20M-2, OAR-Br

8691. Deh vieni alla finestra
Opera: DON GIOVANNI or IL DISSOLUTO PUNITO, 1787 (K. 527),
libretto by Lorenzo da Ponte.   Part of Don Giovanni, Act II.   Common title: Don Giovanni's serenade.   d2-e3   f♯2-d3   Sustained in
moderate tempo.   Lyric throughout.   Requires simplicity.   Short.
Acc: 3-4   (VS)GS, GR, CP.   OPA-4 (Spicker; Adler), 20M-1, OAR-
Br.   (S)GR

8692. Finch' han dal vino
Opera: DON GIOVANNI or IL DISSOLUTO PUNITO.   Part of Don
Giovanni, Act I.   d2-eb3   f2-eb3   Animated in fast tempo.   Requires
fluent enunciation.   High tessitura.   Acc: 3-4   (VS)GS, GR, CP.
OPA-4 (Spicker; Adler), 20M-1, OAR-Br.   (S)GR

8693. Ho capito, Signor, si
Opera: DON GIOVANNI or IL DISSOLUTO PUNITO.   Part of Masetto,
Act I.   c2-c3   d2-c3   Lively and animated.   Requires fluent enuncia-
tion.   Has quasi-recitative style.   Climactic ending.   Acc: 3-4   (VS)
GS, GR, CP.   20M-1.   (S)GR

8694. Meta di voi qua vadano
Opera: DON GIOVANNI or IL DISSOLUTO PUNITO.   Part of Don
Giovanni, Act II.   c2-e3   e2-c3   Animated in moderate tempo.

Requires fluent enunciation.   Has some quasi-recitative passages.
Acc: 4 (VS)GS, GR, CP.   OAR-Br

8695.   A forza del martelli
        Opera: LA FINTA GIARDINIERA, 1775 (K. 196), libretto by Ranieri
        Calzabigi (?).   Part of Nardo, Act I.   d2-e3 g2-d3 Animated in
        lively tempo.   Requires fluent enunciation and some flexibility.   Has
        some slightly slower sections.   Climactic ending.   Acc: 4 20M-1

8696.   Con un vezzo all'Italiana
        Opera: LA FINTA GIARDINIERA.   Part of Nardo, Act II.   e2-e3
        a2-e3 Animated in varying tempo.   Requires some flexibility.   Has
        humor.   Climactic ending.   Acc: 3-4 20M-2

8697.   Un marito, O Dio
        Opera: LA FINTA GIARDINIERA.   Part of Nardo, Act I.   e2-d3
        f2-d3 Gently animated in moderate tempo.   Graceful and short.
        Acc: 3-4 20M-1

8698.   Con certe persone
        Opera: LA FINTA SEMPLICE, 1768 (K. 51), libretto by Carlo Goldoni.
        Part of Simone, perhaps a supplementary aria for this character.
        a1-e3 d2-d3 Animated in lively tempo.   Requires fluent enunciation.
        Has humor.   Acc: 3-4 20M-2.   (VS)GR

8699.   Ella vuole ed io torrei
        Opera: LA FINTA SEMPLICE.   Part of Cassandro, Act I.   bb1-d3
        e2-c3 Sustained in moderate tempo.   Requires majestic, slightly
        pompous delivery.   Has touch of humor.   Acc: 3-4 (VS)GR.   20M-1

8700.   Non c'e al mondo altro che donne
        Opera: LA FINTA SEMPLICE.   Part of Cassandro, Act I.   a1-e3
        f#2-d3 Animated in lively tempo.   Slightly climactic ending.   Has
        some quasi-recitative passages.   Acc: 3-4 (VS)GR.   20M-1

8701.   Troppa briga a prender moglie
        Opera: LA FINTA SEMPLICE.   Part of Simone, Act I.   g1-e3 c2-
        d3 Animated in first moderate, then lively tempo.   Has several g1's.
        Slightly marked.   Has humor.   Acc: 3-4 (VS)GR.   20M-2

8702.   Vieni, o mia Ninetta
        Opera: LA FINTA SEMPLICE.   Part of Simone, Act II.   g1-f3 e2-
        d3 Animated vocal part in moderate slow tempo.   Requires fluent
        enunciation and some flexibility.   Climactic ending.   Acc: 4 (VS)
        GR.   20M-1

8703.   Ubriaco non son io
        Opera: LA FINTA SEMPLICE.   Part of Cassandro, Act II.   c2-d3
        d2-d3 Animated in lively tempo.   Joyous and outgoing.   Acc: 3-4
        20M-2.   (VS)GR

8704.   R: Tutto e disposto
        A: Aprite un po' quegl' occhi
        Opera: LE NOZZE DI FIGARO, 1786 (K. 492), libretto by Lorenzo da
        Ponte, after Beaumarchais.   Part of Figaro, Act IV.   bb1-eb3 eb2-
        eb3 Sustained aria in moderate tempo.   Descriptive text.   Interpre-
        tatively not easy.   Climactic ending.   Acc: 3-4 20M-2.   (VS)GS,
        CP, GR

8705. Non più andrai
       Opera: LE NOZZE DI FIGARO.   Part of Figaro, Act I.   c2-e3   d2-
       c3   Animated in lively tempo.   Slightly marked, with martial style
       at the ending passage.   The excerpt is Figaro's aria, sung to Cheru-
       bino.   Acc: 3-4   (VS)GS, CP, GR.   20M-2, OPA-5.   (S)GR

8706. Se vuol ballare
       Opera: LE NOZZE DI FIGARO.   Part of Figaro, Act I.   c2-f3   e2-
       d3   Animated in moderate lively tempo.   Faster, animated middle
       section.   Requires simplicity.   Acc: 3-4   (VS)GS, CP, GR.   OPA-
       5, 20M-2

8707. R: Hai gia vinta la causa!
       A: Vedro mentr'io sospiro
       Opera: LE NOZZE DI FIGARO.   Part of Count Almaviva, Act III.
       c# 2-f# 3   e2-d3   Animated in lively maestoso, followed by a slightly
       faster section.   Requires flexibility.   Acc: 3-4   (VS)GS, CP, GR.
       20M-2, OAR-Br

8708. Nur mutig, mein Herze
       Opera: ZAIDE or DAS SERAIL, 1779 unfinished (K. 344), libretto by
       Johann Andreas Schachtner.   Part of Allazim, Act I.   bb1-f3   e2-e3
       Animated in moderate lively tempo.   Requires some maestoso delivery.
       Has passages with high tessitura, and some florid figures.   Requires
       flexibility.   The plot of the opera is similar to that of DIE ENTFÜH-
       RUNG AUS DEM SERAIL.   Acc: 4   20M-1

VICTOR NESSLER, 1841-1890

8709. R: So wird es recht!
       A: Am Ufer blies ich ein lustig Stück
       Opera: DER TROMPETER VON SAKKINGEN, 1884, libretto by J.
       Victor von Scheffel.   Part of Werner, Act II.   b1-f# 3   f# 2-c# 3   Sus-
       tained aria in moderate tempo.   Requires fine P.   Has dramatic pas-
       sages and a climactic high ending (f# 3).   Acc: 3-4   (VS)JS

LOUIS SPOHR, 1784-1859

8710. Der Kriegeslust ergeben
       Opera: JESSONDA, 1823, libretto by Eduard Heinrich Gehe, based on
       Antoine Lemierre's tragedy.   Part of Tristan, Act II.   c2-f3   d2-d3
       Sustained in moderate lively tempo.   Has dramatic climaxes; also re-
       quires some fine P.   Has florid figures and a climactic ending.
       Acc: 3-4   AAB

RICHARD STRAUSS, 1864-1949

8711. Aus einem jungen Mund
       Opera: DIE FRAU OHNE SCHATTEN, 1919, libretto by Hugo von Hof-
       mannsthal.   Part of Barak, Act I.   ab1-f3   gb2-db3   Sustained in
       moderate slow tempo.   Starts gently; generally subdued.   Has a cli-
       mactic passage near the end.   Acc: 3-4   (VS)B-H

RICHARD WAGNER, 1813-1883

8712. Abendlich strahlt der Sonne Auge
Music Drama: DAS RHEINGOLD, 1853-1854, libretto by the composer, in The Prologue of the festival drama, DER RING DES NIBELUNGEN. Part of Wotan, one-act Prologue. b♭1-d3 e♭2-b♭2 Sustained vocal part in moderate lively tempo. Agitated and full-sounding accompaniment. Acc: 4 (VS)GS, CP

8713. Bin ich nun frei?
Music Drama: DAS RHEINGOLD. Part of Alberich, one-act Prologue, Scene 4. f♯1-f♯3 f♯2-d3 Generally sustained in slow tempo. Has dramatic climaxes. In recitative style. Climactic ending. Acc: 3-4 (VS)GS, CP. OGB

8714. R: Die Frist ist um
A: Wie oft in Meeres tiefsten Schlund
Opera: DER FLIEGENDE HOLLÄNDER, 1843, libretto by the composer. Part of the Dutchman, Act I, No. 3. g1-f3 e♭2-e♭3 An extended and dramatic excerpt. Vocally demanding, uses much of the full voice. Interpretatively difficult. In varied tempi and moods. Acc: 4 (VS)GS, CP. OPA-4 (Spicker; Adler), OGB

8715. Euch macht ihr's leicht
Opera: DIE MEISTERSINGER VON NÜRNBERG, 1867, libretto by the composer. Part of Hans Sachs, Act III, Scene 5. b1-f3 e2-d3 Sustained vocal part in generally moderate tempo. Has some climactic passages and a climactic ending. Agitated accompaniment. Acc: 4 (VS)GS, CP. OGB

8716. Jerum! Jerum! Halla hallohe!
Opera: DIE MEISTERSINGER VON NÜRNBERG. Part of Hans Sachs, Act II, Scene 5. Common title: The cobbling song. c2-f3 e♭2-d3 Sustained vocal part in lively tempo. Energetic and strong. Has passages in majestic style. Dramatic ending. Interpretatively not easy. Acc: 4 (VS)GS, CP. OGB

8717. Verachtet mir die Meister nicht
Opera: DIE MEISTERSINGER VON NÜRNBERG. Part of Hans Sachs, Act III, Scene 5. c2-e3 f2-d3 A sustained scena in moderate lively tempo. Generally on MF level. Climactic ending. Acc: 4 (VS) GS, CP. OGB

8718. Wahn! Wahn! Ueberall Wahn!
Opera: DIE MEISTERSINGER VON NÜRNBERG. Part of Hans Sachs, Act III, Scene 1. Common title: Hans Sachs' monologue. a1-e3 d2-d3 Generally sustained vocal part in varied tempi and moods. Starts calmly. Has dramatic climaxes and a dramatic ending section. Interpretatively not easy. Acc: 3-4 (VS)GS, CP. OPA-4 (Spicker; Adler), OGB

8719. Was duftet doch der Flieder
Opera: DIE MEISTERSINGER VON NÜRNBERG. Part of Hans Sachs, Act II, Scene 3. Other title: Hans Sachs' monologue. a1-e3 e2-d3 Starts and ends in moderate tempo. Has varied tempi and moods. Interpretatively not easy. Climactic ending. Acc: 3-4 (VS)GS, CP. OPA-4 (Spicker; Adler), OGB

8720. Leb' wohl! du kühnes
       Music Drama: DIE WALKÜRE, 1870, first day of the festival drama,
       DER RING DES NIBELUNGEN, libretto by the composer. Part of
       Wotan, Act III, Scene 3. Common title: Wotan's farewell. a# 1-e3
       e2-d3 Sustained in moderate moving tempo. Dramatic. The last
       section is a little slower and more subdued. Includes the fire music.
       Acc: 5 (VS)GS, CP. OPA-4 (Spicker; Adler), OGB

8721. Dank, König, dir
       Opera: LOHENGRIN, 1850, libretto by the composer. Part of Fried-
       rich, Act I, Scene 1. c2-f3 f2-d3 Sustained vocal part in varied
       tempi. Starts moderately. Has dramatic passages. Generally in
       recitative style. Acc: 3-4 (VS)GS, CP. OGB

8722. Du fürchterliches Weib
       Opera: LOHENGRIN. Part of Friedrich, Act II, Scene 1. c# 2-g3
       f# 2-e3 Sustained vocal part; first in moderate slow tempo, then very
       lively tempo. Dramatic, with passages in high tessitura. Dramatic
       ending. Agitated accompaniment. Acc: 4 (VS)GS, CP. OGB

8723. Mein Vater!
       Music Drama: PARSIFAL, 1882, libretto by the composer. Part of
       Amfortas, Act I. a1-eb 3 d2-c3 Sustained in slow tempo. General-
       ly subdued and solemn. Common title: Amfortas' prayer. Acc:
       3-4 (VS)GS, CP. OPA-4 (Spicker; Adler)

8724. Nein! Lasst ihm unenthüllt!
       Music Drama: PARSIFAL. Part of Amfortas, Act I, Scene 2. b1-
       g3 e2-d3 Sustained vocal part in varied tempi and moods. Has
       dramatic climaxes. Interpretatively not easy. Acc: 4 (VS)GS, CP.
       OGB

8725. Als du in kühnem Sange uns bestrittest
       Opera: TANNHÄUSER UND DER SÄNGERKRIEG AUF DER WART-
       BURG, 1845, libretto by the composer. Part of Wolfram, Act I,
       Scene 4. d2-e3 e2-e3 Sustained in moderate slow tempo. Slower
       middle section. Gentle throughout; requires fine P. Acc: 3-4 (VS)
       GS, CP. OGB

8726. Blick' ich umher
       Opera: TANNHÄUSER UND DER SÄNGERKRIEG AUF DER WART-
       BURG. Part of Wolfram's address, or Eulogy of love. b1-eb 3 eb 2-
       eb 3 Sustained in gentle recitative style. Generally subdued. Cli-
       mactic ending. Acc: 3-4 (VS)GS, CP. OPA-4 (Spicker; Adler),
       OGB

8727. R: O Himmel lass' dich jetzt erflehen
       A: Dir, hohe Liebe
       Opera: TANNHÄUSER UND DER SÄNGERKRIEG AUF DER WART-
       BURG. Part of Wolfram, Act II, Scene 4. Common title: Wolfram's
       second eulogy of love. eb 2-f3 eb 2-eb 3 Sustained in moderate tem-
       po. Very sustained middle section. Generally calm, with some dra-
       matic moments. Acc: 3-4 (VS)GS, CP

8728. R: Wie Todesahnung
       A: O du mein holder Abendstern
       Opera: TANNHÄUSER UND DER SÄNGERKRIEG AUF DER WART-
       BURG. Part of Wolfram, Act III, Scene 2. bb 1-e3 d2-d3 Sustained

and gentle recitative and aria. Very lyric, subdued, almost atmospheric, but warm. Acc: 3-4 (VS)GS, CP. OPA-4 (Spicker; Adler), OGB

8729.   Darf ich die Antwort sagen?
        Opera: TRISTAN UND ISOLDE, 1865, libretto by the composer.
        Part of Kurvenal, Act I, Scene 2. a1-f3 d2-d3 Animated in lively
        tempo. Vigorous, strong, and in certain passages accented. Acc:
        3-4 (VS)GS, CP

CARL MARIA VON WEBER, 1786-1826

8730.   Schweig, damit dich niemand warnt
        Opera: DER FREISCHÜTZ, 1821, libretto by Friedrich Kind, after
        the Gespensterbuch. Part of Caspar, Act I. f♯1-e3 c2-d3 Sustained in moderate tempo. Requires some flexibility. Has dramatic
        passages and two florid passages. Climactic ending. Acc: 3-4
        (VS)GS, CP

8731.   Hier im ird' schen Jammertal
        Opera: DER FREISCHÜTZ. Part of Caspar, Act I. d2-f♯3 d2-d3
        Animated in very fast tempo. Requires flexibility and fluent enunciation. Has some florid figures. Acc: 3-4 (VS)GS, CP

8732.   R: Wo berg' ich mich?
        A: So weih' ich mich
        Opera: EURYANTHE, 1821, libretto by Wilhelmine Helmine von
        Chézy. Part of Lysiart, Act II. g1-f3 e♭2-e♭3 Dramatic recitative and aria. Requires flexibility. In varied tempi and moods.
        Middle section has some rapidly moving scale passages in the accompaniment. Climactic and strong ending. An extended excerpt. Acc:
        4 (VS)NO. OPA-4 (Spicker), OAR-Br

D. American Composers

CARLISLE FLOYD

8733.   I haven't come back here to live
        Opera: WUTHERING HEIGHTS, 1958, libretto by the composer, after
        Emily Brontë. Part of Heathcliff, Act II. d♭2-f3(g3) f2-e3 Generally sustained in varied tempi. Strong and dramatic. Climactic,
        high ending. Acc: 4 (VS)B-H

8734.   Was there ever another place
        Opera: WUTHERING HEIGHTS. Part of Heathcliff, Act I. b1-a♭3
        e2-e♭3 Animated in moderate lively tempo. Quite high tessitura.
        Exultant, dramatic, and strong. Also requires fine P. Climactic
        high ending on a♭3. Acc: 4 (VS)B-H

GIAN-CARLO MENOTTI

Italian by birth. American opera.

8735.   Dearest Amelia
        Opera: AMELIA GOES TO THE BALL, 1937, libretto by the

composer, original text in Italian. Part of the Husband, one-act opera. Common title: Letter aria. b♭1-f3 c2-e♭3 Sustained in moderate slow tempo. Acc: 3-4 (VS)GR

8736. When the air sings of summer
Opera: THE OLD MAID AND THE THIEF, 1937, libretto by the composer. Part of Bob, Scene 8, one-act comic opera. a1-f3 d2-d3 Sustained in moderate slow tempo. Starts calmly and gently. Has some climactic and dramatic passages. Climactic high ending. Acc: 3-4 (VS)GR

DOUGLAS MOORE, 1893-1969

8737. Warm as the autumn light
Opera: THE BALLAD OF BABY DOE, 1956, libretto by John Latouche. Part of Tabor, Act I. b1-e3 d♯2-c♯3 Sustained in moderate slow tempo. Faster middle section. Generally lyric. Subdued ending after high climax. Acc: 3-4 (VS)CC

8738. I wanted clothes... Well, that was a day
Opera: THE DEVIL AND DANIEL WEBSTER, 1938, libretto by Stephan Vincent Benét. Part of Jabez, one-act folk opera. Common title: Jabez's narrative. f♯1-d3 b1-b2 Slightly sustained recitative in slow tempo. Has climactic passages. Requires fluent and fluid enunciation. Acc: 3-4 (VS)B-H

8739. I've got a ram, Goliath
Opera: THE DEVIL AND DANIEL WEBSTER. Part of Webster, one-act folk opera. b♭1-e♭3 e♭2-d3 Sustained in moderate lively tempo in martial style. Faster middle section. Has climactic passages and a dramatic high ending. Acc: 3-4 (VS)B-H

E. British Composer

BENJAMIN BRITTEN

8740. Did you never try taking a girl for a walk?
Comic Opera: ALBERT HERRING, 1947, libretto by Eric Crozier, after Guy de Maupassant. Part of Sid, Act I. a1-g♯3 e2-d3 Animated in lively tempo. Starts in recitative style. Has climactic passages. Requires fine high P and PP. The one g♯3 in the ending phrase is sung falsetto (composer's instruction). Descriptive text. Acc: 3-4 (VS)B-H

8741. Virtue, says Holy Writ
Comic Opera: ALBERT HERRING. Part of Mr. Gedge, the Vicar, Act I. a♭1-g3 f2-d3 Generally animated vocal part in moderate slow tempo. Requires fine PP. Two final phrases in cantabile style. Gently agitated accompaniment on treble range. Acc: 3-4 (VS)B-H

8742. And farewell to ye, old 'Rights o' Man'!
Opera: BILLY BUDD, 1951, libretto by E. M. Forster and Eric Crozier, after Hermann Melville. Part of Billy Budd, Act II. Common title: Billy Budd's farewell. c2-f3 g2-d3 Animated in very lively tempo. Strong and outpouring. Very subdued ending after a dramatic section. Acc: 3-4 (VS)B-H

8743. Look! Through the port comes the moonshine astray!
       Opera: BILLY BUDD. Part of Billy Budd, Act II. c2-e3 d2-c3
       Sustained in moderate slow tempo. Subdued throughout, generally
       marked PP to PPPP. Generally in recitative style. Very subdued
       low ending. Acc: 3-4 (VS)B-H

8744. Thus gamesters united in friendship
       Opera: THE BEGGAR'S OPERA, 1948, libretto by John Gay, adapted
       by Tyrone Guthrie. Part of Lockit, Act III. c♯2-f♯3 f♯2-b2 Ani-
       mated in moderate lively tempo. Strong, bold, and marked. Has
       climactic passages. Acc: 3-4 (VS)B-H

8745. Within this frail crucible of light
       Opera: THE RAPE OF LUCRETIA, 1946, libretto by Ronald Duncan,
       after Andre Obey. Part of Tarquinius, Act II. g1-e3 d2-b2 Sus-
       tained in moderate slow tempo. Tranquil and subdued. Requires
       fine P and PP. Slightly agitated middle section. Very subdued high
       ending--e3 on PPPP. Acc: 3-4 (VS)B-H

8746. When my cue comes, call me
       Opera: A MIDSUMMER NIGHT'S DREAM, 1960, text by William
       Shakespeare, from his drama. Other title: Bottom's dream. Bot-
       tom's scena, Act II. b1-f3 d2-c3 In varied tempi and moods. Has
       some characterization, some dramatic passages, recitative sections,
       and falsetto effects. Ends in parlando, marked PP. Acc: 3-4 (VS)
       B-H, (S)B-H

F. Russian Composers

ALEXANDER PORFIREVICH BORODIN, 1833-1887

8747. R: Fürwahr, so ist's
       A: Wenn ich Fürst, wie Igor
       Opera: PRINCE IGOR, 1869-1887 unfinished, completed by Rimsky-
       Korsakof and Glazunof. Libretto by Vladimir V. Stassof. Part of
       Prince Galitzky, Act I. c♯2-e3(g♭3) e♭2-e♭3 Sustained recitative
       in moderate tempo, and an aria in moderate lively tempo. Has pas-
       sages with high tessitura and dramatic energy. Dramatic high ending.
       The vocal score reviewed has the original Russian, with German and
       French versions. Acc: 3-4 (VS)MB, (S)MB

8748. Umsonst nach Ruhe sucht das trübe
       Opera: PRINCE IGOR. Part of Prince Igor, Act II. b♭1-f3 e♭2-
       d♭3 Sustained in moderate slow tempo. Has dramatic high climaxes.
       Starts and ends subdued. Descending, diminished ending line. Agi-
       tated accompaniment in the middle section. Acc: 3-4 (VS)MB

MODEST PETROVICH MUSSORGSKY, 1839-1881

8749. Now the guards are all asleep
       Opera: KHOVANSHCHINA, 1872-1880, libretto by the composer and
       Vladimir V. Stassof. Part of Shaklovity, Act III. b♭2-f3(g♭3) e♭2-
       e♭3 Sustained in moderate slow tempo, with slower tempo in the
       middle of the excerpt. Generally subdued, with high tessitura in
       many phrases. Vocally difficult. Acc: 3-4 (VS)WB

IGOR FEODOROVICH STRAVINSKY, 1882-1971

8750. In youth the panting slave
Opera: THE RAKE'S PROGRESS, 1951, libretto by W(ystan) H(ugh)
Auden and Chester Kallman, after Hogarth. Part of Nick, Act II.
e♭2-e3 g2-d3 Gently animated vocal part in moderate tempo. Has
climactic passages. Acc: 3-4 (VS)B-H

PETER (PIOTR) ILYICH TCHAIKOVSKY, 1840-1893

8751. If in this world a kindly fortune
Opera: EUGENE ONÉGIN, 1877-1878, libretto by the composer and
Konstantin S. Shilovsky, after Pushkin. Part of Onégin, Act I.   c♯2-
f3 f2-e♭3 Sustained in moderate tempo. Has dramatic passage
toward the end. Very subdued ending. Acc: 3-4 (VS)GS. OPA-4
(Spicker; Adler)

G.   Argentine Composer

ALBERTO GINASTERA

8752. "¡Si consientes esta infamia...."
Opera: DON RODRIGO, 1964, libretto by Alejandro Casona. Part of
Don Julián, Act III. b1-f♯3(a♭3) d2-d3 Generally sustained in lively tempo. Requires dramatic forcefulness, fluent enunciation, and
flexibility. Dramatic high ending. Acc: 4 (VS)B-H

9. BASS-BARITONE and BASSO

Bibliography

CAO-B   Celebri Arie D'Opera.   Bass.   Sixth of six volumes for all voices. Milan: G. Ricordi.

OAB   Opern-Arien für Bass.   Giuseppe Verdi.   Italian texts, with German versions.   Edited by Kurt Soldan.   Frankfurt: C. F. Peters.

OAR-B   Opern-Arien.   Operatic arias in six volumes (two for soprano) in original texts and German versions.   Thirty-four arias for bass, Catalog Number 4235.   Frankfurt: Edition Peters.

OGB   Opern-Gesänge für Bariton.   Richard Wagner.   German texts only. Edited by Kurt Soldan.   Frankfurt & New York: C. F. Peters.

OPA-4   Operatic Anthology.   Volume IV: Baritone.   Edited by Kurt Adler. Original texts, with English versions.   New York: G. Schirmer, Inc.   (The older edition is edited by Kurt Schindler.)

OPA-5   Operatic Anthology.   Volume V: Bass.   Edited by Kurt Adler. Original texts, with English versions.   New York: G. Schirmer, Inc.   (The older edition is edited by Kurt Schindler.)

10M   10 Arias from Operas for Bass.   Wolfgang Amadeus Mozart.   Edited by Sergius Kagen.   Original texts, with separate English translations.   New York: International Music Co.

20M   20 Arias from Operas for Bass and Baritone.   Two volumes. Wolfgang Amadeus Mozart.   Edited by Sergius Kagen.   Original texts, with separate English translations.   New York: International Music Co.

A.   Italian Composers

VINCENZO BELLINI, 1801-1835

8753.   Vi ravviso, o luoghi ameni
      Opera: LA SONNAMBULA, 1831, libretto by Felice Romani.   Part of
      Count Rodolpho, Act I.   g1-eb3   eb2-c3   Sustained in moderate slow
      tempo.   Faster ending (before the entrance of the chorus).   Generally
      subdued, except the allegro moderato section when it becomes more
      climactic.   Acc: 3-4   (VS)GS, GR

ARRIGO BOITO, 1842-1918

8754.   Ecco il mondo
      Opera: MEFISTOFELE, 1868, libretto by the composer.   Part of

Mefistofele, Act II. bb1-eb3(f3) f2-d3 Animated in fast tempo.
Requires flexibility and fluent enunciation. High tessitura. Climactic
ending. Acc: 4 (VS)GR. (S)GR

8755. Son lo spirito che nega
Opera: MEFISTOFELE. Part of Mefistofele, Act I. g1-e3 db2-
db3 Animated in varied fast tempi. Requires flexibility and fluent
enunciation. Outgoing and climactic. Acc: 4 (VS)GR

LUIGI CHERUBINI, 1760-1842

8756. Qui tremar devi tu
Opera: MEDEA, 1797, libretto by François Benoit Hoffmann. Italian
version is reviewed here. Part of Creonte, Act I. a1-f#3 c#2-d3
Animated in lively tempo. Generally strong and dramatic. Climactic ending. The Ricordi edition has an accompaniment which is far
too elaborate for this period. Acc: 4 (VS)GR

GAETANO DONIZETTI, 1797-1848

8757. Ah, un foco insolito
Opera: DON PASQUALE, 1843, libretto by the composer and Michele
Accursi (Giacomo Ruffini), based on Angelo Anelli's novel. Part of
Pasquale, Act I. Common title: Pasquale's cavatina. c2-e3 e2-d3
Animated in very fast tempo. Requires fluent enunciation. Generally
on MF level. Slightly more animated and stronger last section.
Acc: 3-4 (VS)GR. OPA-5

8758. R: Fernando
A: A tanto amor
Opera: LA FAVORITA, 1840, libretto by Alphonse Royer, Gustave
Vaëz, and Eugène Scribe. Part of Alfonso, Act III. c#2-e3 e2-e3
Animated recitative and sustained aria in moderate slow tempo. Re-
quires fine P. Lyric, slightly subdued. Acc: 3-4 (VS)GR. OPA-5

8759. Udite, udite, o rustici
Opera: L'ELISIR D'AMORE, 1832, libretto by Felice Romani. Part
of Dulcamara, Act I. a1-e3 e2-c#3 Animated in moderate tempo.
Requires some fluent enunciation in some passages. Generally in
recitative style, with frequent repeated notes. Has a touch of humor.
Acc: 3-4 (VS)GR, GS. OAR-B. (S)GR

8760. R: Cessi, ah, cessi
A: Dalle stanze, ove Lucia
Opera: LUCIA DI LAMMERMOOR, 1835, libretto by Salvatore Cammarano, after Walter Scott's novel, The Bride of Lammermoor. Part
of Raymond, Act III. a#1-e3 e2-e3 Animated and strong recitative.
Generally sustained aria in moderate tempo. Dramatic, with a more
animated section after the maestoso instrumental interlude. Acc:
4-5 OPA-5. (VS)GS, GR

8761. Vieni! la mia vendetta
Opera: LUCREZIA BORGIA, 1833, libretto by Felice Romani, after
Victor Hugo. Part of Don Alfonso, Act I. bb1-eb3 eb2-eb3 Sustained in slow tempo. Has dramatic passages. Requires some flexibility. Climactic ending. Acc: 3-4 (VS)GS, B-H. (S)GR

ITALO MONTEMEZZI, 1875-1952

8762. Italia, è tutto il mio ricordo!
       Opera: L'AMORE DEI TRE RE, 1913, libretto by the composer,
       after Sem Benelli's tragedy. Part of Archibaldo, Act I. a1-f3 d2-
       d3 Animated in generally lively tempo. Has dramatic passages and
       a climactic ending. High tessitura in several sections. Acc: 3-4
       (VS)GR

AMILCARE PONCHIELLI, 1834-1886

8763. R: Tutto or M'ènoto
       A: Al tuo trono
       Opera: I PROMESSI SPOSI, 1856, unknown librettist, based on Ales-
       sandro Manzoni's novel. g#1(f#1)-e3 c#2-b2 Part of Cristoforo,
       Act II. Recitative and a sustained aria in moderate slow tempo. Re-
       quires fine P and PP. Has climactic passages. Low ending. Acc:
       3-4 (VS)GR

8764. R: Sì, morir ella de'!
       A: Ombre di mia prosapia
       Opera: LA GIOCONDA, 1876, libretto by Arrigo Boito, after Victor
       Hugo. Part of Alvise, Act III. g1-eb3(f3) c2-d3 In varied tempi.
       Aria starts sustained in moderate tempo. Requires fine P and PP.
       Has dramatic passages. Climactic ending section. Acc: 3-4 (VS)
       GS, GR

GIACOMO (ANTONIO DOMENICO, etc.) PUCCINI, 1858-1924

8765. Vecchia zimarra
       Opera: LA BOHÈME, 1896, libretto by Giuseppe Giacosa and Luigi
       Illica, after Henri Murger's novel. Part of Colline, Act IV. b1-
       eb3 e2-c#3 Animated in moderate lively tempo. Requires fine PP.
       Generally subdued. Acc: 3-4 (VS)GS, GR. (S)GR

GIOACCHINO (ANTONIO) ROSSINI, 1792-1868

8766. A un dottor della mia sorte
       Opera: IL BARBIERE DI SIVIGLIA, 1816, libretto by Cesare Sterbini,
       after Beaumarchais' comedy. Part of Bartolo, Act I. bb1-f3 eb1-
       eb3 Animated vocal part, first in moderate slow tempo, then in fair-
       ly fast tempo. Requires considerable flexibility and fluent enunciation.
       Has quite high tessitura, has florid figures, and abounds in repeated
       notes and figures. Extended excerpt. Acc: 4 (VS)GS, GR. OPA-
       5, OAR-B. (S)GR

8767. La calunnia
       Opera: IL BARBIERE DI SIVIGLIA. Part of Don Basilio, Act I.
       c#2-f#3 d2-e3 Animated in lively tempo. Requires fluent enuncia-
       tion. Abounds in repeated notes. Has strong climaxes and ending.
       Acc: 4 (VS)GS, GR. OPA-5, OAR-B. (S)GR

8768. Manca un foglio
       Opera: IL BARBIERE DI SIVIGLIA, 1816, libretto by Cesare Sterbini,
       after Beaumarchais' comedy. Part of Don Bartolo, Act I. eb2-f3(g3)

g2-eb 3 This aria is usually substituted in the place of "A un dottor."
Animated in lively tempo. Requires fluent enunciation. Has passages
with high tessitura and a climactic ending. Acc: 4 (VS)GS, GR.
(S)GR

8769. R: Miei rampolli femminini
A: Mi sognai fra il e il chiaro
Opera: LA CENERENTOLA, 1817, libretto by Jacopo Ferretti, after
Perrault. Part of Magnifico, Act I. a1-f♯ 3 d2-d3 Extended recita-
tive and an animated aria in moderate lively tempo. Requires fluent
enunciation and flexibility. Has passages requiring rapid diction.
Climactic ending. Acc: 3-4 (VS)MR, GR, FC

8770. Sia qualunque delle figlie
Opera: LA CENERENTOLA. Part of Don Magnifico, Act II. c2-f3
e2-c♯ 3 An extended scena in lively tempo. Requires flexibility;
has several short, florid figures. Requires characterization and
fluent enunciation for the fast patter in the second half of the excerpt.
Climactic ending. Acc: 4-5 (VS)FC, MR, GR

8771. Vasto teatro è il mondo
Opera: LA CENERENTOLA. Part of Don Magnifico, Act I. d2-eb 3
f2-eb 3 Animated in moderate lively tempo. Generally strong and
climactic. Acc: 4 (VS)FC, MR, GR

8772. Il mio piano è preparato
Opera: LA GAZZA LADRA, 1817, libretto by Giovanni Gherardini,
after D'Aubigny & Caigniez. Part of Podesta, Act I. a1-e3 c♯ 2-
c♯ 3 Animated in moderate tempo. Faster, more animated middle
section. Requires some fluent enunciation and flexibility. Has florid
passages. Climactic ending. Agitated accompaniment. Acc: 3-4
(VS)EG, GR

8773. Si per voi, pupille amate
Opera: LA GAZZA LADRA. Part of Podesta, Act II. f1-eb 4 c2-
c3 Animated vocal part in moderate slow tempo. Florid, requires
flexibility. Faster last section. Excerpt ends with "piu luogo non
ha." Acc: 3-4 (VS)EG, GR

8774. Duce di tanti eroi
Opera: L'ASSEDIO DI CORINTO, 1826, libretto by Alexandre Soumet
and Luigi Balocchi. Part of Maometto, Act I. Italian version used
here. a1-f3 c2-d3 Animated in lively tempo. Florid, requires
flexibility. Has dramatic passages, and a climactic ending. With
choral part in the score. Acc: 3-4 (VS)GR

8775. Già d'insolito ardore nel petto
Opera: L'ITALIANA IN ALGERI, 1813, libretto by Angelo Anelli.
Part of Mustafà, Act I. bb 1-f3 eb 2-eb 3 Animated in lively tempo.
Requires considerable flexibility. Passages abound in dotted and tri-
plet rhythmic figures. Generally strong. Climactic ending. Florid.
Acc: 3-4 (VS)GR

8776. Ho un gran peso
Opera: L'ITALIANA IN ALGERI. Part of Taddeo, Act II. d1-e3
f♯ 2-d3 Animated in lively tempo. Has passages which require fluent
enunciation. Climactic ending. Acc: 4 (VS)GR

8777.   R: Con tutta la sua boria
        A: Le femmine d'Italia
        Opera: L'ITALIANA IN ALGERI.   Part of Haly, Act II. c2-d3(e3)
        g2-d3 Animated in moderate lively tempo. Slightly agitated accom-
        paniment. High tessitura. Acc: 3-4 (VS)GR

8778.   Deh! ti ferma
        Opera: SEMIRAMIDE, 1823, libretto by Gaetano Rossi, after Vol-
        taire's tragedy. Part of Assur, Act II. g1-eb3 eb2-c3 Animated
        in lively tempo. Has florid passages. Requires flexibility. Excerpt
        ends on ab1, before the second section. Acc: 3-4 (VS)B-H

GIUSEPPE (FORTUNINO FRANCESCO) VERDI, 1813-1901

8779.   Mentre gonfiarsi l'anima
        Opera: ATTILA, 1846, libretto by Temistocle Solera. Part of Attila,
        Act I. c2-f3 f2-c3 An extended aria, first sustained in moderate
        tempo, then animated in fast tempo. Strong, dramatic ending section.
        Tessitura stays high most of the time. Climactic ending on f3. Acc:
        3-4 (VS)GR, OAB

8780.   R: Ella giammai m'amò
        A: Dormirò sol nel manto mio regal
        Opera: DON CARLOS, 1867, libretto by François Joseph Méry and
        Camille du Locle, after Friedrich von Schiller. Part of Filippo
        (King Philip II), Act IV. g1-e3 d2-d3 Sustained in moderate slow
        tempo. Requires fine PP. Has dramatic climaxes. Aria has pas-
        sages in quasi-recitative style. Acc: 3-4 (VS)GS, GR. OPA-5,
        OAB. (S)GR, IM

8781.   R: Che mai vegg' io!
        A: Infelice! e tuo credevi
        Opera: ERNANI, 1844, libretto by Francesco Maria Piave. Part of
        Silva, Act I. g1-eb3(f3) eb2-db3 Animated recitative and a sus-
        tained aria in moderate slow tempo. Has dramatic passages. Low
        ending. At times used with the martial "Enfin che un brando vindice"
        in concert performance. The CP edition has both. Acc: 3-4 (VS)
        GR. OPA-5, OAB. (S)GR

8782.   R: E ancor silenzio!
        A: Ma quando un suon terribile
        Opera: I LOMBARDI ALLA PRIMA CROCIATA, 1843, libretto by
        Temistocle Solera, from a poem by Crossi. Part of Pagano (Ere-
        mita), Act II. c2-eb4 c2-c3 Sustained in slow tempo. Generally
        strong and dramatic. Subdued ending. Agitated accompaniment.
        Acc: 4 (VS)GR. OAB

8783.   R: Vergini, il ciel per ora
        A: Sciagurata, hai tu creduto
        Opera: I LOMBARDI ALLA PRIMA CROCIATA. Part of Pagano, Act
        I. c2-f3 d2-d3 Recitative and a sustained aria in moderate tempo.
        Aria requires some quasi-recitative style. Generally lyric, with dra-
        matic passages toward the end. Slightly climactic ending. Acc: 4
        (VS)GR. OAB

8784.   Un ignoto, tre lune or saranno
        Opera: I MASNADIERI, 1847, libretto by Andrea Maffei, based on

Schiller's drama. Part of Maximilian, Act III. bb1-eb3 eb2-c3
Sustained in moderate slow tempo. Has dramatic passages. Slightly
climactic ending. Acc: 3-4 (VS)GR. OAB

8785. R: O patria, o cara patria
       A: O tu, Palermo
       Opera: I VESPRI SICILIANI, 1856, libretto by E. Caime, after the
       original French by Eugène Scribe and Charles Duveyrier. Part of
       Procida, Act II. f1-eb3 bb2-db3 Generally gentle recitative and
       sustained aria in slow tempo. Lyric, requires fine P. Also has
       dramatic passages and florid passages. Climactic ending. Agitated
       accompaniment. Acc: 4 (VS)GR, CP. OAB. (S)GR

8786. R: La dirò
       A: Di due figli vivea padre beato
       Opera: IL TROVATORE, 1853, libretto by Salvatore Cammarano,
       after Antonio Gutierrez's play. Part of Ferrando, Act I. b1-e3
       c#2-e3 Aria in different tempi and moods, but generally animated.
       Requires fine P and PP, flexibility, and fluent enunciation. Has
       some short florid figures. Acc: 4 (VS)GS, GR. OPA-5, OAB

8787. R: Ah, tutto m'arride
       A: Il mio sangue, la vita darei
       Opera: LUISA MILLER, 1849, libretto by Salvatore Cammarano,
       based on Schiller's tragedy. Part of Walter, Act I. bb1-gb3 bb1-
       c3 Sustained aria in moderate slow tempo. Faster middle section.
       Has dramatic passages. Accented, dramatic ending section with a
       short cadenza at the end. Acc: 3-4 (VS)GR. OAB. (S)GR

8788. R: Studia il passo
       A: Come dal ciel precipita
       Opera: MACBETH, 1847, libretto by Francesco Maria Piave, after
       William Shakespeare. Part of Banco, Act II. a1-e3 b1-e3 Sus-
       tained aria in slow tempo. Has dramatic climaxes and a climactic
       ending. Requires fine P and PP. Agitated accompaniment. Acc:
       3-4 (VS)GR. OPA-5, OAB. (S)GR

8789. R: Sperate, o figli!
       A: D'Egitto là sui lidi
       Opera: NABUCCO, 1842, libretto by Temistocle Solera. Part of
       Zacharias, Act I. g1-f3 e2-d3 A dramatic and slow recitative, and
       a sustained aria in moderate slow tempo. Majestic; has dramatic pas-
       sages. Low ending. Choral background in the full score. Imposing
       ending. Acc: 3-4 (VS)GR. OAB. (S)GR

8790. R: Oh che piange
       A: Del futuro nel bujo discerno
       Opera: NABUCCO. Part of Zacharias, Act III. f#1-f#3 d#2-d#3
       Sustained recitative, and a sustained aria in moderate tempo. Slightly
       faster middle section. Dramatic ending with full-sounding accompani-
       ment. Acc: 4 (VS)GR. OAB

8791. R: Ah, prigioniero io sono!
       A: Dio di Giuda!
       Opera: NABUCCO. Part of Nabucco, Act IV. e2(b#2)-f3 g2-e3
       Strong recitative on high tessitura. Sustained and lyric aria in slow
       tempo. High tessitura; has a good number of d3, e3, and f3. Diffi-
       cult. Has a few florid figures. Acc: 3-4 (VS)GR. (S)GR

8792.   R: Vieni, o Levita!
        A: Tu sul labbro de' veggenti
        Opera: NABUCCO. Part of Zaccarias, Act II. g1-e3 e2-b2 Reci-
        tative and a sustained aria in moderate slow tempo. On MF level,
        generally in lyric style. Low ending on g1. Acc: 3-4 (VS)GR.
        OAB.   (S)GR

8793.   R: A te l'estremo addio
        A: Il lacerato spirito
        Opera: SIMON BOCCANEGRA, 1857, libretto by Francesco Maria
        Piave, after Gutierrez. Part of Fiesco, in The Prologue. f♯1-d3
        b1-c♯2 Recitative in varied tempi and moods. Sustained aria in
        moderate slow tempo. Generally subdued. Descending vocal line
        with f♯1 as last note. Acc: 3-4 (VS)GR. OPA-5.   (S)GR

B.   French Composers

ADOLPHE (CHARLES) ADAM, 1803-1856

8794.   R: Arrêtons-nous ici
        A: Vallons de l'Helvétie
        Opera: LE CHALET, 1834, libretto by Eugène Scribe and Anne
        Honoré Mélesville. Part of Max, one-act opera. b♭1-e♭3 d2-e♭3
        Recitative and sustained aria in moderate slow tempo. Has climactic
        passages and florid passages. Requires flexibility. Has some sus-
        tained high notes. Climactic ending. Acc: 3-4 (VS)SR

8795.   Oui des choristes
        Opera: LE POSTILLON DE LONGJUMEAU, 1836, libretto by Adolphe
        de Leuvon and Leon Brunswick. Part of Alcindor, Act II. a1-e3(f3)
        c2-c3 Animated in lively tempo. Has climactic passages. Requires
        fine P. Outflowing. Acc: 3-4 (VS)BR. OAR-B

8796.   La fleur boit la rosée
        Opera: SI J'ÉTAIS ROI, 1852, libretto by Adolphe Philippe d'Ennery
        and Jules Brésil. Part of the King of Goa, Act II. g2-f3 b♭2-e♭3
        Sustained in moderate tempo. Strong ending on high tessitura. With
        choral part in the score. Acc: 3-4 (VS)AL

HECTOR BERLIOZ, 1803-1869

8797.   Certain rat, dans une cuisine
        Opera: LA DAMNATION DE FAUST, 1846, libretto by the composer,
        after Goethe's drama. A concert opera. Part of Brander, Act II.
        a1-d3 c2-c3 Animated in lively tempo. Climactic ending. Has
        short choral interpolations in the full score. Acc: 3-4 (VS)CT.
        (S)IM

8798.   R: Maintenant, chantons a cette belle
        A: Devant la maisson
        Opera: LA DAMNATION DE FAUST. A concert opera. Part of
        Mephistophele, Act IV. Common title: Méphisto's serenade. b1-
        d♯3 e2-c♯3 Animated aria in waltz tempo and rhythm. Requires
        fine P. Has strong passages. With choral part in the full score.
        Acc: 3-4 (VS)CT

8799.   Voici des roses
        Opera: LA DAMNATION DE FAUST.   Part of Mephistophele, Act III.
        c♯2-e3   e2-c♯3 Sustained in moderate slow tempo.   Graceful and
        gentle throughout.   Acc: 3   (VS)CT

8800.   De quels revers menacestu Carthage
        Opera: LES TROYENS A CARTHAGE, second part of a two-part
        opera, LES TROYENS, 1856-1859, libretto by the composer, based
        on the story of Virgil.   Part of Narbal, Act II.   f1-d3   c2-c3 Sus-
        tained in slow tempo.   Starts subdued, misteriosly.   Has climactic
        passages and a climactic ending.   Acc: 3-4   (VS)EC

GEORGES BIZET, 1838-1875

8801.   Quand la flamme de l'amour
        Opera: LA JOLIE FILLE DE PERTH, 1866, libretto by Vernoy de
        Saint-Georges and Jules Adenis, based on Walter Scott.   Part of
        Ralph, Act II.   b1-e3   e2-d3 Sustained in moderate slow tempo.
        Generally quite strong and energetic.   Has recitative passages and a
        climactic ending.   Starts with the extended "tra la la" section.   Acc:
        3-4   (VS)EC

FÉLICIEN (CÉSAR) DAVID, 1810-1876

8802.   Jusqu'à ce jour
        Opera: LA PERLE DU BRÉSIL, 1851, libretto by J. Gabriel and
        Sylvain Saint-Étienne.   Part of Salvadore, Act I.   g1-e3(f3)   c2-c3
        Sustained in moderate tempo.   Has slower middle section.   Climactic
        ending.   Agitated accompaniment.   Acc: 4   (VS)HC

(ACHILLE) CLAUDE DEBUSSY, 1862-1918

8803.   Maintenant que le père de Pelléas
        Opera: PELLÉAS ET MÉLISANDE, 1892-1902, libretto by Maurice
        Maeterlinck.   Part of Arkel, Act IV.   f1-d♯3   c♯2-c♯3 In recitative
        style throughout.   Generally in moderate tempo.   Has some climactic
        and lyrically sustained passages.   Excerpt begins with "aux côtés de
        la mort...."   Acc: 4   (VS)AD

(CLÉMENT PHILIBERT) LÉO DÉLIBES, 1836-1891

8804.   Lakmé, ton doux regard se voile
        Opera: LAKMÉ, 1883, libretto by Edmond Gondinet and Philippe
        Gille.   Part of Nilakanthe, Act II.   d♯2-f3   e♭2-c3 Sustained in mod-
        erate tempo.   Generally gentle, and requires fine P.   Has passages
        with high tessitura.   Climactic ending.   Acc: 3-4   (VS)HL, IM

CHARLES (FRANÇOIS) GOUNOD, 1818-1893

8805.   Tu t'envas confiant
        Opera: CINQ-MARS, 1877, libretto by Louis Gallet and Paul Poirson,
        based on Alfred de Vigny's novel.   Part of Joseph, Act III.   a1(d1)-
        d3   d2-d3 First part is sustained in moderate tempo.   Middle part

is slightly animated in moderate lively tempo. Has climactic passages. Falling ending line. Extended instrumental postlude. Acc:
3-4 (VS)LS

8806.   Le veau d'or
        Opera: FAUST, 1852-1859, libretto by Jules Barbier and Michel
        Carré, after Goethe.   Part of Mephistophele, Act II.   c2-eb3   eb2-
        eb3   Animated in moderate lively tempo.   Pompous, outgoing, showy.
        Climactic ending.   Agitated accompaniment.   2 verses.   Common
        title: Song of the golden calf.   Acc: 4 (VS)GS, GR.   OPA-5

8807.   R: Il était temps!
        A: Ô nuit, étends sur eux ton ombre!
        Opera: FAUST.   Part of Mephistopheles, Act III.   g1-c3(db3)   g2-
        c3   Sustained aria in slow tempo.   Gentle and somewhat subdued.
        Gently agitated accompaniment.   Acc: 3-4 (VS)GS, GR

8808.   Vous qui faitez l'endormie
        Opera: FAUST.   Part of Mephistopheles, Act III.   g1-g3   d2-d3
        Gently animated in moderate lively tempo.   With sly humor.   Ends
        with laughter two full octaves from highest to lowest note.   Acc:
        3-4 OPA-5.   (VS)GS, GR

8809.   R: Oui, depuis quatre jours
        A: Sous les pieds d'une femme
        Opera: LE REINE DE SABA, 1861, libretto by Jules Barbier and
        Michel Carré, after Gérard de Nerval.   Part of Soliman, Act IV.
        b1(e1)-d3   d#2-c#3   Sustained in slow tempo.   Requires fine P and
        PP.   Has dramatic passages and a climactic low ending.   Acc: 3-4
        (VS)EC

8810.   R: Ah! malheureuse enfant!
        A: Aux jours d'été
        Opera: MIREILLE, 1863, libretto by Michel Carré, after Frédéric
        Mistral.   Part of Ramon, Act IV.   db2-eb3   f2-c3   Sustained aria
        in moderate tempo.   Has dramatic passages.   Acc: 3-4 (VS)EC

8811.   Au bruit des lourds marteaux
        Opera: PHILÉMON ET BAUCIS, 1859, libretto by Jules Barbier and
        Michel Carré.   Part of Vulcain, Act I.   ab1-eb3   d2-c3   Sustained
        in moderate tempo.   Requires fine P.   Climactic ending.   Acc: 3-4
        (VS)EC

8812.   R: Buvez donc ce breuvage
        A: C'est là qu'après un jour
        Opera: ROMÉO ET JULIETTE, 1864, libretto by Jules Barbier and
        Michel Carré, after William Shakespeare.   Part of Friar Laurence,
        Act IV.   g1-d3   eb2-c3   Scena and a sustained aria in moderate slow
        tempo.   Aria is gentle, with no strong contrasts in dynamics.   Acc:
        3-4   (VS)GS, CP

(JACQUES FRANÇOIS) FROMENTAL (ÉLIAS) HALÉVY, 1799-1862

8813.   Art divin qui faisais
        Opera: LA FÉE AUX ROSES, 1847, libretto by Eugène Scribe and
        Vernoy de Saint-Georges.   Part of Atalmuc, Act I.   e1-e3   b1-d3
        Animated in varied tempi.   Starts in lively tempo.   Has dramatic

passages. Climactic high ending. The e1, the lowest note, is sustained. Acc: 3-4 (VS)HL

8814. Non, non, ne crois pas
Opera: LA FÉE AUX ROSES. Part of Atalmuc, Act III. a♭1-e♭3 c2-d♭3 Animated in lively tempo, then followed by a sustained section in moderate slow tempo. Requires some flexibility. Climactic high ending. Acc: 3-4 (VS)HL

8815. Ah! j'implore en tremblant
Opera: LA JUIVE, 1835, libretto by Eugène Scribe. Part of Brogni, Act IV. b1-e3 e2-c3 Animated in fast tempo. Has climactic passages. Detached accompaniment. Acc: 3-4 (VS)HL

8816. Si la rigueur
Opera: LA JUIVE. Part of Brogni, Act I. f1(e1)-c3 c2-c3 Sustained in moderate slow tempo. Lyric, and requires simplicity. Requires fine P. Acc: 3-4 (VS)HL. OPA-5

8817. Vous qui du Dieu vivant
Opera: LA JUIVE. Part of Brogni, Act III. g1-e♭3 d2-d3 Sustained in moderate tempo. Starts in recitative style. Requires fine P. Climactic ending. Acc: 3-4 (VS)HL

VICTOR (FELIX MARIE) MASSÉ, 1822-1884

8818. Tristes amours!
Opera: GALATÉE, 1852, libretto by Jules Barbier and Michel Carré. Part of Pygmalion, Act I. g1-e♭3 e♭2-c3 This part is sung by either Bass-Baritone or Mezzo-Soprano in their respective transposed keys. Sustained in moderate tempo. Faster and more animated ending section. Climactic ending. Acc: 3-4 (VS)CR

JULES (ÉMILE FRÉDÉRIC) MASSENET, 1842-1912

8819. R: Dors, ô cité perverse
A: Astres étincilants
Opera: HÉRODIADE, 1881, libretto by Paul Milliet and Henri Grémont (Georges Hartmann), after a story by Flaubert. Part of Phanuel, Act III. b1-e♭3(f3) d2-d3 Generally sustained in varied moods and tempi. Starts slowly. Has dramatic passages and a climactic ending. Generally in recitative style. Has some agitated accompaniment. Acc: 3-4 (VS)HC

8820. O rage! ô désespoir
Opera: LE CID, 1885, libretto by Adolphe Philippe D'Ennery, Louis Gallet, and Edouard Blau. Part of Don Diègue, Act I. a1-e3 c2-c3 Sustained in generally slow tempo. Requires fine P. Has dramatic passages. Generally in recitative style. Acc: 3-4 (VS)HC

8821. R: Les grands mots que voilà!
A: Épouse quelque brave fille
Opera: MANON, 1884, libretto by Henri Meilhac and Philippe Gille, after Abbé Prévost's novel. Part of the Count, Act III. c2-f3 d2-d3 Animated and strong recitative. Sustained aria in moderate slow tempo. Requires simplicity. Has dramatic climaxes. Acc: 3-4 OPA-5

8822.   Tu songes à l'ami
        Opera: THÉRÈSE, 1907, libretto by Jules Claretie. Part of Andre,
        Act II. c2-eb3 e2-c3 Sustained in moderate tempo. Starts in gen-
        tle recitative style. Climactic ending. Acc: 3-4 (VS)HC

MAURICE RAVEL, 1875-1937

8823.   Evidemment, elle me congédie
        Comic Opera: L'HEURE ESPAGNOLE, 1911, libretto by Franc-
        Nohain. Part of Inigo, one-act opera. g1-eb3(bb3) c2-c3 A buffo
        air, in recitative style. Interpretatively difficult and humorous. The
        bb3 in falsetto (composer's instruction). Acc: 3 (VS)AD

(CHARLES LOUIS) AMBROISE THOMAS, 1811-1896

8824.   Je t'implore
        Opera: HAMLET, 1868, libretto by Jules Barbier and Michel Carré.
        Part of King Claudius, Act III. ab1(eb1)-eb3(f3) eb2-c3 Sustained
        in moderate tempo. Has dramatic and slightly more animated pas-
        sages. Subdued, descending ending after climax. Acc: 3-4 (VS)HC

8825.   R: Je comprends que labelle
        A: Le tambour major tout galonné d'or
        Opera: LE CAÏD, 1849, libretto by M. T. Sauvage. Part of Michel,
        Act I. g1-e3 d2-c3 Sustained recitative and animated aria in mod-
        erate tempo. Rhythmic and marked. Has florid and climactic pas-
        sages. Requires flexibility. Climactic ending. Acc: 3-4 (VS)HC

8826.   De son coeur j'ai calme la fievre
        Opera: MIGNON, 1866, libretto by Michel Carré and Jules Barbier,
        after Goethe. Part of Lothario, Act III. Common title: Berceuse.
        a1-d3 d2-d3 Sustained in moderate tempo. A lullaby, very subdued
        throughout and gentle. Requires considerable vocal control. Short.
        Acc: 3-4 (VS)GS. OPA-5

8827.   Fugitif et tremblant
        Opera: MIGNON. Part of Lothario, Act I. d2-d3 d2-d3 Sustained
        in moderate tempo. Quite lyric and short. Generally on MF level,
        with two somewhat climactic passages. Acc: 3-4 (VS)GS

                          C. German and Austrian Composers

LUDWIG VAN BEETHOVEN, 1770-1827

8828.   Ha! welch' ein Augenblick!
        Opera: FIDELIO, c. 1803-1805, libretto by Joseph Sonnleithner and
        Georg Frederick Treitschke. Part of Pizarro, Act I. ab1-e3 d2-d3
        Sustained vocal part over agitated accompaniment. Strong and dramat-
        ic. Climactic ending. Acc: 3-4 (VS)GS, CP. OPA-5 (Spicker;
        Adler)

8829.   Hat man nicht auch Gold daneben
        Opera: FIDELIO. Part of Rocco, Act I. bb1-d3 eb2-d3 Animated
        in moderate lively tempo alternating with lively tempo. Requires some
        fluent enunciation. Acc: 3-4 (VS)GS, CP. OPA-5, OAR-B

ALBAN BERG, 1885-1935

8830. Was seht Ihr in den Lust.... Sie sehn den Tiger
        Opera: LULU, 1937, libretto by the composer, after Wedekind.
        Part of the Animal Trainer, in The Prologue. g1(f♯1)-f3 c2-d3
        Starts and ends with "rhythmic declamation." Middle sections have
        a more cantabile style. Tessitura here refers to the cantabile sec-
        tions only. f♯1 refers to the parlando range of the excerpt. In-
        terpretatively not easy. Acc: 4 (VS)UE

PETER CORNELIUS, 1824-1874

8831. Mein Sohn
        Opera: DER BARBIER VON BAGDAD, 1858, libretto by the com-
        poser, after the Arabian Nights. Part of Abul, Act I. f♯1(d♯1)-e3
        b1-d♯3 First part is sustained in moderate tempo, then moves on to
        slower and faster tempi. Last section is very fast, animated, and
        requires fluent enunciation. Dramatic and sustained ending. Acc: 4
        (VS)CK. OPA-5

8832. So schwärmet Jugend
        Opera: DER BARBIER VON BAGDAD. Part of Abul, Act I. f♯1-
        e♭3 c2-c3 Sustained vocal part. Generally in moderate lively tem-
        po, with some slower passages. Has dramatic passages and a de-
        scending ending line. Acc: 3-4 (VS)CK. OAR-B

FRIEDRICH (FREIHERR) VON FLOTOW, 1812-1883

8833. Lasst mich euch fragen
        Opera: MARTHA, 1847, libretto by W. Friedrich (Friedrich Wilhelm
        Riese). Part of Plunkett, Act III. g1-f3 e2-d3 Slightly animated in
        moderate slow tempo. Requires fine P. Has dramatic climaxes.
        Outgoing, a drinking song. Common title: Porter song. Acc: 3-4
        (VS)GS, CP. OPA-5, OAR-B

(GUSTAV) ALBERT LORTZING, 1801-1851

8834. O sancta justitia!
        Opera: CZAAR UND ZIMMERMANN or DIE ZWEI PETER, 1837,
        libretto by the composer, after J. T. Merle's play. Part of van Bett,
        Act I. a1(g1)-e3 d2-d3 Animated in lively tempo. Has climactic
        passages. Requires fluent enunciation. Climactic ending. Slightly
        extended excerpt. "O sancta justitia" is used as a quotation. Acc:
        3-4 (VS)CP. AAB, OAR-B

8835. Sonst spielt' ich mit Scepter
        Opera: CZAAR UND ZIMMERMANN or DIE ZWEI PETER. Part of
        the Czaar, Act III. e♭2-f3 g2-e♭3 Sustained in moderate slow tem-
        po. The tessitura stays high most of the time. 3 verses. Acc:
        3-4 (VS)CP

8836. Es wohnt am Seegestade
        Opera: UNDINE, 1845, libretto by the composer, after a story by
        Friedrich de La Motte Fouqué. Part of Kühleborn, Act II, in the
        Finale. a1-e3 e2-c3 Animated in moderate lively tempo. Short
        and graceful. Acc: 3-4 (VS)CP. AAB

GIACOMO MEYERBEER, 1791-1864

8837. R: En chasse!
       A: Le jour est levé
       Opera: LE PARDON DE PLOËRMEL or DINORAH, 1859, libretto by
       Jules Barbier and Michel Carré. Part of Chasseur, Act III. b1-e3
       c2-d3 Animated in moderate lively tempo. Climactic ending. Acc:
       3-4 (VS)BR

8838. Aussi nombreux que les étoiles
       Opera: LE PROPHETE, 1849, libretto by Eugène Scribe. Part of
       Zacharie, Act III. g♯1-e3 c♯2-c♯3 Animated in moderate tempo.
       Requires the majestic approach and fluent enunciation. Has dramatic
       passages and florid passages. With choral ensemble in the score.
       Acc: 3-4 (VS)BR

8839. R: Volontiers
       A: Pour les couvents c'est fini
       Opera: LES HUGUENOTS, 1836, libretto by Eugène Scribe. Part of
       Marcel, Act I. f1-e3 c2-d3 Common title: "Piff, paff," or "Chan-
       son Huguenotte." Quite strong recitative and aria. Dramatic, force-
       ful on rather violent text. Climactic ending. Acc: 3-4 OPA-5

8840. R: Le rovine son queste
       A: Donne, che riposate
       Opera: ROBERTO IL DIAVOLO, 1831, libretto by Eugène Scribe.
       Italian version is reviewed here. Part of Bertram, Act III. b1-d3
       d2-c♯3 Common title: Evocazione. Sustained recitative and an aria
       in moderate tempo. Requires fine P. Has climactic passages. Agi-
       tated accompaniment in the aria. Acc: 3-4 (VS)BR

8841. Io t'ingannai, colpevol sono
       Opera: ROBERTO IL DIAVOLO. Italian version reviewed here. Part
       of Bertram, Act V. a1-e3 e2-c♯3 Animated in very lively tempo.
       Has dramatic passages. Requires fine P. Agitated movement. Acc:
       4 (VS)BR

WOLFGANG AMADEUS MOZART, 1756-1791

8842. Donne mie la fate a tanti
       Opera: COSÌ FAN TUTTE or LA SCUOLA DEGLI AMANTI, 1790
       (K. 588), libretto by Lorenzo da Ponte. Part of Guglielmo, Act II.
       b1-e3 d2-d3 Animated in moderate lively tempo. Requires fluent
       enunciation. Slightly climactic ending. Has touch of humor. Acc:
       4 (VS)GS, CP, GR. 20M-1

8843. R: Le nostre pene
       A: Non siate ritrosi
       Opera: COSÌ FAN TUTTE or LA SCUOLA DEGLI AMANTI. Part of
       Guglielmo, Act I. d2-e3 f♯2-d3 Sustained and gentle aria. Gener-
       ally on MF level. Humorous. Acc: 3-4 (VS)GS, CP, GR. OPA-4
       (Spicker; Adler)

8844. O, wie will ich triumphieren
       Opera: DIE ENTFÜHRUNG AUS DEM SERAIL, 1782 (K. 384), libretto
       by Gottlieb Stephanie II, after C. F. Bretzner's play. Part of Osmin,
       Act III. d1-e3 d2-d3 Animated in quite fast tempo. Requires fluent

enunciation and some flexibility. Has some long-held low notes (a1 and d1). Climactic ending. Acc: 3-4 (VS)CP, B-H. 10M, OAR-B

8845. Solche hergelauf'ne Laffen
Opera: DIE ENTFÜHRUNG AUS DEM SERAIL. Part of Osmin, Act I. f1-f3 c2-d3 Animated in varied tempi. Starts somewhat fast. Requires some flexibility and fluent enunciation. Has touch of humor. Acc: 3-4 (VS)CP, B-H. 10M, OPA-5, OAR-B

8846. Wer ein Liebchen hat gefunden
Opera: DIE ENTFÜHRUNG AUS DEM SERAIL. Part of Osmin, Act I. g1-d3 d2-d3 Gently animated vocal part in moderate slow tempo. Has a "trallalera" refrain. Has touch of humor. Acc: 3-4 (VS)CP, B-H. 10M, OPA-5, OAR-B

8847. In diesen heil'gen Hallen
Opera: DIE ZAUBERFLÖTE, 1791 (K. 620), libretto by Emanuel Schikaneder and Johann Georg Giesecke. Part of Sarastro, Act II. f#1-c#3 b1-b2 Sustained in slow tempo. Has short florid figures. Generally on MF level. Solemn and gently majestic. Acc: 3-4 (VS)GS, CP. 10M, OPA-5, OAR-B

8848. O Isis und Osiris
Opera: DIE ZAUBERFLÖTE. Part of Sarastro, Act II. f1-c3 a1-bb2 Sustained in slow tempo. On MF level. Solemn, with gentle majesty. Has quite a low range. Acc: 3-4 (VS)GS, CP. 10M, OPA-5, OAR-B

8849. Ah, pietà! Signori miei!
Opera: DON GIOVANNI or IL DISSOLUTO PUNITO, 1787 (K. 527), libretto by Lorenzo da Ponte. Part of Leporello, Act II. a1-e3 d2-d3 Animated in lively tempo. Has passages requiring fluent enunciation. Rather subdued ending. Acc: 3-4 (VS)GS, CP, GR

8850. Deh vieni alla finestra
Opera: DON GIOVANNI or IL DISSOLUTO PUNITO. Part of Don Giovanni, Act II. Common title: Don Giovanni's serenade. d2-e3 f#2-d3 Sustained in moderate tempo. Lyric treatment throughout; requires simplicity. Short. Acc: 3-4 (VS)GS, CP, GR. 20M-1, OPA-5 (Spicker; Adler). (S)GR

8851. Finch' han dal vino
Opera: DON GIOVANNI or IL DISSOLUTO PUNITO. Part of Don Giovanni, Act I. d2-eb3 f2-eb3 Animated in fast tempo. Requires fluent enunciation. High tessitura. Acc: 3-4 (VS)GS, CP, GR. 20M-1, OPA-4 (Spicker; Adler). (S)GR

8852. Ho capito, Signor, sì
Opera: DON GIOVANNI or IL DISSOLUTO PUNITO. Part of Masetto, Act I. c2-c3 d2-c3 Animated in lively tempo. Requires fluent enunciation. In quasi-recitative style. Climactic ending. Acc: 3-4 (VS)GS, CP, GR. 20M-1. (S)GR

8853. Madamina! il catalogo
Opera: DON GIOVANNI or IL DISSOLUTO PUNITO. Part of Leporello, Act I. Common title: Catalog aria. a1-e3 d2-d3 Animated in lively tempo, with a slower second half. Requires fluent enunciation. Climactic ending. Humorous text. Acc: 3-4 (VS)GS, CP, GR. 10M, OPA-5, OAR-B

8854. Metà di voi quà vadano
Opera: DON GIOVANNI or IL DISSOLUTO PUNITO. Part of Don
Giovanni, Act II. c2-e3 e3-c4 Animated in moderate tempo. Re-
quires fluent enunciation. Has passages in recitative style. Acc: 4
(VS)GS, CP, GR

8855. Tardi s'avvede d'un tradimento
Opera: LA CLEMENZA DI TITO, 1791 (K. 621), libretto by Caterino
Mazzolà, after Metastasio. Part of Publio, Act II. b1-e3 e2-d3
Animated in moderate lively tempo. Requires some flexibility.
Graceful and short. Acc: 3-4 (VS)CP, IM. 10M

8856. Con certe persone
Opera: LA FINTA SEMPLICE, 1768 (K. 51), libretto by Carlo Goldoni.
Part of Simone, perhaps a supplementary aria for this character. a1-
e3 d2-d3 Animated in lively tempo. Requires fluent enunciation.
Has humor. Acc: 3-4 20M-2. (VS)GR

8857. Ella vuole ed io torrei
Opera: LA FINTA SEMPLICE. Part of Cassandro, Act I. bb1-d3
e2-c3 Sustained in moderate tempo. Requires majesty, somewhat
pompous. Has touch of humor. Acc: 3-4 (VS)GR. 20M-1

8858. Non c'è al mondo altro che donne
Opera: LA FINTA SEMPLICE. Part of Cassandro, Act I. a1-e3
f#2-d3 Animated in lively tempo. Slightly climactic ending. Has
some quasi-recitative passages. Acc: 3-4 (VS)GR. 20M-1

8859. Troppa briga a prender moglie
Opera: LA FINTA SEMPLICE. Part of Simone, Act I. g1-e3 c2-
d3 Animated first part in moderate, then lively tempo. Has several
g1's. Slightly marked. Has humor. Acc: 3-4 (VS)GR. 20M-2

8860. Vieni, o mia Ninetta
Opera: LA FINTA SEMPLICE. Part of Simone, Act II. g1-f3 e2-
d3 Animated vocal part in moderate slow tempo. Requires fluent
enunciation and some flexibility. Climactic ending. Acc: 4 (VS)
GR. 20M-1

8861. Ubriaco non son io
Opera: LA FINTA SEMPLICE. Part of Cassandro, Act II. c2-d3
d2-d3 Animated in lively tempo. Joyous and outgoing. Acc: 3-4
(VS)GR. 20M-2

8862. R: Tutto è disposto
A: Aprite un po' quegl' occhi
Opera: LE NOZZE DI FIGARO, 1786 (K. 492), libretto by Lorenzo da
Ponte, after Beaumarchais. Part of Figaro, Act IV. bb1-eb3 eb2-
eb3 Sustained aria in moderate tempo. Interpretatively not easy.
Climactic ending. Descriptive text. Acc: 3 (VS)GS, CP, GR.
20M-2, OAR-B

8863. La vendetta
Opera: LE NOZZE DI FIGARO. Part of Bartolo, Act I. g#1-e3
d2-d3 Animated in fast tempo. Spirited. Requires fluent enunciation.
Somewhat pompous. Climactic ending. Acc: 4 (VS)GS, CP, GR.
10M, OAR-B

8864. Non più andrai
Opera: LE NOZZE DI FIGARO. Part of Figaro, Act I. c2-e3 d2-c3 Animated in lively tempo. Slightly marked, with martial style at ending passages. The excerpt is sung by Figaro to Cherubino. Acc: 3-4 (VS)GS, CP, GR. 20M-2, OPA-5, OAR-B

8865. Se vuol ballare, Signor contino
Opera: LE NOZZE DI FIGARO. Part of Figaro, Act I. c2-f3 e2-d3 Animated in moderate lively tempo. Faster and animated middle section. Requires simplicity. Acc: 3-4 (VS)GS, CP, GR. OPA-5, OAR-B

8866. Ihr Mächtigen seht ungerührt
Opera: ZAIDE or DAS SERAIL, 1779 unfinished (K. 344), libretto by Johann Andreas Schachtner. Part of Allazim, Act II. a1-f3 bb1-d3 Generally sustained in varied tempi. Starts in moderate slow tempo and ends in moderate lively tempo. Has some long-held low notes and a low ending. Has dramatic passages. The plot of the opera is similar to DIE ENTFÜHRUNG AUS DEM SERAIL. Acc: 3-4 10M

8867. Nur mutig, mein Herze
Opera: ZAIDE or DAS SERAIL. Part of Allazim, Act I. bb1-f3 e2-e3 Animated in moderate lively tempo. Requires somewhat majestic delivery. Has passages with high tessitura, and florid figures. Requires flexibility. Acc: 4 20M-1

8868. Wer hungrig bei der Tafel sitzt
Opera: ZAIDE or DAS SERAIL. Part of Osmin, Act II. c2-f3 f2-d3 Animated in lively tempo. Requires fluent enunciation. Has repeated notes especially on syllables "ha, ha, ha." Climactic ending. A comic air. Acc: 4 10M

VICTOR NESSLER, 1841-1890

8869. Da schlage dich das Wetter
Opera: DER TROMPETER VON SÄKKINGEN, 1844, libretto by Joseph Viktor von Scheffel. Part of Freiherr, Act I. f#1-d3 d2-c#3 Animated in lively tempo. Slower middle section. Requires some flexibility. Low ending. Acc: 3-4 (VS)JS

(CARL) OTTO (EHRENFRIED) NICOLAI, 1810-1849

8870. Als Büblein klein
Opera: DIE LUSTIGEN WEIBER VON WINDSOR, 1849, libretto by Hermann Salomon Mosenthal, after Shakespeare. Part of Falstaff, Act II. Common title: Falstaff's drinking song. e1-e3 b1-c#3 Animated in moderate tempo. Requires some flexibility. Outgoing. Climactic ending. Acc: 3-4 (VS)CP, BH. OPA-5, OAR-B

LOUIS SPOHR, 1784-1859

8871. R: Wie ist mir!
A: Blöder Thor!
Opera: FAUST, 1816, libretto by Josef Karl Bernard, after the

traditional legend. Part of Faust, Act II. e♭2-e3 d2-d3 An extended recitative, and a sustained aria in moderate slow tempo. Faster middle section. Has dramatic passages and florid passages close
to the ending. Interpretatively difficult. Acc: 4 (VS)B-H

8872. R: Der Hölle selbst will ich Segen
       A: Liebe ist der zarte Blüthe
       Opera: FAUST. Part of Faust, Act I. g1-f3(f♯3) c2-d3 Secco
       recitative, and a sustained aria in moderate slow tempo. Generally
       gentle, has florid passages. Extended and florid cadenza at the end.
       Gently animated accompaniment. Acc: 4 (VS)B-H

8873. Der Kriegeslust ergeben
       Opera: JESSONDA, 1823, libretto by Eduard Heinrich Gehe, after
       Antoine Lemierre. Part of Tristan, Act II. c2-f3 d2-d3 Sustained
       in moderate lively tempo. Has dramatic climaxes and florid figures.
       Requires fine P. Climactic ending. Acc: 3-4 AAB

RICHARD STRAUSS, 1864-1949

8874. Aus einem jungen Mund
       Opera: DIE FRAU OHNE SCHATTEN, 1919, libretto by Hugo von Hof-
       mannsthal. Part of Barak, Act I. a♭1-f3 g♭2-d♭3 Sustained in
       moderate slow tempo. Starts gently; generally subdued. Has climac-
       tic passage near the end. Acc: 3-4 (VS)B-H

RICHARD WAGNER, 1813-1883

8875. Abendlich strahlt der Sonne Auge
       Music Drama: DAS RHEINGOLD, the Prologue of the festival drama,
       DER RING DES NIBELUNGEN, 1853-1854, libretto by the composer.
       Part of Wotan, one-act Prologue, Scene 4. b♭1-f3 e♭2-b♭2 Sus-
       tained in moderate tempo. Tranquil and subdued. After a dramatic
       climax, a falling and subdued ending. Acc: 3-4 (VS)GS, CP.
       OGB

8876. Mögst du, mein Kind
       Opera: DER FLIEGENDE HOLLÄNDER, 1843, libretto by the com-
       poser. Part of Daland, Act II, No. 10. a1-d3 d2-d3 Sustained
       vocal part in moderate lively tempo. Has dramatic climaxes. Re-
       quires fine P. Acc: 3-4 (VS)GS, CP. OPA-5

8877. R: Jerum! Jerum!
       A: Als Eva aus dem Paradies
       Opera: DIE MEISTERSINGER VON NÜRNBERG, 1867, libretto by the
       composer. Part of Hans Sachs, Act II, Scene 5. c2-f3 d2-d3 Ex-
       tended scena in varied tempi and moods. Interpretatively difficult.
       Climactic ending. Excerpt is concluded with "ein Schuhmacher und
       Poet dazu." Acc: 3-4 (VS)GS, CP

8878. Euch macht ihr's leicht
       Opera: DIE MEISTERSINGER VON NÜRNBERG. Part of Hans Sachs,
       Act III, Scene 5. b1-f3 e2-d3 Sustained vocal part in generally
       moderate tempo. Has some climactic passages and a climactic end-
       ing. Agitated accompaniment. Acc: 4 (VS)GS, CP. OGB

8879. Jerum! Jerum! Hallahallohe!
Opera: DIE MEISTERSINGER VON NÜRNBERG. Part of Hans Sachs,
Act II, Scene 5. Common title: The cobbling song. c2-f3 eb2-d3
Sustained vocal part in lively tempo. Energetic and strong. Has
passages in majestic style. Dramatic ending. Interpretatively not
easy. Acc: 4 (VS)GS, CP. OGB

8880. Nun hört, und versteht
Opera: DIE MEISTERSINGER VON NÜRNBERG. Part of Pogner, Act
I, Scene 3. Common title: Pogner's address. a1-f4 c2-d3 Ani-
mated in moderate lively tempo. Has some dramatic passages and a
secco recitative. Climactic ending. Acc: 3-4 (VS)GS, CP.
OPA-5

8881. Verachtet mir die Meister nicht
Opera: DIE MEISTERSINGER VON NÜRNBERG. Part of Hans Sachs,
Act III, Scene 5. c2-e3 f2-d3 Sustained vocal part in moderate
lively tempo. Generally on MF level. Climactic ending section.
Acc: 4 (VS)GS, CP. OGB

8882. Wahn! Wahn! Ueberall Wahn!
Opera: DIE MEISTERSINGER VON NÜRNBERG. Part of Hans Sachs,
Act III, Scene 1. Common title: Hans Sachs' monologue. a1-e3
d2-d3 Generally sustained vocal part in varied tempi and moods.
Starts calmly. Has dramatic passages and ending section. Interpre-
tatively not easy. Acc: 3-4 (VS)GS, CP. OPA-4 (Spicker; Adler),
OGB

8883. Was duftet doch oder Flieder
Opera: DIE MEISTERSINGER VON NÜRNBERG. Part of Hans Sachs,
Act II, Scene 3. Other title: Hans Sachs' monologue. a1-e3 e2-d3
Starts and ends in moderate tempo. Has varied tempi and moods.
Interpretatively not easy. Climactic ending. Acc: 3-4 (VS)GS, CP.
OPA-4 (Spicker; Adler), OGB

8884. Leb' wohl! du kühnes
Music Drama: DIE WALKÜRE, 1870, first day of the festival drama,
DER RING DES NIBELUNGEN, libretto by the composer. Part of Wotan,
Act III, Scene 3. Common title: Wotan's farewell. a#1-e3 e2-d3
Sustained in moderate moving tempo. Dramatic. Last section is a
little slower and more subdued. Includes the "fire music." Acc: 5
(VS)GS, CP. OPA-4 (Spicker; Adler), OGB

8885. Nicht send' ich dich mehr aus Walhall
Music Drama: DIE WALKÜRE. Part of Wotan, Act III, Scene 2.
c2-f3 g2-eb3 Sustained in moderate tempo. Starts gently, then
moves into dramatic passages. Acc: 3-4 (VS)GS, CP

8886. Hier sitz' ich zur Wacht
Music Drama: GÖTTERDÄMMERUNG, 1876, third day of the festival
drama, DER RING DES NIBELUNGEN, libretto by the composer.
Part of Hagen, Act I, Scene 2. bb2-d#3 d2-c3 Sustained in moderate tempo. Generally subdued, with a slightly climactic ending. Acc:
3-4 (VS)GS

8887. Dank, König, dir
Opera: LOHENGRIN, 1850, libretto by the composer. Part of Friedrich, Act I, Scene 1. c2-f3 f2-d3 Sustained vocal part in varied

tempi. Starts moderately. Has dramatic passages. Generally in
recitative style. Acc: 3-4 (VS)GS, CP. OGB

8888. Mein Herr und Gott
Opera: LOHENGRIN. Part of King Henry, Act I, Scene 3. f1-eb3
eb2-eb3 Common title: King Henry's prayer. Sustained in slow
tempo. Solemn, requires simplicity and a straightforward approach.
Subdued ending. Acc: 3-4 (VS)GS, CP. OPA-5

8889. Mein Vater!
Music Drama: PARSIFAL, 1882, libretto by the composer. Part of
Amfortas, Act I. a1-eb3 d2-c3 Sustained in slow tempo. Generally subdued and solemn. Common title: Amfortas' prayer. Acc:
3-4 (VS)GS, CP. OPA-4 (Spicker; Adler)

8890. Auf wolkigen Höh'n
Music Drama: SIEGFRIED, 1876, second day of the festival drama,
DER RING DES NIBELUNGEN, libretto by the composer. Part of
the Wanderer, Act I, Scene 2. c2-f3 db2-db3 Sustained in moderate tempo. Generally high tessitura. This excerpt has a strong and
dramatic conclusion and ends on f3. Acc: 3-4 (VS)GS

8891. Tatest du's wirklich?
Opera: TRISTAN UND ISOLDE, 1865, libretto by the composer.
Part of Mark, Act II, Scene 3. g1-e3 c2-d3 In varied tempi and
moods, ranging from lento moderato to vivace. Has some sustained
sections and dramatic passages. Interpretatively difficult. Subdued
ending. Acc: 4 (VS)GS, CP. OPA-5

CARL MARIA VON WEBER, 1786-1826

8892. Hier im ird' schen Jammertal
Opera: DER FREISCHÜTZ, 1821, libretto by Friedrich Kind, after
the Gespensterbuch. Part of Caspar, Act I. d2-f#3 d2-d3 Animated in very fast tempo. Requires flexibility and fluent enunciation.
Has some florid figures. Acc: 3-4 (VS)GS, CP. OAR-B

8893. Schweig, damit dich niemand warnt
Opera: DER FREISCHÜTZ. Part of Caspar, Act I. f#1-e3 c2-d3
Sustained in moderate tempo. Requires some flexibility. Has dramatic passages, and two florid passages. Climactic ending. Acc:
3-4 (VS)GS, CP. OAR-B

8894. R: Wo berg' ich mich?
A: So weih' ich mich
Opera: EURYANTHE, 1821, libretto by Wilhelmine Helmine von
Chézy. Part of Lysiart, Act II. g1-f3 eb2-eb3 Dramatic recita-
tive and aria. Requires flexibility. In varied tempi and moods.
Middle section has some rapidly moving scales in the accompaniment.
Climactic, strong ending. An extended excerpt. Acc: 4 (VS)NO.
OPA-4 (Spicker)

D. American Composers

DAVID AMRAM

8895. If music be the food of love

Opera: TWELFTH NIGHT, in two acts, 1969, text by William Shakespeare. Part of Orsino, Act I. a1-e3 c2-c3 Sustained in moderate slow tempo. Has climactic high passages and a climactic final
phrase with a falling ending. This air opens the opera. Acc: 3
(VS)CP

SAMUEL BARBER

8896. Hark! the land bids me tread no more
       Opera: ANTONY AND CLEOPATRA, 1966, text by William Shake-
       speare. Part of Antony, Act II. a1-f3 e2-c3 Sustained in moder-
       ate slow tempo. Has dramatic passages. Subdued ending with sus-
       tained a1 as the last note. Acc: 3-4 (VS)GS

8897. O sov'reign mistress of true melancholy
       Opera: ANTONY AND CLEOPATRA, 1966, text by William Shake-
       speare. Part of Enobarbus, Act II. bb1-f3 e2-d3 Sustained in
       slow tempo. Much faster, more animated middle section. Generally
       in recitative style. Has dramatic passages and a long-held f3. Sub-
       dued ending. Acc: 3-4 (VS)GS

CARLISLE FLOYD

8898. Hear me, O Lord, I beseech Thee
       Opera: SUSANNAH, 1955, libretto by the composer. Part of Blitch,
       Act III. Common title: Blitch's prayer. g1-e3 c2-d3 Sustained in
       moderate tempo. Declamatory style. Has dramatic passages. Low,
       subdued ending after a dramatic climax. Acc: 3-4 (VS)B-H

GIAN-CARLO MENOTTI

Italian by birth; American by training and musical expression.

8899. Dearest Amelia
       Opera: AMELIA GOES TO THE BALL, 1937, libretto by the com-
       poser, original text in Italian. Part of the Husband, one-act opera.
       Common title: Letter aria. bb1-f3 c2-eb3 Sustained in moderate
       slow tempo. Acc: 3-4 (VS)GR

8900. When the air sings of summer
       Opera: THE OLD MAID AND THE THIEF, 1937, libretto by the com-
       poser. Part of Bob, Scene 8. a1-f3 d2-d3 Sustained in moderate
       slow tempo. Starts calmly and gently. Has some climactic and dra-
       matic passages. Climactic high ending. Acc: 3-4 (VS)GR

DOUGLAS MOORE, 1893-1969

8901. Warm as the autumn light
       Opera: THE BALLAD OF BABY DOE, 1956, libretto by John La-
       touche. Part of Tabor, Act I. b1-e3 d#2-c#3 Sustained in moder-
       ate slow tempo. Faster middle section. Lyric in style. Subdued
       ending after high climax. Acc: 3-4 (VS)CC

8902. I wanted clothes.... Well, that was a day
       Opera: THE DEVIL AND DANIEL WEBSTER, 1938, libretto by

Stephan Vincent Benét. Part of Jabez, one-act folk opera. Common
title: Jabez's narrative. f♯1-d3 b1-b2 Slightly sustained recitative
in slow tempo. Has climactic passages. Requires fluent and fluid
enunciation. Acc: 3-4 (VS)B-H

8903. I've got a ram, Goliath
Opera: THE DEVIL AND DANIEL WEBSTER. Part of Webster, one-
act folk opera. b♭1-e♭3 e♭2-d3 Sustained in moderate lively tempo in martial style. Faster middle section. Has climactic passages,
some high tessitura, and a dramatic high ending. Acc: 3-4 (VS)
B-H

E. British Composer

BENJAMIN BRITTEN

8904. When the cue comes, call me
Opera: A MIDSUMMER NIGHT'S DREAM, 1960, text by William
Shakespeare, from his drama. b1-f3 d2-c3 In varied tempi and
moods. Has some characterization, some dramatic passages, recita-
tive sections, and falsetto effects. Ends in parlando marked PP.
Acc: 3-4 (VS)B-H, (S)B-H

8905. Albert Herring's clean as new-born hay
Comic Opera: ALBERT HERRING, 1947, libretto by Eric Crozier,
after Guy de Maupassant. Part of Superintendent Budd, Act I. f2-e3
a2-d3 Animated in very fast tempo. Requires fluent enunciation.
High tessitura. Dramatic high ending on d3. Short. Acc: 3-4
(VS)B-H

8906. And farewell to ye, old 'Rights o' Man'!   Bass-Baritone
Opera: BILLY BUDD, 1951, libretto by E. M. Forster and Eric
Crozier, after Hermann Melville. Part of Billy Budd, Act II. Common title: Billy Budd's farewell. c2-f3 g2-d3 Animated in very
lively tempo. Strong and outpouring. Very subdued ending after a
dramatic section. Acc: 3-4 (VS)B-H

8907. Look! Through the port comes the moonshine astray! Bass-Baritone
Opera: BILLY BUDD. Part of Billy Budd, Act II. c2-e3 d2-c3
Sustained in moderate slow tempo. Subdued throughout, generally
marked PP to PPPP. Generally in recitative style. Very subdued
low ending. Acc: 3-4 (VS)B-H

8908. O beauty
Opera: BILLY BUDD. Part of Claggart, Act I. g1-f♯3 c2-d3
First part is sustained in moderate agitated tempo. Second part is
animated in quite fast tempo. Dramatic and strong. Musically not
easy. Requires flexibility. Acc: 4-5 (VS)B-H

F. Russian Composers

ALEXANDER PORFIREVICH BORODIN, 1833-1887

8909. Wie geht es, Fürst?
Opera: PRINCE IGOR, 1887, libretto by Vladimir V. Stassof. Unfinished opera, completed by Rimsky-Korsakof and Glazunof. Part of

Kontschak, Act II. f1-d3 d2-d3 Animated in moderate lively tempo. Has recitative passages, dramatic passages, and a strong, descending ending line. Agitated accompaniment in the middle part. Acc: 3-4 (VS)MB, (S)MB

MODEST MUSSORGSKY, 1839-1881

8910. A peaceful monk
Opera: BORIS GODUNOV, 1874, libretto by the composer, after Alexander Sergeyevich Pushkin and Nikolai Mikhailovich Karamzin. Common title: Pimen's tale. Part of Pimen, Act IV. c2-e3 e2-d3 Sustained in moderate slow tempo. Requires fine P. Narrative. Slightly climactic ending. Acc: 3-4 (VS)BH, WB, EK. OPA-5

8911. I have attained to power
Opera: BORIS GODUNOV. Part of Boris, Act II. Common title: Boris' monologue. bb1-gb3 eb2-eb3 In varied tempi and moods. Dramatic narrative; interpretatively difficult. Has some high tessitura in certain passages. Acc: 4 (VS)WB, EK, BH. OPA-5

8912. Long ago at Kazan
Opera: BORIS GODUNOV. Part of Warlaam, Act I. f2-e3 f2-d3 Animated in lively tempo. Rather accented, with repeated notes. Has dramatic passages and a climactic ending. Narrative text. In BH and WB scores: 1/2 step higher. Acc: 4 (VS)BH, WB, EK. OPA-5

8913. Here on this spot shall I now proclaim
Opera: KHOVANSHCHINA, 1886, libretto by the composer and Vladimir V. Stassof. Part of Dositheus, Act V. d2-d3 f2-d3 Sustained in moderate slow tempo. Generally subdued. Requires solemnity, quiet majesty, as in a religious song. Ends with a prayer. This aria opens Act V. Acc: 3-4 (VS)WB

IGOR FEODOROVICH STRAVINSKY, 1882-1971

8914. In youth the panting slave
Opera: THE RAKE'S PROGRESS, 1951, libretto by W(ystan) H(ugh) Auden and Chester Kallman, after Hogarth. Part of Nick, Act II. eb2-e3 g2-d3 Gently animated vocal part in moderate tempo. Has climactic passages. Acc: 3-4 (VS)B-H

PETER (PIOTR) ILYICH TCHAIKOVSKY, 1840-1893

8915. All men should once with love grow tender
Opera: EUGENE ONÉGIN, 1878, libretto by the composer and Konstantin S. Shilovsky, after Pushkin. Part of Gremin, Act III. In the GS score the first line is: All men surrender to love's power. gb1-eb3 db2-eb3 Sustained in moderate slow tempo. Slightly faster middle section. Has dramatic climaxes. Low ending on gb1. Acc: 3-4 (VS)GS. OPA-5

G.   Czechoslovakian Composer

BEDŘICH SMETANA, 1824-1884

8916. Lovers everywhere
       Opera: THE BARTERED BRIDE (PRODANÁ NEVĚSTA), 1866, libret-
       to by Karel Sabina.   Part of Kezal, Act II.   b1-d3   d2-d3 Animated
       in moderate lively tempo.   Climactic ending.   Has some dramatic
       passages.   Acc: 3-4   (VS)GS.   OPA-5

CHAPTER XII

FLORID DISPLAY SONGS, RECITAL VOCALISES, AND ALLELUIAS

Introduction

The inclusion of this chapter is prompted by the need of some singers for variety in building recital programs. Most of the material here is for coloratura sopranos and lyric sopranos, and was mostly designed to give further evidence of what the human voice is capable of doing. There is nothing wrong with the performance of works for mere vocal display as long as it is not overdone. Most composers have written works of this nature, not only for the voice but also for the mechanical instruments. The alleluias, however, are not wholly display material, but are expressions of sacred joy and exaltation. Their role is of a much more serious nature; the word itself always implies religious rejoicing.

A good number of composers have written vocalises, both for pedagogical purposes and for performances. The limited number given here is mainly for concert work. Vocalises are not all confined to the coloratura soprano voice. There are vocalises for voices other than soprano. Any voice should be able to present itself in vocalise; it is healthy both for the voice and for the general well-being.

15A 15 Arias for Coloratura Soprano. Edited by Estelle Liebling. New York: G. Schirmer, Inc.

A. Florid Display Songs

LUIGI ARDITI, 1822-1903, Italian

8917. Parla   Coloratura Soprano
Poet: Anon. c#3-f#5 g3-a4 Animated in waltz tempo. Bright. Starts very gently. Has climactic and florid passages. Requires flexibility. Short cadenza in the middle. Climactic high ending on sustained d5. Acc: 3-4 KAS

JULIUS BENEDICT, 1804-1885, German-born English composer

8918. Carnival of Venice   Coloratura Soprano
Poet: Anonymous Italian. d3-eb5 ab3-bb4 A shortened version of the original composition which uses themes from a popular Italian tune. A showy, very florid, highly ornamented song. Generally animated in moderate lively tempo. Requires considerable flexibility. Climactic high ending. Revision by Estelle Liebling. Acc: 3-4 15A

HENRY (ROWLEY) BISHOP, 1786-1855, British

8919. Pretty mocking bird   Coloratura, Lyric Soprano
       Poet: T. Morton. d3-ab4 g3-f4 Animated in moderate lively tem-
       po. Very florid, requires flexibility and agility. Ends with extended
       and florid cadenza. Acc: 3 SOE-1

8920. Should he upbraid   Coloratura, Lyric Soprano
       Poet: William Shakespeare, in The Taming of the Shrew. c#3-g4
       g3-g4 Bright, florid, with a sustained vocal line. Requires flexi-
       bility. An extended, showy song. Shortened version edited by Estelle
       Liebling and published by G. Schirmer. Acc: 3-4 OHS, TSB (Ch.
       1-A, Bishop). (S)GS

THOMAS BROWN, dnk, British

8921. Shepherd! Thy demeanor vary   Coloratura, Lyric Soprano
       Poet: Anon. e3-c5 f3-f4 Animated in lively tempo. Spirited,
       bright, has florid passages, requires flexibility. Requires fluent
       enunciation. Climactic ending. Acc: 3-4 OEM

KARL ANTON FLORIAN ECKERT, 1820-1879, German

8922. Er liebt nur mich allein   Coloratura Soprano
       Poet: Anon. Common title: Swiss echo song. d3(a2)-b4(d5) f3-a4
       Animated in moderate lively tempo. Very florid, requires consider-
       able flexibility. Has added cadenza by Estelle Liebling. Climactic
       ending. Texts in German, English (None he loves but me), and
       French (Il n'aime que moi!). Acc: 3-4 15A. (S)GS-two keys

POLISH TRADITIONAL SONG

8923. Mother dear   Coloratura Soprano
       Poet: Yvonne Ravell. d3-d5(e5) a3-b4 Animated in moderate tem-
       po. Waltz rhythm. Graceful. Climactic high ending, with slightly
       florid cadenza. Acc: 3-4 15A

JOHANN STRAUSS, 1825-1899, Austrian

8924. Frühlingsstimmen   Coloratura Soprano
       Poet: Anon. d3-c5 f3-bb4 Animated in lively tempo. Requires
       considerable flexibility, fluent enunciation, and very fine high PP. A
       waltz, rhythmic and bright. Has florid, showy, climactic passages,
       and generally high tessitura. Climactic ending. Acc: 3-4 KAS

RICHARD STRAUSS, 1864-1949, German

8925. Amor   Coloratura Soprano
       Poet: Clemens Maria Brentano. d3-d5 a3-a4 Op. 68, No. 5. Ani-
       mated in moderate slow tempo. Joyous and florid. Requires flexi-
       bility, very fine high P and PP, and a very fine command of high
       notes. Extended high trills at the end. Generally agitated accompani-
       ment. Acc: 4 RSL-2 (Ch. VIb--Strauss)

SWEDISH TRADITIONAL SONG

8926. When I was seventeen   Coloratura Soprano
Poet: H. Lilljebörn. Swedish first line: När jag blef sjutton år.
c3-bb4 eb3-g4 Animated in moderate slow tempo. Generally subdued, 3 verses. Has added cadenza refrain and two coloratura variants by Marcella Sembrich. An ornamented arrangement of the simpler folk melody. Acc: 3 ART-3

B. Recital Vocalises

PAUL BEN-HAIM, Israel

<u>Three Songs Without Words.</u> For high voice (or instrument) and piano.
Tel-Aviv: Israeli Music Publications, P.O. Box 6011.

8927. (1) Arioso   High Voices
Text: Any open vowel. c3(a2)-a4 g3-d4 Sustained in moderate
tempo. Very subdued, sustained ending marked PPPP in the last
measure. Mainly chordal accompaniment. Acc: 3

8928. (2) Ballad   High Voices
Text: Any open vowel. eb3-bb4 f3-f4 Sustained vocal part in moderate lively tempo. Requires flexibility for the florid passages, and
some fine P. Has some dramatic high passages. Sustained, very
subdued ending. Acc: 3-4

8929. (3) Sephardic melody   High Voices
Text: Any open vowel. a#2-a4 e3-g4 A traditional melody, arranged by Ben-Haim. Sustained in slow tempo. Has many high passages and some wide intervalic skips. Starts strongly. Has both
strong and subdued passages. Requires considerable flexibility and
some low tessitura. Very subdued high ending. Not for light voices.
Acc: 4

WILBUR CHENOWETH, American

8930. Vocalise   Coloratura, Lyric Soprano
Text: "ah" vowel, or variation. d3-b4(d5) g3-a4 Sustained, florid
vocalise. Requires flexibility and a very fine command of high P and
PP. Subdued, high ending on g4. Rhythmic chordal accompaniment
throughout. Has version for solo and men's chorus. Acc: 3 (S)LG

AARON COPLAND, American

8931. Vocalise   High Voices
Text: open vowel. c3-bb4(a4) e3-g4 A vocalise, requires flexibility and agility. Acc: 4 (S)B-H, AL

GABRIEL FAURÉ, 1845-1924, French

8932. Vocalise-Étude   High Voices
Text: open vowel. b2-g4 e3-e4 Sustained in slow tempo. General-
ly tranquil, subdued. Has florid passages. Requires flexibility.
Subdued, high ending. Acc: 3 (S)AL

NIKOLAI MEDTNER, 1880-1951, Russian of German descent

8933. Sonate-Vocalise   Coloratura, Lyric Soprano
       Text: open vowel. c3-ab4 g3-g4 Introduced by the "Moto:
       Geweihter Platz. " An extended vocalise in generally moderate lively
       tempo. Starts and ends very gently and subduedly. Composer's in-
       structions on which vowels to use (generally "ah") are included in
       the score. Acc: 4 (S)JZ

OLIVIER MESSIAEN, French

8934. Vocalise-Étude   High Voices
       Text: open vowel. d3-a4 f#3-f#4 Sustained in moderate tempo.
       Starts gently. Requires fine P. Has climactic passages. Subdued
       ending after dramatic high climax. Agitated accompaniment. Acc:
       4-5 (S)AL

ANDRZEJ PANUFNIK, Polish, now British citizen

8935. Hommage à Chopin. Five vocalises for soprano and piano. eb3-ab4
       g3-g4 May be performed as one work or separately. Soloist is giv-
       en full liberty in the use of vowels and breathing marks. The first
       and last songs may be transposed a minor third. Requires flexibility
       and a good command of high notes. Duration: 15 minutes. London:
       Boosey & Hawkes.

FRANCIS POULENC, 1899-1963, French

8936. Vocalise-Étude   High Voices
       Text: open vowel. d3-bb4 g3-g4 Sustained in moderate tempo.
       Has florid passages, climactic high passages, and a subdued ending.
       Generally chordal accompaniment. Acc: 3 (S)AL

SERGEI RAKHMANINOF, 1873-1943, Russian

8937. Vocalise   Coloratura, Lyric Soprano
       Text: open vowel. c#3-g#4(c#5) g#3-e4 Sustained in slow tempo.
       Very lyric. Has some climactic passages. Subdued ending. Sung
       on vowels ah, oh, or oo, or a mixture of these sounds. Subdued
       ending. Acc: 3-4 GAS, SSR (Ch. IX--Rakhmaninof)

MAURICE RAVEL, 1875-1937, French

8938. Piece en forme de habanera   High Voices
       Text: open vowel. c3-a4 g3-g4 Agitated vocal part in slow tempo.
       Florid, requires flexibility. Has trills, portandos, and climactic
       passages. Starts gently. Ends with descending portando, after trill
       on g4-a4. Acc: 3-4 (S)AL

JOSÉ SEREBRIER, Uruguayan

8939. Canción sin nombre y sin palabras   High Voices

Text: open vowel. eb3-bb4 g3-g4 Sustained in moderate tempo.
Vocalized "ah" vowel throughout, ending on "m" in final measure.
Generally subdued. Acc: 3 (S)SM

IGOR STRAVINSKY, 1882-1971, Russian

8940. Pastorale   High Voices
Text: open vowel. c#3-f#4 e#3-f#4 Sustained in somewhat slow
tempo. Florid, requires flexibility. Generally gentle, subdued. Requires very fine P and PP. Graceful and delicate. Gently agitated
accompaniment. Acc: 3-4 50A

C. JOSÉE VIGNERON-RAMAKERS, French

8941. Vocalise   All Voices
Text: open vowel. c#3-a4(b4)H f#3-f#4 Sustained in varied tempi.
Starts slowly and gently. Has contrasting dynamics. Requires con-
siderable flexibility. Subdued and calm ending. Also issued for
Medium (the original key) and Low Voices. Acc: 4-5 (S)SF, 1972

C. Alleluias

JOHANN SEBASTIAN BACH, 1685-1750, German

8942. Alleluja   Coloratura, Lyric Soprano
Work: CANTATA 51--Jauchzet Gott in allen Landen. The second part
of the aria "Sei Lob und Preis mit Ehren." c3-c5 g3-e4 Animated
in moderate lively tempo. Very florid, requires considerable flexibility. Has some wide intervalic skips. Climactic ending. Scored for
soprano voice, strings, trumpet, and continuo. Piano-vocal score is
available. Acc: 4 (VS)BH

GEORGE FRIDERIC HANDEL, 1685-1759, German

8943. R: O king of Kings
A: Alleluia   Soprano
Work: ESTHER, oratorio 1732 second version, text by Alexander
Pope and John Arbuthnot. Part of Esther. e3-a4 g3-g4 Short and
majestic recitative, and an animated, florid alleluia in very rapid
tempo. Joyous, bright, requires considerable flexibility. An extended alleluia aria. Climactic ending. Acc: 3-4 CSH-2 (See VII)

ISSACHAR MIRON, Israeli

8944. Halleluiah   All Voices
d3-e4 f3-d4 Animated in very fast tempo. Requires some flexibility.
Joyful and generally strong. Climactic ending. Acc: 3-4 GSI
(Ch. X)

CLAUDIO MONTEVERDI, 1567-1643, Italian

8945. Alleluja   High, Medium Voices

d3-g4 e3-d4 Animated in lively tempo. Bright and joyous. Florid,
requires flexibility. Climactic ending. The final movement in the
solo motet "Exulta Filia," and appears in the motet, not published
separately. Acc: 3 (SC)SC

WOLFGANG AMADEUS MOZART, 1756-1791, Austrian

8946. Alleluja   Soprano
f3-a4(c5) a3-g4 Third movement in the solo motet of three movements, "Exsultate, Jubilate." Animated in lively tempo. Bright,
joyous, and quite brilliant. Florid, requires flexibility. Climactic
ending. In Mozart's original score, the ending line of this movement
goes down (sequence: f4-g3-c4-f3) instead of up. The high C (c5),
usually appearing as an optional note in modern editions of the score
and heard in recordings and performances, must not be taken as
absolute, but the singer's preference. Acc: 4-5 (S)CF (three keys),
GS (three keys), FC, CP

HENRY PURCELL, 1659-1695, British

8947. Alleluia   High Voices
Text: Alleluia. f3-g4 a3-eb4 Animated in lively tempo. Brilliant,
has florid passages. Requires flexibility. Starts gently. Dramatic
high ending in slower tempo and broader delivery. A charming alleluia. Acc: 3-4 TDH (Purcell)

NED ROREM, American

8948. Alleluia   High Voices
b2-g♯4 f♯3-f♯4 Animated in fast tempo. Dramatic and brilliant.
Marked "somewhat hysterical." Agitated, with some accents. Ends
with a "shout." Acc: 4 (S)HM

CHAPTER XIII

TRADITIONAL SONGS AND SPIRITUALS

(Recital Arrangements for Study and Performance)

Introduction

Thousands of folk songs exist. Traditional material cannot be considered unimportant in the development of the solo art song or in recital, for the folk idiom has influenced every major composer in every country through the centuries. It has been the major source of historical continuity in music, vocal or instrumental. Every great composer has learned from and used folk material as a basis for the start of a personal musical style. It should not be necessary to mention that Bach, Brahms, Beethoven, Haydn, and Mozart, to mention a few, greatly respected the lowly folk melody whose subjects cover every known human activity and emotion, and whose texts cover the widest range of any musical material.

Folk songs have a place on concert programs in the form of recital arrangements whose accompaniments are generally more elaborate than the authentic and simple chordal accompaniment, usually with some string instrument, and now popularly with the guitar. Most of the titles in this chapter are of the type just mentioned. The accompaniments of settings like several by Manuel de Falla, Joseph Canteloube, and Heitor Villa-Lobos require accomplished pianists, and on the whole, deserve the attention one gives to the accompaniment of art songs.

The best guide in the performance of concert settings of art songs is simplicity. Without this most important aspect, the result will appear insincere and musically fraudulent. Unless done by master composers, accompaniments are better set also in simplicity. All of us have attended recitals of well-known artists whose performances of folk songs are done in the so-called "operatic" style. An approach in this direction, regardless of who does it, is definitely questionable, and should never be emulated and imitated.

The accompaniments of traditional material from Italo-Iberian cultures are generally more elaborate than their central northern European counterparts. This is mainly due to the virtuoso gypsy guitar-playing that has so influenced the vivacity and sensuousness attached especially to Hispanic arts. Some of this may be felt in the compositions and arrangements of de Falla and the Spanish compositions of Ravel.

Negro spirituals and sacred ballads are a special type of folk songs, and are typically American. With an eventful historical background, these songs are all deeply religious and serious. This author encourages their inclusion in more recital programs by all nationalities, for they have become part of an international song literature. It must be conceded that only the American Negro can give a fluent and most convincing performance of the dialect. Anybody else who is not at home with it would fare better by using

standard American English diction rather than trying to mimic a Negro singer and thus sound ridiculous.   Henry T. Burleigh, Hall Johnson, and Margaret Bonds are among those who have written the most musical and admirable recital arrangements of Negro spirituals.

This chapter on folk songs is by no means complete, for a listing of
all music of this genre would become encyclopedic and thus impractical for
this purpose.   However, this chapter gives those who are interested many
fine recital settings to choose from.   As in the other chapters of this work,
what appears here is what was made available to the author.   Information in
each folk song entry is minimal compared to entries in other chapters because most folk material is best rendered in a less elaborate manner, and
the material itself makes no unusual demands on the voice.   Generally, folk
song melodies are confined to a range of one octave, except those of the
Irish which are wider.   Dynamics are generally few and less subtle and con-
trasty.   Folk songs may be performed in any key that is comfortable for the
performer and which affords him the greatest freedom with the text.   The
ranges given here are mostly those of the high keys published.   Folk song
performance is ahead of the performance of art songs and operatic arias in
one way: it has been found that in a recital, the folk song arrangement often
exhibits the singer's best tone, easily produced, whereas he may be tense
and drive his tone with other types of literature.   There is something to
learn vocally from the simplicity of the folk song approach.   Or is it a mat-
ter of simple and plain psychology?

In alphabetizing the titles and first lines of folk material, the articles
the, a and an are not considered (as they are in other chapters) since traditional material is not constant, but changes according to time and region,
although the basic melody and texts are retained.

This chapter is arranged under the following headings:

United States	Hungary
General & American Negro	Israel
England	Greece
Scotland	Italy
Hebrides	France
Ireland	General & Auvergne
Wales	Spain
Canada	Argentina
Norway	Brazil
Denmark	Chile
Sweden	Colombia
Germany	Mexico
Poland	West Indies
Russia	Other Iberian-American Countries
Czechoslovakia	Japan

General Bibliography

ART   Art Songs for School and Studio.   Two volumes, high, low.   Edited
         by Mabelle Glenn and Alfred Spouse.   Bryn Mawr: Oliver Ditson.

FSM   Folk Songs in Settings by Master Composers.   Forty-four songs:

English, Irish, Scottish, Welsh, and American. All in English versions. Edited by Herbert Haufrecht. Only one key, mostly high and medium. One of the best collections. With notes. New York: Funk and Wagnalls, 1970.

JTA   John Charles Thomas Album of Favorite Songs and Arias. Baritone. New York: G. Schirmer.

MAA   Marian Anderson Album of Songs and Spirituals. Edited by Franz Rupp. With English versions on the foreign languages. New York: G. Schirmer.

POS   Pathways of Song. Four volumes, revised edition. High, low. Edited by Frank LaForge and Will Earhart. English songs, and songs in foreign languages with English versions. M. Witmark, Inc. (Note: POS-1 means: Pathways of Song, Vol. 1.)

SCS   Seven Centuries of Solo Song. High, low. Six volumes, with volume 4 devoted to recital arrangements of folk songs. Edited by James Woodside. Thirteenth to 20th century song literature. Boston: Boston Music Co.

SLS   Songs My True Love Sings. Compiled by Beatrice Landeck; arranged by Charity Bailey. New York: Edward B. Marks Corp.

SVR   Standard Vocal Repertoire. High, low. Two volumes. Edited by Richard D. Row. New York: R. D. Row, c/o Carl Fischer, Inc.

WFF   A Treasury of the World's Finest Folk Song. Collected and arranged by Leonhard Deutsch. Thirty-four cultures. Original languages and English versions. New York: Crown Publishers. (Note: A very fine collection.)

4FS   4 Folk Songs. Spanish, French, Italian, and Hebrew folk songs arranged by Maurice Ravel. Original texts, with English and French versions. New York: International Music Co.

25F   25 Favorite Latin-American Songs. Arranged by Miguel Sandoval. Original texts, with English versions. New York: G. Schirmer, Inc. (A very fine collection of recital arrangements of Latin-American songs.)

56S   Fifty-six Songs You Like to Sing. No editor. General collection issued in one key although songs are for voices of different ranges. New York: G. Schirmer.

Other Available Collection:

Volkslieder Baltischer Länder. Lithuanian, Lettische, Esthonian, and Finnish folk songs. Arranged by Dr. Heinrich Möller. Original texts, with German versions. Mainz: B. Schott's Söhne. (Note: A very fine collection of folk songs unknown in western Europe and America.)

1. UNITED STATES

A. General

Bibliography

AEI   Folk Songs American-English-Irish. Arranged by John Edmunds. High, Low. New York: R. D. Row Music Co.

AFB   American-English Folk-Ballads from the Southern Appalachian Mountains. Six songs, medium key. Set 22. Arranged by Cecil J. Sharp. New York: G. Schirmer, Inc.

AUR   Along Unpaved Roads. Eight American folk songs arranged by Ernst Bacon. Los Angeles: Delkas Music Publishing Co., c/o Broude Bros. Also published by Leeds Music Corp., New York.

OAS   Old American Songs. Two sets. Arranged by Aaron Copland. Three songs in each set. One key. New York: Boosey & Hawkes.

SAF   Schirmer's American Folk-Song Series. Available sets: 2, 3, 8, 11, 12, 13, 14, 16, 17, 18, 20, 21, 22, 24, 25, 26, 27. Collected and arranged by different people. New York: G. Schirmer, Inc.

20A   20 American Songs and Negro Spirituals. Arranged by Gerard Hengeveld. Amsterdam: Broekmans & Van Poppel.

8949.   Across the Western Ocean   Men
Origin: Sea Chanty, arranged by Celius Dougherty. d3-d4 d3-d4
Sustained in moderate slow tempo. Broad, with climactic passages.
Acc: 3 (S)GS

8950.   Adam and Eve   High, Medium Voices
d3-f4 f3-d4 Sustained in moderate slow tempo. Narrative text.
Generally on MF level. Setting by Ernst Bacon. Also issued in low
key. Acc: 3 (S)CF

8951.   Ah, Suzette, dear   Men
Region: Louisiana. French title: Ah, Suzette, chere. eb3-f4 f3-
d4 Animated in moderate lively tempo. Texts in French, French
dialect, and English. Acc: 3 SAF-2

8952.   At the river   All Voices
Origin: Hymn tune. eb3-eb4 g3-c4 Sustained in moderate tempo.
Somewhat majestic. Marked "with dignity." Acc: 3 OAS-2

8953.   The ball of Monsieur Preval   All Voices
Region: Louisiana. French dialect title: Michie Preval. c#3-b3
c#3-a3 Animated in moderate lively tempo. Graceful. 12 verses.
Acc: 3 SAF-2

8954. The banjo   Men
Region: Southern states. Other titles: "'Twill never do to give it
up" and "The camptown races." c#3-f#4 f#3-c#4 Animated in
moderate tempo. 4 verses and refrain. Setting by Louis Moreau
Gottschalk. Acc: 4 FSM

8955. Banjo Sam   All Voices
Region: North Carolina. eb3-bb3 eb3-g3 Best for men. Animated in lively tempo. A diction narrative. Requires fluent enunciation. Acc: 3 SAF-3

8956. Berceuse   All Voices
Region: Louisiana. Bayou French title: Guê-gue Solingaie. In
French, Bayou French, and English. c3-d4 f3-bb4 Sustained in
moderate slow tempo. Subdued. Acc: 3 SAF-2

8957. Billy boy   All Voices
Origin: Sea chanty. c3-f4 f3-d4 Animated in brisk tempo. Requires fluent enunciation. 4 verses. Acc: 3 AEI

8958. Bird courtships   All Voices
d3-f4 f3-d4 Animated in lively tempo. Narrative, with some characterization. Setting by James Woodside. Acc: 3-4 SCS-4

8959. Black is the color of my true love's hair   Men
d3-g4 f3-eb4 Sustained in moderate slow tempo. Gentle. 4
verses. Issued in three keys by G. Schirmer, Inc. , arranged by
John Jacob Niles. Oliver Ditson edition is arranged by Clifford Shaw.
Requires fine P and PP. Subdued high ending. Acc: 3 (S)GS, OD.
SAF-17, SLS

8960. The blackbird and the crow   All Voices
b2-d4 e3-b4 Animated in moderate lively tempo. Has humor. 4
verses. Acc: 3 SAF-3

8961. Blow, ye winds   Men
c3-d4 c3-c4 Very animated in fast tempo. Generally light, requires
fluent enunciation. Setting by Celius Dougherty. Acc: 4 (S)GS

8962. The boatman's dance   All Voices
e3-f#4 e3-f#4 Rhythmic, joyous, and dance-like. 3 verses and refrain. Acc: 3 OAS-1

8963. De boll weevil   All Voices
c3-f4 f3-f4 Animated in moderate lively tempo. Narrative, with
characterization. Generally on MF level. Humorous. Accompaniment "in phony habanera style. " Setting by Ernst Bacon. Acc: 3
AUR

8964. Bring my Lulu home   Men
c3-d4 eb3-c4 Sustained in slow tempo. Generally on MF level.
Subdued, sustained ending. Acc: 3 (S)GS

8965. Buffalo gals   All Voices
a2-c4(L) bb2-bb3 Animated in lively tempo. Narrative, 2 verses.
Issued in medium and low keys. Setting by Ernst Bacon. Acc: 3
(S)CF

8966. Butterfly love   Men
Original Spanish title: Es el amor mariposa. d3-e4 f3-d4 Animated in moderate tempo. 2 verses; Spanish and English texts.
Acc: 3 SAF-11

8967. Careless love   All Voices
c3-d4 f3-c4 Sustained in moderate tempo. Light. 4 verses. Acc:
3 SLS

8968. Careless love   All Voices
e3-f♯4 e3-e4 Sustained in moderate slow tempo. Requires simplicity. Generally subdued, with sad texts. May be transposed for
lower voices. Setting by Ernst Bacon. Acc: 3 AUR

8969. The cherry-tree   All Voices
Region: Kentucky. g3-e4 a3-d4 Sustained in moderate slow tempo.
A Christmas carol, 9 verses, narrative. Acc: 2-3 SAF-8

8970. Ching-a-ring chaw   All Voices
d3(a2)-d4(f♯4) d3-d4 A minstrel song. Animated in lively tempo.
Marked, requires fluent enunciation. Outgoing. Acc: 3-4 OAS-2

8971. Cindy   Men
d3(b2)-f4 e3-e4 Animated in lively tempo. Has climactic passages.
Requires some fluent enunciation. Climactic ending. Setting by
Reginald Boardman. Acc: 3-4 SVR-2

8972. Clémentine   Men
Region: Louisiana. In French, French dialect, and English. d3-e4
f3-c4 Animated in moderate lively tempo. Generally light. Acc:
2-3 SAF-2

8973. Colorado trail   Men
c3-e♭4 e♭3-c4 Sustained in moderate tempo. Setting by Celius
Dougherty. Acc: 3 (S)GS

8974. Come all ye fair and tender ladies   All Voices
Region: North Carolina. c3-e4 g3-e4 Sustained in moderate slow
tempo. 4 verses. See the Kentucky version. Acc: 3 SAF-21,
AEI

8975. Come all ye fair and tender ladies   Women
Version: Kentucky. e3-g4 a3-e4 Sustained in moderate tempo. 4
verses. See the North Carolina version. Acc: 3 SAF-8

8976. Come dance Codaine   All Voices
Region: Louisiana. French title: Dansez Codaine. f3-d4 a3-d4
Animated in moderate lively tempo. Graceful. In French, French
dialect, and English. Acc: 3 SAF-2

8977. Common Bill   Women
b2-e4 e3-c4 Generally sustained in moderate tempo. Generally on
MF level. Has some strong passages. Gently humorous. Setting
by Ernst Bacon. Acc: 3 AUR

8978. The crawfish song   All Voices
Region: Creole. c3-f4 f3-e♭4 Gently animated in moderate tempo.
Requires some fluent enunciation. 2 verses. Acc: 3 AEI

8979. The cruel brother   All Voices
Region: North Carolina. f3-d4 f3-d4 Sustained in moderate tempo.
Narrative, 16 verses. Acc: 2 AFB

8980. The cuckoo   All Voices
Region: North Carolina. b♭2-e♭4 e♭3-b♭4 Animated in moderate
lively tempo. Requires fluent enunciation. Narrative, 2 verses.
Acc: 3 SAF-3

8981. The dear companion   Women
Region: North Carolina. f3-c4 f3-c4 Sustained in moderate tempo.
Sad text, 4 verses. Acc: 3 SAF-21

8982. Dearest Bille   Women
Region: North Carolina. e3-e4 e3-d4 Gently animated in moderate
tempo. 3 verses. Acc: 3 SAF-3

8983. The death of Queen Jane   All Voices
Region: Kentucky. f3-f4 f3-c4 Sustained in slow tempo. Sad,
narrative text. 5 verses on the death of Jane Seymour, third wife
of Henry VIII. Acc: 2-3 SAF-20

8984. The dodger   Men
g3-d4 g3-d4 Other title: Campaign song. Animated, marked,
rhythmic, and humorous. 3 verses and refrain. Acc: 3 OAS-1,
FSM

8985. Down in that valley   All Voices
Region: Kentucky. e3-e4 g3-d4 Gently animated in moderate tempo. Different tune from the well-known melody. 6 verses. Acc:
2-3 SAF-14

8986. Down in yon forest   All Voices
Region: North Carolina. A Christmas (Eucharistic) carol. c3-f4
f3-c4 Sustained in moderate tempo. 7 verses. Acc: 2 SAF-16

8987. Edward   All Voices
Region: Tennessee. d3-d4 d3-d4 Sustained in moderate tempo.
Conversation between two characters. 6 verses. Acc: 2 AFB

8988. Ef I had a ribbon bow   Women
Region: Kentucky. g3-f4 a3-d4 Animated in moderate tempo. Generally light. 2 verses. Acc: 3 SAF-8

8989. The enchantress   Men
Region: California. Original Spanish title: La mágica mujer. d3-
f♯4 f♯3-c4 Animated in moderate tempo. Graceful. Spanish and
English texts. Acc: 3 SAF-11

8990. The Erie Canal   Low Voices
d3-c4 d3-a3 Other title: Low bridge. Generally sustained in moderate tempo. Has climactic passages. Rhythmic. Requires fine P
and PP. Best for men. Setting by Ernst Bacon. Acc: 3 (S)CF

8991. Every night when the sun goes in   All Voices
Region: Appalachia. c3-f4 f3-d4 Sustained in moderate tempo.
Generally subdued. 2 verses. Acc: 3 AEI

8992. The false knight upon the road   All Voices
Region: Tennessee, originally English. b2-e4 e3-b3 Sustained in
slow tempo. Narrative, 7 verses. The setting in OX is by Howard
Boatwright, mainly for baritone. Acc: 3 AFB, (S)OX

8993. The false young man   All Voices
Region: Tennessee. b2-d4 d3-d4 Sustained in moderate tempo.
Requires some flexibility, 5 verses. Acc: 3 SAF-21

8994. Fare you well   All Voices
f3-ab4 f3-f4 First line: If I had wings like Nora's dove. Sustained in slow tempo. Requires simplicity. 2 verses. Acc: 3-4
AEI, SVR-1

8995. Farewell, o love, forever   All Voices
Original Spanish title: Adios, adios, amores. e3-e4 f♯3-c♯4 Sustained in slow tempo. 3 verses. Spanish and English texts. Acc:
3 SAF-11

8996. The farmer's curst wife   All Voices
Region: Kentucky. e3-e4 a3-c♯4 Animated in fairly lively tempo.
Narrative, 11 verses. Acc: 2-3 SAF-20

8997. Forward march, grenadiers!   Men
Region: Louisiana. French dialect title: En avant, grenadiers!
eb3-gb4 gb3-eb4 Animated in march tempo. Energetic, best for
men. In French, French dialect, and English. Acc: 3 SAF-2

8998. Geordie   All Voices
Region: Virginia. e3-e4 e3-c4 Gently animated in moderate tempo.
Tragic narrative, 9 verses. Acc: 3 SAF-14

8999. Georgie, O   All Voices
Region: North Carolina. d3-d4 d3-d4 Animated in moderate tempo. Requires some fluent enunciation. Narrative. Acc: 3 SAF-3

9000. Go to sleep   All Voices
Region: East Texas. c3-c4 d3-c4 Animated in moderate tempo.
Generally subdued. A lullaby. Acc: 2-3 SAF-25

9001. Go 'way from my window   All Voices
c3-g4 eb3-eb4 Sustained in moderate tempo. Generally on MF
level. Generally gentle. 4 verses and refrain. Descending ending
line. Issued in two keys. Setting by John Jacob Niles. Acc: 3
(S)GS

9002. The golden willow tree   All Voices
d3(g2)-e4(f♯4) d3-d4 An Anglo-American ballad. Animated and fast.
Requires fluent enunciation. Acc: 3-4 OAS-2

9003. Grandma Grunts   Men
Region: North Carolina. f3-c4 f3-c4 Animated in moderate tempo.
Requires some fluent enunciation. 4 verses. Acc: 3 SAF-3

9004. The hammock   All Voices
Region: California. Original Spanish title: La hamaca. c3-f4 f3-
d4 Animated in moderate tempo. 2 verses. Spanish and English
texts. Acc: 3 SAF-11

9005. He's gone away   Women
Region: North Carolina. c3-e4 c3-c4 Sustained in slow tempo.
In free style. Generally on MF level. Subdued ending. Setting by
Clifford Shaw. Acc: 3 (S)OD

9006. Home on the range   Men
Region: Texas. bb2-eb4 eb3-c4 Sustained in moderate slow tempo. Generally on MF level. The GS edition is a slightly elaborate
recital arrangement. Setting by David W. Guion. Acc: 3 JTA

9007. I bought me a cat   All Voices
c3-d4 f3-c4 A children's nursery rhyme. Animated in moderate
lively tempo. Gently humorous. Acc: 3 OAS-1

9008. I know my love   Women
bb2-eb4 d3-c4 Animated in lively tempo. Bright. Acc: 3 SLS

9009. I wonder as I wander   All Voices
Region: North Carolina. eb3-g4 g3-eb4 Sustained in moderate
slow tempo. Pastorale; gently graceful. A Christmas song. Issued
in two keys. Acc: 3 (S)GS. SAF-14

9010. I'm going to get married next Sunday   Men
Region: North Carolina. c3-d4 d3-c4 Animated in moderate lively
tempo. Requires fluent enunciation. 4 verses. Acc: 3 SAF-3

9011. I'm sad and I'm lonely   Women
c#3-f#4 e3-f#4 Sustained in slow tempo. Generally on MF level.
Sad texts. Acc: 3 20A

9012. In Springtime   All Voices
Region: California. Original Spanish title: La primavera. bb2-d4
eb3-c4 Animated in moderate tempo. Graceful. Spanish and English texts. Acc: 3 SAF-11

9013. Jack o' Diamonds   Women
Region: North Carolina. eb3-c4 e3-c4 Sustained in moderate slow
tempo. 3 short verses. See the Kentucky version (f3-d4 f3-c4) in
SAF-20. Acc: 2-3 SAF-3

9014. Jesus born in Beth'ny   All Voices
Region: Virginia. d3-d4 e3-b3 A Christmas song. Sustained in
moderate tempo. Narrative, 10 verses. Acc: 2-3 SAF-16

9015. Jesus, Jesus, rest your head   All Voices
Region: Kentucky, Hardin County. Setting by John Jacob Niles. A
Christmas song. d3-g4 g3-e4 Sustained in moderate tempo. Gently
subdued. Issued in two keys. A lullaby. Acc: 3 (S)GS, SAF-16,
AEI

9016. Jesus the Christ is born   All Voices
Region: Tennessee. c3-d4 f3-c4 A Christmas song. Animated in
moderate tempo. Majestic. 5 verses. Acc: 3 SAF-16

9017. Jimmy Randal   All Voices
Region: Kentucky. f3-e4 g3-d4 Sustained in slow tempo. Sad text.
7 verses. Acc: 2-3 SAF-20

9018.   John Reilly   All Voices
        Region: Kentucky. c3-d4 f3-c4 Animated in lively tempo. Narra-
        tive. 8 verses. Acc: 2-3 SAF-20

9019.   Lady Ishbel and the elfin-knight   All Voices
        Region: North Carolina. c3-d4 d3-c4 Gently animated in moderate
        tempo. Narrative. 10 verses. Acc: 2-3 SAF-20

9020.   The lady who loved a pig   All Voices
        c3-f4 f3-c4 Animated in moderate lively tempo. Narrative, humor-
        ous. Setting by Celius Dougherty. Acc: 3 (S)GS

9021.   The lass from the low countree   All Voices
        Region: North Carolina. b2-d4 f♯3-c♯4 Sustained in moderate
        tempo. Narrative, 3 verses. Acc: 3 SAF-20

9022.   The little horses   Women
        b2-e4 e3-d4 A lullaby. Sustained and generally slow. Subdued,
        descending ending. Acc: 3 OAS-2

9023.   The lonesome grove   All Voices
        eb3-g4 f3-eb4 Sustained in moderate slow tempo. Gentle and
        charming. Issued in two keys. Acc: 3 (S)CF

9024.   Long time ago   Men
        f3-f4 f3-d4 Sustained in moderate slow tempo. A lyric ballad. 2
        verses. Acc: 3 OAS-1

9025.   Look down that lonesome road   All Voices
        d3-bb3 d3-bb3 Sustained in moderate slow tempo. Gentle and sub-
        dued. 3 verses. Acc: 2-3 SLS

9026.   Lulle lullay   All Voices
        Region: Tennessee. c3-d4 e3-c4 A Christmas song. Sustained in
        moderate slow tempo. Graceful and gentle. 5 verses. Acc: 2-3
        SAF-16

9027.   Marianne's loves   All Voices
        Region: Louisiana. Bayou French title: Z'Amours Marianne. d3-
        eb4 d3-d4 Sustained in moderate tempo. A conversation between
        two characters. In French, French dialect, and English. Acc: 3
        SAF-2

9028.   Midnight special   Men
        d3-d4 d3-d4 Sustained in moderate tempo. Generally gentle; on MF
        level. Setting by Ernst Bacon. Acc: 3 AUR

9029.   The milk-maid   All Voices
        Region: Kentucky. d3-f4 g3-b3 Sustained in moderate slow tempo.
        Narrative, 6 verses. Acc: 2-3 SAF-20

9030.   Mobile Bay   Men
        Region: Southern Negro chanty. bb2-eb3 eb2-eb3 Animated in
        moderate fast tempo. Joyous and carefree. May be transposed for
        higher voices. Setting by Celius Dougherty. Acc: 3-4 (S)GS

9031.   My horses ain't hungry   All Voices
        Region: Kentucky. b2-e4 e3-d4 Best for women. Animated in
        moderate lively tempo. 5 verses. Acc: 3 SAF-14

9032. My little Mohee   Men
Region: Kentucky. d♯3-e4 e3-c♯4 Sustained in moderate tempo.
Narrative text, 5 verses. See the North Carolina version in SAF-3.
Acc: 3 SAF-14, 3

9033. My Lulu   Men
c3-c4 f3-c4 Animated in lively tempo. Requires some fluent enunciation. Setting by Ernst Bacon. Acc: 3 AUR

9034. My shepherd will supply my need   All Voices
d3-f♯4 d3-d4 The text is Isaac Watt's paraphrase of Psalm 23.
Sustained vocal part in lively tempo. Subdued middle section. Setting by Virgil Thompson. 3 verses. Acc: 3 FSM

9035. Never was a child so lovely   All Voices
Region: Kentucky. d3-d4 f3-c4 Sustained in moderate slow tempo.
Gentle. A Christmas carol. 6 verses. Acc: 2-3 SAF-18

9036. Now once I did court   Men
Region: Tennessee. e♭3-d4 f3-c4 Animated in moderate lively
tempo. 5 verses. Acc: 3 SAF-21

9037. On the first day of Christmas   All Voices
Region: Appalachian version of the English carol, "The twelve days
of Christmas." c3-d4 f3-c4 Animated in moderate tempo. Generally sung without accompaniment. Acc: None SAF-16

9038. On top of old smokey   All Voices
Region: Appalachia. e3-f4 f3-d4 Sustained in slow tempo. Generally gentle and subdued. 6 short verses. Acc: 3 AEI

9039. One morning in May   All Voices
Region: Kentucky. d3-e4 f3-c4 Animated in fast tempo. Narrative, 6 verses. Acc: 3 SAF-14

9040. Pity poor Mam'zelle Zizi   All Voices
Region: Louisiana. Bayou French title: Pauv' piti Mom'zelle Zizi.
d3-d♭4 e♭3-c4 Sustained in moderate tempo. In French, French
dialect, and English. Acc: 3 SAF-2

9041. 'Possum tree   Men
Region: North Carolina. d3-d4 d3-d4 Animated in fast tempo. Requires fluent enunciation. 2 verses and refrain. Acc: 3 SAF-3

9042. Pretty Polly   All Voices
Region: Kentucky. b♭2-e♭4 e♭3-b♭3 Slightly animated and subdued.
A tragic ballad. 10 short verses. Acc: 2-3 SAF-17

9043. Pretty Saro   Men
Region: North Carolina. d3-d4 d3-d4 Sustained in moderate tempo.
Generally gentle, 3 verses. Acc: 3 SAF-3

9044. The rejected lover   Men
Region: Virginia. d3-d4 f3-d4 Animated in moderate lively tempo.
6 verses. Acc: 3 SAF-21

9045. The riddle song   All Voices
Region: Kentucky. e3-e4 e3-e4 Sustained in moderate tempo. 3
verses. Acc: 3 SAF-21

1178

9046. Rio Grande   Men
       Region: Sea chanty. e♭3-e♭4 e♭3-c4 Slightly sustained in moder-
       ate tempo. Setting by Celius Dougherty. Acc: 3 (S)GS

9047. The rosewood casket   All Voices
       Region: North Carolina. c♯3-d4 d3-a3 Sustained in moderate tem-
       po. 3 verses. Acc: 3 SAF-3

9048. Rosie Nell   Men
       b♭2-f4 e3-c4 Animated in moderate lively tempo. Rhythmic and
       happy. Requires some fluent enunciation. Acc: 3 20A

9049. See Jesus the Saviour   All Voices
       Region: Kentucky. A Christmas song. e3-c♯4 e3-c♯4 Sustained
       in moderate slow tempo. 8 one-line verses each ending with vocal-
       ized passage. Acc: 2-3 SAF-16

9050. Serenade   Men
       Region: California. Original Spanish title: La noche 'sta serena.
       d♭3-d♭4 f3-c4 Sustained in slow tempo. Tranquil. Spanish and
       English texts. Acc: 3 SAF-11

9051. The seven joys of Mary   All Voices
       Region: North Carolina. A Christmas carol. b2-e4 e3-c♯4 Sus-
       tained in moderate tempo. 7 verses and refrain. Acc: 3 SAF-16

9052. Shenandoah   Men
       Region: Sea chanty. Setting by Celius Dougherty. a2-d4 d3-b3
       Sustained in slow tempo. Generally gentle. May be transposed for
       tenor. Acc: 3 (S)GS

9053. The shoemaker   All Voices
       Region: California. Original Spanish title: El zapatero. c3-d4 f3-
       c4 Animated in moderate tempo. Humorous. Spanish and English
       texts. Acc: 3 SAF-11

9054. Simple gifts   All Voices
       Other title: Shaker song. e♭3-e♭4 e♭3-e♭4 Sustained in moderate
       tempo. Short. Acc: 3 OAS-1

9055. Sinful shoe   All Voices
       c3-d4 c3-c4 Animated in moderate fast tempo. Generally on MF
       level. Climactic ending. Acc: 3 AUR

9056. Sinner man   All Voices
       Region: Southern Appalachian; originally English. c3-c4 c3-c4 Sus-
       tained in moderate tempo. Slightly declamatory. 7 verses. Setting
       by Howard Boatwright. Acc: 3 (S)OX

9057. A son of a gambolier   Men
       g3-a4 c3-g4 Animated in fast tempo. Should be transposed to a
       lower key. 5 verses. Setting by Charles Ives. Acc: 3-4 FSM

9058. Sourwood mountain   Men
       e♭3-e♭4 e♭3-c4 Animated in moderate lively tempo. Rhythmic,
       joyful, requires some fluent enunciation. Has humor. Setting by
       Ernst Bacon. Acc: 3 AUR

9059. Stewball   Men
g3-g4 g3-c4 Animated in lively tempo. Bold and outgoing. Setting
by Celius Dougherty. Acc: 3 (S)GS

9060. Sucking cider   Men
g3-d4 g3-d4 Generally sustained in moderate tempo, with some
variations. Has gentle humor. Setting by Ernst Bacon. Acc: 3-4
AUR

9061. Suzanne, Suzanne, pretty one!   Men
Region: Louisiana. French dialect title: Suzanne, Suzanne, j'olie
femme! b2-c♯4 e3-b3 Animated in moderate lively tempo. Humorous. Acc: 3 SAF-2

9062. A teamster's song   Men
Region: California. Original Spanish title: Peña hueca. e3-c4 f3-
c4 Sustained in moderate tempo. Spanish and English texts. Acc:
3 SAF-11

9063. Three little pigs   All Voices
Region: Virginia. f3-d4 g3-c4 Animated in lively tempo. Has
tra-la refrain. 4 verses. Acc: 3 SAF-14

9064. To the pines   Men
Region: North Carolina. d3-a3 d3-a3 Sustained in slow tempo.
Short melody. Subdued. 3 verses. Acc: 2 SAF-25

9065. The two brothers   All Voices
Region: Kentucky. d3-e4 g3-d4 Animated in moderate lively tempo. Graceful. Narrative, 17 verses. Acc: 3 AFB

9066. The two sisters   All Voices
Region: Kentucky. Other title: The old Lord by the northern sea.
c3-d4 e3-c4 Animated in moderate tempo. 13 short verses. Acc:
2 SAF-17

9067. Waillie waillie!   All Voices
d3-e4 g3-d4 Sustained in moderate slow tempo. Generally on MF
level. Subdued ending. Acc: 3 20A

9068. The water-cresses   Men
Region: Kentucky. c3-f4 f3-d4 Animated in moderate tempo.
Graceful. Narrative, 3 verses. Acc: 3 SAF-20

9069. Wayfaring stranger   All Voices
Source: The Sacred Harp, a song collection. d3-e4 e3-c4 Sustained in moderate slow tempo. Generally on MF level. Subdued
ending. Setting by John Jacob Niles. Acc: 3 (S)GS

9070. The weep-willow tree   All Voices
Region: Kentucky. Other title: The golden vanity. c3-e4 e3-c4
Sustained in moderate tempo. Narrative, 8 verses. Acc: 2-3 SAF-
20

9071. What you gonna do when the meat gives out   Men
c3-f4 f3-c4 Animated in lively tempo. Requires fluent enunciation.
Setting by Celius Dougherty. Acc: 2-3 (S)GS

9072. Whistle, daughter, whistle   Women
       Region: North Carolina. c♯3-e4 e3-d4 Animated in moderate fast
       tempo. Has a whistle interlude in the second verse. 2 verses.
       Acc: 2-3 SAF-14

9073. The white hawk   All Voices
       Region: California. Original Spanish title: El quelêle. d3-d4 f3-
       c4 Animated in moderate tempo. Light. Spanish and English texts.
       Acc: 3 SAF-11

9074. The wife wrapt in wether's skin   Men
       Region: Kentucky. c3-d4 d3-d4 Animated in moderate tempo.
       Narrative, 10 verses. Acc: 3 AFB

9075. The wind blew up, the wind blew down   Men
       Region: Kentucky. b2-d4 e3-a3 Sustained in moderate slow tempo.
       8 verses. May be transposed for tenors. Acc: 2-3 SAF-17

9076. Young hunting   All Voices
       Region: Kentucky. c3-d4 c3-c4 Animated in moderate lively tem-
       po. Narrative, 12 verses. Acc: 3 AFB

9077. You've got to cross that lonesome valley   All Voices
       Region: North Carolina. a2-f4 f3-f4 Sustained in moderate tempo.
       Has climactic passages. Gentle ending section. Setting by John
       Jacob Niles. Acc: 3 (S)GS

9078. Zion's walls   All Voices
       Source: A revivalist song. c3-f4 d3-d4 Gently animated. Climac-
       tic ending. Acc: 3 OAS-2

B. American Negro Spirituals and Ballads

Bibliography

ANS   Album of Negro Spirituals. Arranged by J. Rosamond Johnson. Me-
       dium voice and piano. Twenty-six songs. New York: Edward B.
       Marks Music Corp.

BAN   The Book of American Negro Spirituals. The Second Book of Negro
       Spirituals. Two volumes in one, 61 songs in each book. Collected
       and arranged by James Weldon Johanson and J. Rosamond Johnson.
       New York: The Viking Press, 1956.

GPS   The Green Pastures Spirituals. Arranged by Hall Johnson. Twenty-
       five songs, mostly medium and high keys. New York: Carl Fischer
       Co. (Note: This collection leans toward the use of considerable dia-
       lect.)

NSB   Album of Negro Spirituals. Arranged by H. T. Burleigh. High, low.
       Twelve songs. New York: Franco Colombo, 1969.

TNS   Thirty Negro Spirituals. Arranged by Hall Johnson. High voice and piano. New York: G. Schirmer, Inc. (Note: May be transposed for lower voices.)

TSH   Three Spirituals. Arranged by Philip Hattey. London: Oxford University Press.

Note: See General Bibliography following the Preface to this chapter for titles of general collections which also have spirituals.

9079. Ain't got time to die   All Voices
c3-g4 eb3-eb4 Animated in moderate tempo. In declamatory style.
Strong. Climactic ending section. Setting by Hall Johnson. May also be transposed. Acc: 3 (S)GS

9080. De band of Gideon   All Voices
d3-d4 f3-c4 Animated in lively tempo. Generally on MF level.
Acc: 3 ANS

9081. De blind man stood on de road and cried   All Voices
Text: Mark 10:46, 52. f3-f4 f3-f4 Sustained in slow tempo.
Starts gently. Generally on MF level. Setting by H. T. Burleigh.
Acc: 3 NSB

9082. By an' by   All Voices
eb3-f4 eb3-eb4 Sustained in moderate slow tempo. Starts strongly.
Also requires fine P and PP. Setting by H. T. Burleigh. Acc: 3
NSB

9083. Crucifixion   All Voices
c3-c4 g3-c4 First line: They crucified my Lord. Very sustained
in slow tempo. Requires simplicity. Intense, but generally subdued
dynamics. Very subdued ending. Setting by John Payne. Acc: 2-3
MAA

9084. Crucifixion   All Voices
b2-c4 f#3-b3 Sustained in moderate slow tempo. Gentle, requires
simplicity. 4 verses. Acc: 3 WFF

9085. Deep river   All Voices
c3-a4 d3-d4 Very sustained in slow tempo. Generally subdued.
Has slightly strong middle section. Acc: 3 NSB, ANS

9086. Didn't it rain!   All Voices
ab2-db4 db3-bb3 Animated in moderate lively tempo. Starts
strongly. Has climactic passages and some low tessitura. 3 verses.
Setting by Margaret Bonds. Acc: 3 (S)MM

9087. Didn't my Lord deliver Daniel?   All Voices
eb3-c4 f3-c4 Animated in lively tempo. Vigorous. 4 verses.
Acc: 3 ANS

9088. Done written down my name   All Voices
eb3-g4 g3-eb4 Animated in moderate tempo. Generally strong.
Acc: 3 TNS

9089. Every time I feel the spirit   All Voices
c3-eb4 eb3-eb4 Animated in moderate lively tempo. Joyful. 3
verses. Acc: 3 TNS, NSB

9090. Ezekiel saw the wheel   All Voices
d3-e4 f3-b3 Sustained in moderate tempo. Generally on MF level.
The MM setting is by Margaret Bonds. Acc: 3 ANS, (S)MM

9091. Fix me, Jesus   All Voices
bb2-db4 db3-ab3 Sustained in slow tempo. Requires adherence to
strict rhythm. May be transposed for other voices. Generally subdued, requires fine P and PP. Setting by Hall Johnson. Acc: 3
MAA

9092. Git on board little children   All Voices
eb3-c4 f3-c4 Animated in lively tempo. Requires fluent enunciation. The title in NSB: The gospel train. Acc: 3 ANS, NSB

9093. Give me that old time religion   All Voices
c3-c4 c3-a4 Animated in moderate tempo. Generally on MF level.
2 verses. Acc: 3 ANS

9094. Go down, Moses   All Voices
d3-d4 d3-d4 Sustained in slow tempo. Majestic, with some intensity.
Acc: 3 ANS, GPS

9095. Go tell it on the mountain   All Voices
eb3-f4 eb3-f4 A Christmas spiritual. Sustained in moderate tempo.
Issued in two keys. Setting by John W. Work. The MM setting is
by Margaret Bonds. Acc: 3 (S)GA, MM

9096. Going to shout all over God's heaven   All Voices
d3-b3 d3-b3 Other title: I got shoes. Animated in lively tempo.
Generally on MF level. 3 verses. Acc: 3 ANS

9097. Great day!   All Voices
gb3-gb4 bb3-eb4 Animated in march tempo. Starts and ends with
refrain. 4 verses. Acc: 3 TNS

9098. Hallelujah!   All Voices
f3-f4 f3-c4 Animated in lively tempo. Bright. Generally strong.
Acc: 3 GPS

9099. Hallelujah! King Jesus   All Voices
eb3-f4 f3-c4 Animated in moderate tempo. Majestic. Generally
strong and climactic. Acc: 3 GPS

9100. He's got the whole world in his hand   All Voices
c#3-b3(a4) f#3-b3 Animated in moderate tempo. Bright, exultant.
The high range from c4 to a4 is an added arrangement rather than
part of the original melody. Climactic ending. Setting by Margaret
Bonds. Acc: 3 (S)MM

9101. Hold on   All Voices
c3-eb4 c3-c4 Sustained in moderate tempo. Has some strong passages. Descending ending line after high climax. Setting by Margaret
Bonds. Acc: 3 (S)MM

9102. Honor, honor   All Voices
eb3-g4 f3-g4 Animated in moderate lively tempo. Bright, exultant.
Has some climactic high passages. Slightly climactic ending. Setting by Hall Johnson. Also issued in low key. Acc: 3 (S)CF

9103. How long train been gone?   All Voices
e3-g4 g3-e4 Sustained in moderate tempo. Sad text. 3 verses and
refrain. Acc: 3 TNS

9104. I been in the storm, so long   All Voices
d3-d4 g3-d4 Animated in moderate tempo. Generally on MF level.
Acc: 3 ANS

9105. I couldn't hear nobody pray   All Voices
d3-f4(a4) f3-d4 Animated in moderate tempo. Generally subdued.
3 verses. Acc: 3 TNS

9106. I got a robe   All Voices
e3-c#4 f#3-c4 Animated in lively tempo. Joyful and rhythmic.
Acc: 3-4 TSH

9107. I want to be ready   All Voices
c3-f4 f3-c4 Animated in moderate lively tempo. Energetic. Acc:
3 GPS

9108. I'm a-rolling   All Voices
bb2-eb4 eb3-bb3 Generally sustained in moderate tempo. Generally on MF level. Acc: 3 ANS

9109. In bright mansions above   All Voices
f3-g4 f3-d4 Sustained in moderate lively tempo. Short. Acc: 3
GPS

9110. Jesus walked this lonesome valley   All Voices
d3-g4 d3-g4 Sustained in moderate slow tempo. Generally subdued.
Has one climactic passage. Setting by William L. Dawson. Issued
in two keys. Acc: 3 (S)RM

9111. Joshua fit the battle of Jerico   All Voices
c#3(a2)-d4(f4) d3-d4 Animated in moderate lively tempo. Vigorous
and descriptive. Has climactic passages. Acc: 3 ANS, GPS, TSH

9112. Let us break bread together   All Voices
d3-g4 d3-g4 Sustained in moderate slow tempo. Gently majestic.
Setting by Noah Francis Ryder. May be transposed. Acc: 3 (S)JF

9113. Let's have a union   All Voices
bb2-ab4 eb3-eb4 Animated in moderate tempo. Rhythmic. Has
climactic passages. May be transposed for lower voices. Setting by
Hall Johnson. Acc: 3 (S)GS

9114. Listen to the lambs   All Voices
d3-f4 f3-c4 Sustained in moderate slow tempo. Slightly lively middle section. Generally on MF level. Acc: 3 ANS

9115. Little David play on your harp   All Voices
c3-f4 f3-c4 Animated in moderate tempo. Joyous. Acc: 3 ANS

9116. Lord, I don't feel noways tired   All Voices
       bb 2-f4 db 3-db 4 Sustained in slow tempo. Generally marked and
       joyous. Acc: 3 GPS

9117. Mary had a baby   All Voices
       d3-e4 g3-d4 Gently animated in moderate slow tempo. A lullaby,
       subdued. 6 verses. Acc: 2-3 TNS

9118. Mobile Bay   Men
       Region: Southern Negro chanty. bb 2-eb 4 eb 3-eb 4 Animated in
       moderate fast tempo. Joyous and carefree. May be transposed for
       tenor. Acc: 3-4 (S)GS

9119. My God is so high   All Voices
       f3-f4 f3-d4 Sustained in moderate tempo. Generally strong. 2
       verses and refrain. Acc: 3 GPS

9120. My Lord what a morning   All Voices
       Text: Matthew 24:29, a paraphrase. f3-f4 f3-eb 4 Sustained in
       moderate slow tempo. Very subdued ending. Issued in two keys.
       Setting by William L. Dawson. Acc: 3 (S)FS. TNS

9121. Nobody knows the trouble I see   All Voices
       d3-d4 d3-d4 Sustained in slow tempo. Has climactic passages.
       Bright ending. Acc: 3 ANS, TSH, NSB

9122. Now let me fly   All Voices
       d3-e4 d3-d4 Animated in lively tempo. Generally on MF level.
       3 verses. Acc: 3 ANS

9123. O, rocks, don't fall on me   All Voices
       c3-g4 eb 3-eb 4 Sustained in slow tempo. Generally subdued. 2
       verses. Acc: 3 ANS

9124. Oh, graveyard   All Voices
       c# 3-e4 f# 3-e4 Sustained in moderate slow tempo. Generally sub-
       dued. Acc: 3 TNS

9125. Oh, Mary, don't you weep   All Voices
       f3-eb 4 g3-d4 Animated in moderate lively tempo. Rhythmic. Acc:
       3 GPS

9126. Oh, rise and shine   All Voices
       eb 3-eb 4 g3-eb 4 Sustained in moderate slow tempo. Generally
       strong. 3 verses. Acc: 3 GPS

9127. Oh, what a beautiful city!   All Voices
       f3-g4 f3-f4 Animated in moderate tempo. Joyous and very rhythmic.
       Issued in two keys. Setting by Edward Boatner. Acc: 3 (S)GS.
       MAA

9128. Over Jordan   All Voices
       b2-d4 e3-b3 A Negro version of a white spiritual: A poor wayfar-
       ing stranger. Sustained in moderate slow tempo. Acc: 3 WFF

9129. Peter, go ring-a them bells   All Voices
       c3-f4 f3-d4 Animated in lively tempo. Generally on MF level. 2
       verses. Acc: 3 ANS

9130. Peter on the sea, sea, sea   All Voices
       d3-c4 f3-c4 Animated in very lively tempo. Narrative. Generally
       on MF level. 4 verses. Acc: 3 ANS

9131. Po' mo'ner got a home at last   All Voices
       eb3-ab4 f3-ab4 Sustained in slow tempo. Has climactic passages.
       May be transposed for lower voices. Setting by Hall Johnson. Acc:
       3 (S)GS

9132. Ride on, Jesus!   All Voices
       c3-f4 a3-f4 Animated in march tempo. Starts and ends with re-
       frain. 3 verses. Acc: 3 TNS

9133. Roll Jordan, roll   All Voices
       d3-d4 d3-d4 Animated in lively tempo. Descending ending line.
       Acc: 3 ANS, MAA

9134. Scandalize my name   All Voices
       e3-e4 a3-c#4 Animated in moderate tempo. 3 verses. Acc: 3
       TNS

9135. Sometimes I feel like a motherless child   All Voices
       c3-f4 f3-c4 Sustained in slow tempo. Intense and subdued. 3
       verses. Acc: 3 ANS, NSB

9136. Stand still, Jordan   All Voices
       e3-e4 e3-d4 Sustained in slow tempo. Requires some flexibility.
       2 verses. Acc: 3 TNS, NSB

9137. Standing in the need of prayer   All Voices
       bb3-g4 bb3-d4 Sustained in moderate tempo. 3 verses. Acc: 3
       TNS

9138. Steal away to Jesus   All Voices
       bb2-c4 eb3-c4 Sustained in moderate slow tempo. Has some cli-
       mactic passages. Very gentle beginning. Acc: 3 ANS

9139. Swing low, sweet chariot!   All Voices
       e3-f#4 a3-e4 Sustained in moderate tempo. Generally subdued.
       Acc: 3 TNS

9140. Talk about a child that do love Jesus   All Voices
       g3-g4 g3-g4 Animated in moderate lively tempo. Rhythmic. Set-
       ting by William L. Dawson. Acc: 3 (S)FS

9141. There is a balm in Gilead   All Voices
       bb3-f4 bb3-f4 Sustained in moderate slow tempo. Tranquil, 2
       verses. Acc: 2 TNS

9142. There's no hiding place down there   All Voices
       g3-e4 g3-d4 Animated in moderate tempo. Energetic. 3 verses.
       Acc: 3 GPS

9143. They led my Lord away   All Voices
       c#3(g2)-c#4 e3-c#4 Other title: Passion spiritual. Sustained in
       moderate slow tempo. Intense, generally on MF level. Has climac-
       tic passages. May be transposed for high voices. Setting by Elmo
       Dorsey. Acc: 3 (S)GS

9144. This is the healing water   All Voices
c3-f♯4   d3-b♭3   Animated in moderate tempo.   3 verses and refrain.
Acc: 3 TNS

9145. Wade in the water   All Voices
b2-e4   e3-b3   Sustained in moderate tempo.   An elaborate setting.
2 verses. Setting by Samuel Coleridge-Taylor. Acc: 4 FSM, NSB

9146. Weeping Mary   All Voices
Text: Adapted from John 22:11.   f3-f4   f3-c4   Sustained in moderate
tempo. Starts gently. Generally on MF level. Requires simplicity.
Acc: 3 NSB

9147. Were you there?   All Voices
d3-g4   g3-e4   Sustained in moderate slow tempo.   Generally subdued.
4 verses. Acc: 3 TNS, NSB

9148. When I lay my burden down   All Voices
f3-f4   g3-d4   Animated in moderate lively tempo.   Exultant.   7
verses. Acc: 3 TNS

9149. When the saints come marching in   All Voices
f3-d4   f3-c4   Animated in moderate tempo.   Generally strong, rhythmic.   3 verses and refrain.   Acc: 3 GPS

9150. Witness   All Voices
f3-d4   f3-d4   Animated in moderate tempo.   Has some climactic passages. Acc: 3 GPS

2. BRITISH ISLES

Bibliography for the British Isles

(England, Scotland, Hebrides, Ireland, Wales)

AEI   Folk Songs American-English-Irish. Arranged by John Edmunds. High, low. Recital arrangements. New York: R. D. Row Music Co.

CFS   Seven Cheshire Folk-Songs. Collected by Dorothy Dearnley. Arranged by Freda Brislee. London: Oxford University Press.

FAB   Folksong Arrangements. Vol. 3 & Vol. 5: British Isles. Arranged by Benjamin Britten. High, Medium. London: Boosey & Hawkes.

FSB   Folk Songs of the British Isles. Vol. I, Medium Voices. Edited by Benjamin Britten. London: Boosey & Hawkes.

NNB   The New National Song Book. Edited by Charles Villiers Stanford and Geoffrey Shaw. Simplified settings for schools. London: Boosey & Hawkes.

OHF   One Hundred English Folksongs. Edited by Cecil J. Sharp. Medium voice. Bryn Mawr: Oliver Ditson, c/o Theodore Presser.

SBI   Songs of the British Isles. Arranged by Healy Willan. Boston: Boston Music Co. (A collection of both art and folk songs.)

SCF   A Selection of Collected Folk-Songs. Vol. 1. Arranged by Cecil J. Sharp and Ralph Vaughan Williams. Thirty-six songs with piano accompaniment. London: Novello & Co.

SFN   Six Folk Songs from Norfolk. Collected and arranged by Ernest J. Moeran. London: Augener Ltd.

2a. ENGLAND

See Bibliography for the British Isles.

9151. Barbara Allen   All Voices
f3-f4 f3-f4 Sustained in moderate slow tempo. Narrative. Acc: 3 SBI, SLS, NNB

9152. The basket of eggs   All Voices
c3-f4 f3-d4 Animated in moderate lively tempo. Requires some fluent enunciation. Narrative, 6 verses. Setting by Ralph Vaughan Williams. Acc: 3 FSM

9153. Bobbin' around   Women

c3-f4 f3-c4 Animated in very lively tempo. Requires fluent enunciation. Joyous. 3 verses. Acc: 3 CFS

9154. The brisk young widow   All Voices
d3-f♯4 f♯3-d4 Animated in brisk tempo. Requires some fluent enunciation. Narrative, 5 verses. Acc: 3 FAB-5

9155. Cheshire Mayday carol   All Voices
c3-d4 d3-c4 Animated in quite lively tempo. Joyous and bright. 2 verses. Acc: 3 CFS

9156. Come you not from Newcastle?   Women
From Hullah's Song Book. b2-e4(M) d3-d4 Animated in lively tempo. Generally subdued. Acc: 3 FAB-3

9157. The country girl's farewell   Women
Anon. 18th century. d3-e4 f3-eb4 Animated in moderate lively tempo. Generally strong. Acc: 3-4 (S)OX

9158. The crystal spring   All Voices
c3-f4 f3-d4 Gently animated in moderate lively tempo. Narrative, 4 verses. Setting by Cecil Sharp. Acc: 3 SCF-1

9159. The cuckoo   All Voices
d3-e4 g3-d4 Animated in lively tempo. Bright, requires some flexibility. 5 verses. Acc: 3 CFS

9160. Down by the riverside   All Voices
d3-e4 g3-d4 Sustained in moderate tempo. Narrative, 3 verses. Setting by Ralph Vaughan Williams. Acc: 3 SCF-1, SFN

9161. Early one morning   All Voices
c3-f4 f3-c4 Animated in moderate lively tempo. Requires simplicity. Narrative. Acc: 3 SBI, FAB-5

9162. The false knight   All Voices
e3-b3 e3-b3 Sustained in slow tempo. A conversation between two characters. Acc: 3 CFS

9163. A farmer's son so sweet   All Voices
Region: Somerset. d3-e4 g3-d4 Sustained in moderate tempo. Narrative, 7 verses. Setting by Cecil Sharp. Acc: 3 SCF-1

9164. The female highway man   All Voices
e3-e4 e3-c♯4 Sustained in moderate slow tempo. Has humor. Narrative, 6 verses. Setting by Ralph Vaughan Williams. Acc: 3 SCF-1

9165. The foggy, foggy dew   Men
Region: Suffolk. d3-d4(M) d3-b3 Sustained in moderate tempo. Narrative. Acc: 3 FAB-3

9166. Ae fond kiss   All Voices
bb2-eb4 eb3-c4 Sustained in slow tempo. 4 verses. Acc: 3 SBI

9167. Fortune, my foe   All Voices
Text: William Chappell. f♯3-f♯4 g3-d4 Best for men. Sustained

in moderate tempo.   2 verses.   Setting by Jan Pieterszoon Sweelinck.
Acc: 3-4   FSM

9168.   Go from my window   All Voices
        Text: William Chappell.   d3-c4   g3-b3 Sustained in moderate tempo.
        4 verses and refrain.   Setting by Thomas Morley.   Acc: 3-4   FSM

9169.   Golden slumbers   All Voices
        Other title: May fair.   c3-db4   eb3-c4 Sustained in moderate tem-
        po.   A lullaby; subdued.   Acc: 3 NNB

9170.   Greensleeves   Men
        e3-g4 a3-e4 Sustained in moderate slow tempo.   Issued in two keys.
        Setting by Ralph Vaughan Williams.   The tune is used in his opera,
        SIR JOHN IN LOVE.   Acc: 3 (S)OX

9171.   Harvest home   Men
        c3-f4 f3-c4 Animated in lively tempo.   4 verses.   Setting by Henry
        Purcell, and used in his opera, KING ARTHUR (Act V, Scene 2).
        Acc: 3 FSM

9172.   Heave away, my Johnny   Men
        c#3-e4 e3-c#4 A sea chanty.   Animated in moderate lively tempo.
        6 verses and chorus.   Setting by Cecil Sharp.   Acc: 3 SCF-1

9173.   How should I your true love know?   All Voices
        d3-d4 g3-c4 Sustained in slow tempo.   Acc: 3 SBI, SLS

9174.   I will give my love an apple   Men
        c3-e4 e3-c4 Sustained in moderate slow tempo.   Gentle, 2 verses.
        Setting by Ralph Vaughan Williams.   Acc: 2 SCF-1

9175.   If the heart of a man   All Voices
        a2-e4 e3-c4 Animated in moderate lively tempo.   Best for men.
        May be transposed for high voices.   Acc: 3 SBI

9176.   I'm seventeen come Sunday   Men
        Region: Somerset.   d3-e4 f#3-d4 Animated in lively tempo.   Spir-
        ited.   7 verses.   Setting by Cecil Sharp.   Acc: 3 SCF-1

9177.   King Herod and the cock   All Voices
        Region: Worcestershire.   d3-d4 g3-d4 Sustained in moderate tem-
        po.   Narrative, 4 verses.   Setting by Cecil Sharp.   Acc: 3 SCF-1

9178.   The lark in the morn   All Voices
        Region: Somerset.   d3-e4 d3-d4 Animated in moderate lively tem-
        po.   Graceful and bright.   Setting by Cecil Sharp.   Acc: 3 SCF-1

9179.   The lawyer   All Voices
        Arranged for voice and violin by Ralph Vaughan Williams; see "Two
        English Folk-Songs." c3-e4 e3-c4 Animated in lively tempo.   Has
        some characterization.   Violin: 3 (S)OX

9180.   The Lincolnshire poacher   All Voices
        e3-g4 e3-d4 Animated in lively tempo.   Marked "boisterously."
        Generally strong and marked.   Narrative.   Acc: 3 FAB-5

9181.   Little Sir William   All Voices

Region: Somerset.   d3-d4   d3-d4   Animated in moderate lively tempo.   5 verses.   Acc: 3 FSB-1

9182. Lonely waters   Men
Region: East Norfolk.   c3-d4   c3-d4   Sustained in moderate tempo.
Narrative.   Acc: 3 CFS

9183. The merry wooing of Robin and Joan   All Voices
Text: from "Wit Restored."   e3-e4   g3-d4   Generally sustained.   A
conversation between two characters.   10 verses.   Setting by William
Byrd.   Acc: 3 FSM

9184. The miller of Dee   Men
g3-g4   g3-g4   Animated in moderate lively tempo.   3 verses.   Setting by Ludwig van Beethoven.   In FAB, three steps lower.   Acc:
3-4 FSM, FAB-3

9185. My boy Billy   All Voices
d3-e4   d3-e4   Animated in moderate lively tempo.   Has characterization.   Setting by Ralph Vaughan Williams.   Acc: 3 SCF-1

9186. My gentle harp   All Voices
Text: Thomas Moore.   bb2-eb4   eb3-c4   Sustained in slow tempo.
Gentle, subdued, and lyric.   4 verses.   Setting by Geoffrey Shaw.
Acc: 3 NNB

9187. Near Woodstock town   All Voices
c3-e4   e3-d4   Sustained in moderate tempo.   6 verses.   Acc: 3
SBI

9188. O no, John!   All Voices
d3-d4   g3-d4   Animated in moderate lively tempo.   Narrative, has
humor, 7 verses.   Setting by Cecil Sharp.   Acc: 3 ART-1

9189. O waly, waly   All Voices
Region: Somerset.   d3-d4(M)   d3-c4   Best for men.   Animated in
moderate lively tempo.   The OX setting is by Howard Boatwright.
Acc: 3 FAB-3, (S)OX

9190. Oliver Cromwell   All Voices
c3-c4   c3-c4   Animated in very lively tempo.   A nursery rhyme.
Acc: 3 FSB-1

9191. Praise we the Lord   All Voices
Text: Steuart Wilson.   f3-f4   f3-f4   Animated in lively tempo.
Strong, exultant, and in 3 verses.   Acc: 3 AEI

9192. Salisbury Plain   All Voices
c3-d4   g3-c4   Sustained in moderate tempo.   Narrative, 6 verses.
Setting by Ralph Vaughan Williams.   Acc: 2 FSM

9193. Sally in our alley   Men
d3-g4   a3-d4   Gently animated in moderate slow tempo.   7 verses.
Setting by Ludwig van Beethoven.   Acc: 3 FSM, FAB-5

9194. Searching for lambs   Men
Setting by Ralph Vaughan Williams for voice and violin in "Two English Folk-Songs."   e3-e4   g3-d4   Sustained in moderate tempo.
Violin: 3 (S)OX

9195. The shooting of his dear   All Voices
d3-e4 e3-d4 Sustained in moderate slow tempo. Narrative. Acc:
3 CFS

9196. Sing ovy, sing ivy   Men
a2-d4 d3-c4 Animated in moderate lively tempo. Narrative, 9
verses. Acc: 3 WFF

9197. Spanish ladies   Men
Region: Somerset. d3-e4 e3-d4 A sea chanty. Animated in mod-
erate lively tempo. 5 verses. Setting by Cecil Sharp. Acc: 3
SCF-1

9198. The spring's acoming   All Voices
d3-e4 f#3-c#4 Animated in moderate lively tempo. Bright and
joyous. Acc: 3 WFF

9199. Sweet Polly Oliver   All Voices
b2-e4(M) d3-d4 Animated in moderate lively tempo. Narrative, 5
verses. Acc: 3 FAB-3

9200. The three ravens   All Voices
d3-f4 g3-d4 Animated in moderate tempo. Narrative, 2 verses.
Requires some fluent enunciation. Acc: 3 SBI

9201. To all you ladies   Men
d3-d4 f3-d4 Animated in very fast tempo. Requires fluent enunciation. Bright, joyous, and outgoing. Acc: 3-4 SBI

9202. What Child is this   All Voices
Text: William C. Dix. Melody: Greensleeves. c3-eb4 f3-eb4
Has climactic passages. Sustained in moderate tempo. Setting by
Ernst Victor Wolff. Acc: 3 (S)GS

9203. When the bright god of day   All Voices
d3-f4 g3-d4 Animated in moderate lively tempo. Narrative, 5
verses. Acc: 3 SBI

9204. William Taylor   All Voices
d3-d4 g3-d4 Animated in very lively tempo. Has humor. Narrative, 9 verses. Setting by Cecil Sharp. Acc: 3 SCF-1

9205. Would God I were a tender apple blossom   All Voices
Text: Katharine Tynan Hinkson. Original tune: O Danny boy. a2-
e4 c3-c4 Sustained in slow tempo. Acc: 3 56S

9206. Yarmouth fair   Men
Region: Norfolk. d3-g4 g3-g4 Animated in lively tempo. Bright
and joyful. Issued in three keys. Setting by Peter Warlock. Acc:
3 (S)OX

2b. SCOTLAND

FSR Four Scottish Songs. Settings by Ottorino Respighi. English texts,
with German versions. Vienna: Universal Edition.

TSO   The Scottish Orpheus.   Three volumes.   Arranged by J. Michael
         Diack.   London: Paterson's Publications, Ltd.

Note: In addition, see Bibliography for the British Isles, page 1187.

9207.   Afton water   All Voices
         Text: Robert Burns.   This is the melody for which Burns wrote his
         poem "Flow gently, sweet Afton."   bb2-eb4   eb3-c4   Sustained in
         moderate slow tempo.   4 verses.   Acc: 3 TSO-2

9208.   Aye waukin', O!   All Voices
         eb3-f4 g3-eb4 Sustained in slow tempo.   3 verses and refrain.
         Acc: 3 TSO-1

9209.   Baloo, baloo   Women
         Text: Richard Gall.   g3-e4 g3-c4 Sustained in moderate slow tem-
         po.   A lullaby; subdued.   3 verses and refrain.   Acc: 3 TSO-2

9210.   Barbara Ellen   All Voices
         e3-e4 e3-e4 Animated in moderate lively tempo.   Narrative.   Acc:
         3 OHF

9211.   The Bonny Earl o' Moray   All Voices
         e3-e4 e3-e4 Sustained in slow tempo.   Grave and generally subdued.
         2 verses and refrain.   Acc: 3 FSB-1

9212.   Bonny Laddie, highland laddie   All Voices
         Text: James Hogg.   c3-f4 f3-c4 Animated in very fast tempo.   4
         verses.   Setting by Ludwig van Beethoven.   Acc: 3-4 FSM

9213.   Ca' the yowes   All Voices
         Text: Robert Burns.   d3-f#4 f#3-d4 Sustained in moderate tempo.
         Marked "broadly."   Requires some fine P to PPP.   3 verses.   Acc:
         3 FAB-5

9214.   Cockoo of the grove   All Voices
         b2-e4 e3-c4 Animated in moderate lively tempo.   Requires some
         fluent enunciation.   2 verses.   Acc: 3 WFF

9215.   Come fill, fill, my good fellow   All Voices
         Text: William Smyth.   Other titles: "Three gude fellows" and "The
         town drummer."   c3-g4 f3-d4 Animated in fast tempo.   3 verses
         and refrain.   Setting by Ludwig van Beethoven.   Acc: 3-4 FSM

9216.   For the sake o' somebody   All Voices
         Text: Robert Burns.   d3-f#4 g3-d4 Animated in moderate tempo.
         2 verses.   Setting by Johann Nepomuk Hummel, 1778-1835.   Acc: 3
         FSM

9217.   Green grow the rashes, O   All Voices
         Text: Robert Burns.   bb2-e4 f#3-b3 Best for men.   Animated in
         lively tempo.   5 verses and refrain.   Setting by Joseph Haydn.   Acc:
         3 FSM

9218.   Hey tutti, taiti   Tenor
         Text: Robert Burns.   g3-g4 g3-e4 Animated in lively tempo.   Ener-
         getic.   Responsorial: tenor and chorus.   Setting by Max Bruch.
         Acc: 3-4 FSM

9219. Hieland laddie   All Voices
c3-f4   f3-c4   Animated in march tempo.   Requires some fluent enunciation. Acc: 3 TSO-2

9220. I lo'e ne'er a laddie but ane   All Voices
e♭3-e♭4   e♭3-d4   Gently animated in moderate slow tempo.   Graceful, 2 verses. Setting by Joseph Haydn. Acc: 3 SCS-4

9221. Jockey and Jenny   All Voices
Text: Thomas D'Urfey.   g3-c5   g3-e4   Animated in lively tempo.
A conversation between two characters.   May be transposed to lower
keys. Setting by Henry Purcell. Acc: 3 FSM

9222. John Anderson my jo   Women
d3-f4   g3-c4   Sustained in moderate slow tempo.   2 verses.   Setting
by Carl Maria von Weber. Acc: 3 FSM

9223. Kind Robin lo'es me   Women
c3-f4   f3-c4   Sustained in moderate slow tempo.   3 verses. Acc:
3 TSO-2

9224. The lea rig   All Voices
b♭2-e4   e♭3-c4   Animated in moderate lively tempo.   5 verses.
Acc: 3 WFF

9225. Loch Lomond   All Voices
d3-e4(g4)   g3-e4   Sustained in moderate tempo.   Slightly climactic
ending, 3 verses. Setting by Carl Deis. Acc: 3 (S)GS

9226. Lord Gregory   All Voices
Other text: Oh, Mirk, Mirk is this midnight hour (Robert Burns).
d3-f4   g3-d4   Sustained in moderate slow tempo.   4 verses.   Setting
by Max Bruch. 4 verses. Acc: 3 FSM

9227. Maggie Lauder   All Voices
b2-f♯4   f♯3-d4   Animated in lively tempo.   Requires fluent enunciation. 5 verses. Setting by Joseph Haydn. Acc: 3 FSM

9228. My faithful fair one   Men
Text is from the Gaelic, translated by Henry Whyte.   e♭3-f4   g3-e♭4
Gently animated in moderate tempo. 3 verses. Acc: 3 TSO-1

9229. My heart's in the highlands   All Voices
Text: Robert Burns.   c3-f4   f3-d4   Animated in moderate lively tempo. Spirited, with optional high ending. 3 verses. The FSR setting
by Ottorino Respighi. Acc: 3-4 TSO-3, FSR

9230. O bonnie was yon rosy brier   All Voices
Text: Robert Burns.   c3-e4   e3-c4   Sustained in moderate slow tempo. Graceful, 2 verses. Acc: 3 TSO-3

9231. O can ye sew cushions   All Voices
b♭2-e♭4   e♭3-c4   Gently animated in moderate tempo.   2 verses.
Acc: 3 FSB-1, TSO-1

9232. O gin my love were yon red rose   All Voices
d3-e4   e3-c4   Sustained in moderate slow tempo.   2 verses. Acc:
3 TSO-2

9233. O my love is like a red, red rose   Men
       Text: Robert Burns. b♭2-f4 b♭2-c4 Sustained in moderate tempo.
       See the art song by John Koch. Acc: 3 TSO-2

9234. O Nancy's hair is yellow like gowd   All Voices
       b♭2-e♭3 b♭2-c3 Animated in moderate march tempo. Acc: 3
       TSO-3

9235. Oh, had I a cave   All Voices
       Text: Robert Burns. Also sung to the tune "Robin Adair" by Robert
       Burns. g3-g4 a3-c4 Sustained in moderate tempo. 2 verses. Set-
       ting by Joseph Haydn. Acc: 2-3 FSM

9236. On a bank of flowers   All Voices
       Text: Robert Burns. b2-f♯4 d3-d4 Sustained in moderate lively
       tempo. Narrative, 4 verses. Acc: 3 WFF

9237. Peggy, I must love thee   Men
       Other title: Weel my Willie lo'es me. d3-g4 g3-c4 Animated in
       moderate tempo. 4 verses. Setting by Henry Purcell. Acc: 3
       FSM

9238. Pibroch of Donvil Dhu   Men
       Text: Walter Scott. f3-f4 a3-c4 Animated in martial rhythm.
       Energetic. 5 verses. Setting by Johan Nepomuk Hummel. Acc: 3
       FSM

9239. The piper of Dundee   All Voices
       e3-f4 e3-e4 Animated in lively tempo. Narrative. Generally strong
       and bright. Has intervalic skips of a ninth. Setting by Ottorino
       Respighi. Acc: 4 FSR

9240. Saw ye my father   Women
       e♭3-f4 g3-c4 Sustained in moderate slow tempo. 7 verses. Setting
       by Max Bruch. Acc: 3 FSM

9241. There was a lad   All Voices
       Text: Robert Burns. c3-e4 c3-c4 Animated in moderate lively
       tempo. Narrative, 5 verses and refrain. Acc: 3 TSO-1

9242. There's none to soothe   All Voices
       Text: from Hullah's Song Book. b2-d4 d3-b3 Sustained in slow
       tempo. 2 short verses. Acc: 2 FAB-3

9243. There's none to soothe my soul to rest   All Voices
       b♭2-d4 b♭2-c4 Sustained in slow tempo. Subdued and sad. Acc:
       3 TSO-3

9244. The trees that grow so high   Women
       b♭2-d4 b♭2-d4 Sustained in moderate tempo. In this arrangement,
       the first lines are unaccompanied. Narrative. Acc: 2-3 FSB-1

9245. True-hearted was he the sad swain   All Voices
       Text: Robert Burns. b2-f4 e3-d4 Animated in moderate lively tem-
       po. Graceful, 2 verses. Setting by Carl Maria von Weber. Acc: 3
       FSM

9246. 'Twas within a furlong of Edingborough town   All Voices

Text: Thomas D'Urfey. d3-g4 a3-e4 Animated in moderate tempo. 3 verses. Setting by Henry Purcell. Acc: 3 FSM

9247. Up in the morning early   All Voices
Text: Robert Burns. Other title: The Scotchman outwitted. d3-g4 g3-d4 Animated in lively tempo. 4 verses. Setting by Joseph Haydn. Acc: 3 FSM

9248. When the kye come hame   All Voices
db3-f4 f3-eb4 Best for men. Generally sustained in moderate slow tempo. Generally on MF level. Setting by Ottorino Respighi. The spelling of "hame" is correct. Acc: 3-4 FSR

9249. Where ha'e ye been a' the day?   All Voices
Text: Hector MacNeill. c3-f4 f3-e4 Animated in moderate lively tempo. 7 verses. Setting by Carl Maria von Weber. Acc: 3 FSM

9250. Within a mile of Edinburgh town   All Voices
b2-g4 d3-e4 Animated in moderate tempo. Narrative, with some climactic passages. Has a wide range for a folk song. Setting by Ottorino Respighi. Acc: 3-4 FSR

2c. HEBRIDES

Bibliography

SOH Songs of the Hebrides. Three volumes, new edition. Collected, arranged, and translated by Marjory Kennedy-Fraser and Kenneth Macleod. Gaelic texts and English versions. London: Boosey & Co.

TSH Twelve Songs from the Hebrides. Gaelic and English texts. Settings by Marjory Kennedy-Fraser and Kenneth Macleod. London: Paterson's Publications Ltd.

TSS Twelve Selected Songs of the Hebrides. Vol. 3. Collected, arranged, and translated by Marjory Kennedy-Fraser and Kenneth Macleod. London: Boosey & Hawkes.

9251. A Barra love lilt   All Voices
bb2-eb4 eb3-eb4 Sustained vocal part in fast tempo. Graceful 3/4. Joyous. Acc: 3 SOH-3

9252. The Christ-Child's lullaby   All Voices
g2-g4 c3-f4 Sustained in gentle, slow 3/4. Second verse ending with a low "halleluia" section. Acc: 2 SOH-1

9253. The cockle gatherer   All Voices
eb3-eb4 eb3-eb4 Animated in very fast tempo. Requires fluent enunciation. Acc: 3 SOH-3

9254. Deirdre's farewell to Scotland   All Voices
g3-e4 g3-d4 Text: from traditional sources and Glenmasen manuscript, 1238. Gaelic title: Deirdre a Fagail na h-Albann. Sustained

in moderate tempo. Has climactic passages. Acc: 3 TSH

9255. An Eriskay lullaby   All Voices
b2-e4 e3-d4 Sustained in moderate tempo. Generally gentle, graceful, subdued. Acc: 3 SOH-1

9256. The fairy's love song   All Voices
c3-d4 d3-d4 Sustained in moderate tempo. Melody has octave intervalic skips. Descending ending. Acc: 3 SOH-1

9257. Fionn's keening for his grandson, Oscar   Men
Gaelic title: Laoidh Oscair. eb3-eb4 g3-c4 Sustained in moderate
tempo. Has climactic passages. Acc: 3 TSH

9258. The harper   All Voices
eb3-eb4 g3-c4 Sustained in moderate slow tempo. Subdued ending.
Acc: 3 TSS-3, SOH-3

9259. Heart o' fire-love   All Voices
eb3-f4(ab4) eb3-eb4 Sustained vocal part in moderate fast tempo.
Very agitated accompaniment, mostly on treble range. Climactic
ending. Acc: 4 SOH-2

9260. A Hebridean seafaring song   All Voices
d3-d4 f3-d4 Best for men. Animated in moderate tempo. Acc: 3
SOH-1

9261. Isle of my heart   All Voices
c3-ab4 eb3-eb4 Animated in moderate tempo. Requires fine high
P. Sustained high ending. Acc: 3-4 SOH-2

9262. Kirsteen   All Voices
c3-eb4 eb3-c4 Sustained in moderate slow tempo. Short and gentle.
Acc: 3 TSS-3, SOH-3

9263. Land of heart's desire   All Voices
bb2-eb3 eb3-eb4 Sustained in moderate lively tempo. Calm, with
arpeggiated accompaniment. Acc: 3 SOH-2

9264. The peat-fire flame   All Voices
Text: Kenneth Macleod. bb2-eb4 c3-c4 Animated in moderate tempo. Requires some fluent enunciation. Acc: 3 SOH-3

9265. The return from the fairy hill   All Voices
c3-eb4 eb3-bb3 Animated in moderate tempo. Short. Uses mostly
the cry "Ho ro lail o." Acc: 3 TSS-3, SOH-3

9266. The road to the isles   All Voices
Texts: Kenneth Macleod. d3-e4 f#3-e4 Animated in march tempo.
Has dotted rhythms. 3 verses and refrain. Acc: 3 SOH-2

9267. Sail hoisting chanty   Men
Gaelic title: Taobh thall a chuilinn. d3-d4 d3-d4 Animated in moderate lively tempo. Bold and outgoing. 3 verses. Acc: 3 TSH

9268. Sea feast   Men
Region: Barra. Gaelic texts attributed to Mary MacLeod, 16th-17th
century: Cuirm-Mhara. c3-f4 f3-eb4 Sustained in moderate tempo.
In strict rhythm. Acc: 3 TSH

9269. Sea sorrow   All Voices
eb3-c4 eb3-c4 Sustained in moderate tempo. Generally on MF
level. Acc: 3 SOH-1

9270. Sea-longing   All Voices
d3-e4 d3-d4 Sustained in slow tempo. In gentle graceful 3/4 meter.
Acc: 3 SOH-2

9271. Sleeps the noon in the deep blue sky   All Voices
d3-d4 e3-b3 Sustained in moderate slow tempo. Tranquil, requires
simplicity. 3 verses. Acc: 2 TSS-3, SOH-3

9272. To Iona   All Voices
Region: Skye. c3-f4 f3-c4 A processional. Animated in moderate
tempo. 3 verses. Acc: 2 TSH

9273. To people who have gardens   All Voices
Text: Agnes Mure Mackenzie. f3-c4 f3-c4 Best for men. Animated in lively tempo. Joyous. Requires fluent enunciation. Acc:
3 SOH-3

9274. To the Lord of the Isles   All Voices
f3-f4 f3-c4 Sustained in moderate tempo. Majestic. Has strong
bold passages. Acc: 3 SOH-2

9275. A wandering shade   All Voices
db3-eb4 eb3-db4 Sustained in slow tempo. Very subdued and delicate. Acc: 3 SOH-3

9276. The wind on the moor   All Voices
d3-b3 d3-a3 Sustained in slow, quasi-recitative style. Narrow
range. Acc: 3 TSS-3, SOH-3

9277. Ye highlands and ye lowlands   All Voices
Text: Kenneth Macleod. d3-f4 f3-d4 Sustained in moderate tempo.
Majestic, Nationalistic text. Acc: 3 SOH-2

2d. IRELAND

Bibliography

AEI   Folk Songs American-English-Irish. High, low. Arranged by John
       Edmunds. Recital arrangements. New York: R. D. Row Music
       Co.

FAB-4 Moore's Irish Melodies. Folksong Arrangements, Vol. 4. Settings
       by Benjamin Britten. London: Boosey & Hawkes.

ICS   Irish Country Songs. Two volumes. Collected and edited by Her-
       bert Hughes. London: Boosey & Co.

IFF   Irish Folksongs. Five songs. Arranged by Howard Ferguson.
       Medium keys. London: Boosey & Co. , Ltd.

MFE   Music for Everyone. Folk Songs of Ireland, No. 9 of a series.

Over 100 songs.   New York: Remick Music Corp.

OIM   Old Irish Melodies.   Vol. 1.   Edited by Herbert Hughes.   Twelve
           songs from the Bunting MS.   Medium high keys.   London: Boosey
           & Hawkes.

SOI   Songs of Old Ireland.   Fifty songs.   Arranged by C. Villiers Stan-
           ford.   London: Boosey & Hawkes.

Note: In addition, see Bibliography for the British Isles, page 1187.

———————————

9278.   Ancient lullaby   Women
        eb3-c4   eb3-bb3 Sustained in moderate slow tempo.   Gentle and
        subdued.   Very subdued ending.   Acc: 3 SOI

9279.   The apron of flowers   Women
        c3-db4   db3-db4 Sustained in slow tempo.   Generally on MF level.
        Acc: 3 IFF

9280.   As I went a-walking one morning in Spring   Men
        d3-e4   g3-d4 Sustained in moderate tempo.   Narrative, 4 verses.
        Acc: 3 MFE

9281.   At the mid hour of night   All Voices
        Irish title: Molly, my dear.   e3-g4   g3-e4 Sustained in very slow
        tempo.   Generally subdued, with movement.   Subdued ending.   May
        be transposed for lower voices.   Acc: 4 Setting by Benjamin Britten.
        FAB-4

9282.   Avenging and bright   High Voices
        Irish title: Crooghan a venee.   d3-f#4   f#3-d4 Animated in very
        fast tempo.   Generally strong; marked "fierce."   Requires fluent
        enunciation.   4 verses.   Setting by Benjamin Britten.   Acc: 3-4
        FAB-4

9283.   Barbey Ross   Women
        Belfast street song.   eb3-f4   f3-f4 Animated in fast tempo.   Re-
        quires fluent enunciation.   2 verses.   Acc: 3-4 AEI

9284.   Believe me if all those endearing young charms   All Voices
        Text: Thomas Moore.   eb3-eb4   eb3-eb4 Sustained in moderate
        slow tempo.   2 verses.   Acc: 3 MFE

9285.   Beltane night   All Voices
        Text: after the Irish, by Harold Boulton.   d3-g4   d3-g4 Gently ani-
        mated in moderate tempo.   Delicate and light.   Acc: 3 OIM-1

9286.   The Boreens of Derry   All Voices
        Text: after the Irish, by Harold Boulton.   bb2-eb3   bb2-eb3 Sus-
        tained in moderate tempo.   Gentle.   Acc: 3 OIM-1

9287.   Calen-O   All Voices
        Text: Translated from the Gaelic by Douglas Hyle.   c3-c4   f3-c4
        Gently animated in moderate tempo.   Generally on MF level.   Acc:
        3 IFF

9288.   Cockles and mussels   All Voices g3-g4   g3-g4   Animated vocal part in moderate tempo. Requires fluent enunciation. Setting by R. D. Row. Acc: 3 SVR-1

9289. Come over and dance with me, Eily   All Voices
Text: from the Irish, by Harold Boulton. d3-d4   d3-d4   Animated in fast tempo. Rhythmic in 6/8. Acc: 3 OIM-1

9290. Come rest in this bosom   All Voices
c#3-e4   e3-c#4   Sustained in moderate tempo. 3 verses. Acc: 3 WFF

9291. Danny boy   All Voices
Text: Fred. E. Weatherly. a2-e3(L)   c3-c4   Sustained in moderate slow tempo. Generally subdued. Acc: 3 (S)B-H

9292. Dear harp of my country   All Voices
Irish title: Kate Tyrrel. c3-g4   f3-f4   Gently animated in slow tempo. Generally on MF level. May be transposed. Setting by Benjamin Britten. Acc: 3 FAB-4

9293. Dermot and Shelah   All Voices
Text: T. Toms. d3-e4   f#3-d4   Animated in moderate lively tempo. Arranged for string trio by Beethoven. This vocal setting is by Beethoven. 3 verses. Acc: 3-4 SCS-4

9294. Eileen Aroon   All Voices
Text: Gerald Griffin. f3-f4   f3-d4   Sustained in moderate slow tempo. 7 verses. Setting by Will Earhart. Acc: 3 POS-2

9295. The forlorn queen   All Voices
Text: from the Irish, by Harold Boulton. d#3-e4   d#3-e4   Sustained in slow tempo. Requires some flexibility. 2 verses. Acc: 3 OIM-1

9296. Grania's lament for Dermot   All Voices
Text: from the Irish, by Harold Boulton. a2-f#4   a2-f#4   Sustained in moderate tempo. Low ending. Acc: 3 OIM-1

9297. The harp that once through Tara's halls   All Voices
Text: Thomas Moore. c3-e4   e3-c4   Sustained in moderate slow tempo. 2 verses. Acc: 3 MFE

9298. He promised me at parting   Women
Air: Killeary. Text: William Smyth. d3-g4   f3-d4   Gently animated in moderate tempo. 3 verses and refrain. Setting by Ludwig van Beethoven, arranged by Gerald Moore. Acc: 3 (S)OX (Two Irish Songs)

9299. Her brow is like the lily   Men
d3-eb4   d3-d4   Sustained in moderate tempo. Slightly climactic ending. 4 verses. Acc: 3 SOI

9300. How sweet the answer   All Voices
Irish title: The wren. f#3-f#4   f#3-d#4   Sustained in moderate tempo. Gracefully flowing. Generally subdued. Setting by Benjamin Britten. Acc: 3 FAB-4

9301. I know my love   Women

d3-g4   f3-d4   Animated in fast tempo.   Requires some fluent enunciation.   2 verses.   Acc: 3 AEI

9302. I'm from over the mountain   Men
eb3-eb4   eb3-c4   Animated in lively tempo.   Requires fluent enunciation.   Narrative.   Acc: 3 IFF

9303. Irish girl   Men
b2-d4   d3-c4   Animated in moderate lively tempo.   Narrative, 5
verses.   Acc: 3 WFF

9304. Irish lullaby   All Voices
Other title: The angel's whisper.   c3-eb4   eb3-c4   Sustained in
moderate slow tempo.   Gentle, subdued, has 3 verses.   A song about
a lullaby, not the lullaby itself.   Acc: 3 SBI

9305. Johnny O'Reilly   All Voices
Text: from the Irish, by Harold Boulton.   a2-e4   a2-e4   Animated
in very fast tempo.   Requires fluent enunciation.   Acc: 3 OIM-1

9306. Kathleen O' More   Men
Text: George Nugent Reynolds.   f3-eb4   f3-d4   Sustained in moderate slow tempo.   Descriptive text.   Acc: 3 ICS-2

9307. Kitty of Coleraine   Men
c#3-f#4   e3-e4   Animated in very rapid tempo.   Requires fluent
enunciation.   2 verses.   Edited by Frank LaForge.   Acc: 3 POS-3

9308. Kitty Traill   All Voices
Text: from the Irish, by Harold Boulton.   c3-f4   c3-f4   Animated in
lively tempo.   Graceful and rhythmic.   Acc: 3 OIM-1

9309. Lady, be tranquil   All Voices
Text: from the Irish.   d3-d4   d3-d4   Animated in lively tempo.
Graceful and light.   Acc: 3 OIM-1

9310. The lark in the clear air   Men
Poet: Samuel Ferguson.   db3-f4   eb3-eb4   Sustained in moderate
tempo.   Generally on MF level.   Very lyric.   Issued in two keys.
Setting by Phyllis Tate.   Acc: 3 (S)OX

9311. The last rose of summer   All Voices
Irish title: The groves of Blarney.   eb3-ab4   eb3-eb4   Sustained in
slow and free tempo.   Generally subdued and gentle.   A highly ornamented setting, requires some flexibility.   Setting by Benjamin Britten.   Acc: 3 FAB-4

9312. Lesbia hath a beaming eye   Men
Text: Thomas Moore.   f3-eb4   f3-eb4   Animated in moderate lively
tempo.   3 verses.   Acc: 3 MFE

9313. Lilliburlero   All Voices
f3-a4   g3-e4   Animated in lively tempo.   May be transposed for lower voices.   12 short verses.   One step lower in AEI.   Setting by
Henry Purcell.   Acc: 3 FSM, AEI

9314. Little boats   All Voices
Text: from the Irish, by Harold Boulton.   eb3-eb4   eb3-eb4   Sustained in moderate slow tempo.   Graceful lullaby.   Acc: 2 OIM-1

9315. The little red lark   All Voices
c3-f4 f3-f4 Animated in moderate lively tempo. Generally gentle
and graceful. One step higher in SVR (high). Acc: 3 SBI, SVR-2

9316. Loving dark maid   All Voices
Text: from the Irish, by Harold Boulton. b♭2-f4 b♭2-f4 Sustained
in moderate tempo. Requires some flexibility. Has some climactic
passages. Acc: 3 OIM-1

9317. The maid with the bonny brown hair   Men
d3-e4 f♯3-d4 Animated in moderate lively tempo. Narrative. Acc:
3 ICS-2

9318. The minstrel boy   Men
Irish title: The moreen. c♯3-f♯4 f♯3-f♯4 Animated in broad
march tempo. Has contrasts of strong and light passages. 2 verses.
Setting by Benjamin Britten. Acc: 3 FAB-4

9319. My grandfather died   Men
b♭2-d♭4 d♭3-d♭4 Animated in lively tempo. Requires fluent enunciation. Narrative text. Acc: 3 IFF

9320. My love's an arbutus   Men
Poet: Alfred Perceval Graves. e♭3-f4 e♭3-e♭4 Sustained in mod-
erate tempo. Has some climactic passages. Subdued low ending.
Acc: 3 ART-1

9321. O the sight entrancing   All Voices
Irish title: Planxty Sudley. b2-g4 e3-e4 Animated in fast tempo.
Brilliant, marked, and strong. Not for lighter voices. Setting by
Benjamin Britten. Acc: 3-4 FAB-4

9322. O would I were but that sweet linnet!   All Voices
Text: William Smyth. d3-g4 g3-d4 Gently animated in moderate
slow tempo. Graceful. Setting by Ludwig van Beethoven, arranged
by Gerald Moore. Acc: 3 (S)OX (Two Irish Songs)

9323. Oft in the stilly night   All Voices
e♭3-d♭4 e♭3-d♭4 Sustained in slow tempo. Generally very subdued.
Marked "dreamily. " Setting by Benjamin Britten. Acc: 3 FAB-4

9324. Oh! Where are the swifts and the swallows gone?   All Voices
Text: from the Irish, by Harold Boulton. f3-e♭4 f3-e♭4 Sustained
in moderate tempo. Gentle. Acc: 3-4 OIM-1

9325. Oh! Who my dear Dermot   All Voices
e3-f♯4 a3-d4 Sustained in moderate slow tempo. 4 verses. Setting
by Ludwig van Beethoven. Acc: 3 FSM

9326. An old Derry air   All Voices
Text: Will Ransom. a♭2-f4 e♭3-b♭3 Gently animated in moderate
tempo. 2 verses. Acc: 3 SBI

9327. On and on   Women
d3-d4 f♯3-d4 Sustained in moderate tempo. Generally gentle. 5
verses. Acc: 3 WFF

9328. The pulse of an Irishman   All Voices
Tune: St. Patrick's Day. c3-f4 f3-d4 Animated in very fast tempo.

1202 Solo Voice Repertoire

Requires fluent enunciation. 2 verses. Setting by Ludwig van
Beethoven. Acc: 3 FSM

9329. The rejected lover   Men
d3-eb4 eb3-c4 Animated in moderate tempo. 4 verses. Acc: 3
SOI

9330. Reynardine   Women
e3-f#4 a3-d4 Animated in moderate lively tempo. Legendary text.
Acc: 3 ICS-1

9331. Rich and rare   All Voices
Irish title: The summer is coming. d3-f#4 f#3-e4 Sustained in
moderate tempo. Starts very gently. Has climactic passages. Low
ending. Setting by Benjamin Britten. Acc: 3 FAB-4

9332. The rose of Kildare   All Voices
Text: Harold Boulton. db3(bb2)-gb4 db3(bb2)-gb4 Sustained in
moderate slow tempo. Very lyric. Acc: 3 OIM-1

9333. Sail on, sail on   All Voices
f3-f4 f3-d4 Best for men. Sustained in moderate tempo. Marked
"quietly rocking." Generally subdued. A sea chanty, 2 verses.
Other title: The humming of the ban. Setting by Benjamin Britten.
Acc: 3 FAB-4

9334. The Sally Gardens   Men
Text: William Butler Yeats. db3-eb4 db3-eb4 Sustained in moderate slow tempo. Narrative. Acc: 3 FSB-1

9335. She moved thro' the fair   Men
Text: Old ballad, edited by Padraic Colum. db3-eb4 eb3-eb4
Sustained in moderate tempo. Has some climactic passages. Narra-
tive. Acc: 3 ICS-1

9336. The snowy-breasted pearl   Men
f3-a4 f3-f4 Sustained in moderate slow tempo. Generally on MF
level. Issued in two keys. Setting by Phyllis Tate. Acc: 3 (S)OX

9337. The soldier   Men
Text: William Smyth. c3-f4 f3-d4 Other title: The minstrel boy.
Animated in moderate tempo. 3 verses. Setting by Ludwig van
Beethoven. Acc: 3 FSM

9338. Spinning-wheel song   Women
d3-d4 g3-d4 Animated in moderate lively tempo. Requires some
fluent enunciation. 2 verses. Acc: 3-4 SOI

9339. The swan   Men
First line: On the lonely banks of Bann. bb2-eb4 d3-d4 Sustained
in moderate slow tempo. Tranquil and gentle. Acc: 3 IFF

9340. 'Tis believed that this harp   All Voices
Text: Thomas Moore. d3-e4 e3-c4 Sustained in moderate tempo.
Narrative, 4 verses. Acc: 3 MFE

9341. 'Tis the last rose of summer   All Voices
Text: Thomas Moore. Tune: The groves of Blarney. eb3-eb4

e♭3-e♭4 Sustained in moderate slow tempo. Used in Flotow's opera,
MARTHA, Act II. 3 verses. The FSM setting is by Felix Mendels-
sohn. See the entry of the same song, "The last rose of summer."
Acc: 3 MFE, FSM

9342. When thro' life unblest we rove   All Voices
Text: Thomas Moore. c3-g4 e3-e4 Sustained in moderate tempo.
Acc: 3 ICS-1

9343. The willow tree   Women
c3-e♭4 e♭3-c4 Sustained in moderate slow tempo. Generally subdued, sad text. 3 verses. Acc: 3 SOI

2e. WALES

SWM Sixteen Welsh Melodies. Edited and arranged by J. Lloyd Williams
and Arthur Somervell. Original Welsh texts, with English versions
by Alfred Perceval Graves. Two volumes. London: Boosey &
Hawkes.

Note: In addition, see Bibliography for the British Isles, page 1187.

———————

9344. The ash grove   Men
b♭2-d4 d3-c4 Sustained in moderate tempo. Generally gentle and
subdued. Acc: 3 FSB-1

9345. Away to the oaken grove   All Voices
Text: Anne Hunter. d3-e4 g3-d4 Animated in very fast tempo.
Setting by Joseph Haydn. Acc: 3 FSM

9346. The bard's dream   All Voices
Text: Ceiriog. d3-d4 d3-d4 Sustained in slow tempo. Generally
subdued and narrative. Setting by Arthur Somervell. Acc: 3 SWM-
2

9347. The bells of Aberdovey   All Voices
Text: Ceiriog. d3-g4 g3-d4 Animated in moderate lively tempo.
Requires fluent enunciation. Acc: 3 SWM-1

9348. The blossom of the thorn   All Voices
c3-f4 f3-c4 Sustained in moderate slow tempo. Graceful. 3 verses.
Setting by Joseph Haydn. Acc: 3 SCS-4

9349. The blueing of the day   All Voices
e3-f4 f3-d4 Sustained in moderate tempo. Descending ending line.
Acc: 3 SWM-1

9350. The dove   Men
c♯3-e4 e3-c♯4 Gently animated in moderate slow tempo. Graceful.
Setting by Arthur Somervell. Acc: 3 SWM-2

9351. The dream   All Voices
Text: David ap Gwillim. e♭3-f4 f3-e4 Sustained in moderate slow

tempo. Generally gentle. Set to music by Ludwig van Beethoven, arranged for solo voice and piano by Gerald Moore. Acc: 3 (S)OX

9352. Farewell, Mari   Men
Text: Llew Tegid. e3-g4 g3-e4 Sustained in moderate slow tempo.
Acc: 3 SWM-1

9353. Gwendoleen's repose   All Voices
d3-f♯4 d3-d4 Best for women. Sustained in moderate tempo.
Acc: 3 SWM-1

9354. Hunting the hare   All Voices
c3-f♯4 f3-c4 Animated in moderate lively tempo. Setting by Joseph
Haydn. Acc: 3 FSM

9355. The live long night   All Voices
e3-f♯4 e3-c♯4 A lullaby. Sustained in moderate slow tempo. 3
verses. Setting by Joseph Haydn. Acc: 3 FSM

9356. The loom   All Voices
b♭2-e♭3 d3-d4 Sustained in moderate tempo. Subdued high ending.
Setting by Grace Williams. 3 verses. Acc: 3 (S)OX

9357. Lullaby   All Voices
Text: Robert Bryan. g3-g4 g3-d4 Best for women. Sustained in
moderate slow tempo. Gentle and subdued. 2 verses. Acc: 3
SWM-1

9358. Men of Harlech   Men
Text: Ceiriog. f3-g4 g3-f4 Animated in lively tempo. Spirited
and strong. Climactic ending. Acc: 3 SWM-1

9359. Merch megan   Men
Other title: Peggy's daughter. b♭2-f4 e♭3-e♭4 Animated in mod-
erate lively tempo. 3 verses. Setting by Ludwig van Beethoven.
Acc: 3 FSM

9360. O let the kind minstrel   All Voices
c3-e4 e3-e4 Animated in moderate lively tempo. Setting by Arthur
Somervell. Acc: 3-4 SWM-2

9361. The rising of the lark   All Voices
Text: Ceiriog. e3-e4 g3-e4 Animated in moderate tempo. Gen-
erally gentle and subdued. Setting by Arthur Somervell. Acc: 3-4
SWM-2

9362. Sir Watkyn's dream   All Voices
Text: Anne Hunter. c3-g4 g3-d4 Animated in moderate lively tem-
po. 4 verses. Tune: The ash grove. Setting by Joseph Haydn.
Acc: 3-4 FSM

9363. The song of the thrush   Men
Text: Ceiriog. b♭2-f4 e♭3-e♭4 Sustained in moderate tempo. Descending ending line. Setting by Arthur Somervell. Acc: 3 SWM-2

9364. Waken, lords and ladies gay   All Voices
Text: Walter Scott. d3-f♯4 a3-e4 Animated in lively tempo. Joyous. Setting by Ludwig van Beethoven. 4 verses. Acc: 3-4 FSM

9365. Watching the wheat   Men
     Welsh title: Bugeilio'r gwenith gwyn. English translation by Grace
     Williams. d♯3-f♯4 e3-c♯4 Sustained in moderate slow tempo.
     Tranquil and subdued. 4 verses. Setting by Grace Williams. Acc:
     3 (S)OX

9366. When I was a shepherd   All Voices
     Text: Ceiriog. d3-f♯4 f♯3-d4 Best for men. Sustained in mod-
     erate slow tempo. Narrative. Setting by Arthur Somervell. Acc:
     3 SWM-2

3. CANADA

Bibliography

SRC   Six Regional Canadian Folk Songs. Arranged by Carey Blyton. Lon-
        don: J. Curwen & Sons Ltd., 1963.

TSQ   Three Songs of Old Quebec. Edited by C. K. Offer. Includes only
        the English versions of the original French texts. Arranged by
        Phyllis Tate. London: Oxford University Press.

4LS   4 Love Songs. Arranged for baritone and piano by John Beckwith.
        Toronto: Berandol Music Limited.

9367.   Auction block   All Voices
        Region: Ontario. g3-eb4 g3-c4 Sustained in moderate tempo. In-
        tense. A song of slavery referring to the Negro's escape to Canada
        from the U.S. 4 verses and refrain with religious text. Setting by
        Carey Blyton. Acc: 3 SRC

9368.   C'est l'aviron   All Voices
        Region: Quebec. English: Pull on the oars. c#3-d4 d3-a3 Sus-
        tained in moderate tempo. Low ending. Narrative texts. 12 verses.
        Setting by Carey Blyton. Acc: 3 SRC

9369.   Donkey riding   Men
        Other title: The maritimes. eb3-c4 eb3-bb3 A sailor's song.
        Animated in brisk tempo. Rhythmic. 3 verses and refrain. Setting
        by Carey Blyton. Acc: 2 SRC

9370.   Drimindown   Baritone or Tenor
        Region: Nova Scotia. A Gaelic song. First line: There was an
        old man. c3-f4 d3-d4 Slightly animated in moderate tempo. De-
        scending ending. Narrative text. Setting by John Beckwith. Acc: 3
        4LS

9371.   An Eskimo lullaby   All Voices
        Region: Baffinland. db3-ab3 db3-gb3 Sustained in moderate slow
        tempo. Subdued; requires simplicity. 3 verses. Setting by Carey
        Blyton. Acc: 2 SRC

9372.   Go to the market, daughter fair   Women
        Region: Quebec. e3-d4 g3-c4 Animated in lively tempo. Joyous,
        requires some fluent enunciation. 5 verses. Acc: 3 TSQ

9373.   Kelligrews soiree   Men
        Region: Newfoundland. d3-c4 d3-c4 Animated in rapid tempo.
        Joyous, outgoing, rhythmic. Five narrative texts and refrain. Set-
        ting by Carey Blyton. Acc: 3 SRC

1206

9374. L'Amant malheureux   Baritone or Tenor
Region: Quebec. c3-e4 e3-d4 Sustained in moderate tempo. Requires some flexibility. Much of the accompaniment is for left hand
only. French text. Setting by John Beckwith. Acc: 3 4LS

9375. Lukey's boat   Men
Region: Nova Scotia. d3-b3 d3-b3 Animated in moderate lively
tempo. Rhythmic; perhaps once a sailors' song. 8 verses and refrain. Setting by Carey Blyton. Acc: 3 SRC

9376. Nass River dance song   Baritone
Region: Tsimshian Indian culture. a2-e4 f3-c4 Animated in lively
tempo. Free, irregular meter. In the Tsimshian dialect. Setting
by John Beckwith. Acc: 3 4LS

9377. The St. John's girl   Baritone or Tenor
Region: Lower Labrador. e3-d4(g4) e3-d4 Animated in lively tem-
po. Requires some fluent enunciation. Narrative text. Setting by
John Beckwith. Acc: 3 4LS

9378. The shepherd boy's song   All Voices
Region: Quebec. f3-c4 f3-c4 Animated in fast tempo. Generally
light. Generally on MF level. 5 verses and refrain. Setting by
Phyllis Tate. Acc: 3 TSQ

9379. Though I'm my father's only child   All Voices
Region: Quebec. c3-f4 f3-c4 Animated in moderate tempo. Has
strong passages. Subdued ending. A sea chanty; narrative. Setting
by Phyllis Tate. Acc: 3 TSQ

4. SCANDINAVIA

4a. NORWAY

Bibliography

NOR   Norway Sings. English-Norwegian edition. No editor. Oslo: Norsk Musikforlag.

9380. Among the rocks by the North Sea's blue waters   All Voices
Region: Sunnmöre. Norwegian title: Millom bakkar og berg ut med havet. d3-e4 g3-c4 Animated in lively tempo. 4 verses. Acc: 2-3 NOR

9381. Astri, my Astri   Men
Norwegian title: Astri, mi Astri. Text: from Horace's "Ode to Lydia," freely translated by Hans Hanson. g2-e4 c3-c4 Sustained in moderate slow tempo. 5 verses. Acc: 2-3 NOR

9382. Cowherd's song   All Voices
Norwegian title: So lokka me over den myra. d3-e4 g3-d4 Best for men; a peasant's song. Animated in moderate lively tempo. Acc: 3 WFF

9383. The dream song   All Voices
Norwegian title: Draumkvaedet. Region: Telemark. Text: Medieval poem, c. 1250. c3-d4 d3-bb3 Gently animated in moderate tempo. Tune is one of four traditionally used. Acc: 2 NOR

9384. A girl fifteen   All Voices
Norwegian title: Når gjenta bare blir femten å. d3-d4 d3-bb3 Animated in moderate lively tempo. A conversation between boy and girl. 4 verses. Acc: 3 WFF

9385. Homecoming from summer pastures   Men
Norwegian title: Os ha gjort ka gjerast skulde. Text: E. Storm. d3-eb4 eb3-c4 Animated in moderate tempo. Has dotted rhythms. Acc: 3 WFF

9386. The Hulder and Elland   All Voices
Norwegian title: Huldra å'en Elland. d3-eb4 d3-c4 Animated in moderately fast tempo. Requires some flexibility. Acc: 3 NOR

9387. I climbed to the farm one day   Men
Norwegian title: Eg gjekk meg opp til saeterli. Region: Kvikne. e3-d4 e3-d4 Animated in rapid tempo. Humorous, 4 verses. Acc: 3 NOR

9388. Ich legte mich zur Ruh   All Voices
German text by Heinrich Möller. f3-f4 a3-e4 Animated in moderate tempo. May be transposed. 3 verses. Acc: 3 LIU (Ch. VI)

9389. In Finne Castle how wondrous fair   All Voices
Norwegian title: Det er så fagert i Finne-slottet. Region: Vosse-
vangen. f♯3-d4 g3-d4 Animated in moderate tempo. Joyous.
Acc: 3 NOR

9390. In heaven above, in heaven above   All Voices
Norwegian title: I himmelen, i himmelen. Religious folk hymn from
Heddal. e3-d4 e3-c♯4 Sustained in moderate tempo. Hymn-style,
4 verses. Acc: 2-3 NOR

9391. It was me and it was you   All Voices
Norwegian title: Det var je og del var du. Region: Elverum. d3-
e♭4 g3-d4 Animated in moderate lively tempo. Graceful, 3 verses.
Acc: 2-3 NOR

9392. The lad up the hill   Women
Norwegian title: Vesle guten oppi bakken. Region: Valdres. e♭3-
e♭4 e♭3-b♭3 Animated in lively tempo. Generally strong. Acc:
3 NOR

9393. Let me sing you a merry ballad   All Voices
Norwegian title: Gamal vise frå Lom. Region: Lom. c3-e♭4 e♭3-
c4 Animated in moderate tempo. Humorous narrative. Acc: 2-3
NOR

9394. Lo, who are these a dazzling band   All Voices
Norwegian title: Den store hvite flokk, å se. e3-d4 f3-d4 Religious folk song from Heddal. Sustained in moderate slow tempo. 3
verses. Acc: 3 NOR

9395. Lullaby   All Voices
Norwegian title: Vuggetrall. Region: Aker. d3-d4 d3-b♭3 Only
the first two and the last two measures have text. The extended
section between is hummed. Unusual, a very fine lullaby. One of
the best lullaby's examined. Acc: 3 NOR

9396. My Tulla   All Voices
Norwegian title: Eg gjaette Tulla. Region: Heddal. c3-e4 e3-c4
Gently animated in moderate tempo. Narrative, 4 verses. Acc: 2-3
NOR

9397. Now listen to me, Katie   Men
Norwegian title: Velan du vesle Karl. Region: Flatdal. b♭2-d4
f3-c4 Sustained in moderate tempo. Subdued, low ending. Acc:
2-3 NOR

9398. Oh, I want to marry, that I do, sir   Men
Norwegian title: Je sku' au ha løst å gifte mei, san. Region: Byg-
land. f♯3-e♭4 g3-d4 Animated in moderate lively tempo. Strong
ending. 4 verses. Acc: 3 NOR, WFF

9399. Oh, Ole, Ole, I loved you dearly   All Voices
Norwegian title: A, Ola, Ola, min eigen unge. Region: Vegårshei.
b2-d4 c3-a3 Sustained in moderate slow tempo. 4 verses. Acc:
3 NOR

9400. Our little Kate   All Voices
Norwegian title: Å vesle Kari vår. Region: Valdres. c3-d4 f3-c4

1210 Solo Voice Repertoire

Animated in moderate lively tempo. Narrative. Acc: 3 NOR

9401. Sjugar and the troll All Voices
Norwegian title: Å kongen han stod på høgelofts svòl. Region: Hal-
lingdal. d3-eb4 f3-c4 Sustained in moderate slow tempo. Narrative. 3 verses. Acc: 2-3 NOR

9402. Solvejg's song All Voices
Norwegian title: Solveigs Sang. e3-a4 g#3-f#4 Sustained in moderate slow tempo. The second verse ends with a florid cadenza. Setting by Edvard Grieg, who used it in Op. 23; see Chapter VIII.
Acc: 3 FSG, 20S, GSS, & RSG-3 all Grieg Bibliography. ART-2,
56S

9403. Sunfair and the dragon king All Voices
Norwegian title: Solfager og Ormekongen. e3-d4 e3-b3 Sustained
in slow tempo. 5 verses. Acc: 3 NOR

9404. To folk, ye lambkins All Voices
c#3-ab4 f#3-f4 Generally sustained in moderate slow tempo. Has
some strong passages. The setting and the English version are by
James Woodside. Acc: 3 SCS-4

9405. Tom Fiddler All Voices
Norwegian title: Per spelmann. c#3-d4 d3-c#4 Animated in mod-
erate lively tempo. Descending ending line. 3 verses. Acc: 2-3
NOR

4b. DENMARK

Bibliography

DNS Denmark Sings. Danish and English texts. Copenhagen: Wilhelm
Hansen.

9406. Agnete and the merman All Voices
Danish title: Agnete hun stander. c3-d4 f3-c4 Animated in moderate lively tempo. Narrative. Seventeen two-line verses. Only the
first seven have English versions. Acc: 2-3 DNS

9407. Good evening, my pretty All Voices
Danish title: God Aften, min Pige! b2-e4 e3-c4 Sustained in mod-
erate slow tempo. A conversation between two characters. 5 verses.
Acc: 3 WFF

9408. On Saturday, towards evening All Voices
Danish title: Det var en Lørdag Aften. Region: Sjaellandsk. c3-d4
e3-a4 Animated in moderate tempo. Text: Ved Svend Grundtvig.
4 verses. Acc: 2-3 DNS

9409. Osborn Snare's courtship All Voices
Danish title: Dankonning og Herr Asbjørn Snare. d3-d4 g3-d4 Gen-
tly animated in moderate tempo. A ballad; narrative. 2 verses.
Acc: 3 WFF

9410. Our mother-tongue is beautiful   All Voices
       Danish title: Vort Modersmaal er dejligt. Text: Advard Lembcke.
       c♯3-e4 e3-c♯4 Animated in moderate tempo. Acc: 2-3 DNS

9411. Roselil   All Voices
       Danish title: Roselil. e3-f4 f3-d4 Animated in moderate tempo.
       Narrative, 7 verses. Acc: 2-3 DNS

4c. SWEDEN

                            Bibliography

SOS   Songs from Sweden. Collected by Gustav Hägg. Original Swedish
       texts, and English versions by Henry Grafton Chapman. New York:
       G. Schirmer, Inc.

SWS   Sweden Sings. Ballads, folk songs, and dances. Arranged by Josef
       Jonsson. Original texts, with English versions by Noel Wirén and
       Leonard B. Eyre. Stockholm: Nordiska Musikførlaget.

9412. All day while I'm at work   All Voices
       Swedish title: Om dagen vid mitt arbete. Text: Lundquist. b2-d4
       d3-ab4 Sustained in slow tempo. Grave and slightly melancholic.
       2 English verses. Acc: 3 WFF

9413. Come, pretty   Men
       Swedish title: Jag tror jag får. b2-d4 e3-b3 Animated in moderate
       lively tempo. Dancelike, 2 verses. Acc: 3 WFF

9414. Come with me   Men
       Swedish title: Ack, hör du lilla flicka. a2-f4 d3-d4 Animated in
       rapid tempo. Requires fluent enunciation. Has a wide range for a
       folk song. Acc: 3 SWS

9415. Do you think that I   Men
       Swedish title: Tänker du, att jag förlorader är. d3-e4 f3-c4 Ani-
       mated in moderate tempo. Joyous, ends with "fa la la" refrain.
       Acc: 3 SWS

9416. The first time in my life   All Voices
       Swedish title: Den första gång i världen. d3-d4 f♯3-b3 Sustained
       in moderate slow tempo. Acc: 3 SOS

9417. Flowers of joy   All Voices
       Swedish title: Glädjens blomster. d3-d4 f♯3-c4 Sustained in mod-
       erate slow tempo. Tranquil and subdued. Acc: 3 SWS, WFF

9418. Fourteen years, I should say, was my age   Women
       Swedish title: Fjorton år tror jag visst att jag var. b2-f♯4 d3-d4
       Animated in rapid tempo. Wide range. 3 verses with "fa la la" re-
       frain. Acc: 3 SWS

9419. Here in our grove   All Voices
       Swedish title: Uti vår hage. c3-eb4 f3-c4 Sustained in moderate

tempo. Graceful. 3 verses and refrain. Acc: 3 SWS

9420. I know a rose so comely   Men
       Swedish title: Jag vet en dejlig rosa. f#3-eb4 g3-d4 Sustained in
       slow tempo. Tranquil. 4 verses and refrain. Acc: 3 SWS

9421. I see by your eyes   Men
       Swedish title: Jag ser uppå dina ögon. d3-f4 f3-d4 Sustained in
       moderate tempo. Climactic ending. Acc: 3 SOS

9422. I sit alone   Women
       Swedish title: Jag sitter ensam och är förskjuten. c3-db4 c3-ab3
       Sustained in moderate slow tempo. Sad texts, 2 verses. Acc: 3
       WFF

9423. I walked abroad at eventide   Women
       Swedish text: Jag gick mig ut an aftonstund. e3-e4 g3-d4 Sus-
       tained in moderate slow tempo. Generally subdued. 2 verses. Acc:
       3 SOS

9424. I would go to that eastern country   Women
       Swedish text: Till Österland vill jag fara. e3-e4 a3-d4 Sustained
       in moderate slow tempo. Tranquil, 2 verses. Acc: 3 SWS

9425. In heaven's vault above me   Women
       Swedish title: Allt under himmelens fäste. d#3-e4 f#3-d4 Sus-
       tained in slow tempo. Ends with subdued florid passage. 2 verses.
       Acc: 2-3 SOS

9426. In summer the sun shines so clearly   All Voices
       Swedish title: I sommarens soliga dagar. c3-eb4 eb3-bb3 Sus-
       tained in generally march, moderate tempo. Joyous. 4 verses and
       refrain. Acc: 3 SWS

9427. It cannot be   Men
       Swedish title: Av hjärtat jag dig älskar i all min levnadstid. b2-c4
       f3-b3 Gently animated in moderate slow tempo. 2 verses. Acc:
       3 WFF

9428. The lonely clouds blow across the sky   All Voices
       Swedish title: Sa ödsligt monen pa fästet gå. d3-eb4 f#3-c4 Sus-
       tained in moderate lively tempo. Charming melody, 2 verses. Acc:
       2-3 SOS

9429. The maiden to the well has gone   Women
       Swedish title: Och jungfrun gick åt killan. Region: Skåne. b2-e4
       f#3-c#4 Sustained in moderate slow tempo. 5 verses. Acc: 3
       SWS

9430. O listen, pretty Dora   All Voices
       Swedish title: Och hör du unga Dora. d3-d4 g3-c4 Animated in
       moderate tempo. A conversation between boy and girl. 2 verses.
       Acc: 3 SWS

9431. O Värmeland, thou lovely   Men
       Text: Anders Fryxell. Swedish title: Ack, Värmeland, du sköna.
       b2-f#4 e3-e4 Gently animated in moderate slow tempo. Acc: 3
       SOS, WFF

9432. Perhaps when lilies bloom   Women
Swedish title: Och inte vill jag sörja. c♯3-c♯4 f♯3-c♯4 Sustained
in moderate tempo. Two verses in English. Acc: 3 WFF

9433. Remember what you promised me   All Voices
Swedish title: Och mins du hvad du lofvade.   d3-e4   f♯3-d4 Sustained in moderate tempo. Acc: 3 SOS

9434. Soft winds sigh   All Voices
Swedish title: Vindarna sucka uti skogarna.   d3-d4   f♯3-c4 Sustained in slow tempo. 2 verses. Acc: 3 SWS

9435. Song of the North   All Voices
Swedish title: Du gamla, du fria, du fjällhöga Nord.   f3-e♭4   a3-d4
Sustained in moderate tempo. Majestic. 2 verses. Acc: 3 SOS

9436. The stars above me   All Voices
Swedish title: Som stjärnan uppå himmelen so klar. f♯3-e♭4 g3-d4
Sustained in slow tempo. Generally gentle. Acc: 3 SOS

9437. Sweet angel, still I wish thee well   All Voices
Swedish title: Jag unnar dig ändå allt godt.   c3-e4   e3-c4 Sustained
in moderate slow tempo. Tranquil. Acc: 2 SOS

9438. A thousand things I ponder   All Voices
Swedish title: Jag går i tusen tankar. f3-f4 g3-d4 Sustained in
moderate slow tempo. 2 verses. Acc: 2 SOS

9439. Through crystal shines fairly   Men
Swedish title: Kristallen den fina. e3-e4 e3-b3 Gently animated
in moderate tempo. 2 verses and refrain. Acc: 3 SWS

9440. The watersprite   All Voices
Swedish title: Neckens polska. d3-f4 f3-d4 Sustained in moderate
tempo. Acc: 3 SOS

9441. What I have promised, that will I hold to   All Voices
Swedish title: Hvad jag har lofvat, det skall jag hålla. c♯3-d4 d3-
b3 Animated in moderate lively tempo. Acc: 2 SOS

9442. When I was seventeen   Women
Swedish title: När jag blef sjutton år. Text: Lilljebörn. c3-b♭4
e♭3-g4 Animated in moderate slow tempo. Generally subdued, 3
verses. Has an added cadenza and two coloratura variants by Marcella Sembrich for use in concert. Best for coloratura soprano or
lyric soprano. Acc: 3 ART-2

5. GERMANY

Bibliography

DDK   Das Deutsche Kunstlied. Three volumes; no editor. Medium keys. German texts only. Mainz & London: B. Schott's Söhne.

DLL   Das Leben in Liedern. High, Medium, Low. Edited by Paul Losse. Sixty songs by different composers. Frankfurt & New York: C. F. Peters.

DLS   Deutscher Liederschatz. Over 100 art and folk songs. Leipzig: C. F. Peters. (A very fine collection.)

FSG   Folk Songs. Deutsche Volkslieder. Two volumes, high and low. Arranged by Johannes Brahms. German texts, with English versions by Regina Winternitz. New York: International Music Co. (Twenty-one songs in each volume, for voice and piano.)

KDL   Klassiker des Deutschen Liedes. Two volumes. Edited by Hans Joachim Moser. Frankfurt & New York: C. F. Peters.

LIU   Das Lied im Unterricht. High, medium (or low). Edited by Paul Lohmann. Sixty-one art and folk songs in German. Mainz: B. Schott's Söhne.

LJB   Lieder-Auswahl Johannes Brahms. High, low. German texts. Mainz: B. Schott's Söhne.

UNT   Unterrichtslieder. High, medium, low. Edited by Paul Losse. Sixty old and modern German songs. Frankfurt & New York: C. F. Peters.

Note: All entries of German folk songs are in the German language. English titles and first lines are those which actually appear in the editions reviewed and are not necessarily the literal and exact translations. All articles are included in the alphabetization of German titles since German literature is generally constant.

9443. Ach, englische Schäferin   All Voices
English: Ah my gracious shepherdess. d3-e4 g3-e4 Animated in moderate tempo. Narrative: a conversation between hunter and shepherdess. 6 verses. Arranged by Johannes Brahms. Acc: 3 FSG-1

9444. Ach Gott, wie weh tut Scheiden   Men
English: To part, ah grief unending. e♭3-f4 f3-e♭4 Sustained in moderate tempo. Graceful, 4 verses. Setting by Johannes Brahms. English version by Will Earhart. Acc: 3 POS-4, FSG-1

9445. Ach könnt' ich diesen Abend   Men
English: To woo my love, this evening. d3-e4 a3-d4 Animated in
lively tempo. 4 verses. Arranged by Johannes Brahms. Acc: 3
FSG-2

9446. All' mein' Gedanken   All Voices
From the Lochheimer Liederbuch, 1460. e♭3-f4 g3-e♭4 Sustained
in moderate tempo. Generally on MF level. May be transposed.
3 verses. Setting by Helmut Spittler. The setting in FSG is by
Brahms and is in 4 verses. Acc: 3 LIU

9447. Da unten im Tale   All Voices
English: Below in the valley (POS title). e3-d4 g3-c4 Sustained
in moderate tempo. 4 verses. One step lower in UNT. Setting by
Johannes Brahms. Acc: 3 POS-2, UNT, FSG-1

9448. Das Mühlrad   Men
English: The mill-wheel. a♭3-f4 a♭3-e♭4 Animated in moderate
tempo. 5 verses. Setting by Will Earhart. Acc: 3 POS-2

9449. Das Schäfermädchen und der kuckuck   All Voices
c3-e4 g3-c4 Animated in moderate lively tempo. Narrative.
Dated 1820. 5 verses. Acc: 3 DLS

9450. Der Reiter   Women
English: The horseman spread his greatcoat. d3-f♯4 f♯3-d4 Sustained in moderate tempo. Has climactic passages. 3 verses. Arranged by Johannes Brahms. Acc: 3 FSG-2

9451. Der Sandmann   All Voices
Region: Lower Rhine. d3-e4 f♯3-d4 Sustained in moderate tempo.
Subdued. English: The sandman. Arranged and the English version
by Frank LaForge. German text is not provided in POS. Acc: 3
POS-1

9452. Der Tod als Schnitter   All Voices
Dated 1637. c3-c4 f3-c4 Sustained in generally moderate tempo.
Has strong passages. 4 verses. Acc: 3 DLS

9453. Des Abends kann ich nicht schlafen geh'n   Men
English: When night does fall I cannot sleep. e3-e4 a3-d4 Sustained in moderate slow tempo. Generally subdued. 4 verses. Setting by Johannes Brahms. Acc: 3 FSG-2

9454. Die Nachtigall im Tannenwald   All Voices
d3-e♭4 f3-d4 Animated in moderate lively tempo. Has humor. 2
verses. Acc: 3 DLS

9455. Die Sonne scheint nicht mehr   All Voices
English: Now shines the sun no more. d3-g4 g3-g4 First part is
sustained in moderate tempo; second part is animated in lively tempo.
2 verses. Setting by Johannes Brahms. Acc: 3 FSG-1

9456. Dort in den Weiden steht ein Haus   All Voices
English: There, 'neath the willows stands a house. d3-g4 g3-e4
Animated in lively tempo. Graceful. 3 verses. Setting by Johannes
Brahms. Acc: 3 FSG-2

9457. Du mein einzig Licht   All Voices
English: To my soul, your light. e3-e4 e3-d4 Sustained in moder-
ate tempo. Generally strong. 2 verses. Setting by Johannes
Brahms. Acc: 3 FSG-2

9458. Erlaube mir, feins Mädchen   Men
English: Now suffer me, fair maiden (POS). d3-f♯4 f♯3-e4 Gently
animated in moderate tempo. Gentle. Two steps lower in WFF.
Setting by Johannes Brahms. Acc: 3 POS-4, WFF, FSG-1, UNT
(German only)

9459. Es ging ein Maidlein zarte   All Voices
English: A maiden young and tender. e3-g4 e3-e4 Sustained in
moderate tempo. Narrative: the story of maiden and death. 4
verses. Setting by Johannes Brahms. Acc: 3 FSG-1

9460. Es ist auf Erd kein schwerer Leiden   All Voices
Melody is dated 1603; text is dated 1582. g3-f4 b♭3-e♭4 Sustained
in moderate tempo. Has some climactic passages. 4 verses. Setting by Helmut Spittler. Acc: 3 LIU

9461. Es reit' ein Herr und auchsein Knecht   All Voices
English: A master with his servant was riding. e♭3-g♭4 g♭3-d♭4
Animated in lively tempo. Narrative. 8 verses. Setting by Johannes
Brahms. Acc: 3 FSG-2

9462. Es ritt ein Ritter   All Voices
English: A knight was riding. g3-g4 b3-f♯4 Animated in moderate
tempo. Narrative. A conversation between a knight and a princess.
5 verses. Setting by Johannes Brahms. Acc: 3 FSG-1

9463. Es steht ein' Lind   All Voices
English: A linden tree stands. g3-g4 g3-e4 Sustained in moderate
slow tempo. Sad texts. 3 verses. Setting by Johannes Brahms.
Acc: 3 FSG-2

9464. Es war ein Markgraf' überm Rhein   All Voices
English: There lived a Markgrave on the Rhine. e3-e4 e3-d4 Sustained in moderate slow tempo. Generally subdued. 4 verses. Setting by Johannes Brahms. Acc: 3 FSG-2

9465. Es war eine schöne Jüdin   Women
English: There once was a ravishing Jewess. e3-e4 g♯3-e4 Ani-
mated in moderate tempo. Narrative text. 5 verses. Setting by
Johannes Brahms. Acc: 3 FSG-1

9466. Es wohnet ein Fiedler   All Voices
English: There once lived a fiddler. e3-e4 g♯3-d4 Animated in
moderate lively tempo. 4 verses. Setting by Johannes Brahms.
Acc: 3 FSG-2

9467. Feinsliebchen, du sollst mir nicht barfuss gehn   All Voices
c3-e4 e3-c4 Animated in lively tempo. Requires some fluent enunciation. Bright. 8 verses. Setting by Johannes Brahms. Acc: 3
DDK-1, FSG-1

9468. Gang zur Liebsten   Men
f3-f4 g3-c4 Sustained in moderate slow tempo. Requires simplicity.
4 verses. Acc: 3 DLL, (S)AU

9469. Gar lieblich hat sich gesellet   Men
       English: But lately my heart has spoken. f♯3-e4 g3-e4 Animated
       in moderate tempo. Graceful. 4 verses. Setting by Johannes
       Brahms. Acc: 3 FSG-1

9470. Gunhilde   All Voices
       English: Gunhilde. d3-e4 e3-e4 Animated in moderate tempo.
       Narrative text. Requires fluent enunciation. 10 verses. Setting by
       Johannes Brahms. Acc: 3 FSG-1

9471. Guten Abend, mein tausiger Schatz   All Voices
       English: Good evening, I bid you my dear. f♯3-f♯4 f♯3-f♯4 Ani-
       mated in moderate tempo. A conversation between two characters.
       6 verses. Setting by Johannes Brahms. Acc: 3 FSG-1

9472. Herzlich tut mich erfreuen   All Voices
       Attributed to Georg Rhaw, dated 1545. f3-f4 f3-d4 Sustained in
       very fast tempo. Descending ending line. 3 verses. Setting by
       Franz Willms. Acc: 2-3 LIU

9473. Ich hab die Nacht   All Voices
       English: I heard a scythe. c3-e♭4 f3-c4 Best for women. Gently
       animated. 3 verses. Acc: 3 WFF

9474. Ich hab die Nacht geträumet   All Voices
       English: The dream. c3-f4 f3-c4 Sustained in moderate slow tem-
       po. Descending ending line. 4 verses. Acc: 3 WFF

9475. Ich stand auf einem hohen Berg   All Voices
       English: Count and nun. b♯2-b3 e3-a3 Sustained in moderate tem-
       po. Narrative, 9 verses. Acc: 3 WFF, FSG-2

9476. Ich weiss mir'n Maidlein   Men
       English: I know a maiden sweet and fair. e3-e4 e3-e4 Animated
       in moderate lively tempo. 5 verses. Setting by Johannes Brahms.
       Acc: 3 FSG-2

9477. In stiller Nacht   All Voices
       d3-g4 g3-c4 First line: In stiller Nacht, zur ersten Wacht. Sus-
       tained in slow tempo. Gentle, generally subdued. 2 verses. Setting
       by Johannes Brahms. Also issued in different keys and editions.
       Acc: 3 LIU, DLS, FSG-2

9478. Jungfräulein, soll ich mit euch gehn   All Voices
       English: Young maiden, may I go with you. d3-e4 g3-e4 Animated
       in lively tempo. Narrative text: a conversation between a boy and a
       girl. 5 verses. Setting by Johannes Brahms. Acc: 3 FSG-1

9479. Klage   Men
       Text: from Niederrheim. f3-f4 a♭3-d♭4 Sustained in moderate
       tempo. Generally subdued. 3 verses. Acc: 3 UNT

9480. Maria ging aus wandern   All Voices
       English: The virgin went forth walking. e3-e4 e3-e4 Sacred text
       on Jesus' crucifixion. Sustained in moderate slow tempo. Subdued
       and narrative. 4 verses. Setting by Johannes Brahms. Acc: 3
       FSG-1

9481. Marias Wanderung   All Voices f♯3-f♯4   f♯3-f♯4   Sustained in moderate tempo.   Generally calm, subdued.   5 verses.   Setting by Johannes Brahms.   Acc: 3   DKL (Ch. VI)

9482.   Mein eigen soll sie sein   Men
Dated 1823.   c3-d4   f3-c4   Sustained in moderate tempo.   4 verses.
Acc: 3   DLS

9483.   Mein Mädel hat einen Rosenmund   Men
English: Yon maiden's lips are rosy red (SCS).   d3-f4   g3-e♭4   Animated in very lively tempo.   Requires fluent enunciation.   Melody is probably by Wilhelm von Zuccalmaglio.   4 verses and refrain.   Setting by Johannes Brahms.   Acc: 3   SCS-4, POS-2, (German only); UNT, KDL-2, LJB-H, FSG-2

9484.   Mir ist ein schön's braun's Maidelein   Men
English: A handsome maid of nut-brown skin.   d3-f4   g3-c4   Sustained in moderate tempo.   4 verses.   Setting by Johannes Brahms.
Acc: 3   FSG-2

9485.   Morgenlied der schwarzen Freischar   All Voices
Text: Gustav Adolf Salchow.   b2-e4   e3-c♯4   Animated in moderate tempo.   Joyous and bright.   5 verses and a "tra la la" refrain.
Acc: 3   DLS

9486.   Nur ein Gesicht auf Erden lebt   Men
English: There's but one face upon this earth.   g3-g4   c3-f4   Sustained vocal part in moderate lively tempo.   Generally high tessitura.   3 verses.   Setting by Johannes Brahms.   Acc: 3   FSG-1

9487.   Och Moder ich well en Ding han   Women
English: I have a wish, dear Mother!   b2-f♯4   g♯3-c♯4   Animated in lively tempo.   4 verses.   In Köln dialect.   Setting by Johannes Brahms.   Acc: 3   FSG-2

9488.   Sagt mir, o schönste Schäf'rin mein   Men
English: Tell me, my pretty shepherdess.   g3-g4   g3-f4   Animated in lively tempo.   Generally light.   4 verses.   Setting by Johannes Brahms.   Acc: 3   FSG-1

9489.   Schnitter Tod   All Voices
Dated 1638.   f3-f4   a♭3-e♭4   Sustained in moderate tempo.   Strong ending.   3 verses.   Setting by Helmut Spittler.   Acc: 3   LIU

9490.   Schöner Augen schöne Strahlen   Men
English: Eyes of sparkle, eyes of beauty.   e3-e4   g3-e4   Sustained in moderate tempo.   Generally strong.   6 verses.   Setting by Johannes Brahms.   Acc: 3   FSG-2

9491.   Schönster Abendstern, ei, wie seh   All Voices
c♯3-d4   f♯3-c♯4   Gently animated in moderate slow tempo.   4 verses.   Acc: 3   WFF

9492.   Schönster Schatz, mein Engel   Women
English: Beauteous one, my angel.   g3-e4   g3-d4   Sustained vocal part in lively tempo.   Bright.   4 verses.   Setting by Johannes Brahms.   Acc: 3   FSG-1

9493. Schwesterlein   All Voices
       f3-f4 f3-db4 Sustained in moderate tempo. Generally on MF level.
       3 verses. A conversation between two characters. Setting by
       Johannes Brahms. Acc: 3 LIU, LJB-L, FSG-1 (one step lower)

9494. Sehnsucht   Women
       e3-g4 g3-e4 Sustained in moderate slow tempo. Short. Setting by
       Johannes Brahms. Acc: 2-3 UNT

9495. So will ich frisch und fröhlich sein   Men
       English: I want to be both young and gay. d3-g4 g3-d4 Animated
       in lively tempo. Joyous. 3 verses. Setting by Johannes Brahms.
       Acc: 3 FSG-2

9496. So wünsch ich ihr ein' gute Nacht   Men
       English: Good night I say to you. c3-f4 f3-c4 Animated in lively
       tempo. 4 verses. Setting by Johannes Brahms. Acc: 3 FSG-1

9497. Soll sich der Mond nicht heller scheinen   All Voices
       c#3-e4 g#3-c4 Sustained in moderate slow tempo. Narrative.
       Acc: 3 WFF, FSG-2

9498. Vergissnichtmein   All Voices
       c3-eb4 eb3-c4 Animated in moderate tempo. 3 verses. Acc: 3
       DLS

9499. Wach' auf mein' Herzensschöne   All Voices
       English: Awake my lovely sweetheart. f3-g4 a3-f4 Gently animated
       in moderate tempo. Lyric. 4 verses. Setting by Johannes Brahms.
       Acc: 3 FSG-1

9500. Wach' auf, mein Hort   All Voices
       English: Awake my love. d3-e4 g3-d4 Animated in lively tempo.
       Generally strong. Narrative, has three characters in the song. 6
       verses. Setting by Johannes Brahms. Acc: 3 FSG-1

9501. We kumm ich dann de Poots eren?   All Voices
       English: How can I enter in your house. e3-e4 a3-e4 Animated in
       lively tempo. A conversation between a boy and a girl. In Köln dia-
       lect. 4 verses. Setting by Johannes Brahms. Acc: 3 FSG-2

9502. Wie komm ich denn zur Tür herein   Men
       f#3-f#4 f#3-f#4 Animated in quite fast tempo. Gentle and subdued.
       Requires fine high PP. 4 verses. Setting by Johannes Brahms.
       Acc: 3 LIU

9503. Wo gehst du hin, du Stolze?   All Voices
       English: Where do you go so proudly? d3-e4 g3-d4 Animated in
       lively tempo. Generally strong. 2 verses. Setting by Johannes
       Brahms. Acc: 3 FSG-2

9504. Wohl heute noch und morgen   All Voices
       a2-d4 f3-bb3 English: When will you come again? Sustained in
       moderate slow tempo. 6 verses. Acc: 2 WFF

6. POLAND

9505. Homage a Chopin   Soprano
Five vocalises for soprano and piano, based on Polish folk melodies.
e♭3-a♭4 g3-g4 May be performed separately. The singer is given
full liberty in the use of vowels and breathing marks. The first and
last songs may be transposed a minor third lower. All require flexibility and a good command of high notes. Setting and arrangement by
Andrzej Panufnik. Duration: 15 minutes. Acc: 3-4 (SC)B-H

9506. Love oracle   All Voices
Original first line: W polu lipeńka, w polu zielona. d3-d4 e3-c4
Sustained in moderate tempo. 8 short verses. Acc: 2 WFF

9507. Mother dear   Coloratura Soprano
Text: Yvonne Ravell. d3-d5(e5) a3-b4 Animated in moderate tem-
po. In waltz rhythm. Graceful. Ends with a slightly florid cadenza.
An arrangement for recital. Acc: 3 15A (Ch. XII)

9508. Rosemary, lovely garland   All Voices
Original first line: O jezioro, jezioro. b♯2-e4 f♯3-c♯4 Sustained
in moderate slow tempo. Generally gentle. 4 verses. Acc: 3
WFF

9509. Wind of night   Women
Original first line: Leci glos po rosie. e3-f4 f3-c4 Sustained in
moderate slow tempo. 3 verses. Acc: 3 WFF

7. RUSSIA

9510. Ah, no stormy wind   All Voices
e♭3-f4 f3-e♭4 Sustained in moderate tempo. Has some florid figures. Setting by Alexander Borodin, who used it in his opera,
PRINCE IGOR. In POS-4 only an English version by Will Earhart.
Acc: 3 POS-4

9511. Ah, that day   Men
Region: Ukraine. Original first line: Pijšov ja raz na ulycju. a♯2-
b3 a♯2-a3 Animated in moderate lively tempo. One verse in Russian; two verses in English translation. Acc: 3 WFF

9512. Cossack cradle song   All Voices
d3-f4 g3-d4 Sustained in moderate tempo. Gently graceful and subdued. 4 verses. Setting by James Woodside. Acc: 3 SCS-4

9513. Elder blooming   All Voices
Region: Ukraine. Original first line: Červonaja kalynon'ka. d3-e♭4
g3-d4 Animated in moderate lively tempo. 2 verses. Acc: 2-3
WFF

9514. The jailer's slumber song   All Voices
d3-f4 f♯3-e♭4 Sustained in moderate slow tempo. Has strong and
gentle passages. 2 verses. Setting by Alexander Borodin. English
version by Will Earhart. Acc: 3 POS-4

9515. One is high and one is low   Men
       Region: Ukraine. Original first line: Odna hora vysokaja. d♯3-e4
       e3-b3 Animated in moderate lively tempo. Requires some fluent
       enunciation. 3 verses in English. Acc: 3 WFF

9516. Snowdrops   High Voices
       e3-a4 g♯3-f♯4 Animated in lively tempo. Strong beginning and end-
       ing sections. Climactic high ending on a4. Setting by Sergei Pro-
       kofiev (B-H edition). In 50A, the English version is by Lorraine
       Noel Finley. Acc: 3-4 50A, (S)B-H

9517. Snowflakes   High Voices
       e3-g4 f♯3-f♯4 Sustained in moderate slow tempo. Gentle, delicate,
       and subdued. In 50A, the English version is by Lorraine Noel Finley.
       Setting by Sergei Prokofiev in the B-H edition, with texts in Russian,
       French, English, and German. Acc: 3 50A, (S)B-H

9518. Song of the Volga boatman   Men
       f3-f4 a3-f4 Sustained in slow tempo. Rhythmic. Setting by Sig-
       mund Spaeth. 56S has the Russian text. Acc: 3 56S

9519. Take me, earth   Men
       Original first line: To ne veter vetku klonit. e3-e4 e3-c4 Sus-
       tained in moderate slow tempo. Sad texts, 3 verses in English and
       4 verses in the original Russian. Acc: 2 WFF

8. CZECHOSLOVAKIA

Bibliography

TBS   Three Bohemian Songs. Arranged by Phyllis Tate. Only English
       versions. London: Oxford University Press.

TSS   Three Slovak Songs. Arranged by Phyllis Tate. Only English ver-
       sions. London: Oxford University Press.

9520. The cuckoo   All Voices
       Slovak song. d3-e4(g4) f♯3-d4 Sustained in moderate tempo. Gen-
       erally on MF level. Has passages for humming or whistling. Acc:
       3 TSS

9521. Dance song   All Voices
       d3-d4 g3-c4 Animated in moderate lively tempo. Rhythmic and
       bright. 3 verses. Setting and English version by Frank LaForge.
       Acc: 3 POS-1

9522. The falling dew   Men
       e3-f4 a3-c4 Animated in moderate lively tempo. 2 verses. Setting
       and English version by Frank LaForge. Acc: 3 POS-1

9523. The falling dew   Men
       e3-f4 a3-c4 Animated in moderate lively tempo. 2 verses. Setting
       and English version by Frank LaForge. Acc: 3 POS-1

9524. I had a darling dove   All Voices
Bohemian song. g3-e4 g3-c4 Animated in moderate lively tempo.
Light; narrative. Generally on MF level. Acc: 3 TBS

9525. Janko, Janko, better beware!   Men
Slovak song. d3-e4 f♯3-d4 Animated in moderate lively tempo.
Marked, generally strong. Climactic ending. Acc: 3 TSS

9526. The lonely farm on the hill   Men
Bohemian song. Text: C. K. Offer. f3-f4 a3-e4 Sustained in
moderate slow tempo. 3 verses. Acc: 2-3 TBS

9527. Maiden tell me   Women
f♯3-d4 a3-c4 Animated in moderate lively tempo. Rhythmic, 3
verses. Setting and English version by Frank LaForge. Acc: 3
POS-1

9528. Plaint   All Voices
Region: Bohemia. g♭3-e♭4 a♭3-e♭4 Sustained in moderate slow
tempo. 2 verses. Setting and English version by Frank LaForge.
Acc: 3 POS-3

9529. Secret love   Men
c3-f4 a3-d4 Sustained in moderate tempo. Rhythmic, 3 verses.
Setting and English version by Frank LaForge. Acc: 3 POS-1

9530. Sleep, little angel   Women
Region: Bohemia. Original first line: Hajej, muj andílku. e3-f4
f3-f4 Sustained in moderate lively tempo. Subdued, requires fine P
and PP. Setting and English version by Will Earhart. Acc: 3
POS-4

9531. Through our town the Danube flows   All Voices
Slovak song. d3-e4 d3-c4 Sustained in moderate tempo. Generally
on MF level. Narrative. Acc: 3 TSS

9532. Up the river, down the river   All Voices
Bohemian song. d3-e4 e3-c4 A song for two characters: he and
she. Sustained in moderate slow tempo. Graceful. Generally on
MF level. Acc: 3 TBS

9. HUNGARY

Bibliography

EHF   Eight Hungarian Folksongs. Arranged by Béla Bartók. Hungarian
texts, with German and English versions. London: Boosey & Hawkes.

9533. All the lads to war they've taken   All Voices
Hungarian title: Töltik a nagy erdő útját. e3-e4 e3-e4 Sustained
in slow tempo. Generally strong. Acc: 3 EHF

9534. Autumn   All Voices

e3-f4 f3-eb4 Sustained in moderate slow tempo. Setting and English version by James Woodside. 2 verses. Acc: 3 SCS-4

9535. Coldly runs the river   Women
Hungarian title: Istenem áraszd meg a vizet. d3-c4 d3-c4 Sustained in moderate slow tempo. Generally gentle and subdued. Acc:
3 EHF

9536. If I climb the rocky mountains   All Voices
Hungarian title: Ha kimegjek arr' a magos tetore. d3-e4 e3-d4
Animated in lively tempo. Strong. Has extended intervals. Acc:
3-4 EHF

9537. Skies above are heavy with rain   All Voices
Hungarian title: Anynyi bánat az szüvemen. d3-e4 e3-d4 Sustained
in slow tempo. Generally subdued. Sad texts. Acc: 2-3 EHF

9538. Snow is melting   All Voices
Hungarian title: Olvad a ho'. d3-f4 f3-d4 Sustained in moderate
tempo. Strong. Acc: 3 EHF

9539. Snowwhite kerchief   All Voices
Hungarian title: Fekete föd. e3-d4 e3-d4 Sustained in slow tempo.
Generally strong. Acc: 3 EHF

9540. Spring begins to labor   Men
Hungarian title: Eddig való dolgom. eb3-eb4 eb3-eb4 Sustained
in moderate tempo. Generally in quasi-recitative style. Requires
simplicity. Acc: 3 EHF

9541. Women, women, listen   All Voices
Hungarian title: Aszszonyok, had' legyek társatok. c#3-db4 eb3-
bb3 Animated in moderate lively tempo. Generally on MF level.
Acc: 3 EHF

10. ISRAEL

Bibliography

JOG   Jerusalem of Gold. Songs of modern and ancient Israel. Has English translations and versions. New York: Chappell & Co. , Inc.

9542. Artsa Alinu   All Voices
d3-e4 e3-b3 Animated in moderate lively tempo. Generally on MF
level. Setting by Heskel Brisman. Acc: 3 JOG

9543. Chanson hebraïque   All Voices
e3-e4 e3-c4 First line: Mejerke, main Suhn. Animated in moderate lively tempo. Has some characterization and passages in quasi-
recitative style. Has repeated notes, and a strong, driving rhythm
in the left hand accompaniment. Setting by Maurice Ravel. Acc: 3
4FS, (S)AD. 50A

1224 Solo Voice Repertoire

9544. Deux Mélodies Hébraïques All Voices
In Hebrew, with French version. Setting by Maurice Ravel. Also
issued with orchestral accompaniment, which is elaborate.
(1) Kaddisch. c3-g4 eb3-c4 Chantlike, with a few florid passages.
(2) L'Énigme éternelle. e3-f#4 e3-b3 Gentle, simple melody
and setting.
(SC)AD

9545. Emek, emek All Voices
d3-c4 e3-b3 Animated in lively tempo. Requires fluent enunciation.
Generally on MF level. Setting by Heskel Brisman. Acc: 3 JOG

9546. Hatikva All Voices
a2-d4 e3-b3 Sustained in moderate tempo. Majestic. Generally on
MF. Nationalistic texts. Setting by Heskel Brisman. Acc: 3 JOG

9547. Hava nagila All Voices
d3-e4 e3-c4 Animated in very lively tempo. Generally on MF level.
Accented. A popular song among Israeli. Setting by Heskel Brisman.
Acc: 3 JOG

9548. Hava netse b'machol All Voices
d3-c4 e3-b3 English title: Come and let us join the dance. Animated in lively tempo. A spirited dance, very popular among Israeli.
Joyous and bright; has "alleluia" refrain. English version and setting
by Heskel Brisman. Acc: 3 JOG

9549. Israeli lullaby Women
a3-c4 e3-c4 Sustained in moderate slow tempo. Subdued. A lullaby, gently graceful. English version and setting by Heskel Brisman.
Acc: 3 JOG

9550. Lama suka zu All Voices
e3-e4 e3-c4 English title: Song of Succoth. Sustained in moderate
slow tempo. Generally on MF level. 3 verses. Setting by Heskel
Brisman. Acc: 3 JOG

9551. Naale l'artsenu All Voices
f3-d4 g3-c4 Animated in moderate lively tempo. Requires fluent
enunciation. Generally on MF level. Setting by Heskel Brisman.
Acc: 3 JOG

9552. Sephardic melody High Voices
Text: Any open vowel. A vocalise. a#2-a4 e3-g4 Sustained in
slow tempo. Has many high passages and some wide intervalic skips.
Requires considerable flexibility, and some low tessitura. Very sub-
dued ending. Not for light voices. Setting by Paul Ben-Haim. See
Chapter XII: Vocalises, for Ben-Haim's other two songs. Acc: 4
In: Three Songs Without Words, Israeli Music Publ.

11. GREECE

Cinq Mélodies Populaires Grecques. A set of five short songs with texts by
M. D. Calvocoressi. English versions by Nita Cox. Has the Greek

texts, and English and French versions. High, medium. Setting by
Maurice Ravel. Issued as a group by International Music Co. Also
in DCR (see Ravel).

9553.   (1) Chanson de la mariée   High, Medium Voices
g3-eb4(f4)M g3-eb4 Gently animated vocal part in moderate tempo.
Requires fine P and PP. Subdued, somewhat delicate. Agitated accompaniment. Acc: 4

9554.   (2) La-bas, vers l'église   High, Medium Voices
g#3-e4(M) b3-e4 Sustained in moderate slow tempo. Quite subdued
and gentle. Short. Acc: 3

9555.   (3) Quel galant m'est comparable   High, Medium Voices
d3-f4(M) a3-e4 Best for men's voices. Animated in lively tempo.
Generally strong, outgoing, and somewhat free. Short. Acc: 3

9556.   (4) Chanson des cueilleuses de lentisques   High, Medium Voices
a3-e4(M) a3-e4 Sustained in slow tempo. Requires some flexibility.
Has pastoral, chant-like melody. Acc: 3-4

9557.   (5) Tout gai!   High, Medium Voices
eb3-f4(M) ab3-eb4 Animated in lively tempo. Requires some flexibility. Joyous, outgoing, and rhythmic. Second half is sung on "tra
la la." Acc: 3-4

12. ITALY

Bibliography

SOI   Songs of Italy. Sixty-five songs. Edited by Eduardo Marzo. Italian
texts, with English versions. New York: G. Schirmer, Inc.

9558.   All beauty within you   Men
Italian first line: Sei bella negli occhi. b2-d4 e3-c4 Gently ani-
mated in moderate slow tempo. 6 Italian verses; 3 translated into
English. Acc: 3 WFF

9559.   Before I had found a sweetheart   Men
Italian first line: Tenevo una casetta. f#3-d4 a3-c#4 Animated in
moderate tempo. In tango rhythm. 2 English verses. Acc: 3
WFF

9560.   Chanson italienne   Women
c3-eb4(f4) g3-c4 Sustained in moderate slow tempo. In quasi-recitative style. Descending ending line after strong climax. First line:
M'affaccio la finestra. Setting by Maurice Ravel. Acc: 3 4FS,
50A, (S)AD

9561.   Cicerenella   All Voices
Italian first line: Cicerenella, tenea no ciardino. e#3-e4 f#3-e4
Animated in moderate lively tempo. Narrative, 3 verses. Setting
and English version by Will Earhart. Acc: 3 POS-4

9562. The fair maid of Voghera   All Voices
      Italian first line: La biondina di Voghera. d3-f#4 g3-d4 Sustained
      in moderate tempo. 3 verses. Acc: 3 SOI

9563. The gondola   All Voices
      Italian first line: La gondoletta. db3-gb4 ab3-db4 Animated in
      moderate tempo. Graceful, 2 verses. Arranged for voice and string
      trio by Ludwig van Beethoven. English version by James Woodside.
      Acc: 3 SCS-4

9564. If you ever look on love   All Voices
      Italian first line: Se amor mai da vu se vede. f#3-f#4 g#3-d4
      Animated in moderate lively tempo. Climactic ending. Acc: 3 SOI

9565. Lullaby   All Voices
      Italian first line: Fa la nina nina nana. a2-d4 d3-a3 Sustained in
      moderate slow tempo. Tranquil and subdued. 4 Italian verses.
      Acc: 3 WFF

9566. The maiden of Scilla   All Voices
      Italian first line: Vitti na tigra dinta. e3-e4 a3-d4 Animated in
      lively tempo. Has some florid figures. 3 verses. Three steps
      lower in WFF. Acc: 3 SOI, WFF

9567. The pale girl   Women
      Italian first line: La smortina. d#3-d#4 e3-c#4 Sustained in mod-
      erate slow tempo. Acc: 3 SOI

9568. Pimpinella   Men
      Poet: Traditional Italian text. Russian text by P. I. Tchaikovsky.
      English version by Nathan H. Dole. c3-ab4(H) f3-f4 A graceful
      waltz. Has some climactic passages. Setting by P. I. Tchaikovsky,
      from Italian folk songs. Written in Florence. See Chapter IX. Acc:
      3 SFT (Ch. IX, Tchaikovsky)

9569. The poisoned lover   All Voices
      Italian title: L'Avvelenato. b2-c4 e3-a3 Gently animated in mod-
      erate slow tempo. 5 verses. Acc: 3 SOI

9570. Santa Lucia   All Voices
      f3-g4 g3-f4 Gently animated in moderate slow tempo. Graceful.
      Perhaps the best-known Neapolitan song. Acc: 3 SOI

9571. Song of the peasants of Etna   All Voices
      Italian title: Canto decontadini Etnei. a3-f4 a3-d4 Animated in
      moderate slow tempo. 4 verses. Acc: 3 SOI

9572. Thou window that hast shone   Men
      Italian first line: Fenesta che lucivi e mò non luci. c3-eb4 f3-db4
      Gently animated in moderate slow tempo. Sad text. 2 verses. Acc:
      3 SOI

9573. When I raise my eyes   Men
      Italian first line: Te guardando spesso spesso. g#2-e4 c3-c4 Sus-
      tained in slow tempo. Grave. 3 verses. Acc: 3 WFF

9574. While yet a boy, I told you how I loved you   Men

Italian first line: Fanciullo appena, ti parlai d'amore. f3-f4 f3-d♭4
Animated in moderate lively tempo. Graceful. 2 verses and an ending cadenza. Acc: 3 SOI

13. FRANCE

Bibliography

CDA   Chants d'Auvergne. Five books. Voice and piano. Orchestral
accompaniment is available. Collected and arranged by Joseph
Canteloube. Auvergne dialect, with French versions. Paris:
Heugel & Cie.

CFC   Chants de France. Two volumes. Collected and arranged by
Joseph Canteloube. Voice and piano. Orchestral accompaniment
is available. Paris: Durand & Cie.

FAB-2   Folk Song Arrangements. Vol. 2, France. English versions by
Iris Rogers. High, medium. London: Boosey & Hawkes.

TSN   Twelve Songs by Neo-French Composers. Medium voice. French
texts with English versions by Carl Engel. Boston: Boston Music
Co.

Others: Other folk song arrangements by Joseph Canteloube published by
Heugel & Cie.:
       Chants de la Touraine   Chants Paysans
       Chants de Languedoc   Chants de l'Angoumois

Note: Alphabetization of French titles considers the articles due to the
liaison of French words.

A.   General

9575.   Au pre la rose   All Voices
f♯3-d4   g3-d4   Animated in lively tempo.   Generally on MF level.
Acc: 3   CFC-1

9576.   Auprès de ma blonde   All Voices
d3-e4   g3-e4   Sustained in moderate tempo.   Has some climactic passages.   Acc: 3   CFC-1

9577.   Brunete   All Voices
f♯3-d4   g3-c4   First line: Le beau Berger Tircis.   Sustained in
moderate slow tempo.   Generally on MF level.   3 verses.   Setting
by Christophe Ballard, c.1703.   The setting by Michel Pinolet de
Montèclair, also in SSM, is transposed a fifth higher.   Acc: 3   SSM

9578.   Chanson francaise   All Voices
g3-f4   g3-f4   First line: Jeanneton, ou irons nous garder.   Animated
in moderate lively tempo.   Generally on MF level.   In graceful 3/4.
Somewhat delicate.   Setting by Maurice Ravel.   Acc: 3   4FS, 50A,
(S)AD

9579.   Délicieuses cimes   All Voices
f3-f4   f3-d4   Sustained in moderate tempo.   Graceful.   Acc: 3   CFC-1

9580. D'où venez-vous, fillette?   All Voices
g3-e4 g3-d4 Animated in fast tempo. Requires fluent enunciation.
Acc: 3 CFC-1

9581. Du rossigno qui chante   All Voices
English title: O nightingale. eb3-eb4 ab3-eb4 Sustained in moder-
ate slow tempo. Generally gentle. 2 verses. English version by
James Woodside. Acc: 3 SCS-4

9582. Eho! Eho!   All Voices
f#3-e4 g#3-c4 Animated in quite fast tempo. A shepherd's song.
Acc: 3 FAB-2

9583. Fileuse   Women
d3-d4 g3-d4 Animated in very fast tempo. Light, with "Tirouli"
refrains. Acc: 3 FAB-2

9584. Quand j'étais chez mon père   Men
English title: Heigh ho, heigh hi! g3-g4 g3-d4 Animated in lively
tempo. Joyous and outgoing. Narrative. Acc: 3 FAB-2

9585. Il est quelqu'un sur terre   Women
English title: There's someone in my fancy. d3-d4 g3-c4 Animated
vocal part in moderate slow tempo. Requires fluent enunciation.
Acc: 3 FAB-2

9586. La belle est au jardin d'amour   All Voices
English title: Beauty in love's garden. f3-d4 f3-c4 Animated in
moderate slow tempo. 4 verses. Acc: 3 FAB-2

9587. La chanson du tambourineur   Men
English title: The song of the drummer. f3-e4 a3-c4 Animated in
lively tempo. Rhythmic. Eighteenth century song. 6 verses. Setting and English version by Will Earhart. Acc: 3 POS-2

9588. La marche des rois   All Voices
English title: March of the kings. A Provençal noël. d3-eb4 g3-
d4 Animated in march tempo. Generally strong. 5 verses. English version by Will Earhart. Acc: 3 POS-2

9589. La Noël passee   All Voices
English title: The orphan and King Henry. d3-e4 g3-d4 Animated
in moderate lively tempo. Narrative; 3 verses and refrain. Acc: 3
FAB-2

9590. Le chiffonnier   All Voices
English title: The rag picker's bride. Region: Breton. e3-f#4
e3-e4 Animated in lively tempo. Requires fluent enunciation. Setting by P. Ladmirault. Acc: 3 TSN

9591. Le roi s'en va-t'en chasse   All Voices
English title: The king is gone a-hunting. eb3-eb4 ab3-db4 Animated in very fast tempo. Narrative. Acc: 3 FAB-2

9592. L'étoile du matin   All Voices
English title: The morning star. f3-f4 f3-f4 Animated in moderate
lively tempo. Graceful. 3 verses. Acc: 3 CLS

9593. Lizette   All Voices
d3-e4 g3-e4 Animated in quite fast tempo. Requires fluent enunciation. English version by James Woodside. 3 verses. Acc: 3-4
SCS-4

9594. Noël des quêteurs Bressans   All Voices
Text: Maurice Duhamel. English title: Noël of the Bressan. Region: Bressan. f3-f4 f3-f4 Sustained in moderate tempo. Has
strong passages. Setting by Francisque Darcieux. Acc: 3 TSN

9595. Où irai-je me plaindre?   All Voices
e3-f♯4 a3-d4 Sustained in moderate slow tempo. Setting by Joseph
Canteloube. Acc: 3 CFC-1

9596. Réveilles-vous   All Voices
d3-eb4 f3-d4 Sustained in moderate tempo. Acc: 3 CFC-1

9597. Voici le printemps   All Voices
English title: Hear the voice of Spring. f♯3-d4 g3-d4 Animated
in moderate lively tempo. Acc: 3 FAB-2

9598. Voici venir le joli Mai   All Voices
Region: Bressan. English title: Behold, 'tis May. Text: Maurice
Duhamel. e3-f4 a3-e4 Animated in moderate tempo. Setting by
Francisque Darcieux. Acc: 3 TSN

B. Auvergne

9599. Bailero   High, Medium Voices
f3-eb4 f3-d4 Animated in very fast tempo. Simple vocal part.
Arpeggiated accompaniment. Verses with refrain. Acc: 4-5 CDA-1

9600. Brezairola   Women
eb3-eb4 g3-d4 Sustained in slow tempo. A lullaby; subdued. Acc:
3 CDA-3

9601. Chut, chut   All Voices
e3-e4 a3-e4 Animated in fast tempo. Light; requires fluent enunciation. Acc: 3-4 CDA-4

9602. Hé! Beyla-z-y dau fé!   All Voices
French: Hé! Donne-lui du foin! d3-c4 g3-c4 Animated in moderate tempo. Rhythmic. Strong ending. Acc: 3 CDA-5

9603. Jou l'pount d'o Mirabel   All Voices
French: Au pont de Mirabel. f♯3-e4 a3-e4 Sustained in moderate
slow tempo. Slightly faster middle section. Has climactic passages.
Acc: 4 CDA-4

9604. La delaïssado   All Voices
French: La délaissée. eb3-db4 f3-c4 Gently animated vocal part
in slow tempo. Descending ending. Acc: 3 CDA-2

9605. La pastoura als camps   High, Medium Voices
f3-f4 g3-eb4 Animated in very fast tempo. Requires flexibility and
fluent enunciation. Generally light. Acc: 4-5 CDA-1

9606. La pastrouletta è lou chibaliè   Medium Voices
French: La bergère et le cavalier. f♯3-e4 b3-e4 Animated in
moderate lively tempo. 3 verses. Acc: 3 CDA-2

9607. Là-haut, sur le rocher   High, Medium Voices
a♭3-f4 a♭3-d♭4 Generally sustained in moderate tempo, with variations. Acc: 3 CDA-5

9608. L'Antouèno   Medium Voices
French: L'Antoine. b♭3-f4 b♭3-f4 Sustained vocal part in moderate slow tempo. Strong ending section. Acc: 4 CDA-2

9609. Lo calhè   All Voices
French: La caille. e3-e4 a3-d4 Animated in moderate tempo.
Requires some fluent enunciation. Acc: 4 CDA-2

9610. Lo fiolairè   High Voices
d3-g4 g3-e4 Animated in rapid tempo. Light. Climactic high ending. Acc: 4 CDA-3

9611. Lou boussu   All Voices
f♯3-e4 a3-d4 Animated in lively tempo. Spirited, requires fluent
enunciation. Strong ending. Acc: 3 CDA-3

9612. Lou coucut   Medium, High Voices
French: Le coucou. f3-f4 f3-f4 Animated in lively tempo. Requires some fluent enunciation. Acc: 3-4 CDA-4

9613. Lou diziou bè   All Voices
French: On disait bien. b3-e4 g3-d4 Animated in moderate tempo.
Rhythmic. Has stronger middle section. Acc: 3 CDA-5

9614. Malurous qu'o uno fenno   All Voices
e3-f4 f3-e4 A bourrèe. Animated in moderate lively tempo. Requires some fluent enunciation. Acc: 3-4 CDA-3

9615. N'aï pas ièu de mîo   All Voices
French: Je n'ai pas d'amie. f♯3-d4 g3-c4 Animated in moderate
tempo. Acc: 4 CDA-2

9616. Obal, din lo coumbèlo   Medium Voices
French: Au loin, làbas dans la vallèe. f♯3-e4 f♯3-e4 Sustained
in moderate slow tempo. Acc: 4 CDA-5

9617. Oï ayaï   All Voices
d3-f4 g3-d4 Generally sustained in varied tempi. Slightly climactic
ending. Acc: 3 CDA-4

9618. Passo pel prat   All Voices
c♯3-e4 a3-e4 Sustained in moderate slow tempo. Starts and ends
with "lo lo lo" refrain. Strong ending on a3. Acc: 4 CDA-3

9619. Pastorale   All Voices
f♯3-f♭4 b3-e4 Animated in moderate tempo. Requires fluent enunciation. Has many repeated notes. Acc: 4 CDA-4

9620. Pastourelle   Medium Voices
e3-f4 a3-e4 Gently animated in moderate tempo. Generally gentle.
Acc: 3 CDA-2

9621. Postouro, sẽ tu m'aymo   All Voices
       French: Bergere, si tu m'aimes. e3-e4 g3-d4 Animated in mod-
       erate lively tempo. Requires some fluent enunciation and flexibility.
       Acc: 3-4 CDA-5

9622. Pour l'enfant   All Voices
       f3-db4 f3-bb3 Sustained in moderate slow tempo. Gentle and sub-
       dued. A lullaby. Best for women. Acc: 3 CDA-4

9623. Quand z'eyro petitoune   All Voices
       French title: Losque j'ẽtais petite. g3-e4 g3-d4 Animated in mod-
       erate tempo. Graceful and light. Acc: 3 CDA-5

9624. Te, l'co, te!   High, Medium Voices
       French title: Va, l'chien, va! f3-f4 f3-e4 Animated in moderate
       tempo. Strong, bold throughout. Ends with portamento. Requires
       some fluent enunciation. Acc: 3-4 CDA-5

9625. Trois bourẽes   High, Medium Voices
          (a) L'aĩo dẽ rotso
               d3-g4 g3-d4 Animated in fast tempo. Requires fluent enun-
               ciation. Endings of verses are in upward portamento.
          (b) Ound' onorẽn gorda?
               g#3-f#4 a3-e4 Animated in fast tempo. Requires flexibility
               and fluent enunciation.
          (c) Obal, din lou limouzi
               f3-f4 bb3-f4 Animated in fast tempo. Requires flexibility.
               Has high tessitura, and a climactic ending.
       Acc: 4-5 CDA-1

9626. Uno jionto postouro   All Voices
       French: Une jolie bergere. g3-e4 g3-d4 Sustained in moderate
       slow tempo. Has slower middle section. Acc: 3 CDA-5

Bibliography

CBE   Cantos y Bailes Populares de España. Three volumes. Edited by J. Inzenga. Regions: Galicia, Murcia, Valencia. Madrid: Union Musical Española. (One volume per region. The letter appearing after the code indicates the region and volume.)

CEA   Canciones Españolas Antiguas. Collected and arranged by Federico Garcia Lorca. Madrid: Union Musical Española.

CMA   Cuatro Madrigales Amatorios. Arrangements of well-known 16th century Spanish songs. High voice and piano. Orchestral accompaniment is available. London: J. & W. Chester, Inc.

DCC   Douze Chansons Populaires de Catalogne. Edited by Joaquin Nin-Culmell. Catalan language. Paris: Max Eschig.

PCP   Pueblo. Canciones Populares. Collected and arranged by R. Benedicto. Madrid: Union Musical Española.

SCP   Siete Canciones Populares Españolas. Arrangements for voice and piano by Manuel de Falla. In two keys. New York: Associated Music Publishers, and London: J. & W. Chester.

9627. El adios de iparraguirre   All Voices
Region: Vasconia. c3-d4   d3-c4   Animated in moderate tempo. Has dotted rhythms. Acc: 3 PCP

9628. Anda, jaleo   All Voices
d3-e♭4   g3-d4   Animated in moderate lively tempo. Graceful. 3 verses and refrain. Acc: 3 CEA

9629. Aquel pino   All Voices
e3-d4   e3-c4   Animated in moderate lively tempo. Graceful, 2 verses. Acc: 3 PCP

9630. Asturiana   All Voices
f♯3-d4   a3-d4   Sustained vocal part in moderate slow tempo. Generally tranquil style with very controlled, subdued, agitated accompaniment. Acc: 4-5 SCP

9631. Bon cassador   Medium Voices
c3-d4   f3-c4   Animated in moderate tempo. Strong and accented. All phrases have descending contour. 2 verses. Acc: 3 DCC

9632. El cafe de chinitas   All Voices
e3-d4   e3-c4   Animated in moderately lively tempo. 4 verses. Acc: 3 CEA

9633. Canción   All Voices
       e3-f♯ 4   g♯ 3-e4   Animated in moderate lively tempo.   Graceful.   Gen-
       erally somewhat subdued. Requires flexibility.   Agitated accompani-
       ment.   Acc: 3-4 SCP

9634. Canción de cuna   All Voices
       Region: Vasconia.   g3-b3   g3-b3   Sustained in slow tempo.   Gentle
       and subdued.   The narrow range makes this tune reveal that it is
       much older than most in this work.   Acc: 3 PCP

9635. Canción de siega   All Voices
       Region: Salamanca.   e3-d4   g3-d4   Sustained in moderate tempo.
       2 verses and refrain.   Acc: 3 PCP

9636. Canto de cuna   All Voices
       e3-c4   g3-c4   Sustained in moderate tempo.   A short, hummed lulla-
       by.   Acc: 3 CBE-G

9637. Canto de cuna   Women
       d3-d4   d3-c4   Sustained in moderate tempo.   Subdued and gentle.   To
       be sung without accompaniment.   Setting by D. A. Lopez Almagro.
       Acc: None CBE-M

9638. Canto de Granada   All Voices
       Region: Andalucia.   c3-d4   g3-c4   Animated in moderate lively tem-
       po.   Graceful and rhythmic.   3 verses.   Acc: 3 PCP

9639. Canto de la trilla   All Voices
       e3-f4   g3-e4   Gently animated vocal part in moderate slow tempo.
       Florid, requires flexibility.   Subdued, low ending.   Acc: 3 CBE-M

9640. Canto de pescadores   Men
       Region: Galicia.   c3-d4   f3-c4   Animated in lively tempo.   3 verses
       and refrain.   Acc: 3 PCP

9641. Canto popular antiguo   All Voices
       d3-b♭ 3   e♭ 3-b♭ 3   Sustained in moderate slow tempo.   Ends with "la
       la la" section.   Acc: 3 CBE-G

9642. Chanson espagnole   Mezzo-Soprano, Contralto
       d3-b♭ 3   f3-b♭ 3   Sustained in moderate slow tempo.   Graceful and
       rhythmic.   Ends with "la la la" section.   First line: Adios, men
       homino, adios.   Setting by Maurice Ravel.   Acc: 3 4FS, 50A,
       (S)AD

9643. El chiste   All Voices
       e3-e4   f♯ 3-c4   Animated in moderate tempo.   Rhythmic.   Requires
       some flexibility and fluent enunciation.   Acc: 3 CBE-V

9644. Con que la lavare?   All Voices
       f3-a♭ 4   a♭ 3-e♭ 4   Sustained in moderate slow tempo.   Gently animated
       vocal part.   Tranquil and subdued.   Requires very fine high P.   May
       be transposed for lower voices.   Acc: 3 CMA

9645. De dónde venis, amore?   All Voices
       f3-c5   a3-a4   Animated in lively tempo.   Graceful and light.   Best
       for high voices, but may be transposed for the lower ones.   Requires
       some flexibility and fluent enunciation.   Climactic ending section.
       Acc: 3-4 CMA

9646. De los álamos vengo, madre   All Voices
       e♯3-a4   a3-f♯4   Animated in lively tempo. Has some florid pas-
       sages. Requires flexibility, fluent enunciation, and very fine high P.
       Agitated accompaniment. Acc: 4 CMA

9647. Donde vá de mañana   All Voices
       Region: Santander. e3-d♭4 f3-c4 Animated in moderate lively
       tempo. 3 verses. Acc: 3-4 PCP

9648. Dos cantares populares   High, Medium Voices
       c♯3-f♯4 f♯3-c♯4 Sustained vocal part in moderate slow tempo.
       Generally subdued. Very agitated accompaniment. Fine for light
       voices. Setting by Fernando Obradors. Acc: 4-5 CCO-1 (Obradors)

9649. En la Macarenita   All Voices
       Region: Andalucia. d3-e4 a3-d4 Animated in very fast tempo.
       Requires some fluent enunciation. 3 verses. Acc: 3 PCP

9650. En toda la quintana   All Voices
       Region: Asturia. e♭3-e♭4 e♭3-e♭4 Sustained in moderate slow
       tempo. Generally strong and florid. Acc: 3 PCP

9651. Enferma de amor   All Voices
       Region: Mallorca. Castellana version. e3-e4 a3-d4 Gently ani-
       mated in moderate slow tempo. Graceful. 4 verses with interpola-
       tions of "Ay!" Acc: 3 PCP

9652. Fandanguillo   All Voices
       Region: Andalucia. d3-d4 f3-c4 Animated in lively tempo. Re-
       quires flexibility. Has some short and fast florid figures. 3 verses.
       Acc: 3 PCP

9653. L'herèu Riera   Medium Voices
       e♭3-f4 a♭3-e♭4 Animated in moderate tempo. Strong and short.
       2 verses with "la ra la" refrain. Acc: 3 DCC

9654. La huevera   All Voices
       Region: Salamanca. e3-d4 e3-c4 Animated in very lively tempo.
       Requires flexibility. 3 verses. Acc: 3 PCP

9655. Jota   All Voices
       g♯3-f♯4 g♯3-d♯4 Sustained vocal part. Has strong passages,
       lengthy instrumental interludes in agitated, rhythmic dance. Acc:
       4-5 SCP

9656. Lo mariner   Medium Voices
       c3-f4 f3-c4 Animated in moderate lively tempo. 3 verses. Acc:
       2 DCC

9657. Lo noy de la mare   Women
       e♭3-e♭4 f3-c4 A lullaby. Gently animated vocal part in moderate
       tempo. Gentle, subdued, and short. Acc: 3 DCC

9658. Me gustan todas   All Voices
       Region: Pyrenees. English: I like them all. f♯3-f♯4 f♯3-d4
       Animated in moderate tempo. Rhythmic. Setting by Mrs. S. G. C.
       Middlemore. Acc: 3 SCS-4

9659. Las morillas de Jaén   All Voices

Dated XVth century. d3-d4 d3-c4 Animated in moderate tempo,
with variations. Requires some flexibility. Acc: 3 CEA

9660. Mort de la núvia   Medium Voices
e3-d4 e3-c4 Animated in moderate tempo. 2 verses with refrain.
Acc: 3 DCC

9661. Nana   All Voices
e3-f♯4 g3-d4 Sustained in slow tempo. Very subdued, gentle, and
tranquil. Delicate. Requires flexibility and considerable control.
Acc: 3 SCP

9662. Nana de Sevilla   All Voices
d3-b3 d3-b3 Sustained in moderate slow tempo. Has some short
florid figures. Acc: 3 CEA

9663. El niño querido   Women
Region: Cataluña. d3-d4 f♯3-c4 Sustained in moderate tempo.
Generally gentle. 3 verses. Acc: 3 PCP

9664. No quiero casarme   Women
English title: I don't wish to marry. e♭3-e♭4 a♭3-d♭4 Animated
in moderate lively tempo. Requires fluent enunciation. 2 verses.
Setting by F. Campbell-Watson, translation by Frank LaForge. Acc:
3 POS-3

9665. Las palabras, amor mio   All Voices
Region: Santander. c3-e♭4 g3-d4 Sustained in moderate slow tempo. Tranquil, 3 verses. Acc: 3 PCP

9666. El paño moruno   All Voices
g♯3-f♯4 g♯3-d4 Animated in lively tempo. Graceful and outgoing.
Requires some flexibility. Subdued ending. Extended instrumental
prelude. Acc: 3-4 SCP, CBE-M (1/2 step higher)

9667. Picaro molinero   All Voices
Region: Santander. c3-d♭4 f3-c4 Animated in moderate slow tempo.
Has short florid figures. 3 verses. Acc: 3 PCP

9668. Polo   All Voices
f♯3-g4 f♯3-d4 Generally animated vocal part with some sustained
notes. Very fast tempo. Requires fluent enunciation and flexibility.
Climactic passages. Very agitated accompaniment. Acc: 5 SCP

9669. Los reyes de la baraja   All Voices
d3-d4 d3-c4 Animated in moderate tempo. 3 verses. Acc: 3
CEA

9670. Seguidilla Murciana   All Voices
g3-e4 b3-e4 Animated in lively and spirited tempo. Requires fluent
enunciation and flexibility. Climactic ending. Very agitated accompaniment. Acc: 4-5 SCP

9671. Seguidillas Manchegas   All Voices
c3-d4 e3-c4 Animated in moderate lively tempo. Requires some
flexibility. 2 verses. Acc: 3 PCP

9672. El triquitrí   All Voices

Region: Aragon. d3-c4 g3-c4 Animated in moderate lively tempo.
Graceful, has humor. 3 verses with refrain. Acc: 3 PCP

9673. Vos me matásteis   All Voices
a3-a4 a3-e4 Gently animated vocal part in moderate slow tempo.
Very subdued ending. Best for light, high voices. Acc: 3 CMA

15. ARGENTINA

9674. Una vez clavelina   All Voices
Other title: Gato. English title: Sometimes a marigold. f♯3-a4
f♯3-e4 Region: Province of Cuyo. Animated in very lively tempo.
Has some climactic passages. Passages on "ah" vowel were added
at the end. May be transposed for lower voices. Acc: 3-4 25F

9675. Vidalita   Men
g♯3-g4(a4) g♯3-f♯4 Sustained in moderate slow tempo. Generally
subdued, gentle love song. May be transposed for the lower voices.
Vidalita is the name of a girl. Acc: 3 25F

16. BRAZIL

TPI   Tres Poemas Indigenas. Trois Poemes Indiens. Arranged from traditional Indian themes and poems by Heitor Villa-Lobos. Paris:
Editions Max Eschig. (Note: These are elaborate piano arrangements for recital purposes. Themes are from primitive Brazilian
melodies.)

9676. A casinha pequenina   All Voices
English title: Our small house. f♯3-g4 a3-e♭4 Sustained in moderate tempo. Has contrasts in dynamics. Subdued ending. Acc: 3
25F

9677. Adeus Éma   All Voices
d3-e4 e3-a4 Animated in moderate tempo. Requires some fluent
enunciation. Generally subdued. Subdued, high ending. Setting by
Heitor Villa-Lobos. Acc: 3 (S)ME

9678. Canide ioune-sabath   All Voices
c3-a3 d3-f3 Sustained in march tempo. Has some strong passages.
Faster middle section. Very subdued ending. Narrow range, like
most primitive melodies. Setting by Heitor Villa-Lobos. Acc: 3
TPI

9679. Estrella é lua nóva   All Voices
d3-e4 e3-c♯4 Animated in moderate lively tempo. Has strong, intense passages, and incisive rhythms in the accompaniment. Low
ending. Setting by Heitor Villa-Lobos. Acc: 3-4 (S)ME

9680. Iara   Medium, High Voices
       d♭3-g4 f3-e4 Not for light voices. Generally sustained in varied
       tempi. Has dramatic passages. Generally strong, accented, and in-
       tense. Has sustained passages on "ah" vowel. Subdued ending. A
       fine song to end a recital group. Setting by Heitor Villa-Lobos.
       Acc: 4-5 TPI

9681. Mókócê cê-makâ   All Voices
       b♯2-g4 e♯3-b3 Animated in moderate lively tempo. In chant style.
       Each phrase starts strongly, and then immediately goes into a dimin-
       uendo. Very subdued ending. Setting by Heitor Villa-Lobos. Acc:
       3-4 (S)ME

9682. Nozani-nâ   All Voices
       e3-c4 e3-a4 Very animated in lively tempo. Strong, with detached
       bass in the accompaniment. Ends with a yell in upward glissando.
       An Indian chant. Setting by Heitor Villa-Lobos. Acc: 3-4 (S)ME

9683. O' pallida Madona   All Voices
       c3-d4 g3-d4 Sustained in slow tempo. Generally on MF level.
       Subdued low ending. Text in Portuguese. 2 verses. Setting by
       Heitor Villa-Lobos. Acc: 3 (S)ME

9684. Papae curumiassú   All Voices
       c3-c4 e♭3-c4 Sustained in slow tempo. Punctuated in the right
       hand accompaniment with a steady quarter-note, one-tone accented
       pulse. Ends with a yell. Setting by Heitor Villa-Lobos. Acc: 3
       (S)ME

9685. Teirú   Medium Voices
       b2-f♯4 d3-e4 Sustained in varied slow and moderate tempo. A
       funeral chant on the death of an Indian chief. In this setting the basic
       melody is transposed a full octave higher in some passages. Has
       strong, intense passages. Also requires fine PP. Setting by Heitor
       Villa-Lobos. Acc: 4 TPI

9686. Tu passaste por este jardin   All Voices
       Poet: Catullo Cearense.   a2-f4 c3-d4 Sustained in moderate tempo.
       Generally subdued. Requires some flexibility. Subdued ending. Acc:
       3 (S)ME

9687. Vióla quebrada   All Voices
       b2-e4 e3-b3 Animated in moderate lively tempo. Requires fluent
       enunciation. Very subdued ending which is also an optional chorus.
       3 verses. Setting by Villa-Lobos. Acc: 3 (S)ME

9688. Xangô   All Voices
       g3-d4 g3-d4 Sustained vocal part in lively tempo. Incisive rhythms
       and agitated accompaniment. Generally strong. A Makumba chant.
       Setting by Heitor Villa-Lobos. Acc: 3 (S)ME

17. CHILE

9689. Asî amo yo   All Voices
       Other title: Cueca. English title: As I love you. e3-f♯4 g♯3-e4

A dance-song of Chile, northern Argentina, and Bolivia. Animated in moderate lively tempo. Generally on MF level. Has passages for clapping of hands. Acc: 3 25F

9690. Rio, rio   All Voices
Other title: Tonada. English title: River, river. eb3-f4 eb3-eb4
Sustained in moderate slow tempo. Generally on MF level. 2 verses with refrain. Acc: 3 25F

18. COLOMBIA

9691. Mis flores Negras   All Voices
Other title: Pasillo. English title: My sable flowers. e3-f4 f3-e4
Sustained in moderate tempo. Generally on MF level. A dance song. 2 verses. Acc: 3 25F

9692. Por un beso de tu boca   All Voices
Other title: Bambuco. English title: Oh! to kiss your lips. e3-f4
g3-e4 Animated in moderate lively tempo. Generally on MF level. A courtship song and dance-song of the regions of Cundinamarca, Tolima, and Santander. Acc: 3 25F

19. MEXICO

9693. A la orilla del palmar   Men
English title: In the palm grove. eb3-f4(ab4) ab3-eb4 Animated in moderate lively tempo. On MF level, in dance style. Starts gently. Acc: 3 25F

9694. Adelita   Men
Other title: Corrido. c3-e4 a3-d4 A narrative ballad, usually used as a duet. Animated in lively tempo. Generally on MF level. 2 verses. Acc: 3 25F

9695. China del alma   All Voices
English title: O sweetheart mine. c3-f4 f3-d4 Gently animated in moderate slow tempo. Setting by Manuel A. Ponce. Acc: 3 (S)PI

9696. Cielito lindo   All Voices
English title: Dear little heaven. c3-g4 f3-c4 Animated in lively tempo. Graceful, in waltz movement. Climactic ending. Generally on MF level. Acc: 3 25F

9697. Cuatro milpas   All Voices
Other title: Canción ranchera. e3-e4 g#3-d#4 Sustained in moderate tempo. Has strong sections. Subdued ending. English title: Four cornfields. Acc: 3 25F

9698. La golondrina   All Voices
English title: The swallow. c3-a4 f3-d4 Sustained in moderate tempo. Generally on MF level. May be transposed for lower voices.

Spanish texts, with English version. Setting by Narciso Serradell.
Acc: 3 (S)GS. 25F

9699. Hace ocho meses   Men
English title: Unrequited love. d3-d4 d3-d4 Animated in moderate
lively tempo. Setting by Manuel A. Ponce. Acc: 3 (S)PI

9700. Joven divina   Men
b2-e4 f♯3-d♯4 Sustained in moderate tempo. Graceful. Setting by
Manuel A. Ponce. Acc: 3 (S)PI

9701. La malagueña   Men
Other title: Son guasteco. English title: The Malaganian. d3-g4
f3-d4 Originally a Spanish song, transported to Mexico. Gypsy origin. Animated in moderate lively tempo. 2 verses. Acc: 3-4
25F

9702. Las mañanitas   Men
English title: Birthday morning song. f♯3-e4 a♯3-e4 Sustained in
moderate tempo. A serenade by a lover to his sweetheart on her
birthday. Generally on MF level. Subdued ending. Acc: 3 25F

9703. La peña   All Voices
f3-e♭4 f3-d♭4 Sustained in moderate slow tempo. Generally gentle.
Setting by Manuel A. Ponce. Acc: 3 (S)PI

9704. Palomita   Men
First Spanish line: Palomita vamos a la tierra. First English line:
Come away with me, my love. d3-g4 g3-d4 Animated in moderate
lively tempo. Graceful. Setting by Manuel A. Ponce. Acc: 3
(S)PI

9705. Pregúntale a las estrellas   All Voices
English title: Ask all the stars. f♯3-f♯4 f♯3-b3 Origin is uncer-
tain since this song is popular throughout Latin America. Animated
habanera tempo. Generally on MF level. Has one climactic passage.
2 verses. Acc: 3 25F

9706. Qué pronto   All Voices
English title: Love's short memory. b2-f♯4 e3-d♯4 Animated in
moderate lively tempo. Rhythmic. Setting by Manuel A. Ponce.
Acc: 3 (S)PI

9707. La tarde era triste   All Voices
English title: How sad was the evening. d3-g4 f♯3-e4 Origin is
doubtful since this song is very popular throughout Latin America.
Animated in habanera tempo. Has climactic passages. Descending
ending. Acc: 3 25F

9708. Te quiero porque te quiero   All Voices
English title: You are my love, for I love you. a3-g4 a3-e4 Sustained in moderate tempo. Generally on MF level. Climactic high
ending. Acc: 3 25F

9709. El tecolote   All Voices
Other title: Guapango. English title: The owl. f3-f4 f3-e4 Animated in very lively tempo. Generally on MF level. Has the imita-
tion of the owl's cry. Climactic ending. Acc: 3 25F

20. WEST INDIES

WIS   West Indian Spirituals and Folk Tunes.   Arranged by Max Saunders
      and Hal Evans.   English texts only.   London: Boosey & Co.

9710. Death, Oh me Lawd   All Voices
       a2-eb4   eb3-bb3   Sustained in moderate tempo.   Majestic.   Has
       variations in tempo.   Generally on MF level.   Acc: 3   WIS

9711. Jamaicalypso   Men
       c3-f4   f3-d4   Animated in moderate tempo.   Jamaican song.   2
       verses.   Setting by Arthur Benjamin.   Acc: 3   (S)B-H

9712. Jan   All Voices
       c3-db4(f4)   f3-c4   Creole melody.   Sustained in moderate slow tempo.
       Climactic ending.   Jamaican song.   Setting by Arthur Benjamin.
       Acc: 3   (S)B-H

9713. Linstead market   All Voices
       e3-f4   f3-d4   Animated in rumba tempo.   Requires fluent enunciation.
       Climactic high ending.   Jamaican song.   Setting by Arthur Benjamin.
       Acc: 3   (S)B-H

9714. The Lord's prayer   All Voices
       Text: Psalm 23.   bb2-c4   eb3-bb3   Sustained in moderate slow tem-
       po.   Generally subdued.   Subdued ending.   Acc: 3   WIS

9715. Mercy pourin' in   All Voices
       bb2-d4(eb4)   eb3-bb3   Sustained in moderate tempo.   Generally on
       MF level.   Subdued ending.   Acc: 3   WIS

9716. Murder in the market   All Voices
       bb2-c4   eb3-c4   Sustained in moderate tempo.   Starts very strongly.
       Dark.   Strong ending on low tessitura.   Acc: 3   WIS

9717. Ogoun Belele   All Voices
       bb2(g2)-eb4   eb3-c4   Sustained in moderate tempo.   Has some strong
       passages.   Low, subdued ending.   Acc: 3   WIS

9718. Papa din't know   All Voices
       a2-d4   d3-a3   Animated in moderate lively tempo.   Generally on MF
       level.   Has strong passages.   Setting by Hal Evans.   Acc: 3   WIS

9719. Time for man go home   All Voices
       Other title: The monkey song.   bb2-bb3   eb3-bb3   Sustained in mod-
       erate slow tempo.   Generally on MF level.   Uses the dialect.   Setting
       by Hal Evans.   Acc: 3   WIS

9720. The Virgin Mary had a baby boy   All Voices
       c3-eb4   f3-c4   Animated in moderate tempo.   Spirited.   Generally on
       MF level.   Acc: 3   WIS

21. OTHER IBERIAN-AMERICAN COUNTRIES

9721. A las montañas iré   All Voices
    Countries: PERU and BOLIVIA. Other titles: Yaravi and Triste.
    English title: Up to the mountains I'll go. A song of the Incas of
    Peru and Bolivia. d♯3-e4 e3-c♯4 Sustained in slow tempo. Gen-
    erally gentle. Acc: 3   25F

9722. El mishito   All Voices
    Country: GUATEMALA. Other title: Son. English title: The kitten.
    e♭3-f♯4 a♭3-e4 Animated in lively tempo. Has climactic passages.
    Subdued ending. A festive Easter song. The "Son" is a dance form
    of Indian origin. Acc: 3-4   25F

9723. Coco de los Santos   All Voices
    Country: PANAMA. English title: The coconut. c3-a♭4 d3-e♭4
    Animated in moderate lively tempo. Requires fluent enunciation.
    Rhythmic and graceful. Climactic ending. A typical Panamanian
    dance song from the province of Santos. Acc: 3-4   25F

9724. Riqui, riqui, riquirrán   All Voices
    Country: VENEZUELA. English title: Sugar-cane. f♯3-g4 g♯3-e4
    A traditional children's song. Animated in lively tempo. Rhythmic.
    Climactic ending. Acc: 3   25F

22. JAPAN

9725. Kouta   Medium, Low Voices
    a2-e4 e3-c4 Animated in moderate lively tempo, with variations.
    Descending ending line. Setting by Koichi Kishi. Acc: 3 JLK
    (Ch. X--Kishi)

9726. Sakura, sakura   All Voices
    b2-f4 a3-e4 Sustained in moderate tempo. Generally gentle and
    subdued. Probably the best-known Japanese folk song. The Kishi set-
    ting has a German version. Acc: 3 JLK (Ch. X--Kishi)

INDICES

of

THE SOURCES OF TEXTS

and

THE COMPOSERS

The Sources of Texts index is composed of names of
poets, prose writers, playwrights, librettists, and titles
of literary and musical anthologies. An asterisk (*) appearing before a name indicates a source of the librettist's
subject, story, or inspiration, either partly or wholly.
Titles of anthologies and other collections are enclosed in
quotation marks. All index numbers refer to the entry
numbers of songs and arias in the main body of this reference.

The Composers index is placed at the end of the entire
book in order to facilitate handling. All the numbers in
the composer index refer to pages.

Other helpful indices, such as the Index of Titles and
First Lines and the Index of English Translations of Titles,
are reserved for a future supplement.

INDEX OF THE SOURCES OF TEXTS

For practical reasons, the following sources of texts are
not included in this index: 1) poetry by anonymous writers;
2) passages from the many branches of the Roman Catholic
liturgy in Latin; and 3) national folk literature.

Browning, Elizabeth Barrett 702, 1040, 1252, 1891-1895, 2591, 2596

Browning, Robert 1095, 1669

Bruce, V. 6878

Bruchmann, Franz von 4665, 4680, 4862, 4919

Bruère, Charles Antoine Leclerc de La 2894-2897

Brun, Friederike 3908, 3909

Brunn, Carl 6461

Brunswick, Leon 7351, 7352, 7464, 7465, 7567, 7568, 8344, 8373, 8638, 8795

Brüssoff, Valèry Yakovlevich 6611

Bryan, Robert 9357

Buchillot 3322

*Büchner, Georg 7642, 7643, 7905, 7906

Buckton, Alice M. 782

Buddeus 5080

Bulthaupt, Heinrich 4149

Buning, J. Werumeus 7129, 7136

Bunn, Alfred 7426, 7781, 8465

Bunyan, John 906, 908, 1298

Bürger, Gottfried August 3628, 3654, 3661, 3726, 3904, 4488, 5305

Burns, Robert 603, 787, 1048, 1529, 5045, 5120, 5123, 6775, 6778, 6779, 9207, 9213, 9216-9218, 9226, 9229, 9230, 9233, 9235, 9236, 9241, 9245, 9247

Busch, Wilhelm 5354

Busenello, Giovanni Francesco 2094, 2097, 2099, 2103, 2317-2329

Busse, Karl 4493, 5337, 5361

Bussine, Romain 3178

Byron, Eva 1575

Byron, George Gordon Noel 4436, 4450, 5028, 5036, 5044, 5086, 6740, 7533, 7539, 7861, 8322, 8323, 8616

Cadilhe, J. 1932

*Caigniez 7520, 8014, 8311, 8604, 8772, 8773

Caillavet, G. A. de 7630, 8390, 8391, 8517

Caime, E. 7341, 7538, 8327, 8503, 8619, 8785

Cain, Henri 7586, 7626, 7893, 7896, 8046, 8178, 8648

Calamnius, Ilmari 6396

*Calderon 7933

Calderon de la Barca, Pedro 5294, 5295

Callimachus (Greek poet, c. 260 B.C.) 927

Calvocoressi, M. D. 3481-3485, 9553-9557

Calzabigi, Ranieri da 3854, 6200, 6227-6237, 6252, 6259-6266, 6268-6271, 6281, 6283-6285, 6297, 6298, 7414, 7694-7696, 8427, 8695-8697

Cammarano, Salvatore 7323-7325, 7342, 7343, 7346, 7473, 7474, 7477, 7540-7543, 7548, 7549, 7863-7865, 7869, 7998, 8027, 8028, 8153, 8167, 8168, 8265, 8266, 8316, 8328-8330, 8334, 8504-8506, 8577, 8578, 8620-8622, 8627, 8628, 8760, 8786, 8787

Camoens, Luis de 1100

Campbell, Joan 1177

Campbell, Joseph 568, 570

Campe, Joachim Heinrich 3806

Campian (Campion), Thomas 33, 151, 153, 156-159, 162-164, 166-169, 171-176, 179-181, 185, 187, 237, 269, 532, 534, 968, 1423

Campistron, Jean Galbert de 2831

Campoamor, Ramon de 1883-1886, 1903-1906

Campos, Cleomenes 1919, 1921

"Cancionero Popular" 1872

Candidus, Carl 4019, 4065, 4079, 4110, 4121, 5115

Cane, Melville 1750

Canitz, Friedrich R. L. von 3799

Capece, Carlo Sigismondo 2494, 2496-2502, 6146

Capel-Cure, E. 705, 708

Capetanakis, Demetrios 1650-1652

Capoul, Victor 8367

Carducci, Giosuè 1125

Carême, Maurice 3394-3400

Carey, Henry 189

Carossa, Hans 4181, 4183

Carpani, Giuseppe 3665

Carré, Michel 3319, 3520, 3562, 7356, 7357, 7360, 7364-7372, 7377-7379, 7384-7389, 7393-7395, 7577, 7578, 7582, 7588-7601, 7613-7615, 7631, 7636, 7637, 7657-7660, 7884-7887, 7899, 8048-8052, 8057, 8058, 8070-8073, 8180, 8181, 8185, 8194, 8195, 8357, 8358, 8362, 8369-8371, 8392-8396, 8513, 8514, 8645, 8650-8654, 8657, 8668, 8670-8672, 8684, 8685, 8806-8812, 8818, 8824, 8826, 8827, 8837

Saar, Ferdinand von 7015
Sabina, Karel 7803, 8487, 8916
Sacken, Theodore von 6754
Sada-ihe 1393
Saineville, A. de 3563
Saint-Étienne, Sylvain 7359, 7581,
    8361, 8647, 8802
Saint-Georges, Jules H. Vernoy de
    7320-7322, 7373, 7374, 7467-
    7469 7602, 7603, 8055, 8184,
    8260, 8356, 8373, 8376, 8656,
    8801, 8813, 8814
Sakonska, N. 6701
Salchow, Gustav Adolf 9485
Salema, Sylvio 1929
Salis, Johann Gaudenz von 4657,
    4736, 4746, 4784, 4809, 4864
Sallet, Friedrich 5248
*Salvi, Antonio 5882, 5883, 5916,
    5928, 5929
Salvini, A. 1183
Samain, Albert 3179, 3215, 3530
Samain, Alfred 1428
Samuel, Book of 1297
San Geminiano, Folgore de 1470
San Román, José Munoz 1899-1902
Sandburg, Carl 1038, 1254, 1431,
    1432, 1434, 1510, 1511, 1516,
    1581, 1720, 1721
Sandoval, Miguel 1943-1945
Sanskrit, ancient Oriental language
    763-771
Sant'Angioli-Morbilli 3863
"Santissimo Natale" 1998, 2203
Sappho, 6th century B.C. 580,
    4549
Saracinelli, Ferdinando 2035
*Sardou, Victorien 3368, 7327,
    7481-7484, 7508-7510, 7834,
    8272-8274, 8302, 8303, 8583
Sarti, Giuseppe 3746
Sasaki, Nobutsuma 2609
Sassoon, Siegfried 1174, 1175,
    1367, 1756
Sätherberg, H. 6534
Sauter, S. F. 3636, 4771
Sauvage, M. T. 8825
Sbarra, Francesco 2110, 2112,
    2113, 2115
Scève, Maurice 3358
Schachtner, Johann Andreas 7416,
    7711, 7712, 7930, 8430, 8708,
    8866-8868
Schack, Adolf Friedrich Graf von
    4016, 4068, 4112, 4395, 5228-
    5230, 5234, 5237, 5271, 5275,
    5297, 5301, 5309, 5318, 5321,
    5326, 5341, 5345, 5349

Schaffy, Mirza (pseudonym of Fried-
    rich Martin von Bodenstedt) 6753,
    6763, 6765, 6766
Scheffel, Joseph Viktor von 5442,
    7713, 8709, 8869
Schellenberg, Ernst Ludwig 4518
Schenkendorf, Max von 4023, 4024,
    4059, 4064, 5376
Scherbina 6741
Scherer 4145
Schikaneder, Emanuel 7409-7411,
    7674, 8417, 8418, 8689, 8690,
    8847, 8848
*Schiller, Friedrich von 3553-3556,
    3953, 3970, 4419, 4667-4669,
    4718, 4722, 4744, 4745, 4749,
    4756, 4766, 4778, 4782, 4786,
    4792, 4793, 4815, 4848, 4851,
    4910, 5052, 5067, 5069, 7014,
    7330, 7331, 7339, 7340, 7346,
    7516, 7517, 7530, 7536, 7537,
    7548, 7549, 7798, 7857-7859,
    7869, 8025, 8026, 8141, 8235,
    8306, 8320, 8325, 8326, 8334,
    8601, 8611, 8617, 8618, 8627,
    8628, 8780, 8784, 8787
Schilling, Heinar 4261
Schlaf, Johannes 3972, 4582
Schlechta, Franz von 4779, 4823,
    4879, 4935, 4954
Schlegel, August Wilhelm 3957,
    4652, 4790, 4875, 4888, 4927
Schlegel, Friedrich von 4653, 4709,
    4721, 4762, 4763, 4789, 4802,
    4803, 4808, 4831, 4949, 4971
Schmidt, Hans 4042, 4107, 4115
Schmidt, Johann Eusebius 5576
Schmidt, Klamer E. K. 3831
Schneegass, Cyriacus 5804
Schnezler, A. 4328
Schnitzer, Ignaz 7725, 7726
Schober, Franz von 4662, 4681,
    4868, 4906, 4914, 4915, 4940,
    4944, 4947, 4972, 4973, 7044
Schönberg, Arnold 8432
Schopenhauer, Johanna 4855
Schorn, Henriette von 7040
Schott, Paul 7648, 7907
Schreiber, Aloys 4346, 4673, 4714,
    4723, 4734
Schreiber, Heinrich dem 4409
Schroeder, Johann Heinrich 5575
Schubart, Christian Friedrich Daniel
    3898, 4674, 4687
Schubert, Christian 4787
Schubert, Franz 4658
Schulze, Ernst 4688, 4694, 4752,
    4861, 4863, 4877, 4932, 4941, 4942

INDEX OF THE COMPOSERS
AND OTHER MUSICAL SOURCES*

*Index entries include: composer, dates, nationality, and page reference(s).

Clockey, Joseph Waddell, 1890-1960, United States 146
Clough-Leighter, Henry, 1874-1956, United States 146
Colasse, Pascal, 1649-1709, France 345, 360
Coleridge-Taylor, Samuel, 1875-1912, Great Britain 77
Colombia, Traditional Songs 1239
Cone, Edward T., United States 146
Conti, Francesco Bartolomeo, 1681-1731, Italy 269
Cooper, Esther, United States 146
Coperario, Giovanni (John Cooper), c. 1570-1627, Great Britain 25
Copland, Aaron, United States 146, 1001, 1030, 1049, 1095, 1163
Coquard, Arthur, 1846-1910, France 389
Corigliano, John, United States 148
Corkine, William, 16th-17th cent., Great Britain 25
Cornago, Juan, 15th cent., Spain 218
Cornelius, Peter, 1824-1874, Germany 525, 1088, 1149
Cortes, Ramiro, United States 149
Coulthard, Jean, Canada 879
Couperin ("Le Grand"), François, 1668-1733, France 345
Couperin, Gervais-François, 1759-1826, France 346
Courville, Joachim Thibaut de, c. 1570, France 346
Cowell, Henry Dixon, United States 149
Creston, Paul, United States 149
Crist, Bainbridge, United States 150
Crosse, Gordon, Great Britain 77
Cui, César Antonovich, 1835-1918, Russia 831
Cumming, Richard, United States 150
Curran, Pearl Gildersleeve, 1875-1941, United States 150
Czechoslovakia, Traditional Songs 1221

Dalayrac, Nicolas, 1753-1809, France 346
Dallapiccola, Luigi, 1904-1975, Italy 323
Dalvimare, Martin Pierre, 1772-1839, France 347
Damrosch, Leopold, 1832-1885, United States 151
Damrosch, Walter, 1862-1950, United States 151
Dan, Ikuma, Japan 902
Danyel, John, c. 1565-c. 1630, Great Britain 26
Dargomizhsky, Alexander Sergeyevich, 1813-1869, Russia 832
D'Astorga, Emanuele, 1680-c. 1757, Italy 269
Dauvergne, Antoine, c. 1713-1797, France 347
Davico, Vincenzo, Italy 324
David, Félicien (César), 1810-1876, France 389, 949, 979, 1083, 1123, 1145
Davy, John, 1763-1824, Great Britain 27
Daza, Esteban, 16th cent., Spain 218
Debussy, Claude, 1862-1918, France 389, 1040, 1058, 1083, 1145
Dedekind, Constantin Christian, 1628-1715, Germany 466
Deis, Carl, United States 151
Dela, Maurice, Canada 879
Délibes, Léo, 1836-1891, France 396, 949, 979, 1083, 1145
Delius, Frederick, 1862-1934, Great Britain 77
Dello Joio, Norman, United States 151
Denmark, Traditional Songs 1210
Desmarets, Henri, c. 1662-1741, France 347
Destouches, André (Cardinal), 1672-1749, France 348
Diamond, David Leo, United States 153
Dibdin, Charles, 1745-1814, Great Britain 27
Diepenbrock, Alphons, 1862-1921, The Netherlands 911